AMERICA BECOMING

Racial Trends and Their Consequences

Volume II

Neil J. Smelser, William Julius Wilson, and Faith Mitchell, *Editors*

Commission on Behavioral and Social Sciences and Education

National Research Council

NATIONAL ACADEMY PRESS
Washington, D.C.

NATIONAL ACADEMY PRESS 2101 Constitution Avenue, N.W. Washington, D.C. 20418

NOTICE: The project that is the subject of this report was approved by the Governing Board of the National Research Council, whose members are drawn from the councils of the National Academy of Sciences, the National Academy of Engineering, and the Institute of Medicine.

The study was supported by Grant No. SBR-9709489 between the National Academy of Sciences and the National Science Foundation through interagency agreements with the Office of the Assistant Secretary for Planning and Evaluation/U.S. Department of Health and Human Services, Bureau of Transportation Statistics/U.S. Department of Transportation, U.S. Department of Defense, U.S. Department of Energy, U.S. Department of Education, U.S. Department of Labor, Environmental Protection Agency, Economic Research Service/U.S. Department of Agriculture, U.S. Department of Housing and Urban Development, U.S. Department of the Interior, National Institute of Justice/U.S. Department of Justice, President's Initiative on Race, Social Security Administration, U.S. Department of Treasury, and the U.S. Department of Veterans Affairs. The Mellon and Mott foundations provided additiona support. Any opinions, findings, conclusions, or recommendations expressed in this publication are those of the author(s) and do not necessarily reflect the view of the organizations or agencies that provided support for this project.

Suggested citation: National Research Council (2001). *America Becoming: Racial Trends and Their Consequences*. Volume II. Neil J. Smelser, William Julius Wilson, and Faith Mitchell, Editors. Commission on Behavioral and Social Sciences and Education. Washington, DC: National Academy Press.

Library of Congress Cataloging-in-Publication Data

America becoming : racial trends and their consequences / Commission on Behavioral and Social Sciences and Education, National Research Council ; Neil Smelser, William Julius Wilson, and Faith Mitchell, editors.
    p. cm.
Includes bibliographical references and index.
    ISBN 0-309-06839-8 (v. 2) — ISBN 0-309-06840-1 (v. 2 : pbk.)
    1. United States—Race relations—Research—Congresses. 2. United States—Ethnic relations—Research—Congresses. 3. United States—Population—Statistics—Congresses. 4. Minorities—United States—Social conditions—Research—Congresses. 5. Minorities—United States—Economic conditions—Reasearch—Congresses. I. Smelser, Neil J. II. Wilson, William J., 1935- III. Mitchell, Faith. IV. National Research Council (U.S.). Commission on Behavioral and Social Sciences and Education.
    E184.A1 A497 2000
    305.8'00973—dc21

                           00-010549

Additional copies of this report are available from National Academy Press, 2101 Constitution Avenue, N.W., Washington, D.C. 20418

Call (800) 624-6242 or (202) 334-3313 (in the Washington metropolitan area)

This report is also available online at **http://www.nap.edu**

Printed in the United States of America

THE NATIONAL ACADEMIES

National Academy of Sciences
National Academy of Engineering
Institute of Medicine
National Research Council

The **National Academy of Sciences** is a private, nonprofit, self-perpetuating society of distinguished scholars engaged in scientific and engineering research, dedicated to the furtherance of science and technology and to their use for the general welfare. Upon the authority of the charter granted to it by the Congress in 1863, the Academy has a mandate that requires it to advise the federal government on scientific and technical matters. Dr. Bruce M. Alberts is president of the National Academy of Sciences.

The **National Academy of Engineering** was established in 1964, under the charter of the National Academy of Sciences, as a parallel organization of outstanding engineers. It is autonomous in its administration and in the selection of its members, sharing with the National Academy of Sciences the responsibility for advising the federal government. The National Academy of Engineering also sponsors engineering programs aimed at meeting national needs, encourages education and research, and recognizes the superior achievements of engineers. Dr. William A. Wulf is president of the National Academy of Engineering.

The **Institute of Medicine** was established in 1970 by the National Academy of Sciences to secure the services of eminent members of appropriate professions in the examination of policy matters pertaining to the health of the public. The Institute acts under the responsibility given to the National Academy of Sciences by its congressional charter to be an adviser to the federal government and, upon its own initiative, to identify issues of medical care, research, and education. Dr. Kenneth I. Shine is president of the Institute of Medicine.

The **National Research Council** was organized by the National Academy of Sciences in 1916 to associate the broad community of science and technology with the Academy's purposes of furthering knowledge and advising the federal government. Functioning in accordance with general policies determined by the Academy, the Council has become the principal operating agency of both the National Academy of Sciences and the National Academy of Engineering in providing services to the government, the public, and the scientific and engineering communities. The Council is administered jointly by both Academies and the Institute of Medicine. Dr. Bruce M. Alberts and Dr. William A. Wulf are chairman and vice chairman, respectively, of the National Research Council.

v

Foreword

Christopher Edley, Jr.

The President's Race Initiative was launched in June 1997 in the belief that no challenge facing the nation as it enters the new century is as critical and daunting as the challenge of color. Around the world and throughout human history, there have been countless tragedies born of our seemingly innate tendencies toward misunderstanding, distrust, resentment, prejudice, hatred, and even violence—all triggered by racial, ethnic, tribal, and religious differences. It would be hubris to believe that Americans have somehow escaped this human condition, miraculously healed and henceforth immune from our own color-based brand of tribalism. We are unlikely in the next few years to face the upheavals of ethnic cleansing familiar from the Balkans and Central Africa, or the slow burn of ethnicity-based conflict and even terrorism we have witnessed in Sri Lanka, Indonesia, Northern Ireland, Spain, Mexico, and countless other places. The growth of America's diversity is breathtaking. However, unless we in the United States do better to confront and bind our racial and ethnic divisions, the powerful legacy of racial caste will shackle our progress and rend our communities.

Our secular catechism of equality and justice for all, authored at the nation's birth, was belied by practices at the time. Yet these remain the powerful ideals to which we aspire, at least in our nobler moments, and without regard to political party or social status. One could even argue that the essence of being an American has much more to do with allegiance to our conceptions of justice and fairness than it does to proficiency in a common language or devotion to some vague set of cultural practices. (Baseball? Apple pie? Some religion? Television?) When Americans express patriotic pride, we may mention our relative prosperity or some iconic character trait such as self-reliance. But more likely, we boast about our civic institutions and, especially, civic values such as equality and tolerance.

Racial caste in this land is more than twice as old as the nation itself. It began with the campaigns of displacement, killing, and subjugation of native peoples by European settlers, and then expanded to the chattel slavery of imported Africans. Because the roots of American prejudice and racism are some 250 years deeper than the bedrock of our constitutional ideals, it would be yet another form of hubris to believe that the legacy can be undone in a mere generation or two, and the wounds healed. Nonetheless, healing with unflagging determination is precisely what we must be about. The first step must be a better understanding of our history and our present condition. This is where the leaders of the social sciences have an indispensable contribution to make. The Race Initiative asked the National Research Council of the National Academies to provide the nation with an authoritative assessment of where we are. *America Becoming: Racial Trends and Their Consequences* is the result.

America Becoming details demographic changes that have moved America beyond Black and White into a complex multiethnic environment that we still do not understand. Disparities, discrimination, progress, and retrogression within this multilayered economic and social environment demonstrate that the color question is pervasive in our lives, and it is an explicit tension or at least subtext in countless policy debates. These debates range from K-12 school improvement, to criminal justice, to reinvention of the health care system.

The premise is that rational explication, based in research, can make a difference in the pursuit of our ideals. There is, unfortunately, substantial evidence to the contrary when it comes to race and ethnicity. The difficulties are of many sorts. These volumes amply illustrate that there is no shortage of factual, methodological, and conceptual challenges in studying "race"—itself a contingent social construct, rather than a fixed biological or anthropological one. They also illustrate that the research enterprise, try as we might, is almost inextricably tied to our politics—to the currents of public values, interests, and debates. There are contestable judgments implicit in the choice of data we decide to keep, the subjects scholars choose to investigate (and that can attract funding), the questions and variables researchers select, the interpretations and application of the research findings, and so forth. All of this means that research related to race has been the victim of the public's decreased interest in civil rights in the past 25 years, and that even sound research results have often been viewed through lenses shaped by political or ideological agendas.

In the complex agenda of color and ethnicity, it is vital that researchers contribute to a reengagement of both the public and the research community, despite the difficulties and risks. In these papers, researchers repeatedly identify important questions requiring further research. The greatest success of *America Becoming* will be in providing the impetus for a reinvigoration of the social scientific commitment to the cause of racial and ethnic justice: to answer and raise questions, to guide and critique policy actors, to take stock, and, especially, to teach.

America Becoming will be instrumental in feeding thoughtful debate. There is ample nourishment here, to be sure, and one can find in the media and countless communities and institutions reason to hope that the appetite for serious civic discourse on the matter of race is on the rise. In colleges and universities, to take one example, dialogues on race have proliferated, and one must hope that a resurgence of sophisticated course offerings in this field will be a signal achievement of this decade. As we prepare students to live and lead in increasingly diverse communities, it is education malpractice if we fail to provide an understanding of where America is and has been on these troubling matters.

Race is not rocket science; it is harder than rocket science. Race demands an intellectual investment equal to the task. It also demands relentlessness in research and teaching that will overwhelm the human tendency to let our differences trigger the worst in our natures.

Acknowledgments

The editors would like to acknowledge the role that many people and agencies played in contributing to the success of the Research Conference on Racial Trends in the United States and the report based on that conference, *America Becoming: Racial Trends and Their Consequences*.

The conference grew out of discussions between the National Research Council (NRC) and the President's Initiative on Race. Judith Winston, the executive director of the Initiative, and her staff, including Lin Liu and John Goering, were engaged and helpful throughout the process. The additional support of Christopher Edley, Jr. (special adviser to the Initiative), Rebecca Blank (Council of Economic Advisers), Peter Rundlet (White House), and Katherine Wallman (Office of Management and Budget), was indispensable. Their ability to demonstrate the importance of the documentation of racial trends persuaded many agencies to support the conference. An advisory committee, made up of representatives of the sponsoring agencies and chaired by Rebecca Blank, met several times with NRC staff during the conference planning period. This committee provided the NRC with very helpful feedback and advice.

The sponsors of the conference included the Bureau of Transportation Statistics of the U.S. Department of Transportation, the Economic Research Service of the U.S. Department of Agriculture, the Environmental Protection Agency, the National Institute of Justice of the U.S. Department of Justice, the Office of the Assistant Secretary for Planning and Evaluation of the U.S. Department of Health and Human Services, the

President's Initiative on Race, the U.S. Department of Defense, the U.S. Department of Education, the U.S. Department of Energy, the U.S. Department of Housing and Urban Development, the U.S. Department of the Interior, and the U.S. Department of Labor. A generous Mellon Foundation grant provided support for the dissemination of *America Becoming*. Thanks to the paper authors, discussion leaders, and other presenters, the intellectual content and tone of the conference were of the highest quality from beginning to end. We would like to thank: Bruce Alberts, chairman of the National Research Council and president of the National Academy of Sciences, Richard Alba, Marcus Alexis, Rebecca Blank, Alfred Blumstein, Lawrence Bobo, Frank Bonilla, Thomas Boston, John Sibley Butler, Albert Camarillo, Ken Chay, Beverly Coleman-Miller, Cecilia Conrad, Christopher Edley, Jr., Reynolds Farley, Ronald Ferguson, Roberto Fernandez, Rodolfo de la Garza, Peter Gottschalk, Darnell Hawkins, Jennifer Hochschild, Harry Holzer, James S. Jackson, Paul Jargowsky, Gerald Jaynes, Renée Jenkins, James Jones, Thomas Kane, Randall Kennedy, Raynard Kington, Sanders Korenman, Betsy Lozoff, Anthony Marx, Douglas Massey, Vonnie McLoyd, Robert Moffitt, Charles Moskos, Don Nakanishi, the late Herbert Nickens, Eugene Oddone, Michael Omi, Manuel Pastor, Laura Petersen, Sharon Robinson, Gary Sandefur (with Molly Martin, Jennifer Eggerling-Boeck, Susan E. Mannon, and Ann M. Meier), Thomas Shapiro, Daryl Smith, James Smith, Matthew Snipp, Carol Swain, Russell Thornton, Mary Waters, Morris Weinberger, David Williams, and Min Zhou.

This report was reviewed in draft form by individuals chosen for their diverse perspectives and technical expertise, in accordance with procedures approved by the NRC's Report Review Committee. The purpose of this independent review was to provide candid and critical comments that assist the institution in making the published report as sound as possible and to ensure that the report meets institutional standards for objectivity, evidence, and responsiveness to the study charge. To protect the integrity of the deliberative process, the review comments and draft manuscript remain confidential.

We are indebted to the following individuals for their helpful comments on a previous draft of *America Becoming*: Robert Bates (Harvard University), Lawrence Friedman (Stanford University), Jack Geiger (CUNY Medical School), Robert M. Hauser (University of Wisconsin), Christopher S. Jencks (Harvard University), Eleanor E. Maccoby (Stanford University), Cora B. Marrett (University of Massachusetts), Robert A. Moffitt (Johns Hopkins University), T. Paul Schultz (Yale University), Tim Smeeding (Syracuse University), and Kenneth I. Wolpin (University of Pennsylvania). However, responsibility for the final content of this report rests entirely with the editors and the National Academy of Sciences.

We would like to thank the Committee on National Statistics of the Commission on Behavioral and Social Sciences and Education for their involvement in this project. In addition, many commission staff either volunteered their time during the conference or worked on bringing the report to completion. Margo Cullen, Myrna McKinnon, Brenda McLaughlin, Janet Overton, and Ronné Wingate from the Commission's Division on Social and Economic Studies all contributed to finalizing the manuscript, under the masterful guidance of CBASSE reports editor Christine McShane.

Finally, Barbara Boyle Torrey, executive director of CBASSE, has been an essential player throughout, contributing her fine intelligence, humor, and insight to the planning and execution of this enormous endeavor.

Neil J. Smelser
William Julius Wilson
Faith Mitchell

Contents

APPENDIXES

TABLES AND FIGURES

Tables

Figures

Contents
Volume I

NEIGHBORHOOD AND GEOGRAPHIC TRENDS

APPENDIXES

Terminology Used in This Report

As many of the authors point out, the term "race" as used to categorize ethnic origins of human beings is a social construct and has no biological basis. Nevertheless, we have come to identify certain terms and names with certain groups of people. The variety of those terms was reflected in the various authors' usage choices; often, more than one term was used for the same group in the same paper. For the purposes of these volumes, we will use the terms as recommended by the U.S. Office of Management and Budget (OMB) in 1999: it coded race into five single-race groups: White, Black, American Indian or Alaska Native, Asian or Pacific Islander, and Other. These terms are defined the terms as follows:

American Indian or Alaska Native. A person having origins in any of the original peoples of North and South America (including Central America), and who maintains tribal affiliation or community attachment.

Asian. A person having origins in any of the original peoples of the Far East, Southeast Asia, or the Indian subcontinent including, for example, Cambodia, China, India, Japan, Korea, Malaysia, Pakistan, the Philippine Islands, Thailand, and Vietnam.

Black or African American. A person having origins in any of the black racial groups of Africa. Terms such as "Haitian" or "Negro" can be used in addition to "Black or African American."

Native Hawaiian or Other Pacific Islander. A person having origins in any of the original peoples of Hawaii, Guam, Samoa, or other Pacific Islands.

White. A person having origins in any of the original peoples of Europe, the Middle East, or North Africa.

Hispanic or Latino. With respect to ethnicity, is defined as: Hispanic or Latino. A person of Cuban, Mexican, Puerto Rican, South or Central American, or other Spanish culture or origin, regardless of race. The term "Spanish origin" can be used in addition to "Hispanic or Latino." (Note: A Hispanic person can be Black or White.)

Again, for the purposes of brevity and consistency, the terms used throughout these volumes are those recommended by OMB—American Indian or Alaska Native, Asian or Pacific Islander, Black, Hispanic, and White. Where necessary to distinguish, non-Hispanic Black and non-Hispanic White are used.

SOURCE: Tabulation Working Group, Interagency Committee for the Review of Standards for Data on Race and Ethnicity. 1999. Draft Provisional Guidance on the Implementation of the 1997 Standards for the Collection of Federal Data on Race and Ethnicity (3-5,65; February 17, 1999). Washington, D.C.: Executive Office of the President, Office of Management and Budget.

AMERICA BECOMING

1

Racial Trends in the Administration of Criminal Justice

Randall Kennedy

N o area in American life is more volatile than the point at which charges of racial injustice intersect with the administration of criminal law (Kennedy, 1997; Cole, 1998; Tonry, 1995; *Chicago Kent Law Review*, 1998; *Harvard Law Review*, 1988). Examples include the Watts, California, riot of 1965; the Liberty City, Florida, riot of 1980; and the Los Angeles, California, riot of 1992—all of which were ignited by incidents that dramatized, or were at least perceived as involving, racial unfairness in criminal-law enforcement. The Los Angeles riot is characteristic. It followed the acquittal of police officers charged with criminally assaulting a Black motorist, the now-legendary Rodney King, by a jury that contained no Black members. The outpouring of violent anger following that acquittal reflected, to a large extent, a deep-seated belief on the part of many Blacks that the judicial process is unfairly stacked against them, whether they be defendants or victims of crime. In a 1995 Gallup Poll, more than one-half of the Black people questioned said that they believed the administration of criminal justice is racially biased against them. Two-thirds indicated that, in their view, anti-Black police racism is common throughout the country (Gallup Poll, 1995).

The racial demographics of criminal-law enforcement provide ample nourishment for these impressions. Blacks are victimized by crime at rates that are dramatically higher than the rates at which Whites are victimized, and at every income level, except for the poorest (annual household income less than $7,500). Whereas White victimization rates decline as income increases, Black victimization rates rise as income increases.

Whites in the highest income bracket ($75,000 or more) are the least victimized by crimes of violence, with a rate of 36.6 crimes per 1,000 persons; Blacks in the highest income bracket are the most victimized group, with a rate of 104 reported crimes per 1,000 persons (U.S. Department of Justice, 1996). As regards homicide, in 1995, there were 5.1 homicide victims per 100,000 non-Hispanic White men; by contrast, there were 57.6 homicide victims per 100,000 Black men—more than 10 times the White rate (Stone, 1998; Rose and McClain, 1990; Hagan and Peterson, 1995). This disparity in victimization extends to other violent crimes and gives rise to the oft-stated assertion that local, state, and federal governments would respond differently if Whites were hit as hard by criminality as Blacks.

At the same time, Blacks are arrested, convicted, and incarcerated at far higher rates than Whites or any other ethnic or racial group. To note one of many disturbing statistical patterns, in the 1990s, the chance that a Black male born in the United States would go to prison for a felony was about 28.5 percent; the chance for a White male was 4.4 percent (Bonczar and Beck, 1997). Against this backdrop, it should not be surprising that frustration, anger, fear, suspicion, even paranoia have seeped into the perceptions of many observers of the criminal justice system across the racial and ideological landscape.

This paper explores racial controversies in three contexts—policing, jury service, and punishment—that have a broad impact on the daily lives of millions of Americans of all races. The goal is to frame the major debates under discussion in these areas, to describe governing law, and to posit the likely course of legal developments in the future.

This paper focuses almost wholly on Black-White conflicts, although racial controversies embrace a wide array of intergroup conflicts. Chris Stone, Director of the Vera Institute of Justice, correctly asserts, however,- that there is a remediable dearth of information about racial issues in the administration of criminal justice outside of the Black-White conflict (Stone, 1999).[1] Careful analysis of racial problems in the United States would be overwhelmed if commentators were forced to deal comprehensively with all complexions of racial conflict anytime they discussed racial injustice. It is also true, however, that too much focus on the Black-White racial paradigm has sometimes led to a debilitating parochialism in analysis and imagination (*Stanford Law Review*, 1995).

The Black-White focus of this paper notwithstanding, much of what is analyzed is applicable to other points of friction along America's varied racial fault-lines. Black-White conflict is placed at center stage here be-

---

[1]For an example of the sort of study that is much needed, see U.S. Department of Justice, Bureau of Justice Statistics, American Indians and Crime (February, 1999).

cause it has been and remains the paradigmatic form of racial conflict in the United States, because it has generated by far the most law governing race relations in the administration of criminal justice, and because concerns about the continued subordination of Blacks in particular prompted the Presidential "conversation on race," from which this paper and this entire Conference stem.

RACIAL PROFILING IN POLICING CITIZENS

Limitations of space preclude detailed consideration of other noteworthy topics such as allegations of racial discrimination in resort to violence by police (Kennedy, 1997:113-125). One reason for focusing on racial profiling by police, as opposed to racially discriminatory police violence is that racial profiling, though less dramatic than racially discriminatory police violence, directly touches more people. Furthermore, as a matter of policy, racial profiling by police is far more controversial than racially discriminatory resort to violence. Although no persons in positions of governmental authority publicly defend racial discrimination in the infliction of force, some officials and commentators do defend some forms of racial profiling (Goldberg, 1999).

Police routinely use a person's race in calculating whether, or to what extent, to subject that person to surveillance, questioning, searching, or perhaps some greater level of investigation (Kennedy, 1997; Cole, 1998; Harris, 1997; Sklansky, 1997; Maclin, 1998). Police use of racial characteristics as probabilistic hints of suspiciousness is widely known as "racial profiling." Critics of racial profiling often portray it as a practice under which police stop, question, and/or search persons "solely" on the basis of their race. In actuality, in profiling, race is typically not the *only* indicator of a need for caution, a level of risk, or a risk of danger. However, race is perceived by police officials doing the profiling as a negative trait that marks the bearer of that trait as a person more likely to cause a criminal problem than similarly situated people without that trait. These police officials thus view and treat Blacks—especially young Black men—differently than similarly situated Whites. This differential treatment on a racial basis is racial discrimination. This is not to say—at least not yet—that this racial discrimination is unjustified. The point, for now, is simply that racial profiling is a type of racial discrimination even though proponents of this practice often decline to use the term "discrimination" when defending it.

That police routinely use racial proxies in making determinations of suspiciousness is well established. Some officers do so, but later claim that they do not. Other officers do so, and candidly admit the nature of their conduct. When courts have been asked to repudiate the practice of using race, along with other variables, in situations in which there exist no obvious signs of an intent to commit a crime, they have generally refused to do so. A statement that mirrors the existing conventional wisdom within the judiciary was made in a finding by a U.S. court of appeals upholding the legality of a search based on racial profiling conducted by Drug Enforcement Agency (DEA) agents. In *United States v. Weaver*, DEA officers were asked to explain why they stopped and questioned a passenger who had deplaned from a flight originating in Los Angeles, California, and terminating in Kansas City, Missouri. The agents explained, under oath, that they investigated the passenger because he was "roughly dressed," young, aboard a flight from a notorious exporting center for drugs to a notorious importing center for drugs, had no checked luggage, possessed two carry-on bags, appeared to be nervous . . . and was Black.

In finding for the United States, the court declared (*United States v. Weaver*, 966 F. 2d 391, CA 8 1992; cert. denied, 506 U.S. 1040, 1992) that, "Large groups of our citizens should not be regarded by law enforcement officers as presumptively criminal based upon their race." However, the court went on to say:

> Facts are not to be ignored simply because they may be unpleasant— and the unpleasant fact in this case is that [the DEA agent] had knowledge, based upon his own experience and upon the intelligence reports he had received from the Los Angeles authorities, that young male members of the Black Los Angeles gangs were flooding the Kansas City area with cocaine. To that extent, then, race, when coupled with the other factors [the agent] relied upon, was a factor in the decision to approach and ultimately detain [the suspect]. We wish it were otherwise, but we take the facts as they are presented to us, not as we would like them to be.

One noteworthy feature of this finding is the casual, impressionistic cast of its empirical underpinnings. A dissenting judge argued that his colleagues lacked the information needed to gauge whether, or the extent to which, Blackness actually correlated with a higher risk of drug trafficking. The judge maintained that, "If we had evidence that young Blacks in Los Angeles were more prone to drug offenses than young Whites, the fact that a young person is Black might be of some significance." He noted, though, that the government had presented no evidence on this point, but had simply relied on common impressions as a basis for a decision. Insisting on a showing of concrete and precise evidence before using race as proxy, the dissenting judge argued that "use of race as a factor [in determining suspiciousness] simply reinforces the type of stereotyping that lies behind drug-carrier profiles. When public officials begin to regard large groups of citizens as presumptively criminal, this country is in a perilous situation indeed."

A second noteworthy feature of the court's statement (as well as that of the dissenting judge) is the assumption that a simple showing of a correlation between the bearing of certain traits, including race, and the commission of certain crimes would justify police use of that trait as a proxy for enhanced risk. This runs counter to strong trends in federal constitutional antidiscrimination law. Generally speaking, any governmental use of racial distinctions is strongly discouraged. Such conduct is presumed to be invalid unless the government can show a compelling reason why the drawing of racial distinctions is necessary, and that the racial lines drawn are narrowly tailored to address the exigency said to necessitate the racial discrimination.

Judicial discouragement of governmental use of racial discrimination has been vigorously pursued against affirmative action programs.[2] That such discouragement is absent, or at a lesser pitch, in the context of police interference with persons of color is itself a revealing anomaly that, perhaps, discloses a line of judicial racial discrimination.

Police use of racial proxies in determining suspiciousness generates anger, humiliation, distrust, and resentment that is deeply felt by large sectors of Black communities. A consequence is lessened respect for the guardians of law and order in many of the communities most in need of effective public policing. Black journalist Don Wycliff states, for example, that notwithstanding his middle-class status and law-abiding character, he feels "an ambivalence tilting towards antipathy for the police." He feels that way, he explains, because "a dangerous, humiliating . . . encounter with the police is almost a rite of passage for a Black man in the United States" (Wycliff, 1987). Similarly, Don Jackson, a Black man and a former police officer, writes that "police have long been the greatest nemesis of Blacks . . . whether we are complying with the law or not. [Police use of racial proxies have signaled to Blacks] that there are cars we are not supposed to drive, streets we are not supposed to walk. [The Black American] finds that the most prominent reminder of his second-class citizenship are the police" (Jackson, 1989:A25).

A large and growing literature repeats and elaborates on the sentiments expressed by Wycliff and Jackson.[3] Henry Louis Gates, Jr. (1995), wrote a particularly instructive article touching on this subject soon after

---

[2] See e.g., *Adarand Constructors, Inc v. Pena*, 115 S. Ct. 2097 (1995); *Shaw v. Hunt*, 116 S. Ct. 1894 (1996); *Hopwood v. Texas*, 78 F. 3d 932 (CA 5 1996), cert. denied , 116 S. Ct. 2581 (1996).

[3] For a report by a statistician that supplies a more objective gloss on these subjective perceptions see John Lamberth, Driving While Black; A Statistician Proves That Prejudice Still Rules the Road, August 16, *Washington Post*, 1998.

the acquittal of O.J. Simpson on charges of murder. Examining responses by elite Blacks to the furor surrounding that acquittal, Gates relates:

> Blacks—in particular, Black men—swap their experience of police encounters like war stories, and there are few who don't have more than one story to tell. Erroll McDonald, one of the few prominent Blacks in publishing, tells of renting a Jaguar in New Orleans and being stopped by the police—simply "to show cause why I shouldn't be deemed a problematic Negro in a possible stolen car." . . . Nor does William Julius Wilson wonder why he was stopped near a small New England town by a policeman who wanted to know what he was doing in those parts. There's a moving violation that many African-Americans know as D.W.B.: Driving While Black.

In the late 1990s, there was a groundswell of attention paid to the issue of "racial profiling" (e.g., *New York Times*, 1999; Holmes, 1999a; *St. Louis Post-Dispatch*, 1999; Drummond, 1999). Legislation that would encourage the collection of data on the racial demographics of police surveillance and investigation has been proposed in Congress.[4] The Report by the Advisory Board to the President's Initiative on Race stated that racial profiling should receive greater scrutiny from the Executive Branch (The President's Initiative on Race Advisory Board, 1998). In 1999, President Clinton promulgated an Executive Order instructing federal law enforcement agencies to collect racial data on persons stopped or arrested and commented that, in his view, racial profiling "is wrong . . . destructive and . . . must stop" (Holmes, 1999b; Fletcher, 1999).

Although these developments may seem, at first blush, clear and encouraging, the reality of the controversy surrounding racial profiling is ambiguous and sobering. A major problem is that the term "racial profiling" is quickly and quietly becoming defined all too narrowly as merely the most blatant and indefensible version of racial profiling—an exclusive or heavy emphasis on race in determining suspiciousness, a practice that a consensus of opinion already condemns. At the same time, the more widespread practice of using race as a probabilistic marker, along with other indicia of suspiciousness, is being insulated from scrutiny and reform by a widespread failure to acknowledge that it, too, constitutes racial profiling and thus racial discrimination. As racial discrimination, racial profiling is a form of social differentiation and should be made to bear a very heavy burden of justification. Unfortunately, racial profiling is

---

[4]See, e.g., the proposed Traffic Stops Statistics Act of 1997, H.R. 118, 105th Congress (1997), which would require the collection of information about drivers stopped for traffic offenses, including the race of the driver, the reason for the stop, and the rationale for any search following the stop.

likely to continue as a lawful form of police practice for the foreseeable future, so long as it is implemented with sufficient politeness and subtlety to avoid a clear confrontation with the racial logic that it embodies.

PREEMPTIVE CHALLENGE IN JURY SELECTION

Jury service is a second area in which both real and perceived racial discrimination have nourished distrust of the administration of criminal justice. A successful challenge to a state law that expressly excluded Blacks on a racial basis marked the first time that the Equal Protection Clause of the Federal Constitution was interpreted in a race-relations context (*Strauder v. West Virginia*, 100 U.S. 303 1879). Since 1880, hundreds of cases have stemmed from allegations of racial discrimination in the selection of jurors (Kennedy, 1997; Colbert, 1990; Schmidt, Jr., 1983). Such allegations maintain a significant presence on the dockets of state and federal courts. Things have changed considerably since the 1950s when, in the southern United States, well-known, officially sponsored customs purposefully excluded Blacks en masse from jury service.[5] Blatant, large-scale campaigns to bar Black jurors have largely been erased by statutory reforms, along with rigorous judicial enforcement of antidiscrimination norms.

It is still true, however, that purposeful racial discrimination continues to play a substantial role in the selection of jurors. The entry point for the discrimination is a device called the peremptory challenge—a privilege, granted by statute, that generally enables attorneys to reject the seating of a certain number of otherwise eligible jurors without having to convey reasons for doing so. Until 1986, attorneys could lawfully take race into account in deploying their peremptory challenges. If a prosecutor believed that he was more likely to obtain a conviction by using his peremptory challenges to exclude all Blacks from a jury, courts ruled that he could properly do so under the federal constitution. In 1986, however,

---

[5]In 1959, the U.S. Court of Appeals for the Fifth Circuit took judicial notice not only of continuing widespread racial discrimination, but also of the fact that "lawyers residing in many southern jurisdictions rarely, almost to the point of never, raise the issue of systematic exclusion of Negroes from juries." See *United States ex rel Goldsby v. Harpole*, 263 F. 2d 71, 82 (CA 5 1959). Five years later, the same Court of Appeals noted that it understood "what happens when a white attorney for a Negro defendant raises the exclusion issue in a county dominated by segregationist patterns and practices: both the defendant and his attorney will suffer from community hostility." *Whitus v. Balkom*, 333 F. 2d 496 (CA 5 1964) cert. denied, 379 U.S. 931 (1964). Thirty years later, community pressures continued to dissuade some defense attorneys from raising jury discrimination claims in the Deep South. See *Gates v. Zant*, 863 F. 2d 293, cert denied, 493 U.S. 945 (1989) (see also Bright, 1995).

in *Batson v. Kentucky* (476 U.S. 79 [1986]), the Supreme Court changed course, ruling that prosecutors could no longer lawfully take race into account in calculating how to deploy peremptory challenges. The Court did not abolish peremptory challenges; it simply declared that race could no longer lawfully be among that vast universe of variables used to reject prospective jurors—e.g., age, occupation, place of residence, too much education, too little education, pure whimsy, etc.

Given this breadth of discretion left to attorneys, some observers anticipated from the outset of *Batson* that many attorneys would continue their racially discriminatory ways. After all, the wholly unregulated peremptory challenge had a long and cherished lineage. Many attorneys believe that "race matters" in courtrooms and that, therefore, taking race into account in choosing the ultimate arbiters of a dispute is eminently "reasonable" and not merely "prejudiced." Many attorneys believe, moreover, that it is difficult to detect a racially discriminatory peremptory challenge as opposed to a peremptory challenge based on some other, nonracial, basis. For these and other reasons, the fear that the new rule on peremptory challenges would be substantially underenforced has largely been confirmed. Many observers of courtrooms across the nation report that, behind a thin disguise of well-rehearsed pretexts, attorneys continue to deploy racially discriminatory peremptory challenges.

Quantifying the incidence of racial discrimination in this area is difficult. Perpetrators of the unlawful conduct have strong reasons to cover their tracks.[6] It is clear, though, that the extent of the unlawful racial discrimination is considerable. In *People v. McDonald* (530 N.E. 2d 1351, Ill. 1988), for example, three Black men were prosecuted for kidnapping and rape. At trial, the prosecution used 16 of its peremptory challenges to remove all of the Blacks in the pool of potential jurors. An all-White jury then proceeded to convict the defendants. Although *Batson* had not been announced at the time of the trial, it was available by the time their convictions were appealed. Pursuant to a Supreme Court ruling on retroactivity, the Supreme Court of Illinois decided that the defendants should have an opportunity to prove that the prosecutors had been racially discriminatory in their deployment of peremptory challenges. The defendants easily established a prima facie case of discrimination, given the conspicuous racial pattern of the prosecution's peremptory challenges.

---

[6]Prior to the Supreme Court's ruling in *Batson v. Kentucky,* Judge Leonard D. Wexler noted that many attorneys confronting a rule prohibiting them from using racially discriminatory peremptory challenges "will be under enormous pressure to lie regarding their motives . . . . Indeed, it is even possible that an attorney will lie to himself in an effort to convince himself that his motives are legal"—i.e., nonracial (*King v. County of Nassau*, 581 F. Supp. 493, 501-502, E.D. N.Y. 1984).

The prosecution was then asked whether it could give nonracial explanations for its actions. Inasmuch as the prosecution had been initiated prior to *Batson*, it would have been understandable for the prosecutor to have stated candidly that, relying on precedent, he had racially discriminated in his use of peremptory challenges. That, however, is not how the prosecutor responded. Instead he offered nonracial explanations that were transparently specious. For example, the prosecutor claimed to have challenged a 34-year-old Black man because of his youth, yet he had refrained from challenging an 18-year-old White man. He claimed to have peremptorily challenged a 63-year-old Black man on the basis of his advanced age, yet he had refrained from challenging a 67-year-old White man. The Supreme Court of Illinois agreed with a trial court that, regardless of the prosecutor's denials, he did in fact engage in prohibited racial discrimination. In many other cases, however, in which the racial discrimination is evident, judges have for various reasons declined to make a finding of racial discrimination (Raphael and Ungvarsky, 1993).

Surveying all reported decisions of federal and state courts between April 30, 1986 (the date of the *Batson* decision), and December 31, 1993, one researcher uncovered 165 cases in which judges determined that prosecutors used peremptory challenges in a racially discriminatory fashion. This figure amounts to a little more than 10 percent of the 1,101 cases in which criminal defendants alleged that prosecutors were discriminating racially (Melilli, 1996). By itself this figure is troubling. It is an indication of the extent to which some influential persons, including public servants, believe that they can openly evade prohibitions against racial discrimination, *People v. McDonald* being a case in point. More troubling still is that this figure probably undercounts the actual amount of racial discrimination, because it is likely that judges tend to find violations of the *Batson* ruling only when the evidence of discrimination is clear—a condition that a well-schooled attorney can often avoid.

The difficulty of enforcing *Batson*, along with concern that underenforcement will exacerbate public distrust of the criminal justice system, has prompted some observers to demand either a decrease in the number of peremptory challenges available to attorneys or elimination of peremptory challenges altogether. That, however, is unlikely. Courts evince little inclination to invalidate the laws authorizing peremptory challenges; and legislatures evince little inclination to eliminate statutorily a practice that many attorneys continue to embrace as an essential feature of the American adversarial system of litigation.

A second major issue involving the racial demographics of juries involves the question of whether affirmative, race-conscious measures ought to be undertaken to ensure the presence of at least some racial minorities on every jury (or at least every jury deciding a case in which racial minorities are parties). This question is posed because, in many jurisdictions, even in the absence of any purposeful racial discrimination, conventional modes of recruitment and selection yield disproportionately small numbers of prospective Black jurors (Kairys et al., 1977; *Cornell Law Review*, 1997). The underrepresentation of Blacks on juries is attributable to a variety of factors. Voter registration lists are the most commonly used source for lists of prospective jurors. Many Blacks are not registered to vote, and hence do not appear on these lists. Further, to be eligible for jury service, one must receive, complete, and return a questionnaire sent to all prospective jurors. Because Blacks tend to move more often than Whites, a larger percentage of Blacks never receive questionnaires that have been mailed to outdated addresses. When questionnaires are received, Blacks, on average, return them at lower rates than Whites. Finally, among those who do return the questionnaires, larger percentages of Blacks than Whites are disqualified for such things as language deficiencies or conviction for a felony.

A consequence of this small pool is the likelihood that in a substantial number of cases, all-White juries (or juries with no Black participants) will decide cases in which Blacks or other racial minorities are defendants or victims. In a county in Minnesota, for example, 9 percent of the adult population in 1990 were people of color, yet racial minorities constituted only 5.3 percent of the people who sat on grand juries. In 40 percent of the cases, all-White grand juries determined whether to indict suspects; and in this jurisdiction, 71 percent of the criminal suspects and 66 percent of the victims of criminality were people of color (Alschuler, 1995). This is a circumstance that strikes some observers as inherently unfair (Ramirez, 1994; Van Ness, 1994; Potash, 1973). Professor Albert W. Alschuler contends, for example, that "few statements are more likely to evoke disturbing images of American criminal justice than 'the defendant was [indicted or] tried by an all-White jury' " (Alschuler, 1995).

Critics of procedures that yield underrepresentation of Blacks and other people of color have responded in several ways. One response has been to challenge the legality of criteria—e.g., registration as a voter or absence of a felony conviction—that disproportionately exclude Blacks from jury service, albeit with no racial purpose to do so. Courts, however, have generally rebuffed such challenges (Kennedy, 1997; Williams, 1990). Another approach is to take affirmative, race-conscious steps to recruit greater numbers of colored prospective jurors or, going further, to ensure a minimum number of colored jurors in any given proceeding (King, 1993).

One proposal would have judges take racial demographics into account in determining the locale to which cases should be transferred when they conclude that defendants cannot receive a fair hearing at the original place of trial. A judge proceeded in this fashion in the recent trial of the White man accused of murdering Medgar Evers, a Black civil rights activist. Judge L. Breland Hilburn of the Hinds County, Mississippi Circuit Court, moved the trial from Jackson, Mississippi, because of prejudicial pretrial publicity. Faced with the task of determining where to move the trial to, Judge Hilburn chose a jurisdiction with "close to the same racial balance" as Hinds County (Kennedy, 1997).

A second proposal would have court administrators use racially targeted mailings of jury questionnaires to predominantly minority residential areas, organizations, and churches, in an effort to elevate the number of eligible minority jurors. A third proposal would involve subtracting from a jury pool the names of prospective jurors of a majority race in order to make the pool racially "balanced." A fourth proposal would involve reserving a certain number of seats for racial minorities on juries. These proposals have been put into operation in various parts of the country. That this is so indicates that a substantial number of Americans want not only the absence of purposeful racial exclusion in the process of selecting juries, but also want racially mixed juries—even if obtaining that result means using race as a factor in the selection process. There is a trend, in other words, favoring methods of jury selection that facilitate, if not require, the creation of juries that "look like America." On the other hand, there also exists a counter trend that is resistant to race-specific selection schemes. These reforms have been tested judicially to a surprisingly small extent. The existing case law suggests, however, that the future of these reforms is dim. Here, as elsewhere in the controversial area of race-relations law, courts are becoming increasingly skeptical of the legitimacy of policies that take race into account in seeking to redress past inequities or to ensure racial diversity within institutions that might lack a significant presence of people of color.[7]

RACIAL DISPROPORTIONS IN PUNISHMENT

The race question in punishment is another subject with respect to which opinions conflict sharply. Everyone would concede that, for a long period of American history, Blacks were formally discriminated against

---

[7]See, *United States v. Greene*, 971 F. Supp. 1117, 1142 n. 25, E.D. Mich. 1997 (noting without deciding that race-dependent plan "to increase Black representation on the jury is, essentially, a modified system of racial preference, which, regardless of . . . good-faith motivations . . . might be violative of equal protection guarantees."); *State v. Moore*, 404 S.E. 2d. 845, N.C. 1991 (North Carolina Supreme Court invalidates conviction based on race-dependent selection of black grand jury foreman) (see, also, Kennedy, 1997:253-255; King, 1993:27).

in the setting of punishments. Before the Civil War, statutes expressly prescribed more severe punishments for a Black person who engaged in prohibited conduct than for a White person who engaged in the same conduct. Many would concede that, despite formal prohibitions against racial discrimination, informal but blatant racial discrimination played a major role in the imposition of criminal punishments until the civil rights revolution of the 1950s and 1960s. The most striking instance of this sort of discrimination involved capital punishment, especially capital punishment for rape.

In 1949, for example, a group of seven Black men in Virginia were convicted of, and sentenced to death for, raping a White woman. On appeal, the defendants' attorneys showed that between 1908 and 1949, no White man had been executed for rape, though 45 Black men had been put to death for that crime. During those same years, almost twice as many Blacks as Whites convicted of rape were sentenced to life imprisonment (Rise, 1995). The Virginia courts concluded that racial discrimination played no role in the sentence imposed on the seven Black men, and shortly thereafter they were put to death (*Hampton v. Commonwealth*, 58 S.E. 2d 288, 1950). This court decision has been followed by scores of others in which state and federal tribunals have consistently declined to acknowledge racial discrimination in punishment, even in the face of the most provocative statistical patterns (Kennedy, 1997; Wolfgang and Riedel, 1976; Dorin, 1981).

That racial discrimination in punishment once existed as a widespread and easily discernible phenomenon is not controversial. Nor is it controversial to say, now, that judges and other authoritative decision makers erred in dismissing as unfounded allegations of racial discrimination in punishment. What is intensely controversial, however, is the charge that these older patterns persist, that racial discrimination continues to infect sentencing, and that decision makers continue to close their eyes and ears to this invidious practice. The two contexts in which this charge emerges most saliently today involve the imposition of the death penalty and the enforcement of the "war on drugs," particularly that arena of the drug war focused on the eradication of "crack" cocaine.

The leading contemporary case concerning allegations of racial discrimination in the administration of capital punishment is *McCleskey v. Kemp* (481 U.S. 279, 1987), which was decided by the U.S. Supreme Court in 1987. A decade previously, a jury in Georgia—constituted by 11 Whites and 1 Black—sentenced Warren McCleskey, a Black man, to death for the murder of a White police officer, Frank Schlatt, during the course of a robbery. On appeal, McCleskey's attorneys challenged the legality of Georgia's regime of capital punishment on the grounds that it was infected by racial bias, as revealed in striking disparities in sentencing. Even after taking into account a wide range of nonracial variables that would likely affect sentencing—e.g., age, level of education, criminal record, military record, method of killing, motive for killing, relationship of defendant to victim and so forth—researchers, led by Professor David Baldus, determined that the race of the victim continued to have a statistically significant correlation with the imposition of capital punishment (Baldus et al., 1983). Professor Baldus concluded that the odds of being condemned to death were 4.3 times greater for defendants who killed Whites than for defendants who killed Blacks—a variable nearly as influential as a prior conviction for armed robbery, rape, or even murder.

By a bare majority (five to four), the Supreme Court ruled against McCleskey. It concluded that, "At most the Baldus study indicates a discrepancy that appears to correlate with race." The opinion of the Court noted several considerations of policy that influenced the majority's reasoning. One was the need to allow ample latitude in sentencing and use of discretion in making the unique decision of whether to end the life of an individual as a punishment for criminal conduct. Another concern was that ruling in favor of McCleskey would open a Pandora's box of litigation. The Court declared, "McCleskey's claim, taken to its logical conclusion, throws into serious question the principles that underlie our entire criminal justice system [because, if accepted, the Court] could soon be faced with similar claims as to other types of penalty" from members of other groups alleging bias.[8] Finally, the Court invoked considerations of institutional competence and judicial restraint as reasons to avoid intervention; "McCleskey's arguments are best presented to legislative bodies. . . . It is the legislatures, the elected representatives of the people, that are constituted to respond to the will and consequently the moral values of the people."

After the *McCleskey* decision, critics of it did attempt to address the problem of unexplained racial disparities in capital sentencing with a statutory solution. Proposed legislation, dubbed the Racial Justice Act, would have established as *prima facie* evidence of racial discrimination the type of statistical showing that McCleskey had relied on (Schoeman, 1995; Berger et al., 1989). The Supreme Court held that, in order to prevail on a constitutional claim, a defendant would have to show purposeful racial discrimination *in his own particular case*. The Court was unwilling to allow a defendant to prevail on the basis of inferences generated by unexplained and therefore suspicious racial patterns in other cases. By contrast, the proposed Racial Justice Act would have created for a defendant the rebuttable presumption that a statistically significant racial disparity in death

---

[8]Id. at 315.

sentences in a given locale meant that wrongful racial discrimination tainted his sentence, too. The defendant would not automatically win at that point; the disparity would count only as a rebuttable presumption. The locale would be prevented from carrying out the execution, unless it could come forward and show either (a) that there were nonracial reasons that persuasively explained the apparently racial sentencing disparities or (b) that, even in the absence of racial discrimination, the defendant at issue would still have been sentenced to death in light of the enormity of his crime.

Although the House of Representatives twice passed the Racial Justice Act, it failed to win the support of the Clinton Administration, was strenuously opposed by vocal critics (mainly Republicans) in the Senate, and bears little chance of enactment in the foreseeable future. Opponents of the Racial Justice Act contend, as did the dissenting members of the House Committee on the Judiciary, that "While it may be true that killers of White victims are more likely to receive the death penalty than killers of Blacks, this statistical disparity is easily explained by the presence of mitigating or aggravating factors which account for the differences in sentences" (U.S. Congress, House Committee on the Judiciary, 1994); however, in light of the data regarding capital punishment for rape, the Baldus study, and the many other investigations that have consistently reached similar conclusions, it cannot reasonably be said that the racial disparities in question are "easily explained" by nonracial variables. Indeed, given the past and present realities of racial sentiment in the United States, it would be extraordinary if racial bias did not appreciably affect sentencing, including—or perhaps, especially—capital sentencing. This is not to minimize the changes that have significantly improved race relations since the 1950s. It is to note, however, that alongside notable discontinuities in American race relations are certain continuities as well, including myopia when it comes to recognizing invidious racial discrimination in punishment.

The war on drugs frames another hotly contested area in which many allege, and many deny, that racial discrimination substantially affects punishments. That this arena of crime policy would become a principal site of bitter discord should not be at all surprising. On the one hand, minority communities have been peculiarly disrupted by commerce in hard drugs. On the other hand, minority communities have been peculiarly disrupted by efforts to suppress this commerce, especially the imposition of long-term incarceration for drug trafficking. These trends have nourished various apprehensions. One is that the war on drugs is purposefully ineffective because "The White Establishment" actually wants people of color to be dependent on illicit drugs. Another is that the war on drugs is too dependent on punishment and has become a virtual war against colored people, especially young Black men.

No single site in the war on drugs more vividly focuses these tensions than the front on which the U.S. government seeks to obliterate trafficking in crack cocaine. A federal statute enacted in 1986 criminalizes the distribution of crack cocaine with unusual severity. Under that law, a person convicted of possession with intent to distribute 50 grams or more of crack must be sentenced to no fewer than 10 years in prison; by striking contrast, a person has to be convicted of possession with intent to distribute at least 5,000 grams of powder cocaine before being subject to a mandatory minimum of 10 years—a 100:1 ratio in terms of intensity of punishment. Moreover, under a federal statute enacted in 1988, a person caught merely possessing 1 to 5 grams of crack cocaine is subject to a mandatory minimum sentence of 5 years in prison, which makes crack the only drug for which there exists a mandatory minimum penalty for a first offense of simple possession (Anti-Drug Abuse Act of 1988, P.L. 100-690, 102 Stat. 4181, 1988).

Many see this dramatic difference in punishment in racial terms. For one thing, in the perception of many, there exists a fundamental similarity between trafficking in crack and powder: cocaine is cocaine, this argument runs. For another, there exists a clear difference in the racial composition of the pools of people arrested, prosecuted, convicted, and imprisoned for these apparently similar drug offenses. In 1992, 92.6 percent of the defendants convicted for crack cocaine offenses nationally were Black, and only 4.7 percent were White. In comparison, 45.2 percent of defendants sentenced for powder cocaine offenses were White and only 20.7 percent were Black. To many observers, the difference in punishment conjoined with the racial difference in rates of prosecution and incarceration indicates, or at least suggests, racial inequity.

Some jurists have argued that the crack-versus-powder distinction in sentencing violates the Equal Protection Clause of the federal constitution. That argument, though, has been rejected by almost all of the courts that have ruled on the question. The Minnesota Supreme Court did invalidate that state's analogue to the federal crack-versus-powder distinction. Several judges have castigated the 100:1 distinction as excessive and needlessly provocative. Several former Congressional supporters of the crack-versus-powder distinction have changed their minds. In 1995, the U.S. Sentencing Commission recommended eliminating the sentencing differential distinguishing traffickers in crack from traffickers in powder. The Commission suggested a level-down equalization, under which traffickers in crack would have been punished no more harshly than traffickers in powder. The Commission's recommendations would have gone into effect automatically, absent specific disapproval from both Houses of

Congress. With the support of President Clinton, however, the Congress did disapprove—the first time it had done so in the Commission's history.

There is good reason to eschew charges that Congress sought purposefully to target Blacks by enacting the crack-versus-powder distinction. Black members of Congress with long records of attentiveness to claims of racial justice initiated and supported "cracking down on crack." No charges of racism were heard when the crack-versus-powder sentencing differential was initially enacted. Sensational reports in newspapers and on television about the crack epidemic understandably galvanized public opinion and, with it, congressional desires to control this perceived new menace. Moreover, apart from perceptions, there were real differences between crack and powder and other illicit drugs, differences that could reasonably justify punishing trafficking in crack cocaine more harshly than trafficking in powder cocaine.

Putting aside controverted scientific testimony about the relative addictiveness and toxicity of crack versus powder, one difference between the two is accepted universally—crack is sold in smaller quantities at lesser prices in a more convenient form and is, therefore, more accessible to larger groups of people. Crack democratized the cocaine high. It "reinvigorated the cocaine market and greatly increased the population of cocaine abusers" (Duke and Gross, 1993; Kleiman, 1992).[9] That distinction alone could provide a basis for distinguishing crack and powder for purposes of punishment, notwithstanding their common cocaine lineage. Even if crack and powder were otherwise identical, the greater marketability of crack means that it has more potential reach than powder and can thus be sensibly perceived as more socially dangerous.

This is not an endorsement of the crack-versus-powder distinction. There are weighty, perhaps compelling, arguments against it, especially in light of information gained from more than a decade's worth of experience with existing crack penalties. It seems patently wrong to punish a small-scale crack dealer equally, or even more harshly, than a large-scale trafficker in powder cocaine. Moreover, even if racial discrimination played no active role in establishing the crack-versus-powder differential, the appearance of racial unfairness generated by its results forms an important part of an argument in favor of reform. Furthermore, there exists the assertion that (predominantly White) policy-making bodies would

---

[9]According to Professor Kleiman, in 1978 "cocaine was something between a curiosity and a menace . . . . By 1988, cocaine had become the drug problem par excellence, with a retail market nearly equal to those for heroin and marijuana combined . . . . How did a minor drug become so major, a seemingly benign drug so horrible? In a word, crack happened." Id.

react differently if the racial shoe were on the other foot—if more than 90 percent of crack offenders were White instead of Black. If that were so, this speculation runs, policy would be changed because of the clamorings of politically influential constituents terrified by the prospect of their sons and daughters facing 5- and 10-year mandatory minimum prison sentences for relatively low-level drug offenses.

There exist developments that run counter to this speculation. For example, Whites predominate in the trafficking and use of methamphetamine. Yet a federal law was recently enacted that enhanced the punishment for dealing this drug to levels comparable to the sentences imposed on crack dealers (Comprehensive Methamphetamine Control Act of 1996, 21 U.S.C. 801, Pub. L. 104-237, 101 Stat. 3099 [October 3, 1996]). After the Minnesota Supreme Court invalidated that state's crack-versus-powder sentencing differential under the state constitution, the state legislature was put to the test of either leveling up (raising the criminal penalty on powder offenses to that reserved for crack offenses) or leveling down (lowering the penalty on crack offenses to that reserved for powder offenses). The legislature chose to level up, which can be taken as an indication that, regardless of the racial composition of those imprisoned for long periods, policy makers are insistent and consistent in their attack on illicit drugs.

On the other hand, leveling up to equalize punishments will probably not completely negate the suspicions of some skeptics who will continue to believe that racial selectivity accounts, at least in part, for the continuation of severe sentencing policies that have the effect of incarcerating disproportionately large numbers of Blacks. That is, the number of Whites incarcerated for longer periods because of leveling up would remain relatively small in comparison with the overall total White population. Skeptics would likely contend that this small number of marginalized Whites would merely serve as a sacrifice to legitimate a policy that would continue to burden Blacks disproportionately. These skeptics would embrace the contention of Professor Alfred Blumstein who has hypothesized that

> A major factor contributing to [the de facto decriminalization of marijuana] was undoubtedly a realization that the arrestees were much too often the children of individuals, usually White, in positions of power and influence. Those parents certainly did not want the consequences of a drug arrest to be visited on their children, and so they used their leverage to achieve a significant degree of decriminalization (Blumstein, 1993:4).

Critics of the war on drugs in general, and the crack-versus-powder distinction in particular, assert, echoing Blumstein, that punitive policies would be different, less severe, if as large a percentage of White people as

Black people were incarcerated pursuant to these policies (Cole, 1998). Perhaps those who espouse this view are wrong, but one cannot dismiss their claim as wholly implausible. That one cannot do so indicates disturbingly that, despite advances toward racial justice that have been made in the United States of America since 1950, there remains much work to do, much ground to cover.

REFERENCES

Alschuler, A.
    1995   Racial quotas and the jury. *Duke Law Journal* 44(4):704-743.
Baldus, D., C. Pulaski, and G. Woodworth
    1983   Comparative review of death sentences: An empirical study of the Georgia experience. *Journal of Criminal Law and Criminology* 74(3):661-753.
Berger, V., N. Walthour, A. Dorn, D. Lindsey, P. Thompson, and G. von Helms
    1989   Comment, Too much justice: A legislative response to *McCleskey v. Kemp. Harvard Civil Rights—Civil Liberties Law Review* 24(2):437-528.
Blumstein, A.
    1993   Making rationality relevant: The American Society of Criminology 1992 Presidential Address. *Criminology* 31(1):1-16.
Bonczar, T., and A. Beck
    1997   Lifetime Likelihood of Going to State or Federal Prison, NCJ-160092 (March). Washington, D.C.: U.S. Department of Justice, Office of Justice Programs.
Bright, S.
    1995   Discrimination, death and denial: The tolerance of racial discrimination in infliction of the death penalty. *Santa Clara Law Review* 35(2):433-483.
Bueker, J.
    1997   Note, Jury source lists: Does supplementation really work? *Cornell Law Review* 82(2):390-431.
Colbert, D.
    1990   Challenging the challenge: Thirteenth Amendment as a prohibition against the racial use of peremptory challenges. *Cornell Law Review* 76(1):1-128.
Cole, D.
    1999   *No Equal Justice: Race and Class in the American Criminal Justice System.* New York: New Press.
Dorin, D.
    1981   Two different worlds: Criminologists, justices and racial discrimination in the imposition of capital punishment in rape cases. *Journal of Criminal Law and Criminology* 72(4):1667-1698.
Drummond, T.
    1999   It's not just in New Jersey; Cops across the U.S. often search people just because of their race, a study says. *Time* (June 14).
Duke, S., and A. Gross
    1993   *America's Longest War: Rethinking Our Tragic Crusade Against Drugs.* New York: Putnam.
Fletcher, M.
    1999   Clinton orders data collection in effort to halt "racial profiling." *Washington Post* (June 10).
Gallup Poll Monthly
    1995   October.

Gates, H., Jr.
1995 Thirteen ways of looking at a black man. *New Yorker* (October 23).
Goldberg, J.
1999 The color of suspicion. *New York Times Magazine* (June 20).
Hagan, J., and R. Peterson
1995 Criminal inequality in America: Patterns and consequences. In *Crime and Inequality*, J. Hagan and R. Peterson, eds. Stanford, Calif.: Stanford University Press.
Harris, D.
1997 "Driving While Black" and all other traffic offenses: The Supreme Court and pretextual traffic stops. *Journal of Criminal Law and Criminology* 87(2):544-582.
Harvard Law Review
1988 Developments in the law—Race and the criminal process. *Harvard Law Review* 101(7):1472-1641.
Holmes, S.
1999a The stark reality of racial profiling. *New York Times* (June 13).
1999b Clinton orders investigation on possible racial profiling. *New York Times* (June 10).
Jackson, D.
1989 Police embody racism to my people. *New York Times* (January 23).
Kairys, D., J. Kadane, and J. Lehoczky
1977 Jury representativeness: A mandate for multiple source lists. *California Law Review* 65(4):776-827.
Kennedy, R.
1997 *Race, Crime and the Law.* New York: Pantheon Books.
King, N.
1993 Racial jurymandering: Cancer or cure? A contemporary review of affirmative action in jury selection. *New York University Law Review* 68(4):707-776.
Kleiman, M.
1992 *Against Excess: Drug Policy for Results.* New York: Basic Books.
Lamberth, J.
1998 Driving while Black; A statistician proves that prejudice still rules the road. *Washington Post* (August 16).
Maclin, T.
1998 Race and the Fourth Amendment. *Vanderbilt Law Review* 51(2):333-393.
McAdams, R, ed.
1998 Symposium on race and criminal law. *Chicago Kent Law Review* 73:467.
Melilli, K.
1996 *Batson* in practice: What we have learned about *Batson* and peremptory challenges. *Notre Dame Law Review* 71(3):447-503.
New York Times
1999 Getting the facts on racial profiling. *New York Times* (June 11).
Potash, D.
1973 Mandatory inclusion of racial minorities on jury panels. *Black Law Journal* 3(1):80-95.
President's Initiative on Race Advisory Board
1998 *One America in the 21st Century: Forging a New Future—The Initiative on Race Advisory Board's Report to the President.* Washington, D.C.: U.S. Government Printing Office.
Ramirez, D.
1994 The mixed jury and the ancient custom of trial by jury *de medietate linguae*: A history and a proposal for change. *Boston University Law Review* 74(5):777-818.

Raphael, M., and E. Ungvarsky
    1993   Excuses, excuses: Neutral explanations under *Batson v. Kentucky. University of Michigan Journal of Law Reform* 27(1):229-275.
Rise, E.
    1995   *The Martinsville Seven: Race, Rape, and Capital Punishment.* Charlottesville: University Press of Virginia.
Rose, H., and P. McClain
    1990   *Race, Place, and Risk: Black Homicide in Urban America.* Albany: State University of New York Press.
Schmidt, Jr., B.
    1983   Juries, jurisdiction, and race discrimination: The lost promise of *Strauder v. West Virginia. Texas Law Review* 61(8):1401-1499.
Schoeman, P.
    1995   Note, Easing the fear of too much justice: A compromise proposal to revise the Racial Justice Act. *Harvard Civil Rights—Civil Liberties Law Review* 30(2):543-576.
Sklansky, D.
    1997   Traffic stops, minority motorists, and the future of the Fourth Amendment. *Supreme Court Review* 271-329.
Stanford Law Review
    1995   Symposium, Race and remedy in a multicultural society. *Stanford Law Review* 47(5):819-1026.
St. Louis Post-Dispatch
    1999   An end to racial profiling. *St. Louis Post-Dispatch* (June 14).
Stone, C.
    1998   *Race, Crime, and the Administration of Justice: A Summary of the Available Facts.* Vera Institute of Justice.
    1999   Race, crime, and the administration of justice: A summary of available facts. *National Institute of Justice Journal* (April).
Tonry, M.
    1995   *Malign Neglect—Race, Crime, and Punishment in America.* New York: Oxford University Press.
U.S. Congress, House Committee on the Judiciary
    1994   Dissenting Views on Racial Justice Act, Report 103-458 of the 103rd Congress, 2d Sess., March 24.
    1996   Comprehensive Methamphetamine Control Act of 1996, 21 U.S.C. 801, Pub. L. 104-237, 101 Stat. 3099 (October 3, 1996).U.S. Department of Justice
U.S. Department of Justice
    1996   Criminal Victimization in the United States, 1993—A National Crime Victimization Survey. Report 23, 26-27 (May). Washington, D.C.: U.S. Government Printing Office.
Van Ness, D.
    1994   Preserving a community voice: The case for half-and-half juries in racially-charged criminal cases. *John Marshall Law Review* 28(1):1-56.
Williams, C.
    1990   Jury source representativeness and the use of voter registration lists. *New York University Law Review* 65(3):590-634.
Wolfgang. M., and M. Riedel
    1976   Rape, racial discrimination, and the death penalty. Pp. 99-121 in *Capital Punishment in the United States,* H. Bedau and C. Pierce, eds. New York: AMS Press, Inc.
Wycliff, D.
    1987   Blacks and blue power. *New York Times* (February 8).

2

Race and Criminal Justice

Alfred Blumstein

The interaction between race or minority status and the criminal justice system is a particularly salient aspect of the racial problems in the United States, and it represents one of the crucial issues that must be addressed as the nation tries to deal with its racial conflicts. There is a large disproportionate representation of minorities, especially Blacks, involved in all aspects of the criminal justice system; and this disproportionality alone, regardless of its legitimacy, conveys a profound sense of unfairness to the overrepresented groups. That sense of unfair treatment is certainly reflected in many polls that show a sharp difference between minority groups and others in their assessment of the fairness of the system. By its very name, the "justice" system carries a particularly heavy burden—it must not only be fair, but it must also be seen as being fair. These concerns are undoubtedly why one of the four missions President Clinton posed to the Race Initiative Advisory Board was to "address crime and the administration of justice."

There are clearly profound differences in the involvement of different racial groups with the criminal justice system. The differences are most stark between Blacks and non-Hispanic Whites. For example:

This critique is based on Randall Kennedy's paper, "Racial Trends in the Administration of Criminal Justice," prepared for the Research Conference on Racial Trends in the United States. National Research Council, Washington, D.C., October 15-16, 1998.

- Blacks' incarceration rate in 1999 was 2.8 times their rate in 1980.
- Blacks' incarceration rate in 1999 was 8.2 times the incarceration rate for non-Hispanic Whites.
- Of the Black population, 1.6 percent was incarcerated in state and federal prisons in 1999 (Blumstein and Beck, 1999: Table 2).
- Of Black males in their 20s, 8.3 percent are in prison in 1999 (Blumstein and Beck, 1999: Table 2).
- It is likely that 28.5 percent of Black males will serve time in a state or federal prison; whereas it is likely that 4.4 percent of non-Hispanic White males will serve time in a state or federal prison (Bonczar and Beck, 1997).
- Of Black males in their 20s, 30 percent were under control of the criminal justice system—prison, jail, probation, or parole (Mauer, 1990)
- In some cities, the rate of Black males in their 20s under control of the criminal justice system exceeds 50 percent (Miller, 1996).

Anyone who looks at these high rates of involvement must find them most distressing, especially for the social control system that is intended to be a last resort for engendering proper behavior in a civil society. Even if they represented totally even-handed administration of justice, the high rates of intrusiveness—and especially the glaring disparities between Blacks and Whites—must raise profound concerns and an intense search for means of reducing the racial disparities. It is then critical to examine the sources of the disparities in order to know where to focus attention to alleviate the problems.

The paper by Randall Kennedy (1998) highlights a number of important examples of policies and practices that contribute to the racial disparities in the criminal justice system.

FACTORS CONTRIBUTING TO THE DISPARITIES

It is important to isolate factors contributing to the disparity, because different factors will lead to different approaches for improvement. We can identify three different contributors:

- individual acts of discrimination,
- policies that have differential racial effects, and
- racial differences in participation in the crimes that lead to involvement with the criminal justice system.

Discrimination

The first and most obvious cause is individual acts of discrimination by police, prosecutors, judges, corrections agencies, or parole authorities. Discrimination is often difficult to identify in an individual case, but statistical patterns of discriminatory decision making can be ascertained. There is little doubt that any such discriminatory behavior should be highlighted, routed out, and guilty officials appropriately dealt with. There can be little doubt that such acts of discrimination occur; but the racial disparities are so great that it strains credulity to believe that in the United States, at the end of the twentieth century, the bulk of the disparities can be attributed to individual acts of discrimination.

Policies with Differential Racial Impact

The second major source of disparity is policies, reflected in statutes or formal administrative actions, that have a racially disparate consequence. For example, sentences meted out for violent crimes, like robbery or homicide, tend to be higher than those for property crimes like burglary. It would be discriminatory if White robbers received shorter sentences than Black robbers, controlling for other legitimate factors that enter into judicial decision making. There should be serious challenge if the sentence for robbery was made more severe than for burglary because Blacks were more disproportionately involved in robbery than in burglary. On the other hand, because society views robbery as a more serious offence than burglary, it is not discriminatory if the respective sentences reflect only that difference in seriousness.

Given the complexity of discerning intentions in the establishment of any policies, it will often be difficult to distinguish clear and simple reasons for any particular policy. But any policy that results in significantly different racial outcomes, that does not have a strong rational basis, must be suspect and should be challenged.

Differential Involvement in Crimes

The third consideration (aside from discrimination and policies with racial consequences) is the differential involvement in the kinds of crimes that give rise to serious punishment. To the extent that the racial disproportionality in prison is a consequence, not of discrimination by the criminal justice system, but rather because more Blacks commit the serious crimes that give rise to incarceration, then we must search outside the criminal justice system for means of changing that behavior, and recognize that improvements within the criminal justice system will fail to diminish those differences.

That again raises the question of whether we punish certain crimes more severely because we consider them to be more serious, or because they are disproportionately engaged in by Blacks or other minority groups. With the exception of drug offenses—and this is an important exception because drug prisoners currently comprise 23 percent of state prisoners and 60 percent of federal prisoners (Blumstein and Beck, 1999)—there seems to be strong evidence that there is a high ordinal association between people's perception of the seriousness of the offense and the time served for them (Blumstein and Cohen, 1980). This poses a research challenge of finding a basis for assessing the rates of commission of various crimes by members of different racial groups.

POLICE PROFILING BASED ON RACE

Kennedy highlights one important policy that is sometimes formal and more often informal—the use of race as a factor in police "profiling," or the use of an individual's attributes to make him a suspect of a particular violation, such as being a drug courier. Here again, there is widespread agreement that use of race alone is entirely inappropriate in any police action. The issue raised in Kennedy's paper is whether race may be used at all, even if it is only one of a number of other factors in profiling. Obviously, the argument for including race requires the presence of a solid empirical basis for strong differences in involvement in certain crimes based on race that are not accounted for by other observable characteristics. Certainly, in the absence of a strong empirical basis, then it would be entirely inappropriate for race to be taken into consideration.

But even if there is an empirical difference, it seems entirely reasonable never to permit race to become a factor in profiling. If it were, then it would open the door to the considerable potential for enhancing racial stereotyping, which can create severe problems in a society working hard to eliminate the remnants of past racism.

Furthermore, with changing conditions, there could well be important changes in the empirical bases linking race to the crime outcome, potentially even eliminating the correlation. Because race has no theoretical meaning in this context, bringing about this change in the profiling would be most difficult in the face of the considerable inertia inhibiting revision of the factors used in profiling.

A further danger of using race in profiling is the relative difficulty in measurement of the different factors in the profile. Race is one of the most readily observed attributes of an individual, so that, even if it is not one of the most important factors in a profile, it can easily become far more salient than other more salient attributes that are more difficult to measure. As a result, it is likely to be given far more weight in the profiling decision than would be warranted, based on its empirical support. Kennedy has noted that courts have generally upheld the use of race in profiling, but one can see strong reasons why it should be prohibited.

In this context, it is useful to note the observation by civil rights leader, Rev. Jesse Jackson, that "there is nothing more painful to me at this stage in my life, than to walk down the street and hear footsteps, and start thinking about robbery—then look around and see somebody White and feel relieved." This provides a clear indication that, even though the use of racial information in profiling may not be inherently irrational, one can find powerful public-policy reasons for precluding its use. The pain to Rev. Jackson, and to the society more broadly, can be far more insidious than whatever crime-control benefit is attained that cannot be attained virtually as well by using other, more acceptable indicators.

PUNISHMENT POLICIES

Perhaps the strongest concerns about racial differences are associated with the ways in which punishment is meted out. The case is made even more conspicuous in the case of capital punishment, which, even if infrequent, is our most extreme sanction, and one that is extremely symbolic because of its connection to the abhorrent traditions of lynching.

Capital Punishment

Kennedy highlights the dilemma of the *McCleskey* case, in which the strong analytic work of Baldus et al. (1983) was presented to the U.S. Supreme Court. Baldus showed that decisions for capital punishment took account of the race of the victim as a salient consideration—i.e., murderers who killed White victims were sentenced to execution more often than those who killed Black victims. The Court chose not to take account of this finding of clear differential treatment based on race because they claimed there was no proof that that consideration applied in the *McCleskey* case.

Another important finding in the Baldus research was the recognition that the race of the offender was not significantly associated with a capital sentence. That finding is a source of some degree of comfort; failing to find that would certainly raise serious concerns about the discriminatory treatment of offenders. The joint effect of these two findings—no effect associated with the race of the offender but a racial bias (often labeled as "victim discounting") associated with the race of the victim—raises a difficult dilemma. The great majority of murders are between people of the same race, with the largest exception being murders committed in the course of a felony such as a robbery. If capital-punishment decisions were purged of victim discounting, that would lead to an increase in the already distressingly high racial disproportionality on death row, regardless of whether capital-punishment rates were reduced to the rates associated with Black victims (thereby freeing many White offenders from capital punishment) or increased to the level associated with White victims (thereby passing a death sentence on many more Black offenders). We have no way of knowing to what extent this dilemma entered the consideration of the Supreme Court in their review of the *McCleskey* case and contributed to their choice not to accommodate the claims that were raised.

Drug Sentencing Policies

Perhaps the most visible of the policies with differential racial impact is the striking disparity highlighted by Kennedy of the federal statute (Anti-Drug Abuse Act of 1988, P.L. No. 100-690, 102 Stat. 4181, 1988 [from Kennedy, 1998]) prescribing mandatory-minimum sentences for possession of cocaine with an intent to deliver. The same mandatory-minimum sentence of 10 years is prescribed for both 50 grams of crack cocaine and for 5,000 grams of powder cocaine, a 100:1 ratio. The underlying presumption is that crack cocaine is more often associated with violence than is powder cocaine. It is also the case, however, that individuals convicted of crack cocaine charges are predominantly Black (according to Kennedy, 92.6 percent compared to 4.7 percent White), while individuals convicted of powder cocaine charges are predominantly White (45.2 percent compared to 20.7 percent Black).

This difference must raise the question of whether this extreme 100:1 disparity is based on rational consideration of violence or whether it is a subterfuge for specifically being more punitive to Blacks, or perhaps some combination. The U.S. Sentencing Commission was sensitive to these concerns and several times asked for changes in this particular racially disparate policy, but Congress rejected those proposals, and so the policies still stand. This is in the face of decisions by other courts, such as the Minnesota Supreme Court, which declared that any treatment difference between crack cocaine and powder cocaine was a violation of at least the Minnesota State Constitution.

Differences in Incarceration Rate

The two previous examples—capital punishment decisions and the drug mandatory-minimum sentences—are certainly important, but they represent a relatively small fraction of the total prison population. But the ratio of 8.2:1 between the incarceration rate for Blacks compared to non-Hispanic Whites applies to the entire prison population, and must raise important concerns. Here, it is important to be able to distinguish how much of this difference is attributable to racial differences in involvement in crime, especially the kinds of serious crime that leads to imprisonment, and how much is attributable to some mixture of discrimination and policies within the criminal justice system that have differential racial impact.

The initial challenge, then, is finding some means of estimating the involvement of different racial groups in the kinds of serious crimes that lead to incarceration. Self-report studies typically have too few of those events. The National Crime Victimization Survey (NCVS), conducted annually by the Bureau of Justice Statistics since 1973, asks victims about the race of the offender who victimized them. That information is helpful for crimes involving a personal confrontation like robbery, assault, or rape, but not very useful for property crimes where there was no direct confrontation. Hindelang (1978), in a classic study, compared the victim reports of the race of the offender in a number of cities with the race of the arrestees for robbery and aggravated assault (offenses in which the victim could observe the offender), and found a strong correspondence between the two. This suggests the reasonableness of using arrest information for the serious crimes that give rise to prison, as a proxy for race information on the offenders themselves.

I published such a study in 1982 (Blumstein, 1982) and found for two of the most serious offenses, robbery and murder, that the Black/White ratio of arrestees was close to the race ratio in prison; and so arrest accounted for about 100 percent of the prison disproportionality. As one examines the less-serious offenses, where there is more discretion at the various stages of the criminal justice system, the race ratio at arrest accounts for less of the racial disproportionality in prison. The race ratio in drug arrests in particular accounted for only about 50 percent of the prison disproportionality for drug offenses. Aggregating across the various offenses, weighting them by their relative proportion of prisoners, about 80 percent of the racial difference in prison is accounted for by the racial differences in arrest. The other 20 percent includes other factors that may be different between the races. Some may be factors that judges may legitimately take into account, such as prior record or employment status. Racial discrimination is also a potential factor. We certainly know that discrimination exists at various stages of the criminal justice system, but it would be astonishing if discrimination could be a major explanation of a difference of more than 80 percent.

In a 1993 update of that earlier study (Blumstein, 1993), the prison disproportionality accounted for by arrest dropped from 80 percent to 76 percent. The dominant reason for that drop was the growing prevalence of drug offenders in prison. In the 1982 study, based on data from the 1970s, drug offenders accounted for only 5.7 percent of prisoners. By the 1993 update, based on a survey of prisoners in 1991, drug offenders had become 21.5 percent of all prisoners. Race differences in the arrest of drug offenders still accounted for only 50 percent of the racial disproportionality of drug prisoners, but because drug prisoners had increased so significantly, their presence diminished the ability of arrest disproportionality to explain the total prison disparity.

When we look at the individual states, we also find some striking results. The aggregate Black/White incarceration ratio for the total United States is about 7 to 1. The individual states display a considerable range, from 20.4 at one end to 4.0 at the other. The five states at one extreme are Tennessee, South Carolina, Georgia, Mississippi, and Alabama—generally southern states. The five states at the other extreme are Minnesota, Connecticut, Utah, New Jersey, and Nebraska—generally progressive states. The interesting observation is that the southern states have a low incarceration ratio and the progressive states have the high incarceration ratio. This clearly conflicts with the stereotypical presumption that the southern states, with their history of discrimination, should be at the high end rather than the low end. This difference could well be associated with different rates of offending of Blacks in the South, inasmuch as those rates could be associated, perhaps, with greater socialization through residential stability and more rural residency. Also, the typically higher incarceration rates in the southern states could result from more punishment for less-serious offenses, where racial differences are less than in the most serious offenses.

These studies of prison disproportionality show that the bulk of the disparity is attributable to factors outside the criminal justice system. That makes it particularly important to address the many other factors that contribute to differential involvement in crime, and particularly the most serious crimes. These are the issues addressed by all the other sessions of this conference.

SOME RESEARCH NEEDS

Explanation of the Factors Contributing to the Disparities

Given the importance of the problem of race and criminal justice, it is striking to note how little research attention has been paid to the fundamental task of isolating the factors contributing to the important racial differences in the criminal justice system. Generating such empirical knowledge should be a high priority in order to help address and effectively reduce the problems of racial disparity.

Further efforts are needed to isolate the factors contributing to the radical racial differences in incarceration rates. Information about racial differences by crime type in arrest and, where possible, on victimization through the NCVS, will be important in contributing to such analyses. It is important that differences by state be explored. Other relevant factors taken into account by judges, such as type of defense counsel, prior record, employment status, and other factors, should be addressed wherever possible.

It is also important to distinguish how racial disparities differ between the adult and juvenile systems. There are strong indications that the disparities are much greater in the juvenile system, especially in distinguishing placements in private, versus public, institutions. It is important to identify the sources of those disparities and their legitimacy.

Existence and Impact of Police Profiling

A second important theme is examining the degree to which police profiling occurs. Some initial studies of this issue are already being pursued by Mastrofski et al. (1998) in two cities (St. Petersburg, Florida, and Dayton, Ohio) under a National Institute of Justice grant. In addition, there have been a variety of reports of traffic stops and drug searches carried out with a strong suggestion of racial profiling.

Role of the Drug War in Contributing to Racial Differences

The strongest candidate for a policy area that does have strong racial implications has been the efforts to pursue drug abuse through enforcement and incarceration. It would be desirable to assess the form and degree of racial impact associated with the nation's drug enforcement efforts. Any such study should focus first on differential effects on individuals, reflecting the degree to which the racial disproportionality in prison is attributable to differential involvement in arrest for drug offenses and the racially different punishment associated with drugs. In particular, it is important to isolate the degree to which the distinctions made between powder cocaine and crack cocaine, especially in mandatory-minimum sentencing, have contributed to these differences. It would also be desirable to examine the degree to which the high incarceration rates of young Black males, many of whom are in prison on drug charges, have contributed both to significant disruption within their communities as well as to a reduction in those communities in the deterrent effect associated with the threat of incarceration.

Interactions Between the Police and Minority Communities

A fourth major theme should pursue the issue of interactions between the police and minority communities. So often, it is the interaction between the police and minority individuals that serves to escalate the tensions and, thereby, deteriorate interaction between the two groups. A highly publicized confrontation, whether appropriate or not, gives rise to hostility by members of the group, leading to their withholding support from the police when and where they need it, and aggressive or excessively defensive action in their interactions with the police. All of this contributes to putting the police on the defensive, and results in police acting more aggressively and more defensively when they interact with members of these groups. This process of escalating conflict and tension is not easy to extinguish. It is certainly exacerbated by those individual police officers who display a persistent pattern of racism. It is in the interest of every police department to develop procedures for identifying such individuals and appropriately punishing or dismissing them from the department. Symmetrically, it is important that leadership groups in the minority communities be recruited to work with the police to help reduce these tensions.

Research in this area should attempt to measure the level of tension between the police and various minority groups, and relate that level of tension to various aspects of police operations. It should also include consideration of recent incidents of conflict between the police and members of the minority communities. It is likely that these tensions increase considerably on both sides following singular incidents of police use of force that is at least arguably excessive. The dynamics of that growth of tension as well as its subsidence can be examined through community and police surveys as well as through ethnographic studies in communities before and after such critical incidents.

REFERENCES

Baldus, D., C. Pulaski, and G. Woodworth
   1983   Comparative review of death sentences: An empirical study of the Georgia experience. *Journal of Criminal Law and Criminology* 74(3):661-753.
Blumstein, A.
   1982   On the racial disproportionality of U.S. prison populations. *Journal of Criminal Law and Criminology* 73(3):1259-1281.
   1993   Racial disproportionality of U.S. prison populations revisited. *University of Colorado Law Review* 64(3):743-760.

Blumstein, A., and A. Beck
   1999   Factors contributing to the growth in U.S. prison populations. Pp. 17-61 in *Crime and Justice: A Review of Research*, M. Tonry and J. Petersilia, eds. Chicago: University of Chicago Press.
Blumstein, A., and J. Cohen
   1980   Sentencing of convicted offenders: An analysis of the public's view. *Law and Society Review* 14(2).
Bonczar, T., and A.J. Beck
   1997   Lifetime likelihood of going to state or federal prison. Bureau of Justice Statistics Special Report No. 160092, March 6.
Hindelang, M.
   1978   Race and involvement in common law personal crimes. *American Sociological Review* 43(1):93+.
Kennedy, R.
   1998   Overview of racial trends in the administration of criminal justice. Paper prepared for the Research Conference on Racial Trends in the United States, Washington, D.C., October 15-16.
Mastrofski, S., R. Parks, C. DeJong, and R. Worden
   1998   Race and everyday policing: A research perspective. Paper delivered at the 12th International Congress on Criminology, Seoul, Korea, August.
Mauer, M.
   1990   *Young Black Men and the Criminal Justice System: A Growing Problem.* Washington, D.C.: The Sentencing Project.
Miller, J.
   1996   *Search and Destroy: African-American Males in the Criminal Justice System.* Cambridge: University Press.

3

Commentary on Randall Kennedy's Overview of the Justice System

Darnell F. Hawkins

M uch evidence suggests that Blacks have made substantial social, political, and economic progress since 1950, despite the persistence of significant barriers to their advancement (Jaynes and Williams, 1989; Farley and Allen, 1989; Collins, 1997; Oliver and Shapiro, 1995). For the most part, however, official crime statistics and data reveal much less change in the level of racial disproportionality in the administration of justice in the United States. Indeed, some have argued that during the 1990s the nation witnessed a pronounced widening of the racial divide in terms of rates of crime and punishment and in public perceptions associated with these disparities (Mann, 1993; Tonry, 1995; Miller, 1996; Walker et al., 1996; Mann and Zatz, 1998; Russell, 1998).

This paradox—the overall social and economic progress of Blacks in contrast to the lack of improvement, and possibly a worsening of their plight, within the context of the American justice system—forms the basis for Randall Kennedy's thoughtful and critical assessment of American criminal law and justice during the 1990s (Kennedy, 1998). Kennedy notes that administration of the criminal law in the United States has changed substantially. Gains have been made both in terms of protection accorded to Blacks against criminality and the treatment accorded to them as suspects, defendants, and convicts (Kennedy, 1998; Kennedy, 1997).

This critique is based on Randall Kennedy's paper, "Racial Trends in the Administration of Criminal Justice," prepared for the Research Conference on Racial Trends in the United States. National Research Council, Washington, D.C., October 15-16, 1998.

It is against this backdrop of significant change in the "letter" and "spirit" of the law that Kennedy presents evidence to support his claim that much remains to be done to make the administration of the criminal law racially just, both in theory and in practice. He cites a 1995 Gallup Poll which reported that one-half of Blacks questioned believe the American criminal justice system is biased against them, and two-thirds believed the police to be anti-Black (Kennedy, 1998:1). For Kennedy, these public perceptions reveal one of two significant dimensions of the racial divide in American justice; the other significant dimension is the racial demographics of both crime and criminal law enforcement in the United States. He notes the wide racial gap in rates of imprisonment for American males and the extreme disparity in rates of homicide and other violent crime victimization for Blacks compared to Whites.

Kennedy uses these statistics to disclose the essence of the dilemma faced by Blacks vis-à-vis the justice system—that not only are Blacks more likely than Whites to be arrested and punished for crime, they are also more likely to be crime victims. Thus, in comparison to other racial and ethnic groups, Blacks are in greater need of the protection afforded by the justice system and would, therefore, stand to gain most from a justice system that provides effective crime deterrence and expeditious punishment. According to Kennedy, the current reality is that the ability of the American justice system to provide the protection needed by Blacks is severely compromised by the persistence of racial bias and discrimination on the part of the protectors.

Kennedy discusses three major areas of justice administration: (1) tactics used by the police for the surveillance of persons suspected of committing crime, (2) use of peremptory challenges in jury selection, and (3) sentencing and punishment for crime, particularly the imposition of the death penalty. This essay examines the social science and jurisprudential evidence of racial bias in each of these areas.

RACE AND AMERICAN CRIMINAL JUSTICE IN THE 1990s: A CASE OF HEIGHTENED EXPECTATIONS?

After 1950, Americans of all races came increasingly to believe that the nation had finally come to grips with the legal and social problems stemming from its racist past. Many social analysts and activists believed that the civil rights and due process "revolutions" were capable of eradicating not only the last vestiges of de jure racism, but also of promoting truly equal treatment under the law. It was hoped that civil rights and legal reforms would help promote economic and social equality. In the criminal justice arena, progressive Whites and Blacks concerned with the reduction of racial disparities embraced reforms aimed at (1) ensuring the application of due process and equal protection standards in all legal proceedings, (2) providing judicial scrutiny of the conduct of the police and other system personnel, and (3) minimizing discretion through the adoption of more structured forms of sentencing, variously labeled as determinate, fixed, or mandatory (Tonry, 1988, 1993).

Kennedy's essay is framed against this backdrop of expectations. He observes that, contrary to expectations, the reforms have neither significantly altered the level of racial disparity nor ended racial bias in the operation of the criminal law (Kennedy, 1997). Much of the racial bias with which his essay is concerned can be traced to relatively recent changes in the criminal law and law enforcement, many of which were put in place during the 1980s and early 1990s.

The research questions that appear to guide Kennedy's and other recent studies of race, crime, and justice in the United States are:

1. Why have the legal reforms of the last half-century failed to reduce the level of racial disproportionality?
2. What role does racial discrimination in the administration of justice play in sustaining observed levels of racial disparity?
3. Apart from racial bias in the justice system, what other factors have contributed to the persistence of the racial gap and its seeming widening in recent years?
4. What are the social, political, economic, and legal consequences for American society of the failure to reduce discrimination and disparity in crime and justice?
5. What additional legal reforms or areas of social change are needed to successfully reduce the level of racial inequality in crime and justice?

Public Opinion and Social Change

Public opinion and attitudes play a central role in Kennedy's analysis. He suggests that contemporary law enforcement and criminal justice policies and practices aimed at the Black underclass have not only served to exacerbate the economic and social marginalization of that group, they have also increasingly impacted the lives of those Blacks of higher occupational and socioeconomic standing. Thus, he implies, the spillover of race-based criminal justice practices and policies across social class lines within the Black community accounts for the widespread belief among Blacks of all socioeconomic levels that the American criminal justice system is racially biased.

To the extent that affluent Blacks can exert more influence on policy makers than can poor Blacks, concerted action taken by affluent Blacks might be pivotal in achieving the goal of a nonracist justice system. On the other hand, given the focus on race relations, which is an integral part of the President's Initiative on Race, Kennedy might have provided more discussion of racial differences in perceptions of the American criminal justice system and the effects of those perceptual differences on the likelihood of achieving social change in criminal law and its enforcement.

His introductory remarks highlighted public opinion among Blacks, but did so without explicit reference to the views of Whites and members of other races. Numerous studies have shown that significant differences exist in attitudes and public opinions related to law and justice. Walker and colleagues (1996:2), reporting on data from surveys of the American public, found that there is significant racial polarization in attitudes regarding crime and punishment expressed by respondents. In addition, the lines of racial cleavage they describe largely parallel the areas of bias discussed by Kennedy. Walker et al. (1996:87) note that racial differences in perceptions were especially evident in attitudes toward the death penalty and activities of the police. Other studies of racial differences in public attitude toward a variety of race-related topics also reveal a particularly wide racial divide (Bobo, 1988; Bobo and Hutchings, 1996; Hochschild, 1995).

Whether one accepts the validity of the arguments presented in Kennedy's essay might depend largely on race-linked experiences and perceptions one brings to the reading of it. Middle-class and affluent Whites are seldom the targets, either intentionally or inadvertently, of arbitrary and capricious practices of the justice system that result from consideration of their race or skin color. To the extent that Whites, and members of other races, are out of touch with perceived or real abuses of law enforcement, they may be reluctant to endorse legal and social reforms aimed at addressing them. Obviously, this line of race-linked perceptual discord must be confronted if the goals for a deracialized criminal justice system are to be achieved.

Race and Police Profiles of Crime Suspects

As regards the use of race in police surveillance and scrutiny of citizens suspected of crime, Kennedy suggests that this practice represents one of the most insidious, yet legally sanctioned, forms of racism in contemporary American society because it often inadvertently results in the targeting, and harassment, of Blacks who have no history of criminal conduct. As for the psychological impact on Blacks in general, Kennedy observes that policing practices such as these serve as a reminder for many Blacks of their second-class citizenship. In addition, he observes that despite the obvious potential for fostering interracial animosity, denying equal protection under the law, and further exacerbating racial disparity in crime and punishment, there is an absence of organized opposition to the use of racial profiling.

Kennedy notes the irony in continued support of the use of racial profiles in policing, despite attacks on "racial discrimination" in affirmative action programs. Clearly, racial profiling targets citizens for different treatment on the basis of race, thus constituting governmental racial discrimination. Those who would dismantle affirmative action programs have premised their stance on the fact that such programs target citizens for different treatment on the basis of race, thus constituting governmental racial discrimination. Indeed, the irony prompted Butler (1997) to call for affirmative action in the administration of criminal law. Kennedy sees little chance that such racialist law enforcement procedures will be struck down by the courts, or that legislative remedies aimed at their delegitimization will be approved at the local, state, or federal levels, inasmuch as support for the use of racial profiles in policing has come from the federal courts (*United States v. Weaver*, 966 F. 2d 391, CA 8 1992; cert. denied, 506 U.S. 1040, 1992) and other decision makers.

I am persuaded by most of Kennedy's constitutional and public policy arguments against the use of racial profiles. I think, however, he might have further pushed public-policy reform objectives had he tackled head-on and more systematically the question that undergirds the debate surrounding the use of race-based surveillance tactics: Does the disproportionate rate of Black involvement in crime, as measured by past arrests or other data, provide some logical, commonsensical, or rational basis for police use of racial profiles, even if such profiles are legally and morally dubious on other grounds? Kennedy alludes to the possibility of a rational basis for race-based law enforcement when at one point he says, "This differential treatment on a racial basis is racial discrimination. This is not to say—at least yet—that this racial discrimination is unjustified"(1998:3). Beyond this enticing remark, however, Kennedy gives little insight into what he considers to be the conditions under which race-based police surveillance is justified.

The closest Kennedy comes to addressing this question is in his discussion of *United States v. Weaver* (1992). Kennedy notes the opinion of a dissenting judge who questions the lack of empirical evidence that race should matter in the search for drug suspects. Kennedy (1998:5) cites the judge as saying, "If we had evidence that young Blacks in Los Angeles were more prone to drug offenses than young Whites, the fact that a young person is Black might be of some significance." Both the judge in that case and Kennedy appear to suggest that if empirical evidence, as opposed to anecdote, conjecture, or racial stereotype, is used as the basis for implementing racial profiles, the use might be legally acceptable.

Given such conjecture, and its seeming inconsistency with the main thrust of Kennedy's argument against racial profiling, I would like to have seen more discussion of the problems inherent in an attempt to gather the data needed to meet such an evidentiary standard—i.e., the showing of racial difference in "proneness" to drug offending or other forms of crime.

But how can either supporters or critics of racial profiling use criminal justice system data to bolster their argument and, at the same time, avoid the Catch 22-like conundrum to which use of such data would lead? On one hand, it may be argued that if racial disproportionality is the yardstick, official crime data for a variety of offenses, including drug law violation, could arguably be used to support racial profiling—Blacks have high rates of reported crime, thus justifying greater scrutiny of them. For nearly a century, there has been little debate about the fact that, in comparison to their numbers in the population, Blacks are disproportionately represented in the nation's criminal justice system (Jaynes and Williams, 1989: Chapter 9).

On the other hand, such uncritical acceptance of crime statistics as proof of racial differences in behavior ignores nearly a century of research and statistics delineating the effect of race on detection and punishment of crime in the United States. Indeed, it goes against the major arguments made by Kennedy in this essay and in his earlier work on the subject (1997). The use of racial profiles, based often on social-control objectives that have little to do with the detection or control of criminal conduct, has been commonplace throughout most of American history. So, too, has the use of profiles, based on a legitimate concern for crime control. Both these forms of bias have also contributed to the level of racial disparity seen in official crime statistics in the past, and according to Kennedy (1997), continue to do so today. Thus, any use of potentially "tainted" crime data for the purposes of justifying the current and future use of racial profiles is inherently problematic. Although Kennedy is largely concerned with preventing the future use of racial profiles, I propose that the effects of past profiling and its effects on notions of "proneness" and "propensity" are an inextricable and unavoidable part of the policy and legal debate over its current justification.

RACE AND DRUG-LAW VIOLATIONS

In recent decades, the overrepresentation of Blacks among those charged with and punished for drug offenses—the offense for which the police are most likely to use racial profiling—has been particularly sizeable and rapidly growing (Blumstein, 1982, 1993; Hawkins, 1986; Tonry, 1995; Miller, 1996). Drug-law violations also provide a classic example of the pitfalls involved in the use of official crime statistics in an effort to establish racial differences in the likelihood of engaging in illegal behavior. In comparison to almost every other category of crime perceived as serious, by law and by the public, the detection of illicit drug use and sales is acutely affected by the practices and biases of law-enforcement personnel. Arrests for drug-related offenses, unlike crimes involving discernible victims, seldom result from citizen complaints. The fact that citizens of all social classes purchase and use illicit drugs, and tend to do so in discrete ways, minimizes their risk of detection. Further, even when drug sales and purchases are more publicly visible, citizens observing sales of drugs often "look the other way." Such patterns of offending obviously mean that direct police surveillance of suspected criminals is often the only viable means of law enforcement.

Although suspected drug offenders have been the most frequent targets of police surveillance, it is clear that the use of racial profiles is not limited to drug offenses. Other offense categories likely to be affected by differential law-enforcement practices based on race include shoplifting and other forms of theft and conversion, weapons offenses, traffic-law violations, and numerous public order offenses. Indeed, the instances of racial profiling that have garnered the most attention in the media have involved the stopping of Blacks who were simply driving or walking through predominantly White, or even their own, neighborhoods.

Thus, we must ask, as Kennedy does, whether police use of racial profiles is based on sound, unbiased evidence of racial differences in offending for the specific offense categories that are targeted. In addition, we must ask whether, after discounting the biasing effects of police-surveillance activities, Blacks are more likely than Whites to be involved in the commission of these crimes. These questions lie, of course, at the center of the perennial debate among criminologists regarding the relationship between race and crime.

Since the beginning of national crime victimization surveys, nearly 25 years ago, many criminological researchers have been inclined to believe that bias in the detection of crime does exist, but that it does not account for all of the differences observed between Blacks and Whites in rates of offending. Racial descriptions of offenders given by persons victimized by serious crime closely match those descriptions found for arrests and crimes known to the police (Hindelang, 1978; Jaynes and Williams, 1989: Chapter 9; Walker et al., 1996). Some researchers have gone so far as to suggest that although bias in the administration of justice might have accounted for a large portion of racial disparity in crime and punishment in the past, such bias is largely nonexistent today (Wilbanks, 1987).

Apart from the question of sufficient proof of racial difference in criminal involvement to legitimize race-based police surveillance, from a public-policy perspective a more significant question might be whether such tactics yield significant returns—i.e., do law enforcement officials actually detect more crime and has public safety been enhanced for all citizens? If so, do the benefits derived from the use of such surveillance outweigh the associated social and political costs—e.g., the fostering of interracial animosity, distrust by minorities of the criminal justice system, and the potential for denying equal protection under the law?

The correct answer to both questions may depend on the specific criminal offense that is the target of surveillance activity. Although Blacks are overrepresented in official and unofficial crime statistics in comparison to their numbers in the general population, the Black share of the pool of known offenders varies substantially from one offense category to another. For 1992, the percentage of arrestees who were Black ranged from 10.1 percent for driving under the influence (DUI), to 33.6 percent for forgery, and as high as 60.9 percent for robbery (Walker et al., 1996:40-41). These are national data, and the actual level of racial disproportionality by offense will vary from one place to another. Nevertheless, they do suggest that, in most locales, a practice of racial profiling aimed at Blacks for the purposes of detecting those committing DUI or forgery will be less rational and potentially less successful than one aimed at robbery.

For the offense categories at which racial profiling is typically aimed—possession, use, or trafficking of drugs—research findings suggest that use of official crime data (arrests, prosecution, and punishment) results in an underestimate of the involvement of Whites and an overestimate of the involvement of Blacks. Surveys (Bachman et al., 1991, National Institute on Drug Abuse, 1991; Rebach, 1992; Lockwood et al., 1995) have shown high use of drugs, including cocaine, among White adults, and unexpectedly low rates of drug use among Black adolescents.

Of course, drug trafficking, as opposed to drug use, is the offense category at which most racial profiling is aimed. There are obvious problems involved in trying to come up with estimates of the "true" extent of racial difference for trafficking, as compared to drug use, for which accurate measurement is problematic in its own right. Yet, it appears likely that the overrepresentation of Blacks in drug trafficking may be limited to the street-level running of drugs in large urban areas, where Black youth predominate. No evidence suggests that Whites, including organized crime, have abandoned their traditional involvement in the trafficking of illicit drugs. Indeed, lucrative drug markets for marijuana, heroin, cocaine, methamphetamines, and other controlled substances exist in both rural and suburban areas, where White traffickers predominate. Further, some Black community activists have insisted that a large portion of the "wholesale" drug dealing within inner-city neighborhoods continues to be under the control of Whites. To the extent that evidence supports such observations and speculation, the differential targeting of Blacks for the purposes of suppressing the flow and purchase of drugs makes little sense from the perspective of either effective law enforcement or protection of the public's health.

Despite failing to come to grips with the thorny evidentiary problems I have briefly described, Kennedy and the dissenting judge in *United States v. Weaver* do raise several important questions of relevance for the making of legal and public policy. Both acknowledge that some form of profiling of criminal suspects is an expected and unavoidable part of law enforcement. They insist, however, that if race is to be the basis for the development of law-enforcement profiles, definitive proof of racial differences in social behavior is required to make such profiles justifiable and rational. In the obvious absence of reliable, unbiased data of the sort I have described, Kennedy suggests that current racial profiling within the criminal justice system likely stems as much from racial stereotyping as from any concrete evidence of racial differences in behavior.

Further, although the police may be expected to use their experiences within given communities to help disentangle the effects of "race" and criminal involvement, some research suggests that their attitudes toward race and crime may stem as much from social forces found in the wider society as from their police work. For example, some early studies of the police in large urban areas found that even seasoned officers overestimated the extent of racial disproportionality in criminal involvement, even in the neighborhoods that they patrolled, and adhered to many of the traditional racial stereotypes (National Advisory Commission on Civil Disorders, 1968).

Further, like all Americans, those who enforce the law are also greatly influenced by the daily media coverage of crime. To the extent they are, research has shown that media depictions seldom reflect an accurate count of the actual incidence of crime or its relative distribution across racial groups or residential areas (Fishman, 1980; Surette, 1984; Donnerstein and Linz, 1995; Johnstone et al., 1994; Hawkins et al., 1995; Hawkins, 1998). Nevertheless, these distorted perceptions derived from the mass media likely affect the racial profiling of crime suspects by the police and the acceptance of such profiling by courts, policy makers, and the public.

RACE AND PUNISHMENT

The "front end" issue of racialized police profiling tactics has elicited much more public notice and debate than the "back end" matters of racial bias in jury selection and the punishment of persons convicted of crime. As Kennedy notes, bias in law enforcement raises concerns that cut across all segments of the Black community; such bias has historically provided a flashpoint for both riots and other forms of social protest, and establishes a case study for civil libertarian critiques of American justice. Critics of American justice, such as Paul Butler, noted, however, that at the level of public policy the three areas of racial bias within American justice outlined by Kennedy are inextricably linked.

As regards serving on juries, much of the impetus for some prosecutors to exclude Blacks may reflect a fear of Black jurists' potential and willingness to "nullify" the harsh penalties now associated with convictions for drug-law violations (Butler, 1995). Further, it is clear that the failure of American courts to prohibit racial profiling, or to enforce the *Batson v. Kentucky* (1986) prohibition against the use of race in peremptory challenges, has relevance for the persistence of racial differences in sentencing, the subject Kennedy tackles in the last part of his essay. Because I believe that few Americans disagree as to the inherent unfairness of jury-selection procedures designed to deny the participation of specific racial groups, I will limit my remaining comments to the question of racial bias in sentencing and criminal punishment.

My own examination of crime and punishment data since 1950, presented here and in Hawkins and Herring (forthcoming), lends support to Kennedy's assertions regarding the continued salience of race for determining the severity of criminal punishment. Table 3-1 lists the racial makeup of the nation's prison population from 1950 through 1995. The first thing one notices is the gradual, then precipitous, increase in the number of prisoners of all races. The percentage of Blacks also increases disproportionately—from slightly more than one-third of all prisoners in 1950 to nearly one-half in the mid-1990s. Indeed, the trend in Table 3-1 suggests a worsening of the plight of Blacks, compared to other racial groups, especially since 1970.

The extent to which Blacks and other racial and ethnic minorities have come to constitute a significantly larger percentage of prison inmates becomes even more evident when one examines changes in the rate of Hispanic confinement. Between 1980 and 1995, the Hispanic percentage of the nation's prison population more than doubled, going from 7.6 percent to 15.5 percent. Thus, at the end of 1995, nearly two-thirds of all state and federal prisoners were either Black, Hispanic, or a member of another non-White racial group.[1]

In comparison to the year-end prison population statistics in Table 3-1, prison-admissions data provide a better picture of temporal change in the racial disproportionality in the nation's prison population. The trend for prison admissions (Table 3-2) reveals a pattern of increase for

---

[1]See periodic imprisonment reports, *Prisoners in State and Federal Institutions on December 31*, from the U.S. Department of Justice. Years used for this data are from 1981 to 1996.

TABLE 3-1 Prisoners Under State and Federal Jurisdiction, by Race, 1950-1995

Year	Total	White	Black	%Black	Other[a]
1950	178,065	NA	NA	34	NA
1960	226,344	NA	NA	37	NA
1970	198,831	NA	NA	41	NA
1980	328,695	169,274	150,249	46	9,172
1981	368,772	190,503	168,129	46	10,140
1982	414,362	214,741	189,610	46	10,011
1983	437,238	225,902	200,216	46	11,120
1984	462,442	239,428	209,673	45	13,341
1985	502,507	253,599	220,700	44	28,208
1986	544,972	274,701	246,833	45	23,438
1987	585,040	291,606	262,958	45	30,476
1988	627,600	308,712	289,462	46	29,426
1989	712,364	343,550	334,952	47	33,862
1990	773,919	369,485	367,122	47	37,312
1991	825,619	385,347	395,245	48	45,027
1992	882,500	409,700	424,900	48	47,900
1993	970,444	444,100	473,300	49	53,044
1994	1,054,774	464,167	501,672	48	88,935
1995	1,126,287	455,021	544,005	48	127,261

[a]Includes other races and persons for whom race was undetermined. Hispanics are typically included with blacks and whites.

SOURCE: U.S. Department of Justice, year-end reports and other periodic publications. Titles vary. Racial breakdowns were not available in most of the reports for the period between 1950 and 1980. The "%Black" data for 1950, 1960, 1970, and 1980 were taken from a special Department of Justice study prepared by Cahalan (1986).

Blacks similar to that seen in Table 3-1. In addition, in Table 3-2, there is evidence of the sharp rise in the non-White percentage of new prisoners during the late 1980s. There was a more-or-less steady increase in the rate of Black admissions between 1950 and 1987, and then a rather sharp increase after 1987. From only 30 percent of all new prison admissions in 1950, Blacks were 41 percent by 1970. By the early 1990s, Blacks were 53 percent of all admissions.

Two important studies published by the Sentencing Commission show the extent of racial differences in criminal justice system control of 20 to 29 year olds in the United States. Between 1989 and 1994, the percentage of White young adults who were either in jail, in a state or federal prison, or on probation or parole, grew from 6.2 to 6.7 percent of all U.S. White males. For the same period, the percentage of Blacks grew from 23 to 30.2 percent (Mauer, 1990; Mauer and Huling, 1995).

The trends in detention of juveniles closely mirror those seen for

TABLE 3-2 State and Federal Prison Admissions, by Race, United States, 1950-1986

Year	Percent White	Percent Black	Percent Other Race
1950	69	30	1
1960	66	32	2
1970	61	39	—
1975	64	35	1
1980	58	41	1
1981	57	42	1
1982	55	44	1
1983	58	41	1
1984	58	41	1
1985	56	43	1
1986	55	44	1
1987	53	45	2
1988	49	50	1
1989	47	52	1
1990	48	51	1
1991	46	53	1
1992	46	53	1
1993	46	53	1
1994	47	52	1
1995	51	48	1

SOURCES: Langan (1991) and U. S. Department of Justice (1997).

young and older adults (Krisberg, 1987; Hawkins and Jones, 1989). Snyder and Sickmund (1995:166) reported that the minority juvenile custody population increased between 1983 and 1991, while the White custody population decreased. By 1991, the long-term custody rate for Black youth in public institutions was 424 per 100,000 Black juveniles in the population—five times the custody rate for White juveniles. For Black youth in Nevada and California, lock-up rates per 100,000 were as high as 1,174 and 1,191, respectively.

Increasing Minority Confinement: A Question of Racial Bias?

A more detailed and nuanced discussion of the issues and debates surrounding the increase since 1950 in overall rates of imprisonment, and in the level of racial disproportionality, is clearly beyond the scope of the present discussion. Blumstein and Beck (1999) explore many of these factors in their recent work on this subject. For our purposes here, however, several observations appear to be warranted. It is clear that a number of historical and demographic trends have come together since 1950 to help shape the rising racial imbalance in levels of imprisonment, particularly the rise in the proportion of inmates who are Black.

The Mainstreaming of White Ethnics

The extent to which America's White ethnics were overrepresented during the past within the nation's criminal justice system is well documented. However, the American criminal justice system of the 1980s and 1990s, in comparison to decades earlier, reflects the successful integration of White ethnics into the American economic, political, and social mainstream. This success has been marked by a sharp decline in the rate of arrests and criminal punishment for members of these groups. Steinberg (1989) reminds us that the successful integration of White ethnics into mainstream American society took much longer than is commonly believed. From the time of their entry into the United States, most immigrant families passed through two to three generations before achieving truly middle-class status. This gradual mainstreaming of White ethnics in part explains the widening of the White-non-White gap in rates of crime and punishment seen since the 1950s.

The Success of Public Policies Aimed at the Exclusion and Marginalization of Non-Black Racial Minorities

Although both American Indians and persons of Asian ancestry were likely to be overrepresented among the nation's prisoners prior to the turn of the century, several governmental policies minimized the likelihood of their continued disproportionate presence; these include the restriction of the immigration of persons of Asian ancestry from the late 1800s into the early decades of the twentieth century. Coupled with the fact that many of the earliest Asian immigrants, like White ethnics, experienced less residential and social segregation, allowing them greater entry to the American economic mainstream, populations of Asian Americans now tend to be underrepresented within the nation's justice system. Similarly, policies during the nineteenth century, which forced American Indians onto reservations and until recently limited the access of immigrants from Latin America, have also minimized their presence within the nation's justice system.

Both of these sets of policies resulted in a greater Black-White contrast in American crime and punishment than might have existed absent such public policies. To assess both the historical and contemporary significance of such public policies, one need only look to recent crime and justice trends in the western United States and major eastern cities where both Asians and Hispanics have immigrated in large numbers. In many of these areas, rates of criminal justice system involvement for Hispanics have recently approached rates seen for Blacks. In addition, many of the various ethnic groupings that comprise the Asian and Pacific Islander populations have rates of involvement quite at odds with past labels of all Asians as "model minorities." Given such trends, it is conceivable that, in the future, members of these groups may experience the kinds of race-based law enforcement tactics now aimed largely at Blacks. The fact that Hispanics are already frequent targets of such surveillance for the purposes of drug law enforcement, and Asian gangs are a source of concern, may not bode well for the future of American race and ethnic relations.

Black Migration from the South

The large-scale movement of Blacks from the rural south to the urban north and west greatly increased the risk of their involvement with the criminal justice system. In addition to setting in motion social forces that led to the rise of the contemporary urban underclass (Wilson, 1987), the increased risk of Black crime and punishment in the urban context is a result of the well-developed institutions of social control found in cities, compared to small towns or rural areas.

The Mainstreaming of White Southerners

Apart from its obvious benefits for Black Americans, among the legacies of the American Civil Rights Movement and the changes it wrought are the social and political reforms that have enabled greater access to the American economic mainstream by Whites living in the South. Although still more likely than their northern counterparts to run afoul of the law today, White working-class southerners were even more disproportionately found in the area's prisons and jails during earlier decades.

The Geographic and Social Marginalization of the White Underclass

Although much attention has been paid to the plight of the Black underclass, the large number of economically marginal Whites has been largely overlooked. It appears that this lack of attention may result partly from their geographic isolation. In comparison to the Black underclass, the tendency of the White underclass to be found in rural and small town America may shield them from some of the forms of crime detection and social control found in the large cities. By comparison, the Black underclass is disproportionately concentrated not only in urban areas, but also within the inner cities of the nation's largest cities.

All of these trends have contributed to the increasingly disproportionate presence of Blacks in the nation's justice system—from arrest through parole. The question posed by Kennedy is whether, in addition to the social forces described, continuing racial bias in the administration of the criminal law also contributes to the levels of racial disparity seen in Tables 3-1 and 3-2. Prompted largely by the precipitous rise in rates of imprisonment in the 1980s, and several widely publicized instances of racial bias in the justice system, a number of other researchers have raised questions similar to Kennedy's.

For example, the idea that the recent increase in the Black percentage of the nation's prison population results from a similar increase during this period in the percentage of serious crime committed by Blacks has been discounted by Tonry (1995:49-80), who notes the relative stability of racial disparity in arrest rates for serious crime (see, also, Hawkins and Herring, forthcoming). Chambliss (1995), Mauer (1990), Mauer and Huling (1995), Miller (1996), and Russell (1998), among others, have all observed that the rather significant increase in the percentage of Blacks admitted to and detained in prisons after 1987 (Table 3-2) appears to reflect the targeting of Black criminal suspects, especially drug offenders. As Kennedy notes, this targeting has taken the form of new federal and state laws aimed at the control of crack cocaine, enacted during the mid-1980s. It has also taken the form of increased police surveillance—at local, state, and federal levels—aimed at drug, and other, offenses.

Given the increase in the marketing of crack cocaine in the 1980s, and its seeming concentration in the nation's inner cities, many social commentators have been inclined to think of rising rates of imprisonment among Blacks as simply a reflection of higher rates of drug trafficking and use in Black communities. However, much of the racial imbalance seen for drug arrests and sentencing predates the advent of the crack cocaine epidemic. Blumstein's (1982) study of the extent to which racial differences in arrests explained levels of imprisonment revealed that, as early as the late 1970s, drug offenses were the crime category for which there was the most unexplained racial disparity. Follow-up studies have also shown significant racial differences in arrest and imprisonment rates for the use and sale of drugs that do not appear to be explained by arrest rates alone (Hawkins, 1986; Blumstein, 1993; Tonry, 1996).

Recent statistics reveal that greater levels of racial disproportionality for drug offenses, compared to other types of offending, are not limited to adult offenders. Snyder and Sickmund (1995:142) reported that during 1992, of all Black juveniles in the United States who were processed though the justice system for varying offenses, 25 percent were detained. This compared to 18 percent of White juveniles, and 22 percent of juveniles of other races. In contrast, the rates of confinement for juveniles charged with drug offenses were 47 percent for Blacks, 26 percent for Whites, and 19 percent for others.

Thus, it seems that for several decades, but especially during the last decade, arrests and punishment for drug-law violations contributed disproportionately to the widening of the racial gap in the justice system. Why drug offenses? Why the focus on Blacks? Given the professed intentions of the war on drugs, how is it that greater attention has not been paid to the drug-law violations of the White population? In light of the consistency of findings reporting greater levels of police surveillance and punishment for Black drug offenders, one wonders what motives—both individual and institutional—undergird that pattern of racial inequality.

It is plausible, as Tonry (1995) and others have noted, that this pattern of inequality represents abuses that arise from the conjoining of ideologies that are a part of both the "get tough" philosophy of the war on drugs and the racist philosophies intrinsic in the nation's heritage. Much of Kennedy's argument (1997, 1998) appears to support this view. I think, however, that one cannot overlook another important purpose that is served by the inordinate attention that is paid to drug offenses by the American criminal justice system. The rigorous enforcement of drug laws is likely seen by many policy makers and law enforcement officials as a form of "selective incapacitation" or "preventive detention" (see, e.g., Miller, 1996).

It is true that drug offenses and offenders possess traits that lend themselves to concerns for incarceration. Drug trafficking, particularly in crack cocaine, has often been highly correlated with an individual's likelihood of involvement in interpersonal violence. Similarly, drug use to the level of addiction has been perennially associated with high rates of both property, and property-related, violent crime. Thus, given the reality and long-term expectation of high rates of property and violent offending by young Black males, the current regime of mandatory and extremely punitive sentencing guidelines for drug offenses may have more to do with the concern of law enforcement and the American public for the prevention of nondrug crime and violence than with the protection of the public's health or economic productivity—goals often cited as justification for punitive stances toward drug use and sales.

Indeed, one of the consequences—perhaps both intended and unintended—of drug law enforcement is the incapacitation through incarceration of legions of lower-class, minority youth who are perceived as having little chance in their lifetimes of joining the economic and social mainstream of American society. As Kennedy observes, however, the price we pay as a society for the legal strategies used to achieve these results may be great, and one that ultimately will cost all of us.

Kennedy concludes by noting that one of the most distressing aspects of the official response to the problems of inequality and injustice is the lack of public concern and attentiveness. Even as the evidence mounts of the persistence of significant forms of racial bias in the administration of American criminal justice, many policy makers and citizens either deny the existence of the problems he describes or tend to de-emphasize their significance. That observation serves to highlight one of the most disheartening features of Kennedy's essay. More than 30 years ago, the Kerner Commission raised similar concerns and reached very similar conclusions in its study of American race relations and administration of justice in the aftermath of the civil disorders of the 1960s (National Advisory Commission on Civil Disorders, 1968); in turn, many of that Commission's observations arose from insights provided nearly a quarter of a century earlier by Gunnar Myrdal (1944) in his treatment of race and the administration of justice.

It is perhaps the recognition and acceptance of the fact that nearly all of the instances of racial bias Kennedy describes have been well documented in earlier studies that prompted him to close his essay by saying that much work awaits all who attempt to move forward to build on the gains in the administration of justice achieved during the last half of the twentieth century. Kennedy's emphasis on racial bias in the administration of justice should not be seen as inconsistent with accounts of race, crime, and justice that attribute the extreme racial disparities in rates of criminal involvement found in the United States today to the operation of other social forces that disdvantage Black Americans.

To his credit, nowhere in his essay does Kennedy suggest that currently high rates of homicide, assault, robbery, and property offenses found in many Black communities can be significantly reduced merely through the implementation of the race-neutral justice administration policies he advocates. Clearly, race trends in crime and violence are responsive to the same economic, social structural, psychological, and ecological forces that shape other manifestations of racial inequality in the United States. Significant progress toward addressing racial disproportionality in crime and justice will depend on progress in these broader social, economic, and political domains. Unfortunately, even as the nation enters a new millennium, these potentially corrective domains also continue to be plagued by problems of racial bias and disparity.

REFERENCES

Bachman, J., J. Wallace, Jr., P. O'Malley, L. Johnston, C. Kurth, and H. Neighbors
    1991   Racial/ethnic differences in smoking, drinking, and illicit drug use among American high school seniors, 1976-89. *American Journal of Public Health* 81:372-377.

Blumstein, A.
1982   On the racial disproportionality of United States' prison populations. *Journal of Criminal Law and Criminology* 73:1259-1281.
1993   Racial disproportionality of U.S. prison populations revisited. *University of Colorado Law Review* 64:743-760.
Blumstein, A., and A. Beck
1999   Factors contributing to the growth in the U.S. prison populations. In *Crime and Justice: A Review of Research*, M. Tonry, ed. Chicago: University of Chicago Press.
Bobo, L.
1988   Group conflict, prejudice, and the paradox of contemporary racial attitudes. Pp. 85-114 in *Eliminating Racism: Profiles in Controversy*, P. Katz and D. Taylor, eds. New York: Plenum.
Bobo, L., and V. Hutchings
1996   Perceptions of racial group competition: Extending Blumer's theory of group position to a multiracial social context. *American Sociological Review* 61(December):951-972.
Butler, P.
1995   Racially based jury nullification: Black power in the criminal justice system. *Yale Law Journal* 105:677+.
1997   Affirmative action and the criminal law. *University of Colorado Law Review*. 68(Fall):841-889.
Cahalan, M.
1986   *Historical Corrections Statistics in the United States, 1850-1984*. Washington, D.C.: U.S. Department of Justice, Bureau of Justice Statistics.
Chambliss, W.
1995   Crime control and ethnic minorities: Legitimizing racial oppression by creating moral panics. Pp. 235-258 in *Ethnicity, Race, and Crime: Perspectives across Time and Place*, D. Hawkins, ed. Albany: State University of New York Press.
Collins, S.
1997   *Black Corporate Executives: The Making and Breaking of a Black Middle Class*. Philadelphia: Temple University Press.
Donnerstein, E., and D. Linz
1995   The media. Pp. 237-264 in *Crime*, J. Wilson and J. Petersilia, eds. San Francisco: Institute for Contemporary Studies Press.
Farley, R., and W. Allen
1989   *The Color Line and the Quality of Life in America*. New York: Oxford University Press.
Fishman, M.
1980   *Manufacturing the News*. Austin: University of Texas Press.
Hawkins, D.
1986   Race, crime type, and imprisonment. *Justice Quarterly* 3:251-269.
1995   Race, social class, and newspaper coverage of homicide. *National Journal of Sociology* 9:113-140.
1998   The nations within: Race, class, region, and American lethal violence. *University of Colorado Law Review*. 69(Fall):905-926.
Hawkins, D., and C. Herring
Forth-   Race, crime, and punishment: Old controversies and new challenges. In *New Di-*
coming   *rections: African Americans in a Diversifying Nation*, J. Jackson, ed. Washington, D.C.: National Policy Association Press.

Hawkins, D., J. Johnstone, and A. Michener
 1995   Race, social class, and newspaper coverage of homicide. *National Journal of Sociology* 9(Summer):113-140.
Hawkins, D., and N. Jones
 1989   Black adolescents and the criminal justice system. Pp. 403-425 in *Black Adolescents*, R. Jones, ed. Berkeley, Calif.: Cobb and Henry Publishers.
Hindelang, M.
 1978   Race and involvement in common law personal crimes. *American Sociological Review* 43:93-109.
Hochschild, J.
 1995   *Facing Up to the American Dream: Race, Class, and the Soul of the Nation*. Princeton, N.J.: Princeton University Press.
Jaynes, G., and R. Williams, Jr.
 1989   *A Common Destiny: Blacks and American Society*. Washington, D.C.: National Academy Press.
Johnstone, J., D. Hawkins, and A. Michener
 1994   Homicide reporting in Chicago dailies. *Journalism Quarterly* 71:860-872.
Kennedy, R.
 1997   *Race, Crime, and the Law*. New York: Pantheon Books.
 1998   Overview of racial trends in the administration of criminal justice. Paper prepared for the Research Conference on Racial Trends in the United States, Washington, D.C., October 15-16.
Krisberg, B., ed.
 1987   *Crime and Delinquency*. Special issue on minority youth incarceration and crime. 33(April).
Langan, P.
 1991   *Race of Prisoners Admitted to State and Federal Institutions, 1926-1986*, NCJ-125618. Washington, D.C.: U.S. Department of Justice, Office of Justice Programs, Bureau of Justice Statistics.
Lockwood, D., A. Pottieger, and J. Inciardi
 1995   Crack use, crime by crack users, and ethnicity. Pp. 213-234 in *Ethnicity, Race, and Crime: Perspectives Across Time and Place*, D. Hawkins, ed. Albany: State University of New York Press.
Mann, C.
 1993   *Unequal Justice: A Question of Color*. Bloomington: Indiana University Press.
Mann, C., and M. Zatz
 1998   *Images of Color-Images of Crime*. Los Angeles: Roxbury Publishing.
Mauer, M.
 1990   *Young Black Men and the Criminal Justice System: A Growing Problem*. Washington, D.C.: The Sentencing Project.
Mauer, M., and T. Huling
 1995   *Young Black Americans and the Criminal Justice System: Five Years Later*. Washington, D.C.: The Sentencing Project.
Miller, J.
 1996   *Search and Destroy: African-American Males in the Criminal Justice System*. New York: Cambridge University Press.
Myrdal, G.
 1944   *An American Dilemma*. New York: Harper and Row.
National Advisory Commission on Civil Disorders
 1968   *Report of the National Advisory Commission on Civil Disorders*. New York: Bantam Books.

National Institute on Drug Abuse
  1991   *National Household Survey on Drug Abuse: Population Estimates.* U.S. Department of Health and Human Services publication No. [ADM] 92-1887. Rockville, Md.: National Institute on Drug Abuse.
Oliver, M., and T. Shapiro
  1995   *Black Wealth-White Wealth: A New Perspective on Racial Inequality.* New York: Routledge.
Rebach, H.
  1992   Alcohol and drug use among American minorities. *Drugs and Society* 6:23-57.
Russell, K.
  1998   *The Color of Crime: Racial Hoaxes, White Fear, Black Protectionism, Police Harassment, and Other Macroaggressions.* New York: New York University Press.
Snyder, H., and M. Sickmund
  1995   *Juvenile Offenders and Victims: A National Report.* Washington, D.C.: Office of Juvenile Justice and Delinquency Prevention.
Steinberg, S.
  1989   *The Ethnic Myth: Race, Ethnicity and Class in America.* Boston: Beacon.
Surette, R., ed.
  1984   *Justice and the Media: Issues and Research.* Springfield, Ill.: C.C. Thomas Publishers.
Tonry, M.
  1988   Structuring sentencing. In *Crime and Justice: A Review of Research,* M. Tonry and N. Morris, eds. Chicago: University of Chicago Press.
  1993   Sentencing commissions and their guidelines. In *Crime and Justice: A Review of Research,* M. Tonry and N. Morris, eds. Chicago: University of Chicago Press.
  1995   *Malign Neglect: Race, Crime, and Punishment in America.* New York: Oxford University Press.
  1996   *Sentencing Matters.* New York: Oxford University Press.
U.S. Department of Justice
  1997   *Correctional Populations in the United States, 1995,* NCJ-163916. Washington, D.C.: Office of Justice Programs, Bureau of Justice Statistics.
Walker, S., C. Spohn, and M. DeLone
  1996   *The Color of Justice: Race, Ethnicity, and Crime in America.* Belmont, Calif.: Wadsworth.
Wilbanks, W.
  1987   *The Myth of a Racist Criminal Justice System.* Monterey, Calif.: Brooks/Cole.
Wilson, W.
  1987   *The Truly Disadvantaged.* Chicago: University of Chicago Press.

4

Race and Ethnicity in the Labor Market: Trends Over the Short and Long Term

James P. Smith

O f the many disturbing labor-market trends in recent years, the stagnated wage gap between races may be the most disheartening. Race continues to be America's most persistent area of social and economic disparity. Many Americans were encouraged by the steady and significant economic progress Blacks made after World War II. The recent stagnation, however, challenges that optimism. In addition, the average economic status of Hispanics appears to be deteriorating at an even more alarming rate than that of Blacks.

This paper describes major, long-term trends that have had an impact on the economic status of Blacks and Hispanics, including long-term trends that appear to be influenced mostly by skill-related factors. Also addressed are alternative explanations for the 1960s-to-1990s stagnation in the economic position of minority households; explanations include changes in schooling, quality of students, affirmative action, and rising wage inequality. In addition, the role of immigration in altering the labor-market position of Hispanic workers is analyzed.

LONG-TERM WAGE TRENDS

Since 1940, the American economy has enjoyed substantial economic growth; inflation-adjusted incomes of all its citizens have risen dramatically. For example, real incomes of White men expanded almost threefold between 1940 and 1990, but this improvement was surpassed by even more rapid earnings growth among Black men, whose real incomes more than quadrupled during the same 50-year period (for detailed comparisons, see Smith and Welch, 1989). Not only did the standard of living of Black men improve as measured against earlier Black generations, it rose relative to their White contemporaries.

Table 4-1 shows comparative increases in the relative economic status of Black and Hispanic men from 1940 to 1990. In 1940, the average Black male worker earned only 43 percent as much as his White counterpart; by 1990, it was 75 percent as much. The pace at which Blacks were able to narrow the wage gap, however, was far from uniform. The largest improvement occurred during the 1940s; during the 1950s, advances slowed considerably; during the 1960s and 1970s, the rise in Black men's wages was more than 10 percent higher than the rise in White men's wages; but after 1980, the pace of relative labor-market progress for Blacks slowed considerably.

Although the improvement in the relative economic status of Blacks from 1940 to 1990 was impressive, by 1990 incomes of Black males were still significantly lower than those of White males. The description of the last half century's racial income differences has two messages: (1) considerable progress has been made in eradicating the wage gap between the races; (2) but progress has not eliminated race as an important predictor of an individual's income.

Table 4-1 also shows a remarkably constant wage gap for Hispanics from 1940 to 1990. In 1990, Hispanics earned 67 percent as much as U.S.-born White men, only slightly higher than the Hispanic-White wage gap of 1940. This aggregate stability, however, hides important changes over time. For example, from 1970 to 1990, there was a steady deterioration in the relative economic status of Hispanic men, as their wages decreased by 16 percent compared to White men.

The lack of Hispanic economic progress is most apparent when com-

TABLE 4-1 Minority Male Wages as a Percent of White Male Wages

Minority Group	1940	1950	1960	1970	1980	1990
Blacks	43.3	55.2	57.5	64.4	72.6	74.5
All Hispanics	64.2	73.8	70.2	73.7	70.7	67.3
Mexicans	55.6	71.3	70.0	70.1	68.0	63.0
Puerto Ricans	82.9	71.5	61.3	66.7	66.1	74.5
Cubans	n.a.	n.a.	n.a.	75.6	82.8	86.6
Other Hispanics	82.1	85.4	82.3	82.7	77.6	71.9
Blacks as a percent of Hispanics	67.4	74.8	81.9	87.4	1.03	1.07

pared to Blacks. In 1940, the average Black male worker earned two-thirds as much as the average Hispanic male worker, but in 1990, Black men earned approximately 7 percent more than Hispanic men, on average. One tale of these two minorities is the significant progress achieved by Black men over the last half century. No such story of progress is possible for Hispanics, who seem over the long term to have stagnated and, in recent years, to have deterioriated. This sharp contrast between Hispanics and Blacks suggests that, for Hispanics, forces related to immigration, such as immigration status and English language proficiency, may have played a central role.

Although often viewed as an aggregate, there has always been considerable economic heterogeneity within the Hispanic population. Among the major Hispanic subgroups, Mexicans have always fared the worst economically. In 1940, when the other Hispanic ethnic groups were being paid more than 80 percent of wages paid to U.S.-born White men, Mexican men were earning only 56 percent. By 1950, however, Mexicans were earning 71 percent of what White men earned, a ratio that stayed constant for the next 20 years. After 1970, however, Mexican relative wages declined steadily, expanding their wage disparity to its highest level in more than 40 years.

THE POOR, THE MIDDLE CLASS, AND THE AFFLUENT

Trends in Economic Status

The distribution of this long-term labor-market progress is addressed in Table 4-2. Building on the simplicity of the poverty line, all workers are divided into three wage classes—poor, middle class, and affluent.[1]

Coming out of the Depression era in 1940, 31 percent of working White men had jobs that placed them in the ranks of the poor. The

---

[1]Since the first attempts to measure poverty, debate has continued as to whether poverty is an absolute or relative concept. To determine the percent of the population to be categorized as poor, I used elements of both the absolute and the relative definitions. It turns out that my definition corresponds more closely to most people's notions of what poverty means. Over time, when asked in surveys about the amount of income required not to be poor, the poverty threshold has increased roughly 50 cents for every $1 increase in real income. Based on that observation, my definition of poverty increases the poverty threshold income by 0.5 percent for every 1 percent growth in real income. For 1979, I selected as the initial criterion an income level such that 11 percent of average White male earnings equaled "poor." This poverty threshold was then adjusted for any real income growth or contraction relative to that year. My definition of affluent is asymmetric—i.e., to be affluent, one must have an income equal to 1.33 percent of the White median income for that year (Smith and Welch, 1989).

TABLE 4-2 Income Group Status of Male Workers (percent)

	1940	1950	1960	1970	1980	1990
White Men						
Poor	31	18	13	9	11	12
Middle Class	38	59	63	65	61	60
Affluent	31	23	24	26	28	28
Black Men						
Poor	74	44	37	25	20	23
Middle Class	22	51	58	68	67	64
Affluent	4	5	5	7	13	13
Hispanic Men						
Poor	57	32	27	17	23	27
Middle Class	34	61	66	75	66	62
Affluent	9	7	7	8	11	11
Mexican Men						
Poor	63	37	29	21	24	30
Middle Class	31	57	64	70	65	60
Affluent	6	6	7	9	11	10
Puerto Rican Men						
Poor	33	23	27	15	21	18
Middle Class	49	71	70	80	70	69
Affluent	18	6	3	5	9	13
Other Hispanics						
Poor	45	19	18	13	21	24
Middle Class	40	68	70	73	64	63
Affluent	15	13	12	14	15	13

situation for Blacks and Hispanics was far worse. In 1940, the overwhelming majority of Blacks were poor; three-quarters were destitute, with little hope that their lot or even that of their children would improve. The Black middle class then comprised only one-fifth of all Blacks. On the other extreme, the econmic elite resembled an exclusive White club. Similarly, more than one-half of all Hispanic men in 1940 worked in jobs that confined them and their families within the ranks of the poor; only one in three earned middle-class wages; and the Hispanic affluent comprised one-eleventh of that population. Among Hispanics, Mexicans fared the worst; almost two-thirds of working Mexican men earned wages below the poverty threshold.

The subsequent changes have been dramatic. Driven by economic growth and improvements in the skills of the workforce, poverty rates declined rapidly for the White male majority. Between 1940 and 1970, median White wages grew by 3.2 percent per year, a growth that was fairly uniform across the wage distribution. By 1970, only one in every 11 White male workers earned wages below the poverty threshold, and almost two-thirds earned middle-class incomes. Unfortunately, this historic trend reversed during the 1970s and 1980s. The stagnant economic conditions of those decades, combined with expanding wage inequality, led to an increase in both the percentage of White men who were poor and the percentage who were affluent.

The real story of the 1940s-1990s was the emergence of the Black and Hispanic middle class, whose income gains were real and substantial. Unfortunately, as was true for the White majority, these gains in poverty reduction reversed, but at a more rapid rate for Blacks and Hispanics in the 1970s and 1980s. Since 1980, there has been a more than 10 percent increase in the relative numbers of Black and Hispanic working men who were poor. Notwithstanding these downturns, the growth of the Black middle class was so spectacular that in 1990 it outnumbered the Black poor. In 1990, about two-thirds of Blacks and Hispanics had incomes that met the criteria for middle class. In addition, the odds of a Black man penetrating the ranks of the affluent tripled.

Trends in Education

A basic index of the skill workers bring with them to the labor market is the number of years of schooling completed. Because, on average, Blacks and Hispanics complete fewer years of schooling than Whites, education should play a central role in explaining both levels and trends in their wage gaps. It does. Table 4-3 lists mean years of schooling completed for White, Black, and Hispanic males. To highlight differences, education deficits of Blacks and Hispanics, compared to Whites, are also shown.

Not surprising, among all groups, education levels of each new generation increased from 1940 to 1990. Although this secular improvement exists for men of both races, data in Table 4-3 indicate that improvement was much sharper among Black men. Educational differences still persist between Blacks and Whites, but to a lesser extent in 1990 than at any other time in American history. In 1990, the average Black male had completed 1.1 fewer years of schooling than the average White male, representing a steady and continuous decrease from the 3.7-years difference in 1940. Between 1940 and 1990, almost three-quarters of the education gap between Blacks and Whites was eliminated (Smith and Welch, 1989).

The rate of secular improvement in Hispanic schooling by 1990 was slower and more uneven. Although Black men erased three-quarters of

TABLE 4-3 Education Levels of Males

Year	White	Black	Hispanic	Mexican	Puerto Rican	Cuban	Other Hispanic
A. Average Education Levels of Males							
1990	13.30	12.19	10.57	9.97	11.37	12.28	11.45
1980	12.76	11.37	10.18	9.57	10.09	11.72	11.37
1970	11.84	9.82	9.52	8.76	8.92	10.75	10.82
1960	10.37	7.54	7.88	7.34	7.77	n.a.	9.94
1950	10.23	6.71	6.61	6.08	7.73	n.a.	8.07
1940	9.48	5.74	5.95	5.34	7.95	n.a.	7.15
B. Education Deficits Compared to White Men							
1990	-0-	1.11	2.73	3.33	1.93	1.02	1.85
1980	-0-	1.39	2.58	3.19	2.67	1.04	1.39
1970	-0-	2.02	2.32	3.08	2.92	1.35	1.02
1960	-0-	2.83	2.49	3.03	2.60	n.a.	0.43
1950	-0-	3.52	3.62	4.15	2.50	n.a.	2.16
1940	-0-	3.74	3.53	4.14	1.53	n.a.	2.33

their educational disparity with White men, Hispanics were able to eliminate less than one-third of their initial 1940 deficit. In the process, their education ranking was reversed. Hispanics had a 0.2-year lead over Black men in 1940; by 1990, Black men had more than a 1.5-year schooling advantage. The 1990 Hispanic education gap with White men was nearly two and a half times as large as the schooling gap between Blacks and Whites in that year.

To understand reasons for these disparities, it is necessary to distinguish among Hispanic immigrants and U.S.-born Hispanics. Because immigrants tend to have much less schooling than do U.S.-born Hispanics, secular trends in schooling can be quite sensitive to swings in the size of immigration flows. Some insight into the central role of immigration is suggested by the data in Table 4-4 where Hispanic education levels are listed (and their deficits compared with Whites) by U.S. birth or foreign birth and whether they were recent immigrants—i.e., arrived within the past five years.

Data in Table 4-4 indicate that the changing composition of recent immigration and the increasing percentage of immigrants within the Hispanic population are two dominant underlying trends. Given the better educational opportunities available in the United States, compared to those in their home countries, it is not surprising that U.S.-born Hispanic men have more schooling than their foreign-born counterparts; however, the different secular trends for the U.S.-born and foreign-born Hispanics are more surprising. From 1940 to 1990, the education disparity between

TABLE 4-4　Male Hispanic Years of Schooling Completed, by Nativity

	1990	1980	1970	1960	1950	1940
A. Average Education Levels of Males						
All Hispanics	10.57	10.18	9.37	7.88	6.61	5.95
U.S. born	11.98	10.93	9.80	8.18	7.04	6.18
Foreign born	9.36	9.24	9.26	7.17	5.24	5.27
1-5 years in U.S.	8.96	8.36	9.13	8.47	n.a.	8.21
6 or more years in U.S.	9.50	9.56	9.33	6.75	n.a.	5.23
B. Education Deficits Compared to White Men						
All Hispanics	2.66	2.49	2.47	2.49	3.62	3.53
U.S. born	1.25	1.74	2.04	2.19	3.19	3.30
Foreign born	3.77	3.43	2.58	3.20	4.99	4.21
1-5 years in U.S.	4.27	4.31	2.71	1.90	n.a.	1.27
6 or more years in U.S.	3.73	3.11	2.51	3.62	n.a.	4.25

U.S.-born Hispanics and U.S.-born Whites steadily narrowed. In 1940, U.S.-born White men had a 3.3-year schooling advantage over U.S.-born Hispanic men. By 1990, 60 percent of this deficit had been eliminated, and U.S.-born Hispanics had a deficit of 1.3 years. Similar trends are found for all Hispanic groups, especially for the numerically important Mexican subpopulation.

A far different picture emerges among the foreign-born. Not only are their disparities with White men considerably larger, there is no longer a trend of uniform progress. In particular, from 1970 to 1990, the era of reversal in the aggregate data, the education gap for foreign-born men increased significantly. Indeed, the mean education of foreign-born Hispanic men is little higher now than it was in 1970. Compared to U.S.-born Whites, the education deficit of foreign-born Hispanic workers rose from 2.58 years in 1970 to 3.77 years in 1990.

The force of these changes is most apparent among recent immigrants, who represent a better index of the education of newly arriving immigrants. From 1940 to 1990, there was a steady deterioration in the relative education levels of new Hispanic immigrants. In 1940, compared to U.S.-born White men, new Hispanic immigrants had a deficit of 1.3 years; by 1990, the deficit had risen to 4.3 years. Education deficits of recent immigrants accelerated after 1970.

In sum, the slow rate of Hispanic educational progress largely reflects a changing composition of the Hispanic immigrant workforce. The rising percentage of immigrants in the Hispanic male workforce in recent decades slowed aggregate gains in Hispanic schooling. Increasing numbers of poorly educated Mexicans among Hispanic immigrants also served to lower the mean schooling advances achieved. The aggregate education data for all Hispanics raised an important dilemma best highlighted by comparing limited aggregate Hispanic education gains with the substantial gains achieved by Blacks from 1940 to 1990. If we limit our comparison to Blacks and U.S.-born Hispanics, the dilemma is resolved. Both groups show, in 1990, a substantial narrowing of their education deficits with White men. Hispanics born in the United States seem no less able than Blacks to improve their educational position over time.

RECENT LABOR-MARKET WAGE TRENDS

In a number of important ways, the long-term historical trends begun in 1940 did not continue from the 1960s to the 1990s. In this section, trends in weekly wages by year, race, ethnicity, and gender from the 1960s to 1990 are examined using the yearly March Current Population Surveys (CPS), starting in 1962.

To set an overall context, Figure 4-1 shows yearly trends in mean

A

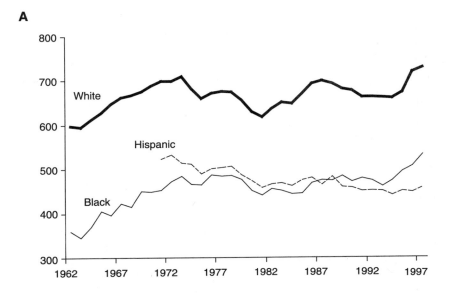

B

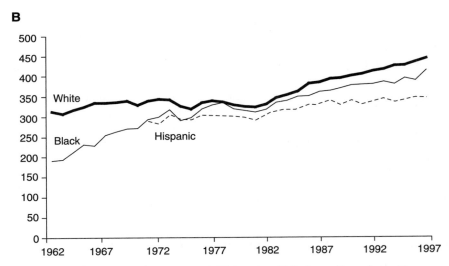

FIGURE 4-1 Yearly trends (1962 to 1997) in mean inflation-adjusted weekly wages for (A) males and (B) females.

inflation-adjusted weekly wages for working Black, Hispanic, and White men and women. Data for White men can serve as an index of what was happening with average wages for all groups. As an approximation, secular trends can be separated into three periods. From 1962 to 1973, real wages grew (1.6 percent per year). Then followed a sharp decline until 1981, when the average real wage of White men fell 14 percent from the 1973 high. This decrease was so steep that real wages in 1981 were only 3 percent higher than in 1962. Fortunately, the years since 1981 were ones of recovery, with real wages of White men in 1996 15 percent higher than at the 1981 trough (1 percent per year growth).

Time-series trends for other groups primarily mimic trends for White men; however, of interest here are those instances of departure from the White male series. These departures are captured in Figure 4-2, which measures yearly wage gaps, as percentages, for Hispanic and Black men and women, relative to White male wages.

Consider, first, working Black men. As was true for White men, real wages among Black men increased from 1962 to 1973, fell from 1973 to 1981, and then gradually rose. Their trends, however, were far from identical. In particular, from 1962 to 1976 the wage gap between Black and White males decreased sharply, from more than 50 percent at the beginning of the period, to about 32 percent at the end. Then, relative progress ceased and actually reversed, as the gap increased to 41 percent by 1986. Given the noise in the data, it is difficult to know with complete confidence what happened since, but a reasonable characterization would be a modest but steady narrowing of the male racial wage gap.

CPS categorization of data based on Hispanic ethnicity began in 1971. Since then, trends in the wage gap among Hispanic men could not be more different. Throughout the 1970s, the Hispanic male wage deficit, using White male data as an index, held steady at about 30 percent. Since the 1980s, however, this wage gap grew, and reached about 45 percent by the mid-1990s. If we examine data for Mexicans alone, the trends are similar, except that the wage gap is about 5 to 8 percent greater than that observed for all Hispanics.

A different pattern again emerges by gender. White female wage gaps expanded from the early 1960s to the mid-1970s—the same years when Black men enjoyed their largest gains. Since the mid-1960s, however, there has been a long, sustained improvement in the wage position of working women. By 1997, the White female wage deficit was about 50 percent, compared to a peak wage deficit of 73 percent in 1973. Black and Hispanic women exhibit their own unique patterns. By far, the largest relative wage gains were made by Black women. The pace of early improvements was staggering. From 1962 through 1973, when real wages among White men increased by 17 percent, real wages of Black women

A

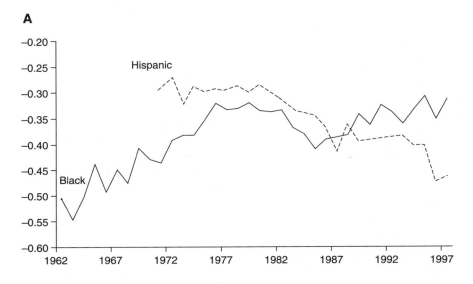

B

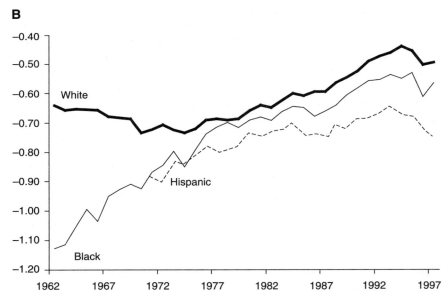

FIGURE 4-2 Percentage wage deficits, relative to White males, for Black and Hispanic (A) males and (B) females.

increased by 50 percent. Although the pace of relative improvement slowed thereafter, it continued steadily until the wage gap for Black women reached about 50 percent, compared to initial levels almost twice that great. In contrast to Hispanic men, Hispanic women did experience some wage gains, but they were relatively small and confined to the 1970s. Similar patterns, with a slightly higher wage gap, exist for Mexican women.

As with the longer-term trends since the 1940s, these more recent trends may also be affected by some well-established, labor-market skill correlate such as schooling. Workers' schooling backgrounds—i.e., where educated and years of schooling completed—changed only gradually as younger, more educated workers replaced less educated workers who retired. Consequently, labor-market conditions among younger workers may be a more sensitive barometer of some of the forces leading to labor-market change. With this in mind, Figures 4-3 and 4-4 plot Black and Hispanic male and female wage gaps, compared with White male wages, based on mean years of schooling completed—exactly 12 years (high school graduates) and 16 years (college graduates). To concentrate on the young, data are shown for workers with 10 or fewer years of labor-market experience.

It is no surprise that male wage gaps are significantly smaller within education groups, which simply speaks to education's always-powerful role as a wage predictor. This smaller gap also results, in part, from the stratification by years of experience, but is mostly a consequence of education stratification. Although sampling variability plays a more important role after these stratifications are made, one can still characterize some trends with some confidence. Among high school graduates, the male racial wage gap has one sharp V-shaped pattern; a steep fall starting in 1976, reaching a trough in the mid-1980s, followed by a subsequent narrowing of the racial wage gap. Despite these impressive cycles, however, the end points are essentially the same, so that the high school racial wage gap was basically unchanged from 1960 to the mid-1980s.

Racial trends among college graduates are clearer. Starting with a relatively large wage gap in the early 1960s, wages of Black male college graduates increased sharply until parity with White male college graduates had almost been reached by 1973. That near parity would, however, be short lived as the male racial wage gap among college graduates eventually expanded until almost coming full circle by 1994.

An important pattern to note among Hispanic males is that their same-education-level wage deficits with White men (see Figure 4-3B) are considerably smaller than the racial wage deficits of Black males. This is another reflection of the general finding that after one controls for a rather small list of standard variables—schooling, age, and English language

A

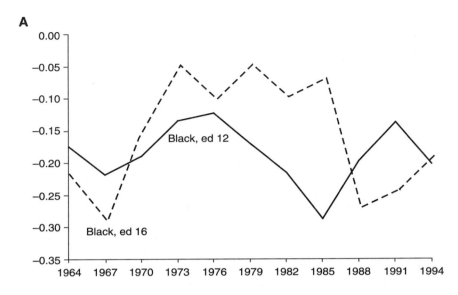

B

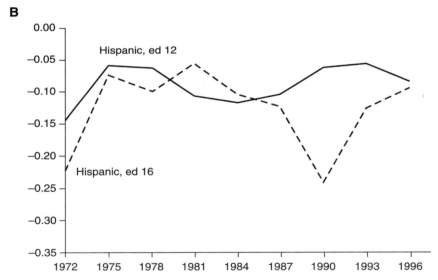

FIGURE 4-3 Percentage wage deficits with comparable White males for (A) Black (1964-1994) and (B) Hispanic (1972-1996) males' average wages for workers with 10 or fewer years of experience. ed 12 = 12 years of schooling (high school graduates); ed 16 = 16 years of schooling (college graduates).

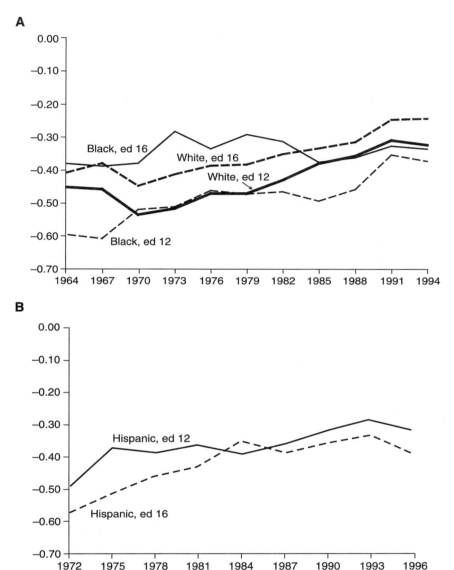

FIGURE 4-4 Percentage wage deficits with comparable White males for (A) Black (1964-1994) and (B) Hispanic (1972-1996) females' average wages for workers with 10 or fewer years of experience. ed 12 = 12 years of schooling (high school graduates); ed 16 = 16 years of schooling (college graduates).

ability—there is little left that is unexplained about the wage differences between Hispanics and Whites—a statement that one would clearly hesitate to make about racial disparities. After controlling for schooling and English language ability, there is no discernible trend in the male wage gap among Hispanics. An implication of this relatively small and constant within-schooling wage gap is that identifying the reasons underlying trends in schooling and age may be enough to account for male Hispanic labor-market trends. But schooling and years of work experience do not comprise a sufficient explanation when the subject turns to race.

Figure 4-4 contains the same-education-level trends for younger Black, Hispanic, and White women compared to younger White men. As a reasonable generalization, among all demographic subgroups, wage gaps with younger White men narrowed in both schooling classes. This indicates that relative schooling trends by sex alone will not account for the narrowing of gender wage differences. Unlike race, the major discriminating variable for women is not schooling but, rather, years of labor-force participation, which leads to greater amounts of labor-market experience (Smith and Ward, 1989). Another point to note is that the narrowing of the gender wage gap in comparison to men was generally more pronounced among college graduates. For example, data begin with 1964 showing higher wage gaps among White female college graduates, but by the mid-1990s this ranking had reversed and the gender wage deficit was greatest among White high school graduates.

So far, all wage comparisons shown here have relied on mean wages across demographic groups. A reliance solely on means is always problematic, but never more so than during the 1960s to 1990s. Whatever was happening to differences among these demographic groups, the major labor-market action was actually occurring elsewhere. During these years, the overriding structural adjustment in the labor market was the rapidly expanding increase in wage inequality. This increase was dramatic even among White men, and can be summarized by a simple rule of thumb— the lower the initial wage or skill, the smaller the subsequent wage growth that took place. Combined with the fact that median wages were relatively flat during most of this period, the end result was that workers earning less than the median wage experienced real-wage losses, and those earning more than the median wage had real-wage gains. Although this structural adjustment was, at its core, not a racial or ethnic issue, the implications of the structural change were decidedly not race or ethnicity neutral.

One graphic glimpse of its legacy is illustrated in Table 4-5 (which parallels Table 4-2). Workers are divided into poor, middle-class, and

TABLE 4-5 Income Group Status of Workers (percent)

	1962	1973	1982	1991	1997
White Men					
Poor	10	11	12	12	12
Middle Class	66	62	57	55	54
Affluent	24	27	31	33	34
Black Men					
Poor	26	17	17	19	16
Middle Class	70	75	70	65	65
Affluent	4	8	13	16	19
Hispanic Men					
Poor	NA	14	14	17	17
Middle Class	NA	66	72	70	69
Affluent	NA	10	14	13	14
Mexican Men					
Poor	NA	15	14	19	18
Middle Class	NA	75	71	70	70
Affluent	NA	8	15	11	12
White Women					
Poor	32	31	30	25	23
Middle Class	65	66	66	64	62
Affluent	3	3	4	11	15
Black Women					
Poor	60	34	30	27	24
Middle Class	39	63	67	65	65
Affluent	1	3	3	8	10
Hispanic Women					
Poor	NA	31	30	31	28
Middle Class	NA	68	67	67	65
Affluent	NA	1	3	6	7
Mexican Women					
Poor	NA	39	29	34	31
Middle Class	NA	60	68	61	63
Affluent	NA	1	3	5	6

affluent groups, based on their wages.[2]   For women especially, this tri-
chotomy is not equivalent to poverty statistics in the conventional sense.
Federal poverty thresholds are based on family incomes (with equiva-
lence-scale adjustments for family composition and size).   Thresholds
here are based on each individual's wages only and simply separated into
three wage classes to determine where different demographic groups end
up in the wage hierarchy and how that separation has changed over time.
The dominant trend among White men is a sharp growth in the percentage of affluent workers. By 1997, more than one-third of all White male
workers were affluent compared to one-fourth in 1962. Using these
thresholds, the relative decrease in middle-class workers shown is the
result of an increasing percentage of affluent workers, rather than any
expansion in the ranks of the poor.

Our central interest centers on the relative status of the other groups.
The principal reductions in the ranks of poor working Black men were
concentrated between 1962 and 1973. Thereafter, the era of stagnation
took over, with Black male poverty rates essentially the same in 1997 as
they were in 1973. Not all was stagnant in the economic status of the
Black community, however. In the 35 years spanned by the data in Table
4-5, there was almost a quintupling in the relative number of affluent
Black male workers. Unlike the working poor data, the trend among the
Black affluent showed no sign of abatement. Growing numbers of Black
male workers not only entered the middle class, they went right past it.

In a more muted way, similar trends exist for Hispanic men. Among
all Hispanic and among Mexican men, the percentage of poor drifted
upward over this period. Simultaneously, the percentage of affluent Hispanic men rose, although, in contrast to Black men, their entry into the
ranks of the affluent was completed by the early 1980s.

Income divisions in Table 4-5 must be interpreted with even more
care with regard to women. As stated earlier, many women whose own
wages may be low live in families with relatively high incomes. These
women would not be classified as poor in any welfare sense. Yet, it is still
of interest to examine how they rank based solely on their wages alone.
Because many women work part time, much larger percentages of them
had weekly wages such that they were categorized as poor; only a relative
handful were able to join the ranks of the affluent. The division into these
three groups changed little for White women until the early 1980s. Thereafter, there was a rapid decrease in the percentage of poor White women,

---

[2]Data are normalized so that 11 percent of White working men in 1979 are defined as
poor. Similar rules as those contained in footnote 1 were used to set the other threshold
values.

and an even more impressive increase in their percentage in the affluent class. In contrast, dramatic upward trends among Black women took place during the 1960s, when their representation among the poor was almost cut in half. At a much reduced pace, these improvements for Black women continued, and in 1997, one-fourth of Black women had weekly wages classifying them as poor, compared with six-tenths of them classified as poor in the early 1960s. In contrast, changes for Hispanic women are modest—a slight reduction in the percentage of poor alongside a more pronounced increase in their percentages among the affluent.

One must be impressed by the diversity in secular wage trends among these different minority group workers. Not only did the size of their wage gaps with White men change at quite different rates, but the periods during which major changes occurred are all over the map. A single factor, common in timing to all groups, apparently will not explain all the changes that have been taking place during the past few decades in the structure of wages across these demographic groups.

EXPLAINING RECENT WAGE TRENDS

To this point, what have been presented mostly are facts that need to be explained. How can such an extraordinarily diverse set of relative wage trends across groups be explained? The potential explanations are (1) differences in schooling, (2) changing quality of minority students, (3) affirmative action, and (4) structural labor-market changes, especially rising wage inequality. For women, to this set must be added (1) the increased entry of women into the labor market and (2) the growing amounts of labor-market experience that go along with it. Finally, additional issues related to their immigrant status arise when the subject turns to Hispanics.

RECENT TRENDS IN EDUCATION

No discussion of trends in the wage gap can proceed far without addressing the role of schooling. Figures 4-5 and 4-6 plot education deficits of each demographic group, with White males as an index. Schooling differences still persist between the races, but to a lesser degree now than at any time in our history. Figure 4-5A shows the education deficit of Black male workers steadily decreased from a more than 2-year schooling deficit, and plateaued at 0.5 year by the mid-1990s. If these schooling trends are compared with trends in the male racial wage gap, the issue is not the early years when the two series (wage gap and schooling deficit) moved in lockstep. Rather, the anomaly involves the past 20 years when schooling deficits continued to narrow while male racial wage gaps stagnated.

If only younger male workers are examined (Figure 4-5B), clearly a steady narrowing of schooling deficits took place in the 20 years between 1962 and 1982. Throughout this century, schooling has been the engine of Black economic progress, but educational progress for men stopped abruptly in the 1980s when the schooling gap of young Black male workers remained constant at about 0.5 year. The 1980s and 1990s cohorts represent the first generation of Black workers who have not decreased schooling gaps with White workers. This end of racial progress is not the result of growing numbers of Black high school dropouts, as the percentage of high school dropouts continued to fall in the 1980s. The problem lies in the transition from high school to college; Black men were no more likely to make that transition in 1990 than 15 years earlier.

These trends could not be any more different among Hispanic workers. For both male workers at all experiential levels and those with 10 or fewer years' experience, their schooling gap with White workers has remained constant at more than two years. Because Black workers had been steadily closing the deficit, by the mid-1990s the average Hispanic worker had a two-year education deficit, compared to his Black counterpart.

From 1962 to 1997, there were never large differences in average schooling between White male and female workers (Figure 4-6A). Gender disparities in schooling among workers depend on both underlying education trends in the full population and on trends in female labor-force participation rates across schooling classes. For both reasons, among workers, White male schooling actually rose faster than White females' until after the early 1980s (see Smith and Ward, 1989). Then, White female workers took the lead until they reclaimed their traditional educational advantage with White males. This resurgence stems from more rapid education gains among women compared to men; gains that were reinforced by more rapid gains in labor-force participation rates among more educated women. Paralleling their rapid relative wage advances, Black female workers steadily narrowed their education disparity with White male workers. It is a remarkable point in American history that, at least among young workers, there were in 1990 essentially no differences in schooling between White men and Black women. Finally, Hispanic women did somewhat better than their male counterparts in that they slightly narrowed their schooling gaps with White men.

To sum up, what role can changing education disparities play in accounting for changing wage disparities across these demographic groups since the 1960s? Until the mid-1970s, schooling continued to assume its historical role as the primary determinant of the male racial wage gap.

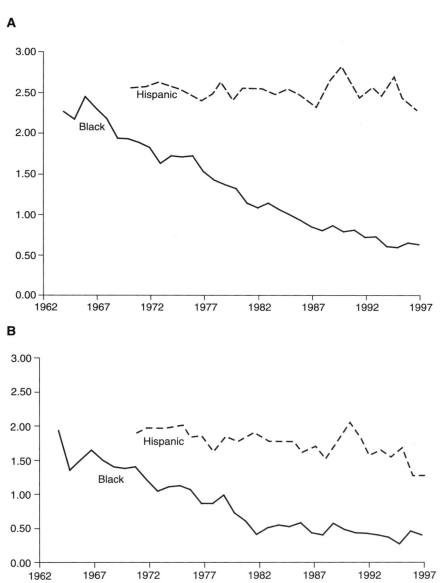

FIGURE 4-5 Education deficits, as percentages, for Black and Hispanic (A) males and (B) males with 10 or fewer years of experience.

A

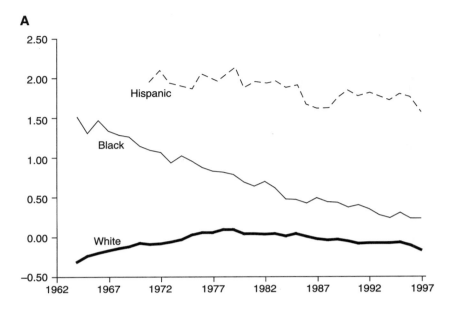

B

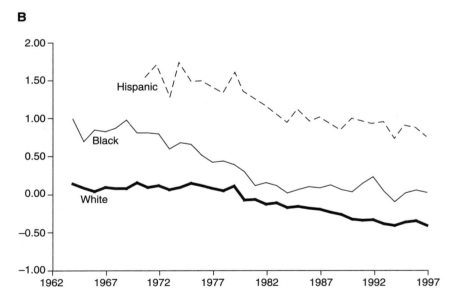

FIGURE 4-6 Education deficits with White men, as percentages, for Black and Hispanic (A) females and (B) females with 10 or fewer years of experience.

Male education differences by race, however, cannot account for the timing and magnitude of the racial stagnation since the mid-1970s; nor can schooling account for the impressive narrowing of the gender wage gap since the 1960s. The stagnation and decrease in Hispanic wages relative to U.S.-born Whites, however, is consistent with the apparent lack of relative educational progress of the average Hispanic worker. The adjective *apparent* is necessary because the absence of progress is mostly the result of a compositional effect of the addition of new Hispanic immigrants with low levels of schooling.

ACHIEVEMENT SCORES

One possible explanation for the stagnation in Black labor-market gains, especially among Black men, that fortunately can be dismissed is that their labor-force quality fell. The origins of any such decrease presumably would lie in the schools. If the quality of minority students had fallen, this would have eventually shown up as lower wages in the labor market. In spite of widespread and legitimate concerns that the quality of contemporary schooling for minority students is low and falling, achievement data tell a different story. Table 4-6 documents a persistent improvement in the achievement of Black high school students compared to that of White students. For both reading and math, achievement scores of White 17-year-olds drifted only slightly upward during the past two decades. In contrast, achievement scores of Black 17-year-olds have consistently improved, and the racial gap has narrowed considerably. To cite examples, 45 percent of the racial gap in reading proficiency, and 33 percent of the gap in math proficiency, between Black and White 17-year-olds has been erased since 1971.

This improvement is not the result of less able Black students dropping out and not taking the exam. Test scores are also presented for 13-year-olds, for whom the high school dropout rate is not an issue. Across math, reading, and science the achievement gap by race among 13-year-olds has been narrowing. Similar evidence of a narrowing in scholastic achievement gaps by race can be obtained from Scholastic Aptitude Test scores of college-bound seniors.

Monitoring trends in student achievement is far more difficult among Hispanics because of the possible skewing of data caused by the continuing influx of new immigrants. If new immigrants perform less well in these tests, average Hispanic scores may decrease without any change in ability of any Hispanic students. In spite of this potential problem, achievement scores of Hispanic students also improved relative to non-Hispanic Whites, albeit at a slower rate of gain than Black students enjoyed.

TABLE 4-6 Achievement Scores of High School Students

Proficiency in	Year				
Reading	1971	1980	1984	1990	1996
White 13 yr old	261	264	263	262	267
Black 13 yr old	222	233	236	242	236
Hispanic 13 yr old	—	237	240	238	240
White 17 yr old	291	293	295	297	294
Black 17 yr old	239	243	264	267	265
Hispanic 17 yr old	—	261	268	275	265
Percent of students rated adept at reading	1971	1980	1984	1990	1996
White	43.2	43.3	46.3	50.1	45.1
Black	7.7	7.1	16.2	16.9	18.0
Hispanic	—	16.5	21.2	27.1	20.0
Science	1973	1977	1986	1990	1996
White 13 yr old	263	256	257	264	266
Black 13 yr old	205	208	221	226	226
Hispanic 13 yr old	—	213	226	232	232
White 17 yr old	304	298	298	301	307
Black 17 yr old	250	240	253	253	260
Hispanic 17 yr old	—	262	259	262	269
Mathematics	1973	1978	1986	1990	1996
White 13 yr old	274	272	274	276	281
Black 13 yr old	228	230	249	249	252
Hispanic 13 yr old	239	238	254	255	256
White 17 yr old	310	306	308	310	313
Black 17 yr old	270	268	279	289	286
Hispanic 17 yr old	277	276	283	284	292
SAT scores of college-bound seniors		1976	1980	1990	1995
Verbal					
White		451	442	442	448
Black		332	330	352	356
Mexican-Americans		371	372	380	376
Mathematics					
White		493	482	491	498
Black		354	360	385	388
Mexican-Americans		410	413	429	426

SOURCE: National Center for Education Statistics: Education Testing Service (1991).

AFFIRMATIVE ACTION

What is the evidence, from 1960 to 1990, of the effect of affirmative action enforcement on the economic position of minorities? Overall, the evidence is mixed with much more consensus on employment effects than on wages, and disagreements on the exact timing and sustainability of impacts.

On one issue, there appears now to be little ambiguity. There is abundant evidence that affirmative action changed where Black men and women worked and the jobs they were able to obtain, especially in the late 1960s and early 1970s (Chay, 1998; Donahue and Heckman, 1991; Holzer and Neumark, 1999; Smith and Welch, 1984). If affirmative action were effective, minority representation should have expanded more among firms required to report to the Equal Employment Opportunity Commission (EEOC). Because they have more to lose, the greatest gains in employment should also have occurred among federal contractors. Finally, the largest minority gains should have been detected within professional and managerial jobs.

The cumulative evidence does show these types of employment effects. For example, Smith and Welch (1984) compared time-series changes in minority employment by whether firms were covered by EEOC and whether the firm was a federal contractor. They show, for 1966, that Black men were 8 percent less likely than White men to work in covered firms; by 1980, however, Black men were 26 percent more likely to work in EEOC-reporting firms. Adding to the suspicion that these were affirmative action-induced changes, these employment shifts were dominated by federal contractors.

As large as these increases in total employment seem, they pale next to changes within professional jobs. Black male professionals were 41 percent less likely than White professionals to work in covered firms in 1966. By 1980, Black male professionals were equally likely to be found in covered firms. A critical issue relates to the timing of effects. The largest employment changes for men occurred between 1966 and 1970, the first four years of required reporting. After 1974, there was little further change in the location of Black male employment by EEOC coverage.

Changes in the sectoral location of employment were even more dramatic and enduring among Black women. In 1966, Black women were 9 percent less likely than White men to be employed in the covered sector. By 1980, they were 54 percent more likely than White men to work in the covered sector. The relocation was more pronounced for officials and managers—39 percent less likely in covered employment in 1966; 54 percent more likely by 1980. Compared to these racial differences, there was a slight expansion in employment of White women (and officials and managers) in covered EEOC employment. Many clerical jobs that had been traditionally held by White women in the covered sector now were held instead by Black women.

In sum, Smith and Welch (1984) demonstrate that the employment effects of affirmative action differ between Black women and Black men. For men, there was a rapid increase in demand for Black workers that appears to have been largely completed, in stock terms, by 1974. For Black women, the increase in demand was even larger and persisted throughout the 1970s.

This evidence of employment effects is supported in other studies. For example, Chay (1998) analyzes the effects of the 1972 expansion of EEOC coverage to employers with 15 to 24 employees and finds that there were shifts in employment favoring Black workers following this expansion in coverage, particularly in the South (where state laws that covered such firms had not previously existed). Similarly, in an important paper, Heckman and Payner (1989) demonstrated that 1965 was a year of an extremely sharp break in the employment of Black men and women in the textile industry in South Carolina. This break was so severe and its timing so precise that there is no other plausible explanation except that it was the consequence of the passage of the Civil Rights Act of 1964.

The wage effects that one can assign to affirmative action are far more controversial and uncertain; however, the rapidity and magnitude of the increases in Black male and female wages during the late 1960s and early 1970s cannot be easily explained by the more slowly evolving changes in the skill distributions between the races. For example, the case that affirmative action pressures, which lead to shifts in employment, contributed to relative gains in Black male wages in the late 1960s and early 1970s is a strong one. For similar reasons, the case is even stronger that affirmative action played an important role in the extraordinary wage gains enjoyed by Black women throughout the late 1960s and 1970s.

Did cutbacks in affirmative action resources and pressures also account for the recent labor-market stagnation especially for Black men? Some feel that affirmative action is the likely culprit behind Black economic stagnation because these policies were significantly changed in the 1980s (Smith, 1993) (Table 4-7). EEOC resources were indeed cut during this period. EEOC inflation-adjusted budgets grew almost 15 percent per year during the 1970s. Although there was some slowdown in the last half of the decade, constant-dollar EEOC budgets expanded by 7 percent per year during the Carter administration; and almost 1,400 budgeted positions were added to the agency (a growth of 50 percent) between 1976 and 1980.

There is no question that during the Reagan administration there was an abrupt end to the growth in EEOC resources. EEOC constant-dollar

TABLE 4-7 Summary Statistics for EEOC

Year	Budget[a] ($1000)	Positions[a]	Charges Resolved[b]	Lawsuits[a]
1966	16,098	314	6,400	NA
1970	55,428	780	8,480	NA
1975	164,319	2,384	62,300	180
1980	242,829	3,777	49,225	326
1985	244,113	3,107	46,411	
1991	237,954	2,796	45,442	495
1995	244,998	2,813	54,464	318
1997	239,740	2,586	62,533	296

NOTE: Budget in 1997 dollars.

[a]Source for 1995 and 1997 data: A Summary of Enforcement Data and Budget and Staffing Information for the U.S. Equal Opportunity Commission. Personal communication, September 1998.

[b]Source: A Title VII of the Civil Rights Act of 1964 Charges FY 1991-1997. From Enforcement Data at EEOC's website.

TABLE 4-8 EEOC Actionable Charges[a]

Year	Race	Sex	Age	Disability
1965	0	0	0	0
1966	3,254	2,053	0	0
1970	11,806	3,572	0	0
1975	33,174	20,205	0	0
1980	44,436	28,171	14	0
1986	47,264	30,576	23,142	0
1992	49,309	41,314	30,064	0
1995	50,879	48,923	28,858	34,282

[a]Prior to 1995, this series was called "Actionable Charges" and taken from EEOC Annual Reports. Subsequently these data are from "Fiscal Year Charge Receipts by Geographic Region EEOC and FEP Agencies," EEOC Annual Report.

budgets fell during this period, and the number of positions declined by almost 1,000. Two presidents later, through the 1990s, there was virtually no resource recovery.

As EEOC resources and personnel decreased during the 1980s, so did measurable output. The sharp break in the 1980s was not so much in the total amount of activity, as in its composition and the resources available per case. Spurred by the passage of the Age Discrimination Act in 1979, age came into its own during this decade. Starting with only 14 cases in the year after passage of the act, the number of age cases increased at an astonishing pace to more than 30,000 by 1992 (Table 4-8). Even without this explosion in age related charges, the significance of race was declining. By 1992, only 40 percent of all EEOC cases involved race issues, compared to 85 percent in 1970. During the 1990s, the new competitor for enforcement resources was cases related to the passage of disability laws. Combined age and disability cases now account for 20 percent more cases than those associated with race.

The declining importance of race on the EEOC's agenda reflects a more general dilution of race as this country's core civil rights concern. Since 1965, the road to equal rights has become very crowded. The quest for racial justice was the clear moral force behind the 1964 Civil Rights Act, with women added in an unsuccessful attempt to scuttle the legislation. Subsequently, Hispanics began to rival Blacks in political clout, and protected minority group status was extended to men older than 40 years old, people with disabilities, and gays. The end result is that more than three-quarters of today's labor force enjoy protected minority group status. Blacks are now a minority in the protected minority class, which itself represents the majority.

Trends in the courts reinforce these changes at the EEOC. In the early years, plaintiffs in employment discrimination cases were the clear winners in the courtroom battles, winning twice as often as defendants did. The odds quickly began to shift throughout the 1970s and 1980s, until firms now win three times as many cases as plaintiffs. Not only were the odds shifting in the courtroom, but one of the most potent weapons in discrimination cases was steadily falling into disuse. A firm's potential financial cost from a discrimination lawsuit was substantially magnified when an individual complaint was filed as representing an entire class of workers. In 1971, 25 percent of employment discrimination cases were class-action suits. Today, less than one in every 200 cases is a class action.

The fact that affirmative action did affect Black employment in the 1970s, and that that policy changed so dramatically in the 1980s, makes it easy to understand why affirmative action retrenchment may also have been responsible for the racial wage stagnation in the 1980s. Although it is plausible, it turns out to be incorrect. The main problem is that the timing of the wage stagnation had little connection to the timing of affirmative action cutbacks. For example, Figure 4-2A shows that the stagnation in aggregate Black male wages began in 1977 and remained so during the Carter years, when EEOC resources were expanding rapidly. Indeed among Black and Hispanic male high school graduates (Figure 4-3), the bulk of the decrease in the racial wage gap took place during the EEOC surge in resources. Among college graduates, the large decrease in the male racial wage gap appears to have taken place well after the cutback in EEOC resources.

During the initial phases of affirmative action, there was a remarkable surge in the incomes of young, college-educated Black men to almost complete wage parity. There is little question that this was an affirmative action-induced benefit. First, the sharp acceleration in Black male wage gains during the late 1960s and early 1970s coincided with the large affirmative action-induced employment effects discussed earlier as Blacks moved in large numbers into the covered sector. Second, the wage gains Blacks achieved during these years are simply too large to be explained by the more slowly evolving historical process of racial skill convergence. This was, however, an ephemeral benefit, as early wage gains exaggerate the permanent affirmative action wage effect. For college graduates, this erosion marked both decades, until we had roughly come full circle with a wage deficit in 1997 little different than the initial wage deficit.

Why did the early gains resulting from affirmative action not persist? By the mid-1970s, the labor-market adjustment to affirmative action had largely taken place. Affirmative action caused many more Black men to be employed in the EEOC-covered sector. But this adjustment was largely finished by the mid-1970s, so that there was little additional reason for these firms to disproportionately hire Black men. In addition, the Black male supply response was rapid and large. In the 10 years after 1967, the number of Black male college graduates in the workforce had more than doubled, while the increase in the number of White college workers was less than half as large. There were lots more college-educated Blacks. This large supply response had two effects. First, it directly produced a decrease in the relative wages of Black male college graduates among new entrants; second, it also eventually eradicated the initial wage benefit received by the generation of Black college graduates most favorably affected by affirmative action.

Another difficulty in assigning a significant wage role to affirmative action is that many other confounding forces were at work that could have altered the racial wage gap. In particular, the labor market was going through a major structural shift, one that was extremely unfavorable to minority workers.

RISING WAGE INEQUALITY

This structural shift involved the substantial widening of wage dispersion (Juhn et al., 1991). Because, as a first approximation during the 1960s, distributions shifted up or down in more or less uniform ways, until the mid-1970s, it was safe to compare groups based on means or medians alone. Now, the median describes almost no one very well.

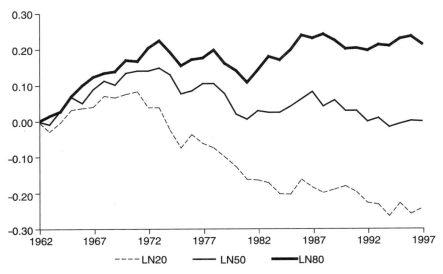

FIGURE 4-7 Wage growth relative to 1962.

Those whose wages were initially less than the median suffered significant real-wage losses, while workers earning more than the median enjoyed inflation-adjusted wage increases.

Figure 4-7 summarizes these changes by plotting percent wage
changes relative to 1962 for White male workers. To see the distributional
character of the changes, these plots are listed for the 20th, 50th, and 80th
percentiles. With a bit of oversimplification, this period can be divided
into three segments—median wage growth of 15 percent between 1962
and 1971, a real wage decrease of 14 percent between 1971 and 1981, and
(with due respect for business cycle variation) constant real wages through
1997.

Using the same time-demarcation points, the world was very different at the bottom than at the top. For example, contrast the 20th and 80th
percentiles. During the first period of sustained economic growth, real
wages were growing for everyone, albeit at a more rapid rate at the top
(17 percent at the 80th, and 8 percent at the 20th percentile). The bottom
truly fell out between 1971 and 1981, with a real wage decrease of 6
percent at the 80th percentile, but a whopping 25 percent at the 20th
percentile. Things improved somewhat after 1981 (wage growth of 10
percent at the top and a decrease of 8 percent at the 20th percentile). The
cumulative effect has been enormous; since 1971, a 37 percent fall in wages
at the 20th percentile compared to wages at the 80th.

Quite appropriately, this structural change has been described without mentioning race, ethnicity, or gender. Although the reasons for this structural labor-market shift have nothing to do with such matters, the consequences were anything but race or ethnicity neutral. The reason is, workers in these demographic groups are found in very different places in the wage distribution than are White males. For example, in 1971 the median Black male worker earned $412 a week—equivalent to what a White worker earned at the 25th percentile of the White male wage distribution. Between 1971 and 1981, wages at the 25th percentile of the White wage distribution declined by 20 percent—quite close to what was happening to the median Black worker.

Given the size of this structural change, it is actually remarkable that, when using means or medians, recent years were only characterized as racial labor-market stagnation and not as a free fall. If Black workers were treated the same as comparable Whites (those in the 25th percentile of the White wage distribution), the median Black male wages would have actually decreased by 27 percent since 1971 instead of increasing by 3 percent. If that 27 percent were added to what actually happened, evaluated at the median, wages of Blacks would be lower than those of Whites by single-digit amounts. These last 20 years were actually a time during which the slowly evolving historical forces continued to close the wage gap between Black and White male workers. These forces were simply overwhelmed by the structural shift of rising wage dispersion.

Hispanic workers also felt the consequences of widening wage dispersion. Figure 4-8A illustrates the process by plotting percent wage changes at each percentile of the wage distribution for Hispanic and U.S.-born White residents of Los Angeles County between 1970 and 1990. Both distributions reveal growing wage dispersion—wages grow more the higher one is in the wage distribution. Although they share that similarity, the Hispanic curve lies well below that of U.S.-born Whites. Although there was virtually no change in White males' median wages, real wages for the Hispanic median-wage male worker fell by almost 40 percent. The distance between the curves is so large that one must get almost to the 90th percentile before any wage gains are registered.

Most, but not all, these differences are the result of rising wage dispersion. Figure 4-8B adjusts the Hispanic curve by subtracting from their observed wage changes the wage change observed for comparable Whites (at the White percentile with the same wage as Hispanics in 1970). The adjusted Hispanic wage-percentiles show about a 10-to-13 percent negative wage change that becomes somewhat smaller above the median. Seventy-five percent of declining wages at the median for Hispanics in Los Angeles was caused by widening wage dispersion in that city. The re-

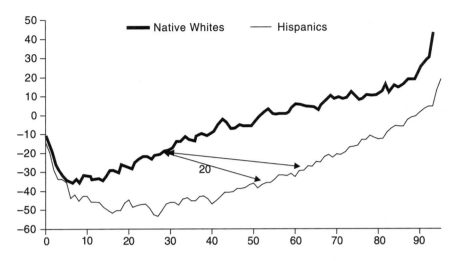

FIGURE 4-8A Wage growth from 1970 to 1990 for U.S.-born male White and Hispanic Los Angeles County residents.

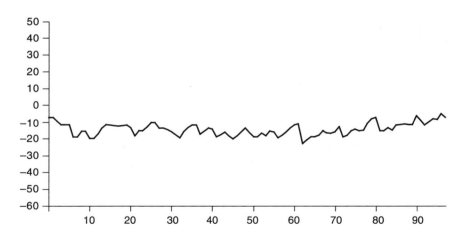

FIGURE 4-8B Adjusted Hispanic wage growth from 1970 to 1990 for Los Angeles County residents.

maining 10-to-12 percent wage deficit was the result of factors unique to the immigrant experience.

SPECIAL ISSUES WITH HISPANIC IMMIGRANTS

There are three overriding issues that have dominated labor-market research about immigrants, and Hispanic immigrants in particular: (1) the changing labor-market skills of new immigrants, (2) life-cycle assimilation, and (3) the extent of generational progress. Despite the extensive available research on these issues, they remain controversial.

The Changing Labor-Market Quality of Immigrants

Although wages of immigrants in the United States typically far exceed wages in their home countries, how do they compare with the wages of U.S.-born workers? A first step toward an index of their changing relative economic status is obtained by looking at relative wages of newly arrived immigrant cohorts. As is the case with most such comparisons, "newly arrived immigrants" are defined as those who immigrated within the past five years, based on the census question about what year respondents came to the United States. Table 4-9 lists wage differentials of newly arrived Hispanic male immigrants compared to U.S.-born Hispanics. Although recent arrivals have always earned much less than U.S.-born workers, this wage gap widened considerably from 1970 to 1990 for both male and female Hispanic immigrants. In 1970 the gap for Hispanic men was 48 percent; by 1990 it had almost doubled to 83 percent. Similarly, the gap for Mexican immigrants rose from 65 percent in 1970 to 94 percent by 1990.

TABLE 4-9 Percent New Arrival Latino Male Wage and Education Gap with Native-Born Men

	Year				
	1940	1960	1970	1980	1990
Hispanic Men					
% wage deficit	−52.2	−47.6	−47.7	−63.3	−82.9
Education deficit (years)	1.27	1.90	2.71	4.31	4.27
Mexican Men					
% wage deficit	−87.0	-55.6	−65.4	−71.1	−93.6
Education deficit (years)	3.31	4.34	5.19	5.73	5.05

Why did relative wages decrease among new Hispanic immigrants? Part of the answer is supplied by the education deficits listed in the same table. Even though recent new Hispanic arrivals are better educated than their predecessors, the education of U.S.-born workers has been rising even faster. Since 1970, the education gap for new Hispanic immigrants increased from 2.7 years to 4.3 years. The reason for the expanding wage gap is not much of a mystery; the gap in their relative skills widened over time. Especially during the most recent decades, as the skill gap widened, the wage gap widened even more. Rising wage inequality implies larger wage differences, holding skill differences constant. Therefore, as skill differences between Hispanic immigrants and U.S.-born Hispanic workers expanded over time, the wage difference expanded even more.

But this is an incomplete story for two reasons. First, Jasso et al. (2000) report, using data from the CPS, that during the 1990s, the relative incomes and schooling of Hispanic immigrants rose rather than decreased, contrary to the common assertion. Second, in virtually all such comparisons of new immigrants, data compiled about relative incomes and schooling rely on census- or CPS-style questions concerning the year of immigration. Jasso et al. (2000) demonstrate that data obtained from such questions are misleading for two reasons. (1) The census question concerning time since immigration is inherently confused in light of the frequent trips made by immigrants back and forth to their home countries.

In addition, many immigrants in the census and CPS files are not legal immigrants. A recent study estimated that only 20 percent of those Mexicans who reported in the 1995 and 1996 CPS that they had immigrated since 1990 were legal immigrants (Passel, 1999). The remainder were either nonimmigrants (those in the United States on a temporary visa; tourists and students are two numerically large examples) or, in the case of Mexicans, primarily illegal immigrants. When data are presented on trends for legal immigrants alone, a quite different picture emerges. During most of the last 25 years, the labor-market quality of all new male legal immigrants (all ethnic groups combined) has been as high as or higher than that of male U.S.-born workers. (2) Although the labor-market quality of all male legal immigrants was indeed decreasing during the 1970s and early 1980s, there has been a steady rise in the labor-market quality of all legal immigrants during the last half of the 1980s and throughout the 1990s. If illegal immigrants comprise an increasing percentage of the Mexican foreign-born in the CPS and the census, this will lead to a steadily rising wage gap with U.S.-born men. The changing composition of Mexican immigrants between those who are legal, those who are non-immigrants, and those who are undocumented, will be an important underlying reason for any changes in immigrant wage differences over time.

Life-Cycle Assimilation

Another central issue concerning immigrants and, hence, the economic status of Hispanics, concerns economic assimilation over the immigrant's lifetime. This issue has been a source of considerable controversy (Borjas, 1985; Chiswick, 1978), but some consensus is now being reached. To address this issue, it is necessary to follow groups of immigrants throughout their lives in the United States. A representative sample of patterns resulting from this tracking of immigrant cohorts is presented in Figures 4-9 and 4-10 (see, also, Smith and Edmonston, 1997). These data plot, for specific cohorts of immigrants defined by time of entry into the United States, their percent wage gap with U.S.-born White workers of comparable age. These figures deal with relatively young immigrants, age 25 to 34, during the census year immediately following their initial entry. For all immigrants, Figure 4-9 plots data for men, Figure 4-10, for women, and both plot data separately for Mexican immigrants.

Consider first the profiles for all immigrants. On average, male and female immigrants narrow their wage gap with U.S.-born workers as their stay in the United States lengthens. Over time, the wage gap closes for some—significantly for immigrants from Europe and Asia and modestly for others. But, as these figures also illustrate, initial gaps at time of entry have been growing; and the time it will take to reach wage parity with U.S.-born workers will take longer.

This positive overall evaluation of within-generation wage assimilation does not pertain to male or female Mexicans, who remain the exception to the general rule. Both female and male Mexican immigrants essentially maintain their initial wage gaps with U.S.-born White workers. It is important, however, to keep the reference group—U.S.-born White males—in mind when interpreting this finding. Our result implies that Mexican immigrants experience wage growth throughout their careers in the United States that is proportionally the same as U.S.-born Whites. Seen in this light, this result could be interpreted more positively as indicating that Hispanic immigrants are assimilating into the same career experiences as U.S.-born Whites.

However, when the reference group is non-Mexican immigrants, careers of Hispanic immigrants do not stand up as well. Why do Mexican immigrants do less well than other immigrant groups? One explanation that actually goes in the other direction stems from the previously mentioned point about the composition of immigrant samples in the census and CPS—i.e., that a large percentage of those whom researchers have labeled new immigrants are actually illegal immigrants or nonimmigrants. This percentage is particularly large (more than a majority) for Mexican immigrants. Because illegal immigrants are, on average, less skilled than

A

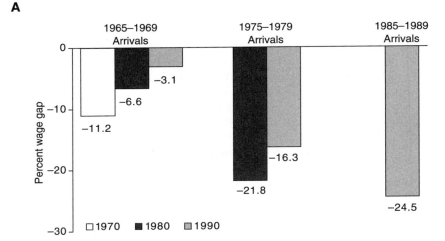

B

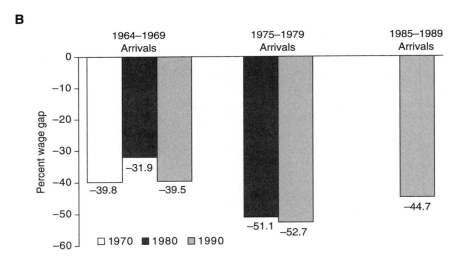

FIGURE 4-9 Career wage growth of new male immigrant cohorts. Each group consists of 25-34 year old males. (A) All new immigrants. (B) New immigrants from Mexico.

other Mexican immigrants, and will probably have a shorter expected duration in the United States, selectivity of out-migrants from the original group alone would imply that the data should show improvement in relative incomes of Mexican immigrants as time since immigration lengthens. Because the data indicate, instead, a basically constant ratio, this

A

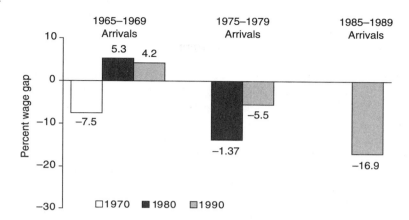

B

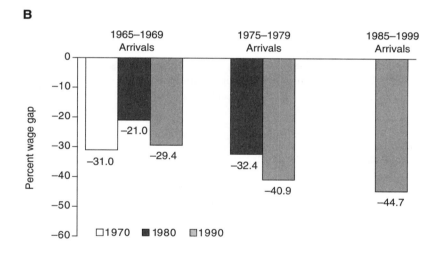

FIGURE 4-10 Career wage growth of new female immigrant cohorts. Each group consists of 25-34 year-old women. (A) All new immigrants. (B) New immigrants from Mexico.

implies that the true relative life-cycle wage progression of Mexican immigrants may actually be even more negative.

Why would this be so? To date, there is no convincing answer to this question, which should receive high priority in the research agenda. One can speculate about the role of language or the implications of the geographic closeness to country-of-origin, but there is little concrete evidence to document any compelling explanation. Other immigrant groups—Asians would be a good example—arrive without complete English language proficiency, and many immigrants have frequent trips back and forth to their home countries.

Part of the problem lies in the inherent ambiguity in using tracking of cohorts across census or CPS files to evaluate life-cycle progress of immigrants. Although cohort tracking has become the standard technique for evaluating economic assimilation, it is problematic as immigrant cohorts are not closed. An initial immigrant cohort can be depleted as some immigrants return home. If, as seems likely, those immigrants who left the country were highly selective, the wage trajectories obtained from cohort tracking will be biased. For example, if high-skill/high-wage immigrants left, average wages of the remaining members of the cohort would decrease even if the wage of every remaining immigrant stayed the same. This problem caused by out-migration from an initial entering immigrant cohort is especially severe among immigrants from Mexico. In the aggregate, roughly one-third of the 1970 Mexican immigrants emigrated by 1980. An even smaller percentage of the 1970 cohort remained by 1990. Until this problem of the nature of the selectivity of emigration of previous Mexican immigrant cohorts can be resolved, one should be cautious about reaching any strong conclusions about the nature of life-cycle labor-market careers of Mexican immigrants.

Generational Assimilation

Regarding the issue of generational assimilation, the conventional wisdom for Hispanics—whom some argue have not enjoyed the same level of success of earlier European immigrants—leans toward the pessimistic side. The reasons for pessimism vary, but one theme is that Hispanic immigrants and their children may be less committed to assimilation than the Europeans were. The data supporting this concern are often derived using cross-sectional comparisons between first-, second-, and third-generation Hispanics of their income and schooling levels. Such comparisons universally show a narrowing of the schooling and income gap between the first and second generation, but either retrogression or little progress between the second and third generation (Smith, 1999). Although conclusions about generational assimilation are often drawn from such data, these inferences are not appropriate. In any cross section, members of the second generation are not sons and daughters of current immigrants, and members of the current third generation in a cross section are not direct descendants of current, second-generation persons.

Fortunately, the conventional wisdom appears to be in error. In Smith

(1999) the data are arrayed in a way that more directly tracks progress made across generations. The schooling deficits of Hispanics are uniformly smaller in the second generation than in the first and smaller still in the third generation. For example, the mean education disparity among all first-generation Mexicans was 4.94 years and decreased to 2.95 years among second-generation Mexicans. The youngest third-generation cohorts had a schooling gap of less than 1 year compared with White men—half as large as their fathers' education deficit.

At least based on the historical record, fears about Hispanic generational assimilation appear to be unwarranted as second- and third-generation Hispanic men have made considerable strides in narrowing their economic disparities with U.S.-born White men, as schooling gains across the generations were translated into generational progress in incomes. Each new Hispanic generation not only had higher incomes than their predecessors, but their economic status converged relative to White men with whom they had to compete.

HOUSEHOLD WEALTH

Until recently, data limitations forced most comparisons of racial economic status to rely only on income differences, but improvements in measuring wealth have made contrasts of household wealth levels feasible. Table 4-10 lists mean and median household wealth levels by race derived from the Panel Study of Income Dynamics (PSID).[3] Racial wealth gaps are extremely large, especially compared to the already sizable household income differences by race. In 1984, mean wealth of non-White households was 22 percent of wealth of White households, and the income ratio was 0.58:1. Wealth differentials are even larger if medians are used as the yardstick; using medians, in 1984 non-White households had less than 10 percent of the wealth of White households. The glimmer of hope is that the relative wealth differentials narrowed over the 10-year period covered in this table. By 1994, mean non-White wealth rose to 31 percent of that of Whites.

Racial and ethnic disparities are even greater in financial assets; these

---

[3]PSID is a longitudinal survey of a representative sample of U.S. individuals (men, women, and children) and the families in which they reside. The study has been conducted at the Survey Research Center, University of Michigan, since its beginning in 1968, with the Inter-University Consortium for Political and Social Research (ICPSR). Wealth modules were included in the 1984, 1989, and 1994 PSIDs. See Juster et al. (1999) for a detailed discussion, and see Browning and Lusardi (1996) for an excellent review of the micro savings literature.

TABLE 4-10 Wealth and Income Levels by Race

	Wealth		Income	
	Mean	Median	Mean	Median
A. Total Household Wealth				
White				
1984	169.0	59.4	48.9	39.1
1989	181.1	59.6	59.6	39.5
1994	178.5	64.7	52.9	41.0
Non-White				
1984	37.1	5.3	28.5	21.7
1989	53.5	6.8	29.9	22.3
1994	54.5	10.4	31.9	23.8
B. Financial Assets				
White				
1984	48.0	6.0		
1989	48.6	7.4		
1994	60.9	13.7		
Non-White				
1984	7.2	0.0		
1989	8.6	0.0		
1994	13.7	0.0		

SOURCE: PSID—1996 dollars. Calculations by author.

more-liquid assets may be a better index of resources a household has on hand to meet emergencies. In 1984, mean financial assets for non-Whites were one-seventh of those of White households. Not only is the ratio of financial assets by race low, the financial assets held by non-White households are meager. In 1984, non-White households had a little more than $7,000 per household in financial assets. But even this number exaggerates their holdings due to the extreme skew in the distribution. In all three years, the median non-White household had no financial assets at all.

A more complete description of racial wealth differences is given in Figure 4-11, which plots, for Whites and non-Whites, household wealth at percentiles of the wealth distribution. These data illustrate the extreme skew in wealth holdings—the top 5 percent of White households have 50 percent more wealth than White households at the 90th percentile, while those at the 90th percentile have more than five times as much as the median White household. This nonlinearity prevails within the lower half of the wealth distribution as well, as the median White household has

A

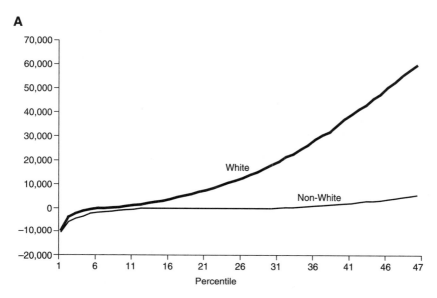

B

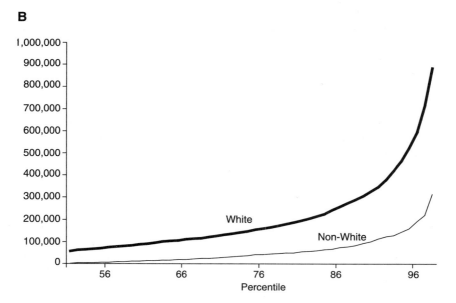

FIGURE 4-11 White and non-White wealth distribution in 1984 (in 1996 dollars). (A) Percentiles 1 to 50. (B) Percentiles 51 to 98.

10 times as much wealth as those at the 20th percentile. A similar extreme skew characterizes the non-White wealth distribution.

Why are racial wealth differentials at least twice as large as household-income differences in the same years? One possibility can easily be dismissed; it is not a consequence of financial wealth being transmitted across generations with the poor unable to give and the affluent ensuring their heirs remain at the top through financial inheritances. Although plausible, this possibility is quantitatively unimportant as the vast majority of households—both White and non-White—do not receive any financial inheritances.[4] Using PSID, mean inheritances (in 1996 dollars) for Black households were about $1,000; for White households about $10,000. Even if these inheritances were completely saved so that they show up in current household wealth, they would account for a small percentage of racial wealth differences documented in Table 4-11. Similarly, two-thirds of all White households and 90 percent of all minority households received no financial inheritances by the time the householders were in their mid-50s. Racial disparities in wealth would be almost the same if we subtracted that part of current wealth derived from past financial inheritances (Smith, 1995).[5]

If not financial inheritances, then all we have left is people saving at different rates from their income and/or experiencing different ex-post rates of return on their savings. The question then becomes, Why do Black and Hispanic households save so much less than White households? This is a much under-researched question partly because of the lack of adequate data. Because wealth disparities far exceed income disparities, there has been some thought that the reasons for the lack of savings behavior must lie in some unique historical events specific to the Black or Hispanic experience. For Blacks, it is sometimes argued that a culture promoting savings was not encouraged or was too difficult to develop. However, the data presented in Figure 4-11 suggest that it is premature to jump to race- and ethnic-specific explanations.

---

[4]This point about the relative unimportance of past bequests in creating wealth differences in the current generation is fundamentally different than the debate about the importance of the bequest motive in accounting for savings behavior of the current generation. The current generation's savings behaviors are forward looking, so that any savings for bequests by the current generation are meant for the subsequent generation. Given the secular rise in bequests, savings for bequests may be a large part of a current generations' savings, while their receipt of past financial inheritances are inconsequential to their own present wealth holdings.

[5]The argument here deals only with bequests and does not speak to the issue of the role of inter-vivos transfers in creating racial and ethnic differences in wealth. See Gale and Scholz (1994) for a good discussion of inter-vivos transfers.

TABLE 4-11 Wealth by Source (000 of dollars)

	Household Wealth	Social Security	Pensions	Total
White	$264	$124	$109	$503
Black	72	94	65	231
Hispanic	80	94	39	218

SOURCE: Smith (1995).

Once again, the reason lies in a concave relation between savings or wealth and household income. This nonlinear relation between savings and income explains a good deal of the racial wealth discrepancies. Although vastly less than average White household wealth, wealth of the median Black household is actually quite similar to Whites with the same income. In 1994, White households with incomes equal to the median Black household lie at the 25th percentile of the White income distribution. If we compare wealth of the median Black to the 25th percentile White, their wealth levels are quite similar. When the nonlinearity is taken into account, income explains a good deal of racial differences in wealth. If low savings behavior is not a racial or ethnic issue, the unanswered question is, Why do low- and middle-income people save so little, no matter what their race or ethnic background?

Different racial groups may also experience different ex-post rates of return to their past savings, which may expand or contract wealth differences between them. For example, the surge in the stock market during the last 15 years increased the wealth of those households with greater amounts of stock market holdings. Because rates of stock ownership and holdings were larger among White households, wealth of White households increased more than wealth of Black households.

This dismissal of financial inheritance as an important source of racial differences in household wealth does not imply that all forms of intergenerational transmission are unimportant. For example, the inheritance of human capital is another source of intergenerational transmission that clearly creates racial and ethnic differences in income. Indeed, one important form in which these differences in inheritances of human capital show up are the education differences discussed earlier.

A second factor distorting racial wealth comparisons is that household wealth represents only part of the wealth households have at their disposal. Despite its widespread use, household wealth ignores large components of wealth that are critical to many households. For example, a household's future expected Social Security benefits are a lifetime annuity that can be discounted to give a present value of Social Security wealth. In a similar vein, private pensions, either directly in defined-contribution plans or indirectly for defined-benefit plans, are an important source of wealth for many households, especially in their pre- and postretirement years. Virtually all households in their 50s anticipate Social Security benefits when they retire, and more than half are counting on income from their pensions. When discounted to the present, these expected income flows translate into considerable wealth.

Table 4-11 demonstrates how large they actually are for families with one member aged 51 to 61. Mean household, Social Security, and pension wealth are listed in the table, providing a better measure of wealth than the conventional concept, which counts only household wealth. For Whites, total wealth is half a million dollars, rather than the quarter of a million in conventional household wealth. More important, the distortion caused by conventional wealth is much larger among minority families. Among Blacks and Hispanics, conventional household wealth is less than one-third of total wealth and Social Security represents the largest part of their wealth. If the enlarged total wealth concept is used, Black households have 46 percent as much as White households do compared to 30 percent for household wealth alone.

CONCLUSIONS

This paper has covered some wide territory in describing the major trends that have impacted on the economic position of Blacks and Hispanics. In addition to long-term trends that appear to be influenced mostly by skill-related factors, I have also evaluated alternative explanations for the recent stagnation in the economic position of minority households. These explanations included changing schooling, quality of students, affirmative action, and rising wage inequality. In addition, the role of immigration in changing the labor-market position of Hispanic workers was evaluated.

Long-term trends in the relative economic status of Blacks and Hispanics appear mainly to reflect long-term trends in their relative skills. For example, relative income differences and education deficits of Blacks compared to Whites are quite closely related. For Hispanics, it is also necessary to distinguish between immigrants and the U.S.-born. The slow rate of Hispanic educational and economic progress largely reflects a changing composition of the immigrant workforce. The rising percentage of immigrants in the Hispanic male workforce in recent decades slowed the aggregate gains in Hispanic schooling.

Until the mid-1970s, schooling continued to assume its historical role as the primary determinant of the male racial wage gap; however, male education differences by race cannot account for the timing and magnitude of the male wage stagnation of the last 25 years. Moreover, there is little evidence that the quality of Black or Hispanic students entering the labor market during the past few decades has declined. Nor can schooling account for the impressive narrowing of the gender wage gap of the last few decades. However, the stagnation and decrease in Hispanic wages relative to U.S.-born Whites is consistent with the apparent lack of relative education progress of the average Hispanic worker. In addition, affirmative action led to changes in the location of minority employment and produced significant early jumps in the wages of Black men; however, these wages gains proved to be temporary.

The bulk of the remaining stagnation in minority group wages since the mid-1970s is the result, principally, of the rising wage inequality in the labor market. Because minority workers' skills place them in the lower part of the wage distribution, increasing wage dispersion across skill levels will decrease their wages more than those of majority workers. The last 20 years were actually a time during which slowly evolving historical forces continued to close the wage gap of Black and White male workers. These forces were simply overwhelmed by the structural shift of rising wage dispersion.

Because of the central role immigration plays in the Hispanic population, some additional factors are relevant when discussing their changing economic status. The well-documented decrease in wages of new Hispanic immigrants appears to reflect three forces. First, a growing skill gap reinforced by an expanding wage gap (conditional on a given skill gap), and possibly an increasing percentage of undocumented Mexican immigrants among all recent immigrants in recent census and CPS surveys. Second, across their careers in the United States, wages of Hispanic immigrants appear to hold steady relative to the White U.S.-born majority. However, Mexican immigrants appear not to do as well over their careers as immigrants from other ethnic groups. There is no consensus explanation as to why this is so. Third, at least based on the historical record, fears about Hispanic generational assimilation appear to be unwarranted as second- and third-generation Hispanic men have made considerable strides in narrowing their education and economic disparities with U.S.-born White men.

Finally, I document in this paper that racial differences in household wealth are extremely large; much larger in fact than racial differences in income. However, in spite of these large racial disparities, the reasons for these large wealth disparities are unlikely to have been produced by factors that are specific to individual racial or ethnic groups. Instead, the reason appears to arise from the more general tendency of low-income households—of either race—to engage in little savings behavior. Because there are more Black and Hispanic than White households in the low-income group, racial and ethnic differences in household wealth will be large.

ACKNOWLEDGMENTS

I thank David Rumpel of RAND and Joseph Lupton of the University of Michigan for expert programming assistance. Funds were provided by a grant from NICHD. Useful comments were made by Gerald Jaynes and an anonymous referee.

REFERENCES

Borjas, G.
  1985   Assimilation, changes in cohort quality, and the earnings of immigrants. *Journal of Labor Economics* 3(4):35-52.
Browning, M., and A. Lusardi
  1996   Household savings: Micro theories and micro facts. *Journal of Economic Literature* XXXIV(4):1797-1855.
Chay, K.
  1998   The impact of federal civil rights policy on Black economic progress: Evidence from the Equal Employment Opportunity Act of 1972. *Industrial and Labor Relations Review* 51(4):608-632.
Chiswick, B.
  1978   The effect of Americanization on the earnings of foreign-born men. *Journal of Political Economy* 86(5):897-921.
Donahue, J., and J. Heckman
  1991   Continuous vs. episodic change: The impact of affirmative action and civil rights policy on the economic status of Blacks. *Journal of Economic Literature* 29(4):1603-1644.
Gale, W., and J. Scholz
  1994   Inter-generational transfers and the accumulation of wealth. *Journal of Economic Perspectives* 8(4):145-160.
Heckman, J., and B. Payner
  1989   Determining the impact of federal antidiscrimination policy on the economic status of Blacks: A study of South Carolina. *American Economic Review* 79:138-177.
Holzer, H., and D. Neumark
  1999   Assessing affirmative action. Unpublished paper.
Jasso, G., M. Rosenzweig, and J. Smith
  2000   The changing skills of new immigrants, recent trends and their determinants. Pp. 185-225 in *Issues in the Economics of Immigration*. Chicago: University of Chicago Press.
Juhn, C., K. Murphy, and P. Brooks
  1991   Accounting for the slowdown in Black-White wage convergence. Pp. 107-143 in *Workers and their Wages: Changing Patterns in the United States*, M. Kosters, ed. American Enterprise Institute Press.
Juster, F., F. Stafford, and J. Smith
  1999   The measurement and structure of wealth. *Labour Economics* 6(2):253-275.

National Center for Education Statistics: Education Testing Service
    1991   *Trends in Academic Progress.*
Passel, J.
    1999   Undocumented immigration to the United States: Numbers, trends, and charac-
            teristics. In *Illegal Immigration in America,* D. Haines and K. Rosenblum, eds.
            Greenwood Publishing.
Smith J.
    1993   Affirmative action and the racial wage gap. *American Economic Review* 83(2):79-84.
    1995   Racial and ethnic differences in wealth. *Journal of Human Resources* 30:S156-S183.
    1999   Progress across the generations. Unpublished paper.
Smith, J., and B. Edmonston
    1997   *The New Americans: Economic, Demographic, and Fiscal Effects of Immigration.* Wash-
            ington, D.C.: National Academy Press.
Smith, J., and M. Ward
    1989   Women in the labor market and the family. *Journal of Economic Perspectives* 3(1):9-
            24.
Smith, J., and F. Welch
    1984   Affirmative action and labor markets. *Journal of Labor Economics* 2(2):269-302.
    1989   Black economic progress after Myrdal. *Journal of Economic Literature* 27:519-564.

5

Racial Differences in Labor Market Outcomes Among Men

Harry J. Holzer

T his paper reviews evidence of racial differences, among men, in labor-market outcomes such as wages, employment, and labor-force participation. Data are presented for trends over time and differences across racial and ethnic groups. Differences between Whites and Blacks are considered, as are some differences involving Hispanic and Asian men, both immigrants and U.S. born. Also considered are various explanations for the noted trends. Possible future trends are discussed, as well as implications for policy and further research.

RELATIVE WAGES AND EMPLOYMENT: TRENDS AND REMAINING DIFFERENCES

Figure 5-1 plots trends in the Black/White wage ratio from 1940 to 1990. Table 5-1 gives a brief list of earnings ratios, based on amounts of labor-market experience, for 1971, 1981, and 1988. The data plotted in Figure 5-1 indicate that the wages of Black men improved dramatically during this time period. In 1940, the wages of Black men were, on average, only 40 percent as high as those of White men; by 1990, they were roughly 75 percent as high. Within this overall trend, however, the rate of progress has been quite uneven. There were two periods of sharp improvement—1940 to 1950 and 1960 to 1975. In contrast, improvements during 1950 to 1960 were much more modest; and since 1975, the relative wages of Black men have stagnated or even declined.

Table 5-1 lists differences in the ratios of relative wages based on

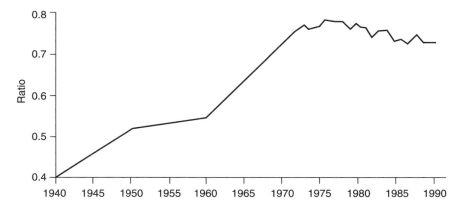

FIGURE 5-1 Relative wages of White and Black males: Trends in Black-White wage ratio, 1940-1990. Reprinted with permission from George Borjas, John F. Kennedy School of Government, Harvard University.

TABLE 5-1 Adjusted Black/White Earnings Ratios Based on Years of Experience, 1971, 1981, 1988

	Years of Experience		
Year	0-9	10-19	20+
1971	0.88	0.78	0.79
1981	0.85	0.80	0.83
1988	0.82	0.84	0.84

Note: Adjusted for differences in education, veteran and marital status, region, urban residence, number of children, and hours worked.

SOURCE: Blau and Beller (1992). Reprinted by permission.

years of experience. Although Black men with 10 or more years of labor-market experience continued to gain in relative wages during the 1980s, the group with the fewest years of experience lost ground relative to Whites. Data indicate that the deterioration in earnings relative to Whites was greatest among young Black men with a college degree; but the deterioration in absolute terms was much greater among the less educated (Juhn et al., 1993; Bound and Holzer, 1996), and reflected the dramatic decline in earnings experienced by less-educated young men of all races during the past 20 years.

The deterioration in relative earnings among young Black men can be observed even after one adjusts for Black-White differences in education, region of residence, etc. In the mid-1970s, young Black men were earning 10 percent less than White men with similar education, age, and area of residence; by the late 1980s, that gap had risen to about 20 percent (Bound and Freeman, 1992). Controlling for differences in other measures of skills, however, such as test scores, will account for at least some of the remaining racial difference (a point addressed below).

Table 5-2 shows differences, by race, in rates of employment, labor-force participation, and unemployment. The data indicate that in 1970, compared to Whites, Blacks' labor-force participation rate was roughly 3 percentage points lower, and their unemployment rate was roughly 3 percentage points higher. But the labor-force activity of Black men deteriorated substantially during the 1970s and 1980s relative to Whites, while unemployment rose. Some of this deterioration in the relative employment of Black men was occurring during the early 1970s, while their relative wages were still improving (Cogan, 1982). Although part of this can be attributed to increases in school enrollment rates among young Black men, the trend can be found even among the nonenrolled. The deterioration continued into the late 1970s and 1980s, during which time relative wages were also deteriorating.

Of course, employment and unemployment rates for both Whites and Blacks follow a strong cyclical pattern, and both groups showed strong improvement in the late 1990s. Unemployment rates during 1998 aver-

TABLE 5-2 Employment Ratios, Labor Force Participation Rates, and Unemployment Rates (percent), by Race

	Employment		Labor-Force Participation		Unemployment	
Year	Blacks	Whites	Blacks	Whites	Blacks	Whites
1970	71.9	77.8	77.6	81.0	7.3	4.0
1975	62.7	73.6	72.7	79.3	13.7	7.2
1980	62.5	74.0	72.1	78.8	13.3	6.1
1985	60.0	72.3	70.8	77.0	15.3	6.1
1990	61.8	73.2	70.1	76.9	11.8	4.8
1994	60.8	71.8	69.1	75.9	12.0	5.4

SOURCE: Bureau of Labor Statistics data from *Employment and Earnings*, January 1971 through January 1998.

TABLE 5-3 Unemployment Rates
(percent) for White, Black, and Hispanic
Males, by Age, 1994

Age (years)	Whites	Blacks	Hispanics
16-17	16.5	39.3	33.3
18-19	14.7	36.5	22.5
20-24	8.8	19.4	10.8
25-54	4.3	9.1	7.7
>55	4.0	6.4	8.0
All ages >16	5.4	12.0	9.4

SOURCE: Blau and Beller (1992). Reprinted by permission.

aged roughly 4 and 9 percent for White and Black men, respectively, even though the absolute decline in unemployment among Blacks during the 1990s was greater. The Black/White unemployment ratio, however, remained roughly constant during this period. Recent gains are important, but how long will they last? Even while they last, they do not fully reverse the strong secular trend toward lower relative employment activity among Black men.

Table 5-3 indicates that overall unemployment rates in 1994 were more than twice as high among Black men as among White men. Unemployment rates were dramatically higher among teenagers than among prime-age (25 to 64 years old) males for each racial group; but the numbers for Blacks were particularly striking, as almost 40 percent of Black teenagers in the labor force were unemployed. In fact, labor-force activity was, in 1994, declining among all racial groups for young men with low levels of education—i.e., high school diplomas only and especially high school dropouts—apparently in response to the decline in real wages they had experienced in the 1970s and 1980s (Juhn, 1992). But, again, the decline among less-educated young Black men was most dramatic.

Table 5-4 presents relative wages for various groups of Hispanic and Asian men in 1979. The unadjusted ratios show raw differences in means between various ethnic groups and White males; the adjusted ratios adjust for differences in education level, age, region of residence, English proficiency, etc. The raw (or unadjusted) data indicate the wide range of earnings across these groups relative to Whites. On the one hand, Asian Indian and Japanese men were earning somewhat more than White men; however, Mexican, Puerto Rican, and Vietnamese men were earning less than two-thirds as much. But, after adjusting for differences in the characteristics mentioned above—education level, age, etc.—the range of rela-

TABLE 5-4 Unadjusted and Adjusted
Ethnic/White Earnings Ratios, 1979

Ethnic Group	Unadjusted	Adjusted
American Indian	0.74	0.92
Asian Indian	1.13	0.98
Chinese	0.89	0.89
Cuban	0.79	0.96
Filipino	0.79	0.92
Japanese	1.05	1.01
Korean	0.89	0.82
Mexican	0.66	0.98
Puerto Rican	0.63	0.95
Vietnamese	0.64	0.98

Note: Adjusted for differences in education, age, hours
worked, marital status, region, knowledge of English,
and place of birth.

SOURCE: Carlson and Schwartz (1988). Reprinted by
permission.

tive earnings narrows dramatically; in fact, virtually all these groups of
men, were, in 1979, earning 90 percent or more of what White men earned.
Differences in educational attainment and language ability seem to account for much of the differences in the raw data, especially for Hispanics
(Reimers, 1983; Trejo, 1997).

Dramatic differences in educational attainment and language proficiency across ethnic groups often reflect a high concentration of immigrants among some of the groups. Figure 5-2 presents wage rates, obtained from the 1990 Census, of U.S.-born Hispanic and Asian men in
comparison to those of Whites. The data reveal much smaller differences
in wages across groups than are shown in the unadjusted data in Table
5-4. Indeed, U.S.-born Chinese and Japanese men were earning more
than White men; and U.S.-born Cuban and Puerto Rican men were earning almost 90 percent as much, even in the raw data.

However, the relative importance of educational and language deficiencies among some groups of Hispanic and Asian men has grown over
the past few decades, as large numbers of less-educated immigrants have
arrived in the United States. This largely accounts for the fact that overall
educational attainment and earnings for Hispanic men fell over the past
20 years (Council of Economic Advisers, 1998). As the children of these
groups assimilate, their relative education and earnings should improve

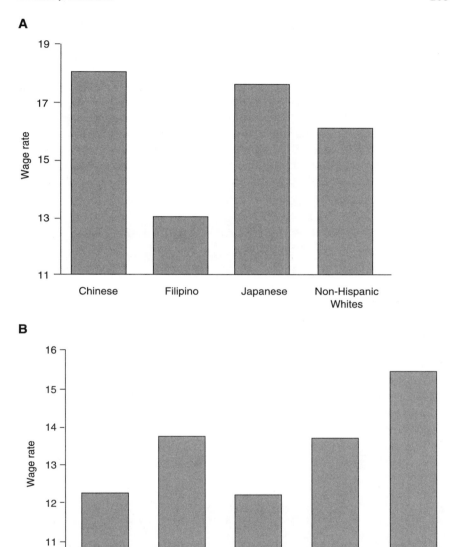

FIGURE 5-2 Relative wage rates in 1990 of U.S.-born Asian and Hispanic men aged 25-64. (A) Asian. (B) Hispanic. Reprinted with permission from George Borjas, John F. Kennedy School of Government, Harvard University.

substantially, although some differences of opinion exist as to whether the convergence in earnings over time for the more recent immigrant groups has been as rapid as for earlier immigrant groups (Chiswick; 1986; Borjas, 1994).

To sum up, these data indicate substantial differences in employment and earnings across groups, and in trends over time. Although the relative earnings of Black men have improved since 1940, the rate of progress has been uneven; and there has been some recent deterioration in their relative earnings. Overall, Hispanic and Asian men earn considerably less than Whites, but much of this is accounted for by lower levels of education and language proficiency, particularly among recent immigrants.

EXPLAINING THE BLACK-WHITE TRENDS

How do we account for the improvements in relative earnings of Black men from, roughly, 1940 to 1975, especially during 1940 to 1950 and 1960 to 1975? And what accounts for the deterioration in relative earnings and employment more recently?

Improvements in the relative earnings of Blacks during the pre-Civil Rights period seem to be explained primarily by their immigration from the rural South to the industrial North and Midwest, and by improvements in the quantity and quality of education attained, particularly in the South (Smith and Welch, 1989; Margo, 1990; Card and Krueger, 1992). Improvements in education, in turn, seem at least partly to reflect political and legal developments, including the Supreme Court decision in *Brown v. Board of Education of Topeka* in 1954 (Boozer et al., 1992; Donohue et al., 1998). Improvements during the 1940s seem to reflect advances made by Black men during World War II, as they moved into more skilled positions vacated by White men who went away to war.

The dramatic progress made by Black men during the 1960s and early 1970s also seems to reflect rapid improvements in their quantity and quality of education and occupational status, as well as in relative earnings within education and occupation groups. Much of this improvement can be tied to social and economic changes induced by the Civil Rights Acts of 1964 and 1972 (Freeman, 1981; Heckman and Payner, 1989; Chay, 1995). Declines in discriminatory behavior seem to be particularly apparent in the South, where discrimination against Blacks had historically been greatest, as Black men began to be increasingly employed in professional/managerial occupations. Other administrative actions and court decisions, such as the implementation of Affirmative Action requirements for government contractors and the "disparate impact" cases brought in the aftermath of *Griggs v. Duke Power* in 1971, likely contributed as well (Brown, 1982; Leonard, 1990).[1]

Given the strong improvements that occurred during 1960 to 1975, what accounts for the stagnation and even deterioration in relative earnings, and employment, since then? A number of developments seem to be responsible for these reversals, on both the demand and the supply sides of the labor market, reflecting both employers/jobs and Black workers. Some of these developments, such as rising employer demand for skills and declining industrialization/unionism, seem to account for the deterioration in employment rates and earnings observed among young Blacks. Other factors, such as labor-market discrimination and social/ spatial factors, have not necessarily worsened over time, but no doubt contribute to the persistence of racial gaps in employment and earnings noted above.

Rising Employer Demand for Skills

During the past two decades, earnings inequality has risen quite dramatically in the labor market. Earnings gaps have risen between educational groups and between those with different levels of cognitive ability, after controlling for education (Levy and Murnane, 1992; Murnane et al., 1995). Although the educational attainment and test scores of Blacks improved somewhat over the past two decades (e.g., Mare, 1995; Hauser and Huang, 1996), large gaps remain relative to Whites. The high school graduation rates of Blacks continued to improve significantly during the 1980s, though their tendency to graduate from college improved much more slowly. Improvements in test scores among students continued until roughly the mid-1980s and have leveled off or mildly deteriorated since then.

Thus, as Blacks remained more concentrated among the less-educated and less-skilled groups, they were likely disproportionately hurt when the relative earnings of men in the less-educated, less-skilled groups declined (Juhn et al., 1993).[2] Furthermore, differences in educational attainment and test scores together may account for most of the racial

---

[1]Although Affirmative Action requirements of federal government contractors were first introduced by Executive Order 11246 in 1965, enforcement of these provisions was limited until the late 1960s and early 1970s. Similarly, changes in the enforcement of the Civil Rights Act, such as the use of class-action suits after 1972, likely contributed to the economic effects of the act as well.

[2]Questions about the extent to which rising returns to unmeasured skills can account for the relative stagnation or deterioration of Black earnings have been raised by Card and Lemieux (1994) and by Chay and Lee (1997), largely on the basis of timing issues and differences in patterns across educational groups.

difference in wages, though less so for differences in employment rates. Ferguson (1993) and Neal and Johnson (1996) provide evidence of lower test scores based on the National Longitudinal Survey of Youth (NLSY). Rodgers and Spriggs (1996) note, however, that racial differences remain in the market returns to these scores and also in their determinants. Significant racial differences in wages remain in other datasets besides the NLSY, even after controlling for education and test scores—e.g., in the High School and Beyond data (Murnane et al., 1995).

Employers continue to be reluctant to hire Blacks for jobs that require significant cognitive skills and credentials, such as specific experience or previous training, even those jobs for which formal educational requirements are not high (Holzer, 1996).

Declining Industrialization and Unionism

Rising demand for skills can account for some of the increase in inequality during the past two decades, but some part of that increase also seems to reflect factors such as declining employment in manufacturing and declining levels of union membership (Levy and Murnane, 1992). Although Black males were no more heavily concentrated in manufacturing jobs nationwide than were White males in the 1960s, they were more heavily concentrated in manufacturing jobs in the urban Midwest. Declines in manufacturing and union membership help account for the particularly strong declines in Blacks' relative employment and earnings in the Midwest since 1970 (Bound and Freeman, 1992; Bound and Holzer, 1993, 1996). Black men have traditionally been more likely to be members of unions than White men, and enjoyed particularly large wage gains from such membership (Freeman and Medoff, 1984). The declining presence of unionism in the economy has, no doubt, hurt Blacks disproportionately.

Persistent Discrimination

Although labor-market discrimination against Blacks has clearly declined over time, there is evidence that it persists. The clearest evidence comes from audit studies, in which matched pairs of Black and White job seekers with comparable credentials, in terms of education and experience, apply for various advertised job openings. These studies found that Blacks are less likely to receive job offers, on average, than Whites (Fix and Struyk, 1994; Bendick et al., 1994).

When comparing the likelihood of White and Black applicants to be employed, clear differences can be found across various kinds of firms: Black applicants are much less likely to be hired by small establishments than by large ones and are less likely to be hired for jobs that involve significant contact with White customers (Holzer, 1998; Holzer and Ihlanfeldt, 1998). The greater degree of informality and subjectivity in the hiring procedures of smaller establishments likely contributes to their more discriminatory behavior (Braddock and McPartland, 1987; Holzer, 1987). Discrimination might also be greater in establishments located in the suburbs than those located in central cities.

The greater tendencies of some of these establishments to discriminate seem to be, at least partly, related to the lower level of monitoring of smaller and/or suburban establishments by Civil Rights enforcement agencies. For instance, only firms with 100 or more employees are required to file Equal Employment Opportunity (EEO)-1 forms with the federal government, unless they have federal contracts. Suburban firms are also less likely to be monitored, and are therefore less likely to be found in violation of antidiscrimination statutes, as they receive fewer Black applicants and have fewer Blacks in their relevant local labor markets (Bloch, 1994).

Discrimination against Blacks seems more clearly pronounced at the hiring stage, perhaps because of how EEO laws are implemented. Donohue and Siegelman (1991) show that most EEO cases involve allegations of discrimination in promotions or discharges, rather than hiring. Thus, some employers might feel they'd face a greater likelihood of being sued if they *do* hire young Blacks than if they don't (Bloch, 1994).

The tendency of employers to discriminate in hiring seems to more clearly impact Blacks than Hispanics, and Black males than Black females (Holzer, 1998b). Kirschenman (1991) provides evidence that employers have a greater fear of Black men than Black women. The greater tendency to discriminate against Blacks seems consistent with ethnographic evidence showing that employers prefer other ethnic groups, especially immigrants, to U.S.-born Blacks, believing that other ethnic groups have a better "work ethic" (Kirschenman and Neckerman, 1991). Although the audit studies suggest that some hiring discrimination against Hispanics remains (Kenney and Wissoker, 1994), Hispanics might be able to avoid the adverse effects of this discrimination by applying for jobs primarily in sectors where it is known that employers do not discriminate against Hispanics and where they have strong networks (Holzer and Reaser, forthcoming [2000]; Waldinger, 1996).

If discrimination against Black men is heavily related to employer (and perhaps customer) fear of crime or violence, it is likely more serious against less-educated than more-educated Blacks. In fact, relative wage gaps are higher among less-educated Blacks (Council of Economic Advisers, 1998). It is possible that such discrimination has grown more serious over the past few decades as crime rates, and their correlation with education levels, have increased in regard to Black men (Freeman, 1992). The growing value that employers seem to put on "soft skills," such as social and verbal skills, might also contribute to a growing reluctance to hire less-educated Black men for jobs where such skills are important (Moss and Tilly, 1995).

Social/Spatial Factors

Although residential segregation between Whites and Blacks has declined modestly over the past few decades, it remains high (Massey and Denton, 1992; Farley and Frey, 1993). Furthermore, economic segregation seems to be rising, especially the tendency of low-income Blacks to live in predominantly Black and poor neighborhoods (Jargowsky, 1997).

These facts are likely to have a number of implications for the labor-market performance of Blacks, especially those with lower incomes. For one thing, residential segregation seems to be associated with lower educational attainment and lower employment outcomes (Cutler and Glaeser, 1997). Economic segregation of Blacks also seems to contribute to these problems (O'Regan and Quigley, 1996). Although the exact mechanisms through which these effects occur are somewhat obscure, data suggest that "social isolation" contributes to a lower quality of education and a variety of problematic behaviors among Blacks.[3] The social isolation of low-income Blacks might also limit their access to employment and/or higher wages because it denies them access to effective employment networks (Braddock and McPartland, 1987; Holzer, 1987).

Another mechanism through which residential segregation appears to limit labor-market opportunities for Blacks is "spatial mismatch," in which inner-city Blacks have difficulty gaining access to jobs located in relatively distant suburbs. Although this notion has been controversial for decades, recent evidence seems largely to bear it out (e.g., Holzer, 1991; Kain, 1992). Blacks are generally located further away from areas of strong employment growth and high job vacancy rates than are Whites, and this distance seems to be associated with lower employment rates for them (Hughes and Sternberg, 1992; Raphael, 1998; Ihlanfeldt, 1998). Black employees at central-city firms are also more likely to quit their jobs when such firms relocate to suburban areas (Zax and Kain, 1996; Fernandez,

---

[3]See Ellen and Turner (1997) for a recent review of the literature on "social isolation" and neighborhood effects. The best micro-level evidence that social contacts affect behavior adversely among young people in poor Black neighborhoods can be found in Case and Katz (1991). Borjas (1992) also presents evidence that neighborhoods may have intergenerational effects across a wide range of ethnic groups.

1994). Among the factors that seem to contribute to "spatial mismatch" are the lack of automobile ownership among lower-income Blacks, and the distance of many suburban firms from public transportation (Holzer et al., 1994; Holzer and Ihlanfeldt, 1996). Limited information about firms and job openings in these areas seems to play some role as well (Ihlanfeldt, 1997; Raphael et al., 1998).

Expectations, Alternative Income, and Illegal Activity

Declining employment rates among young Black men in the 1960s and 1970s, even while their relative wages were improving, suggest that shifts in labor supply away from the low-wage labor market might have contributed to their declining employment in this and later periods. One possible reason might be that wage expectations among young Blacks appear to have risen more rapidly than did the wage offers they received; and "menial" work that was once regarded as acceptable came to be regarded as unacceptable (Anderson, 1980). These notions receive some support from an analysis of self-reported "reservation wages" (or the lowest wages considered acceptable) among young people. Although absolute levels of reservation wages reported by young Blacks are generally lower than those reported by young Whites, they appear to be higher relative to wages actually offered in the market (Holzer, 1986; Petterson, 1996); and this likely contributes somewhat to their longer durations of nonemployment.[4]

The issue of high-wage expectations and unwillingness to accept low-wage employment appears to be one explanation for the high rate of participation of young Black men in illegal activities. These rates are particularly pronounced among Black male high school dropouts (Freeman, 1992), whose earnings have declined dramatically in recent years. Indeed, perceptions that one can do better on the "street" than in a regular job gained popularity during the 1980s, regardless of the overall state of the labor market (Freeman, 1991); and participation in crime seems to be related to this perception of relative returns in the legal and illegal sectors, even after adjusting for risks of incarceration or violence (Viscusi, 1986). Survey evidence suggests that many young men involved in illegal

---

[4]In Holzer's analysis, the higher reservation wages relative to offered wages of Blacks contribute somewhat to their longer spells without employment, although in Petterson's work they do not appear to. But, in both cases, the individuals for whom this is most likely true, such as those who have dropped out of the labor force altogether and are involved in illegal activities or in prison, are not even present in the sample, thus leading to downward biased estimates of effects on employment outcomes.

activities would demand hourly wages of $8 to $10 before they would consider returning to legal work (Freeman, 1992).

WHAT DOES THE FUTURE HOLD?

Given these past trends in Black-White employment outcomes among men, and their causes, what do we expect these trends to look like in the future? There are at least some reasons to be hopeful. For one thing, there continue to be signs of long-term progress in college-enrollment rates and educational attainment in the Black community (Council of Economic Advisers, 1998). Residential segregation, at least for those in the middle class, seems to be slowly but steadily declining, especially in metropolitan areas of the South and West with more racially diverse populations (Farley and Frey, 1993). The impressive drop in urban crime rates of the past few years suggest that fewer young Black men are leaving the labor force for this kind of activity, and might even lead to further declines in segregation and employment discrimination against these young men, as middle-class Whites, and Blacks, become less fearful of them.

Finally, if the current level of labor-market tightness can be sustained for some period of time, it might have longer term effects on labor-market outcomes for Black men, as occurred, for example, during World War II. Discriminatory behavior seems to decline in tight labor markets, as employers are willing to hire workers whom they otherwise would not consider. If their experiences with these groups, and with newer modes of recruiting and screening, are more positive than they expected, their hiring behavior over the longer term might be affected. Also, some young men might gain early labor-market experience during this time that will have positive effects on their future employability and wages.

On the other hand, there are reasons for pessimism as well. The rising costs of postsecondary education make it relatively more difficult for enrollment rates among Blacks to continue to grow (Kane, 1994). Declining political and legal support for affirmative action, especially in university admissions policies, could threaten these enrollment rates as well. Furthermore, children in poor Black families are growing up in more economically segregated neighborhoods, with greater threats from crime and drugs, and less income support from the welfare system, than did those of earlier generations. If family poverty and "neighborhood effects"/social isolation have important causal effects on the educational and employment outcomes of children, this does not bode well for their future. The long-term labor-market prospects of the roughly 1 million Black men who have been incarcerated for illegal activity also look particularly grim.

IMPLICATIONS FOR POLICY

One important implication of the above discussion for policy is the need to maintain, for as long as possible, the labor-market tightness of the past few years. Whether current low rates of inflation can be sustained with unemployment rates lower than 5 percent is unknown, but the important benefits that accrue to disadvantaged groups such as Black men from tight markets must not be lost in the evaluation of these tradeoffs.

Education and Skill Development

Over the long term, enhancing the skills and employment credentials that young Black men bring to the labor market must be a top priority. Of course, there is no single policy intervention that will accomplish this, particularly for those who live in low-income neighborhoods with poor-quality schools. There are, nevertheless, policy options that need to be considered.

Early Childhood Development Programs

The work of Currie and Thomas (1996) suggests that Head Start has had positive long-term effects on cognitive outcomes for poor Whites and Hispanics but generally not for Blacks. Their reasoning is that Head Start is not sufficient to overcome negative family and neighborhood influences that limit the performance of poor Blacks; however, other, more intensive, early-childhood development programs have been more successful for young Blacks—e.g., the Perry Preschool Program and the Child-Parent Centers of Chicago (Reynolds and Temple, 1998). Currie and Thomas (1996) suggest that these programs might merit strengthening and expansion.

School Reforms and Choice

Improving the performance of schools located in the inner city is a high priority, though how to achieve this is not always clear. A number of reform models exist that have shown some promise in various evaluation programs—e.g., Robert Slavin's "Success for All," or James Comer's School Development Program (Barnett, 1996). Using financial incentives to reward schools and teachers who achieve more progress is another approach (Clotfelter and Ladd, 1996). School-choice programs, if implemented in ways that provide inner-city children with real access to good schools, might improve the quality of the education the "movers" receive and also put competitive pressure on the schools they leave behind to become more effective.[5] Finally, some recent evidence suggests that Black inner-city students perform much better academically when they attend Catholic schools (Evans and Schwab, 1995; Neal, 1997). At a minimum, we need to understand better why these effects exist and the extent to which the reasons for them can be emulated in the public schools.

School-to-Work Programs

Establishing more effective links between employers and high schools might overcome early "mismatch" problems, and might improve student performance incentives. Through direct contact with employers, students might more clearly perceive the link between performance and later employment opportunities.

Support for Postsecondary Education

Expansion of Pell Grants and other financial support for postsecondary options is critical for maintaining and improving enrollment rates among Blacks. Combining financial aid with counseling about opportunities (Kane, 1994) might be useful as well.

Second-Chance Training for Out-of-School Youth

Far too many second-chance training programs do not appear to have worked for youth, for example, the Job Training Partnership Act or the National Supported Work Demonstration. A few have, perhaps, been more successful, such as the Job Corps (Lalonde, 1995). Successful programs may require taking young people out of their homes and neighborhood environments, offering a wide range of services and intensive interventions, and providing these over a sustained period of time. The up-front costs of these interventions might be high. Structure and communication of expectations might be critical as well (American Youth Policy Forum, 1997).

---

[5]For the best recent evidence on the effects of school vouchers for inner-city minorities in the well-known Milwaukee program, see Rouse (1997). But these data give us little guidance about what would happen in a larger, city-wide voucher program, where it is much less clear who would choose to move and how the slots at the most desirable schools would be rationed. Also, whether the resulting competition would improve the performance of schools that are losing students remains uncertain; see Hoxby (1996) and Kane (1996) for evidence and discussion of these issues.

Improving Access to Housing and Transportation

Given the evidence that racial and economic segregation generate a wide range of negative outcomes among young Blacks, and that "spatial mismatch" also limits their employment opportunities, improving the access of Blacks to residences and jobs in suburban areas seems critical. Greater residential mobility would likely generate positive outcomes along a wide range of dimensions. Rosenbaum and Popkin (1991) provide such evidence from the well-known Gautreaux experiment, in which central-city residents who moved to suburban areas enjoyed improvements in their employment and earnings relative to those who did not move. Preliminary, and somewhat more ambiguous, evidence from the more recent Moving-to-Opportunity demonstration project is discussed by Katz et al. (1997). Greater residential mobility can be encouraged through greater enforcement of open housing laws, and pressure or incentives for suburban areas to limit zoning and other exclusionary practices (Haar, 1996).

Alternatively, greater job mobility could be provided for those who remain in poorer Black neighborhoods (Hughes and Sternberg, 1992; Harrison and Weiss, 1997), through the efforts of "labor-market intermediaries" who provide job-placement assistance and transportation to suburban employment. The Center for Employment and Training (CET), originally located in San Jose, California, is perhaps the best-known program that relies on a combination of these interventions, along with training that is customized to meet the needs of local employers. Evaluations have indicated positive effects on the employment and earnings of minority participants (Melendez, 1996); however, CET primarily serves disadvantaged Hispanics and their community, and it remains unclear whether this model would work for other groups, such as Black males.

Local economic development assistance, which has traditionally occurred through "enterprise zones," but which more recently can involve support for a broader range of institutions and services, is not inconsistent with this approach (Giloth, 1997). Although enterprise zones have not traditionally been a cost-effective mechanism for improving employment and earnings of disadvantaged zone residents (Papke, 1993), the more recent federally funded "empowerment zones" can potentially be used to fund a much wider array of services to disadvantaged workers who reside in a zone. However, no formal evaluations of the effects of these zones have been performed to date.

EEO Laws and Affirmative Action

Recent evidence suggests that affirmative action raises the employment of minorities and women in establishments that practice it, without generating major losses of economic efficiency or productivity (Leonard, 1984, 1990; Holzer and Neumark, 1998, 1999; Conrad, 1997). Nevertheless, affirmative action remains extremely unpopular with White voters, especially when it is perceived as generating "preferential treatment." There is evidence to support the notion that employment in the affirmative action sector is redistributed from White males to other groups whose educational credentials are lower than their own, even though their productivity is generally comparable. Evidence also suggests that employment of White males in firms that practice affirmative action is about 15 percent lower than it otherwise would be, but that most of this employment is redistributed to White females rather than minorities (Holzer and Neumark, 1999). The "displaced" White males presumably gain employment in the non-affirmative action sector, though perhaps at somewhat lower wages than they otherwise would earn. Holzer and Neumark (1999) also show that firms engaging in affirmative action recruit applicants much more broadly, screen them more intensely, and invest more heavily in training new employees. This, presumably, enables them to hire minorities whose credentials on paper might be weaker but whose actual job performance compares favorably with that of White males.

A clearer public discussion of the benefits as well as costs of affirmative action is desirable, particularly while so many political and legal efforts are under way to dismantle it. Furthermore, some investigation is needed of how alternative university admission mechanisms affect educational and employment outcomes of minorities. One such mechanism is affirmative action based on family income rather than race/gender, which has been analyzed by Kane (1995). Another approach, used at the University of Texas, guarantees admission to all Texas high school students who rank within the top 10 percent of their high school class.

If political and legal restrictions to affirmative action continue to grow, these restrictions should be accompanied by a strong public embrace of EEO principles, and better enforcement of existing EEO laws. More specifically, EEO laws at the hiring stage need to be strengthened precisely in those areas where employment discrimination against Blacks seems to be most serious—i.e., at smaller and/or suburban establishments. This could be done either through more extensive use of the audit methodology, or by relying on real applicants whose access to smaller/suburban establishments is encouraged through the kinds of job mobility policies described above. Because most firms traditionally do not keep records of the race of their job applicants, the courts have generally inferred these numbers from the number of Blacks who reside in the local area (Bloch, 1994). If mobility policies succeed in generating many more Black applicants in areas where few currently live, there would be some need to document exactly where they apply for work and where they are—and are not—being hired.

Job Creation and Wage/Benefit Supports for Low-Wage Workers

Less-educated young Black males face many barriers in the labor market, and some—especially those with poor skills, little work experience, and/or criminal records—may not be employable in the private sector, even under the best of conditions. Therefore, greater use of employer-wage subsidies or public-sector employment to improve job availability for this group is probably warranted (Gottschalk, 1998; Katz, 1998). Some promising models of public-sector employment for young men include the Youth Corps and Youth Build (American Youth Policy Forum, 1997). For young males, these programs combine skills acquisition with employment and the provision of service to communities. When used, public-sector employment should be thought of as "transitional" and providing credentials that might make participants more attractive to private-sector employers.

Ultimately, however, low-wage employment in either the private or public sector will not enable young males to support families or resist the appeals of the illegal job market. Therefore, approaches to improve their earnings and benefits need to be considered. Two methods to directly increase the wages of low-wage workers are to (1) increase the minimum wage or (2) expand the Earned Income Tax Credit, perhaps by making it more generous to adults without custody of children. There remains some controversy among economists about whether minimum-wage increases reduce employment, though relatively modest increases, such as those legislated to date, are likely to generate only small disemployment effects.

Reducing Crime/Helping Incarcerated Youth

As noted above, crime reduction could have quite positive implications for young Black males in the labor market, if employers, both White and Black, become less fearful of them and become willing to employ them. Of course, this assumes that crime reduction can be accomplished in fair and racially unbiased ways (Kennedy, 1997). But it also raises the potential number of incarcerated young Black men, whose labor-market opportunities, once they leave prison, are severely constrained. Special training and job-creation efforts for them, perhaps undertaken with government financial support but administered by the kinds of effective labor-market intermediaries described above, would be an important complement to the kinds of "get tough" policies that have been implemented nationally.

IMPLICATIONS FOR RESEARCH

A number of issues remain unclear in the research literature about the differences in labor-market outcomes of men across racial groups. For many issues, there is a strong need for continued work.

What Are the Specific Mechanisms by Which Differential Labor Outcomes Occur?

Although there seems to be little doubt about the overall importance of factors such as skills, spatial location, and racial discrimination in the labor market for Black men, the exact mechanisms by which these effects operate remain somewhat unclear. For instance, is "spatial mismatch" primarily a function of limited transportation, limited information, or some other factor such as perceived hostility among White suburbanites? Regarding skills, exactly which skills do employers find most deficient among young Black men, and are the perceptions of these employers accurate? Do these deficiencies manifest themselves primarily through Black mens' performance during job interviews, in which case the deficient skills are more "soft" than "hard," through limited and/or unstable work experience, or through other means? And to what extent do their skill deficiencies limit their performance on the job when hired? As for discrimination against young Black men, is it really driven by employer fear of poor work performance, poor attitudes, crime, lawsuits, or some other factor? Answers to these questions are critical for developing effective policy responses; yet our knowledge of these matters remains quite limited.

What Are the Effects of the Interplay Between Personal, Familial, and Neighborhood Factors?

Related to the previous issue is an uncertainty about the extent to which the problems of Blacks in low-income communities are the result of personal, familial, or neighborhood forces. For instance, to what extent are the weaker skills that young Blacks bring to the labor market a result of underfunded schools, a poor social environment in the schools and neighborhood, or limited family educational resources? To what extent is participation in crime influenced by the same set of factors? Even when the right data are available, it is notoriously difficult to sort out neighborhood effects statistically from personal/family factors, given the problems of individual and family sorting (or self-selection) across neighborhoods (Ellen and Turner, 1997). Sorting out the exact causal patterns here is also difficult—e.g., does crime among young Black men lead to residential segregation and discrimination—especially among White suburbanites—or vice versa? And to what extent are the labor-market problems the result of interactions between their skills, social networks, etc.? If that is the case, is addressing these factors separately bound to fail?

Identifying Cost-Effective Policy Responses

In this critical area, our knowledge is perhaps weakest of all. Given the many programs that have failed to generate sustained improvements for disadvantaged Black youth, which ones are effective? When some programs or institutions do succeed for minority men, such as CET for Hispanics, or the Catholic schools for young Blacks, do we know why they work, and can we replicate their success elsewhere? This requires effective evaluation studies, using random-assignment methodology as much as possible, as well as more qualitative analyses of the processes underlying the various interventions.

REFERENCES

American Youth Policy Forum
  1997   *Some Things Do Make a Difference for Youth.* Washington, D.C.: American Youth Policy Forum.
Anderson, E.
  1980   Some observations on Black youth unemployment. In *Youth Employment and Public Policy*, B. Anderson and I. Sawhill, eds. Englewood Cliffs, N.J.: Prentice Hall.
Barnett, S.
  1996   Economics of school reform: Three promising models. Pp. 299-326 in *Holding Schools Accountable*, H. Ladd, ed. Washington, D.C.: The Brookings Institution.
Bendick, M., C. Jackson, and V. Reinoso
  1994   Measuring employment discrimination through controlled experiments. *Review of Black Political Economy* 23(Summer):25-48.
Blau, F.D., and A.H. Beller
  1992   Black-White earnings over the 1970s and 1980s: Gender differences in trends. *Review of Economics and Statistics* 74(2):276-286.
Bloch, F.
  1994   *Antidiscrimination Law and Minority Employment.* Chicago: University of Chicago Press.
Boozer, M., A. Krueger, and S. Wolkon
  1992   Race and school quality since *Brown v. Board of Education.* Brookings Papers on Economic Activity—Microeconomics. Washington, D.C.: The Brookings Institution.
Borjas, G.
  1992   Ethnic capital and intergenerational mobility. *Quarterly Journal of Economics* 107(February):123-150.

1994   The economics of immigration. *Journal of Economic Literature* 32(December):1667-1717.

1996   *Labor Economics*. New York: McGraw Hill.

Bound, J., and R. Freeman
1992   What went wrong? The erosion of relative earnings and employment among young Black men in the 1980s. *Quarterly Journal of Economics* 107(February):201-232.

Bound, J., and H. Holzer
1993   Industrial shifts, skill levels and the labor market for Black and White males. *Review of Economics and Statistics* 75(November):387-396.

1996   Demand shifts, population adjustments and labor market outcomes, 1980-90. Working paper, National Bureau of Economic Research.

Braddock, J., and J. McPartland
1987   How minorities continue to be excluded from equal employment opportunities: Research on labor market and institutional barriers. *Journal of Social Issues* 43:5-39.

Brown, C.
1982   The federal attack on labor market discrimination: The mouse that roared? *Research in Labor Economics* 5:33-69.

Card, D., and A. Krueger
1992   School quality and Black-White relative earnings: A direct assessment. *Quarterly Journal of Economics* 107(February):151-200.

Card, D., and T. Lemieux
1994   Changing wage structure and Black-White wage differentials. *American Economic Review* 84(May):29-32.

Carlson, L., and C. Swartz
1988   The earnings of women and ethnic minorities, 1959-1979. *Industrial and Labor Relations Review* 41(4):530-546.

Case, A., and L. Katz
1991   The company you keep: The effects of family and neighborhood on disadvantaged youth. Working paper, National Bureau of Economic Research.

Chay, K.
1995   Evaluating the impact of the 1964 Civil Rights Act on the economic status of Black men using censored longitudinal earnings data. Unpublished, Princeton University.

Chay, K., and D. Lee
1997   Changes in relative wages in the 1980s: Returns to observed and unobserved skills and Black-White wage differentials. Unpublished, University of California at Berkeley.

Chiswick, B.
1986   Is the new immigrant less skilled than the old? *Journal of Labor Economics* (April).

Clotfelter, C., and H. Ladd
1996   Recognizing and rewarding success in public schools. In *Holding Schools Accountable*, H. Ladd, ed. Washington, D.C.: The Brookings Institution.

Cogan, J.
1982   The decline in Black teenage employment. *American Economic Review* (September).

Conrad, C.
1997   The economic costs of affirmative action. In *Economic Perspectives on Affirmative Action*, M. Simms, ed. Washington, D.C.: Joint Center for Political and Economic Studies.

Council of Economic Advisers

1998 *Changing America: Indicators of Social and Economic Well-Being by Race and Hispanic Origin*. Washington, D.C.: U.S. Government Printing Office.

Currie, J., and D. Thomas

1996 Does subsequent school quality affect the long-term gains from Head Start? Working paper, National Bureau of Economic Research.

Cutler, D., and E. Glaeser

1997 Are ghettoes good or bad? *Quarterly Journal of Economics* 112(August):827-887.

Donohue, J., J. Heckman, and P. Todd

1998 Social action, private choice, and philanthropy: Understanding the sources of improvements in the Black schooling in Georgia. Working paper, National Bureau of Economic Research.

Donohue, J., and P. Siegelman

1991 The changing nature of employment discrimination litigation. *Stanford Law Review* (May).

Ehrenberg, R., and R. Smith

1997 *Modern Labor Economics*. Reading, Mass.: Addison Wesley.

Ellen, I., and M. Turner

1997 Does neighborhood matter? Assessing recent evidence. *Housing Policy Debate* 8(4).

Evans, W., and R. Schwab

1995 Finishing high school and starting college: Do Catholic schools make a difference? *Quarterly Journal of Economics* (November).

Farley, R., and W. Frey

1993 Latino, Asian and Black segregation in multi-ethnic metro areas: Findings from the 1990 Census. Working paper. Population Studies Center, University of Michigan.

Ferguson, R.

1993 New evidence on the growing value of cognitive skills and consequences for racial disparity and returns to schooling. Mimeograph. Kennedy School of Government, Harvard University.

Fernandez, R.

1994 Race, space, and job accessibility: Evidence from a plant relocation. *Economic Geography* 70(October):390-416.

Filer, R., D. Hamermesh, and A. Rees

1996 *The Economics of Work and Pay*. New York: Harper Collins.

Fix, M., and R. Struyk

1994 *Clear and Convincing Evidence*. Washington, D.C.: The Urban Institute Press.

Freeman, R.

1981 Black economic progress since 1964: Who has gained and why? In *Studies in Labor Markets*, S. Rosen, ed. Chicago: University of Chicago Press.

1991 The employment and earnings of disadvantaged young workers in a labor shortage economy. Pp. 103-121 in *The Urban Underclass*, C. Jencks and P. Peterson, eds. Washington, D.C.: The Brookings Institution.

1992 Crime and the employment of disadvantaged youth. Pp. 201-233 in *Urban Labor Markets and Job Opportunities*, G. Peterson and W. Vroman, eds. Washington, D.C.: The Urban Institute.

Freeman, R., and J. Medoff

1984 *What Do Unions Do?* New York: Basic Books.

Giloth, R.

1997 *Jobs and Economic Development*. New York: Sage Publications.

Gottschalk, P.
    1998   The impact of changes in public employment on low-wage labor markets. In *Generating Jobs*, R. Freeman and P. Gottschalk, eds. New York: Russell Sage Foundation.

Haar, C.
    1996   *Suburbs Under Siege: Race, Space and Audacious Judges.* Princeton, N.J.: Princeton University Press.

Harrison, B., and M. Weiss
    1997   *Workforce Development Networks.* New York: Sage Publications.

Hauser, R., and M. Huang
    1996   Trends in Black-White test score differentials. Discussion paper, Institute for Research on Poverty.

Heckman, J., and B. Payner
    1989   Determining the impact of federal antidiscrimination policy on the economic status of Blacks. *American Economic Review* 79(March):138-177.

Holzer, H.
    1986   Reservation wages and their labor market effects for White and Black male youth. *Journal of Human Resources* 21(Spring):157-177.
    1987   Informal job search and Black youth unemployment. *American Economic Review* 77(June):446-452.
    1991   The spatial mismatch hypothesis: What has the evidence shown? *Urban Studies* 28(February):105-122.
    1996   *What Employers Want: Job Prospects for Less-Educated Workers.* New York: Russell Sage Foundation.
    1998   Why do small firms hire fewer Blacks than larger ones? *Journal of Human Resources* 33(4):896-914.

Holzer, H., and K. Ihlanfeldt
    1996   Spatial factors and the employment of Blacks at the firm level. *New England Economic Review* (May/June):65-82.
    1998   Customer discrimination and employment outcomes for minority workers. *Quarterly Journal of Economics* 113:835-867.

Holzer, H., K. Ihlanfeldt, and D. Sjoquist
    1994   Work, search and travel for White and minority youth. *Journal of Urban Economics* 35(May):320-345.

Holzer, H., and D. Neumark
    1998   What does affirmative action do? National Bureau of Economic Research working paper.
    1999   Are affirmative action hires less qualified? *Journal of Labor Economics* 167(July):534-569.

Holzer, H., and J. Reaser
Forth-   Black applicants, Black employees, and urban labor market policy. *Journal of Urban Economics.*
coming
[2000]

Hoxby, C.
    1996   The effects of private school vouchers on schools and students. In *Holding Schools Accountable*, H. Ladd, ed. Washington, D.C.: The Brookings Institution.

Hughes, M., and J. Sternberg
    1992   *The New Metropolitan Reality: Where the Rubber Meets the Road in Antipoverty Policy.* Washington, D.C.: The Urban Institute.

Ihlanfeldt, K.
   1997   Information on the spatial distribution of job opportunities. *Journal of Urban Economics* 41:218-242.
   1998   Is the labor market tighter outside of the ghetto? Unpublished manuscript, Georgia State University.
Jargowsky, P.
   1997   *Poverty and Place.* New York: Russell Sage Foundation.
Juhn, C.
   1992   Declines in male labor force participation: The role of declining opportunities. *Quarterly Journal of Economics* 107(February):79-122.
Juhn, C., K. Murphy, and B. Pierce
   1993   Wage inequality and the rise in returns to skills. *Journal of Political Economy* 101(June):410-442.
Kain, J.
   1992   The spatial mismatch hypothesis three decades later. *Housing Policy Debate* 3(2):371-460.
Kane, T.
   1994   College entry by Blacks since 1970: The role of college costs, family background and the returns to education. *Journal of Political Economy* 102(October):878-911.
   1995   Racial preferences in college admissions. Unpublished, Harvard University.
   1996   Comments on Chapters 5 and 6. In *Holding Schools Accountable*, H. Ladd, ed. Washington, D.C.: The Brookings Institution.
Katz, L.
   1998   Wage subsidies for disadvantaged workers. In *Generating Jobs*, R. Freeman and P. Gottschalk, eds. New York: Russell Sage Foundation.
Katz, L., J. Kling, and J. Leibman
   1997   Moving to opportunity in Boston: Early impacts of a housing mobility study. Unpublished paper, Harvard University.
Kennedy, R.
   1997   *Race, Crime and the Law.* New York: Pantheon.
Kenney, G., and D. Wissoker
   1994   An analysis of the correlates of discrimination facing young Hispanic job seekers. *American Economic Review* 84(June):674-683.
Kirschenman, J.
   1991   Gender within race. Unpublished manuscript, University of Chicago.
Kirschenman, J., and K. Neckerman
   1991   'We'd love to hire them but . . . ' Pp. 203-234 in *The Urban Underclass*, C. Jencks and P. Peterson, eds. Washington, D.C.: The Brookings Institution.
Lalonde, R.
   1995   The promise of public sector-sponsored training. *Journal of Economic Perspectives* 9(2):149-168.
Leonard, J.
   1984   Antidiscrimination or reverse discrimination: The impact of changing demographics, Title VII and affirmative action on productivity. *Journal of Human Resources* 19(Spring):145-174.
   1990   The impact of affirmative action and equal employment opportunity law on Black employment. *Journal of Economic Perspectives* 4(Fall):47-63.
Levy, F., and R. Murnane
   1992   U.S. earnings levels and earnings inequality: A review of recent trends and proposed explanations. *Journal of Economic Literature* 30(December):1332-1381.

Marc, R.
    1995   Changes in educational attainment and school enrollment. In *State of the Union*, R. Farley, ed. New York: Russell Sage Foundation.
Margo, R.
    1990   *Race and Schooling in the South: 1880-1950*. Chicago: University of Chicago Press.
Massey, D., and N. Denton
    1992   *American Apartheid*. Cambridge, Mass.: Harvard University Press.
Melendez, E.
    1996   *Working On Jobs: The Center for Employment and Training*. Boston: Mauricio Gastonia Institute.
Moss, P., and C. Tilly
    1995   Soft skills and race. Working paper, Russell Sage Foundation.
Murnane, R., J. Wilted, and F. Levy
    1995   The growing importance of cognitive skills in wage determination. *Review of Economics and Statistics* 77(May):251-266.
Neal, D.
    1997   The effects of Catholic secondary schooling on educational attainment. *Journal of Labor Economics* 15(January):98-123.
Neal, D., and W. Johnson
    1996   Black-White differences in wages: The role of pre-market factors. *Journal of Political Economy* 104(October):869-895.
O'Regan, K., and J. Quigley
    1996   Spatial effects upon employment outcomes: The case of New Jersey teenagers. *New England Economic Review* (May/June):41-57.
Papke, L.
    1993   What do we know about enterprise zones? Working paper, National Bureau of Economic Research.
Petterson, S.
    1996   Are young Black men really less willing to work? *American Journal of Sociology*.
Raphael, S.
    1998   The spatial mismatch hypothesis of Black youth unemployment: Evidence from the San Francisco Bay area. *Journal of Urban Economics* 43(Spring):79-111.
Raphael, S., M. Stool, and H. Holzer
    1998   Are suburban firms more likely to discriminate against African-Americans? Discussion paper, Institute for Research on Poverty.
Reimers, C.
    1983   Labor market discrimination against Hispanic and Black men. *Review of Economics and Statistics* 65:570-579.
Reynolds, A., and J. Temple
    1998   Extended early childhood development and school achievement: Age thirteen findings from the Chicago Longitudinal Study. Discussion paper, Institute for Research on Poverty.
Rodgers, W., and W. Spriggs
    1996   What does the AFQT really measure? Race, wages, schooling and the AFQT score. *Review of Black Political Economy* 24(Spring):13-46.
Rosenbaum, J., and S. Popkin
    1991   Employment and earnings of low-income Blacks who move to the suburbs. Pp. 342-356 in *The Urban Underclass*, C. Jencks and P. Peterson, eds. Washington, D.C.: The Brookings Institution.

Rouse, C.
    1997   Private school vouchers and student achievement: An evaluation of the Milwaukee Parental Choice program. Working paper, National Bureau of Economic Research.

Smith, J., and F. Welch
    1989   Black economic progress since Myrdal. *Journal of Economic Literature* 27(June):519-564.

Trejo, S.
    1997   Relative earnings of Mexican-Americans. *Journal of Political Economy* 105(December):1235-1268.

Viscusi, W.
    1986   Market incentives for criminal behavior. In *The Black Youth Employment Crisis*, R. Freeman and H. Holzer, eds. Chicago: University of Chicago Press.

Waldinger, R.
    1996   *Still the Promised City? African-Americans and Immigrants in Post-Industrial New York*. Cambridge, Mass.: Harvard University Press.

Zax, J., and J. Kain
    1996   Relocating to the suburbs: Do firms leave their Black employees behind? *Journal of Labor Economics* 14(July):472-504.

6

Racial Trends in Labor Market Access and Wages: Women

Cecilia A. Conrad

I n 1950, Black women earned, on average, sixty cents for every dollar earned by White women.[1] Between 1960 and 1980, this wage gap disappeared. No documented racial trend between 1950 and 1980 is quite as impressive. Unfortunately, the improvement in relative earnings did not continue past 1980; and this post-1980 deterioration in relative earnings was not limited to Black women. The Hispanic/White median weekly earnings ratio for year-round, full-time workers was 0.86:1 in 1980 but only 0.75:1 in 1996. The earnings ratio for Asian[2] women, who have higher average earnings than White women, fell from 1.50:1 in 1988[3] to 1.38:1 in 1996.

Analyzed here are two trends—the improvement in Black-White relative earnings from 1950 to 1975 and the increase in racial inequality after 1980. In the process, trends in employment and in the occupational distribution of women workers will be examined. The ultimate goal is to assess

---

[1]Specifically, a U.S. Civil Rights Commission study (Zalokar, 1990) reports that in 1949, for year-round, full-time female workers between ages 25 and 64, the Black/White hourly wage ratio was 60.4 and the annual wage ratio was 60.5. For all female workers, ages 18 to 64, the hourly wage ratio in 1949 was 64.4, and the annual wage ratio, 55.7.

[2]The earnings ratios reported from the Current Population Survey (CPS) are for Asian and Pacific Islander Americans.

[3]The first year published CPS data on median earnings for Asian Americans are available.

the prospects for racial equality in labor-market status—Are we moving toward equality of opportunity and access?

The experiences of the many racial and ethnic groups represented in the U.S. labor market are individually unique; however, time, space, and data limitations preclude describing each group at the same level of detail. The guiding principle was first to identify interesting trends, then analyze the position of the groups involved in those trends. In some instances, there were too few data or there is too little available research on the experience of a particular group to offer substantive insights.

HISTORICAL TRENDS

There is ample anecdotal evidence of historical employment discrimination. Before 1960, it was difficult for a Black woman to get a job as a clerical worker whatever her credentials. Goldin (1990) observes that the only employers of Black clerical workers were Black-owned insurance companies and Montgomery Ward, then exclusively a mail-order business. In a 1940 Women's Bureau survey, more than 50 percent of employers reported that they had a company policy against hiring Black women as clerical workers (Goldin, 1990). Weaver's classic study of the plight of Black labor documents the exclusion of Blacks from skilled blue-collar jobs, particularly in the South (Weaver, 1946). During World War II, Black women were urged to help the war effort by taking jobs as domestic servants so that White women would be free to work in manufacturing jobs (Jones, 1985b). Discriminatory employment practices and segregation by occupation and industry were extensive, and contributed to differences in pay structure and indirectly to the Black-White female pay gap.

Earnings Inequality

During the 1960s and the 1970s, the median earnings of Black women increased relative to earnings of White women, White men, and Black men (Figure 6-1). Black/White female wages came closest to parity in 1975; from 1980 to 1996, the earnings of Black women relative to those of White women fell. Young Black women, in particular, have seen a reduction in relative earnings (Blau and Beller, 1992; McCrate and Leete, 1994). Blau and Beller (1992) found a reduction in the wages of young Black women, following an adjustment for selectivity bias—in other words, observed wages understate the extent of the wage gap because young Black women with the largest skill deficits had dropped out of the labor market.

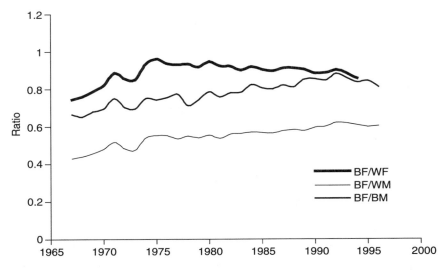

FIGURE 6-1 Ratio of Black women's earnings compared to those of White women, Black men, and White men. SOURCE: March Current Population Surveys, 1967-1996.

Table 6-1 is based on census data of median-income ratios for Hispanic, Asian, and Black women. The Hispanic/White ratio increased between 1960 and 1970, but there was less of an increase than for Black women. Asian (in this instance, Japanese, Chinese, and Filipino) women had higher average earnings than White women in 1960 and retained that advantage in 1980. Filipino women had an increase in relative income greater than that of Black women.

Figure 6-2 charts the earnings of Hispanic, Asian, and Black women, as a ratio of earnings of White women, for year-round, full-time workers since 1974. For Hispanic women, the earnings ratio is relatively stable through the 1980s but decreases in the 1990s. For Asian women, data were not available prior to 1988; since then, however, relative earnings decreased through 1990, rebounded in the early 1990s, and then decreased again.

Figure 6-3 depicts gender differences in earnings. For all races, the ratios of women's to men's earnings increased during the 1980s and have been fairly stable since 1990. The gender gap is smaller for racial and ethnic minority groups than for Whites.

Occupations

The increase in relative earnings of Black women between 1960 and 1975 was accompanied by a shift in their occupational distribution. Before 1960, a White woman without a college degree could find employment as a secretary, a sales clerk, or as a blue-collar operative. A Black woman, particularly in the South, had one option—domestic service. In 1960, more than 33 percent of all Black women worked as domestic servants ("private household workers"); only 3.2 percent of White women held these jobs (statistics cited in this paragraph are from the 1960 and 1980 Censuses). In 1960, of all women with 12 years of schooling, less than 20 percent of Black women, compared to an estimated 54 percent of White women, held jobs as clerical workers; and White women were 1.6 times more likely to be employed as blue-collar operatives than were Black women. In the South, less than 10 percent of all Black women worked as operatives; whereas, 18.5 percent of White women worked in this occupation. By 1980, however, less than 8 percent of Black women worked as domestic servants, the percentage employed as clerical workers had more than tripled, and, in the South, 14 percent of Black women worked as operatives compared to 8 percent of White women.

A U.S. Civil Rights Commission study (Zalokar, 1990) reports indices of occupational dissimilarity for Black and White women in 1940, 1960, and 1980. The index of occupational dissimilarity measures the percentage of Black, or White, women who would have to change occupations in order for the Black-White distribution to be equalized.[4] In 1940, 64 percent of Black women would have had to change occupations to equalize the distribution; in 1960, 51.9 percent; by 1980, 20.4 percent. Among women with 12 years of schooling, 43.7 percent would have had to change jobs in 1960 for equalized occupational distributions; 21.3 percent in 1980; 14 percent in 1990; and 16 percent in 1997.[5]

---

[4] The index of occupational dissimilarity is

$$1/2\sum_i |w_i - b_i|$$

where b_i is the proportion of Black women who work in occupation i, and w_i is the proportion of White women who work in occupation i. If Black and White women were distributed equally across occupations, the value of the index would be 0. If 100 percent of Black women were in one occupation and 100 percent of White women were in another, then the value of the index would be 1 (Zalokar, 1990). This index is commonly used to summarize the extent of occupational segregation in the labor market, but it is sensitive to the level of aggregation.

[5] Author's calculations using data from the U.S. Census of the Population: 1990 and the March 1997 Current Population Survey.

TABLE 6-1 Income Ratios for Hispanics, Asian Americans, and African Americans, 1960-1990

	Median Income, 1960 (All Persons with Income)	Median Income, 1970 (All Persons with Income)	Median Income, 1980 (All Persons with Income)	Median Income, 1980 (Year Round, Full-Time Workers)	Median Income, 1990 (Year Round, Full-Time Workers)
Spanish Surname/ Hispanics		0.93	0.88	0.86	0.79
Puerto Rican Birth or Parentage	1.27	1.24	0.84	0.92	0.90
Mexican American	0.71	0.88	0.85	0.85	0.74
Asian Americans				1.23	1.03
Japanese	1.30	1.36	1.38	1.17	1.20
Chinese	1.37	1.13	1.13	1.17	1.04
Filipino	1.01	1.48	1.54	1.18	1.11
African American	0.60	0.84	0.93	0.92	0.86

Note: The 1960 and 1970 U. S. censuses publish statistics on the Spanish-surnamed population in five Southwestern states: Texas, California, Arizona, New Mexico, and Colorado. These states included 80 percent of all persons of Spanish mother tongue in 1940. A separate report detailed the characteristics of persons of Puerto Rican parentage or birth.

SOURCES: Author's calculations using data from the U.S. Censuses of the Population 1960, 1970, 1980, and 1990. For 1960 data on Asian Americans and African Americans—U.S. Bureau of the Census, *Census of the Population: 960. Subject Reports. Nonwhite Population by Race. Final Report PC(2)-1C.* For 1960 data on Mexican Americans—U.S. Bureau of the Census, *U.S. Census of the Population: 1960. Subject Reports. Persons of Spanish Surname. Final Report PC(2)-1B.* For 1960 data on Puerto Ricans—U.S. Bureau of the Census, *U.S. Census of the Population: 1960. Puerto Ricans in the United States Final Report PC(2)-1D.* For 1960 data on Whites, U.S. Bureau of the Census, *U.S. Census of the Population: 1960. Detailed Characteristics, United States Summary. Final Report PC(1)-1D.* For 1970 data on Asian Americans—U.S. Bureau of the Census, *U.S. Census of the Population: 1970. Subject Reports. Japanese, Chinese and Filipinos in the United States. Final Report PC(2)-1G.* For 1970 data on Whites and African Americans, U.S. Bureau of the Census, *U.S. Census of the Population: 1970. Subject Reports. General Social and Economic Characteristics. United States Summary. PC(1)-C.* For 1970 data on Mexican Americans, U.S. Bureau of the Census, *U.S. Census of the Population: 1970. Subject Reports. Persons of Spanish Surname. 1970 PC(2)-1D.* For 1970 data on Puerto Ricans, U.S. Bureau of the Census, *U.S. Census of the Population: 1970. Subject Reports. Puerto Ricans in the United States. PC(2)-1E.* For 1970 data on Spanish Origin, U.S. Bureau of the Census, *U.S. Census of the Population: 1970. Subject Reports. Persons of Spanish Origin. PC(2)-1C.* For 1980 data U.S. Bureau of the Census, 1984, *1980 Census of the Population General Social and Economic Characteristics. United States Summary. PC80-2-1E.* For 1990 data, U.S. Bureau of the Census, 1993, *1990 Census of the Population: Social and Economic Characteristics, United States. 1990 CP-1-1.*

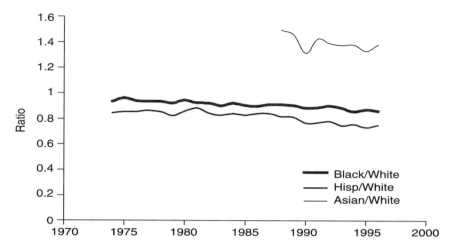

FIGURE 6-2 Earnings of Black, Asian, and Hispanic women as ratios of earnings of White women, 1974-1996. SOURCE: March Current Population Surveys, 1967-1996.

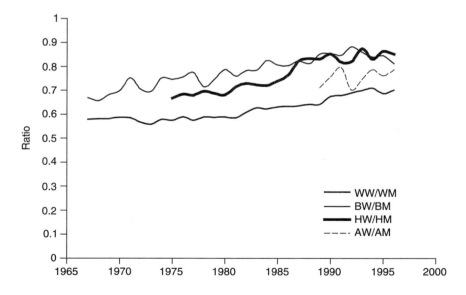

FIGURE 6-3 Female/male earnings ratios by race. SOURCE: March Current Population Surveys, 1967-1996.

TABLE 6-2 Indices of Occupational Dissimilarity for Asian Americans, Hispanics, and African Americans, 1960-1990

	1990	1980	1970	1960
Japanese	0.04	0.03	0.06	0.09
Chinese	0.15	0.14	0.10	0.10
Filipino	0.09	0.09	0.19	0.17
Mexican Americans	0.24	0.22	0.21	0.22
Puerto Ricans	0.14	0.17	0.25	0.48
African Americans	0.16	0.19	0.30	0.41

SOURCES; Author's calculations using data from the U.S. Censuses of the Population 1960, 1970, 1980, and 1990. For 1960 data on Asian Americans and African Americans— U.S. Bureau of the Census, *Census of the Population: 1960. Subject Reports. Nonwhite Population by Race. Final Report PC(2)-1C*. For 1960 data on Mexican Americans—U.S. Bureau of the Census, *U.S. Census of the Population: 1960. Subject Reports. Persons of Spanish Surname. Final Report PC(2)-1B*. For 1960 data on Puerto Ricans—U.S. Bureau of the Census, *U.S. Census of the Population: 1960. Puerto Ricans in the United States Final Report PC(2)-1D*. For 1960 data on Whites, U.S. Bureau of the Census, *U.S. Census of the Population: 1960. Detailed Characteristics, United States Summary. Final Report PC(1)-1D*. For 1970 data on Asian Americans—U.S. Bureau of the Census, *U.S. Census of the Population: 1970. Subject Reports. Japanese, Chinese and Filipinos in the United States. Final Report PC(2)-1G*. For 1970 data on African Americans and Whites—U.S. Bureau of the Census, *U.S. Census of the Population: 1970 General Social and Economic Characteristics. United States Summary. PC80-C1*. For 1970 data on Mexican Americans, U.S. Bureau of the Census, *U.S. Census of the Population: 1970. Subject Reports. Persons of Spanish Surname. 1970 PC(2)-1D*. For 1970 data on Puerto Ricans, U.S. Bureau of the Census, *U.S. Census of the Population: 1970. Subject Reports. Puerto Ricans in the United States. PC(2)-1E*. For 1980 data, U.S. Bureau of the Census, 1984, *1980 Census of the Population General Social and Economic Characteristics. United States Summary. PC80-2-1E*. For 1990, Asians, U.S. Bureau of the Census, *1990 Census of the Population: Asian and Pacific Islander Population in the United States 1990 CP-3-5*. For 1990, Whites and African Americans, U.S. Bureau of the Census, *1990 Census of the Population: Social and Economic Characteristics, United States. 1990 CP-2-1*. For 1990, Hispanics, U.S. Bureau of the Census, *1990 Census of the Population: United States Summary, Persons of Hispanic Origin in the United States, 1990 CP-3-3*.

Table 6-2 lists the indices of occupational dissimilarity for Asian-American (Chinese, Japanese, Filipino), Hispanic (Mexican and Puerto Rican), and Black women. Because the index is sensitive to the definition of occupational categories, the indices for Black women are not identical to those reported by Zalokar (1990), but they are close. The indices for American women of Japanese, Filipino, and Puerto Rican background show the same pattern as for Black women. The occupational distributions have become markedly more similar since 1960. However, for women of Mexican and Chinese background, the distributions have not converged since 1960. In 1960, approximately 24 percent of Mexican-

American women would have had to change jobs to make their occupational distribution identical to that of White women; in 1990, the percentage was unchanged. For Chinese-American women, only 10.5 percent would have had to change jobs in 1960 to make the distributions similar; in 1990, it was 15 percent.

The percentage of Hispanic women employed as clerical workers increased between 1960 and 1980 as it did for Blacks, but the changes were less dramatic. In 1960, 16 percent of Mexican-American women were employed as clerical workers; in 1980, 26.2 percent; and in 1990, 25 percent (U.S. Bureau of the Census). For Puerto Rican women, the percentage employed as clerical workers increased from 13.0 percent in 1960, to 31.9 percent in 1980, to 31 percent in 1990.

Figure 6-4 shows the change in the percentage of female workers employed in administrative and clerical work, by race, between 1960 and 1996. For women of Japanese and Chinese background, and White women, the percentages in this occupation decreased. Meanwhile, percentages increased dramatically for Puerto Rican and Black women. Based on an analysis of data from National Longitudinal Surveys, Power and Rosenberg (1993) suggest that White female clerical workers have more upward mobility than Black female clerical workers. They analyzed the

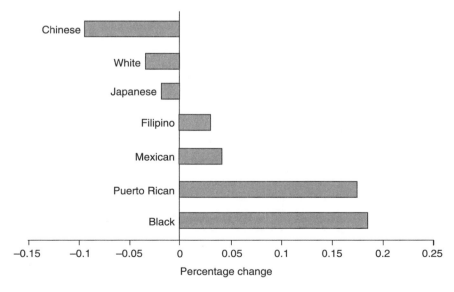

FIGURE 6-4 Change, by race/ethnicity, in the percentage of women employed as clerical workers, 1960-1990. SOURCE: U.S. Censuses of the Population, 1960 and 1990.

occupational positions of young women in 1972 and 1980 and found that among the young Black women who were clerical workers in 1972, 71.6 percent were still employed as clerical workers in 1980. By comparison, only 58.5 percent of the 1972 White clerical workers remained in that occupation. Both Black and White women left clerical work primarily for jobs as professional and technical workers or as managers and administrators (Whites); however, the Black women who moved into professional and technical jobs tended to be more concentrated in low-paying, female-dominated jobs than were White women.

Changes in the occupational distribution of Asian women paralleled the changes for Whites. Figure 6-5 shows the proportion of each racial/ethnic group employed as executives and managers. In 1960, 3.8 percent of Japanese-American women were employed as executives and managers; by 1980, this percentage had increased to 8.3 percent. For Chinese-American women, the percentage increased from 5.4 percent to 10.4 percent; and for Filipino-American women, from 1.6 percent to 6.4 percent. For White women, the percentage employed as executives and managers was 4.3 percent in 1960 and 7.8 percent in 1980.

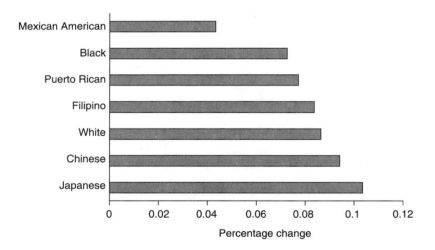

FIGURE 6-5 Change in percentage of women employed as executives and managers, 1960-1990. SOURCE: U.S. Censuses of the Population, 1960 and 1990.

Government Employment

Between 1960 and 1980, the concentration of Black women working in third-sector employment—i.e., government and nonprofit organizations like educational institutions and hospitals—increased relative to that of other groups. Burbridge (1994) reports an increase of 73 percent between 1960 and 1980, while the percentage employed in the for-profit sector decreased 36 percent. In contrast, for all workers, the percentage employed in the for-profit sector decreased only 11 percent. An analysis of 1997 Current Population Survey (CPS) data, shown in Table 6-3, reveals the concentrations of Black and Hispanic women among professions and executives in third-sector employment.

Employment

Ironically, as Black women shifted out of domestic service, White women moved from housework to paid employment. Labor-force participation rates (LFPR) for White women increased rapidly between 1960 and 1980, outpacing increases for other groups. As a result, the LFPR gaps between Black and White women and between Asian and White women narrowed. The gap between White and Hispanic women increased.

Table 6-4 shows LFPR trends between 1960 and 1980 by racial group. For White women, LFPR increased from 40.3 percent in 1960, to 49.6 percent in 1980, to 57.6 percent in 1990. For Black women, LFPR increased from 49.9 percent in 1960, to 52.9 percent in 1980, to 59.3 percent in 1990. Relative decreases in LFPR for Black women were greatest for those who had never been married (who had lower LFPR than their White counterparts) and among younger women (Jones, 1985a). LFPR for women 35 and older increased at a similar rate for Blacks and Whites. Young, never-married Black women remained less likely to be employed or actively looking for work than did their White counterparts, and the gap is increasing. Filipino women's LFPR, in 1960, was the lowest among Asian Americans (Filipino, Japanese, and Chinese). LFPR increases for Filipino women, however, rival those of White women; 36.4 percent of Filipino women were either employed or actively looking for work, compared with 40.3 percent of White women. LFPR for Filipino women increased from 36.24 in 1960 to 72.3 in 1990.

Unemployment rates are higher for Black and Hispanic women than for White women. Between 1975 and 1990, the gap between Black and White women increased, as Figure 6-6 illustrates. Hispanic women, both Mexican-American and Puerto Rican, have exceptionally high rates of unemployment compared to White women.

TABLE 6-3 Proportion Employed in Nonprofit Sector and in Government Sector, 1997

Racial/ Ethnic Group	All Workers		Professions		Executives	
	Third Sector	Government	Third Sector	Government	Third Sector	Government
White	40.6	22.5	69.6	41.1	53.2	37.3
African American	45.0	28.0	77.2	52.5	67.8	57.5
American Indian	54.6	41.6	83.3	53.3	84.3	80.4
Asian and Pacific Islander	33.4	21.3	54.4	36.3	50.8	39.6
Hispanic	36.0	22.2	76.0	49.4	67.4	56.4

SOURCES: Author's calculations from March 1997 Current Population Survey. Third sector combines the class of worker categories local, state, and federal government workers with the industry classifications of hospitals, educational institutions, and social service organizations.

TABLE 6-4 Trend in Labor Force Participation Rates of Women

Year	White	Black	American Indian	Asian				Hispanic			
				All Groups (Includes Pacific Islander)	Japanese Origin	Chinese	Filipino	All Groups	Mexican	Puerto Rican	Cuban
1950	32.9	43.5									
1960	40.3	49.9	25.5		44.1	44.2	36.2		28.8	36.3	
1970	48.8	56.7	35.3		49.4	49.5	55.2		34.9	31.6	
1980	49.6	52.9	48.1	57.1	58.5	58.3	68.1	48.9	49.5	34.8	56.5
1990	57.6	59.3	55.1	60.1	55.5	59.2	72.3	56.3	52.8	42.8	55.9
1996	59.6	59.0		58.6				52.6	51.7	48.9	52.9

Universe: Women 14 and older in 1950-1960; 16 and older 1970-1990 and 1996.

SOURCES: 1996 data for Hispanics, http://www.census.gov/population/socdemo/hispanic/cps96/sumtab-2.txt.
1996 data for Asians, http://www.census.gov/population/socdemo/race/api96/tab-02.txt.
1990 Census data for Whites, Blacks, Asians is from 1990 Census Lookup—http://venus.census.gov/cdrom/lookup/905875740.
Earlier census years are from U.S. Censuses of Population, 1960 to 1980. See citations for Tables 6-1 and 6-2.

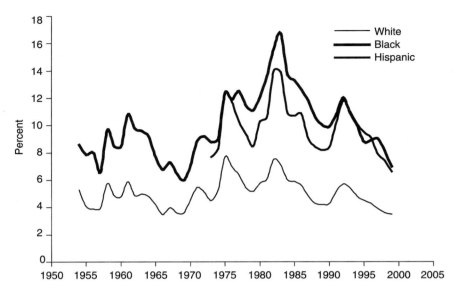

FIGURE 6-6 Unemployment rates for women, age 20 and older. SOURCES: Black (1954-1971), Bureau of Labor Statistics, Series LFU21001722, http://www.bls.gov; Black (1972-1999), Bureau of Labor Statistics, Series LFU21001732, http://www. bls.gov; White, Bureau of Labor Statistics, Series LFU21001712, http://www.bls. gov; Hispanic, Bureau of Labor Statistics, Series LFU21000050, http:// www.bls.gov.

UNDERSTANDING THE TRENDS

Methodology and Data[6]

Neoclassical economic theory emphasizes the importance of human capital in explaining differences in earnings among individuals. The principal tool used to investigate the role of human capital is a regression model. In the standard regression model, the dependent variable is the natural logarithm of earnings, and the set of explanatory variables includes measures of schooling, work experience, and indicators of marital and family status. Controls for occupation and industry may also be included. This estimated model can then be used to explain differences in mean wages by comparing the mean characteristics of two groups. For

---

[6]Altonji and Blank (1999) provide a more thorough and sophisticated discussion of the methodological issues of determining the effects of race and gender on wages.

example, if an additional year of schooling increases earnings by $1,000 per year, and White women have, on average, one additional year of schooling than Black women, then difference in schooling explains $1,000 of the observed earnings difference between Black and White women. Once all relevant productivity characteristics have been included in the model, the remaining pay difference is unexplained and attributable either to unmeasured differences in productivity (that could reflect premarket discrimination) or to labor-market discrimination.[7] Using this methodology, a decrease in the earnings gap between Black and White women might be explained by either (1) changes in the measured productivity characteristics of Black and White women, (2) changes in the return to productivity characteristics, (3) changes in unmeasured productivity, or (4) a decrease in labor-market discrimination.

This methodology has some important limitations. First, the omission of relevant productivity characteristics, or the measurement of some characteristics with error, can bias results. For example, many studies use a measure of potential experience (age minus years of schooling minus six) when data about actual experience are unavailable. For Black and White women of the same age, potential experience might be identical, but actual experience could be quite different. This is a particular problem for the analysis of long-term trends, given racial differences in LFPR. The primary source of data, the Public Use Micro Samples (PUMS) of the decennial U.S. Census, does not have information about actual work experience. In addition, before 1990, the only measure of education available in PUMS was years of formal schooling completed. Hence, with PUMS data, racial differences in the returns to schooling might reflect differences in the rate of degree attainment. If, for the same number of years of schooling, White women are more likely to have earned a degree, then an additional year of schooling will have a bigger effect on their earnings. CPS data have similar problems.

A second limitation is the potential for sample-selection bias. Individual decisions about whether to participate in the labor market will affect the observed structure of pay. For example, if only high-ability White women participate in the wage sector, but high-, medium-, and low-ability Black women work, the observed returns to schooling are likely to be higher for White than for Black women. With a simple-regression model, a researcher might attribute this difference to labor-

---

[7]Some of the unexplained portion of the pay difference will appear as differences in the returns to productivity characteristics. For example, an additional year of schooling might increase the earnings of a Black woman by $1,000 and the earnings of a White woman by $1,100 a year.

market discrimination when, in fact, it reflects differences in productivity. Unfortunately, there are no easy solutions to this problem. Manski (1989) offers a technical discussion of the selection problem and discusses the limitations of the standard solution, a two-stage estimation procedure proposed by Heckman (1976). The results of this procedure are very sensitive to model specification. Alternative approaches, such as the use of robust, nonparametric estimators, have other limitations. According to Greene (1997:983), "the issue remains unsettled."

For the most part, studies reviewed in the following section do not correct for sample-selection bias. Several authors report that they attempted the standard, Heckman two-step estimation procedure: Cunningham and Zalokar (1992) report in a footnote that they found no evidence of sample-selection bias when they attempted the procedure; McCrate and Leete (1994) described their results using the Heckman procedure as "problematic." Blau and Beller (1992) did correct for selection bias in trends in earnings ratios, but not in estimated-wage equations.

Convergence of Earnings of Black and White Women, 1960 to 1975

The studies cited in this section, although not numerous,[8] use different sources of data and different sets of explanatory variables.[9] Nonetheless, they reach remarkably similar conclusions about the contributing factors: essentially that the improvement in relative earnings between 1950 and 1980 is explained primarily by (1) the expansion of employment opportunities outside of private-household service; and (2) a decrease in labor-market discrimination either because of increasing competitiveness of the U.S. economy or enforcement of equal employment opportunity (EEO) laws, or both. Improvements in educational attainment also contributed, but were not the major factor (Zalokar, 1990; Cunningham and Zalokar, 1992; Carlson and Swartz, 1988).[10]

---

[8]The scholarly literature on the economic status of Black women is known to be shallow. Burbridge's count of articles published in 1993 found that of the 7,041 listed, "only 19 had titles indicating an examination of differences by race and sex" (1997:102).

[9]The U.S. Civil Rights Commission study (Zalokar, 1990) and analytical studies (Cunningham and Zalokar, 1992) use three sources of data to analyze racial wage differentials: PUMS, CPS, and Survey of Income and Program Participation (SIPP). Blau and Beller (1992) and Bound and Dresser (1999) also use CPS data. Carlson and Swartz (1988) and Darity et al. (1996) use PUMS. McCrate and Leete (1994) and Anderson and Shapiro (1996) use the National Longitudinal Survey (NLS). The NLS has information on actual work experience as well as greater detail about educational attainment; however, it is not amenable to analysis of long-term trends.

[10]Carlson and Swartz (1988) compare wage inequality in 1969 and 1979; Zalokar and Cunningham (1992) and Zalokar (1990) analyze data from 1940 to 1980.

Behind the expanded opportunities and decrease in labor-market discrimination are three possible explanations. The first is the convergence of unmeasured productivity characteristics, such as the quality of schooling [wage equations estimated by Zalokar (1990) did not include controls for the quality of schooling]. If Black women, on average, attended lower quality schools, then a year of schooling might have a smaller effect on wages for Black women than for White women. If school quality improved for Blacks between 1960 and 1980, differences in the structure of pay could be expected to disappear. A second explanation is a decrease in racial discrimination in wage setting—i.e., when, for a specific job, an employer offers a Black woman lower wages than are offered to a White woman with the same credentials. Legislation at both the state and federal levels made discrimination in wage setting illegal in the 1960s. The third explanation is the convergence of occupational distributions. Findings from Zalokar (1990), Cunningham and Zalokar (1992), and Blau and Beller (1992) suggest that the decrease in occupational segregation between 1960 and 1980 was a major contributing factor to the increase in relative wages of Black women.

Albelda (1986), basing findings on a regression analysis of the determinants of changes in occupational distribution from 1962 to 1981, attributes the convergence of Black-White occupational distributions to educational attainment and to structural shifts in the economy. Zalokar (1990:53) concludes:

> Although Black women's lower educational attainment in 1940 would undoubtedly have limited their occupational opportunities somewhat in any case, the extreme dissimilarity of Black and White women's occupations at that time implies that other factors, such as discrimination against Black women, played a far greater role than racial differences in educational attainment in keeping Black women out of occupations commonly held by White women.

Enforcement of EEO regulations and affirmative action were also factors in the decrease in racial discrimination after 1960. Title VII of the Civil Rights Act of 1964 prohibited discrimination on the basis of sex and race in any aspect of employment. In 1965, Executive Order 11246 required that all federal contractors have affirmative action plans specifying goals and timetables for increasing the representation of women and minorities in their work force. Although there is some debate about the magnitude of the impact of these laws, they appear to have increased employment opportunities for Black women (Leonard, 1990; Heckman and Payner, 1989; Betsey, 1994). Fosu (1992) attributes to Title VII a significant increase in Black women's occupational mobility from 1965 to 1981.

Divergence of Earnings of Black and White Women Since 1975

Although a consensus may have been reached about the convergence in earnings of Black and White women, there is no consensus about the divergence during the 1980s and 1990s. McCrate and Leete (1994), Anderson and Shapiro (1996), and Blau and Beller (1992) find evidence of a divergence in pay structure, particularly in the rates of return to education, but disagree about the causes. Darity et al. (1996) and Blau and Beller (1992) report decreasing, or no, wage discrimination.

Using PUMS data for persons 25 to 54 years old, Darity et al. (1996:420) conclude "there is no systematic evidence of discriminatory differentials affecting the incomes" of Black women after 1980. Blau and Beller (1992) report a decrease in the unexplained wage differential for older women (20 or more years of potential work experience) between 1971 and 1988, but note also an increase for younger women (especially those with 0 to 9 years of experience). Using CPS data, they compare wages earned by an older Black woman with those earned by an older White woman with the same credentials, and estimate that in 1971 the ratio was 80.6:1; in 1981, 90.8:1; and in 1988, 91:1. In contrast, for a Black woman with 0 to 9 years of potential experience, compared to a White woman with equivalent credentials, the ratio was 96.2:1 in 1971; 94.4:1 in 1981; and 93.2:1 in 1988. For the 10-to-19-years-of-experience cohort in Blau and Beller's study (1992), the unexplained wage differential decreases between 1971 and 1981, but increases between 1981 and 1988, perhaps the result of unmeasured characteristics, perhaps indicative of a decrease in school quality for Blacks.

McCrate and Leete (1994:180) express skepticism of this explanation because young Blacks had "recently at least held their own relative to Whites in measures of reading proficiency, scientific knowledge and math achievement."[11] Using data from the 1977 and 1986 NLS, they report a similar divergence in pay structures for women ages 23 to 28; in particular, the rate of return to education for Black women decreased relative to that of White women. Anderson and Shapiro (1996), in an analysis of NLS data for women ages 34 to 44, report that wages were closer to parity and that more of the gap in wages could be explained by differences in characteristics in 1980 than in 1988.

The fact that unexplained differentials go in different directions for

---

[11]James P. Smith's paper in this volume reports achievement test scores by race from 1971 to 1996. In 1971, the difference between the average reading proficiency score of Black 17 year olds and that of White 17 year olds was 52 points. In 1980, it had narrowed to 50 points and in 1990, it was only 30 points. A similar trend characterizes mathematics and science test scores.

different experience groups raises questions about the role of labor-market discrimination in addition to the possible contribution of unmeasured characteristics, such as the quality of schooling. Leonard (1990) argued that the enforcement of EEO regulations effectively ended in the late 1970s; hence, employers with tastes for discrimination might have been able to exercise them with relative impunity. However, Blau and Beller (1992) prefer to attribute the changes to unmeasured characteristics rather than to discrimination.

Bound and Dresser's (1999) results show that college-educated Blacks experienced a greater drop in relative earnings than did women with less than a college degree. They attribute some of the relative decrease in returns to a college degree to the greater occupational mobility of college-educated White women. However, this explanation begs the question, Why are White women more upwardly mobile?

England et al. (1999) attribute racial differences in occupations to differences in skills. Following Neal and Johnson (1996), England et al. use Armed Forces Qualification Test (AFQT) scores as a measure of cognitive skill. Comparing AFQT scores with data on young women from the National Longitudinal Survey of Youth (NLSY), they conclude that differences in cognitive skill contribute to wage differences between Black and White, and Hispanic and White women. Furthermore, they argue that differences in cognitive skill are correlated with occupations. Black women and Hispanics occupy jobs that require fewer cognitive skills than jobs occupied by White women.

The appropriateness of the AFQT score as a measure of cognitive ability is the subject of ongoing debate.[12] If the test is racially biased, as some critics suggest, then the AFQT score is a proxy for race and its inclusion will bias against a finding of discrimination. If the AFQT score does measure a productivity-relevant attribute, its exclusion will bias in favor of finding discrimination. Even if differences in AFQT scores do explain differences in wages, no study has investigated the ability of AFQT scores to explain the erosion of relative wages over time.

Wages of Asian and Hispanic Women

Earnings differentials between Hispanic and Asian and White women appear to be explained primarily by differences in characteristics. Darity

---

[12]Much of this debate has centered on studies of men. Rodgers and Spriggs (1996) show that an adjustment for racial bias substantially reduces the explanatory power of the AFQT. The AFQT is also debated in an exchange between Maume et al. (1996) and Farkas and Vicknair (1996) in the *American Sociological Review*.

et al. (1996) and Carlson and Swartz (1988) report no evidence of racial wage discrimination against Asian women; and Reimers (1985a), Carlson and Swartz (1988), Darity et al. (1996), and Baker (1999)[13] report little evidence of racial wage discrimination against Hispanic women. Hence, it is reasonable to expect that changes in productivity characteristics explain the decrease in relative wages.

Asian women have higher average earnings than White women because they have higher educational attainment and more work experience, and they are more concentrated in professional occupations (Carlson and Swartz, 1988). Some Asian women may have even higher returns to productivity than White women.[14]   Hence, the most likely explanation for the decrease in relative wages of Asian women is a decrease in the size of their human capital advantage. White women have increased their rates of college completion relative to Asian women; and as more White women engage in paid labor, Asian women may lose their edge in work experience.

Reimers (1985a), using data from the 1976 Survey of Income and Education (SIE), attributes the difference in pay between Hispanic and White women to differences in education, family size, and to immigrant status. More recent studies corroborate her findings (Carlson and Swartz, 1988; Darity et al., 1996; Baker, 1999). But there are mixed results regarding the effect of English language ability on earnings. Carlson and Swartz (1988) obtained a statistically significant coefficient on English ability in an earnings equation for Mexican-American women, but not for Cuban-American or Puerto Rican women. In Reimers' estimated equations, the coefficient on English proficiency is never statistically different from 0. Baker (1999), in a study that focused on Mexican-American women in the Southwest, found a positive and statistically significant effect of English ability on earnings in 1980 but not in 1990.

Immigration complicates any analysis of Hispanic/White wage ratio trends. Because immigrant status depresses wages (Reimers, 1985a; Baker, 1999), changes in the percentage of immigrants in the Hispanic population would affect the wage ratio. In addition, the presence of Hispanic immigrants in a labor market might affect the wages of Hispanic women

---

[13]Reimers (1985a) does find evidence of discrimination against Central and South American women using data from the 1976 Survey of Income and Education.

[14]Carlson and Swartz (1988) find that the earnings equations of Filipino, Vietnamese, and Japanese women were higher than the White equation for an equivalent set of characteristics. Darity et al. (1996) also found higher returns to characteristics for some Asian subgroups. Asian Indians and Filipinos had lower returns to their characteristics in 1980, but higher returns in 1990 (Darity et al., 1996).

and White women differently. Baker (1999) analyzed the wages of Mexi-can-American, Black, and other women workers in Southwestern labor markets and found evidence that an increase of Mexican immigrants de-pressed the wages of U.S.-born Mexican women, had no effect on the wages of U.S.-born Black women, but increased the wages of U.S.-born White women.[15]

Given the diversity of experiences among Hispanics, it is conceivable that the decline in relative earnings reflects a change in the composition of the Hispanic female labor force. However, this explanation seems un-likely for several reasons. (1) If immigrants are excluded, the trend in relative wages persists; the Hispanic/White wage ratio decreased for U.S.-born Mexican women and for mainland-born Puerto Rican women after 1980. (2) The percentage of Puerto Rican women workers who are island-born decreased since 1980, but there was no improvement in the relative wage ratio. (3) Baker's analysis of the impact of the size of the immigrant population on the wages of U.S.-born Mexican women estimates a smaller effect in 1990 than in 1980.

A more plausible explanation for the erosion of relative wages for Hispanic women is a change in productivity characteristics. Mexican-American and Puerto Rican women have increased their educational at-tainment; however, the gap in college-completion rates continues to in-crease. Comparable statistics for Mexican-American women having earned a bachelor's degree or higher, compared with White women, are as follows: in 1970, 2.3 percent compared with 13.8 percent; in 1980, 4.9 percent compared with 21.6 percent; in 1990, 6.2 percent compared with 27.9 percent. The gap increased 3 percent between 1980 and 1990 and 8 percent between 1970 and 1990.[16] Given the growing premium paid for college diplomas, it is likely this gap in educational attainment contrib-uted to the decrease in relative earnings of Mexican-American women.

Changes in Labor-Force Participation Rates

In theory, a woman's labor-force participation decision is influenced by (1) the wage she can expect to receive; (2) the productivity of her

---

[15]Baker (1999) estimates separate wage regressions for Mexican immigrant, Mexican, Black, and "other races." The finding for White women described here refers to the "other race" category.

[16]The statistics on educational attainment are from Table 3.1 in Corcoran et al. (1999). Baker (1999) describes a similar if less dramatic pattern in college completion rates for U.S.-born, Mexican-origin women compared with Non-Hispanic Whites in her analysis of south-western urban labor markets.

nonmarket time, as reflected by number of young children, marital status, and living arrangements; and (3) her nonlabor income, including the earnings of her spouse and government transfers. Empirical findings are generally consistent with this theoretical model. The presence of young children and a high-wage earning spouse tend to reduce LFPR among married women; however, factors associated with higher wages, such as education and good health, tend to increase LFPR. Government transfer programs, such as Aid to Families with Dependent Children, tended to reduce formal participation among potentially eligible women.

These factors, however, do not provide a full accounting of racial differences in LFPR among married women (Reimers, 1985b; Goldin, 1977). Using data from the 1976 SIE, Reimers estimates that differences in characteristics explain 95 percent of the gap between U.S.-born White and foreign-born Hispanic married women, and 83 percent of the gap between U.S.-born White and U.S.-born Hispanic married women. Differences in education, family size, language ability, and age of children contribute to lower LFPR in these groups. Differences in characteristics explain 77 percent of the gap between U.S.-born White married women and foreign-born Asians.

Differences in characteristics do not appear to explain historical gaps in LFPR between U.S.-born White, Asian, and Black married women; this gap can be explained by differences in parameters. In other words, given equal education, family size, language ability, and ages of children, the propensity to work is higher for Black and Asian than for White married women. Reimers suggests that cultural factors contribute to this otherwise unexplained differential.

A factor contributing to the slow increase in LFPR of Black women during the 1960s and 1970s was the decrease in LFPR among young single Black women (Jones, 1985a). Jones attributes the gap among young women to differences in the demand for their labor services; she asserts that the relative decrease in Black female LFPR "appears to be a response to inadequate employment opportunities with reasonable wages" (1985a:27). Jones' hypothesis is consistent with the increased demand for skill since the late 1970s. Indeed, in some occupations that opened up to Black women in the 1960s and early 1970s, total employment contracted in the 1990s. Bank tellers provide a case in point; technological change has reduced employment in this occupation just as the number of minority women with these jobs expanded.

It is possible that the factors contributing to the decrease in employment rates among young Black males also contribute to the decrease in labor-force participation for young Black women—lack of skills, geographic concentration in inner cities, low-income communities, and discrimination (Holzer, 1999). Although studies of employers suggest more positive attitudes toward Black women than Black men, young Black women still must overcome skill deficits and the problem of spatial mismatch (Kirschenman and Neckerman, 1991; Holzer, 1996). McLafferty and Preston (1992), in a study of Northern New Jersey, found that Black and Hispanic women have longer commuting times and less localized labor markets than White women. Thus geographic concentration of work outside of central cities may pose an obstacle to employment for young women; childcare needs and concerns about personal safety may discourage them from traveling long distances late at night or early in the morning.

The decrease in the relative LFPR of young Black women may also be linked to their higher rates of teen motherhood, leading younger Black women to have lower relative rates of labor-force participation when they are young and higher relative rates in their late 20s and early 30s. Hispanic women probably confront similar obstacles to employment.

FUTURE TRENDS AND RESEARCH ISSUES

Occupations

The occupational distributions of Black and White women converged between 1960 and 1980, but this trend is unlikely to continue. Initially, because of their more extensive historical participation in the labor force and the barriers to employment they confronted, Black women may have benefited more from the enforcement of EEO laws than White women. Indeed, Epstein (1973) argued that Black women enjoyed an advantage relative to both Black men and White women because they represented a "double-minority"—employers concerned about meeting affirmative action goals and timetables could count a Black woman as two minorities. In addition to this "advantage," the growth in demand for clerical workers and service workers in the 1960s and 1970s created opportunities for Black, White, and Hispanic women on a somewhat equal basis.

Labor in the 1980s, however, favored college-educated workers, and professional and technical workers (Bound and Johnson, 1995; Juhn and Murphy, 1995). White and Asian women, with higher rates of college completion, were able to take advantage of emerging new opportunities; most Black and Hispanic women were not. Yet, even college-educated Black women were increasingly concentrated in low-wage occupations. Occupational comparisons for Black and White college graduates in 1989 are as follows: 29.5 percent of Blacks were clerical workers, compared with 14.5 percent of Whites; 47 percent of Blacks were managerial and professional workers, compared with 63.2 percent of Whites. Bound and Dresser's (1999) study suggests that 18 percent of the increase in the wage

TABLE 6-5 Occupational Distributions, Women 18-64, 1997 (percent)

	White	Black	American Indian	Asian and Pacific Islander	Hispanic
Executives and managers	19.5	13.6	18.0	19.3	16.6
Professional	18.3	11.8	10.6	16.6	8.5
Technical	3.7	3.3	3.5	5.1	2.6
Sales	12.1	9.9	7.8	11.7	10.2
Sales, finance & business, commodities	2.5	1.1	1.4	1.1	0.9
Clerical	24.0	24.7	26.7	18.0	21.9
Private household	0.7	1.2	0.7	0.4	3.4
Service	13.0	21.9	21.1	15.4	18.2
Precision production, crafts and repair	1.9	2.1	2.8	2.4	2.2
All other	1.8	9.3	6.0	8.9	14.6

SOURCE: Author's calculations from March 1997 Current Population Survey.

gap between Black and White college graduates can be attributed to increasing concentration of Black college graduates in low-wage occupations. Table 6-5 provides percentages of occupational distributions of White, Black, Hispanic, and Asian and Pacific Islander women in March 1997.

Future research needs to explore the factors that restrict occupational mobility for Black women and Hispanics. This analysis should investigate decision making by individuals as well as institutional constraints; and the labor-market experiences of Asian groups should not be neglected. Analyses of the labor-market status of Asian women are limited in number; and researchers tend to lump Asians into a single group despite the diversity of characteristics among different national groups.

Greater Inequality Among Younger Women

The trends in occupations suggest that wage inequality is likely to continue to increase, as it has since 1990. The only factors that might offset this trend are a shift in the relative demand for skilled labor or an increase in the college-completion rates of Hispanic and Black women. If the demand for college-educated workers decreases relative to that for other workers, the relative wages of college-educated labor may decrease.

In addition, as noted earlier, Black and Hispanic women have higher rates of unemployment and lower rates of labor-force participation than

White and Asian women. These differences in employment rates will contribute to a relative deficit in experience. Black and Hispanic women also continue to have lower rates of college enrollment, which will further limit the demand for their labor. Finally, welfare reform has increased the supply of low-skilled labor, and minority women appear to be having a more difficult time moving off the welfare rolls (DeParle, 1998).

These observations suggest several questions for future research. (1) What are the obstacles to college completion for Hispanic and Black women? McElroy (1996) and Cardoza (1991) suggest that one obstacle is the higher incidence of teen motherhood among Hispanics and Black women; but, it is not clear whether early childbearing deters college attendance or vice versa. Incentives for early childbearing are poorly understood and require further investigation. (2) How do the employment obstacles confronting young women differ from those confronting young men? For example, neighborhood segregation is likely to impact women differently from men, but few studies have examined the spatial mismatch hypothesis for young women. (3) How do the employment prospects of young men affect decision making by young women? Although several authors have suggested a link between male employment status and family formation, none has explored the potential link between employment prospects of young men and schooling and employment choices of young women. (4) To what extent does discrimination by employers limit opportunities? Racial differences in employment rates and in occupational distribution might reflect differences in tastes or in unobserved productivity characteristics. On the other hand, the persistence of occupational and employment disparities may reflect institutional factors, including discrimination in the employment process. One method of assessing the role of discrimination is the employment audit in which matched pairs of testers (one minority, one White) respond to advertised job openings to develop comparisons of treatment at each stage of the application process. Although there have been a number of employment audits involving Black and Hispanic men, there have been no employment audits involving minority women.

CONCLUSIONS

Are we moving toward equality of opportunity and access? The answer is uncertain. Once women are in the same jobs, they appear to earn the same pay. However, there persist racial differences not only in the distribution of women by occupations but also in employment status; and the widening gap in college-completion rates and the deterioration in the relative returns to schooling among younger women threaten future progress.

ACKNOWLEDGMENTS

Special thanks to Kenneth Chay, William Spriggs, William Darity, Margaret Hwang, and Rebeccca Blank for their advice as this manuscript was in progress. It has also benefited from the suggestions of an anonymous referee.

REFERENCES

Albelda, R.
    1986   Occupational segregation by race and gender, 1958-1981. *Industrial and Labor Relations Review* 39:404-411.

Altonji, J., and R. Blank
    1999   Race and gender in the labor market. In *Handbook of Labor Economics, Volume 3C*, O. Ashenfelter and D. Card, eds. New York: North Holland.

Anderson, D., and D. Shapiro
    1996   Racial differences in access to high-paying jobs and the wage gap between Black and White women. *Industrial and Labor Relations Review* 49(2):273-286.

Baker, S.
    1999   Mexican-origin women in southwestern labor markets. In *Latinas and African American Women at Work: Race, Gender and Economic Inequality*, I. Brown, ed. New York: Russell Sage Foundation.

Betsey, C.
    1994   Litigation of employment discrimination under Title VII: The case of African American women. *American Economic Review* 84(2):98-107.

Blau, F., and A. Beller
    1992   Black-White earnings over the 1970s and 1980s: Gender differences in trends. *The Review of Economics and Statistics* 74(2):276-286.

Bound, J., and L. Dresser
    1999   Losing ground: The erosion of the relative earnings of African American women during the 1980s. In *Latinas and African American Women at Work: Race, Gender and Economic Inequality*, I. Brown, ed. New York: Russell Sage Foundation.

Bound, J., and G. Johnson
    1995   What are the causes of rising wage inequality in the United States. *Federal Reserve Bank of New York Economic Policy Review* 1(1):9-17.

Brown, I., and I. Kennelly
    1999   Stereotypes and realities: Images of Black women in the labor market. In *Latinas and African American Women at Work: Race, Gender and Economic Inequality*, I. Brown, ed. New York: Russell Sage Foundation.

Burbridge, L.
    1994   The reliance of African-American women on government and third-sector employment. *American Economic Review* 84(2):103-107.
    1997   Black women in the history of African American economic thought: A critical essay. In *A Different Vision: African American Economic Thought, Volume One*, T. Boston, ed. New York: Routledge.

Cardoza, D.
    1991   College attendance and persistence among Hispanic women: An examination of some contributing factors. *Sex Roles A Journal of Research* 24:133-147.

Carlson, L., and C. Swartz
   1988   The earnings of women and ethnic minorities. *Industrial and Labor Relations Review* 41:530-552.
Corcoran, M., C. Heflin, and B. Reyes
   1999   The economic progress of Mexican and Puerto Rican women. In *Latinas and African American Women at Work: Race, Gender and Economic Inequality*, I. Brown, ed. New York: Russell Sage Foundation.
Cunningham, J., and N. Zalokar
   1992   The economic progress of Black women, 1940-1980: Occupational distribution and relative wages. *Industrial and Labor Relations Review* 45:540-555.
Darity, W., D. Guilkey, and W. Winfrey
   1996   Explaining differences in economic performance among racial and ethnic groups in the USA: The data examined. *American Journal of Economics and Sociology* 55(4):411-426.
DeParle, J.
   1998   Shrinking welfare rolls leave record high share of minorities. *The New York Times* July 27:A1+.
England, P., K. Christopher, and L. Reid
   1999   Gender, race, ethnicity, and wages. In *Latinas and African American Women at Work: Race, Gender and Economic Inequality*, I. Brown, ed. New York: Russell Sage Foundation.
Epstein, C.
   1973   Positive effects of the multiple negative: Explaining the success of Black professional women. *American Journal of Sociology* 78(4):912-935.
Farkas, G., and K. Vicknair
   1996   Appropriate tests of racial discrimination require controls for cognitive skill: Comment on Cancio, Evans, and Maume. *American Sociological Review* 61(August):557-560.
Fosu, A.
   1992   Occupational mobility of Black women, 1958-1981: The impact of post-1964 antidiscrimination measures. *Industrial and Labor Relations Review* 45(2):281-294.
Goldin, C.
   1977   Female labor force participation: The origin of Black-White difference, 1870 and 1880. *Journal of Economic History* 37(1):87-108.
   1990   *Understanding the Gender Gap: An Economic History of American Women*. New York: Oxford University Press.
Greene, W.
   1997   *Econometric Analysis*. Upper Saddle River, N.J.: Prentice Hall.
Heckman, J.
   1976   The common structure of statistical models of truncation, sample selection, and limited dependent variables and a simple estimator for such models. *Annals of Economic and Social Measurement* 5:479-492.
Heckman, J., and B. Payner
   1989   Determining the impact of federal antidiscrimination policy on the economic status of Blacks: A study of South Carolina. *American Economic Review* 79(1):138-177.
Holzer, H.
   1996   *What Employers Want: Job Prospects for Less-Educated Workers*. New York: Russell Sage Foundation.

1999   The barriers to higher employment rates among African Americans. In *Job Creation Prospects and Strategies*, W. A. Leigh and M. C. Simms, eds. Washington, D.C.: Joint Center for Political and Economic Studies.

Jones, B.
1985a   Black women and labor force participation: An analysis of sluggish growth rates. *Slipping Through the Cracks: Review of Black Political Economy* 14(special issue):11-31.

Jones, J.
1985b   *Labor of Love, Labor of Sorrow: Black Women, Work, and the Family from Slavery to the Present.* New York: Basic Books.

Juhn, C., and K. Murphy
1995   Inequality in labor market outcomes. *Federal Reserve Bank of New York Economic Policy Review* 1(1):26-34.

Kirschenman, J., and K. Neckerman
1991   'We'd love to hire them, but . . . ': The meaning of race for employers. In *The Urban Underclass*, C. Jencks and P. Peterson, eds. Washington, D.C.: The Brookings Institution.

Leonard, J.
1990   The impact of affirmative action regulation and equal employment law on Black employment. *The Journal of Economic Perspectives* 4(4):47-64.

Manski, C.
1989   Anatomy of the selection problem. *Journal of Human Resources* 24:343-360.

Maume, D., A. Cancio, and T. Evans
1996   Cognitive skills and racial wage inequality: Reply to Farkas and Vicknair. *American Sociological Review* 61(August):561-564.

McCrate, E., and L. Leete
1994   Black-White wage differences among young women, 1977-86. *Industrial Relations* 33:168-183.

McElroy, S.
1996   Early childbearing, high school completion, and college enrollment: Evidence from 1980 high school sophomores. *Economics of Education Review* 15:303-324.

McLafferty, S., and V. Preston
1992   Spatial mismatch and labor market segmentation for African American and Latina women. *Economic Geography* 68(4):406-431.

Neal, D., and W. Johnson
1996   The role of premarket factors in Black-White wage differences. *Journal of Political Economy* 104:869-895.

Power, M., and S. Rosenberg
1993   Black female clerical workers: Movement toward equality with White women? *Industrial Relations* 32(2):223-237.

Reimers, C.
1985a   A comparative analysis of the wages of Hispanics, Blacks, and non-Hispanic Whites. In *Hispanics in the U.S. Economy*, G. Borjas and M. Tienda, eds. New York: Academic Press.
1985b   Cultural differences in the labor supply among married women. *American Economic Review* 75:252-255.

Rodgers, W., III, and W. Spriggs
1996   What does the AFQT really measure: Race, wages, schooling and the AFQT score. *The Review of Black Political Economy* 24(4):13-46.

U.S. Bureau of the Census
1963a   *U.S. Census of the Population: 1960. Subject Reports. NonWhite Population by Race, Final Report PC (2)-1C.* Washington, D.C.: U.S. Government Printing Office.

1963b *U.S. Census of the Population: 1960. Subject Reports. Puerto Ricans in the United States. Final Report PC(2)-1D.* Washington, D.C.: U.S. Government Printing Office.

1963c *U.S. Census of the Population: 1960. Subject Reports. Persons of Spanish Surname. Final Report PC(2)-1B.* Washington, D.C.: U.S. Government Printing Office.

1963d *U.S. Census of the Population: 1960. Detailed Characteristics: United States Summary. Final Report PC(1)-1D.* Washington, D.C.: U.S. Government Printing Office.

1973a *U.S. Census of the Population: 1970. Subject Reports. Japanese, Chinese and Filipinos in the United States. Final Report PC(2)-1G.* Washington, D.C.: U.S. Government Printing Office.

1973b *U.S. Census of the Population: 1970. Detailed characteristics: United States Summary. Final Report PC(2)-1G.* Washington, D.C.: U.S. Government Printing Office.

Weaver, R.

1946 *Negro Labor: A National Problem.* New York: Harcourt, Brace and Company.

Zalokar, N.

1990 *The Economic Status of Black Women: An Exploratory Investigation.* Washington, D.C.: U.S. Commission on Civil Rights.

7

Ethnic and Racial Differences in Welfare Receipt in the United States

Robert A. Moffitt and Peter T. Gottschalk

T he general public in the United States has long linked welfare and race. This association has played a major role in attitudes toward the welfare system and in the politics of welfare reform. Attitudes toward welfare spending are correlated with racial attitudes (Bobo and Smith, 1994:389), and opposition to welfare among White voters has been shown to be related to attitudes toward race (Gilens, 1995, 1996). Many analysts have noted that the general popular perception that minority racial and ethnic groups dominate the welfare rolls has been historically incorrect, for minorities have historically accounted for no more of the welfare caseload than White families. Ethnic minorities do, however, have higher rates of participation in the welfare system than does the majority White population, given their lesser total numbers. Thus, the popular perception has some basis in fact, if interpreted to mean that minorities have higher propensities to make use of the welfare system.

A natural question to which this observation gives rise concerns the source of the ethnic and racial differences in welfare receipt rates. The research in this area has noted that there are two conflicting general views. One is that the differences arise from differences in the underlying risk factors associated with welfare receipt—rates of single motherhood, poverty, low earnings capability and job skills, high rates of unemployment, low levels of education, and similar variables. The other is that there are inherent differences in the propensity to take up welfare by different ethnic and racial groups, usually thought to arise from different cultural and social norms for the acceptability of being on welfare and different degrees of stigma associated with welfare receipt. This stigma can be either transmitted across families in a given neighborhood or city or transmitted across generations, as children of welfare recipients themselves learn to find welfare receipt more acceptable.

This study documents and explores racial and ethnic differences in welfare-participation rates in the United States in two ways. First, we examine what those differences are today and how they have changed over the last decade. We find that substantial racial and ethnic differences in welfare participation exist, regardless of how they are measured, but we also find that these differences have not changed much over this period. Second, we explore the alternative sources for this difference by quantifying the relative importance of measurable risk factors, which differ across race and ethnic groups, on the one hand, and immeasurable differences, which include differences in cultural and social norms, on the other. We find that the majority of most differences in welfare receipt can be explained by measurable risk factors, including differences across race and ethnic groups in earnings and other forms of nonwelfare income, in family structure, in education, and in other variables representing disadvantaged status more generally. This implies that it is these underlying risk factors, and their underlying causes, that require policy attention if racial and ethnic disparities in welfare receipt are to be reduced.

THE U.S. WELFARE SYSTEM

The U.S. welfare system is composed of several distinct components. The most well known is the program that provides cash assistance to families with dependent children—defined as families in which one or both parents are not present—currently called the Temporary Assistance to Needy Families (TANF) program and called Aid to Families with Dependent Children (AFDC) prior to 1996. The AFDC program was created by the Social Security Act in 1935. It originally provided benefits primarily to poor widows, but in the 1960s its caseload shifted toward benefit provision to poor divorced and separated women with children, and has more recently shifted toward poor never-married women who have had out-of-wedlock births.[1] These shifts in the composition of the caseload undoubtedly explain some of the changes in public attitudes toward the program. Eligibility for the program also requires low income and low levels of assets. Currently, the TANF program has strict work requirements and a maximum five-year time limit as well.

---

[1]The AFDC-UP (for unemployed parent) program provided benefits to families with children in which both parents are present, but restrictive eligibility conditions in the program limited its size to only a small fraction of the AFDC caseload.

More important in both dollar and caseload terms today are the programs providing noncash benefits to low-income families. These include Food Stamps, Medicaid, low-income housing assistance, and a host of other programs including job training, Head Start, and a variety of food assistance programs other than Food Stamps. By one authoritative account, there are upwards of 80+ programs in the United States providing cash or noncash assistance to low-income families (Burke, 1995). Eligibility for all the programs is restricted to those with low income and assets, and usually there are additional restrictions on eligibility. The three largest noncash programs are Food Stamps, Medicaid, and housing assistance. The Food Stamp program is unique in providing benefits to families and individuals regardless of family structure, for neither the presence of children nor the absence of a parent, for example, is required. The Medicaid program historically provided benefits primarily to AFDC families but today provides significant benefits to children of poor, nonwelfare families, resulting from a series of legislative expansions of eligibility in the late 1980s and early 1990s.[2] Housing assistance is the only major noncash program that is not an entitlement, and serves all family types who are low income; however, priority has historically been given to AFDC families, which has resulted in a caseload that is disproportionately composed of unmarried women with children.

Aside from AFDC-TANF, the only major remaining cash-benefit program is the Supplemental Security Income (SSI) program, which provides cash benefits to aged, blind, and disabled adults and to blind and disabled children. Although it is not a transfer program, the Earned Income Tax Credit, if counted as a cash program, is also very large. Families with children and with earnings below certain thresholds receive tax credits and reductions in tax liability under the program.

Figure 7-1 shows the trend in the per capita caseloads of four major programs—AFDC, Food Stamps, Medicaid, and SSI—over the last 30 years.[3] The AFDC rolls grew tremendously during the late 1960s and early 1970s, a growth often attributed to relaxation of eligibility requirements and increased generosity of the benefit "package" associated with being on AFDC, but partly also a result of reductions in the stigma of welfare receipt. The AFDC rolls then flattened out from 1973 through 1989, a result usually thought to be attributable to decreasing real AFDC

---

[2]Medicaid also provides benefits to the elderly and disabled. We do not discuss those groups in this study.

[3]Other programs are much smaller than these four. The Job Training Partnership Act and Head Start programs, for example, are less than 15 percent as extensive as SSI, the smallest of the four. Note that the Medicaid caseload numbers illustrated in Figure 7-1 include only dependent children and adults, not the elderly.

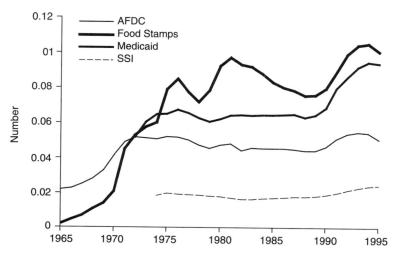

FIGURE 7-1 Number of welfare recipients per capita, 1965 to 1995. SOURCE: U.S. Social Security Administration (1991, Table 7.E; 1997, Tables 7.A9, 9.G1, 9.H1, 8.E2), U.S. Department of Commerce (1996:8).

benefits during the period, and to 1981 legislation that restricted eligibility for the program. The AFDC caseload then grew substantially, starting in the late 1980s and early 1990s, for reasons not fully understood, but has been decreasing since around 1993. The latter decrease has been judged to be partly the result of favorable economic conditions and partly the result of policy changes, both those subsequent to the August 1996 Personal Responsibility and Work Reconciliation Act (PRWORA), as well as similar state policies that began before that legislation (Council of Economic Advisers, 1997).

Created by Congress in 1964, the Food Stamp Program caseload grew rapidly from the late 1960s through the early 1970s, and then grew more slowly in the late 1970s. The early 1970s growth resulted from a 1973 mandate that the program be extended nationwide, and the late 1970s growth was partly the result of the elimination of the purchase requirement (i.e., the requirement that families "buy" their Food Stamps with their own cash). The caseload decreased through most of the 1980s, but then grew again in the late 1980s and early 1990s, along with AFDC. Like that of the AFDC program, the Food Stamp caseload has recently decreased. Since 1975 the Food Stamp caseload has been larger than that of both AFDC and Medicaid.

The Medicaid program was created in 1965. Figures for the caseload of dependent children and adults with dependent children are available only from 1975, and are shown in Figure 7-1. The caseload was relatively flat until the late 1980s, at which time it began to grow rapidly. Much of that growth was the result of expanded eligibility enacted by Congress that allowed coverage for many children who were not on the AFDC rolls. The Medicaid caseload has, like that of AFDC and Food Stamps, decreased since 1993.

The SSI program is considerably smaller than the other three but has grown markedly in percentage terms. Its caseload has doubled since 1974 and has grown by 50 percent since 1989 alone. This growth has been almost entirely among disabled adults and children, and larger for disabled children than adults. The numbers who qualify based on old age or blindness have remained constant or have even decreased. This growth was also partly a target of the 1996 PRWORA legislation.

WELFARE PARTICIPATION RATES BY
RACE AND ETHNIC GROUP

Table 7-1 shows participation rates of U.S. households in four means-tested programs—AFDC, Food Stamps, Medicaid, and Housing assistance—during 1994 to 1996.[4] Rates are shown for five broad race-ethnic groups: Hispanics, non-Hispanic Whites, non-Hispanic Blacks, American Indians and Alaska Natives, and Asian and Pacific Islanders. Participation rates vary markedly across the groups. American Indians and Alaska Natives have the highest rates of participation in all programs except housing assistance, and non-Hispanic Blacks have the second highest. Hispanics have high rates of participation in all programs except housing, and their rates overall are not far below those of non-Hispanic Blacks. Non-Hispanic Whites, and Asians and Pacific Islanders, on the other hand, have the lowest rates, with Asians and Pacific Islanders having somewhat higher rates of participation in most of the programs, especially Medicaid, than non-Hispanic Whites.

Figure 7-2 shows the rates of "any welfare participation"—i.e., receipt of benefits from any one of the four welfare programs—for 1985 and 1995. Slightly more than 50 percent of all American Indians and Alaska Natives received at least one type of benefit, and more than 30 percent of Hispanic and non-Hispanic Black households did. These groups are very broad and disguise much intragroup variation, but such high participation nev-

---

[4]Three years of the March Current Population Survey are pooled to increase sample sizes of the smaller race-ethnic groups. Participation in a program is defined as having any income from that program during the year. Housing assistance includes public housing and rent-subsidized housing.

TABLE 7-1 Participation Rates of Households in Means-Tested Welfare
Programs, 1994-1996 (percent)

	AFDC	Food Stamps	Medicaid	Housing Assistance
Hispanic	11.8	20.1	24.5	9.1
Non-Hispanic White	2.7	5.7	8.3	3.5
Non-Hispanic Black	14.0	23.3	27.0	15.3
American Indian and Aleut. Eskimo	15.6	24.5	43.8	11.4
Asian and Pacific Islander	4.9	7.1	13.5	5.3

SOURCE: Authors' tabulations from the March 1994, 1995, and 1996 Current Population
Surveys.

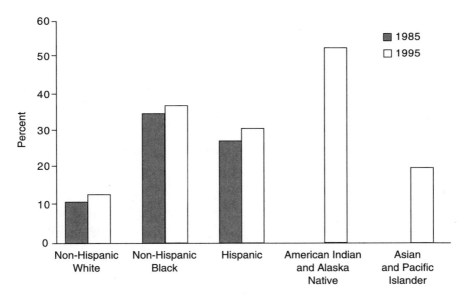

FIGURE 7-2 Percentage of benefit usage from any of the welfare programs,
by race, 1985-1995. SOURCE: Authors' tabulations from Current Population Survey.

ertheless signals racial and ethnic usage differences that should be a policy
concern. That more than one-half of all American Indians and Alaska
Natives, and more than one-third of non-Hispanic Blacks and Hispanics,
receive benefits from at least one type of program reflects a disadvantaged status and degree of dependency that have to be regarded as very
high.

TABLE 7-2 Persons with Welfare Income, 1992 (percent)

| | Persons with 50 Percent or More of Their Income from a Welfare Source | | | Persons with any Welfare Income from AFDC, FS, or SSI |
	AFDC or Food Stamps	SSI Only	AFDC FS, or SSI	
All persons	3.8	0.7	4.9	16.9
Non-Hispanic White	1.8	0.4	2.4	11.0
Non-Hispanic Black	12.3	2.1	15.9	41.0
Hispanic	8.9	1.2	10.5	33.3

SOURCE: U.S. Department of Health and Human Services (1997: I-5 to I-6).

Tables 7-2 and 7-3 illustrate this dependency in different ways. Table 7-2 shows the percentage of the population of different groups for whom benefits from welfare exceed 50 percent of income. This distinction helps separate those for whom welfare is merely a minor supplement to income from those for whom it is a major source of support. The figures in Table 7-2 are much lower than those in Table 7-1.[5] In 1992, only 15.9 percent of non-Hispanic Blacks received more than 50 percent of their income from AFDC, Food Stamps, and SSI; and only 10.5 percent of Hispanics did. This puts a more favorable light on the degree of dependence, although these figures still represent millions of individuals. Moreover, the racial and ethnic differences are still large, which is a cause of concern. The rate of dependency for non-Hispanic Blacks is more than six times that of non-Hispanic Whites, and that of Hispanics is more than four times as high.

Table 7-3 illustrates welfare participation and dependence over a much longer period—1985 to 1992—and therefore represents something closer to what we might call "long-term" dependence. The figures represent dependence on one of several welfare programs (primarily AFDC, Food Stamps, and SSI). Over the eight-year period, almost 50 percent of non-Hispanic Black women and 36 percent of Hispanic women received benefits at some point; on average, the former were on welfare for 28 percent of the eight years and the latter were on for 17 percent of the period. The average rates of income dependence are quite low, however. When income dependence is examined, the rates remain high for non-

---

[5]Table 7-1 illustrates rates for households, whereas Table 7-2 illustrates rates for persons; and data are three years apart. But these differences account for only a small amount of the difference in participation rates.

TABLE 7-3 Welfare Participation Over an Eight-Year Period Among U.S. Women Ages 15-44, 1985-1992

	Percent Ever on Welfare	Percent of the Eight-Year Period on Welfare		Percent of Income from Welfare Over the Period		Percent with at Least 50% of Income from Welfare Over the Period	
		All Persons	Persons Ever On	All Persons	Persons Ever On	All Persons	Persons Ever On
Non-Hispanic White	11.9	4.9	41.0	2.0	16.7	1.2	10.3
Non-Hispanic Black	49.7	28.2	56.7	20.2	40.6	14.5	29.3
Hispanic	36.2	17.8	49.2	7.3	20.1	2.8	7.7
Other	17.8	5.4	30.1	2.1	11.6	2.3	13.0

SOURCE: Authors' tabulations from the Michigan Panel Study on Income Dynamics. Welfare includes AFDC, AFDC-UP, GA, Food Stamps, and SSI.

TABLE 7-4 Trends in Welfare Recipiency Among Households 1985-1995 (percent)

	AFDC	Food Stamps	Medicaid	Housing Assistance
Hispanic				
1995	11.8	20.1	24.5	9.1
1985	11.8	17.3	20.0	7.7
Non-Hispanic White				
1995	2.7	5.7	8.3	3.5
1985	2.8	5.3	6.4	2.6
Non-Hispanic Black				
1995	14.0	23.3	27.0	15.3
1985	15.3	23.7	26.0	12.8

SOURCE: Authors' tabulations from the March 1984, 1985, 1986, 1994, 1995, and 1996 Current Population Surveys.

Hispanic Black women, but drop considerably for Hispanic women. Non-Hispanic Black women received, on average, 20 percent of their income over the eight-year period from welfare; and almost 15 percent of this group received at least 50 percent of their total income over the period from welfare. Respectively, the same numbers for Hispanic women are 7 percent and 3 percent, however.

Table 7-3 also illustrates, in a way that the other tables have not, how serious the degree of dependence is for those who receive some benefits. Non-Hispanic Black women who received some benefits during the eight years were on welfare for more than half of those years (56 percent of the period) and received more than 40 percent of their income from welfare. Hispanic women who received some benefits were on welfare for 49 percent of the period and received more than 20 percent of their income from this source. These figures suggest that although long-term dependence on the program is not always extensive, the dependence among those who do participate is often quite substantial for the groups with the highest participation rates.

Table 7-4 shows how participation rates among U.S. households have changed over the past decade.[6] Participation rates in AFDC have been quite stable for all race-ethnic groups, while Food Stamp participation has grown slightly for all groups. Interesting to note is that participation in housing assistance has grown over the period as well, by almost 3 percent

---

[6]The CPS in the mid-1980s did not separately identify American Indians and Alaska Natives, or Asians and Pacific Islanders, so these two groups are omitted from the table.

for non-Hispanic Blacks and 1.5 percent for Hispanics. Medicaid participation has also grown over the decade, usually more than any of the other
programs, no doubt reflecting the expanded eligibility noted earlier.[7] Figure 7-2 shows participation rates in 1985 for the three race-ethnic groups.
Rates rose slightly, as the figure indicates.

The major conclusion from Table 7-4 and Figure 7-2 is that relative
race-ethnic differentials in welfare participation have been fairly stable
over the last decade. Although a somewhat greater increase in Medicaid
and Food Stamp participation by Hispanics than by non-Hispanic Blacks
and by Whites led to a somewhat higher rate of growth of overall welfare-
program participation over the decade, the three race-ethnic groups did
not change relative position. In both 1985 and 1995, participation rates
among Hispanics and non-Hispanic Blacks were in the same ballpark,
with Hispanic rates somewhat or slightly below those of non-Hispanic
Blacks, and rates among non-Hispanic Whites far below that. Thus, it is
reasonable to conclude that race and ethnic differentials in welfare-program participation have been relatively stable over time.

Although relative welfare-receipt rates were stable from 1985 to 1995,
the AFDC-TANF caseload began to decrease precipitously for all races
around 1993; and the decrease accelerated in 1996. In part, this decrease is
a result of the improvement in the economy, and in part it is a result of the
1996 PRWORA legislation and the state waiver reforms that began prior
to that. The decrease implies that all participation rates in AFDC-TANF
have fallen from those shown in the tables as of 1995. There have been no
significant changes in the racial-ethnic distribution of the caseload, however; hence, the relative participation rates shown in Tables 7-1 and 7-4
are still accurate.[8]

Finally, Figure 7-3 shows related trends, namely in the percent of
different race-ethnic groups on AFDC (similar figures for the other welfare programs are not available). The percents of the AFDC caseload composed of White and Black families have been very close to one another
over the period, but both have slowly decreased relative to that of Hispanics. But the growth of the Hispanic representation on AFDC is not, as
Table 7-4 indicates, reflective of an increase in the propensity of the His-

---

[7]The Medicaid question changed in 1988; hence, there is some noncomparability between the figures at the two dates.

[8]In 1995, White parents constituted 35.6 percent of the AFDC caseload, and the respective percents for Blacks and Hispanics were 37.2 percent and 20.7 percent (U.S. Department
of Health and Human Services, 1998:Table 3.8). As of mid-1997 (the most recent data
available), the respective percents for TANF adults were 36.0, 35.4, and 21.2 (U.S. Department of Health and Human Services, 1999: Table 11).

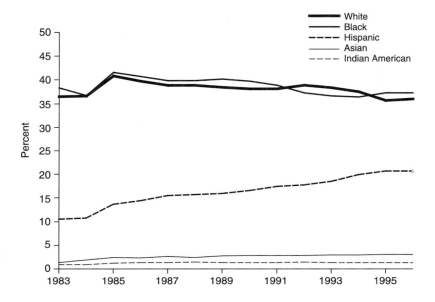

FIGURE 7-3 Distribution of AFDC families by race of parent, 1983 to 1996.
SOURCE: U.S. Department of Health and Human Services (1998).

panic population to receive AFDC; instead, the growth is, simply, the
result of growth in the size of the Hispanic population in the United
States. This serves to illustrate the more general point that the percentages
of different race-ethnic groups among welfare recipients are not very
reliable indicators of the propensity of different groups to receive welfare,
because those percentages reflect, in part, differences in relative population size. The participation rates shown in Tables 7-1 through 7-4 are more
reliable indicators of the propensities that are the more important subjects
of policy interest.

CORRELATES AND RISK FACTORS

An important question is why the differences in welfare-participation
rates across race and ethnic groups are so large. A number of factors are
known to be associated with welfare-program participation in general
(for reviews, see Blank, 1997; Moffitt, 1992). Factors include low income
and poverty, most obviously, but also family structure—in particular,
whether the household is headed by an unmarried woman with children—as well as labor-force participation and earnings, urban-rural loca-

tion, educational levels, and other variables. The most conventional conceptual model of welfare participation presumes eligible women with children choosing between going onto welfare or not based on relative income and other circumstances on and off the rolls. The level of the benefit, the greater level of Medicaid coverage, possibly greater child-care support, and more free time to care for children are among the attracting forces of going onto welfare. The level of potential earnings and the availability of income from other sources (family, friends, etc.) affects the feasibility and desirability of being off welfare, together with the health insurance coverage and child care costs that result along with decreased time with children.

Many studies of welfare participation have examined whether racial differences in participation exist after these and similar variables measuring the risk factors for receipt and the relative incomes on and off the rolls are controlled for. The evidence to date is mixed. For example, of the studies of welfare participation through 1992 reviewed by Moffitt (1992: Tables 6 and 7), approximately two-thirds found no significant differences in participation across race groups after accounting for measurable variables. However, these studies usually did not examine race and ethnic differences fully; and in those studies that more fully explored race and ethnic differences, significant differences were found even after accounting for the measured variables (e.g., Fitzgerald, 1991).[9] More recent studies have continued to find mixed results (see references in Edin and Harris, 1999).

We will report a new, updated examination of this issue, using a limited number of major risk factors and income variables but allowing these factors and variables free rein to "explain" race and ethnic differences in welfare receipt. The risk factors we use to explain welfare receipt are listed in Table 7-5, which shows the association of several risk factors with welfare-program participation by households, and also the composition of the population of each race and ethnic group relative to each risk factor. For example, the first four rows of the first column of the table show that household type is highly correlated with welfare participation, for almost 54 percent of all female heads of households with children— not restricted by income or any other characteristic—received either AFDC, Food Stamps, Medicaid, or housing assistance in the mid-1990s. This high rate reflects primarily the extremely low income of such households. Not surprising is the fact that households headed by unmarried

---

[9]The distinction being referred to here is the regression specification difference between allowing only race dummies in the participation equation, versus stratifying the equation by race and thereby allowing all coefficients to differ.

TABLE 7-5 Welfare Participation Rates by Risk Factors and Distribution of Risk Factors, 1994-1996

	Welfare Participation Rates (All)	Percent Distribution				
		Non-Hispanic White	Non-Hispanic Black	Hispanic	American Indian/Eskimo	Asian Pacific
Household Type						
Female Head w. children	53.7	5.5	24.1	15.3	18.8	5.4
Married w. children	13.9	26.8	18.9	38.4	28.3	39.9
Unmarried w/o children	7.0	31.7	41.7	18.3	15.5	25.7
Other	18.9	36.0	15.3	28.1	37.5	29.0
Nonwelfare Household Income (quartile interval)						
0-25th quartile	42.9	21.5	41.1	35.8	39.7	21.5
25th-50th quartile	14.8	24.4	26.4	28.5	27.0	20.1
50th-75th quartile	7.1	26.3	19.1	21.4	20.0	24.0
75th-100th quartile	3.4	27.8	13.4	14.3	13.4	34.4
Household Earnings (quartile interval)						
0-25th quartile	33.8	25.3	31.0	21.6	26.6	17.6
25th-50th quartile	24.4	21.5	32.2	36.7	35.6	21.0
50th-75th quartile	7.9	25.9	22.7	26.2	23.2	26.7
75th-100th quartile	3.1	27.4	14.1	15.6	14.3	34.7

Employment Status of the Head						
Working	11.6	71.1	65.2	72.3	71.2	77.0
Not Working	30.5	28.9	34.8	27.7	28.8	23.0
Education of the Head						
<12 years	35.5	14.8	26.6	43.4	27.0	13.4
12 years	17.8	33.6	35.7	27.9	33.5	22.7
13-15 years	13.2	25.7	24.9	18.8	30.2	21.5
16+ years	5.1	25.8	12.8	9.9	9.3	42.5
Age of the Head						
<25	31.0	4.5	6.0	7.9	8.0	6.0
25-45	17.2	40.2	45.4	54.1	49.9	51.59
45+	15.6	55.3	48.6	38.0	42.1	42.6
Urban-Rural						
Rural	17.1	46.4	26.6	23.8	69.0	16.2
Urban	17.1	53.6	73.4	76.2	31.1	83.8

Notes: Welfare participation is defined as receipt during the year of benefits from any of the four programs shown in Table 7-1. SOURCE: Authors' tabulations from the March 1994, 1995, and 1996 Current Population Surveys.

individuals without children had low participation rates (7.0 percent); other household types were in between these two extremes. The other columns in Table 7-5 show that race-ethnic groups differ markedly in their relative numbers comprising the different household types. More than 24 percent of non-Hispanic Black households and almost 19 percent of American Indian and Alaska Native families were headed by unmarried women with children, as compared to less than 6 percent for non-Hispanic White households. Interesting to note is that Hispanic households, despite their relatively heavy welfare-participation rates, as shown in prior tables, are not as likely to be headed by unmarried females, and are much more likely to be married with children, relative to non-Hispanic Blacks and American Indians. Marriage rates for Hispanics are, with those of Asians, the highest among the groups. Thus, household type is a less powerful indicator of welfare participation for Hispanics than it is for some of the other race-ethnic groups.

The other major risk factors are income and earnings. Table 7-5 shows the distribution, across nationwide quartiles, of household nonwelfare income and earnings of the different race-ethnic groups as well as how welfare-participation rates vary with such income.[10] Nonwelfare income and earnings are strongly and negatively correlated with receipt of benefits, as would be expected. At the same time, the different groups have significantly different distributions of income and earnings. There are differences particularly between non-Hispanic Whites and Asians, on the one hand, and non-Hispanic Blacks, Hispanics, and American Indians and Alaska Natives, on the other. For example, about 20 percent of the former groups are in the lower quartile of the nonwelfare income distribution, whereas approximately 35 to 40 percent of the latter groups are. It is interesting to note that the differences are not nearly so large for household earnings, where, for example, there are more non-Hispanic Whites than Hispanics in the lowest quartile. The earnings differences, however, show up primarily in the second lowest quartile (between the 25th and 50th quartile points), where non-Hispanic Blacks, Hispanics, and American Indians and Alaska Natives have the greatest concentration. Still, because the differences in welfare-participation rates between the second-lowest earnings quartile interval (24.4 percent) and that in the next highest interval (7.9 percent) are so large, household earnings still go a long way toward explaining the higher welfare-participation rates among these three groups.

---

[10]The quartile points are defined from the income and earnings distributions of all races pooled together. Consequently, the percentages across each row must necessarily center about 25 percent.

The other risk factors listed in Table 7-5 show the importance of the other factors in explaining the race-ethnic differences. There are differences in employment status of household heads across the groups, although not as large as one might have expected. Welfare participation rates do, however, correlate strongly with such status, with working heads of households having much lower rates (11.6 percent vs. 30.5 percent). Heads of households who have attained higher education levels also have much lower welfare receipt rates. At the same time, education levels are much lower among non-Hispanic Blacks and American Indians—especially among Hispanics—as compared to non-Hispanic Whites and Asians. Thus, education may prove to be a factor that is more important in explaining welfare-participation rates for Hispanics (which may also counter the lesser importance of family structure mentioned above). Age differences across the groups are not dramatic, although they are not minor either. Combined with the strong correlation of age with welfare participation, age difference explains some of the variance in rates across the groups; Hispanics and American Indians are the youngest, for example. On the other hand, urban-rural residential status, while differing strongly across the race-ethnic groups, is not correlated with welfare participation.

The degree to which these risk factors can explain welfare receipt across the various race and ethnic groups can be quantified using well-known statistical methods. Working with a fixed set of measurable risk factors—those in Table 7-5, for example—one can determine how those risk factors correlate with welfare-participation rates for a particular race-ethnic group, say, Hispanics. This correlation is generally accomplished with a multivariate regression analysis, which yields an estimate of the "effect" of each risk factor on welfare-participation rates, holding all other factors fixed. The second step is to estimate welfare-participation rates for any specific group—Hispanics, for example—and what the rates would be if the levels of their risk factors were the same as those of the majority White population. Table 7-5 shows the difference in those levels. These predicted, "as if," or "adjusted" welfare-participation rates, for the Hispanic population will be closer to those of Whites than the unadjusted rates shown in Table 7-1; but they will not be entirely equal to those of Whites, in general, because some of the differences in the welfare-participation rates of the two groups is a result of different propensities to be on welfare, even for households with the exact same levels of all the risk factors. The importance of the risk factors themselves, as opposed to differences in propensities to be on welfare across groups for the same levels of risk factors, is measurable quantitatively by how close the adjusted participation rates of each are to those of the majority White population.

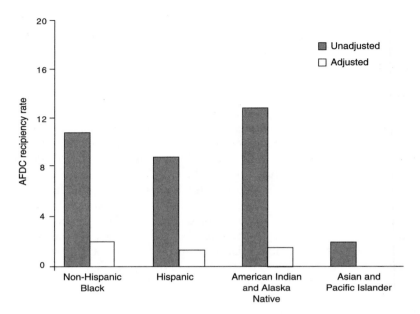

FIGURE 7-4 Adjusted and unadjusted race-ethnic differences in AFDC recipiency rates, relative to the White population, 1995.

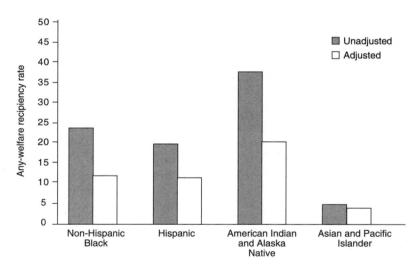

FIGURE 7-5 Adjusted and unadjusted race-ethnic differences in any welfare recipiency rate, relative to the White population, 1995. SOURCE: Authors' tabulations from Current Population Survey.

Figures 7-4 and 7-5 show the results of such calculations.[11] Figure 7-4 illustrates the results for the AFDC receipt rate, showing the unadjusted differences in AFDC-receipt rates between the group in question and the White population; for example, non-Hispanic Blacks have approximately 11 percent higher AFDC participation rates than non-Hispanic Whites (14.0 – 2.7 = 11.3, from Table 7-1). Also shown are adjusted rates—i.e., the difference in the participation rates of the two groups after adjusting for differences in levels of risk factors. The result immediately apparent from Figure 7-4 is that the vast majority of the differences are explainable by the risk factors; very little remains after the adjustment. Approximately 89 percent of the gap between non-Hispanic Blacks and non-Hispanic Whites is so-explained, and more than 95 percent is explained for Hispanics, American Indians and Alaska Natives, and Asians and Pacific Islanders. Thus, the differences across groups in factors that can be identified and measured—income, family structure, and related variables—provide the explanation for the higher welfare-participation rates of the four minority groups. This is, to some extent, a favorable result for policy because at least these variables provide mechanisms through which policy levers might be able to reduce the disparity in race-ethnic welfare-participation rates.

Figure 7-5 shows the unadjusted and adjusted differences in rates of "any welfare" recipiency. Although the adjusted differences are still considerably smaller than those for AFDC alone, the amount of reduction is not nearly so large. For most of the groups, the adjustments explain approximately 60 percent of the unadjusted gap. Nevertheless, this is still a sizable degree of explanation and implies that the majority of the differences are so-explained.

The remaining differences in welfare receipt, even though small, can be interpreted as a measure of the differences resulting from cultural and social norms toward welfare across the different groups. Some of these factors are, in principle, measurable but are not available in the census data, such as whether an individual's parents were on welfare, an indication of intergenerational transmission of preferences for welfare; whether the community and neighborhood in which an individual resides has high numbers of welfare recipients, possibly leading to a reduction in stigma of welfare receipt; and so on.[12] On the other hand, many risk factors are also omitted from Table 7-5, and these could, if measured and accounted for, lead to even higher explanatory power for such factors. For

---

[11]The Appendix describes some of the technical details.

[12]These variables are not without problems, if interpreted solely as taste shifters, however. This issue has been discussed extensively in the research literature among studies able to use data sets that measure these variables.

example, one major risk factor omitted from the analysis (because it is not measurable in our data) is social networks—i.e., income and other forms of support from family, friends, and others in the community. The work of Edin and Lein (1997) and Edin and Harris (1999) suggests that there are major differences across the races in what they term the "private safety net," and that this can explain much of the racial difference in welfare-participation rates. Also omitted from the list of risk factors are those that would enable a more accurate accounting for job availability and options in the labor market, including residential location and distance from jobs; variables measuring health and disability status; and variables measuring capital market constraints and constraints on ability to borrow.

There is a sense that estimates of percentage explained in Figures 7-4 and 7-5 are too high because the risk factors used for the adjustment are themselves, to some degree, a result of individual and household choices. This raises questions about the direction of causality in the relationship between welfare participation and the risk factors. If single mothers withdraw from the labor force when they go onto welfare, or if they have a child prior to marriage and simultaneously go onto welfare, it is not clear which event is causing which, or the degree to which the decisions are jointly made rather than one causing another. Although this issue is important for some purposes, the direction of causality is not a major issue here. The question addressed by the calculations shown in Figures 7-4 and 7-5 is whether, given the other decisions made by the different racial and ethnic groups, there is any remaining difference in their welfare-participation decisions, even if the other decisions are jointly made with the welfare decision. Thus the question addressed is whether there are any "pure" differences in welfare-participation propensities, holding fixed the propensities to make other decisions.

The policy implications to be drawn from the calculations are not necessarily that policies be implemented that directly alter income or female heading of households (it is difficult to imagine policies that would alter the latter, in any case). Rather, policy implications are that the underlying determinate of low income and earnings, and of females heading households—such as education, job skills, wage rates; and policy variables such as benefit levels, tax rates, and public programs for training—should be the subjects of policy attention. The results of the calculations here imply that if these underlying determinants of both welfare participation and low income and female heading of households were altered by policy, welfare-participation decisions would necessarily, and perforce, change as well. Thus, race and ethnic differences in welfare dependency could be greatly reduced by reducing the differentials in the underlying determinants of the risk factors.

SUMMARY

We have found in this study racial and ethnic disparities in welfare-program participation that are disturbingly large. American Indians and Alaska Natives have the highest probabilities of receiving benefits; more than one-half receive one of four major types of benefit. Non-Hispanic Black households and Hispanic households also have very high rates of receipt. For the populations of these three groups as a whole, long-term dependence on benefits is not extensive in either a participation or a monetary sense (i.e., the percentage of income coming from welfare sources); however, those in each group who do end up participating in the welfare system have relatively heavy dependence. These racial differences have been quite stable over the last decade, which is at least favorable if one were expecting them to widen (as some other racial differences have), but is still discouraging because it is desirable to see those differences reduced in magnitude.

We have found that most of the difference in welfare engagement across race and ethnic groups can be "explained" by differences in income, in family structure, in employment, and in the education and age of the head of household. We have found little evidence for an important role for differences in social norms, cultural attitudes, or differences in the stigma of welfare receipt across race-ethnic groups in explaining differentials in welfare dependency. Most of these risk factors for welfare participation are addressable by public policies. Although it does not seem likely that race-specific welfare policies are either likely in the near future or desirable, reducing the disparities in the underlying risk factors, or in their underlying causes, should have the beneficial by-product of reducing disparities in welfare receipt as well.

ACKNOWLEDGMENTS

We thank Zhong Zhao and Kevin Moore for research assistance and Sanders Korenman and Timothy Smeeding for their comments.

APPENDIX

The data used for the analysis are the pooled March Current Population Surveys for 1994, 1995, and 1996. The unit of observation is the household, and the survey universe is all U.S. households. The dependent variable in the regressions is either receipt of AFDC income by at least one member of the household in the prior calendar year, or receipt of income from one of the four programs shown in Table 7-1. Separate ordinary least-squares regressions are estimated for each of the five race-ethnic groups.[13] The independent variables in the regressions include dummies for the three household types shown in Table 7-5; third-order polynomials in nonwelfare household income and household earnings; an urban-rural dummy; the number of household members; a third-order polynomial in age; three education dummies (12, 13-15, and 16+ completed years); eight regional dummies; and interactions between the education and age variables, the household type and household size variables, and the two income variables and a female-head dummy. The adjusted participation rates were obtained by inserting the non-Hispanic White means for these regressors into the estimated equation for each of the four minority groups. The estimated regression coefficients are available upon request.

REFERENCES

Blank, R.
    1997   *It Takes a Nation*. New York: Russell Sage Foundation.
Bobo, L., and R. Smith
    1994   Antipoverty policy, affirmative action, and racial attitudes. In *Confronting Poverty*, S. Danziger, G. Sandefur, and D. Weinberg, eds. Cambridge: Harvard University Press.
Burke, V.
    1995   *Cash and Noncash Benefits for Persons with Limited Income: Eligibility Rules, Recipient and Expenditure Data, FYs 1992-1994*. Washington, D.C.: Congressional Research Service.
Council of Economic Advisers
    1997   *Technical Report: Explaining the Decline in Welfare Receipt, 1993-1996*. Washington, D.C.: U.S. Government Printing Office.
Edin, K., and K. Harris
    1999   Getting off and staying off: Racial differences in the work route off welfare. In *Latinas and African American Women at Work: Race, Gender, and Economic Inequality*. New York: Russell Sage Foundation.
Edin, K., and L. Lein
    1997   *Making Ends Meet: How Single Mothers Survive Welfare and Low-Wage Work*. New York: Russell Sage Foundation.
Fitzgerald, J.
    1991   Welfare durations and the marriage market: Evidence from the survey of income and program participation. *Journal of Human Resources* 25(Summer):545-561.
Gilens, M.
    1995   Racial attitudes and opposition to welfare. *Journal of Politics* 57:994-1014.
    1996   "Race coding" and White opposition to welfare. *American Journal of Political Science* 90:593-604.

---

[13]Probit equations were also estimated, and yielded the same relative importance of the regressors as shown in Figures 7-4 and 7-5. Probit equations, however, do not fit the mean of the dependent variable at the mean of the regressors; hence, they are less easily exposited for the decompositions.

Moffitt, R.
  1992   Incentive effects of the U.S. welfare system: A review. *Journal of Economic Litera-
         ture* 30(March):1-61.
U.S. Department of Commerce, Bureau of the Census
  1996   *Statistical Abstract of the United States: 1996.* Washington, D.C.: U.S. Government
         Printing Office.
U.S. Department of Health and Human Services
  1997   *Indicators of Welfare Dependency: Annual Report to Congress.* Washington, D.C.
  1998   *Aid to Families with Dependent Children: The Baseline.* Washington, D.C.
  1999   *Characteristics and Financial Circumstances of TANF Recipients, July-September 1997.*
         Washington, D.C.
U.S. Social Security Administration
  1991   *Annual Statistical Supplement to the Social Security Bulletin, 1991.* Washington, D.C.:
         U.S. Government Printing Office.
  1997   *Social Security Bulletin: Annual Statistical Supplement, 1997.* Washington, D.C.: U.S.
         Government Printing Office.

8

Labor Force Trends:
The Military as Data

John Sibley Butler and Charles C. Moskos

> One major American institution . . . contradicts the prevailing [failure]
> race paradigm. It is an organization unmatched in its level of racial
> integration. It is an institution unmatched in its broad record of Black
> achievement. It is a world in which the Afro-American heritage is part
> and parcel of the institutional culture. It is the only place in American
> life where Whites are routinely bossed around by Blacks. The institu-
> tion is the U.S. Army.
>
> (Moskos and Butler, 1996:1-3)

This paper explores the participation of Blacks in the military, with
an emphasis on the Army. Although most analyses of labor-force
participation of excluded groups emphasize increasing the number of previously excluded persons (Hill and Jones, 1993; Feagin, 1989;
Blauner, 1972), the military has a history of utilizing groups excluded by
the larger society. This has been especially true for Blacks.

Blacks' participation in the military on these shores predates the inception of the America Republic. Indeed, Blacks have participated in all
of this country's wars and conflicts. A further distinction is that Blacks
have never, as a group, participated in conflicts against the United States.
The history of Black service to country, and the by-product of labor-market participation, is certainly a unique story. Black service in the armed
forces, moreover, involves participation with the institution charged with
defense of the country, the highest form of citizenship. Focusing on Blacks
in the Army also means giving a strong consideration to Black females,
especially because there is a strong interaction between race and gender
in the Army.

The military stands at the forefront of organizations representative of
Black achievement. It is worthy of note that the disproportionately Black
armed forces stand out as the most respected institution in American
society.

LABOR-FORCE PARTICIPATION: A UNIQUE HISTORY

The participation of Blacks in the military is not unique to the contemporary period. Rather, Blacks have a history of participation in the armed forces that is unmatched in the annals of racial and ethnic participation in the armed forces of America. In 1760, 16 years before the Revolutionary War, people of African descent participated in the defeat of the Yamassee Indians, as the New England colonies were struggling to mature. In the French colony of Louisiana, free and enslaved Black people participated in the defeat of the Chickasaw and Natchez Indians. In all four wars pitting the British colonists against the French, Blacks were used as scouts and soldiers (Foner, 1974).

This early participation of Blacks, which predated the development of the United States and mass ethnic immigration from Europe by more than 100 years, was developed as a strategy of necessity. Colonists granted Blacks the privilege of participation, but feared they might turn their weapons on colonists and try to put an end to slavery. After a slave revolt in 1739, Carolina colonists noted that "there must be great caution used, least our slaves when armed might become our masters" (Foner, 1974:4-5). The reality of manpower needs, however, ensured Blacks a role in all colonial conflicts.

By the time the Revolutionary War ended, the free Black population had settled into the process of developing small enterprises, to create a degree of economic stability (Walker, 1998). One of the more famous Philadelphia entrepreneurs was James Forten, whose experience in the Revolutionary War was the prototypical experience of Blacks who served. In 1780, Forten embarked on the *Royal Louis*, a man-of-war ship, as a powder boy. After a victory over an English ship, he received part of the honors bestowed on the crew for their valiant and successful fighting. Later, his vessel was captured by three English ships, and he was held as a prisoner of war. The captain of the English ship offered to free him if he would go to England and become a part of the English military. Forten replied, "No, no. I am here a prisoner for the liberties of my country. I never shall prove a traitor to her interests" (Minton, 1913). James Forten was one of more than 5,000 Blacks who participated in the Revolutionary War for freedom from British rule.

In spite of the fact that Blacks made up an estimated 20 percent of the 2.5 million colonial population at the start of the "rebellion," the Continental Congress issued four orders forbidding free Blacks and slaves from joining the Army. Recognizing that slavery was a divisive issue for the colonists, the British solicited Black recruits, offering freedom to slaves who would fight for the British crown. In 1777, John Murray, Earl of Dunmore and Royal Governor of Virginia, proclaimed:

> All indentured servants, Negroes, or other (appertaining to Rebels), free,
> that are able and willing to bear arms, they joining His Majesty's Troops,
> as soon as may be, for the more speedily reducing the colony to a proper
> sense of their duty, to His Majesty's crown and dignity (U.S. Depart-
> ment of Defense, 1981:28).

More than 200 Blacks answered the British call, inscribed their uniforms with the words "Liberty Slaves," and served in a unit called Lord Dunmore's "Ethiopian Regiment" (U.S. Department of Defense, 1981:4).

In response to the British action, General George Washington autho-rized the recruitment of Blacks. Washington's army averaged 54 Blacks in each well-integrated battalion. Some colonies, such as Massachusetts and Rhode Island, raised all-Black battalions. After the defeat of the British, however, free Blacks were not allowed to remain in the military; and those who had been in slavery prior to the conflict were sent back into bondage (Butler and Holmes, 1982). This policy toward Blacks, after the Revolutionary War, started a pattern that has come to be called recruit-retain-and-reject, which lasted until the Korean conflict. Blacks would be recruited (sometimes after protesting for the right to fight) only when manpower shortages were apparent, retained during the conflict, and dismissed thereafter.

The Civil War produced an enthusiastic response from Blacks; how-ever, the Secretary of War, Edward M. Stanton, declared, "This depart-ment has no intention to call into service any colored soldiers." Only after the Emancipation Proclamation, in 1863, were Blacks allowed, officially, to fight against the Confederacy. Nearly 180,000 were formed into sepa-rate units called "United States Colored Troops." They engaged in crucial battles, won 14 congressional medals of honor, and helped liberate Peters-burg and Richmond. At least half a million of the Confederacy's 3,500,000 slaves came within the Union lines during the war, and many of them worked for the North (McPherson et al., 1971:113-114).

A fact not frequently discussed is the participation of Blacks in the Confederate military. Blacks constituted more than one-third of the Con-federate population, and without Black labor—free and bondage—the South would not have been able to wage war. In the war's early stages, the Confederate congress passed an act that guaranteed equal pay for those Blacks who served. The following applied to musicians:

> The Congress of the Confederate States of America do enact, that when-
> ever colored persons are employed as musicians in any regiment or com-
> pany, they shall be entitled to the same pay now allowed by law to
> musicians regularly enlisted; Provided that no such persons shall be so
> employed except by the consent of the commanding officer of the bri-
> gade to which said regiments or companies may belong (Nalty and
> MacGregor, 1981).

The above quotation testifies, ironically, to the relationship between military service and equal pay—even in a situation of racial hostility, the officiating Congress voted for equality in the pay scale.

After the Civil War, official Army policy was that Black soldiers who fought would not be retained, and no effort would be made to enlist Blacks in peace-time service. In response to tension and battles with Indians in the West, however, and after much debate, Congress, in 1866, approved legislation creating six all-Black regiments: two cavalry and four infantry (there had been 120 units during the Civil War). These units played major roles in the Indian Wars from 1870 to 1890; the soldiers who participated in these units became known as Buffalo Soldiers (Hoover, 1968).

The Spanish-American war began when the battleship *Maine* was sunk in Havana Harbor; 22 Black sailors were in its hull. Though Blacks were barred from state militia, North Carolina, Virginia, Illinois, and Kansas permitted Blacks to organize volunteer units. The war lasted only 10 weeks, and few of these units saw action; but the units of the Buffalo Soldiers were in the heat of the conflict. The Twenty-Fifth Infantry and Tenth Cavalry fought at El Caney, and the Tenth received honors; the Twenty-Fourth Infantry helped in the assault on San Juan Hill (U.S. Department of Defense, 1981).

More than 200,000 Blacks served in World War I, heeding President Woodrow Wilson's call to make the world "safe for democracy." Georgia Congressman Frank Parks's bill to make it unlawful to appoint Blacks as noncommissioned officers (NCOs) was defeated, and Blacks served in all ranks (Butler, 1992).

After World War I the Army instituted a quota system to restrict the number of Blacks to their proportion in the population. By 1940, only 500 remained, mostly serving in all-Black units. There were only 5 Black officers; White officers commanded most Black troops, as they had done in the segregated army of the Civil War and World War I.

During World War II, the relationship between Blacks and the military was renegotiated. Civilian social issues were now explicitly tied to Blacks' role in the defense industry and the military. A. Philip Randolph called for a march on Washington on July 1, 1941, to end racial segregation in the military and to open defense jobs to Blacks. Racial discrimination by defense contractors was ended—in principle, if not practice—by President Roosevelt's Executive Order 8802 in June 1941. Truman followed this action with Executive Order 9981 in 1948, which ended official segregation in the military. More than 900,000 Blacks served in segregated units during World War II (Dietz et al., 1991).

The end of the Korean War saw the end of the segregated military. By the mid-1950s, the services were totally integrated officially. In 1962, on the eve of the war in Vietnam, Blacks comprised 12.2 percent of all Army enlisted personnel, 9.1 percent of the Air Force, 7.6 percent of the Marine Corps, and 5.2 percent of the Navy. In that same year, however, Blacks accounted for only 1.6 percent of all commissioned officers (3.2 percent in the Army).

During the Vietnam War, the proportion of Blacks increased slightly. In 1971, Blacks accounted for 15.6 percent of Army enlisted personnel, 12.5 percent of the Air Force, 12.3 percent of the Marine Corps, and 5.7 percent of the Navy. In 1971, Blacks made up 2.3 percent of commissioned officers (4.2 percent in the Army). Some 70,000 Black soldiers saw action in the Vietnam conflict. Over the course of the Vietnam War, Blacks made up 12.1 percent of all combat deaths, a number proportionate to the general population.

After the Vietnam War, conscription ended, in 1973. The change to an all-volunteer force was accompanied by a significant rise in the Black composition of the armed forces, especially the Army, as shown in Table 8-1. The Army has, proportionately, approximately twice as many Black personnel as any of the other three military services. This applies at both officer and enlisted levels. Since conscription ended, Blacks have comprised close to 30 percent of the Army's enlisted force; twice as many as when the draft was enforced. It should be pointed out, however, that the actual number of Blacks entering the armed forces has decreased since the end of conscription. In 1964, some 50,000 Black men entered the armed forces, compared to 28,000 in 1997. Considering that the national cohort of Black men was considerably smaller in 1964, the proportionate decrease of Black male enlistees is even more precipitous than actual numbers indicate.

There has been, however, a sharp growth in the number of Black officers—again, especially in the Army. Blacks comprised 7 percent of officers (both commissioned and warrant) in 1980 compared with 15 percent in 1998. What is particularly noteworthy is the number of Black generals—approximately 9 percent—a figure for senior leadership that would be hard to match in any other mainstream organization. Data from other services also show increases in the number of Black officers between 1980 and 1998: from 2.4 to 6.3 percent in the Navy, and from 4.9 to 8.1 percent in the Marine Corps. The Air Force, with approximately 6 percent Black officers, has not shown a major increase for the past 30 years.

Attention here is focused on enlisted participation, as these ranks comprise about 85 percent of all military personnel. Since the 1950s, the Army has had a significant Black NCO core. In 1998, more than 33 percent of senior NCOs in the Army were Black; the proportion in the Marine

Corps was about 25 percent; in the Air Force, about 20 percent; and in the Navy, about 11 percent.

The large percentage of Blacks discussed above seemingly poses a "peacetime benefit" versus "wartime burden" dilemma. For decades critics have earnestly claimed that the United States uses Blacks as cannon fodder—a charge that is untrue. For example, during the Vietnam War, Black fatalities amounted to 12.1 percent of all Americans killed in Southeast Asia—a figure proportionate to the percentage of Blacks in the general population and lower than the percentage of Blacks in the military during that time period (Moskos and Butler, 1998). Further, the racial data on combat deaths of U.S. soldiers during the conflicts in Mayaguez, Lebanon, Grenada, Panama, the Persian Gulf and Somalia—all post-Vietnam deployments—show that Blacks accounted for 14 percent of all combat deaths. No case can be made that Blacks suffer disproportionate casualties in America's wars and military interventions (Moskos and Butler, 1998).

In light of the controversies surrounding the issue of Black casualties in time of war, it should be noted that the contemporary era has seen a sharp decrease in the number of Blacks in the combat arms. This corresponds with a higher concentration of Blacks in support and logistics service branches and a lower concentration among the infantry (see Table 8-2). Percentages of Blacks in the infantry decreased from approximately 30 percent in 1980, to 20 percent in 1990, to 15 percent in 1997. Some assert the cause for this trend is that more civilian-transferable skills are acquired in logistics specialties; but this has been true for the past 10 to 20 years, and so does not explain the recent phenomenon. In any event, this finding is worth noting in assessing participation of Blacks in the military.

Black women have an even more significant participation rate in the armed forces than Black men. Attention here is focused on the Army, where the trend has been most marked. As shown in Table 8-3, at the commissioned-officer level, the proportion of Black women just about doubled from 1980 to 1990, from approximately 11 to 20 percent. The trend among enlisted women is even more striking; in 1980 the composition of female enlistees was 56 percent White, 37 percent Black. By 1998, the composition was 47 percent Black, 39 percent White. A contributing factor may be that Black women have a much lower rate of attrition than do White women (attrition referring to the inability, for whatever reason, to complete the term of enlistment). Table 8-4 shows attrition rates by race and gender for the various services. In all four services, Black women have significantly lower attrition rates than White women. Again, the Army is most notable; whereas 35 percent of Black females fail to complete their enlistments (a figure correspondent to males of any race), the figure for White females is 54 percent.

TABLE 8-1 Blacks as a Percentage of Total Personnel by Grade and Service 1980, 1990, 1998

Grade[a]	1980				
	Army	Navy	Air Force	Marine Corps	DoD Total
Total Commissioned Officers	7.2	2.4	4.5	3.7	4.8
0-7 and above (Generals)	5.3	0.1	0.2	0.3	0.3
0-6 (Colonel)	4.5	0.7	1.8	N/A	2.3
0-5 (Lt. Colonel)	4.9	0.5	2.0	0.5	2.6
0-4 (Major)	4.4	1.2	2.4	1.6	2.7
0-3 (Captain)	7.5	3.0	4.3	4.4	5.1
0-2 (1st Lieutenant)	10.2	3.8	8.0	5.4	7.1
0-1 (2nd Lieutenant)	10.4	3.3	8.3	4.4	7.6
Warrant Officers	5.9	4.6	N/A	6.8	5.7
All Officers	7.1	2.5	5.7	3.9	4.9
Enlisted					
E-9 (Sergeant Major)	20.5	5.7	9.0	13.3	11.9
E-8 (Master Sergeant)	25.3	5.7	17.7	15.2	15.8
E-7 (Sergeant 1st Class)	24.7	5.5	13.6	14.8	15.9
E-6 (Staff Sergeant)	23.9	6.0	14.8	18.6	15.5
E-5 (Sergeant)	31.2	8.2	18.3	18.4	20.5
E-4 (Specialist)	37.2	11.4	16.1	17.8	24.2
E-3 (Private 1st Class)	39.0	14.9	15.9	25.1	24.1
E-2 (Private)	37.0	16.6	17.7	27.5	26.5
E-1 (Private Recruit)	27.0	15.7	13.5	23.6	21.0
Subtotal	32.5	11.2	16.0	22.0	21.6
Total	29.2	10.1	14.0	20.5	19.3

Note: DoD = U.S. Department of Defense.

[a]Army titles given in parentheses have equivalent pay grades in other services.

SOURCE: U.S. Department of Defense.

OVERCOMING RACE:
ARMY LESSONS FOR CIVILIAN SOCIETY

Although Blacks participate in all services, the above analysis clarifies the Army's role as the prototype for Black opportunity. In *All That We Can Be: Black Leadership and Integration the Army Way* (Moskos and Butler, 1996), the Army is emphasized because it is the largest of the armed services and the one with the highest proportion of Blacks. The Army's numbers and trends have entered the country's everyday dialogue on

1990				
Army	Navy	Air Force	Marine Corps	DoD Total
11.2	3.9	5.6	4.6	6.8
6.4	1.1	1.2	N/A	3.0
4.6	0.8	2.1	1.4	2.5
5.3	2.1	2.6	2.3	3.3
9.5	3.3	6.0	4.3	6.2
14.0	4.2	6.6	4.9	8.1
12.9	4.6	6.0	5.2	7.7
11.8	5.8	5.5	5.6	7.8
11.0	7.5	N/A	9.9	8.9
11.0	4.0	5.6	5.1	6.9
30.5	5.7	17.5	13.3	16.0
24.8	5.7	20.1	15.2	16.5
30.7	7.5	20.9	18.7	20.0
37.6	12.3	25.9	18.2	23.2
36.7	16.1	24.3	19.0	24.1
32.5	17.8	19.5	19.2	23.7
28.3	23.6	19.2	14.5	21.9
25.6	21.6	19.9	12.5	21.3
25.2	24.9	20.4	14.2	24.0
29.1	17.3	20.8	17.6	22.7
26.8	15.6	19.2	15.4	20.4

race. President Clinton has also built the success of the military into his dialogue on race and, during his 1998 State of the Union Address, referred to the military as a model of racial progress. The questions now are, What are the lessons for American society as a whole? How can the country build into its fabric the illusive idea of opportunity? In this section, the analysis first presented by Moskos and Butler (1996), of military lessons for American society, is expanded. This is done with the understanding that the military has never been perfect, but is an institu-

TABLE 8-1 (*Continued*)

Grade[a]	1998				
	Army	Navy	Air Force	Marine Corps	DoD Total
Total Commissioned Officers	11.0	6.0	6.0	6.1	7.6
0-7 and above (Generals)	8.8	3.2	3.3	4.8	5.3
0-6 (Colonel)	6.7	2.9	3.5	4.0	4.4
0-5 (Lt. Colonel)	10.0	3.4	6.7	4.3	6.8
0-4 (Major)	12.4	5.0	5.9	4.5	7.6
0-3 (Captain)	11.9	6.7	5.9	5.3	7.9
0-2 (1st Lieutenant)	10.5	8.3	6.4	7.7	8.4
0-1 (2nd Lieutenant)	10.7	7.9	6.9	9.9	8.8
Warrant Officers	15.3	14.8	N/A	14.1	15.1
All Officers	12.7	6.3	6.0	6.9	8.1
Enlisted					
E-9 (Sergeant Major)	33.5	7.6	19.3	26.6	21.0
E-8 (Master Sergeant)	36.6	9.8	19.3	29.7	24.7
E-7 (Sergeant 1st Class)	37.5	12.9	17.9	26.7	25.5
E-6 (Staff Sergeant)	38.4	17.3	19.9	26.1	25.7
E-5 (Sergeant)	32.4	21.7	18.4	18.8	23.3
E-4 (Specialist)	25.5	20.7	15.3	13.2	20.3
E-3 (Private 1st Class)	25.2	23.5	16.4	13.7	20.2
E-2 (Private)	24.2	20.6	18.0	14.1	20.1
E-1 (Private Recruit)	21.9	21.4	19.0	14.1	19.9
Subtotal	29.6	19.8	17.7	16.7	22.2
Total	26.6	17.8	15.4	15.7	19.9

NOTE: DoD = U.S. Department of Defense.

[a]Army titles given in parentheses have equivalent pay grades in other services.

SOURCE: U.S. Department of Defense.

tion that has dealt with, and continues to deal with, the issue of racial equality.

One of the major questions about the transfer of lessons revolves around differences between the Army and the civilian world. Critics point out that the Army commands methods of surveillance and coercion unavailable to civilian institutions and is, thus, less democratic. They also point to the fact that Army personnel have a degree of economic stability as well as access to both decent housing and medical benefits, unavailable to many in civilian society, where race and poverty (among all groups) confound procurement of basic life necessities. It has also been pointed out that criteria for becoming a soldier exclude members of society considered to be at the very bottom rungs; thus, the most severe social prob-

TABLE 8-2 Percentage in Army Infantry
Enlisted, by Race, 1980, 1990, 1997

Race	1980	1990	1997
White	57.0	69.2	71.0
Black	29.7	20.6	15.1
Hispanic	5.3	5.3	7.8
Other[a]	8.0	4.9	6.1
Total	100	100	100

[a]Includes unknown.

SOURCE: U.S. Department of Defense.

TABLE 8-3 Percentage of Women by Race, Army and U.S. Department
of Defense Total, 1980, 1990, 1998

	Commissioned Officers		Enlisted	
	Army	DoD Total	Army	DoD Total
1980				
White	82.4	85.1	56.4	69.9
Black	11.4	9.3	37.5	25.2
Other	6.2	5.6	6.1	5.9
Total	100	100	100	100
1990				
White	72.2	80.6	44.2	58.1
Black	21.2	13.2	48.2	33.3
Other	6.6	6.2	7.6	8.6
Total	100	100	100	100
1998				
White	69.2	76.6	39.5	52.8
Black	19.9	13.6	47.1	34.9
Other	10.9	9.8	13.4	12.3
Total	100	100	100	100

SOURCE: U.S. Department of Defense.

TABLE 8-4 Enlisted Attrition (at 36 months) by Race and Gender (FY 1993 Accessions)

	Male		Female	
Branch	White	Black	White	Black
Army	34	32	54	35
Navy	34	36	39	30
Marine Corps	28	29	51	38
Air Force	20	28	31	24

SOURCE: U.S. Department of Defense.

lems are not brought into the Army (Moskos and Butler, 1996). Certainly it is undeniable that there are differences between military and civilian life. The point is, the Army's willingness to change as needed for the good of the institution has broadly applicable implications for overcoming racial inequality in America.

Certainly the Army is not a democracy, but neither are most other organizations in American life. The Army relies more on around-the-clock, weekly, and daily accountability than most civilian organizations; but accountability and control in and of themselves cannot force good race relations. The racial situation is far worse in prisons, where coercive authority regulates accountability and control much more heavily than the military. Moreover, racist norms and behaviors can prevail in any large organization, including those with quasi-military structures. Indeed, the Army of the 1970s was torn with racial turbulence, even though there were significant numbers of Black personnel, a situation which most American institutions at that time could not match. Something other than submersion of individual rights must have been involved in the Army's progress from a racially tense arena to the relative harmony of the present.

It should also be noted that once in the Army, not even the lowest soldier is "underclass." A private receives base pay of $10,000 a year, in addition to room and board, medical care, and other benefits; and, of course, rewards increase as one moves up the rank structure. But the solid economic status of most soldiers does not explain the dynamics of race relations in the Army. After all, racial tensions have sharpened in the larger society at all income levels. Even Blacks who have achieved high education and income must deal with, and have issues with, the "racist" society (Cose, 1993).

Certainly the most salient objection to treating the Army as a model for racial equality relates to the troops recruited; as stated, they do not come from the very bottom rungs of American society and tend to be less jaded and psychologically scarred by the vicissitudes of abject poverty. And the fact that Army personnel are made up of more physically and socially stable people may account for the fact that race relations are better in the armed forces than in other institutions; including those that presumably recruit the highest-quality youths in America—our institutions of higher learning, where campuses are divided by racial isolation and sometimes by racial hostility (Moskos and Butler, 1996).

Perhaps the question to ask is, "How do Whites and Blacks perceive the racial climate in the military?" This question goes beyond numbers to the heart of everyday life. When one examines Army opinion surveys, Black soldiers are nearly twice as likely (64 percent) to discern racial discrimination in the military as are Whites (34 percent). Even so, Blacks are more likely (83 percent) than White career soldiers (73 percent) to express satisfaction with their Army experience. In addition, a survey of Army veterans revealed that almost twice as many Blacks (69 percent) wished they had stayed in the Army (Moskos and Butler, 1998).

During times of war, the disproportionate number of Blacks in the Army is seen as inflicting casualties on America's most victimized group. In times of peace, these same numbers are viewed as employment opportunities for Blacks (Moskos and Butler, 1998). Something of a paradox is the fact that both "liberals" and "conservatives" have noted that the Army is a model of racial integration and Black achievement. Below are lessons that we hope will become standard in other American institutions as they struggle with the task of providing opportunities for Blacks.

Lesson One

Blacks and Whites do not have to hold identical views of the racial situation in order to succeed. Research has shown that, during the last four decades, Blacks in the military see the racial situation differently, and, indeed, stress different things as being important in the racial organizational climate (Moskos, 1966; Brink and Harris, 1967; Butler and Wilson, 1978; Moskos and Butler, 1996). Holding different views of the racial situation should not block the participation of Blacks in organizations.

Lesson Two

Organizations should focus on Black opportunity channels rather than on eradicating racism. The core issue is not White racism but Black opportunity. If there must be a trade-off between Black advancement coexisting with White racism on the one hand and fewer Blacks in a presumed nonracial setting on the other, the former situation is preferable. The Army model, which stresses opportunity, is preferable to the state of affairs at most universities where antiracism is promulgated, but Black presence is limited. In no way should the absence of racism be considered a precondition of Black achievement. Racism did not deter Blacks from creating and maintaining institutions of higher learning. An emphasis on education has always been a strong characteristic among Blacks. It is interesting that the South, where structured racism was most prevalent, is the region that encompasses the most Black colleges and graduates. The combination of historically Black schools and the value structure of Blacks in regard to education has made the South a producer of Black talent (Butler, 1992). Spelman College, Dillard University, and Morehouse College, all Black institutions of higher learning located in the South, have concentrated on Black opportunity rather than attitudes of White racism. And these schools have produced some of this country's most celebrated and talented citizens: Martin Luther King, Oprah Winfrey, Spike Lee are among the many Black achievers who graduated from historically Black colleges and universities. The new century demands a strategy that has worked; that strategy is to concentrate on opportunity for Blacks.

Lesson Three

Organizations should be ruthless about eradicating discriminatory behavior. Although racist attitudes are not central, racist behavior cannot be tolerated. Individuals who display such tendencies must not be promoted to positions of responsibility. In the Army, racist behavior (not racist attitudes) can terminate a soldier's career (Moskos and Butler, 1996).

Lesson Four

Affirmative action must be linked to standards and the qualified pool. Although Blacks have been members of the military since its inception, and Truman's desegregation order predated *Brown vs. Board of Education* in 1954, the military's efforts to ensure fair treatment are linked to the present debate on affirmative action (Butler, 1992). It is understood that promotion goals must be based on the relevant pool of qualified candidates, both Blacks and Whites, not on percentage of Blacks and Whites in the organization or the general population. Efforts to improve opportunities must acknowledge that compensatory action may be needed to help members of disadvantaged groups meet the standards of competition. It is counterproductive to suspend those standards—for either race—in the selection process. Any organization that promotes the less qualified in the name of "diversity" invites long-term disaffection (Moskos and Butler, 1996).

Lesson Five

A level playing field is not always enough. The Army has demonstrated that youths with disadvantaged backgrounds can be trained to meet demanding academic as well as physical standards. The Army has successfully introduced programs to bring young people up to enlistment standards, to raise enlisted soldiers to NCO standards, to bring undergraduates up to officer commissioning standards, and to raise high school graduates to U.S. Military Academy admission standards. These programs, though not targeted exclusively to minority soldiers, are disproportionately Black (Moskos and Butler, 1996).

Lesson Six

Enhancing Black participation is good for the effectiveness of the organization. Participation of Blacks in the military, from the Truman desegregation order to the present, has not been smooth, and there will be difficult times ahead. The important thing is that the army experience has proved that race relations can best be transformed by an absolute commitment to nondiscrimination coupled with uncompromising standards of performance. As noted by Moskos and Butler (1996), the military is perhaps the only organization in America where prestige of the organization increased as the number of Blacks increased.

Lesson Seven

Participation of the Blacks in the Army is a by-product of the need to defend the country and not an end unto itself. One of the major realities evolving from the military experience is that Black participation has always been connected to the defense of the country (Moskos and Butler, 1996). Neither the military nor the Army set out to produce great opportunities for Blacks, but rather to defend the country. Thus, excellent opportunities are a by-product of a major goal—the defense of America.

CONCLUSION

Blacks are and have always been an intrinsic part of America, its society and culture; a notable indication of this is their participation in the armed forces. The realities of legal segregation as well as the realities of racial discrimination have interfered with, rather than halted, this participation. Like all Americans who have participated in the armed forces, Blacks have put their lives on the line and also partaken of the joy of victory. It is not surprising that the armed forces is the institution that stands out when looking at both participation and achievement of Blacks. Other organizations can learn from this model. The emphasis must be placed on organizational goals and Black opportunity channels rather than racist attitudes. It is in the interests of American business and the country to ensure that all Americans—regardless of race or ethnicity— have the foundation and the opportunity to become highly skilled, productive contributors to their communities and the country. The organizational goal of America should be that every citizen must be able to and allowed to perform to high degrees of professionalism and citizenship at every opportunity. This is what Black labor-force participation should ultimately come down to.

REFERENCES

Blauner, R.
  1972   *Racial Oppression in America.* New York: Harper and Row.
Brink, W., and L. Harris
  1967   *Black and White: A Study of U.S. Racial Attitudes Today.* New York: Simon and Schuster.
Butler, J.
  1991a *Entrepreneurship and Self-Help Among Black Americans: A Reconsideration of Race and Economics.* New York: State University of New York Press.
  1991b The military as a vehicle for social integration. P. 38 in *Ethnicity, Integration, and the Military,* H. Dietz, J. Elkin, and M. Roumani, eds. Boulder, Col.: Westview Press.
  1992   Affirmative action in the military. *Annals of the American Academy of Political and Social Science* 526(September):196-206.
Butler, J., and M. Holmes
  1982   Changing organizational structure and the future of race relations in the military. Pp. 167-177 in *Conscripts and Volunteers,* R. Fullinwider, ed. New York: Rowan & Littlefield.
Butler, J., and K. Wilson
  1978   The American soldier revisited: Race and the military. *Social Science Quarterly* (Autumn):628-638.
Cose, E.
  1993   *The Rage of a Privileged Class.* New York: Harper Collins.
Dietz, H., Elkin, J., and Roumani, M., eds.
  1991   *Ethnicity, Integration, and the Military.* San Francisco: Westview Press.
Feagin, J.
  1989   *Racial and Ethnic Relations.* Englewood Cliffs, N.J.: Prentice-Hall.
Foner, J.
  1974   *Blacks in the Military in American History.* New York: Praeger.
Hill, H., and J. Jones, Jr.
  1993   *Race in America: The Struggle for Equality.* Madison: University of Wisconsin Press.
Hoover, D.
  1968   *Understanding Negro History.* Chicago: Quadrangle Books, p. 270.

McPherson, J., L. Holland, J. Banner Jr., N. Weiss, and M. Bell
   1971   *Blacks in America: Bibliographical Essays.* New York: Doubleday.
Minton, H.
   1913   Early History of Negroes in Business in Philadelphia. A paper read before the American Historical Society, March.
Moskos, C.
   1966   Racial integration in the Armed Forces. *American Journal of Sociology* 72(September):132-148.
Moskos, C., and J. Butler
   1996   *All That We Can Be: Black Leadership and Racial Integration the Army Way.* New York: Basic Books.
   1998   Racial integration the Army way. *Army Magazine* (July): 29-31.
Nalty, B., and M.J. MacGregor
   1981   Blacks in the Military: Essential Documents. Wilmington: Scholarly Resources, Inc.
U.S. Department of Defense
   1981   *Black Americans in Defense of Our Nation.* Washington, D.C.: U.S. Department of Defense.
Walker, J.
   1998   *The History of Black Business in America: Capitalism, Race, Entrepreneurship.* New York: Prentice Hall International.

9

Trends in Minority-Owned Businesses

Thomas D. Boston

During the past quarter century, minority-owned businesses have undergone a significant transition. Small-scale, personal-service businesses—beauty salons, barber shops, etc.—no longer predominate; they have been replaced by businesses in a diverse array of industries from which Blacks had, heretofore, been excluded for reasons of education, experience, or race. Between 1960 and 1980, minority-owned, personal-service businesses decreased by 49.1 percent, while minority-owned finance, insurance, and real estate businesses increased by 185.7 percent; business services increased by 175 percent; and wholesale industries increased by 111.8 percent (Bates, 1987; see Table 9-1).

One factor that may have helped accelerate this trend, from the mid-1960s through the 1980s, was public-sector, affirmative-action programs in contracting and procurement. These programs created important points-of-entry for minority entrepreneurs, allowing Blacks unprecedented opportunities for diversification in choice of business ventures. This new stage in minority business ownership began with the abatement of racial segregation in the 1960s. Accelerating factors during the 1970s and 1980s were education and experience; Blacks were quickly gaining managerial and executive-level experience in the corporate sector, pursuing business degrees in greater numbers, and, in general, accumulating greater endowments of human-capital attributes closely associated with self-employment activities.

By the late 1980s and early 1990s, decreases in the percentage of personal-service establishments among Black-owned businesses bottomed

TABLE 9-1 Percentage of Minority Self-Employment in Various Industries, by Industry Group, 1960 and 1980

Industry	1960	1980	Percent Change
Construction	16.7	16.5	−1.2
Manufacturing	4.1	6.0	46.3
Transportation, communication, and utilities	3.9	6.0	53.8
Wholesale	1.7	3.6	111.8
Retail	25.4	25.4	0.0
Finance, insurance, and real estate	1.4	4.0	185.7
Business services	2.4	6.6	175.0
Repair services	5.2	6.9	32.7
Personal services	28.9	14.7	−49.1
Other services	10.3	10.3	0.0
Total	100.0	100.0	—

SOURCE: Bates (1987). Reprinted by permission.

out as the new generation of Black business owners emerged—younger, better educated, and with more managerial and supervisory experience. And these new owners relied, to a great extent, on public-sector markets. For the first time, a significant number of Black businesses emerged in large-scale, public-works construction contracting and subcontracting, architectural and engineering services, management and consulting services, data processing, computer sales and services, public relations, and other industries closely tied to public-sector procurement opportunities. These opportunities, in turn, expanded the diversification, revenue sources, and employment capacity of Black-owned businesses.

By the 1980s, obtaining public-sector contracting and procurement was a fundamental business strategy for a significant portion of successful minority business owners, because public-sector affirmative-action programs afforded minority entrepreneurs substantial growth and revenue opportunities. In 1987, Black-owned firms with revenues of $1,000,000 or more earned 12.8 percent of their gross revenue from the public sector, while nonminority male-owned businesses of a similar size earned only 6.1 percent of their revenue from such sources (U.S. Bureau of the Census, 1991:204); for firms with revenues between $500,000 and $999,999, percentages of revenue from the public sector were 9.3 percent for Black-owned and 5 percent for nonminority male-owned businesses.

In 1995, I mailed a survey to 1,412 businesses owned by ethnic minorities and White women located in the Atlanta metropolitan area to determine the number and kinds of industries/businesses owned, and their sources of income (Boston, 1998). The survey population was drawn from databases maintained by public and private agencies in the Atlanta metropolitan area.[1] Of the 1,412 surveys mailed, 316 responses were received (approximately 22 percent response rate), including 223 from Black-owned businesses.

Industries represented and percent of total sample were as follows: services, 40 percent; construction, 24 percent; wholesale,14 percent; manufacturing, 7 percent; transportation and communications, 5 percent; retail, 4 percent; finance, insurance, and real estate, 2 percent; and nonclassified industries, 2 percent. Among the firms in service industries, the largest concentrations were in computer and data processing followed by engineering and architecture, services to buildings, management and public relations, commercial printing, personnel supply, other business services, and advertising. Of the businesses responding to the survey, 71 percent were owned by Blacks; 14 percent, by White women; 7 percent, by Hispanics; 5 percent, by Asian and Pacific Islanders; and 1 percent, by Native Americans.

The survey results for Black-owned businesses revealed that 42.5 percent are located within the city limits of Atlanta. Among those businesses, in response to why they chose their present location, 25.4 percent gave cost considerations as the most important factor, 14.7 percent cited the need to be close to their customers and clients, 12.8 percent said convenience and accessibility was most important, and 12.6 percent said that they did so to be close to home. Among businesses located in the suburbs, 25.7 percent indicated they did so to be close to their customers and clients, 16.8 percent cited convenience and accessibility, 14.1 percent indicated cost considerations, and 9.8 percent indicated that they worked from a home office. In regard to employment, 45.7 percent of all workers employed by the Black-owned businesses lived in the city. Data also reveal that Black-owned businesses hired 21.5 percent of their workforce from low-income, inner-city neighborhoods. More precisely, 24.6 percent of employees in businesses located in the city lived in low-income, inner-city neighborhoods, and 19.2 percent in suburban businesses were from low-income neighborhoods. Finally, survey results indicate that 83.6 percent of employees in Black-owned firms were Black. Among businesses located in the city, 81.8 percent of their employees were Black, and 84.9

---

[1]The Atlanta Business League, the City of Atlanta Office of Contract Compliance, Atlanta Public Schools Office of Contract Compliance, Fulton County Office of Contract Compliance, Georgia Minority Supplier Development Council, Dekalb County Office of Contract Compliance, Grady Health Systems Disadvantaged Business Enterprise Program, and the Metropolitan Atlanta Rapid Transit Authority.

percent of employees in Black-owned businesses located in the suburbs were Black.

The survey also revealed a significant reliance on government contracting. In 1995, in particular, the mean percentage of revenue derived from the government sector, for all groups, was 31.5 percent. Of that, the highest amount, 34.4 percent, went to Black-owned businesses; and the lowest amount, 19.1 percent, went to businesses owned by White women (Table 9-2). Dependence on the government as a source of revenue varied considerably by industry. For example, 50.9 percent of the gross revenue of construction firms came from the public sector, whereas public-sector revenue totaled 11.5 percent for manufacturing (Table 9-3).

Minority participants in the city of Atlanta's minority business programs are among the most successful in the metropolitan area. In 1993, the average revenue of 770 Black-owned businesses participating in the City of Atlanta and Fulton County's program was $606,208.00; in contrast, the U.S. Bureau of the Census (USBC) (1996) indicates that the average revenue of all 23,488 Black-owned businesses in the Atlanta metropolitan area, in 1992, was $44,668.00.

MAJOR IMPROVEMENTS FROM THE PAST

Aldrich and Waldinger (1990) assert that minority business success is built on the interaction between opportunity structures and group char-

TABLE 9-2 Mean Percentage of Minority-Owned Revenue from the Government Sector, by Group, 1995 Survey

Minority Group	Mean Percent	Respondents to Question	Number of Respondents to Survey	Percent of Survey Respondents
Black	34.4	207	223	70.6
American Indian/ Alaskan Native	ND[a]	3	3	0.9
Asian American/ Pacific Islander	33.2	16	17	5.4
Hispanic American	28.6	20	21	6.6
White women	19.1	41	45	14.2
Unclassified	13.7	6	7	2.2
Total	31.5	293	316	100

Note: Ownership lists based on businesses registered with seven public agencies in Metropolitan Atlanta, Georgia. Survey conducted by Thomas D. Boston.

[a]Not determined.

TABLE 9-3 Mean Percentage of Minority-Owned Business Revenue from the Government Sector by Industry, 1995 Survey

Industry	Mean Percent	Number of Respondents to Survey	Percent of Survey Respondents
Agriculture	0.0	2	0.6
Construction	50.9	52	16.5
Manufacturing	11.5	13	4.1
Transportation, communication, utilities	20.6	18	5.7
Wholesale	27.0	35	11.1
Finance, insurance, real estate	24.9	14	4.4
Retail	35.0	18	5.7
Consumer services, repair, health	32.4	42	13.3
Business services, law, computer	28.2	111	35.1
Other	29.2	11	3.5
Total	31.5	316	100

Note: Ownership lists based on businesses registered with seven public agencies in Metropolitan Atlanta, Georgia. Survey conducted by Thomas D. Boston.

acteristics. Opportunity structures include favorable market conditions, the ability to provide products and services beyond those aimed at specifically ethnic markets, and the ease of access to business opportunities, competitive environments, and government policies. Group characteristics include selective migration, culture, aspirations, ethnic and social networks, organizing capabilities, ability to mobilize resources, and the extent to which government facilitates or constrains resource acquisition by/for the group. During the 1960s, these conditions were not favorable for minority entrepreneurs, especially Blacks; but as conditions improved, so did the aggregate characteristics of minority-owned businesses.

In 1960, few Blacks occupied the kinds of managerial, administrative, and technical jobs in the corporate sector that typically equip employees with the experience needed to become successful entrepreneurs. As recently as 1987, only 18.5 percent of Black business owners reported having prior managerial, executive, and supervisory experience; whereas 30.0 percent of nonminority male business owners reported having such experience. Similar figures for Hispanic business owners and other minorities were 18.8 and 26.6 percent, respectively. In addition, 48 percent of nonminority male business owners had close relatives who were business owners or were self-employed; this was true for only 27.8 percent of Black business owners (U.S. Bureau of the Census, 1991:50, 58).

During the 1960s, Blacks were excluded from the nation's prestigious country clubs and business associations—i.e., places where networking and important deal making occur. Blacks were educated in second-rate schools, confined mainly to segregated neighborhoods, and constituted a disproportionate percentage of low-wage, low-skill workers. As a result, Blacks' access to capital, credit, and business opportunities was lower compared to Whites. This deficit directly affected the types of businesses Blacks were able to start and operate.

During the time that segregation was legal, it was not uncommon for Blacks to encounter racial barriers even when they attempted to service Black consumers. This was particularly true in certain industries outside of personal service and retail. T.M. Alexander, Georgia's first Black licensed insurance agent, recounted how segregation created both legal and psychological barriers between Black entrepreneurs and Black consumers (Alexander, 1992:66).

> For many years, Blacks had been shrewdly taught to place their confidence in Whites and to look with doubt and suspicion upon their own race. This was a sad but true fact of life that hampered many Black companies. My White competitors would stress the unavoidable failures of Black business in an effort to capture the Black market. White salesmen of all kinds could enter large numbers of Black homes with little sales resistance. I could not. Ironically, the White agents would enter Black homes without the usual courtesy one would expect essential to good salesmanship.

Coleman and Cook observed (1976:46):

> It is not unreasonable to assume that during the nineteenth century and until the 1960s, prospective Black businessmen were rather reluctant to start a business beyond the "mom-and-pop" variety. For indeed, any large-scale enterprise would have been, in all probability, dependent in some way upon White suppliers and/or White consumers either or both of which would have probably proved hostile. Furthermore, Black entrepreneurs faced the very real possibilities of receiving either physical harm or destruction of their property by antagonistic White competitors or bigots.

In 1972, at least 35 percent of all Black-owned businesses operated in just four industries—food stores (6.3 percent), eating and drinking establishments (7.6 percent), personal-service establishments (18.5 percent), and auto repair/garages (2.9 percent) (Table 9-4), typically thought of as "mom and pop" enterprises. In 1972, average revenue of the 34,693 personal-service establishments was only $9,223. The average for businesses

TABLE 9-4 Characteristics of Black-Owned Businesses in Selected Industries, 1972 to 1992

Characteristic	1972	1977	1982	Percent Change 1972 to 1982
Total Black-owned firms	187,602	231,203	339,239	80.8%
Receipts of Black-owned firms $ (000), Total	$5,534,000	$8,645,000	$12,444,000	124.9%
Number of Black-Owned Firms in Selected Industries	**66,273**	**65,620**	**68,688**	3.6%
Food stores	11,887	10,679	9,187	−22.7%
Eating and drinking	14,346	13,008	11,629	−18.9%
Personal service	34,693	35,035	40,394	16.4%
Auto repair and garages	5,347	6,898	7,478	39.9%
Percent of All Black-Owned Firms	**35.3%**	**28.4%**	**20.2%**	−42.7%
Food stores	6.3%	4.6%	2.7%	−57.3%
Eating and drinking	7.6%	5.6%	3.4%	−55.2%
Personal service	18.5%	15.2%	11.9%	−35.6%
Auto repair and garages	2.9%	3.0%	2.2%	−22.7%
Receipts of Black-Owned Firms in Selected Industries	**$1,432,805**	**$1,941,936**	**$2,349,686**	64.0%
Food stores	$570,572	$785,776	$882,737	54.7%
Eating and drinking	$437,088	$572,331	$675,230	54.5%
Personal service	$320,125	$399,274	$560,809	75.2%
Auto repair and garages	$105,020	$184,555	$230,910	119.9%
Percent of All Receipts in Black-Owned Firms	**25.9%**	**22.5%**	**18.9%**	−27.1%
Food stores	10.3%	9.1%	7.1%	−31.2%
Eating and drinking	7.9%	6.6%	5.4%	−31.3%
Personal service	5.8%	4.6%	4.5%	−22.1%
Auto repair and garages	1.9%	2.1%	1.9%	−2.2%
Average Revenue of Black Firms				
All black firms	$29,499			
Selected firms	$21,620			
Food stores	$48,000			
Eating and drinking	$30,468			
Personal service	$9,227			
Auto repair and garages	$19,641			

[a]Data adjusted by the U.S. Census Bureau to exclude 1120C corporations (Internal Revenue Service Tax Form 1120C).

1982	1987[a]	1992[a]	1982[a] to 1992[a]
308,260	424,165	620,912	101.4%
$9,619,000	$19,763,000	$32,197,000	234.7%
66,312	**89,359**	**114,100**	72.1%
8,919	8,952	8,466	−5.1%
11,406	11,834	13,832	21.3%
38,709	56,772	76,988	98.9%
7,278	11,801	14,814	103.5%
21.5%	**21.1%**	**18.4%**	−14.6%
2.9%	2.1%	1.4%	−52.9%
3.7%	2.8%	2.2%	−39.8%
12.6%	13.4%	12.4%	−1.3%
2.4%	2.8%	2.4%	1.1%
$2,214,792	**$3,472,210**	**$4,785,902**	116.1%
$820,155	$1,001,462	$979,773	19.5%
$619,093	$1,084,468	$1,785,569	188.4%
$551,099	$959,696	$1,468,760	166.5%
$224,445	$426,584	$551,800	145.9%
23.0%	**17.6%**	**14.9%**	−35.4%
8.5%	5.1%	3.0%	−64.3%
6.4%	5.5%	5.5%	−13.8%
5.7%	4.9%	4.6%	−20.4%
2.3%	2.2%	1.7%	−26.6%
		$51,854	
		$41,945	
		$115,730	
		$129,090	
		$19,078	
		$37,249	

in all four industries was $21,620, compared to $29,499 for all Black-owned businesses.

Between 1972 and 1982, the industry composition of Black-owned businesses changed significantly. Although the total number of Black-owned businesses increased by 80.8 percent, and Black-business revenues increased by 124.9 percent, the number of businesses in the four predominant industries increased by only 39.9 percent, and their total revenue increased by only 64 percent. As a result, the share of all Black-owned businesses decreased from 35.3 percent to 20.2 percent (a 42.7 percent decrease), and their share of business revenue decreased from 25.9 percent to 18.9 percent (a 27.1 percent decrease). The share of food stores decreased by 57.3 percent; eating and drinking establishments, by 55.2 percent; personal-service establishments, by 35.6 percent; and auto repair/garages, by 22.7 percent. Similarly the share of revenues accounted for by both food stores and eating and drinking establishments decreased by 31 percent, personal-service establishments, by 22.1 percent; and auto repair/garages, by 2.2 percent.

Between 1982 and 1992, the number of Black-owned personal-service and retail establishments continued to fall, but not as dramatically as in the previous decade. Black-owned businesses comprising the four predominant industries decreased from 21.5 percent in 1982 to 18.4 percent in 1992 (a 14.6 percent decrease). During the previous 10 years, their industry share decreased by 42.7 percent. By contrast, the loss of Black business revenue accounted for by these industries was greater between 1982 and 1992 than it was in the previous decade. Revenue share decreased from 23.0 percent to 14.9 percent between 1982 and 1992 (a 42.6 percent decrease), compared to 27.1 percent the previous decade.

The changing character of Black-owned businesses mirrored changes in the Black population. Desegregation and affirmative-action policies in higher education allowed a significant increase in the proportion of Blacks who attained business and engineering degrees. Bates (1997:9) reports that between 1976 and 1992, the number of Blacks receiving education degrees decreased by 63.2 percent (from 14,209 to 5,226); in contrast, the number receiving business degrees increased by 92.9 percent (from 9,489 to 18,304); and the number receiving engineering degrees increased by 161.3 percent (from 1,370 to 3,580). At the same time, major corporations initiated affirmative-action policies to recruit more minorities into managerial and professional positions.

Coupled with the decline of urban infrastructures and the enactment of open housing policies, a growing number of middle- and upper-income Blacks moved to the suburbs. At the same time, major chain stores and franchises (e.g., fast-food chains, convenience stores, drug stores, commercial dry cleaners, one-stop gas stations, etc.) moved into Black urban communities and captured consumer markets that heretofore were the exclusive domain of Black business owners. Thus, traditional Black-owned businesses lost their "protected" markets to population dispersion and stiffer competition from non-Black businesses.

As minority-owned businesses diversified, more minorities also entered the business arena. Between 1987 and 1992, Hispanic-owned businesses had the highest rate of increase at 82.7 percent (from 422,373 to 771,708), while businesses owned by minorities other than Blacks and Hispanics increased 61.0 percent (from 376,711 to 606,426); and businesses owned by Blacks increased 46.4 percent (from 424,165 to 620,912). In total, minority-owned businesses increased by 63.4 percent, whereas businesses owned by nonminority males increased by only 26.9 percent during the same period. In 1987 the ratio of nonminority male-owned businesses to minority-owned businesses was 7.16:1; in 1992, 5.56:1 (U.S. Bureau of the Census, 1991, 1997).

Between 1982 and 1992, the number of Black-owned businesses grew at a rate of 7.25 percent annually—twice the growth rate of all small businesses. In addition, the employment capacity of Black-owned businesses grew at 11.02 percent annually. Because of this, the 620,912 Black-owned firms in 1992 had an employment capacity equal to 2.3 percent of the Black workforce.

LOTS OF ROOM FOR IMPROVEMENTS YET TO COME

Although minority-owned businesses have experienced high growth rates, they still account for only 11.4 percent of all small businesses in the United States and only 6.1 percent of small business revenue. In contrast, businesses owned by nonminority males constitute 58.6 percent of all small businesses and 76.0 percent of small business revenue. Current figures are an improvement over 1987, when the 424,165 Black-owned firms comprised 3.1 percent of all small firms and accounted for just 1 percent of all small business revenue, and the average gross revenue per Black business, $46,593, was exactly 25 percent of the gross revenue of businesses owned by nonminority men and 32 percent of the average revenue of all U.S. firms. Blacks also had smaller annual revenues than Hispanics ($58,555) and other minorities ($93,222). By 1992, there had been some marginal growth; the 621,912 Black-owned firms comprised 3.6 percent of all small businesses, but their gross revenue was still only 1 percent of all small business revenue. Average 1992 revenues ranged from $249,800 for nonminority male-owned firms; $192,680 for all small businesses; $94,400 for Hispanic-owned businesses; $164,400 for businesses owned by other minorities; and $51,855 for Black-owned firms.

The relative disparity for Blacks was wider than other minorities in a number of key areas. For example, in 1996, only 60.1 percent of Blacks still owned the business they owned in 1992, whereas the average for all the other groups was 68.9 percent. The next lowest percentage was women-owned businesses at 66 percent; the highest was nonminority males at 70.5 percent. In regard to the reason for the change in ownership, 26.0 percent of Blacks indicated that their business no longer existed, as opposed to being sold or transferred to another owner; overall, 18.3 percent of ex-owners cited this as the reason. Further, 20.7 percent of Blacks indicated that their business was unsuccessful at the time it was discontinued, compared to 14.1 percent of all ex-owners. Finally, 23.9 percent of Black ex-owners indicated that the reason their business was unsuccessful was because they lacked access to business or personal loans or credit, whereas only 11.5 percent of all ex-owners cited this as a reason. The differential rate of Black business terminations and the reasons given for it are signs that Blacks continue to encounter problems not experienced by Whites or other minorities. Finally, although 44.5 percent of all small businesses earned $10,000 or less in 1992, this was true for 46.6 percent of Hispanic-owned businesses, 35.1 percent of businesses owned by other minorities, 38.5 percent of businesses owned by nonminority males, and 56.1 percent of businesses owned by Blacks (U.S. Bureau of the Census, 1991, 1997).

STRENGTHS AND WEAKNESSES OF DATA AVAILABLE FOR DESCRIBING TRENDS

Trends noted above are based on two data sets—the Survey of Minority-Owned Business Enterprises (SMOBE) and the Characteristics of Business Owners (CBO). USBC compiles SMOBE, the data set most widely used to study minority-business trends, for businesses owned by Blacks, Hispanics, Asians, Pacific Islanders, Native Americans, Alaska Natives, and White women. The data are compiled from income tax returns and surveys, and include industry type, size of firm, number of firms, legal form of organization, gross receipts, number of paid employees, annual payroll, and geographic location. The first survey was conducted in 1969; since 1977, it has been conducted every five years. Income tax data are derived from any of three Internal Revenue Service business tax forms— 1040 Schedule C (sole proprietorship, i.e., unincorporated business or self-employed person), 1065 (partnership), or 1120 or 1120 S[2] corporation.

---

[2]An 1120 S corporation is an IRS designation for legally incorporated businesses with 35 or fewer shareholders. One advantage of the S corporation is that its shareholders do not face the double tax liability encountered by shareholders of regular corporations for whom

Social Security numbers from the forms are forwarded to the Social Security Administration, which supplies the race of the owners for sole proprietorship and for the majority of owners for partnerships and S corporations. SMOBE is widely accessible and reliable for areas with large numbers of minority firms. Reliability estimates for sampling errors are provided with the reports, and measures are also taken to reduce nonsampling errors. The disadvantage of the data is that, over time, USBC has redefined criteria for inclusion in, and methodology of, the survey.

These changes complicate comparison of older and newer surveys, as do other changes, including the way in which various minority groups have been disaggregated; the Standard Industrial Classification used to categorize firms by industries; the enumeration of establishments of a firm, as opposed to the entire firm; the business-receipt threshold used as a benchmark to include or exclude firms; and the incorporation status of firms—i.e., 1120 S or regular corporations.

Prior to 1982, a self-identified minority person had only to file one of the business tax returns noted above to be counted in the survey cohort. Since 1982, only businesses with gross receipts of $500.00 or more were included. Based on past history, it is safe to assume that Black businesses are disproportionately concentrated among businesses earning less than $500 in revenue; that being the case, the size of the decrease of Black businesses, specifically personal-service businesses (as noted in Table 9-4) is likely overstated simply because of the change in the revenue threshold.

In 1987 a second significant redefinition of the survey cohort occurred; USBC excluded regular corporations but maintained inclusion of 1120 S corporations. Thus, the 1987 and 1992 SMOBEs do not include information for regular corporations, the legal form of most incorporated Black businesses. Because of this, census data significantly understate total employment and revenue in small businesses. When the change was made in 1987, the survey results for 1982 were retabulated using the 1987 methodology, excluding regular corporations; hence, survey results exist for 1982 data both with and without regular corporations. Before regular corporations were dropped from the 1982 survey, total revenue for Black-owned firms was $12.4 billion, and total employment was 165,765; after regular corporations were dropped, total revenue was $9.6 billion and

---

both corporate earnings and dividends are taxed. All earnings of the S corporation are distributed to the shareholders and treated as individual income. Apart from the restriction on the number of shareholders, S corporations are prohibited from operating in financial service industries and international markets and they cannot be held by or hold other companies. For tax purposes, these corporations are treated as individuals.

TABLE 9-5 Number and Percentages of Minority-Owned Firms by Legal Form of Organization, 1995 Survey

Legal Form of Organization	Black		American Indian/ Alaska Native		Asian American/ Pacific Islander	
	No. of Firms	Percent of Total	No. of Firms	Percent of Total	No. of Firms	Percent of Total
Proprietorship	51	22.9			1	5.9
Partnership	7	3.1				
Subchapter S Corporation	61	27.4			8	47.1
Regular Corporation	99	44.4	3	100	8	47.1
Franchise	5	2.2				
Total	223	100	3	100	17	100

Note: Ownership lists based on businesses registered with seven public agencies in Metropolitan Atlanta, Georgia. Survey conducted by Thomas D. Boston.

total employment was 121,373. Thus, removing regular corporations from the survey cohort reduced Black business revenue by 22.6 percent and reduced employment in Black-owned businesses by 26.8 percent. Other research indicates that employment and revenue may be understated by as much as 50 percent (Boston, 1995).

Using survey data from Atlanta, as viewed in Table 9-5, the significance of omitting regular corporations is clear: 99 of the 160 Black-owned corporations are regular corporations. For the survey as a whole, 137 of the 232 corporations are regular corporations. In fact, 57.9 percent of all businesses certified to participate in Atlanta's and Fulton County's affirmative-action programs are corporations; 72.6 percent of these are regular corporations. This same trend prevails in other minority business programs across the country.

Table 9-6 indicates the mean and median employment in firms according to their legal form of organization. Although the mean employment in regular and S corporations is similar, the median employment in regular corporations is greater—S corporations employed 2,062 workers, regular corporations employed 2,859 workers.

The 1992 SMOBE survey cohort included businesses filing 1040 C, 1065, and 1120 S forms in that year. According to the 1992 SMOBE, Black-

Hispanic American		White Women		Ethnicity Unclassified		Group Total	
No. of Firms	Percent of Total	No. of Firms	Percent of Total	No. of Firms	Percent of Total	No. of Firms	Percent of Total
1	4.8	14	31.1	3	42.9	70	22.2
2	9.5					9	2.8
9	42.9	13	28.9	4	57.1	95	30.1
9	42.9	18	40.0			137	43.4
						5	1.6
21	100	45	100	7	100	316	100

owned S Corporations comprised just 4 percent of all Black-owned businesses but accounted for 38 percent of all business revenue and 51 percent of all employees in Black-owned firms. Black-owned regular corporations have an even larger average employment and revenue capacity. Since 1992, USBC has changed its survey methodology again to include subchapter regular corporations in the 1997 SMOBE.

CBO is similar to SMOBE, but has the added advantage of providing information about the characteristics of businesses—age of the business, capital invested, net income, current assets, markets, and survival—and personal information about the owners—age, education, experience, marital status, and gender. CBO has been published every five years since 1982. Its disadvantages as a data source center primarily on the lack of accessibility of the data and the inconsistency in survey methodology between survey periods (see Nucci, 1992; Bates, 1990, 1991).

Bates (1997), Farlie and Meyer (1996), Borjas and Bronars (1989), and Evans and Leighton (1989) examined minority-owned business trends by using self-employment data from population censuses; however, these data are of limited use because they lack employment and revenue information about businesses (Bates, 1997:3).

TABLE 9-6 Mean and Median Employment by Legal Form of
Organization, 1995 Survey

Legal Form of Organization	Number of Firms	Mean	Median	Total
Proprietorship	70	3.89	3	249
Partnership	9	46.44	7	418
Subchapter S Corp	95	22.41	7	2,062
Regular Corp	137	22.16	10	2,859
Franchise	5	31.60	30	158
Total	316	19.22	7	5,746

Note: Ownership lists based on businesses registered with seven public agencies in Metropolitan Atlanta, Georgia. Survey conducted by Thomas D. Boston.

PUBLIC POLICIES THAT WORKED

As noted earlier, a fundamental element in the industry diversification and growing capacity of minority-owned businesses is their access to
local, state, and federal procurement opportunities. Government contracting was pivotal, especially given the difficulties encountered by minorities in gaining access to opportunities in the private sector.

In 1964, Congress passed the Civil Rights Act authorizing the Attorney General to enforce the Fourteenth Amendment to the Constitution,
adopted in 1868 to prevent states from denying equal protection to freed
slaves. Titles II and III of the Civil Rights Act prohibited discrimination in
public accommodations; Title IV authorized implementation of the 1954
U.S. Supreme Court decision, *Brown v. Board of Education,* which outlawed
segregation in public schools.

In 1965, President Lyndon Johnson issued Executive Order 11246
(amended in 1976 by Executive Order 11375), which obligated recipients
of federal contracts in excess of $50,000 to file written affirmative-action
plans, not to discriminate in employment, and to undertake steps to recruit and upgrade their employment of minorities and women. The U.S.
Department of Labor was empowered to enforce the Order and to impose
penalties for noncompliance. The Economic Opportunity Act of 1964 directed the Small Business Administration (SBA) to assist small businesses
owned by low-income individuals. In 1967, the federal government
amended this Act and provided the first statutory assistance to minority-
owned small businesses.

In March of 1969, President Richard Nixon issued Executive Order
11458, which outlined arrangements for developing and coordinating a
national program for minority businesses. The order did not prescribe

specific goals, but directed the Secretary of Commerce to develop and coordinate activities at the federal, state, and local levels aimed at promoting minority business development. The head of each federal department, or a designated representative, was responsible for submitting reports to the Commerce Secretary about the department's budget, plans, and programs to assist minority businesses. These activities led to the establishment of the Office of Minority Business Enterprise.

To increase awards of federal contracts to minority businesses, Section 8(a) of the Small Business Act was enacted to authorize SBA to enter into contracts with federal agencies and, in turn, award these contracts to small businesses. Section 8(a) became one of the primary means of increasing the use of minorities in federal procurement. In fiscal year 1969, $8.9 million was awarded under the 8(a) program; in 1971, $64.5 million; and in 1973, $208 million. Between 1968 and 1977, $2.2 billion was awarded under this program (Walker, 1986).

The Public Works Employment Act of 1977 (Public Law 95-28; 91 Stat. 117) and the 1978 Omnibus Small Business Act (Public Law 95-507[92 Stat. 1757]) established percentage goals in procurement for minority-owned firms for the first time, requiring at least 10 percent of all federal grants for local public-works projects to be expended to minority businesses. The two Acts also directed the Secretary of Commerce, in cooperation with federal departments and agencies, to develop comprehensive minority-enterprise programs and institute specific goals for minority firms in federal procurement. Monitoring and evaluation procedures were established to assess performance against these goals. A new subcontracting program was introduced under section 8(d) of the Small Business Act that required recipients of federal contracts exceeding $1 million for the construction of a public facility to establish percentage goals for the use of minority subcontractors. In 1981, minority-owned firms received 3.4 percent of all federal procurement expenditures. In 1987, total federal procurement with minorities was $7.5 billion. This was equivalent to 10 percent of the $77.8 billion in gross revenue received by all minority firms. In 1992, minority-owned firms received $11.7 billion in federal procurement, equivalent to 5.7 percent of minority business revenue for that year. In 1994 they received $14.4 billion (8.3 percent) of federal procurement; and in 1995, $11.2 billion (5.5 percent) (Clayton, 1996:75).

Until 1980, the federal government made the biggest push of all governmental agencies for minority business inclusion. In contrast, little or nothing was happening in the private sector or at state and local government levels. This changed when Mayor Maynard Jackson pushed the city of Atlanta to adopt an aggressive minority-business affirmative-action plan.

Mayor Jackson's affirmative-action initiative grew out of the 1974 "Atlanta Plan," designed in response to Presidential Executive Order 11246 and intended to ensure equal employment opportunity in all city activities. In 1975, Jackson extended the scope of the plan by issuing an administrative order mandating the use of minority contractors on the construction of the proposed Hartsfield International Airport as a means to achieve the goals of Title VII. Opposition to the plan was intense because the airport was one the largest capital construction projects in the South at the time. In 1976, the Atlanta City Council formally adopted a resolution mandating that 25 percent of the funds expended on the design and construction of the new airport go to minorities as joint-venture partners, prime contractors, or subcontractors. Soon afterward, this minority business initiative was extended by an executive order to cover all city contracting.

Minority business utilization by the city of Atlanta increased substantially following the implementation of the Plan. According to the *Annual Reports of the Office of Contract Compliance of the City of Atlanta*, total minority procurement was 0.13 percent in 1973, 3 percent in 1974, 14.3 percent in 1975, 19.9 percent in 1976, and 24.1 percent in 1977. By 1978, the end of Jackson's first term, the city boasted of having achieved 38.5 percent minority participation. The *Annual Reports* show that during Mayor Jackson's term in office, which began in 1974, minority procurement increased significantly; however, actual percentages were less than those claimed made by the city (Boston, 1996). In an independent examination of contracts awarded between 1979 and 1989, it was determined that ethnic minorities and White women, representing 359 firms, received $191 million (15.5 percent) of all dollars awarded, including 11.4 percent of all prime contracts, 17.5 percent of all subcontracts, and 27.6 percent of all joint ventures. An examination of bid activity indicates that Blacks submitted 29 percent of all construction bids during this period (Boston, 1996). During the 1980s, dozens of cities followed Atlanta's lead. By the mid-1980s, more than 200 local and state programs existed nationwide (Minority Business Enterprise Legal Defense and Education Fund, 1988).[3] Most, at the local level, were patterned after Atlanta's program.

Boston (1998) recorded information about cities with at least 200 Black-owned businesses in 1982. The data, for 1982 through 1992 (Table 9-7), included the number of firms, their combined total sales and combined total employment, the year an affirmative-action plan was initiated,

---

[3]This report lists all local programs created prior to the 1989 Croson decision (discussed later). It also gives the legislative authority creating them, the general category of purchasing activity they were designed to cover, and the percentage goal for the program.

if one was, prior to 1987,[4] industries covered by the plan, percentage goal of the plan, and changes in the number of businesses over time. Of these 88 cities, 76 percent implemented affirmative-action plans prior to 1987. Although the growth rate is greater in cities with affirmative-action programs than in cities without programs, the difference, about 5 percent, is not statistically significant.

Because 1987 SMOBE data do not include information for regular corporations, the more prevalent legal form of organization among affirmative-action programs, it is not possible to evaluate the impact of affirmative-action policies on changes in revenue and employment for these companies. Nevertheless, firms registered in these programs usually have much greater revenues and employment capacities.

PUBLIC POLICIES THAT NEED TO BE IMPROVED

Given the role affirmative-action programs play in the changing character of minority-owned businesses, public policies are needed to clear up the ambiguity surrounding the "strict scrutiny" standard being used to dismantle these programs. In 1977, the Public Works Employment Act mandated that 10 percent of federal funds appropriated for local public-works projects must be used by state and local grantees to procure services or supplies from minority businesses. Soon after the Act was passed, H. Earl Fullilove, and several associations of construction contractors, challenged its constitutionality,[5] and their case became the first legal challenge to a federal set-aside program to reach the Supreme Court. The suit alleged that Fullilove and others incurred injury because of the enforcement of the minority business requirement. They argued that the requirement violated the Equal Protection Clause of the Fourteenth Amendment and the Due Process Clause of the Fifth Amendment.

On July 2, 1980, a plurality of U.S. Supreme Court justices found the program to be constitutional, allowing federal departments and agencies as well as state and local agencies to operate minority business programs, and by 1988 there were programs at 190 local governmental agencies and 36 state agencies. Justice Burger, writing the plurality opinion, concluded that Congress need not establish specific findings of discrimination because it has the broad authority as well as the affirmative duty to react to

---

[4]The cut-off at 1987 is used because it predates the 1989 U.S. Supreme Court decision in the case of the *City of Richmond v. J. A. Croson Co.* Following the Croson decision, numerous programs were disbanded. The details of this decision are discussed later in this paper.

[5]*H. Earl Fullilove, et al., Petitioners, v. Philip M. Klutznick, Secretary of Commerce of the United States, et al.* No. 78-1007, 448 U.S. 448, 65 L.Ed.2nd 902.

TABLE 9-7 Statistics for Black-Owned Businesses in Cities, 1982 to 1992

City	State	Number of Firms, 1982	Number of Firms, 1987	Number of Firms, 1992	Total Sales, 1982 (000)	Total Sales, 1987 (000)	Total Sales, 1992 (000)	Total Employment 1982	Total Employment 1987	Total Employment 1992	Date Affirmative Action Plan Initiated
AKRON	OH	628	679	940	10,556	14,034	20,922	164	140	312	1984
ANCHORAGE	AK	312	347	518	11,907	11,334	32,321	217	161	832	1984
ATLANTA	GA	3,496	3,869	5,762	238,549	290,702	280,701	4,162	3,230	3,299	1982
AUGUSTA	GA	294	272	391	18,518	12,326	12,736	472	187	343	1982
AUSTIN	TX	815	1,111	1,579	19,704	31,689	45,026	397	731	871	1982
BALTIMORE	MD	4,077	5,044	7,542	241,024	165,350	233,164	2,411	1,898	2,409	1982
BATON ROUGE	LA	1,177	1,196	1,791	45,022	56,261	67,623	700	629	680	1986
BIRMINGHAM	AL	1,145	1,437	2,105	47,107	48,281	77,364	892	778	1,103	1980
BOSTON	MA	1,214	1,860	2,583	59,224	86,220	182,525	-----	928	639	1987
BUFFALO	NY	717	735	1,011	25,993	31,484	36,321	697	345	906	-----
CAMDEN	NJ	264	270	356	5,771	9,103	28,514	41	116	629	1983
CHARLESTON	SC	490	456	703	14,838	15,825	26,251	218	234	951	1979
CHARLOTTE	NC	1,308	1,880	3,216	48,470	75,885	123,654	576	945	519	1983
CHATTANOOGA	TN	485	584	793	17,712	16,110	23,502	-----	211		-----
CINCINNATI	OH	1,636	1,753	2,431	45,389	58,008	94,881	642	901	1,166	1983
CLEVELAND	OH	2,407	2,359	2,943	131,494	107,098	125,170	1,492	1,516	1,247	1984
COLUMBIA	SC	629	743	1,225	16,104	41,016	-----	259	622	922	1986
COLUMBUS	GA	618	866	1,255	16,151	43,707	98,384	257	1,115		1984
COLUMBUS	OH	1,906	2,301	3,314	37,419	64,996	188,630	604	1,074	2,265	1983
DALLAS	TX	4,883	5,633	7,071	134,357	157,962	330,354	1,875	1,992	5,191	-----
DAYTON	OH	908	879	1,122	20,123	33,134	31,716	336	644	432	1987
DENVER	CO	1,325	1,383	1,916	53,076	52,155	121,622	664	438	1,636	-----
DETROIT	MI	6,798	7,116	9,275	272,405	258,375	486,092	2,877	3,861	4,528	-----
DURHAM	NC	693	936	1,589	69,929	27,506	43,805	1,808	512	649	1984
EAST ORANGE	NJ	659	938	1,132	21,386	26,470	35,936	227	168	336	1982
EL PASO	TX	266	305	503	8,308	19,632	16,570	-----	814	210	1985
EVANSTON	IL	337	451	679	6,963	13,120	43,182	81	99	578	1973
FLINT	MI	634	683	960	26,481	21,018	22,309	218	230	259	-----
FORT LAUDERDALE	FL	472	620	643	12,201	34,337	26,200	194	365	267	1986
FORT WAYNE	IN	293	350	544	9,445	22,584	25,177	197	381	274	1984
FRESNO	CA	306	359	486	9,377	14,403	21,725	133	191		1986
GARDENA	CA	322	316	488	6,905	10,534	31,940	65	70	187	1984
GARY	IN	1,103	1,051	1,274	49,005	77,456	84,777	171	894	854	-----

City	Affirmative Action Plan Coverage	Percent Goal of Plan	Percent Change In the No. of Businesses 1982-92	Percent Change in the No. of Businesses 1987-92
AKRON	Construction	15%	50%	38%
ANCHORAGE	Construction	10%	66%	49%
ATLANTA	Goods and Services	25%	65%	49%
AUGUSTA	No Plan		33%	44%
AUSTIN	Construction	8%	94%	42%
BALTIMORE	Construction Contracts	25%	85%	50%
BATON ROUGE	Construction	10%	52%	50%
BIRMINGHAM	Procurement	13%	84%	46%
BOSTON	Goods and Services	23%	113%	39%
BUFFALO	Construction	10%	41%	38%
CAMDEN	No Plan		35%	32%
CHARLESTON	No Plan		43%	54%
CHARLOTTE	Construction Grants	10%	146%	71%
CHATTANOOGA	Construction Grants	12%	64%	36%
CINCINNATI	Construction	15%	49%	39%
CLEVELAND	Construction	30%	22%	25%
COLUMBIA	No Plan		95%	65%
COLUMBUS	Procurement	4%	103%	45%
COLUMBUS	Construction Contracts	10%	74%	44%
DALLAS	No Plan		45%	26%
DAYTON	Construction Contracts	20%	24%	28%
DENVER	Construction Contracts	20%	45%	39%
DETROIT	No Plan		36%	30%
DURHAM	Services Construction	28%	129%	70%
EAST ORANGE	Construction Contracts	25%	72%	21%
EL PASO	Construction	20%	89%	65%
EVANSTON	No Plan		101%	51%
FLINT	Construction Contracts	18%	51%	41%
FORT LAUDERDALE	No Plan		36%	4%
FORT WAYNE	Procurement	10%	86%	55%
FRESNO	Construction	25%	59%	35%
GARDENA	Procurement	10%	52%	54%
GARY	No Plan		16%	21%

TABLE 9-7 Continued

City	State	Number of Firms, 1982	Number of Firms, 1987	Number of Firms, 1992	Total Sales, 1982 (000)	Total Sales, 1987 (000)	Total Sales, 1992 (000)	Total Employ-ment 1982	Total Employ-ment 1987	Total Employ-ment 1992	Date Affirmative Action Plan Initiated
GRAND RAPIDS	MI	252	312	494	7,419	13,719	16,594	84	107	144	1982
GREENSBORO	NC	897	1,094	1,617	22,460	30,751	45,201	312	461	915	—
HAMPTON	VA	660	936	1,179	17,110	61,310	22,729	189	531	353	1985
HARRISBURG	PA	258	328	384	7,193	12,817	10,541	96	232	144	1982
HARTFORD	CT	436	526	751	23,570	32,758	26,551	236	480	218	1983
HOUSTON	TX	10,019	10,025	13,592	283,724	288,897	537,490	2,470	2,561	6,191	
JACKSON	MS	1,251	1,738	2,560	38,093	71,603	93,616	593	1,235	1,623	1985
JACKSONVILLE	FL	1,703	1,967	2,507	53,755	80,913	112,765	1,031	1,156	1,710	1984
KANSAS CITY	KS	601	670	778	28,776	29,239	19,688	246	775		—
KANSAS CITY	MO	1,552	1,812	2,243	60,594	78,673	84,997	767	1,568	1,565	
LAKE CHARLES	LA	416	490	644	10,780	13,876	16,124	168	185		1980
LOS ANGELES	CA	12,197	11,607	15,371	459,754	721,958	2,628,903	5,727	5,527	13,138	1983
LOUISVILLE	KY	973	1,097	1,465	44,056	32,882	94,997	1,294	567	1,038	1983
MACON	GA	393	663	932	9,925	52,225	27,694	193	478	417	1983
MEMPHIS	TN	3,119	4,225	5,662	139,902	147,861	183,665	2,164	2,337	2,257	
MIAMI	FL	1,142	1,164	2,155	59,358	78,989	86,584	676	852	876	1985
MILWAUKEE	WI	1,516	1,741	2,423	59,807	73,002	176,966	664	870	2,112	1987
MINNEAPOLIS	MN	554	603	1,114	43,970	44,147	68,217	823	773	964	
MONROE	LA	270	350	429	8,117	35,512	16,369	165	231	90	1986
NEW HAVEN	CT	333	448	570	37,705	15,348	14,608	142	127	119	1963
NEW YORK CITY	NY	17,350	25,256	35,120	641,187	1,065,032	1,466,994	8,010	8,727	8,779	
NEWARK	NJ	918	1,231	1,500	60,781	124,118	144,114	1,067	901	1,200	1984
NORFOLK	VA	922	1,165	1,248	45,222	46,546	35,911	1,069	872	621	
OAKLAND	CA	3,633	3,445	4,282	181,179	137,159	215,057	2,861	1,711	2,612	1980
OMAHA	NE	538	633	975	32,901	21,899	47,110	163	469		1985
ORLANDO	FL	427	463	811	13,068	29,800	37,030	125	425	647	
PASADENA	CA	573	642	901	13,227	23,341	35,260		206	301	1980
PHILADELPHIA	PA	5,017	5,540	7,183	215,337	255,907	549,414	2,316	2,474	5,962	1984
PHOENIX	AZ	685	776	1,204	22,352	47,150	64,438	330	937	617	1981
PLAINFIELD	NJ	384	519	659	12,154	13,795	15,088	452	178	112	—
PORTSMOUTH	VA	614	687	770	10,421	16,658	16,168	133	296	232	—
RALEIGH	NC	655	984	1,619	16,717	37,804	56,653	298	721	718	1983
RICHMOND	VA	1,563	1,838	2,630	45,360	57,420	95,777	815	821	1,596	1983

City	Affirmative Action Plan Coverage	Percent Goal of Plan	Percent Change In the No. of Businesses 1982-92	Percent Change in the No. of Businesses 1987-92
GRAND RAPIDS	Construction Contracts	10%	96%	58%
GREENSBORO	Construction	10%	80%	48%
HAMPTON	No Plan		79%	26%
HARRISBURG	Construction	15%	49%	17%
HARTFORD	Construction Contracts	10%	72%	43%
HOUSTON	Construction	10%	36%	36%
JACKSON	No Plan		105%	47%
JACKSONVILLE	Goods and Services	10%	47%	27%
KANSAS CITY	Contracts	10%	29%	16%
KANSAS CITY	Construction	16%	45%	24%
LAKE CHARLES	Procurement	10%	55%	31%
LOS ANGELES	Construction	16%	26%	32%
LOUISVILLE	Credit-MBE Bids	15%	51%	34%
MACON	No Plan		137%	41%
MEMPHIS	No Plan		82%	34%
MIAMI	Goods and Services	50%	89%	85%
MILWAUKEE	All Projects	15%	60%	39%
MINNEAPOLIS	Construction Supplies	10%	101%	85%
MONROE	Goods and Services	10%	59%	23%
NEW HAVEN	Construction Projects	15%	71%	27%
NEW YORK CITY	Construction Contracts	10%	102%	39%
NEWARK	Construction	25%	63%	22%
NORFOLK	No Plan		35%	7%
OAKLAND	DOT Funded	30%	18%	24%
OMAHA	Construction	20%	81%	54%
ORLANDO	Construction/Services/Supplies	18%	90%	75%
PASADENA	No Plan		57%	40%
PHILADELPHIA	Construction Services.	15%	43%	30%
PHOENIX	All Areas	12%	76%	55%
PLAINFIELD	Contracts	25%	72%	27%
PORTSMOUTH	No Plan		25%	12%
RALEIGH	Construction--SW Raleigh	9%	147%	65%
RICHMOND	Construction	30%	68%	43%

TABLE 9-7 Continued

City	State	Number of Firms, 1982	Number of Firms, 1987	Number of Firms, 1992	Total Sales, 1982 (000)	Total Sales, 1987 (000)	Total Sales, 1992 (000)	Total Employment 1982	Total Employment 1987	Total Employment 1992	Date Affirmative Action Plan Initiated
RICHMOND	CA	623	660	874	29,402	25,465	29,703	351	407	405	------
ROCHESTER	NY	498	655	926	17,999	21,001	23,699	244	366	365	1985
SACRAMENTO	CA	843	809	1,313	12,424	21,652	42,511	150	226	359	1980
SAN ANTONIO	TX	989	1,273	1,477	25,597	41,865	68,583	363	602	1,073	1984
SAN FRANCISCO	CA	1,980	1,965	2,230	80,193	99,296	220,799	1,264	1,209	2,005	1984
SAN JOSE	CA	998	961	1,351	30,516	36,739	48,252	515	295	567	1983
SEATTLE	WA	1,063	1,040	1,569	36,011	37,997	83,569	719	722	1,498	1986
SHREVEPORT	LA	827	1,018	1,216	27,063	29,054	32,066	477	385	697	1980
SPRINGFIELD	MA	265	429	515	8,441	13,748	13,058	69	105	95	1984
ST PETERSBURG	FL	566	788	919	17,889	29,158	26,528	219	343	198	1981
ST. LOUIS	MO	2,164	2,235	2,481	89,543	83,826	98,443	1,307	1,255	1,060	1979
STOCKTON	CA	260	299	374	6,478	11,901	15,855	79	139	180	1971
TACOMA	WA	287	287	442	5,451	10,719	13,144	72	101	190	1982
TALLAHASSEE	FL	310	501	799	12,885	41,893	33,944	158	597	371	1985
TAMPA	FL	606	800	1,118	20,263	88,342	70,478	392	695	845	1981
TULSA	OK	680	738	1,114	12,368	26,533	31,751	139	379	431	1986
TUCSON	AZ	259	247	448	7,863	7,592	10,521	150	126	137	------
WASHINGTON D.C.	DC	8,966	8,275	10,111	268,488	411,941	451,861	3,417	4,085	4,277	1981
WILMINGTON	DE	332	377	544	12,485	16,991	41,932	223	286	1,488	------
WINSTON-SALEM	NC	513	703	1,061	15,052	26,305	34,285	302	399	324	1981
WICHITA	KS	588	601	746	18,068	71,164	18,709	------	335	------	1983
YOUNGSTOWN	OH	330	337	451	7,650	7,910	17,300	113	113	298	1980

City	Affirmative Action Plan Coverage	Percent Goal of Plan	Percent Change In the No. of Businesses 1982-92	Percent Change in the No. of Businesses 1987-92
RICHMOND	No Plan		40%	32%
ROCHESTER	Construction Projects	10%	86%	41%
SACRAMENTO	Procurement	20%	56%	62%
SAN ANTONIO	Construction	14%	49%	16%
SAN FRANCISCO	Public Works	30%	13%	13%
SAN JOSE	No Plan		35%	41%
SEATTLE	Construction Consulting	21%	48%	51%
SHREVEPORT	Construction	10%	47%	19%
SPRINGFIELD	Construction Contracts	5%	94%	20%
ST PETERSBURG	Construction	5%	62%	17%
ST. LOUIS	Contracts	10%	15%	11%
STOCKTON	Procurement	15%	44%	25%
TACOMA	Contracts Purchasing	15%	54%	54%
TALLAHASSEE	Contracts Over $100,000	15%	158%	59%
TAMPA	No Plan		84%	40%
TULSA	No Plan		64%	51%
TUCSON	Construction	17%	73%	81%
WASHINGTON D.C.	Construction	35%	13%	22%
WILMINGTON	Construction	15%	64%	44%
WINSTON-SALEM	No Plan		107%	51%
WICHITA	Construction	10%	27%	24%
YOUNGSTOWN	Construction	20%	37%	34%

SOURCE: Statistical data collected from the U.S. Bureau of the Census, 1985, 1990, 1996. Data on local area goals provided by Minority Business Enterprise Legal Defense and Education Fund, "Report on the Minority Business Enterprise Programs of State and Local Governments, 1988."

and address discrimination as a matter of national concern. The test is whether there is a "rational relationship" between the remedy and the government's interest. Congress subsequently wrote affirmative-action provisions into the Surface Transportation Assistance Act of 1982, the Foreign Assistance Act of 1983 as well as its 1985 extension, and the Surface Transportation and Uniform Relocation Assistance Act of 1987.

STRICT SCRUTINY BECOMES THE LEGAL STANDARD

In April 1983, the Richmond, Virginia, City Council voted to enact an affirmative-action plan in contracting (National Cooperative Highway Research Program, 1992; Dixon, 1990; Stoelting, 1990; Rice, 1991). The purpose of the plan was to increase the participation of minority-owned businesses in public construction contracts awarded by the city. In the course of the public hearings, evidence was introduced indicating that (1) even though the city had a 50 percent Black population, over the previous five years only 0.67 percent of the city's prime construction contracts went to minority firms; (2) six local construction associations had virtually no minority members; (3) widespread discrimination existed in the local, state, and national construction industries; and (4) the proposed ordinance was consistent with the *Fullilove* decision. The plan was enacted for a period of five years and included Blacks, Hispanics, Asians, and Alaska Natives. It required recipients of prime construction contracts to subcontract at least 30 percent of the contract's value to minority firms. A waiver from the goal was provided in cases where no suitable minority firms were available.

Five months after the enactment of the plan, the city invited bids for the installation of plumbing fixtures at the city jail. The J.A. Croson Company submitted the only bid on the project. Prior to doing so, the company contacted several minority businesses. One, Continental Metal Hose, expressed an interest in serving as a subcontractor on the project, but had to obtain a price quotation for fixtures before it could submit its bid. The supplier Continental contacted for a bid had already submitted a bid to Croson and refused to provide a quote to Continental. Another supplier refused to provide Continental a quote until it had obtained a credit check, a procedure that would take a minimum of 30 days. Because of this, Croson submitted its bid without the minority requirement. Shortly after the bid opening, Croson submitted a waiver requesting release from the minority requirement. Continental learned of this and informed the city that it could supply the fixtures. Continental's quoted price, however, was $6,183.29 higher than the price Croson had stipulated in its proposal. Croson was given 10 days to comply with the minority requirement. Instead the company argued for a waiver or the right to increase the contract price. The city rejected both requests and decided to rebid the contract. Croson filed suit in the district court claiming that the program was unconstitutional.

The District Court upheld the constitutionality of the city's program. The U.S. Court of Appeals, using *Fullilove* as a standard, affirmed the district court's decision. Croson then appealed to the U.S. Supreme Court. The Supreme Court vacated the earlier decision and remanded the case back to the Fourth Circuit Court where the district court's decision was reversed; the Fourth Circuit Court ruled that the plan violated the equal protection clause of the Fourteenth Amendment because the city's plan did not conform to the "strict scrutiny standard"—meaning that the "factual predicate" underlying racial preference programs must be supported by adequate and specific findings of past discrimination; generalized findings are not sufficient.

The City of Richmond then appealed the Fourth Circuit Court's decision to the U.S. Supreme Court. This time the Supreme Court affirmed the Circuit Court's decision. It was the first time a majority, rather than a plurality, agreed that strict scrutiny would be applied to racial preference programs. In 1987, the majority ruled that Sections 1 and 5 of the Fourteenth Amendment limit the powers of states, in contrast to the more sweeping powers of Congress—i.e., Congress is not required to meet the strict scrutiny standard, but states and localities are. The decision held that the program denied certain citizens the opportunity to compete for a fixed percentage of contracts based solely on their race. Justice Sandra Day O'Connor argued that all classifications based on race, whether benefiting or burdening minorities or nonminorities, will be subject to strict scrutiny.

In establishing its program, the city of Richmond initially relied on statements of minority business owners attesting to their exclusion from the skilled trades and encounters with discrimination in the industry and the fact of only 0.67 percent of contracts being awarded to minority businesses. The Supreme Court ruled, however, that the city's findings did not provide a strong enough basis of evidence to implement a remedial race-based program, because the evidence did not point to specific discrimination. Richmond was also criticized for including Hispanics, Asians, American Indians, and Alaska Natives in its plan when there was no evidence of past discrimination against them. The Court was also critical of the city's plan because it allowed all minorities to be eligible no matter where they resided, and the Court viewed the 30 percent minority requirement as a quota.

The *Croson* decision left little doubt about how the Court would rule on state and local affirmative-action programs that did not conform to the strict scrutiny standard. The only question was whether it would apply the same standard to programs of the federal government. The distinction between the powers of federal, state, and local agencies to implement racial mandates was dissolved in June 1995 by the Supreme Court's decision in *Adarand Constructors v. Pena and the U.S. Department of Transportation*. The Supreme Court ruled in a 5-to-4 vote that strict scrutiny must be the standard of review for race-based programs of the federal government as well (Greenhouse, 1995). In making this shift, the Court voided all previous rulings that interpreted the equal protection clause of the constitution as having a different application at different levels of government.

By the time the *Croson* decision was rendered, Atlanta had become the focal point for cities interested in implementing affirmative-action programs. By the mid-1980s, Atlanta's program, established in mid-1970, had become the model for most of the nation's municipal affirmative-action programs. Atlanta's leaders viewed *Croson* as a challenge to the achievement of civil rights. As a result, the expense of complying with the decision's strict scrutiny standard was secondary in importance to the need to demonstrate nationally that the strict scrutiny standard could be met and that affirmative action is a legal remedy for past injustices. In 1989, the city of Atlanta commissioned a disparity study supervised by economists Andrew Brimmer and Ray Marshall; it was commissioned at more than $500,000 and completed in 1990. The study covered contracting and procurement in the city of Atlanta and Fulton County.

In an effort to ensure compliance with strict scrutiny standards, state and local governments also began to commission disparity studies. Unfortunately, the Supreme Court's decision left numerous questions unanswered regarding, specifically, what evidence is required to meet strict scrutiny standards; thus, the evidentiary standard is being redefined constantly. Uncertainty about appropriate evidence, along with the absence of a standard measure of cost, led to a situation whereby the very extensive, and expensive Atlanta Disparity Study set the initial methodology, and the market price.

Other public agencies gave in to a classic case of what economist Joseph Stiglitz calls "the dependence of quality on price"—i.e., using price as an indicator of quality. Agencies all over the country used Atlanta as a yardstick. Eventually, state and local governments spent more than $13 million on disparity studies; the Urban Mass Transit Administration spent an additional $14 million between January 1991 and June 1992 (La Noue, 1993). In 1990, 34 disparity studies were commissioned at an average cost of $243,913, according to the Joint Center for Political and Economic Studies. The University of Maryland, Baltimore County, maintains a clearinghouse of disparity studies. In 1996, their inventory consisted of 102 studies conducted in 27 different states and the District of Columbia. La Noue

(1994) found that by the summer of 1994, state and local governments had spent more than $40 million on disparity studies.

Persistent legal challenges forced agencies to add more and more dollars to the disparity-study coffers to patch up weaknesses in existing studies or conduct new ones. For example, nine agencies in the Memphis metropolitan area paid $1.3 million for a disparity study. The cities of Miami and St. Louis spent hundreds of thousands of dollars on disparity studies and were forced to repeat these expenditures because the initial studies did not withstand court challenges.

The difficulty in meeting the standard resides in the fact that the kind of evidence required has not been clarified. Oddly, the Supreme Court imposed the strict scrutiny standard in the *Croson* decision, but did not take the opportunity in the subsequent *Adarand* decision to clarify its specific evidentiary requirements. What is needed is a Judicial Commission to set the guidelines for compiling evidence and to determine which methods are acceptable and which are not. In the meantime, the *Croson* requirement has become practically impossible to meet and as a result federal, state, and local programs are being dismantled.

The vagueness of the guidelines for meeting strict scrutiny and the exorbitant (sometimes extortionist) cost of complying with the *Croson* decision are major impediments to equal treatment. By March 1991, just two years after *Croson*, of the slightly more than 200 programs nationally, 66 had been challenged legally, 33 had been voluntarily terminated, and 65 were under reevaluation. Between 1982 and 1992, cities with affirmative-action plans saw Black businesses increase 65 percent; cities without plans, 61 percent. After *Croson*, between 1987 and 1992, cities with affirmative-action plans saw Black businesses increase 41 percent; cities without plans, 36 percent. Although a 5 percent differential may not be statistically significant, these numbers represent livelihoods. Strict scrutiny is indeed both "strict in theory" and "fatal in fact."

Despite the obstacles, by the late 1980s and early 1990s, a new Black entrepreneurial class had emerged in metropolitan areas across the country. And, despite the growing challenges to minority business programs, local governments and the federal government continued to support these programs and to appropriate funds in an attempt to have them comply with legal guidelines.

POSSIBLE FUTURE TRENDS

At the dawn of a new century, it is a good time to take stock of the economic progress of minority-owned businesses. Another reason to do this is because the economy is experiencing one of the most vigorous and long-lasting periods of growth in peacetime history. The current recovery, which began in 1991, has brought unemployment to its lowest level in a quarter of a century. Equally important is the fact that growth has accelerated, while core inflation, now just 2.2 percent, is the lowest in 32 years.

In general, the economic status of Blacks has improved during this period of growth. In particular, poverty among Blacks is at the lowest level since the government began tracking the figures in 1959. In 1998, the average household income of Blacks increased by 3.6 percent, while the income of Whites increased by 2.2 percent. But these general improvements hide the fact that there are still large employment and income disparities between Blacks and Whites. Even though average household income among Blacks improved, it is still only 63 percent that of Whites. Even though the poverty rate among Blacks might be the lowest on record, 30 percent of Black families still live below the poverty line. And while the rate of unemployment among Whites is 3.7 percent, it is 9.2 percent for Blacks. Twenty years ago, Blacks comprised 20 percent of all unemployed workers; that percentage has not changed, even though Blacks now constitute only 11.2 percent of the labor force. In fact, racial disparities have not changed significantly over the last 20 years.

The current economic expansion forces the government to face a rather unsettling reality: the economy is now posting its best performance in peacetime history, yet large racial disparities in income and employment still remain; thus economic growth is necessary but not sufficient to reduce these disparities.

Between 1982 and 1992, the number of Black-owned businesses grew at a rate of 7.25 percent annually, and their employment capacity grew at a rate of 11.02 percent annually. If the current growth rate is maintained between 1992 and 2010, there will be about 2 million Black-owned firms. Likewise, if employment in these firms continues to grow at 11.02 percent annually, these firms will employ approximately 2.3 million workers by 2010. That will be equivalent to 12.1 percent of the projected 2010 Black workforce. Now, if we add subchapter regular corporations, the total employment capacity of Black firms will be even greater. If current trends hold, approximately 80 percent, or 2.5 million, of the new jobs Black firms create will go to Blacks. This trend, if sustained through the first decade of the next century, has important implications for Black unemployment and upward mobility. It will be useful to check the validity of this theory by examining the 1997 census of Black-owned business data when they are released around the year 2000.

If these trends are valid, promoting the growth of Black-owned businesses means reducing society's unemployment burden, providing jobs where they are most needed, and improving the income status of people who are too often trapped below the poverty line.

Assisting Blacks in creating employment opportunities through supporting business development initiatives is a fundamental strategy for the new century. The changes currently taking place among these businesses are significant, and the possibility of reducing racial disparities through promoting their continued growth is promising. Past policies, centering on promoting general economic growth with the assumption that employment growth will "trickle down" to Blacks, have reduced Black unemployment in terms of absolute numbers but failed to narrow the racial income and employment gap. Promoting Black-owned businesses has the potential to succeed where other policies have failed. Not only do such policies help remedy past injustices, but they also make good sense, economically and socially.

IMPORTANT QUESTIONS FUTURE RESEARCH MUST ANSWER

The U.S. Supreme Court has not disallowed the use of race-based remedies to redress identified discrimination, though it has made it exceedingly difficult to do so. Nevertheless, the possibility still exists. Objective research is needed to establish the criteria and the methodology for meeting the strict scrutiny standard.

From a practical standpoint, many successful minority-owned businesses are dependent on government programs. In the short run, gaining equal access to government contracting and subcontracting in the absence of such programs, or replacing this revenue source, will be difficult. As such, the decrease of affirmative action is likely to have some significant adverse consequences on a rather large sector of minority-owned businesses. It is, therefore, important for researchers to measure the magnitude of this impact and estimate the costs and benefits of alternative strategies for minority business development.

The current growth trend of Black-owned businesses, projected to the year 2010, has some significant employment implications. Research is needed to examine this trend more rigorously.

Black-owned businesses are growing at twice the rate of all small businesses, but some are experiencing limits to their continued growth as a result of their more limited access to equity and debt capital. Many of these business owners are now willing to give up equity for growth, but potential investors are not convinced that there is adequate capacity and profitable outlets for investments in Black-owned businesses. Researchers can facilitate this process through publishing and disseminating findings that accurately document the state of Black-owned businesses.

Disposable income of Black households is approaching $0.5 trillion. In addition, Blacks comprise a significant percentage of some major urban markets and are trendsetters in other industries such as specialty clothing, sports, and entertainment. Thus research regarding the income, spending, and demographic patterns of minorities is worth further consideration. Such research will aid in the identification of business opportunities and serve the unmet needs of minority households and is worthy of a university research center for minority business strategies and dynamics.

REFERENCES

Aldrich, H., and R. Waldinger
    1990   Ethnicity and entrepreneurship. *Annual Review of Sociology* 16:111-135.
Alexander, T., Sr.
    1992   *Beyond the Timber Line: The Trials and Triumphs of a Black Entrepreneur.* Edgewood, Md.: M. Duncan.
Bates, T.
    1987   Self-employed minorities: Traits and trends. *Social Science Quarterly* 68(3):539-551.
    1990   The characteristics of business owners database. *Journal of Human Resources* 25(4): 752-756.
    1991   *Major Studies of Minority Business: A Bibliographic Review.* Washington, D.C.: Joint Center for Political and Economic Studies.
    1997   *Race, Self-Employment and Upward Mobility: An Illusive American Dream.* Baltimore: The Johns Hopkins University Press.
Borjas, G., and S. Bronars
    1989   Consumer discrimination and self-employment. *Journal of Political Economy* 97(3): 581-605.
Boston, T.
    1995   Characteristics of Black-owned corporations in Atlanta: With comments on the SMOBE undercount. *Review of Black Political Economy* 23(4):85-99.
    1996   Five-year review of the equal opportunity program of the City of Atlanta. Report to the Atlanta City Government (September). Unpublished report.
    1998   *Affirmative Action and Black Entrepreneurship.* New York: Routledge.
Clayton, E.
    1996   Statement of Congresswoman Eva Clayton before the U.S. House of Representatives. Committee on Small Business, Hearing on H.R. 3994, The Entrepreneur Development Act of 1996. Appendix, pp. 73-77.
Coleman, L., and S. Cook
    1976   The Failures of Minority Capitalism: The Edapco Case. *Phylon* 37(1):44-58.
Dixon, D.
    1990   The dismantling of affirmative action programs: Evaluating *City of Richmond v. J.A. Croson Co. Journal of Human Rights* VII:35-57.
Evans, D., and L. Leighton
    1989   Some empirical aspects of entrepreneurship. *The American Economic Review* 79(3): 519-535.
Farlie, R., and B. Meyer
    1996   Ethnic and racial self-employment differences and possible explanations. *The Journal of Human Resources* xxxi(4):757-793.

Greenhouse, L.
    1995   By 5-4 justices cast doubt on U.S. programs that give preferences based on race. *New York Times* (Dec. 6):1, 21.
La Noue, G.
    1993   Social science and minority set-asides. *The Public Interest* 111:49-62.
    1994   Standards for the second generation of *Croson*-inspired disparity studies. *The Urban Lawyer* 26(3):485-540.
Minority Business Enterprise Legal Defense and Education Fund
    1988   *Report on the Minority Business Enterprise Programs of State and Local Governments.* Unpublished report.
National Cooperative Highway Research Program
    1992   Minority and disadvantaged business enterprise requirements in public contracting. *Legal Research Digest* 25(September):1-28.
Nucci, A.
    1992   The characteristics of business owners database. Discussion paper, Center for Economic Studies, U.S. Bureau of the Census. CES 92-7.
Rice, M.
    1991   Government set-asides, minority business enterprises, and the Supreme Court. *Public Administration Review* 51(2):114-122.
Stoelting, D.
    1990   Minority business set-asides must be supported by specific evidence of prior discrimination. *Cincinnati Law Review* 58:1097-1135.
U.S. Bureau of the Census
    1985   *Survey of Minority-Owned Business Enterprises: Black, 1982, MB82-1.* Washington, D.C.: U.S. Government Printing Office.
    1990   *Survey of Minority-Owned Business Enterprises: Black, 1987 (SMOBE) MB87-1.* Washington, D.C.: U.S. Government Printing Office.
    1991   *Characteristics of Business Owners, 1987, CBO87-1.* Washington, D.C.: U.S. Government Printing Office.
    1996   *Survey of Minority-Owned Business Enterprises: Black, 1992, MB 92-1.* Washington, D.C.: U.S. Government Printing Office.
    1997   *Characteristics of Business Owners, 1992, CBO92-1.* Washington, D.C.: U.S. Government Printing Office.
Walker, M., Jr.
    1986   The SBA 8(a) programs, minority set-asides, and minority business development. Paper prepared for Race, Values and American Legal Process, April 11, Georgia State University, pp.1-78.

10

Wealth and Racial Stratification

Melvin L. Oliver and Thomas M. Shapiro

*I*ncome is what the average American family uses to reproduce daily existence in the form of shelter, food, clothing, and other necessities. In contrast, *wealth* is a storehouse of resources, it's what families own and use to produce income. Wealth signifies a control of financial resources that, when combined with income, provides the means and the opportunity to secure the "good life" in whatever form is needed—education, business, training, justice, health, material comfort, and so on. In this sense, wealth is a special form of money not usually used to purchase milk and shoes or other life necessities; rather it is used to create opportunities, secure a desired stature and standard of living, and pass class status along to one's children.

Wealth has been a neglected dimension of social science's concern with the economic and social status of Americans in general and racial minorities in particular. Social scientists have been much more comfortable describing and analyzing occupational, educational, and income distributions than examining the economic bedrock of a capitalist society—"private property." During the past decade, sociologists and economists have begun to pay more attention to the issue of wealth. The growing concentration of wealth at the top, and the growing racial wealth gap, have become important public-policy issues that undergird many political debates but, unfortunately, not many policy discussions. Our work takes up this challenge. This paper begins with a summary of the social science findings on race and wealth. The data are strongest regarding

Black-White differences, but reference is made to findings and data that refer to Hispanics, Asians, and American Indians as well.

This paper focuses on three key contributions. First, an indispensable contribution to the current understanding of racial stratification is an examination of wealth, distinct from labor-market indicators, which this paper offers. Second, the paper makes an evidentiary contribution to the theory that current racial trends in inequality result, to a significant extent, from past racial policies and practices; and that the racial inequality of today, if left unattended, will contribute to continued racial stratification for the next generation. Third, by looking at new evidence concerning wealth and racial stratification, this paper contributes an impetus to push forward the research and policy agenda concerned with America's racial wealth gap. Thus, a wealth perspective provides a fresh way to examine the "playing field." Consequently, a standard part of the American credo—that similar accomplishments result in roughly equal rewards—may need reexamination.

RACIAL STRATIFICATION AND THE ASSET PERSPECTIVE

Understanding racial inequality, with respect to the distribution of power, economic resources, and life chances, is a prime concern of the social sciences. Most empirical research on racial inequality has focused on the economic dimension, which is not surprising considering the centrality of this component for life chances and well-being in an industrial society. The concerted emphasis of this economic component has been labor-market processes and their outcomes, especially earnings, occupational prestige, and social mobility. Until recently, the social sciences and the policy arena neglected wealth, intergenerational transfers, and policy processes that result in differential life chances based on racial criteria. Our ongoing work attempts to redress this severe imbalance.

The data and the social science understanding are strongest for income inequality in relation to race. For most, income is a quintessential labor-market outcome indicator. It refers to a flow of resources over time, representing the value of labor in the contemporary labor market and the value of social assistance and pensions. As such, income is a tidy and valuable gauge of the state of present economic inequality. Indeed, a strong case can be made that reducing racial discrimination in the labor market has resulted in increasing the income of racial minorities and, thus, narrowing the hourly wage gap between minorities and Whites. The command of resources that wealth entails, however, is more encompassing than income or education, and closer in meaning and theoretical significance to the traditional connotation of economic well-being and access

to life chances as depicted in the classic conceptualizations of Marx, Weber, Simmel, and Tawney.[1]

As important is the fact that wealth taps not only contemporary resources, but also material assets that have historic origins and future implications. Private wealth thus captures inequality that is the product of the past, often passed down from generation to generation. Conceptualizing racial inequality through wealth revolutionizes the concept of the nature and magnitude of inequality, and of whether it is decreasing or increasing. Although most recent analyses have concluded that contemporary class-based factors are most important in understanding the sources of continuing racial inequality, a focus on wealth sheds light on both the historical and the contemporary impacts not only of class but also of race. Income is an important indicator of racial inequality; wealth allows an examination of racial stratification.

A wealth perspective contends that continued neglect of wealth as a dimension of racial stratification will result in a seriously underestimated racial inequality. Tragically, policies based solely on narrow differences in labor-market factors will fail to close that breach. Taken together, however, asset-building and labor-market approaches open new windows of opportunity.

HISTORICAL TRENDS AND CONTEXT OF WEALTH DISTRIBUTION IN THE UNITED STATES

Wealth inequality is today, and always has been, more extreme than income inequality. Wealth inequality is more lopsided in the United States than in Europe. Recent trends in asset ownership do not alleviate inequality concerns or issues. In general, inequality in asset ownership in the United States between the bottom and top of the distribution domain has been growing. Wealth inequality was at a 60-year high in 1989, with the top 1 percent of U.S. citizens controlling 39 percent of total U.S. household wealth. The richest 1 percent owned 48 percent of the total. These themes have been amply described in the work of Wolff (1994, 1996a, 1996b). Household wealth inequality increased sharply between 1983 and 1989. There was a modest attenuation in 1992, but the level of wealth concentration was still greater in 1992 than in 1983.

Until recently, few analyses looked at racial differences in wealth

---

[1]See Marx, K., and F. Engels, 1947, *The German Ideology*, New York: International Publishers; Weber, M., 1958, *The Protestant Ethic and the Spirit of Capitalism*, New York: Scribner's; Simmel, G., 1990, *The Philosophy of Money*, London: Routledge; Tawny, R.H., 1952, *Equality*, London: Allen and Unwin.

holding. Recent work, however, suggests that inequality is as pronounced—or more pronounced—between racial and ethnic groups in the
dimension of wealth than income. The case of Blacks is paradigmatic of
this inequality. Eller and Fraser (1995) report that Blacks had only 9.7
percent of the median net worth (all assets minus liabilities) of Whites in
1993 ($4,418 compared to $45,740); in contrast, their comparable figure for
median family income was 62 percent of White income. Using 1988 data
from the same source, Oliver and Shapiro (1995a) established that these
differences are not the result of social-class factors. Even among the Black
middle class, levels of net worth and net financial assets (all assets minus
liabilities excluding home and vehicle equity) are drastically lower than
for Whites. The comparable ratio of net worth for college-educated Blacks
is only 0.24; even for two-income Black couples, the ratio is just 0.37.
Clearly there are factors other than what we understand as "class" that
led to these low levels of asset accumulation.

   Black Wealth/White Wealth (Oliver and Shapiro, 1995a) decomposed
the results of a regression analysis to give Blacks and Whites the same
level of income, human capital, demographic, family, and other characteristics. The rationale for this was to examine the extent to which the
huge racial wealth gap was a product of other differences between Whites
and Blacks. Given the skewness of the wealth distribution, researchers
agree that median figures best represent a typical American family; however, it should be noted, that regressions conventionally use means. A
potent $43,143 difference in mean net worth remains, with 71 percent of
the difference left unexplained. Only about 25 percent of the difference in
net financial assets is explained. Taking the average Black household and
endowing it with the same income, age, occupational, educational, and
other attributes as the average White household still leaves a $25,794
racial gap in mean net financial assets. These residual gaps should not be
cast wholly to racial dynamics; nonetheless, the regression analyses offer
a powerful argument to directly link race in the American experience to
the wealth-creation process.

   As important is the finding that more than two-thirds of Blacks have
no net financial assets, compared to less than one-third of Whites. This
near absence of assets has extreme consequences for the economic and
social well-being of the Black community, and of the ability of families to
plan for future social mobility. If the average Black household were to
lose an income stream, the family would not be able to support itself
without access to public support. At their current levels of net financial
assets, nearly 80 percent of Black families would not be able to survive at
poverty-level consumption for three months. Comparable figures for
Whites—although large in their own right—are one-half that of Blacks.
Thinking about the social welfare of children, these figures take on more

urgency. Nine out of ten Black children live in households that have less than three months of poverty-level net financial assets; nearly two-thirds live in households with zero or negative net financial assets (Oliver and Shapiro, 1989, 1990, 1995a, 1995b).

Because home ownership plays such a large role in the wealth portfolios of American families, it is a prime source of the differences between Black and White net worth. Home ownership rates for Blacks are 20 percent lower than rates for Whites; hence, Blacks possess less of this important source of equity. Discrimination in the process of securing home ownership plays a significant role in how assets are generated and accumulated. The reality of residential segregation also plays an important role in the way home ownership figures in the wealth portfolio of Blacks. Because Blacks live, for the most part, in segregated areas, the value of their homes is less, demand for them is less, and thus their equity is less (Oliver and Shapiro, 1995b; Massey and Denton, 1994). (Because the area of home ownership is so central to the wealth accumulation process, the most current data will be analyzed in a later section of this paper.)

Similar findings on gross differences between Hispanics and Whites also have been uncovered (Eller and Fraser, 1995; Flippen and Tienda, 1997; O'Toole, 1998; Grant, 2000). Hispanics have slightly higher, but not statistically different, net worth figures than Blacks, based on the 1993 Survey of Income and Program Participation (SIPP); however, these findings are not sufficiently nuanced to capture the diversity of the Hispanic population. Data from the Los Angeles Survey of Urban Inequality show substantial differences in assets and net financial assets between recent immigrants who are primarily from Mexico and Central America and U.S.-born Hispanics (Grant, 2000).

Likewise, place of birth and regional differences among Hispanic groups also complicate a straightforward interpretation of this national-level finding. For example, Cuban Americans, we would hypothesize, have net worth figures comparable to Whites because of their dominance in an ethnic economy in which they own small and medium-sized businesses (Portes and Rumbaut, 1990). They have a far different set of economic life chances than Blacks and other recent Hispanic immigrants by way of their more significant wealth accumulation. For recent Hispanic immigrants, these figures suggest real vulnerability for the economic security of their households and children.

Finally, it is important to point out findings by Flippen and Tienda (1997) that attempt to explain the Black-White and Hispanic-White gap in wealth. Substituting White means for all the variables in a complex Tobit model, Flippen and Tienda found that the model "reduces asset inequality more for Hispanics than for Blacks." This is particularly the case for housing equity; for Hispanics, mean substitution reduced the gap by 80 percent, compared to only 62 percent for Blacks. As Flippen and Tienda note, "This suggests the importance of residential segregation and discrimination in the housing and lending market in hindering the accumulation of housing assets for Black households" (1997:18). Although their findings for Hispanics may be true for "White Hispanics," they may not apply to Black Puerto Ricans, who share social space with non-Hispanic Blacks and, therefore, may also be targeted for institutionalized racism in housing markets and financial institutions. Preliminary data from the Greater Boston Social Survey suggest that Hispanics in that region, the majority of whom are Puerto Rican, have even lower levels of net worth and financial assets than Blacks (O'Toole, 1998).

The case of Asians is quite similar to that for Hispanics, in that it is necessary to be mindful of their diversity, in terms of both national origin and immigrant status. Changes in immigration rules have favored those who bring assets into the country over those without assets; as a consequence, recent immigrants, from Korea, for example, are primarily individuals and families with assets, and once they arrive, they convert these assets into other asset-producing activities—e.g., small businesses. Bates' (1998) analysis of SIPP points out that Koreans who started businesses had significant assets and were able to use those assets to secure loans for business startups. Data from Los Angeles again underscore the importance of immigrant status and place of birth. U.S.-born Asians have both net worth and net financial assets approaching those of White Los Angelenos; foreign-born Asians, however, report lower wealth than U.S.-born Asians but higher wealth than all other ethnic and racial groups (Grant, 2000).

American Indians form a unique case when it comes to assets. They are asset rich but control little of these assets. Most Indian assets are held in tribal or individual Indian trust (Office of Trust Responsibilities, 1995). Thus, any accounting of the assets of individual Indian households is nearly impossible to calculate, given their small population and these "hidden" assets.

The dearth of studies of wealth in the United States has hampered efforts to develop both wealth theory and information. For more than 100 years, the prime sources concerning wealth status came from estate tax records, biographies of the super rich, various listings of the wealthiest, and like sources. In other words, something was known about those who possessed abundant amounts of wealth, but virtually nothing was known about the wealth status of average American families. During the 1980s, several data sources were developed based on field surveys of the American population. Most notable are SIPP, the Panel Study of Income Dynamics (PSID), the Federal Reserve Board's Survey of Consumer Finances (SCF), and the Health and Retirement Study (HRS). Thus, it is only relatively recently that any data at all were available to characterize the asset well-being of American families.

RACE, INCOME, AND WEALTH

The empirical presentation begins with a fundamental examination of the most current income and wealth data for Whites, Blacks, Hispanics, and Asians. The data displayed in Table 10-1 are taken from the 1993 SIPP, Wave 7. Drawing attention first to income comparisons, the household income ratio of Blacks, compared to Whites, is 0.61:1, and the Hispanic ratio, 0.67:1. Asians fare considerably better in this comparison, earning close to 125 percent of White income. (It is important, here, to mind the caution from the literature review: the Hispanic and Asian data are aggregated, subsuming important dimensions of country of origin and immigrant status.) These income comparisons closely match other national data and provide an effective indicator of current racial and ethnic material inequality. Changing the lens of analysis to wealth dramatically shifts the perspective. Black families possess only 14 cents for every dollar of wealth (median net worth) held by White families. The issue is no longer how to think about closing the gap from 0.61 but how to think about going from 14 cents on the dollar to something approaching parity. Nearly half of all Black families do not possess any net financial assets, compared to $7,400 for the average White family. These figures represent some asset accumulation for both Whites and Blacks between 1988 and 1994; nonetheless, the wealth perspective reveals an economic fragility for the entire American population, as it demonstrates the continuing racial wealth gap.

TABLE 10-1 Income, Wealth, Race, and Ethnicity: 1994

	Median Income	Median NW[a]	Mean NW	Median NFA[b]	Mean NFA
White	$33,600	$52,944	$109,511	$7,400	$56,199
Black	$20,508	$6,127	$28,643	$100	$7,611
Ratio to White	0.61	0.12	0.26	0.01	0.14
Hispanic	$22,644	$6,723	$40,033	$300	$15,709
Ratio to White	0.67	0.13	0.37	0.03	0.27
Asian	$40,998	$39,846	$117,916	$4,898	$57,782
Ratio to White	1.22	0.67	1.02	0.51	0.98

[a]Net worth
[b]Net financial assets.

SOURCE: 1993 SIPP, Wave 7.

The data for Hispanics resemble the Black-White comparisons in one important respect and diverge in another. The median figures for both net worth and net financial assets reveal similar gaps in comparison with Whites, but the mean figures for net worth and net financial assets bump Hispanics "ahead" of Blacks. This apparent peculiarity most likely illustrates differences in experiences, country of origin, and immigrant status referred to earlier.

Mindful that the Asian data also are grouped, the figures for Asian wealth show an even more exaggerated pattern. The median-wealth figures indicate that Asians possess about three-quarters of the net worth and two-thirds of the net financial assets that Whites own. Commentators could seize on this piece of the story, noting that Asian family income is greater than Whites', and wonder why the wealth gap exists. An examination of mean wealth figures proves this exercise unnecessary—indeed, the data indicate parity in wealth between White and Asian families. Like the Hispanic data, but to an even greater extent, the Asian aggregate data mask different historical immigrant experiences, country of origin, and immigration status. The divergence between median and mean figures also most likely indicates that a sizable portion of the Asian community is relatively well off alongside a sizable portion of the community whose asset resources are far less than the average White family's. In other words, in parts of the Asian community, the wealth resources more closely resemble Black and Hispanic wealth profiles, while some segments of the Asian community virtually mirror the White profile.

These data provide a baseline of information regarding racial and ethnic differences in income and wealth resources. Not only do they update previous analyses in a simple way, they also bolster the previous findings. More important, the wealth data consistently indicate a far greater chasm in and pattern of racial and ethnic inequality than when income alone is examined.

INCOME AND WEALTH

A starting point for building on the basic analysis is a further examination of the connection between income and wealth. One leading economic perspective contends that the racial wealth gap predominantly results from income inequality. Do differences in income explain nearly all the racial differences in wealth? If so, then policies need to continue a primarily labor-market orientation that further narrows income inequality. If not, however, then social policy must address dynamics outside the labor market as well as income-generating, labor-market dynamics. Thus, it is critically important to address whether the wealth of Blacks is similar to Whites with similar incomes.

The strong income-wealth relationship is recognized in previous analysis of the 1984 SIPP data. *Black Wealth/White Wealth* (Oliver and Shapiro, 1995a) identified income as a significant variable determining wealth accumulation, next only to age in the wealth regressions. Looking at wealth by income ranges, however, showed that a powerful racial wealth gap remained. A regression analysis similarly indicated a highly significant differential wealth return to Whites and Blacks from income. The idea that wealth is quite similar when controlling for income, nonetheless, still holds some currency; so a direct empirical examination that uses the most recently available data should provide some evidence of, and resolution of, this issue. An empirical examination can be done in two ways.

The first way to address this issue can be demonstrated by using the data in Table 10-2, which show median measured net worth and net financial assets by income quintile, race, and Hispanic origin. White households in every income quintile had significantly higher levels of median wealth than Black and Hispanic households in the same income quintiles. In the lowest quintile, the median net worth for White households was $17,066, while that of Black and Hispanic households was $2,500 and $1,298, respectively. For the highest quintile households, median net worth for White households was $133,607; significantly lower was the median for Black households, $43,806. The median net financial assets data are just as revealing. At the middle quintile, for example, the median net financial assets for White households were $6,800, which was markedly higher than for Black ($800) and Hispanic ($1,000) households.

It is important to observe that controlling for income in this manner does, indeed, significantly lessen the Black-White/Hispanic-White wealth ratios. The overall median Black-White net worth ratio was 0.14:1, but this narrows when comparing White and Black households in similar income quintiles. The gap, as expressed in ratios, stays about the same for the two lowest income quintiles but narrows to 0.3:1, 0.45:1, and 0.33:1 for the next three income quintiles. In brief, as shown by this comparative procedure, controlling for income narrows the gap; but a significantly large gap persists, even when incomes are roughly equal. This evidence does not support the proposition that Whites and Blacks at similar income levels possess similar wealth.

Another way to address the income and wealth connection is to examine wealth at precisely similar income points for Whites and Blacks. Net worth for Whites and Blacks is examined first at distribution percentiles—i.e., leaving income uncontrolled. Figures 10-1 and 10-2, drawn from 1994 SIPP data, show that median White wealth totaled $7,671 and Black wealth totaled $0 at the 25th percentile of each distribution. At the 50th percentile, White net worth was $52,944, compared with $6,126 for Blacks.

TABLE 10-2 Wealth by Race and Hispanic Origin and Income Quintiles: 1994

	Total		White		Black		Hispanic	
	NW[a]	NFA[b]	NW	NFA	NW	NFA	NW	NFA
All households								
Median	$40,172		$52,944	$7,400	$7,400	$100	$6,723	$ 300
Ratio to white:					0.14		0.13	
Lowest income quintile								
Median	8,032	185	17,066	551	2,500		1,298	0
Ratio to white:					0.15	0.07	0.08	0
Second income quintile								
Median	27,638	1,848	39,908	3,599	6,879	249	5,250	250
Ratio to white:					0.17	0.07	0.13	0.07
Third income quintile								
Median	40,665	4,599	50,350	6,800	14,902	800	12,555	1,000
Ratio to white:					0.30	0.12	0.25	0.15
Fourth income quintile								
Median	59,599	10,339	65,998	13,362	29,851	2,699	26,328	2,125
Ratio to white:					0.45	0.20	0.4	0.16
Highest income quintile								
Median	126,923	36,851	133,607	40,465	43,806	7,448	91,102	11,485
Ratio to white:					0.33	0.18	0.68	0.28

[a]Net worth.
[b]Net financial assets.

SOURCE: 1993 SIPP, Wave 7.

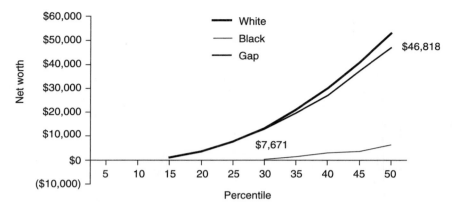

FIGURE 10-1 Wealth gap in 1994 with no control of income: $0-$60,000.
SOURCE: 1993 SIPP, Wave 7.

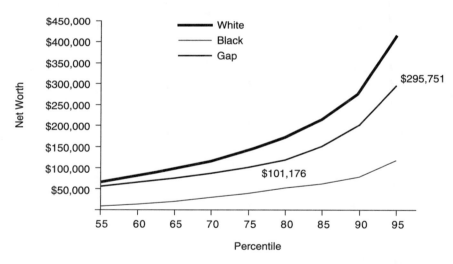

FIGURE 10-2 Wealth gap in 1994 with no control of income: $0-$450,000.
SOURCE: 1993 SIPP, Wave 7.

At the 75th percentile, White net worth was $141,491 versus $40,315 for
Blacks. How much of this gap is closed by controlling for income? Will
Black-White wealth become actually quite similar, or will substantial, dramatic racial wealth inequality persist? At stake here is a test of two con-
tending claims—(1) wealth inequality fundamentally derives from income

inequality versus (2) wealth inequality derives from accumulations within historically and racially structured contexts. The claim is that Black wealth would be near parity with Whites' if incomes were equal; therefore, the logic is to compare net worth while controlling for income. Calibrating the White-to-Black income distributions means, for example, comparing the 25th percentile of the White wealth data to the 45th percentile of the Black distribution, the 50th White to the 70th Black, and the 75th White to the 88th Black.

Figures 10-3 and 10-4 graph this income-wealth relationship. A summary that captures some major data points should guide any interpretation. At the 25th percentile for Whites, median net worth is $7,671; controlling for income, the Black net worth adjusts upward to $3,548. At the 50th percentile for Whites, net worth is $52,944, compared to $30,000 for Blacks earning equivalent incomes. At the 75th percentile for Whites, wealth stands at $141,491 versus $72,761 for Blacks.

At the 50th percentile, then, the original uncontrolled gap weighs in at $46,817 with a ratio of 0.12:1. Controlling for income reduces this gap to $22,944. The Black/White wealth ratio closes as well to 0.57. Let us be clear: controlling for income significantly reduces the wealth gap; at the same time, however, even if incomes are equal, a consequential racial wealth gap remains. Indeed, after controlling for income, it is prudent to note that the remaining wealth gap is about as large as the racial income inequality gap. So if this exercise is correct, something akin to the original racial income gap remains unexplained after equalizing incomes.

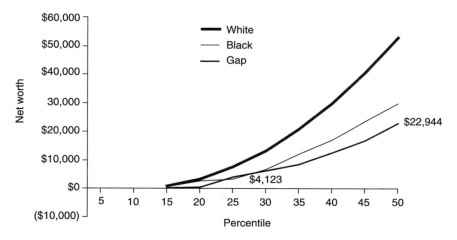

FIGURE 10-3 Wealth gap in 1994 controlled for income: $0-$60,000. SOURCE: 1993 SIPP, Wave 7.

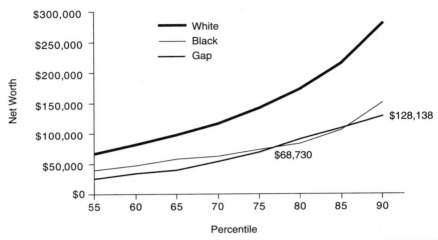

FIGURE 10-4 Wealth gap in 1994 controlled for income: $0-$300,000. SOURCE: 1993 SIPP, Wave 7.

RACIAL STRATIFICATION BY AGE COHORTS

The social science analysis of wealth is still, at this point, in its beginning stages. Particularly hampering progress, thus far, is the general lack of longitudinal analysis, which is critically important in examining the dynamics of family wealth accumulation over time. We know, for example, that Blacks start far behind Whites in accumulation of asset resources, but does this gap close or widen throughout the life course? Does it reflect the pattern of income, or does it provide evidence of a social process that is more independent of income and savings? We know from cross-sectional analyses, for example, that the racial wealth gap is increasing; but we do not yet know what is happening for the same cohort of families over long periods of time. PSID allows for longitudinal tracking of a family's economic resources across the life course; however, PSID has only been collecting detailed data on family asset and liabilities since 1984. Every five years this information is brought up to date; 1994 is the latest year these data were gathered. Thus, PSID opens a 10-year longitudinal window for tracking family asset resources.

Following family income and wealth by age cohorts from 1984 to 1994 produces some engaging results. As shown in Table 10-3, the Black-White income gap increases for the two younger age cohorts and decreases for the two older ones. Among Whites, retirement from the labor force, and the resulting decrease in income, is a likely contributor to the sizeable gap decrease during the last five-year period in the oldest cohorts. For all

TABLE 10-3   Income Gap and Age Cohorts

	Income Gap (adjusted, 1994 = 100)		
Age cohort 1			
20-29 in 1984	$14,468	base	
25-34 in 1989	$21,072	increase	$6,604
30-39 in 1994	$18,850	decrease	($2,222)
1984-1994 gap		increase	$4,382
Age cohort 2			
30-39 in 1984	$20,253	base	
35-44 in 1989	$24,131	increase	$3,878
40-49 in 1994	$21,207	decrease	($2,924)
1984-1994 gap		increase	$954
Age cohort 3			
40-49 in 1984	$21,634	base	
45-54 in 1989	$30,692	increase	$9,058
50-59 in 1994	$20,433	decrease	($10,259)
1984-1994 gap		decrease	($1,201)
Age cohort 4			
50-59 in 1984	$25,894	base	
55-64 in 1989	$24,202	decrease	($1,692)
60-69 in 1994	$13,129	decrease	($11,073)
1984-1994 gap		decrease	($12,765)

SOURCE: PSID.

cohorts, the income gap narrowed between 1989 and 1994. If the oldest cohort is excluded, the changes are quite moderate and no distinguishable pattern emerges. The income gap for the youngest age cohort, those 20 to 29 years old in 1984, widens by $4,382, starting at a base inequality of $14,468 and increasing to $18,850 by the time they reach 30 to 39 years old. The racial income gap increased slightly, $954, for the next oldest cohort; and the gap decreased by $1,201 for the next cohort. The income action is hardly startling.

The racial wealth gap is another story. In Table 10-4, the racial wealth gap increases at every marker for all age cohorts; and it does so systematically and spectacularly. The net worth gap for the youngest age cohort begins at $8,733 and increases $23,926 in the 10-year period. Among those age 40 to 49 in 1984, the base net worth wealth gap is a hefty $70,290 and increases to $107,000 in just 10 years. In the 10-year period, then, the income gap for this age cohort actually narrows by $1,201, although the wealth gap widens by more than $36,710. The decrease in the income gap

TABLE 10-4 Net Worth Gap and Age Cohorts

	Net Worth Gap (adjusted 1994 = 100)		
Age cohort 1			
20-29 in 1984	$8,733	base	
25-34 in 1989	$18,585	increase	$9,852
30-39 in 1994	$31,900	increase	$13,315
1984-1994 gap		increase	$23,167
Age cohort 2			
30-39 in 1984	$42,174	base	
35-44 in 1989	$61,095	increase	$18,921
40-49 in 1994	$63,360	increase	$2,265
1984-1994 gap		increase	$21,186
Age cohort 3			
40-49 in 1984	$70,290	base	
45-54 in 1989	$78,677	increase	$8,387
50-59 in 1994	$107,000	increase	$28,323
1984-1994 gap		increase	$36,710
Age cohort 4			
50-59 in 1984	$100,501	base	
55-64 in 1989	$127,381	increase	$26,880
60-69 in 1994	$126,005	decrease	($1,376)
1984-1994 gap		increase	$25,504

SOURCE: PSID.

is notable in its own right, but the magnitude of the increasing wealth gap is cause for concern.

The net financial assets data in Table 10-5 are just as revealing; they show the financial asset gap increasing at least twofold for three of the age cohorts. The gap for the oldest age cohort increases "only" by $17,532 between 1984 and 1994. For the younger cohorts, the irony is that in absolute terms the Black wealth data reveal steady but modest improvement in absolute life chances against a background of dramatically ratcheted-up Black-White wealth inequality. In this sense, life chances improve modestly, while inequality grows rapidly. A notable exception in even the humble improvement in life chances is seen in decreasing liquid assets for the oldest Black cohort. In sum, tracking resource data by age cohorts across a 10-year window provides more empirical evidence that important parts of the wealth-accumulation process are not governed by income dynamics. As White and Black families traverse the American life course, the differential opportunities afforded by increasingly dispar-

TABLE 10-5 Net Financial Assets and Age Cohorts

	Net Financial Assets (adjusted, 1994 = 100)		
Age cohort 1			
20-29 in 1984	$6,068	base	
25-34 in 1989	$9,556	increase	$3,488
30-39 in 1994	$14,000	increase	$4,444
1984-1994 gap		increase	$7,932
Age cohort 2			
30-39 in 1984	$13,064	base	
35-44 in 1989	$23,895	increase	$10,831
40-49 in 1994	$29,750	increase	$5,855
1984-1994 gap		increase	$16,686
Age cohort 3			
40-49 in 1984	$25,205	base	
45-54 in 1989	$41,890	increase	$16,685
50-59 in 1994	$58,000	increase	$16,110
1984-1994 gap		increase	$32,795
Age cohort 4			
50-59 in 1984	$39,618	base	
55-64 in 1989	$61,522	increase	$21,904
60-69 in 1994	$57,150	decrease	($4,372)
1984-1994 gap		increase	$17,532

SOURCE: PSID.

ate financial resources continue to compound racial inequality. This process is a good illustration of the sedimentation of inequality.

UNDERSTANDING THE TRENDS

A review of the literature, and the findings thus far, point to several important considerations. First, racial differences are important in terms of wealth. In the case of Blacks, for whom there is the most clear-cut data, it is obvious that racial factors are implicit in these findings. Second, national origin and immigration status may explain a great deal of the differences among Hispanic and Asian groups; but this is a key area of research that needs to be explored further. Third, American Indians pose a different set of challenges for understanding wealth accumulation because the Indian community has significant wealth in terms of land and assets, but those assets are under federal government control. The public policies needed to address economic inequality for American Indians would require a legal solution.

The analytical power derived from examining racial stratification through the lens of wealth is most obvious in the case of Blacks. How do we explain the sources of the enormous racial wealth disparity? By focusing on a sociology of wealth that situates the social context in which wealth generation occurs, it is clear that a significant part of this difference is explained by the unique and diverse social circumstances that Blacks and Whites face. Blacks and Whites face different structures of investment opportunity, which have been affected historically and contemporaneously by both class and race. Three concepts can be used to provide a sociologically grounded approach to understanding racial differences in wealth accumulation. These concepts highlight the ways in which this opportunity structure has disadvantaged Blacks and helped contribute to massive wealth inequalities between the races in America.

The first concept, "racialization of state policy," refers to how state policy has impaired the ability of many Blacks to accumulate wealth—and discouraged them from doing so—from the beginning of slavery throughout American history. From the first codified decision to enslave Blacks, to the local ordinances that barred Blacks from certain occupations, to the welfare-state policies of the recent past that discouraged wealth accumulation, the state has erected major barriers to Black economic self-sufficiency. In particular, state policy has structured the context within which it has been possible to acquire land, build community, and generate wealth. Historically, policies and actions of the U.S. government have promoted homesteading (Oubre, 1978), land acquisition, home ownership (Jackson, 1985), retirement, pensions (Quadagno, 1994), education (National Research Council, 1989), and asset accumulation (Oliver and Shapiro, 1995a; Sherraden, 1991) for some sectors of the population and not for others. Poor people—Blacks in particular—generally have been excluded from participation in state-sponsored opportunities. In this way, the distinctive relationship between Whites and Blacks has been woven into the fabric of state actions. The modern welfare state has racialized citizenship, social organization, and economic status, while consigning Blacks to a relentlessly impoverished and subordinated position within it (Mink, 1990).

One of the key policies of the federal government that encourages home ownership is the deductibility of mortgage interest on homes (a companion is the deferral of capital gains on the sale of principal residences). The state subsidizes home ownership by allowing the marginal tax rate to be deducted from a family's income taxes. Housing policies that encourage ownership are a part of the "hidden" welfare state that cost the federal government about $94 billion in fiscal expenditures (Howard, 1997). Home ownership may very well be sound social policy, but it is an uneven process that clearly benefits some groups over others (Jackman and Jackman, 1980; Ong and Grigsby, 1988). Howard (1997) calculates that 88 percent of this "hidden" welfare goes to families earning more than $50,000, with 44 percent accruing to those earning more than $100,000. This class bias has clear racial ramifications as well. Only 1.2 percent of Black families earn enough to qualify for 44 percent of the mortgage interest deduction benefits, compared to 6.6 percent of White families.

The second concept, the "economic detour," helps explain the relatively low level of entrepreneurship among, and the small scale of the businesses owned by, Black Americans. Although Blacks have traditionally sought out opportunities for self-employment, they have faced an environment, especially from the postbellum period to the middle of the twentieth century, in which they were restricted by law from participation in business as free economic agents (Butler, 1991). These policies had a devastating impact on the ability of Blacks to build and maintain successful enterprises—the kind that anchor communities and spur economic development. Not only were Blacks limited to a restricted Black market, to which others also had easy access, but they were unable to tap the more lucrative and expansive mainstream White market. When businesses were developed that competed in size and scope with White businesses, intimidation and, in many cases, violence were used to curtail their expansion or destroy them altogether. The lack of major assets and indigenous community economic development has thus played a crucial role in limiting the wealth-accumulating ability of Blacks.

The past certainly casts a long shadow on the economic status of Blacks, but discrimination is not limited to the past. Recent studies of housing discrimination (Yinger, 1995, 1998), consumer markets (Yinger 1998), employment practices (Darity and Mason, 1998), and mortgage lending (Ladd, 1998) indicate pervasive and persistent discrimination—individual and institutional—in the last years of the twentieth century; in fact, the "economic detour" concept still operates in the most important way typical American families accumulate assets—home equity, as will be discussed in the next section.

The third concept, the "sedimentation of racial inequality" is synthetic in nature. The idea is that, in pivotal ways, the cumulative effects of the past have ostensibly cemented Blacks to the bottom of society's economic hierarchy. A history of low wages (Leiberson, 1980), poor schooling, and segregation affected not one generation of Blacks but practically all Blacks well into the twentieth century. The best indicator of this is wealth—or lack thereof. Wealth is one indicator of material disparity that captures the historical legacy of low wages, personal and organizational discrimination, and institutionalized racism. The low level of wealth accumulation evidenced by current generations of Blacks best represents the economic status of Blacks in the American social structure. In contrast, Whites in general—but well-off Whites in particular—had far greater structured opportunities to amass assets and use their secure financial status to pass their wealth and its benefits from generation to generation. What is often not acknowledged is that the same social system that fosters the accumulation of private wealth for many Whites denies it to Blacks, thus forging an intimate connection between White wealth accumulation and Black poverty. Just as Blacks have had "cumulative disadvantages," many Whites have had "cumulative advantages." Because wealth builds over a lifetime and is then passed along to kin, it is an essential indicator of Black economic well-being.

An understanding of the trends focuses attention on how past racial inequality in policy and practices translates into current racial stratification in the form of vastly different wealth resources for Black and White families, even among those with roughly equal accomplishments. Social injustice is not just an artifact of the past; contemporary institutional discrimination contributes to generating and maintaining the racial wealth gap. One key area is housing, perhaps the most important institutional sphere in which this inequality is passed along.

GENERATING CONTEMPORARY RACIAL STRATIFICATION: THE INSTITUTIONAL CONTEXT OF HOUSING, REAL ESTATE, AND FINANCIAL MARKETS

Home ownership is without a doubt the single most important means of accumulating assets for the typical American family. Home equity constitutes the largest share of net worth, accounting for about 44 percent of total measured net worth (Eller and Fraser, 1995). Federal housing, tax, and transportation policies have traditionally reinforced racial residential segregation. Continuing segregation has had an enduring impact on Blacks' quest for asset accumulation; and continuing institutional and policy discrimination serve to intensify that impact. Three areas in which discrimination is known to be a factor are obtaining credit, assignment of interest rates, and assessment of property values. The first, access to credit, is important because whom banks deem to be creditworthy determines who owns homes, and institutional racial bias in the process of securing home ownership has had, and will have, lasting consequences. The second area of potential discrimination concerns the interest rates attached to loans for those approved for buying homes. Blacks are generally slotted for higher rates. Third, as is well known, housing values climbed

TABLE 10-6 Homeownership, Mortgages, Home Equity, and Race: 1994

	Homeowner	Mortgage Rate	Home Equity	
			Mean	Median
White	61.5%	8.12%	$74,859	$58,000
Black	41.4%	8.44%	$46,254	$40,000
Difference	20.1%	0.32%	$28,605	$18,000

SOURCE: 1993 SIPP, Wave 7.

steeply during the 1970s and 1980s, far outstripping inflation, and created a large pool of assets for those who already owned homes. Did all home-owners share equally in the appreciation of housing values, or is housing inflation color-coded?

Table 10-6 shows that the home ownership rate in 1994 for Blacks was about 20 percent lower than rates for Whites. Oliver and Shapiro, in *Black Wealth/White Wealth* (1995a), contended that this difference was not merely the result of income differences, but, rather, was a product of the histori-cal legacy of residential segregation, redlining, Federal Housing Author-ity and Veterans' Administration (FHA/VA) policy, and discrimination in real estate and lending markets (Yinger, 1995; Massey and Denton, 1994). How does this historical legacy and contemporary state of affairs contribute to the racial gap in wealth resources?

In order to purchase a home, families must pass the first stage—qualification for a home mortgage. Several Federal Reserve Board studies, based on the outcome of all loan applications (the release of which is mandated by federal legislation), show that even when applicants are equally qualified—i.e., "creditworthy"—Black families are still rejected for home loans 60 percent more often than equally qualified White fami-lies (Oliver and Shapiro, 1995a; Ladd, 1998). Thus, as egregious as past discrimination may have been in this sector, the intensity of covert con-tinuation of racial discrimination is no less alive in the financial mortgage markets.

The second stage, for those fortunate enough to be approved for a home loan, is determining a mortgage rate. Oliver and Shapiro, in *Black Wealth/White Wealth* (1995a), showed that there is a mortgage rate differ-ence for Blacks compared to Whites that is not determined by where the home is located, the purchase price, or when the home was bought. On average, Black families pay about 0.33 percent, or a third of a percent, more in mortgage interest rates than White families. Consider that the median home purchase price is about $120,000 with, say, $12,000 down payment, leaving a mortgage of $108,000. One-third of 1 percent may not sound like much, but on a typical 30-year loan this amounts to a $25-amonth difference—for 360 months. Thus, over the loan period, a typical Black homebuyer will pay $9,000 more in interest to financial institutions than the average White homebuyer.

Bankers contend that they do not discriminate in setting mortgage interest rates on home loans. Instead, they say, it is more typical for Whites than Blacks to use larger down payments and financial "gifts" from family members to secure lower mortgage rates.[2] But many people, Blacks particularly, cannot afford large down payments or do not have access to in vivo transfers; and based on accumulated evidence, we are firmly convinced that this process reveals a key to understanding how past inequality is linked to the present, and how present inequalities will project into the next generation. Essentially, past injustice provides a disadvantage for most Blacks and an advantage for many Whites in how home purchases are financed. Because similar home mortgages cost Black families $9,000 more, Blacks pay more to finance their homes and end up with less home equity in the future.

The third stage brings home equity into the analysis. The 1994 SIPP data on home equity show that buying a home seems to increase the wealth assets for all able to afford one; however, the valuing of homes and home equity is color-coded. (This analysis includes only those currently still paying off home mortgages and, thus, provides a very conservative estimate of the dynamics.) As seen in Table 10-6, the mean value of homes owned by White families increased $28,605 more than the value of homes owned by Black families. Again, Oliver and Shapiro (1995a) found that region, length of ownership, purchase price, when the home was purchased, and so on, did not explain the racial differential in home equity. The explanation lies in how the dynamics of residential segregation impact housing markets—a contemporary illustration of the economic detour Blacks confront.

A White family attempting to sell its house in a relatively homogeneous White community is limited only by market forces, that is, economic affordability. A similar Black family attempting to sell its home in

---

[2]In the course of this research project, we have had the opportunity to talk about these results before many different groups, including Federal Reserve Board conferences attended by bankers. The ensuing discussions have been heated and frank, and they provided a key research clue. Bankers insisted that they do not discriminate by charging different rates to Black customers. Instead, they contend, it is far more typical for Whites to bring greater assets to the table, use them to lower the amount of the loan or to pay "points" on the loan, and consequently receive a lower interest rate on their mortgage. Indeed, in interviews gathered for *Black Wealth/White Wealth* and projects currently being conducted, we find that extraordinary proportions of young, first-time homebuyers receive financial assistance from their parents. Both White and Black young couples use this in vivo transfer to help with the down payment and/or to pay points.

a community that is more than 20 percent non-White faces normal market limits plus effects of racial dynamics: the pool of potential buyers is no longer 100 percent of the market because most potential White buyers are not interested in mixed neighborhoods (Yinger, 1995; Massey and Denton, 1994); thus the pool of potential buyers has evaporated to mainly other Blacks who can afford the home, and possibly other minorities. The economic detour idea shows how the path to home equity can shift for Black home owners. A diminished pool of potential buyers composed of buyers with more limited financial assets also helps explain why housing values do not rise nearly as quickly or as high in Black communities or in those with more than 20 percent non-White residents.

TRANSLATING INEQUALITY INTO STRATIFICATION 1: PASSING IT ALONG

The role of intergenerational transfers in asset accumulation is certainly one of the most significant and controversial areas regarding wealth. How important are intergenerational transfers in the accumulation of assets? This question is important because if significant portions of assets are acquired as gifts from others, then a large part of the reason some people do not have assets can be traced to phenomena outside their control; and if this is the case, it could provide a strong basis for the normative argument for spreading asset ownership opportunities based on a principle of equal opportunity. For many years, the consensus viewpoint was that people save to smooth out undesirable consumption fluctuations and, in large part, to maintain comfortable living standards during the postretirement years (Modigliana and Brumberg, 1954). Financial inheritance has been dismissed as a source of the racial wealth gap on the theory that inheritance is quantitatively unimportant because the vast majority of households do not receive financial inheritances. Further, some claim that racial wealth disparities would be almost the same if wealth derived from past financial inheritances were subtracted out of current wealth.

Some economists, however, have challenged this view (e.g., Koltikoff and Sommers, 1981), concluding that intergenerational transfers were responsible for between 52 and 80 percent of accumulated wealth. Gale and Scholz (1994) calculate that 21 percent of wealth comes from in vivo gifts and 31 percent from bequests. McNamee and Miller (1998:200) conclude that "meritocracy is superimposed on inheritance rather than the other way around." Wilhelm (1998) reviewed this literature and concluded that a great deal of wealth—at least one-half but likely more—is inherited. The bulk of these intergenerational transfers go to Whites who are well educated and work as professionals and managers. Disagreements remain, but our reading of the evidence suggests that intergenerational transfers account for a very substantial share of total wealth; just how substantial remains to be determined empirically. In this spirit, we contribute some modest and preliminary findings.

White and Black families have a fairly realistic grasp of their economic circumstances and fortunes. It is interesting to note the expectations and hopes these families have regarding receiving and giving financial help and inheritances. In 1994, PSID families were asked about the likelihood that they would give financial assistance totaling $5,000 or more to their children, relatives, or friends over the next 10 years. This taps a double expectation—that they will be in a position to give help to people who need it and will be willing to do so. The figures, in Table 10-7, show high expectations for both groups—52 percent for Whites and 44 percent for Blacks. Table 10-7 also contains data regarding families' beliefs about their chances of leaving inheritances totaling $10,000 or more and $100,000 or more. The study questions probe, among other things, assumptions about present asset circumstances and optimism about future wealth accumulation. The data reveal some rather dramatic racial differences. Just about 25 percent of White families say they plan to leave an inheritance of $10,000 or more; 13.4 percent say they will bequeath more than $100,000 to their heirs. The grasp of present circumstances and optimism about future wealth among Black families is considerably more circumspect; less than 10 percent of Black families expect to leave an inheritance of $10,000 or more, and only 3.1 percent say their financial bequest will be $100,000 or more.

As noted, the above data reflect attitudes, expectations, and perhaps hopes. Actual receipt of inheritances is an interesting complement to these beliefs and expectations. Table 10-8 shows actual inheritances of $10,000

TABLE 10-7 Bequests and Race

| | Likelihood of Leaving Money[a] | | | |
	Get >$5,000	Give >$5,000	Leave >$10,000	Leave >$100,000
Sample	18.9%	49.1%	19.1%	9.7%
White	17.2%	52.1%	24.5%	13.4%
Black	22.9%	43.7%	9.5%	3.1%

[a]Chances are better than 50 percent.

SOURCE: 1994 PSID.

TABLE 10-8 Inheritance and Race

	Inheritance	Value of Inheritance	
	Past 5 Years	Mean	Median
Sample	3.8%	$68,999	$30,000
White	5.30%	$74,219	$30,000
Black	1.6%	$33,363	$25,000
Difference	3.7%	$40,856	$5,000

SOURCE: 1994 PSID.

or more bequeathed from 1989 to 1994. Note that the amount is larger than the median net financial assets of American families (see Table 10-2). These data give a glimpse into a primary method by which wealth is passed along. Among White families, 5.3 percent were the beneficiaries of inheritances, compared to just 1.6 percent of the Black families. Thus, in the limited time period shown, Whites are more than three times as likely as Blacks to benefit from a substantial inheritance. Among Whites who received them, the mean inheritance amounted to nearly $75,000 compared to $33,400 among Blacks. Not only then are Whites much more likely to inherit, but the amounts are considerably larger, by $40,856. The difference between the mean and median inheritance among Whites indicates the extreme top heaviness of this distribution. This is not the case among the few Blacks that inherited, as the mean and median figures are comparatively close.

Wilhelm (1998) makes an important contribution to this discussion. Using PSID data, he adds further evidence of the importance of inheritance, especially when "inheritance" includes broader forms of intergenerational transfers. His summary evidence from 1984 and 1989 PSIDs shows that 22 percent already had inherited substantial amounts, with the average heir receiving $140,000. Those in the top quintile are more likely to inherit than those in the bottom quintile (26 to 15 percent); and it is not surprising that heirs in the top quintiles received considerably larger amounts, $289,000 to $60,000. He also looks at in vivo gifts from the 1988 PSID. About one in five families received such gifts in the previous year, averaging $2,540. Wilhelm's data also show that inheritances and in vivo gifts occur among poor families to a much larger extent than previously acknowledged; and it is projected that the annual flow of transfers through inheritance will grow eightfold as the parents of baby-boomers pass on (Avery and Rendell, 1993).

TRANSLATING INEQUALITY INTO STRATIFICATION 2:
THE FUTURE OF THE CHILDREN

Shapiro is presently conducting a research project examining how assets are used to pass racial stratification along, in the context of how families choose communities and select schooling for their children. This project is collecting nearly 250 in-depth interviews with families with young children in three cities. Based on preliminary insights and emerging trends from this early phase of the research, it is clear that there are those whose assets give them a multitude of options and opportunities, and those who have very limited options from which to choose. More remarkable is how families consciously use or plan to use assets to solidify their class status and racial identification, and, at the same time, consciously plan to improve the life chances of their children.

White, upper-middle class respondents with significant wealth are generally the ones "making choices." Some of them have "prime choice"; in other words, they can live pretty much anywhere they choose, and they often choose stable, solidly middle-class neighborhoods. One mother explained her move from an integrated middle-class community to a better-off, virtually all-White suburb: "We always wanted to live on a street like this, with a big lot and all brick, two car garage, Sappington zip code 63128." The zip code was attractive but she was moving because "I'm afraid of them. I am afraid of them. I want to shelter my kids until they're older and they can handle it better. . . . I don't want them being exposed to that type of situation. . . . those poor inner city kids whose parents are on crack . . . and have drugs and guns laying around for them to bring to school."

One single White mother used her assets, inherited from her family, to move to a better community. This way she does not "have to worry about [my child] being abducted . . . I don't have to worry so much about drive-by shooting . . . [that]something terrible is going to happen to him just because he was out in the street."

At the other end of the spectrum are those who are "making do" with very limited choices, usually working class Blacks. Many describe how they are "doing the best they can," living in a "bad, but not so bad" neighborhood. They would prefer to live elsewhere, but are glad they are not in the "worst" neighborhood. Others just feel "stuck."

The interview analysis thus far clearly shows that families are putting a lot of thought, time, and energy into "navigating the school system." The strategies they are able to use and the options available to them are clearly wealth-related, in that more money buys "better" schools or, at least, schools perceived as better. Whether those better schools are private, or public schools in expensive, prestigious neighborhoods, having assets allows some to elude the most troublesome aspects of America's urban ills. A Black mother is considering moving "because if I can't afford to pay for private school, then I may think in terms of selling the house and moving to a community . . . [where] the school system is a little bit better." She is illustrative of families who move or want to move to a community specifically for its school system, clearly planning to use family assets to increase the life chances of their children.

Often people plan to move from a community or send their children to private school once their children reach middle or junior high school age; people's perceptions of public junior high schools revolve around gangs, drugs, negative peer influence, and so on. In our sample, families have fled, or plan to flee, urban public school systems much earlier—i.e., when their children reach fifth or sixth grade. Many adults in our sample who attended private schools as children are adamant in their desire to send their own children to private schools, stating repeatedly that "public school wasn't an option" and often going to great lengths to ensure that their children attend private schools. Of course, for most of these families, their assets make this choice possible; but for these families and those with more limited choices, these interviews are highly suggestive of how families use assets to pass advantages along to their children.

BREAKING WITH THE PAST

A wealth perspective shows how past and contemporary institutional discrimination casts a long shadow on the economic status of Blacks. The challenge now is to explore how a wealth perspective might inform social policy. Bold and creative initiatives are needed to link the opportunity structure to policies that promote asset formation and begin to close the wealth gap. We can all help to build this agenda. Two approaches are needed. First, we must directly address both the historically generated and the current institutional disadvantages that limit the ability of Blacks and other racial groups to accumulate wealth resources. Second, we must resolutely promote asset acquisition among those at the bottom of the social structure who have been locked out of the wealth-accumulation process. Legislation at the federal level and in many of the states has been enacted to frame Individual Asset Accounts (IDAs) (Sherraden, 1991). These accounts offer a high set of structured incentives, in the form of matching payments, for poor families to save money for specific purposes, like buying a home, home repairs, starting a business, or education, health, and retirement.

Discussions promoting asset accumulation and IDA policy discussion were presented at the NRC Racial Trends Conference in October 1998. Since then, legislation has been considered and passed that structures this policy option. In addition, President Clinton, in his 1999 State of the Union Address, incorporated this recommendation into his proposal for Universal Savings Accounts (USA; see Corporation for Enterprise development, 1996). As of this writing, the idea of promoting asset development is on the policy agenda. It should also be noted, however, that the ability of the social sciences to contribute evidence to this discussion or to shape policy design lags far behind the policy discussions and legislation.

Another positive step would be to democratize the 84 percent of welfare expenditures (Sherraden, 1991) that are targeted for the nonpoor and promote asset accumulation for the middle and upper classes—e.g., mortgage interest deduction and capital gains taxes. Making the "hidden" welfare state (Howard, 1997) subject to the democratic process puts social policy in an entirely different resource and policy context. These efforts would benefit minorities as well as many White Americans who are asset poor, making them potential allies in the fight for economic and racial justice.

Finally, the pronounced rise in wealth inequality during the 1980s is another source of policy urgency. Virtually all the growth in wealth between 1983 and 1989 accrued to the top 20 percent of households (Wolff, 1994).

RESEARCH ISSUES

Interest in wealth studies is growing rapidly; the field is young and the promise is great. A key challenge is to provide institutional incentives for this field to develop and attract top researchers. The task is twofold: technical and substantive. Technically we must ensure that the current databases continue to produce high-quality information about household asset formation and expenditures, and that other databases receive strong encouragement to include modules on assets and liabilities. As more data are collected and examined by researchers and policy makers, the information and knowledge base improves, thus measures and methodologies for change can also improve. Private foundations and the federal government should be encouraged to provide support for efforts in this direction. Longitudinal data will be especially useful for examining many of the complex issues regarding wealth accumulation and inequality, some of which have been identified in this paper. In terms of racial stratification, we offer a modest beginning by offering framework questions:

- What accounts for the wealth gap over time?
- How do families use assets to plan for social mobility?
- In what way does acquiring assets affect behaviors, social psychology, future orientation, family violence, and ambitions?

- What do more nuanced data analysis for Hispanics, Asians, and other minorities reveal about the American experience?
- What is the role of savings in accumulating assets?
- What is the relationship between home ownership and civic participation?
- Will poor families save? Under what conditions?
- What are the claims of different family members on family assets? Gender differences? Gender preferences?
- How do families use assets to reproduce class standing for themselves and their children?
- How important are intergenerational transfers in wealth accumulation?
- How important are intergenerational transfers in perpetuating the racial wealth gap?

Other possible explanations of racial differences in wealth should be fully explored.

REFERENCES

Avery, R., and M. Rendell
  1993 Estimating the size and distribution of the baby boomers' prospective inheritances. Pp. 11-19 in *American Statistical Association: 1993 Proceedings of the Social Science Section*. Alexandria, Va.: American Statistical Association.
Bates, T.
  1998 *Race, Self-Employment, and Upward Mobility: An Illusive American Dream*. Baltimore: Johns Hopkins University Press.
Butler, J.
  1991 *Entrepreneurship and Self-Help Among Black Americans: A Reconsideration of Race and Economics*. Albany, N.Y.: State University of New York Press.
Corporation for Enterprise Development
  1996 *Universal Savings Accounts—USAs: A Route to National Economic Growth and Family Economic Security*. Washington, D.C.: Corporation for Enterprise Development.
Darity, W., Jr., and P. Mason
  1998 Evidence on discrimination in employment: Codes of color, codes of gender. *Journal of Economic Perspectives* 12(2):63-90.
Eller, T., and W. Fraser
  1995 Asset Ownership of Households: 1993. *U.S. Bureau of the Census. Current Population Reports, P70-47*. Washington, D.C.: U.S. Government Printing Office.
Flippen, C., and M. Tienda
  1997 Racial and Ethnic Differences in Wealth Among the Elderly. Paper presented at the 1997 Annual Meeting of the Population Association of America, Washington, D.C.
Gale, W., and J. Scholz
  1994 Intergenerational transfers and the accumulation of wealth. *Journal of Economic Perspectives* 8(4):145-160.

Grant, D.
    2000   A demographic portrait of Los Angeles, 1970-1990. In *Prismatic Metropolis: Ana-lyzing Inequality in Los Angeles*, L. Bobo, M. Oliver, J. Johnson Jr., and A. Valenzuela, eds. New York: Russell Sage Foundation.
Howard, C.
    1997   *The Hidden Welfare State: Tax Expenditures and Social Policy in the United States.* Princeton: Princeton University Press.
Jackman, M., and R. Jackman
    1980   Racial inequalities in home ownership. *Social Forces* 58:1221-1233.
Jackson, K.
    1985   *Crabgrass Frontier: The Suburbanization of the United States.* New York: Oxford University Press.
Koltikoff, L., and L. Sommers
    1981   The role of intergenerational transfers in aggregate capital accumulation. *Journal of Political Economy* 89:706-732.
Ladd, H.
    1998   Evidence on discrimination in mortgage lending. *Journal of Economic Perspectives* 12(2):41-62.
Leiberson, S.
    1980   *A Piece of the Pie.* Berkeley: University of California Press.
Massey, D., and N. Denton
    1994   *American Apartheid: Segregation and the Making of the Underclass.* Cambridge: Harvard University Press.
McNamee, S., and R. Miller, Jr.
    1998   Inheritance and stratification. In *Inheritance and Wealth in America*, R. Miller, Jr., and S. McNamee, eds. New York: Plenum Press.
Mink, G.
    1990   The lady and the tramp: Gender, race, and the origins of the American welfare state. Pp. 92-122 in *Women, the State, and Welfare*, L. Gordon, ed. Madison: University of Wisconsin Press.
Modigliana, F., and R. Brumberg
    1954   Utility analysis and the consumption function: An interpretation of cross-section data. In *Post-Keynesian Economics*, K. Kurihara, ed. New Brunswick: Rutgers University Press.
National Research Council
    1989   *A Common Destiny: Blacks and American Society*, G. Jaynes and R. Williams, eds. Washington, D.C.: National Academy Press.
O'Toole, B.
    1998   Family net asset levels in the greater Boston region. Paper presented at the Greater Boston Social Survey Community Conference, John F. Kennedy Library, Boston, Mass., November.
Office of Trust Responsibilities
    1995   *Annual Report of Indian Lands.* Washington, D.C.: U.S. Department of the Interior.
Oliver, M., and T. Shapiro
    1989   Race and wealth. *Review of Black Political Economy* 17:5-25.
    1990   Wealth of a nation: At least one-third of households are asset poor. *American Journal of Economics and Sociology* 49:129-151.
    1995a   *Black Wealth/White Wealth: A New Perspective on Racial Inequality.* New York: Routledge.
    1995b   Them that's got shall get. In *Research in Politics and Society*, M. Oliver, R. Ratcliff, and T. Shapiro, eds. Greenwich, Conn.: JAI Press Vol. 5.

Ong, P. and E. Grigsby
    1988   Race and life cycle effects on home ownership in Los Angeles, 1970 to 1980. *Urban Affairs Quarterly* 23:601-615.
Oubre, C.
    1978   *Forty Acres and a Mule: The Freedman's Bureau and Black Land Ownership.* Baton Rouge: Louisiana State University Press.
Portes, A., and Rumbaut, R.
    1990   *Immigrant America.* Berkeley: University of California Press.
Quadagno, J.
    1994   *The Color of Welfare.* New York: Oxford University Press.
Sherraden, M.
    1991   *Assets and the Poor: A New American Welfare Policy.* New York: Sharpe.
Wilhelm, M.
    1998   The role of intergenerational transfers in spreading asset ownership. Prepared for *Ford Foundation Conference on The Benefits and Mechanisms for Spreading Assets,* New York, December 10-12.
Wolff, E.
    1994   Trends in household wealth in the United States, 1962-1983 and 1983-1989. *Review of Income and Wealth* 40:143-174.
    1996a   *Top Heavy: A Study of Increasing Inequality of Wealth in America.* Updated and expanded edition. New York: Free Press.
    1996b   International comparisons of wealth inequality. *Review of Income and Wealth* 42:433-451.
Yinger, J.
    1995   *Closed Doors, Opportunities Lost: The Continuing Costs of Housing Discrimination.* New York: Russell Sage Foundation.
    1998   Evidence on discrimination in consumer markets. *Journal of Economic Perspectives* 12(2):23-40.

HERBERT W. NICKENS
1947-1999

The health section of America Becoming: Racial Trends and Their Consequences *is dedicated to the memory of Herbert W. Nickens, M.D., M.A., who passed away on March 22, 1999. In his all too brief lifetime, Dr. Nickens devoted his academic and professional interests toward improving the health status of racial and ethnic minorities in the United States. After serving on the staff of the landmark Secretary's Task Force on Black and Minority Health, Dr. Nickens became the first director of Department of Health and Human Services' Office of Minority Health. In that role, he was pivotal in crafting the programmatic themes for that office—many of which continue to this day. As the first Vice President for Community and Minority Programs for the Association of American Medical Colleges (AAMC), Dr. Nickens devoted much of his professional energy to increasing the number of underrepresented minority applicants to medical school. His passion for social justice brought forth the Project 3000 by 2000, which reignited the institution's long-standing commitment to increasing minority representation in medicine. Dr. Nickens's interests did not, however, focus solely on the educational pipeline. He continued to maintain his focus on eliminating minority health disparities in his scholarly writings, such as the co-authorship of one of the chapters in this report, and in AAMC programming, such as the Health Services Research Institute for Minority Medical School Faculty. Herbert W. Nickens will be remembered for many things—but most importantly for his pursuit of equity in health.*

11

Racial and Ethnic Differences in Health: Recent Trends, Current Patterns, Future Directions

Raynard S. Kington and Herbert W. Nickens

The volume of research addressing racial and ethnic differences in health has grown dramatically in recent decades as more and better data have become available. Health results from the interaction of intrinsic genetic and biological factors with environmental and social factors distributed throughout every facet of life. Health also influences every facet of life: it affects one's ability to work, to socialize, to think, to learn, to communicate, to reproduce. Because of the complex causal pathways and widespread influences, no single discipline is sufficient to address the problem of racial and ethnic differences in health status.

All of the behavioral and social sciences—anthropology, psychology, sociology, economics, and demography—have contributed to the understanding of racial and ethnic health differentials. The public health and medical sciences provide different and often complementary perspectives. Researchers grounded in epidemiology, genetics, molecular biology, physiology, and clinical medicine have all described aspects of health and disease that differ by race or ethnicity and have posited theories to account for those differences. In attempting to synthesize these data into a coherent whole, we have decided against presenting our findings within a single theoretical framework. Instead, we chose an ecumenical approach, accepting core insights from multiple disciplines to understand the evidence on why racial and ethnic groups differ in health status and what can be done to address the disparities.

HISTORICAL PERSPECTIVE

Over the past century, a series of reports have addressed the health of minorities in the United States: from the health-related papers in the Atlanta University Series (1896, 1906), to the comprehensive review by Dorn (1940) on the health of Blacks written as a background paper for Gunnar Myrdal's *An American Dilemma,* to the groundbreaking 1985 *Report of the Secretary's Task Force on Black and Minority Health* (U.S. Department of Health and Human Services, 1985). Until the 1960s and 1970s, minority health studies in the United States focused on Blacks. The exception was an extensive body of anthropological literature on American Indian health, dating from the 1920s (see the review in Young, 1994, pp. 25-28). Much of it suggests that the introduction of infectious diseases from European colonists led to a significant decline in the American Indian population; that decline did not begin to reverse itself until the end of the nineteenth century. Other studies of the health status of non-Black minorities in the nineteenth and early twentieth centuries were likely carried out, but probably limited to a single locale.

Systematic registration of deaths in the nation began only about 50 years ago when all of the United States was included in the Death Registration Area[1] (Ewbank, 1987), and all of the historic studies show that Black death rates were substantially higher than those for Whites. Disparities lessened somewhat, however, when Blacks and Whites at similar socioeconomic position (SEP) were compared (e.g., Holland and Perrott, 1938). In the nineteenth century, Black death rates decreased along with those for Whites. Although Black death rates remained at a higher level, there were fewer deaths overall from infectious diseases because of improvements in factors such as water and sanitation and in child care. Ewbank (1987) concludes that in the second half of the nineteenth century, declines in Black mortality were minimal, but life expectancy increased from about 35 to 54 years between 1900 and 1940; thus, life expectancy for Blacks in 1940 was approximately equal to what life expectancy was for Whites in 1920.

Race as a Concept in Health Studies

Race as a factor in health care and health outcomes is increasingly being recognized and addressed by researchers. The modern concept of

---

[1]Begun in 1880, the national Death Registration Area included only Massachusetts, New Jersey, and the District of Columbia. The other states were gradually included; and by 1933 all 48 contiguous states and the District of Columbia were included; Alaska and Hawaii were added when they became states.

race was developed during a period of intense global exploration and European colonialism. Hierarchical schemes of classification rooted in dubious theories of biology and genetics were invented to classify individuals as both foreign and inferior. This strategy served as a scientific and moral enabler of colonial economic activity, for which enslaving people was accepted as an economic expedient. The concept of race, however, has been under increasing assault in the last half of the twentieth century from at least two different fronts. First, the Civil Rights Movement and its aftermath led to the end of legal segregation. Subsequently, since the 1960s, there has been increasing racial integration in the U.S. mainstream. Second, intense and sustained immigration has led to a more diverse U.S. population, resulting in a society so multiracial, simplistic racial classification and hierarchies are no longer sustainable.

The concept of "race" as it has been typically used in health research, however, has at least five flaws:

1. "Race" does not reflect meaningful biological or genetic distinctions. Race classifications are based on an individual's appearance; and although physiognomic differences are genetic, the vast proportion of genetic variation is not so visible, and occurs within races, not between them (Lewontin, 1972).

2. Race classification schemes are highly imprecise (LaVeist, 1994; Williams et al., 1993; Williams, 1996). In the case of determining the race of a child, such a classification may rely on arbitrary rules based on factors such as race or nationality of the mother, race or nationality of the father, or the race the mother or father if either was non-White, etc. In determining race on a death certificate or health record, judgment is often made visually by a clerk or a funeral director.

3. Our current concept of race is distorted by America's Black-White experience. This is especially problematic with regard to trying to classify "Hispanics," who may be either Black or White, though the vast majority of Hispanics self-describe as White (U.S. Bureau of the Census, 1999).

4. The idea of a pure race is problematic. Each human being more than likely embodies a variety of racial groups. U.S. citizens who self-identify as Black, for example, are likely genetic admixtures of White, American Indian, and African in widely different proportions.

5. The widespread analysis of data by race may steer investigators away from thinking more deeply about actual underlying variables of interest such as SEP, disenfranchisement, and cultural values. In an examination of the use of "race" in the journal *Health Services Research* over a 25-year period, Williams (1994) noted that about 66 percent of empirical studies included "race," but only 13 percent defined the term or had a justifiable reason for using it.

Quality of Health and Health-Care Data

One of the primary challenges in research addressing racial and ethnic health disparities is the quality of data on the health status and health
care of many minority populations. Data accuracy is especially problematic for Hispanics, Asian and Pacific Islanders, and American Indians and
Alaska Natives. In the 1980s, fewer than half of the states recorded Hispanic ethnicity on death certificates. By 1996, the District of Columbia and
all states except Oklahoma reported Hispanic ethnicity on death certificates (National Center for Health Statistics, 1998). Sorlie and colleagues
(1992a) compared reported race and ethnicity from study data with death
certificate data for 21,000 deaths in the National Longitudinal Mortality
Survey and found that while agreement on race was 99.2 percent for
Whites and 98.2 percent for Blacks, agreement for American Indians and
Alaska Natives was 73.6 percent and for Asians and Pacific Islanders 82.4
percent. Agreement for ethnicity was 89.7 percent for Hispanics. Hahn
and Eberhardt (1995) analyzed 1990 death certificate data, correcting for
both census undercount and race misclassification. Changes in the estimates of American Indian and Alaska Native mortality were particularly
striking; estimated life expectancy at birth decreased from 73.8 years to
71.0 years for men and from 81.6 years to 79.4 years for women. The
change resulted in this population going from having a reported health
advantage compared to Whites to having a disadvantage. Mortality rates
that are not adjusted for misclassification underestimate the mortality of
these populations and lead to overestimates of life expectancy.

Protocols for collecting racial and ethnic data also change over time.
Kovar and Poe (1985) considered changes in data collection for the National Health Interview Survey (NHIS). From its inception in 1957 until
1976, NHIS racial categorization depended on interviewer observation,
and all racial and ethnic categories other than Black and White were
identified as "Other Races." In 1976, in addition to interviewer-observed
race, the NHIS added a single question allowing the respondent to identify one of the following categories as his or her national origin or ancestry: countries of Central or South America, Chicano, Cuban, Mexican,
Mexicano, Mexican-American, Puerto Rican, Other Spanish, Other European (such as German, Irish, English, or French), Black/Negro/Afro-
American, American Indian/Alaskan Native, and Asian and Pacific Islander (such as Chinese, Japanese, Korean, Filipino, Samoan). In 1978, to
comply with guidelines established by the U.S. Office of Management
and Budget (OMB) Directive 15, that question was then changed to two
parts: the first addressed Hispanic ethnicity; the second addressed race.
Persons who self-identified as being of Hispanic ancestry could report
any of the following groups: Puerto Rican, Cuban, Mexican/Mexicano,

Mexican American, Chicano, "Other Latin American," or "Other Spanish." Racial categories to choose from were American Indian or Alaska Native, Asian and Pacific Islander, Black, White, or other. In 1992, NHIS expanded the subgroups of Asians and Pacific Islanders; in addition to Chinese, Filipino, Korean, and Japanese, respondents could choose Vietnamese, Asian Indian, Samoan, Guamanian, and "Other Asian and Pacific Islander." (Beginning with the 2000 Census, all federal data systems will over several years change to comply with the revised OMB Revision directive that mandates federal agencies that collect data on race to allow persons to self-identify as being a member of more than one racial group [Office of Management and Budget, 1997].)

Although data from longitudinal cohort studies or interview surveys that rely on self-report of race and ethnicity should not be subject to significant misclassification errors, these longitudinal data sets do not allow assessment of trends in differences between races and ethnic groups.

Measures of Health Status

"Health" extends far beyond simple measures of the risk of disease and death. It encompasses an array of quality-of-life dimensions that include physical and social functioning and mental well-being. The primary measures of health we used in this overview are life expectancy, all-cause mortality, and, when available, respondent-rated general health status. Life expectancy is the estimated average number of years of life remaining for a person at a given age, and life expectancy at birth is a good summary measure of mortality differences across the life cycle. We use age-adjusted mortality rates,[2] wherever possible, to allow appropriate comparisons because the age structure varies substantially across racial and ethnic groups. We use only all-cause mortality because subsequent chapters address cause-specific rates. Respondent-rated[3] general health status is measured by the response to a standard survey question that asks a person to grade his or her overall health, usually on a scale of excellent, very good, good, fair, and poor. How a respondent answers

---

[2]Age-adjusted rate: statistically, a weighted average of age-specific rates, where the weights represent the fixed proportion by age; thus, age-specific rates provide the adjusted rates for all ages combined. For example, comparing the 1980 death rates for Whites and Blacks, the age-adjusted formula would account for the fact that a certain percentage of Whites were 75 years or age or older, where significantly fewer Blacks were in that age group.

[3]We use the term "respondent-rated" rather than "self-rated" or "self-reported" because in some surveys a household respondent may answer for another individual in the household.

that single question captures many dimensions of health including health-related quality-of-life and functional status; how a respondent answers has also proved to be a significant predictor of mortality even after accounting for standard socio-demographic factors (Idler and Benyamini, 1997).

PATTERNS OF RACIAL AND ETHNIC DIFFERENCES IN MORTALITY AND GENERAL HEALTH STATUS

The story of health in the United States in the twentieth century can be summarized by two central findings. First, simply and clearly, across age groups, across racial and ethnic groups, among males and females, by almost all indicators, the health of the U.S. population has improved dramatically. Second—and complex to the degree that it defies straightforward description—in spite of the improvements, there have been remarkably persistent differences in health status by race and ethnicity, with the members of many, but not all, racial and ethnic minorities experiencing worse health than the majority population but also with substantial heterogeneity within any one group. Both findings are illustrated by statistics listed in Table 11-1.

Members of the largest minority group of the twentieth century, Blacks, have experienced poorer health compared to Whites throughout the century. Members of the fastest growing minority group in absolute numbers, Hispanics, have enjoyed relatively good health by some measures but contain within their ranks substantial variation—e.g., health of

TABLE 11-1 Age-Adjusted Death Rates, 1980-1996 (per 100,000 person years)

	1980	1990	1996
White	559.4	492.8	466.8
Black	842.5	789.2	738.3
Hispanic	—	400.2	365.9
American Indian/ Alaska Native	.564.1	445.1	456.7
Asian or Pacific Islander	315.6	297.6	277.4

SOURCE: National Center for Health Statistics (1998).

Puerto Ricans is comparatively poorer, whereas health of Mexican Americans and Cubans is comparatively better. For Asians and Pacific Islanders the picture is varied as well, though many Asian and Pacific Islander subgroups have comparatively good health. American Indians and Alaska Natives, like Blacks, continue to experience poorer health than Whites, though in recent periods the health gap between Whites and American Indians and Alaska Natives has narrowed considerably.

Black Americans

Over the course of the twentieth century, life expectancy at birth for Blacks has more than doubled; for Whites it increased by about 60 percent. In 1900, life expectancy for a Black person was 33 years and 47.6 years for a White person; by 1950, life expectancy had risen to 60.7 years for Blacks and 69.1 years for Whites (National Center for Health Statistics, 1998). The Black-White gap had decreased to its lowest point, 5.8 years, around 1984, and then began to increase due to high death rates among Blacks from HIV, homicides, diabetes, and pneumonia. (A decrease in life expectancy was extremely unusual for a large subpopulation in a developed country.) Another factor in the increased differential was that mortality from heart disease decreased at a much faster rate for Whites than for Blacks (Kochanek et al., 1994). By 1989 the gap was at 7.0 years, where it remained until 1995. By 1996 life expectancy increased to 70.2 years for Blacks and 76.8 years for Whites (National Center for Health Statistics, 1998). Comparison of age-adjusted all-cause mortality rates for Blacks presents a similar picture. In 1950, the mortality rate for Blacks was 1,236.7 per 100,000; the rate for Whites was 800.4. As shown in Table 11-1, by 1996, the rate for Blacks had fallen by almost 40 percent to 738.3; the rate for Whites was 466.8 (National Center for Health Statistics, 1998).

One fact is true for all groups: women live longer than men. Relative gains in mortality and life expectancy have not been experienced equally, however, by Black men and women. In 1900, the life expectancy at birth of Black females was 1 year greater than for Black males; for White females life expectancy was 2.1 years longer than for White men. Among Blacks the differential increased to 3.8 more years for females in 1950, 8.3 more in 1970, and peaked at about 9.2 years in 1991. In 1996 it decreased to 8.1 years. Among Whites the differential peaked in 1970 at 7.6 years and has steadily declined since then, primarily because of reductions in cardiovascular disease among men (National Center for Health Statistics, 1998; Waldron, 1993).

National survey data on respondent-reported general health status also suggest a poorer health-related quality of life for Blacks compared to Whites. The age-adjusted percentage of Blacks who reported "fair" or "poor" health in 1995 was 15.4 percent compared to 8.7 percent for Whites (National Center for Health Statistics, 1998), and it has remained around 15 to 17 percent during the last decade. Among the elderly age 75 or older, the Black-White gap in the percentage reporting "fair" or "poor" health narrowed from 18.8 percent to 13.1 percent between 1987 and 1995. Among Black persons age 75 and older the percentage dropped from 52.4 to 44.4; among Whites, from 33.2 percent to 31.2 percent.

Although the Black population is often thought of as a culturally distinctive, homogenous group, there are in fact significant differences among subgroups. Several studies have described wide variation in mortality rates among Blacks in different parts of the county, with some areas far behind others in recent improvements in health (McCord and Freeman, 1990; Geronimus et al., 1996). A growing literature has also described differences in health between Blacks who were born in the South and Blacks born in other parts of the country (Fang et al., 1996; Schneider et al., 1997; Kington et al., 1998). Most, but not all, of this literature has found worse health for Blacks born in the South even if they have migrated. These findings may be related to poor early-life health conditions in the South or perhaps to more subtle psychosocial factors (Schneider et al., 1997).

A related body of literature is now describing the health of recent immigrants of African descent, most notably those from the Caribbean but more recently those from sub-Saharan Africa. In 1980, approximately 3.1 percent of Black Americans were foreign born. It is estimated that by 2010, over 10 percent of the Black population in the United States will be recent immigrants or their descendants (Reid, 1986). We know of no national studies of West Indian or African immigrants, but Fang and colleagues (1997) analyzed data on mortality in New York and found that U.S.-born Blacks had between 1.5 and 2 times the age-adjusted mortality rate of foreign-born Blacks (67 percent of whom were from the West Indies, 12 percent from South America, and 5 percent from Africa). David and Collins (1997) analyzed data on the birth weight of infants, a potent indicator of infant mortality risk, and found that among infants born in Chicago between 1985 and 1990, those born to African-born Black women were likely to have a birth weight more similar to infants of U.S.-born White women rather than to babies born to U.S.-born Black women. Literature on the relatively good health of foreign-born Blacks in the United States has been used to dispel the idea that Black health status is genetically based. Comparisons across Black subgroups may provide important additional insights into the causes of racial and ethnic differences in health.

Hispanic Americans

By some measures of general health status, Hispanics experience relatively good health, but closer scrutiny of the data reveals a more complicated pattern. Life expectancy at birth for Hispanics in 1990 was estimated to be 79.1 years, 3 years longer than the 76.1 years estimated for Whites (Erikson et al., 1995). That 79.1 years, however, is almost certainly an overestimate because it is based on data that exclude several states, including New York, where over 40 percent of Puerto Ricans live, and this group generally has poorer health status than other Hispanic subgroups. NCHS mortality data also suggest that the health of the Hispanic population has improved. Between 1985 and 1994-1996, the age-adjusted mortality rate for Hispanic males decreased from 524.8 to 501.1, and for Hispanic females from 286.6 to 270.3[4] (National Center for Health Statistics, 1998). For non-Hispanic White males over this period, the mortality rate dropped from 669.7 to 602.8 and for females from 385.3 to 365.5. Analyses by Sorlie et al. (1993) and Liao et al. (1998) of longitudinal data on national sample cohorts revealed a similar pattern of lower mortality rates for Hispanics compared to non-Hispanic Whites.

In 1990, Mexican Americans comprised the largest subpopulation of Hispanics, 63 percent, Puerto Ricans comprised 11 percent, Cubans, 5 percent, and a combined category of "all other Hispanics" including immigrants from Central and South America comprised the remaining 21 percent (US. Bureau of the Census, 1991). Analyses of data sets that have included a sufficient number of members of each subgroup to compare have found substantial differences across the Hispanic subgroups. For example, Sorlie and colleagues (1993) analyzed data from the National Longitudinal Mortality Study and compared the age-adjusted mortality rate of Hispanic subpopulations and the non-Hispanic population; they found that the ratio for Hispanics compared to non-Hispanics was 0.74:1 for men and 0.82:1 for women (ratios less than 1 indicate better health than Whites), but the ratio varied substantially across age groups. For example, among men older than age 65, Mexicans, Puerto Ricans, Cubans, and a final category of "all other Hispanics" each had substantially lower mortality rates than non-Hispanics. In contrast, among those aged 25 to 44, no Hispanic subgroup had a mortality risk significantly different than Whites. Liao and colleagues (1998) analyzed linked mortality data from the 1986-1990 NHIS and describe a similar pattern of overall lower

---

[4]Again, these trend data must be viewed with caution because the 1985 rates are based on data from 17 states and the District of Columbia (90 percent of the Hispanic population) while the 1994-1996 rates are based on data from 49 states plus the District of Columbia (99.6 percent of the Hispanic population) (National Center for Health Statistics, 1998).

mortality for Hispanics, but with a pattern of significantly higher mortality among young Hispanic men and lower mortality among older Hispanics.

Mortality data present a picture of relatively good health for Hispanics on average; however, survey data on respondent-reported general health present a different picture. Data from the 1992-1994 NHIS revealed that Hispanics were more likely to report "fair" or "poor" health (14.7 percent) than non-Hispanic Whites (10.4 percent). Among Hispanic subgroups, Puerto Ricans were more likely to report "fair" or "poor" health (17.4 percent) than Mexicans (15.3 percent) or Cubans (13.3 percent). A similar pattern of relatively poor respondent-rated health status for Hispanics was found in the 1987-1988 National Survey of Families and Households (Ren and Amick, 1996).

American Indians and Alaska Natives

Much of the data on the health of American Indians and Alaska Natives comes from the Indian Health Service (IHS), which provides health-care services primarily to the American Indian and Alaska Native populations living on or near reservations (Indian Health Service, 1996; Kunitz, 1996)—about 60 percent of all Native Americans residing in the United States. The consensus is that American Indians and Alaska Natives have significantly poorer health than Whites, and data from the IHS, which generally provides a reasonable picture of its service population, corroborate that consensus. Their data also suggest that the gap between American Indians and Alaska Natives and Whites is narrowing.[5] In 1940, life expectancy at birth for American Indians and Alaska Natives was 51 years compared to 64.2 years for Whites, a gap of 13 years (Indian Health Service, 1991). By the period of 1972 to 1974, life expectancy for the IHS population had increased to 63.5, leaving about an 8-year gap. By 1991-1993, the gap had narrowed to about 3.3 years, with a life expectancy of 73.2 years for the IHS population (Indian Health Service, 1996).

Although more than half of American Indians live in urban areas, IHS provides services in relatively few urban areas (Indian Health Service, 1996). Because the IHS data are the primary source of high-quality data on the health of American Indians, little is known about the health of urban American Indians and Alaska Natives. In one of the few studies of urban American Indians, Grossman and colleagues (1994) compared health indicators among urban American Indians, Blacks, and Whites in

---

[5]Even IHS data probably underestimate mortality and overestimate life expectancy for American Indians and Alaska Natives (Indian Health Service, 1991).

the Seattle, Washington, metropolitan area and American Indians in seven rural Washington counties with reservation lands. In general, urban American Indians in this study had a pattern of health similar to that of Blacks—i.e., poorer than Whites; but no consistent differences were found between urban and rural American Indians.

Asian Americans and Pacific Islanders

Immigrants from Asia and the Pacific Islands have been a part of this country for more than a century, but national data on the relative health status of this population have been collected only within the past thirty years (Yu and Liu, 1992). Although national vital statistics are likely to underestimate mortality for Asians and Pacific Islanders, it is still accepted that as a group Asian Americans live longer than Whites. In 1992, the estimated life expectancy for Asian Americans between birth and age 1 was estimated to be 80.3 years compared to 75.1 years for Whites (Hoyert and Kung, 1997). Such a statistical comparison, however, masks the diversity of among Asian and Pacific Islander subgroups. The only reasonable summary statement about the relative health of Asian and Pacific Islander populations is that some of the subgroups enjoy good health compared to the country as a whole, while other subgroups have poorer health.

In 1990 the three largest subgroups among Asian Americans were Chinese Americans (24 percent), Filipinos (20 percent), and Japanese (12 percent) (U.S. Bureau of the Census, 1993). The remaining 44 percent included Vietnamese, Koreans, Hawaiians, Samoans, and Guamanians, and smaller subgroups such as Cambodians and Hmong. Each of these subgroups has a distinctive culture, language, and immigration history. Not surprisingly, health status varies substantially across these groups, as demonstrated by an analysis of 1992 mortality data from seven states that account for 73 percent of the Asian and Pacific Islander population (Hoyert and Kung, 1997). At one extreme, Japanese, Asian Indians, and Koreans had mortality rates of 298.8, 272.2, and 292.3, respectively, substantially lower than the population-wide average of 523.6. At the other extreme, Hawaiians and Samoans had rates of 901.4 and 907.7, respectively. A similar pattern of significantly lower mortality rates for Chinese, Asian Indians, and Japanese was found in California from 1985 to 1990 (Wild et al., 1995).

Wide variations in respondent-rated general health status were in data from the 1992-1994 NHIS (Kuo and Porter, 1998). Compared to 8.9 percent of non-Hispanic Whites reporting "fair" or "poor" general health, 17.2 percent of Vietnamese reported "fair" or "poor" health. The rate for Asian Indians was similar to that for non-Hispanic Whites; for Chinese it was 7.4 percent, for Filipinos, 7.4 percent, and for Japanese, 6.1 percent.

Specific Measures of Mortality and General Health Status

Infant Mortality

Infant mortality has long been considered a key indicator of a population's well being. Low birth weight (LBW) is the most important risk factor for infant mortality. Neonatal infant mortality is generally believed to result from factors intrinsic to the overall health of the pregnancy, whereas postneonatal mortality is considered to be more related to environmental factors in the infant's first year of life. Low birth weight is the most important risk factor for infant mortality and may result because an infant is born too small (small for gestational age [SGA]) and/or too soon (preterm). Data patterns of LBW, SGA, and preterm births are complex and vary among various racial and ethnic groups and subgroups, a full discussion of which is beyond the scope of this overview.

Less complex are data patterns indicating that infant mortality rates are dropping in the United States. As with other health data, it is not possible to establish historical trends for most non-Black minorities because such information has only been available recently; but recent data given in Table 11-2 show current patterns illustrating substantial variation in rates between both groups and subgroups. What is startling is that in 1996 Blacks still had the highest rates at 14.7 per 1,000 live births compared to 6.1 for Whites (National Center for Health Statistics, 1998; MacDorman and Atkinson, 1998). More startling is the fact that the ratio of Black-to-White infant mortality has increased— from 1.6:1 in 1950 to about 2.4:1 in the 1990s (National Center for Health Statistics, 1998). Historical data for American Indians and Alaska Natives documents a substantial improvement in the infant mortality rates, and, in particular, the neonatal infant mortality rates (Indian Health Service, 1996). The neonatal infant mortality rate for American Indians and Alaska Natives remains somewhat higher than that of Whites, but the postneonatal infant mortality rates for American Indians and Alaska Natives are about 2.5 times that of Whites (National Center for Health Statistics, 1998).

Mortality Among the Elderly

The fastest growing age group of the U.S. population is people 85 years old and older, and the growth rate for racial and ethnic minorities is substantially higher than for Whites (Angel and Hogan, 1994; U.S. Bureau of the Census, 1996). The elderly are most likely to experience health problems and, because of their burgeoning number, are likely to consume more and more health-care resources. An increasing percentage of research over the last two decades has addressed the health of the elderly,

TABLE 11-2 Infant, Neonatal, and Postneonatal Mortality Rates by Race or Hispanic Origin of Mother: United States, 1995

Hispanic Origin/ Race of Mother	Infant Mortality Rate	Neonatal Mortality Rate	Postneonatal Mortality Rate
Total Hispanic	6.3	4.1	2.1
Mexican	6.0	3.9	2.1
Puerto Rican	8.9	6.1	2.8
Cuban	5.3	3.6	1.7
Central and South American	5.5	3.7	1.9
Other and unknown Hispanic	7.4	4.8	2.6
Total Non-Hispanic	7.8	5.0	2.8
Non-Hispanic White	6.3	4.0	2.2
Non-Hispanic Black	14.3	9.6	5.0
Asian or Pacific Islander	5.3	3.4	1.9
Chinese	3.8	2.3	1.5
Japanese	5.3	3.3	a
Hawaiian	6.6	4.0	a
Filipino	5.6	3.4	2.2
Other Asian or Pacific Islander	5.5	3.7	1.9
American Indian and Alaskan Native	9.0	3.9	5.1

aFigure does not meet standard of reliability or precision.

SOURCE: MacDorman and Atkinson (1998).

minority elderly in particular; and it has found that patterns of differences in health across racial and ethnic groups persist into old age.

In 1960, life expectancy at age 65 was 14.4 years for Whites and 13.9 years for Blacks—a gap of 0.5 years (National Center for Health Statistics, 1998). By 1990, life expectancy for both groups at this age had increased: at age 65 life expectancy was 17.3 years for Whites and 15.4 years for Blacks, an increase in the gap to 1.9 years.

There has been some debate as to whether the health disadvantages of minorities increase in old age because of a compounding of the effects of age and race, the "double jeopardy" hypothesis (Dowd and Bengston, 1978). Evidence of this hypothesis is inconsistent. Ferraro and Farmer's (1996) longitudinal analysis of national data found that at every age Blacks had poorer health than Whites but did not find Blacks becoming more worse off, relative to Whites, as they age. Gibson (1991) reviewed analyses of several national data sets and described a bimodal distribution of health among older Blacks—a younger group was, on average, relatively sick and an older group was, on average, relatively hardier. For many years, analyses of mortality data have suggested that at older ages, the Black-White mortality gap narrows and eventually crosses over so that the life expectancy of Blacks older than age 75 to 80 exceeds that of Whites. Preston et al. (1996) ascribed mortality cross-over results primarily to differential misreporting of age; Corti and colleagues (1999) suggest that the cross-over may be real.

Mortality rates for elderly Hispanics consistently have been found to be lower than rates for elderly Whites (Sorlie et al., 1993; Liao et al., 1998; National Center for Health Statistics, 1998). Among those age 65 to 74, mortality rates in 1994-1996 for Hispanic males was 2,307.8, for Hispanic females, 1,387.0, for White males, 3,225.0, and for White females, 1,940.8 (National Center for Health Statistics, 1998). Two recent national surveys, however, one of persons age 50 to 60 and another of persons age 70 and above, indicate poorer respondent-rated general health for older Hispanics compared to Whites (Smith and Kington, 1997b).

Mortality data on American Indians and Alaska Natives older than age 65 suggest relatively small differences in health compared to Whites. In 1991-1993, the mortality rate for American Indians and Alaska Natives age 65 and older was 4,255.2; for Whites in this age group, it was 4,871.2 (Indian Health Service, 1996). The general pattern of overall better health for Asians and Pacific Islanders and wide differences among these subgroups persists in old age. For example, life expectancy for persons between ages 65 and 74 in 1992 was 17.2 years for Whites and 19.9 years for all Asians and Pacific Islanders. Among Asian and Pacific Islander subgroups, Chinese, Japanese, Asian Indians, and Filipinos in the older age groups have longer life expectancies than Whites; Hawaiians and Samoans have lower life expectancies (Hoyert and Kung, 1997).

Disability and Functional Status

Disability addresses the impact of disease and poor health on a person's ability to handle demands made on that person in particular environments. One of the most widely accepted frameworks for understanding disability was proposed by Nagi (see review, Nagi, 1976). It describes disability as the end result of a process that leads from pathology in a bodily function, to impairment of a physical structure or function, to a limitation in the ability to perform tasks, and finally to a limitation in performing an expected role. Although disability has a much higher prevalence among the elderly, its impact on individuals and families may be even greater when it occurs in working-age adults (DeJong et al., 1989). Most of the data related to disability and the closely related concept of physical function are from elderly populations.

NHIS is a primary source of data on disability rates. One general measure of disability is activity limitation—i.e., a long-term reduction in the ability to perform the usual age-appropriate activities because of chronic disease or impairment. In 1995 Blacks were more likely than Whites to report an activity limitation (age-adjusted percentage 17.4 percent versus 13.6 percent) (National Center for Health Statistics, 1998). For this paper we analyzed NHIS data for 1992-1994 and found Hispanics overall reported a major activity limitation at a rate similar to non-Hispanic Whites, at about 15 percent age-adjusted, with Puerto Ricans at 15.9 percent, and Cubans and Mexicans at about 10 percent. In general, Asian and Pacific Islanders are less likely to report a disability compared to Whites. Kuo and Porter (1998) report that among Asians and Pacific Islanders, in the NHIS 1992-1994 surveys, an age-adjusted 9.3 percent reported an activity limitation, compared to about 15 percent for non-Hispanic Whites. Although there was variation among Asian and Pacific Islander subgroups, all had percentages less than Whites. The highest percentage was for Vietnamese at 13.2 percent. John (1996) reports high rates of disability among American Indians and Alaska Natives. Across age groups, American Indians and Alaska Natives report higher rates of activity limitations caused by chronic medical conditions (Centers for Disease Control and Prevention, 1992). Among persons age 60 and older, 44 percent report a work disability compared to 29 percent of non-Hispanic Whites (U.S. Bureau of the Census, 1994).

A growing amount of evidence suggests an overall lowering of disability rates among older Americans (e.g., Freeman and Martin, 1998). Relatively few studies have specifically addressed trends in relative disability rates across racial and ethnic groups. Clark (1997) compared data from the 1982, 1984, and 1989 National Long Term Care Surveys and found that Black-White disparities in disability increased substantially over this period. Freeman and Martin (1998), using data from the 1984 and 1993 Survey of Income and Program Participation, present a different pattern. Their findings suggest that disability rates for persons more than 49 years old were higher for both Blacks and Hispanics compared to Whites, but that disability rates in all groups have decreased since the 1980s.

CAUSAL PATHWAYS FOR DIFFERENCES IN HEALTH STATUS

Over the past 20 years, research on differences in health status among racial and ethnic groups has shifted from descriptive studies of differences in outcomes toward analytical studies of potential underlying causes for the differences. Delineating the causal pathways requires pursuing an often frustratingly ill-defined course and piecing together an array of scientific clues. The evidence is overwhelmingly observational and often cross-sectional, with all of the attendant limitations of those types of data; and measures of many important variables are imprecise. Long periods of time generally separate the initiation of a causal factor and its impact on health; to date, no comprehensive studies trace the consequences of any one factor through the complete pathway to the clinical and biological manifestations of impaired health. Therefore, the process of reaching reasonable conclusions about why Blacks have poorer health than Whites, or why Mexican Americans have overall better health than Puerto Ricans, or why Japanese but not Vietnamese have relatively good health requires intellectual leaps, and this literature has been criticized for that reason (e.g., Kaufman and Cooper, 1995).

That said, in the following sections, we review evidence relating observed racial and ethnic differences in health to SEP; health-risk behaviors; psychosocial factors, including stress and racism; access to health care; acculturation; genetic factors; and environmental and occupational exposures to the observed racial and ethnic differences in health. These groups of factors are addressed separately, but many are intimately related to each other. For example, dietary patterns are closely related to socioeconomic position, which in turn may be related to environmental exposures.

Socioeconomic Position

In his groundbreaking 1899 study *The Philadelphia Negro*, DuBois compared mortality rates of Blacks and Whites at different socioeconomic levels. One hundred years later, with increasingly more complex statistical techniques and more comprehensive data sets, the basic premise of DuBois's analysis remains a cornerstone of research efforts to understand racial and ethnic differences in health in the United States.

We use the term socioeconomic position (SEP), as defined by Krieger, Williams, and Moss (1997) and Haan and Kaplan (1985), to capture the range of dimensions that describe an individual's relative and absolute position in society—financial and human resources such as income, wealth, and educational skills; social position or class; occupational prestige; and contextual variables such as neighborhood poverty concentration. SEP also captures the dynamic nature of these dimensions over the life stages from fetal life to old age. Although the range of concepts covered by the term is wide, SEP has been measured, in almost all studies until very recently, by a few relatively simple variables—yearly gross income, education, and occupation. One common analytic approach for studying racial and ethnic differences in health has been first to describe unadjusted differences in a health outcome and then statistically to adjust for SEP and assess whether the differences remain. Unfortunately, when differences in health between groups persist after controlling for standard SEP measures—such as educational attainment—residual differences are often inappropriately attributed to genetic or biologic differences (Kaufman et al., 1997).

Attention has focussed on SEP as a factor in racial and ethnic differences in health for two reasons. First, over the past 150 years, a strong relationship between SEP and health has been found in an overwhelming amount of research (Antonovsky, 1967; Marmot et al., 1987; Bunker et al., 1989; Williams, 1990; Feinstein, 1993; Adler et al., 1994; Evans et al., 1994; Preston and Taubman, 1994; Anderson and Armstead, 1995; Blane et al., 1996; Wilkinson, 1996). The evidence is succinctly summarized in the opening sentence to a recent editorial in *The Lancet* (1995): "The rich are healthy; the poor are not." Second, many racial and ethnic groups with poorer health are also more likely to have low SEP.

Although an association between socioeconomic position and health is well-documented, questions remain about the relative contribution of the two causal directions of the relationship. Lower SEP may lead to poor health, and conversely, poor health may also lead to low SEP. We focus here on the causal direction from SEP to health. (For a discussion of theoretical and analytic implications of this issue, see Garber, 1989, Smith and Kington, 1997b, and Ettner, 1996.)

Measurement and Conceptualization of SEP

Most health databases include only simple measures of SEP such as income and education. The lack of comprehensive measures of SEP in health databases limits researchers' ability to make definitive determinations about the extent to which differences in health status are related to SEP (Kreiger et al., 1997; Kaufman et al., 1997). For example, relatively few health studies include data on wealth, even though wealth may be a better measure of lifetime economic resources than income. Presently, racial and ethnic differences in wealth in the United States are significant, exceed the differences in income, and appear to be growing (e.g., Wolff, 1998, Smith, Volume II, Chapter 4). A person's SEP may also change over time. Most research on the relationships between SEP, race, ethnicity, and health relies on assessments of SEP at a single point in time, overlooking the cumulative and dynamic nature of SEP (Singer and Ryff, 1997); and recent analyses of data sets that include longitudinal data on SEP suggest that duration of SEP matters (Lynch et al., 1997; McDonough et al., 1997; Hart et al., 1998). Health status today may reflect circumstances or exposures decades old. Conditions in early childhood or even *in utero* may set health trajectories for chronic conditions much later in life (Barker, 1994; Peck, 1994). Given the dramatic changes in SEP among racial and ethnic groups in this century, particularly for Blacks, the lack of long-term measures of SEP is especially problematic and could prove detrimental to addressing racial and ethnic disparities.

The characteristics of the area where a person lives may also be SEP determinants of an individual's health (Haan and Camacho, 1987; Anderson et al., 1997). Community-level characteristics encompass factors such as environmental risks and housing quality, and thus are relevant within the context of understanding the role of SEP. Community-level characteristics related to SEP may be especially important for understanding differences in health status because of the persistent degree of residential segregation among some racial and ethnic groups. A growing body of literature has described a strong correlation between various measures of societal-level inequality and mortality. Wilkinson (1996) and other researchers have proposed that inequality at the societal level rather than at the individual level may be the primary pathway for the relationship between SEP and health. Understanding the role of societal-level inequality may be especially relevant in light of growing income inequality between and within some racial and ethnic groups (Pappas et al., 1993).

Summary of Findings on SEP

The bulk of the research addressing the role of socioeconomic position in explaining racial and ethnic differences in health has focused on differences between Blacks and Whites (Williams and Collins, 1995; Smith and Kington, 1997b; Dressler, 1993; Kaufman et al., 1997, 1998; Lillie-Blanton et al., 1996). Most of the reviews—including studies of all-cause mortality as well as infant mortality, general health and function, and specific disease prevalence and incidence—come to the conclusion that SEP (typically education and income) accounts for a substantial part of the observed Black-White differences in health status. Many studies of all-cause mortality (Menchik, 1993; Keil et al., 1992; Rogers, 1992; Sorlie et al., 1992b; Otten et al., 1990) and studies of functional status and general health in adults (Schoenbaum and Waidmann, 1997; Smith and Kington, 1997a; Kington and Smith, 1997; Guralnik et al., 1993) have found that SEP is an important underlying factor. SEP as typically measured, however, appears to play a more limited role in explaining Black-White differences in infant mortality and prevalence of specific diseases such as hypertension and diabetes (Lillie-Blanton et al., 1996; Smith and Kington, 1997b; Williams and Collins, 1995; Schoenbaum and Waidmann, 1997).

Less attention has focused on Hispanics, probably because the health disadvantage is not as consistent. In one of the few studies addressing the role of SEP in explaining health status differences between Hispanics and Whites, Wei and colleagues (1996) analyzed longitudinal data from the San Antonio Heart Study and found that although foreign-born Mexican Americans had mortality rates similar to non-Hispanic Whites, U.S.-born Mexican Americans had a significantly higher mortality rate. Controlling for SEP measured by income, education, and an occupational prestige index accounted for all of the mortality disadvantage for U.S.-born Mexican Americans. In their analysis of mortality data from the National Longitudinal Mortality Study, Sorlie and colleagues (1993) found that the overall Hispanic mortality advantage increased after adjusting for family income. Given the lower SEP of Hispanics in general, this finding suggests that SEP operates within the Hispanic population as it does in general but that other factors are likely to account for the patterns of mortality advantage. To explain this finding of better health among some Hispanic subgroups in spite of worse SEP—what has been called the "Hispanic paradox"or "epidemiological paradox"—several theories have been proposed including selective migration to this country of relatively healthier immigrants, strong social networks of Hispanic immigrant communities, and better diets (Markides and Coreil, 1986). Hayes-Bautista (1992) and Liao and colleagues (1998) have questioned the pervasive acceptance of the intellectual foundations of the "paradox" nomenclature, suggesting that it is based on a simplistic model of causation and a narrowly defined and measured notion of SEP.

SEP also plays a role in rates of low birth weight (LBW) in babies, but the effect of SEP is variable. Among Blacks, Whites, and American Indians and Alaska Natives, LBW rates are inversely related to the mother's level of education: i.e., the higher the level of education, the lower the rate of LBW. American Indians and Alaska Natives have less of a gradient than Blacks or Whites. Hispanics and Asians and Pacific Islanders in general do not show this pattern; they tend to have similar and low rates of LBW across the educational spectrum. Within these minority groups, however, Hawaiians do show a strong inverse relationship, as do Puerto Ricans and Cubans. To further illustrate the complex interactions of race and SEP, LBW rates are higher among the most educated segment of Blacks than among the least educated segment of any other race or ethnic group (National Center for Health Statistics, 1998).

Health-Risk Behaviors

Four health behaviors—smoking, dietary intake, physical activity, and alcohol intake—are particularly important determinants of health. Another important determinant of health, though not a behavior, is obesity.

Obesity, however, is related to both diet and physical activity behaviors; it is also related to the risk for conditions such as diabetes and hypertension, which are important contributors to racial and ethnic differences in health status. A substantial body of evidence suggests significant differences across racial and ethnic groups for a range of health behaviors; increasing attention has been focused by government and private health care entities on public health interventions to discourage risk-increasing health behaviors and promote risk-lowering behaviors (U. S. Department of Health and Human Services, 1990).

Smoking

Cigarette smoking is a causal factor for some cancers, respiratory disease, and cardiovascular disease; and different racial and ethnic groups have distinctly different risks for these diseases. Scientific evidence on racial and ethnic differences in smoking was extensively reviewed in a report from the Office of the Surgeon General (U.S. Department of Health and Human Services, 1998); that report is considered to be the definitive synthesis of evidence on this topic and is, therefore, summarized here.

Among racial and ethnic groups, rates of smoking are highest among American Indians and Alaska Natives, high among Blacks and Southeast Asian men, and lowest among Asian and Pacific Islander and Hispanic women. Among adults during 1994 and 1995, age-adjusted percentages for current smoking among adults were: American Indian and Alaska Native, 36; Blacks 26.5; Whites, 26.4; Hispanics, 18.0, and Asians and Pacific Islanders, 14.2. From 1978 through 1995, smoking declined among Blacks, Asian, and Pacific Islanders, and Hispanic adults. After a period of several years of decline among all groups, however, during the 1990s smoking increased among Black and Hispanic adolescents. Particularly relevant to Hispanic health and the health of other largely immigrant populations is the finding that as immigrant populations acculturate they adopt the smoking habits of the broader community. For example, evidence suggests that smoking increases among Hispanic women as they become more acculturated (Haynes et al., 1990).

The Surgeon General's report concluded that differences in smoking patterns across racial and ethnic groups were directly related to differences in patterns of diseases related to smoking such as lung cancer, but there is little research on how much of the racial and ethnic differences in various smoking related diseases can be attributed to the behavior (Chen, 1993).

Dietary Intake

We know of no research that has specifically addressed the relationship between observed racial and ethnic differences in health and differences in diet. In the face of growing evidence relating diet to health risks, the National Academy of Sciences developed guidelines to promote healthy dietary intake; they recommend that people consume less fat, cholesterol, sodium, and red meat, and more carbohydrates and fiber from fruits, vegetables, grains, and legumes (National Research Council, 1989). In recent years, Americans in general have improved their dietary habits, with notable decreases in fat and cholesterol intake (Norris et al., 1997); however, the overall dietary quality remains low for all groups.

The analysis of racial and ethnic differences in diet is complicated by large differences in diet among persons of differing SEP (James et al., 1997). Popkin and colleagues (1996, 1997) compared survey data for Whites and Blacks between 1965 and 1989-1991 and calculated a diet quality index that scores overall compliance with eight dietary recommendations of the National Academy of Sciences; they found that in 1965 the dietary quality of Whites and Blacks was similar and that overall quality improved for both Blacks and Whites. There were only small differences across racial and socioeconomic groups, and Blacks at high socioeconomic levels had the highest quality diets.

Data from NHIS in 1987 and 1992 indicate Hispanics consumed the least fat as a percentage of energy in both time periods and reduced fat and cholesterol intake more than Whites or Blacks. Blacks reduced fat and cholesterol intake substantially less than Whites. There was little change for the population as a whole in fiber intake, but Hispanics in 1992 consumed more fiber than Whites or Blacks (Norris et al., 1997).

Few studies have comprehensively described the dietary habits of either American Indians and Alaska Natives or Asians and Pacific Islanders, and we found none that described trends. The studies that have addressed these groups typically have been restricted to one subgroup such as a single American Indian and Alaska Native tribe or an Asian and Pacific Islander group in one city. A recent review of studies of dietary habits of American Indians and Alaska Natives concluded that in general this population has a diet that is moderately high in total fat and saturated fat and low in polyunsaturated fat and fiber, but it was noted that in spite of these patterns, American Indians and Alaska Natives overall have low rates of two common diet-related diseases, heart disease and cancer (Bell et al., 1997).

Although most research on racial differences in dietary habits has focused on consumption of high-risk foods such as fat and cholesterol and related risks for obesity and cardiovascular disease, insufficient food intake may also be an important health-risk factor, especially for women of child-bearing age and children. From 1988 through 1994, the overall prevalence of food insufficiency, as measured by reports of a family sometimes or often not having enough food to eat, was about 4.1 percent (Alaimo et al., 1998). Insufficiency was primarily related to poverty, but there were differences across racial and ethnic groups. Non-Hispanic Black families were more likely to report food insufficiency than non-Hispanic White families, primarily due to income and other socio-demographic differences. Even after controlling for these factors, however, Mexican families were twice as likely to report food insufficiency as non-Hispanic White families. It is not known to what extent differences in food insufficiency contributed to differences in health outcomes.

Physical Activity

The relationship between physical activity and good health has been clearly demonstrated (U.S. Department of Health and Human Services, 1990, 1996). Lack of physical activity has been shown to be related to overall mortality as well as to the risk of chronic diseases such as cardiovascular disease, non-insulin dependent diabetes, osteoarthritis, and depression (U.S. Department of Health and Human Services, 1996). Rates of physical activity clearly differ across racial and ethnic groups. In 1990, only 34.3 percent of Blacks and 34.9 percent of Hispanics older than age 18 reported exercising or playing sports regularly compared to 41.5 percent of Whites and 41.2 percent of all non-Hispanics older than age 18 (Piani and Schoenborn, 1993). The one exception to this general pattern across age groups and genders was among men between ages 18 and 29; in this group Blacks were more likely to report regular exercise or playing sports than Whites.

Relatively little is known about the physical activity patterns of American Indians and Alaska Natives and Asians and Pacific Islanders. An analysis of national data from the 1991-1992 Behavioral Risk Factor Surveillance System compared across racial and ethnic groups the percentage of persons with a sedentary lifestyle, defined as reporting fewer than three 20-minute sessions of leisure-time physical activity per week (*Morbidity and Mortality Weekly Report*, 1994). The study found sedentary lifestyle rates of 64 to 65 percent for both Asians and Pacific Islanders and American Indians and Alaska Natives, compared to 56 percent for Whites, 62 percent for Hispanics, and 68 percent for Blacks. In all groups, with the exception of Asian and Pacific Islander men, the prevalence of sedentary lifestyle was lowest among those with the highest education. We found no comprehensive analyses comparing rates of physical activity across subgroups of Asians and Pacific Islanders or American Indians and Alaska Natives.

Obesity

Obesity, defined as a body-mass index of ≥30.0, although not a behavior, is an important risk factor for a range of important chronic diseases and is likely related to both dietary intake and physical activity behaviors. With obesity, genetic factors are also likely to play a causal role (Rosenbaum et al., 1997a). The prevalence of overweight and obesity has increased considerably across the U.S. population since at least 1960, and the general trends have been similar across racial and ethnic groups for whom trend data are available (Flegal et al., 1998). National data on body weight for Blacks and Hispanics have been available only since the late 1970s, and there are few data sets on body weight for Asians and Pacific Islanders and American Indians and Alaska Natives. Non-Hispanic Blacks and Mexicans are substantially more likely to be obese, with most of the difference among women. During 1988 through 1994, 22.4 percent of non-Hispanic White women were obese, compared to 37.4 percent of non-Hispanic Black women and 34.2 percent of Mexican women (Flegal et al., 1998). Furthermore, analysis of data on adolescents suggested that the rate of obesity increases in second- and third-generation immigrants (Popkin and Udry, 1998). Although data from other racial and ethnic groups are more limited, they suggest a high prevalence of obesity as well among Puerto Ricans, American Indians and Alaska Natives, Native Hawaiians, and Samoans, again with strikingly higher rates among women (Kumanyika, 1993; McGarvey, 1991; Aluli, 1991; Broussard et al., 1991).

Few studies have specifically addressed the contribution of racial and ethnic differences in obesity to the differences in prevalence of chronic medical conditions. Obesity is a particularly important risk factor for adult-onset diabetes, and Blacks, Hispanics, and American Indians all are at increased risk (Centers for Disease Control and Prevention, 1992). Two studies of the contribution of obesity to Black-White differences in diabetes found that the obesity contributed to, but did not explain all of, the differences in diabetes (O'Brien et al., 1989; Cowie et al., 1993).

Alcohol

Excessive alcohol intake is an important health-risk factor related to numerous health outcomes including chronic diseases such as cirrhosis, pancreatitis, and cardiomyopathy as well as injuries and sexually transmitted diseases. Alcohol is also a factor in a range of adverse pregnancy outcomes and fetal abnormalities. There are substantial differences in alcohol intake across racial and ethnic groups. In 1990, Blacks were less likely than Whites (4.3 percent versus 5.8 percent) and Hispanics were less likely than non-Hispanics (4.6 percent versus 5.6 percent) to report excessive alcohol intake (here defined as an average of one ounce or more of alcohol per day in a two-week period) (Piani and Schoenborn, 1993); likewise, Blacks were less likely than Whites (46.4 percent versus 63.1 percent) to report at least one drink of beer, wine, or liquor over two weeks, and Hispanics were less likely than non-Hispanics (52.3 percent versus 61.4 percent) to report at least one drink of beer, wine, or liquor over a two-week period. Data from the 1982-1984 Hispanic Health and Nutrition Examination Survey suggest that among Hispanic subgroups, Mexican and Puerto Rican men have the highest rates of excessive alcohol intake (Aguirre-Molina and Caetano, 1994).

Excessive alcohol intake is a particularly important problem among American Indian and Alaska Native populations. From 1991 through 1993 their mortality rate from alcoholism was 38.4, 6.3 times the rate among Whites (Indian Health Service, 1996). Though the rate remains high, both the absolute alcoholism mortality rate and the rate relative to Whites has decreased in recent years. From 1979 through 1981, the alcoholism mortality rate among American Indians was 59.0, 8.6 times the rate in Whites. Although there is no question that alcoholism has a significant impact on the health of American Indian populations, surveys of drinking patterns, most of which are restricted to a single tribe or reservation, present a complex picture. A recent review of the epidemiologic evidence on drinking among American Indians concluded that (1) there is wide variation in drinking patterns across subgroups and periods of time, (2) some recent studies suggest less drinking on average among American Indians compared to the general U.S. population, (3) urban Indian populations tend to have a higher prevalence of drinking than reservation populations, (4) Indian women are more likely than other U.S. women to abstain, and (5) among those Indians who drink, there is a high prevalence of heavy drinkers, particularly binge drinkers (May, 1996).

Although the deleterious health effects of excessive alcohol intake are clear, the overall health implications of alcohol intake for a population are complicated by the well-described relationship between moderate alcohol intake and decreased mortality, especially for cardiovascular disease.

Summary

The evidence suggests significant differences in favorable and unfavorable health-related behaviors across racial and ethnic groups (Myers et al., 1995). Relatively few studies have attempted to estimate the contribution of behavioral differences to differences in outcomes such as mortality. Otten and colleagues (1990) analyzed longitudinal data beginning in 1971 through 1975 for a national cohort of persons and estimated the percentage of the Black-White differential in mortality that could be attributed to six risk factors: smoking, alcohol intake, cholesterol level, body-mass index, and systolic blood pressure. They found that 31 percent of the mortality difference could be attributed to these factors, 38 percent to family income, and the remaining 31 percent was unexplained. Berkman and Mullen (1997) analyzed data from the Established Population for Epidemiologic Studies of the Elderly in New Haven and concluded the Black-White differences in health behaviors were unlikely to account for Black-White differences in health status. Similarly, an analysis of mortality differences between U.S.-born and foreign-born Mexicans and non-Hispanic Whites in the San Antonio Heart Study found that health-risk factors, including smoking, physical activity, and alcohol intake, added little to explaining differences beyond SEP (Wei et al., 1996). Lantz and colleagues (1998) attempted to assess the contribution of risk behaviors to health differences among socioeconomic groups and also found that smoking, alcohol intake, sedentary lifestyle, and relative body weight did not account for those differences in mortality. Though the importance of reducing unfavorable health behaviors and promoting favorable health behaviors throughout the general population is unquestioned, and differences in health behaviors probably contribute to racial and ethnic differences in health, health behaviors alone are unlikely to account for the bulk of the racial and ethnic differences in general health status.

Psychosocial Factors: Stress and Racism

Researchers also have long speculated that the stressful effects of racial and ethnic discrimination and marginalization in American society could underlie some of the racial differences in health. Indeed, in recent decades, studies have begun to describe increasingly complex physiologic pathways that connect stress with adverse health outcomes (Weiner, 1992). Much of the literature on the relationship between stress and racial differences in health has specifically addressed the role of stress in the risk for hypertension, which has a much higher prevalence among Blacks and is thought to be causally related to a range of psychological factors.

One issue that has been examined is whether race or SEP is the source of stress; conflicting results have been reported (Kessler and Neighbors, 1986; Cockerham, 1990; Fiscella and Franks, 1997). A substantial body of work has arisen from surveys in which people are asked about their perceptions related to racism or discrimination; then the correlation between their responses and an objective health outcome is measured. One of the principal barriers to this area of research is the subjective nature of stress, and the circular reasoning associated with it: something is stressful if it makes someone feel stressed and vice versa. Again the results of these studies are inconclusive. It is also difficult to determine the direction of the causal relationship: poor health can create a predisposition to experience life as stressful (Kennedy et al., 1997; Jackson et al., 1996).

Another group of studies have examined patterns of coping styles and their relation to health outcomes (Krieger and Sidney, 1996; Strogatz et al., 1997). However, a complication of interpreting this research is that coping styles are not value free. In general, American society favors active coping, even in a situation in which one is lower in the power structure. Perhaps the most colorfully described coping style explored has been John Henryism (named for the folk hero) (James, 1994)—i.e., the tendency on the part of some Black men to adapt by overcompensating, to overcome racial stereotypes by laboring self-destructively and then succumbing to ill health from overwork.

A related set of studies looked at the effect on health outcomes of what might be termed an imposed coping style: workplace conditions. One study examined job-related decision latitude and job strain; for Black men, but not Black women, high decision latitude was associated with a lower prevalence of hypertension (Curtis et al., 1997). Another body of research has addressed whether similar measures of control in the workplace also underlie socioeconomic differences in health outcomes (e.g., Marmot et al., 1997). Finally, there are a substantial number of studies that have tried to reverse the causal chain, for example, using stress reduction as a treatment for hypertension (e.g., Schneider et al., 1995).

Access to Health Care

Historically, much of the public policy discussion about differences in health across sociodemographic groups has been devoted to the role of health care, especially differences in access—i.e., the extent to which an individual is able to obtain a reasonable level of medical services given his or her medical care needs. Although health insurance is an important determinant of access, it is not the only determinant. Other access factors include willingness of providers to accept certain forms of insurance, insurance co-payments, travel costs, the cultural competence of health care providers, and the knowledge of, and attitudes toward, the patient and the health of patients and their families. All these factors affect access regardless of whether an individual has health insurance. One of the primary reasons for focusing on health insurance, however, is the prominent role that the federal and state governments have played in providing health insurance, especially for vulnerable populations including the elderly and the poor.

We know of no empirical research that has attempted to estimate explicitly how much racial and ethnic differences in access contribute to differences in health status. For decades, the conventional wisdom in the public health community has been that most of the improvements in health in this century were the result of society-level improvements in nutrition and housing and public health activities such as improved sanitation, rather than the result of medical interventions (e.g., McKeown, 1979; McKinlay and McKinlay, 1977). More recently, however, researchers have criticized these conclusions, suggesting that, in fact, a significant part of the recent improvements in health are indeed the result of medical interventions (Bunker, 1995; Andrulis, 1998). Furthermore, a number of studies suggest that lack of insurance coverage is related to a range of clinical outcomes, including mortality (Braveman et al., 1989; Shea et al., 1992; Franks et al., 1993a, 1993b; Ayanian et al., 1993; Braveman et al., 1994).

Prenatal care is often a prominent part of discussions of LBW and infant mortality in part because prenatal care is one of the few direct interventions available in attempting to lower LBW and infant mortality rates. The percent of live births in which prenatal care began during the first trimester is 84 percent for Whites, 81 percent for Asians, 72 percent for Hispanics, 71 percent for Blacks, and 67.7 percent for American Indians (National Center for Health Statistics, 1998). Unfortunately the data do not support the assertion that prenatal care even if universally provided would dramatically change infant mortality rates (Mustard and Roos, 1994; Fiscella, 1995). In addition to representing a set of health-care services, use of prenatal care may also be an indicator of women who differ along a number of dimensions from women who obtain prenatal care late or not at all.

Clearly, there is wide consensus in this country in favor of providing reasonable access to health care for everyone, to maximize health and quality of life and minimize pain and suffering. The fundamental question of the role of medical care in eliminating differences across groups is important because it may predict the relative effectiveness of alternative strategies targeted to reduce racial and ethnic differences overall. There is a growing compilation of high-quality evidence of the impact of both medical and public health interventions on a range of diseases that are major determinants of mortality and likely causal factors in racial and ethnic differences in health. A reasonable conclusion is that access to effective medical interventions plays a role in the differences in health. How much of a role is unclear.

In the United States, health insurance is probably the major determinant of access, and health insurance serves primarily by reducing the out-of-pocket cost of medical services. Most working-age Americans are insured by private insurance obtained through employment, and racial and ethnic differences in employment patterns underlie some of the differences in insurance patterns. The vast majority of elderly persons are primarily insured by Medicare with most elderly having secondary coverage by private insurance, often related to previous employment. The majority of children receive insurance coverage through their parents' employment-obtained insurance, but a large minority of children are covered by Medicaid. The type of health insurance coverage a person has may be another important determinant of access because reimbursement rates vary by insurance type. In particular, Medicaid reimbursement rates are substantially lower than those of private insurers. As a result, providers may limit access to Medicaid recipients and the quality of services may also be lower (Braveman et al., 1994; Medicaid Access Study Group, 1994).

Hispanics

Among racial and ethnic minority groups in the United States, Hispanics have the lowest rates of health insurance coverage. In 1995, 30.8 percent of Hispanics younger than age 65 were uninsured, compared to 12.7 percent of non-Hispanic Whites (National Center for Health Statistics, 1998). Furthermore, there is substantial variation across Hispanic subpopulations; 17.8 percent of Puerto Ricans, 21.6 percent of Cubans, 35.4 percent of Mexican Americans, and 29 percent of other Hispanics were uninsured in 1995 (National Center for Health Statistics, 1998). As is true for the elderly in every racial and ethnic group, the vast majority of Hispanic elderly, though still a lower percentage than Whites and Blacks, are covered by Medicare; for example, in 1989, of those age 65 and older, 96 percent of non-Hispanic Whites, 95 percent of non-Hispanic Blacks, and 91 percent of Hispanics were covered by Medicare (General Accounting Office, 1992). There are also substantial differences in insurance coverage among Hispanic subgroups correlated with foreign birth. During 1989 and 1990, 40.8 percent of foreign-born Hispanics age 18 or older were uninsured compared to 24.8 percent of U.S.-born Hispanics (Thamer et al., 1997).

The distinctive pattern of insurance coverage among Hispanics below age 65 results from two factors (Valdez et al., 1993; General Accounting Office, 1992); first, Hispanics are more likely to work in lower paying jobs in smaller firms and in industries less likely to offer health insurance coverage; second, as a group, Hispanics, and especially Mexicans (only 19 percent of whom were covered by Medicaid), are more likely to reside in states with more stringent Medicaid eligibility criteria—e.g., Texas and Florida. Puerto Ricans, on the other hand, 36.3 percent of whom are covered by Medicaid, are concentrated in New York and New Jersey—two states with less restrictive Medicaid eligibility requirements.

Another indicator of access to health care is whether one has a regular source of medical care. By this measure as well, Hispanics have less access to care compared to Whites. In 1993, among persons ages 18 to 64, 71.9 percent of Hispanics reported a regular source of care compared to 84.2 percent of non-Hispanic Whites; for Mexicans the number was 69.5 percent (Bloom et al., 1997).

Blacks

With the enactment of the legislation creating Medicare and Medicaid in 1965, substantially more Americans in general, Blacks in particular, began to enjoy the benefits of health insurance coverage. That legislation, along with the 1964 Civil Rights Act, played an important role in eliminating segregation in health-care facilities (Halperin, 1988; Thomson, 1997). Implementation of Medicare and Medicaid effected a substantial narrowing of gaps between Blacks and Whites in coverage and access (Davis et al., 1987). Nevertheless, some differences remain, mostly in the types of insurance coverage. Among persons younger than age 65 in 1996, 55.4 percent of non-Hispanic Blacks and 78.5 percent of non-Hispanic Whites had private insurance, 24.2 percent of Blacks and 7.5 percent of Whites had public insurance, and 18.9 percent of Blacks and 12.9 percent of Whites had no insurance (National Center for Health Statistics, 1998). Of those older than age 65, 42 percent of non-Hispanic Blacks and 77.9 percent of non-Hispanic Whites had private insurance in addition to Medicare.

Black adults report having a regular source of care at frequencies similar to Whites. Between ages 18 and 64, about 83.1 percent of non-Hispanic Blacks and 84.2 percent of non-Hispanic Whites report having a regular source of care, while above age 64, about 94 percent of both Whites and Blacks report having a regular source of care (Bloom et al., 1997; Cohen et al., 1997).

Asians and Pacific Islanders

Asians and Pacific Islanders in general are more likely to be uninsured than Whites. In 1996, 18.6 percent of Asians and Pacific Islanders younger than age 65 were uninsured compared to 15.4 percent of Whites (National Center for Health Statistics, 1998). In 1996, Asians and Pacific Islanders were slightly more likely (12.4 percent) to report coverage by Medicaid or another public program compared to Whites (9.3 percent) under age 65 and were less likely to have private insurance (67.8 percent versus 74.2 percent). As with Hispanics, where a person was born also was a factor in the percentage uninsured. In 1989 and 1990, of those older than age 18, 20.9 percent of foreign-born Asians and Pacific Islanders were uninsured. Of that same age group, about 11 percent of both U.S.-born Asians and Pacific Islanders and U.S.-born Whites were uninsured (Thamer et al., 1997).

As with health status, there is significant variation in access across Asian and Pacific Islander subgroups. Comparing pooled data from the 1993-1996 NHIS on age-adjusted insurance rates for those younger than age 65, we found the variation striking. On average, about 19.2 percent were uninsured in this period and 68.1 percent had private insurance. Of the subgroups, Japanese had the highest rate of private insurance (86.5 percent) and the lowest rate of uninsured (10.3 percent). The rate of private insurance among Korean Americans was 56.7 percent; uninsured was 36.8 percent. An alternative measure of access is the length of time since a person last saw a physician; analysis of 1992-1994 NHIS data on this access measure revealed similar variation across Asian and Pacific Islander subpopulations (Kuo and Porter, 1998). Japanese and Vietnamese had the highest age-adjusted percentage of persons who had been seen by a physician within a year (76.7 percent); Koreans and Chinese had the lowest percentage (69.7 percent). On average, Asians and Pacific Islanders reported a slightly longer period of time since the last physician visit compared to Whites. Adjusting for age, 73.4 percent of Asians and Pacific Islanders had seen a physician within the last year compared to 79.6 percent of Whites.

American Indians and Alaska Natives

American Indians and Alaska Natives have had the option of receiving health care from the federal government since the early nineteenth century. In 1995, IHS operated 38 hospitals and 112 health centers, which, in general, offer a more limited range of services than other community health settings (Kunitz, 1996). Relatively little is known about the access to health care services for Native Americans who are not covered by the IHS. In 1987, the National Medical Expenditures Survey (NMES) was used to obtain information about American Indians and Alaska Natives eligible for IHS services. Results showed that 55 percent had no health insurance other than the IHS. Even the elderly population was less well covered than other elderly populations; only 85 percent were covered by Medicare, compared to over 96 percent for other groups (Cunningham and Schur, 1991).

Trends in Insurance Coverage

Analyses of gross trends in insurance coverage suggest an increase in the percentage of persons without insurance in recent decades. Determining detailed trends in insurance coverage across racial and ethnic groups, however, is difficult because different surveys often ask different questions about coverage, which may affect estimates, and because surveys may lack sufficient sample sizes to estimate changes in coverage over time for small groups. Estimates of the extent of the change in insurance coverage across racial and ethnic groups in recent decades vary depending on the data source and the time period. Berk and colleagues (1996) compared data from the 1977 National Medical Care Expenditures Survey, the 1987 NMES, and the 1989 and 1992 NHIS and found that for the entire U.S. population, although the percentage of uninsured increased (from 12.2 percent in 1977 to 17.1 percent in 1992), the rate of increase varied substantially across racial and ethnic groups. They estimated that the increase in uninsured Hispanics accounted for almost 40 percent of the total increase over the covered time periods, with Mexican Americans alone accounting for 27 percent of the increase.

Since the 1980s, the changes in the number of Americans without health insurance are not as striking. Comparison of data from the 1987 NMES with 1996 Medical Expenditures Panel Survey data on similar questions reveals increases in the rates of uninsured among the non-institutionalized population of Hispanics. In 1987, percentages were: Hispanics 31.5 percent and Blacks 22.0 percent. The comparable 1996 percentages were: Hispanics, 33.5 percent and Blacks, 22.9 percent (Short et al., 1989; Vistnes and Monheit, 1997). Comparison of NHIS data over a similar time period: in 1984, the percentages uninsured were Hispanics 29.0 percent, Asians and Pacific Islanders 17.8 percent, non-Hispanic Blacks 19.2 percent, and non-Hispanic Whites 11.6 percent; in 1996, Hispanics 31.6 percent, Asians and Pacific Islanders 18.6 percent, non-Hispanic Blacks 18.9 percent, and non-Hispanic Whites 12.9 percent (National Center for Health Statistics, 1998).

Analyses of data from the Current Population Survey between 1989 and 1996 revealed that the largest increase in percentage of persons uninsured was among Blacks (2.4 percent) (Carrasquillo et al., 1999). Among Hispanics, the percentage uninsured did not change significantly over this period, but because of the increase in the overall size of the Hispanic population, Hispanics accounted for a large increase in the absolute number of uninsured.

Quality of Care

Because of concerns about the rising costs of health care, public attention has expanded beyond access to address the issue of the quality of
health-care services, and with increased attention has come increasing
evidence of differences in the quality of health care provided across racial
and ethnic groups. A large number of studies have documented differences in the usage of a range of health-care services among racial and
ethnic groups, and most have found that Blacks are less likely to receive a
number of procedures (Escarce et al., 1993; McBean and Gornick, 1994;
Carlisle et al., 1995; Ford and Cooper, 1995). Schulman et al. (1999) conducted a study involving physicians and identical presentations of patients with chest pain; the only variation in the presentation was the
patient's race and gender. Differences by race and gender were found in
the proportion of patients referred for cardiac catheterization. This compelling evidence suggests that bias at the level of the health-care system
may be a reflection of biases in physicians' clinical judgments and diagnoses. Differences in usage, however, can also be the result of a range of
other factors including differences in access, differences in clinical characteristics of diseases, and differences in patient preferences. (An overview
of racial and ethnic differences in utilization is included in the paper by
Oddone and colleagues in this volume).

Relatively few studies have explicitly compared the quality of care
across racial and ethnic groups. In an analysis of data based on the review
of more than 30,000 New York State medical records in 1984, Burstin and
colleagues (1992) found that compared to a reference group of Whites and
others, Blacks were not more likely to experience substandard care as
measured by the overall rate of adverse medical events, but were more
likely to experience adverse medical events due to negligence. The difference, however, was no longer significant after accounting for lack of insurance and low income, both of which were related to greater likelihood
of substandard care.

In another study based on reviews of medical records of a sample of
Medicare recipients between 1981 and 1986, Kahn and colleagues (1994)
found that within each category of hospital (rural, urban teaching, and
urban non-teaching), Blacks were more likely to have poorer processes of
care even after controlling for a range of patient and hospital characteristics. An interesting finding of this study was that overall both Blacks and
patients from poor neighborhoods did not experience poorer care because they tended to receive care in urban teaching hospitals, which delivered better care than the other types of hospitals. More recently, Pappas
and colleagues (1997) analyzed data on the 1990 rates of hospitalization
for conditions that may be avoidable if appropriate ambulatory care were

provided and found that even among persons privately insured, Blacks under age 65 were more likely than Whites to experience avoidable hospitalizations.

There is little research addressing the quality of care of Hispanics, Asians and Pacific Islanders, or American Indians and Alaska Natives. In one of the few assessments of quality of care specifically addressing Hispanics, researchers at UCLA reviewed medical records from emergency room patients with isolated long-bone fractures and found that even after controlling for a range of potentially confounding factors, Hispanic patients were twice as likely to receive no pain medication (Todd et al., 1993). Another small study of pain control among cancer patients found a similar pattern of insufficient pain control for Hispanics and other minorities (Cleeland et al., 1997). A small number of the studies of utilization of procedures have also addressed racial and ethnic differences other than Black-White differences. For example, Carlisle and colleagues (1995) reviewed hospital discharge data for use of invasive cardiac procedures in Los Angeles between 1986 and 1988 and found that, as in other study samples, controlling for a range of sociodemographic and clinical variables, Blacks and Hispanics were also less likely to receive the procedures compared to Whites and Asians.

Managed care has raised new concerns. As more and more persons have become covered by managed-care organizations, fears have been raised that by placing barriers to access, managed-care organizations will exacerbate existing racial and ethnic differentials in access to health care and possibly increase differentials in quality of care, although few data are available on this topic (Rosenbaum et al., 1997b).

Any conclusion regarding the contribution of differences in health care access to differences in health requires substantial speculation. In general, many racial and ethnic minority groups have less access to health care than the majority population, and these differences are probably related to differences in health outcomes.

The Role of Minority Health-Care Professionals in Access and Provision

The relationship between an available supply of minority physicians and access to care has been buttressed by several studies that support the conclusion that minority physicians are much more likely to serve minority patients, and to serve poorer patients (Moy and Bartman, 1995; Komaromy et al., 1996). Advocates for increasing minority representation among health-care professionals make the case that minority professionals have a broad salutary effect on minority patients' health (Nickens, 1991). For that reason, among others, underrepresentation of minorities in the health professions has occupied a substantial part of the discussion of minority access to health care and minority health in general, particularly since the Civil Rights movement of the 1960s.

In 1964, only 2.2 percent of the 32,000 students enrolled in the nation's then 83 allopathic medical schools were Black. The only two Black medical schools then in existence, Howard and Meharry, enrolled 76 percent of these students—i.e., on average, each of the other 81 schools enrolled only 1 Black student every two years (Hutchins et al., 1967). In 1971, the first year for which there are data for minority groups other than Blacks, only 19 Mexican Americans, 14 mainland Puerto Ricans, and 2 American Indian physicians graduated from U.S. medical schools. (These groups plus Blacks are the four groups considered by the Association of American Medical Colleges to be underrepresented in medicine). Such low enrollment numbers provided an obvious target for physicians and others seeking to obtain racial equity in the health profession; since then, substantial energy has been directed toward increasing minority representation in medicine (Nickens et al., 1994).

One way of quantifying racial and ethnic representation in medical professions is by calculating race/ethnic-specific physician-population ratios. For example, Libby et al. (1997) estimate that in 1990 there were 124 Hispanic, 69 Black, 46 American Indian, 875 Asian, and 241 non-Hispanic White active physicians per 100,000 persons. This would seem to create a somewhat artificial, some would say objectionable, implication—i.e., that only those of a given racial/ethnic group can or should treat members of that group. Obviously, that is not true. By quantifying minority representation, an indication of access to care is provided, and considering the fact that medical professions tend to rate high on professional indexes, an indication of the group's progress on the socioeconomic ladder.

Although arguments over what is the appropriate physician-population ratio are far from settled, Hispanic, Black, and American Indian and Alaska Native physician supply numbers are far below any that could reasonably be advanced as adequate. At the other extreme, Asians now represent about one in five new entrants to U.S. allopathic medical schools, about six times their representation in the population at large (Association of American Medical Colleges, 1998a).

Health professions across the board have similar levels of underrepresentation of Hispanics, Blacks, and American Indians and Alaska Natives. Blacks, for example, are 3.6 percent of physicians, 3.1 percent of dentists, 1.7 percent of veterinarians, and 3.4 percent of podiatrists (Association of American Medical Colleges, 1998a). Underrepresented minorities are even more profoundly underrepresented among Ph.D.s in science than within health professions (Malcolm et al., 1998). Though hard data are lacking, many in the health research community believe that minority researchers may be more likely to be interested in problems related to minority and disadvantaged populations than nonminorities. If this is true, then addressing the research agenda implicit in the many unanswered questions we pose in this paper will be much more difficult without a racially and ethnically diverse research workforce.

Acculturation

Acculturation is the process by which members of immigrant or other marginalized groups assimilate into the broader, majority culture. The range of processes for minority groups includes the immigration and assimilation experiences of Hispanics and Asians and Pacific Islanders, the road from slavery to the present for Blacks, the American Indian's history of subjugation and repression, and the incorporation of indigenous Alaska Native and Hispanic populations. Unfortunately, our understanding of the acculturation process and how it affects health is still rudimentary, and researchers have yet to develop a clear and consistent framework that captures the complexity of the processes (Palinkas and Pickwell, 1995).

In contrast to many issues related to minority health, studies of acculturation have been focused primarily on non-Black minorities. Studies have typically used indicators such as foreign versus U.S. birth or fluency in English as measures of acculturation. More elaborate acculturation scales measure factors such as media preferences; friendship networks; ethnic identification of self, mother, and father; and subscription to values that are thought to be associated with the "traditional" culture of origin (e.g., Hazuda et al., 1988).

Typically studies in acculturation and its relation to health status measure the relationship between the degree of acculturation and outcomes such as health behaviors—e.g., smoking and use of prenatal care (Zambrana et al., 1997), obesity (Hazuda et al., 1988), low birth weight (Cobas et al., 1996), and rates of chronic diseases (Palinkas and Pickwell, 1995; Wei et al., 1996). Many of these studies have shown a correlation between adverse health effects and acculturation, but there are suggestions that the overall correlation may mask a more complex process (English et al., 1997). Superficially, it would appear that there is a clear-cut causal link between acquiring health-risk behaviors such as smoking and drug use and the fact that these behaviors are often more common in the United States than in immigrants' countries of origin (Haynes et al., 1990); however, this explanation overlooks the fact that acculturation is not a passive acquisition process. Individuals interact with the majority culture and make choices about which aspects of the new culture to adopt. Immigrants often come to this country seeking the American lifestyle and so may choose elements of that lifestyle that are both obvious and available to them. A more nuanced understanding of acculturation as a reflection of active choices is needed.

Genetic Factors

Perhaps no topic covered in this paper elicits more heated and emotional debate than the question of the role of fundamental biologic and genetic differences as the cause of racial and ethnic differences in health. One reason for concern when this topic is raised is the lengthy history in this country of the misuse of science to support of racism (e.g., see Krieger, 1987). Because of that history, many reviews of racial differences in health have tended to dismiss genetic factors as important determinants of racial and ethnic differences in health. Recent advances in science, however, point to growing evidence that support a role for genetic factors in the etiology of a wide range of diseases, often via complex pathways in which multiple genetic factors are likely to interact with each other and with environmental factors. Although the role of genetic factors in determining the risk of disease in individuals is becoming clearer, the role of genetic factors in explaining differences in health across populations remains quite obscure (Baird, 1994). A detailed discussion of this issue is beyond the scope of this paper. However, worthy of note is that genetic factors alone cannot explain the trends in racial and ethnic differences in health during this century. In diseases in which genetic factors are known to play a role, these trends are likely to be explained by changes in environmental factors which then have their greatest impact on those persons who are at greatest risk genetically.

A recent review of the evidence on the role of genetic factors in explaining racial and ethnic differences in health of the elderly focused on Black-White differences in hypertension and diabetes, two genetically complex and environmentally influenced diseases that differ in risk between Blacks and Whites (Neel, 1997). The review concluded that the interaction of genetic and environmental factors is sufficiently complex that there is little prospect of disentangling the role of genetic factors in explaining racial differences in the near future.

Although clear-cut answers are unlikely to appear for decades, if ever, the volume of research addressing this issue is growing rapidly. For example, the apolipoprotein E (apoE)-ε4 gene allele has been found in several studies to be a risk factor for Alzheimer's disease, an important disease in the elderly population (Jarvik, 1997). Studies, however, have found that the apoE-ε4 allele appears to be less closely related to the disease among Blacks (Farrer et al., 1997). A recent population-based longitudinal study of a sample of elderly in New York City compared the risk for Alzheimer's disease associated with apoE-ε4 allele across racial and ethnic groups and found that although the presence of the allele was a risk factor for Alzheimer's disease among Whites, it was not a risk factor among Hispanics and Blacks (Tang et al., 1998). Furthermore, the study found that both Blacks and Hispanics in the sample were at significantly greater risk of Alzheimer's disease and speculated that other genes may account for this risk. With regard to other health factors, studies have suggested that genetically based racial differences in the metabolism of nicotine might be related to observed Black-White differences in smoking patterns (Perez-Stable et al., 1998; Caraballo et al., 1998). Regarding hypertension, a large body of literature has begun to address the role of various genetic factors in explaining racial differences in the etiology of that disease (Cooper and Rotimi, 1994). The potential for further study addressing the role of genetic factors in racial and ethnic differences in health is likely to increase greatly with the growing number of large population studies that include clinical and genetic data as well as socioeconomic and environmental data on sufficiently large samples of diverse racial and ethnic groups.

Environmental and Occupational Exposures

Over the past few decades, increasing attention has focused on differential environmental and occupational exposures to hazards across sociodemographic groups. Few studies have rigorously assessed the role that exposure to environmental hazards plays in racial and ethnic differences in health status. Several studies have addressed the location of hazardous waste sites. In 1983, the General Accounting Office reviewed the racial and economic characteristics of the communities surrounding four hazardous waste landfills and found that Blacks made up the majority of the population in three of the four sites (General Accounting Office, 1983). Four years later, a frequently cited and controversial report by the United Church of Christ Commission for Racial Justice (1987) also suggested that hazardous waste sites were more likely to be located in areas with large minority populations. A more recent analysis of hazardous waste sites did not find a distinctive pattern of locating these sites in communities with higher concentration of racial and ethnic minorities (Anderton et al., 1994).

Environmental exposures are not confined to hazardous waste sites, however. Exposure of children to lead from a variety of sources in a variety of settings may be an especially important health-risk factor that differs across racial and ethnic groups. Studies suggest that Black and Hispanic children are at much greater risk for exposure to lead than White children (Brody et al., 1994; U.S. Department of Health and Human Services, 1988; Carter-Pockras et al., 1990). Although detailed data are not available for a wide range of environmental risk factors, the preponderance of evidence suggests that racial and ethnic minorities are exposed to higher levels of environmental risks (Institute of Medicine, 1999).

Employment patterns differ substantially across racial and ethnic groups, and some racial and ethnic minorities are more likely to hold jobs that expose individuals to higher risks for injury, illness, and death (Friedman-Jimenez and Ortiz, 1994; Robinson, 1984). Relatively few studies have specifically addressed this issue, however, and none has specifically estimated the contribution of differences in occupation-related risk to overall differences in health. In the few studies that have addressed the issue, the findings vary across data sources, health outcomes, and time periods. National data from the 1970s and 1980s suggested that Blacks had higher rates of disabling occupational injuries than Whites (Robinson, 1984, 1987). Data on work-related injuries and illnesses in California during 1986 also suggested higher rates for Hispanics and Blacks compared to non-Hispanic Whites (Robinson, 1989). A review of occupational cancer epidemiology studies from the mid-1980s found a paucity of data on racial differences in occupational cancer risks but concluded that there was evidence suggesting higher risks for non-Whites (Kipen et al., 1991).

Other studies found mixed results on racial differences in occupational injuries. Data from the 1983-1987 NHIS revealed that working Blacks reported fewer injuries requiring medical attention or restriction of usual activities than Whites and that Blacks and Whites reported similar rates of injuries at work (Wagener and Winn, 1991). An analysis of data on a national sample of persons age 51-61 from 1992-1993 did not find significantly higher reporting of occupational injuries for either Blacks or Hispanics (Zwerling et al., 1996). A recent analysis of data on fatal occupational injuries in North Carolina, however, found that Blacks were more likely than Whites to die from an injury on the job and that much of the difference was due to racial differences in the types of jobs held (Loomis and Richardson, 1998), and national data on fatal injuries during 1980-1985 also found a slightly higher risk for Black workers (Bell et al., 1990).

Although there appear to be racial and ethnic differences in levels of exposure to environmental and occupational risks, there are not enough data to come to any strong conclusion about the relative contribution of exposure to occupational and environmental hazards to overall racial and ethnic differences in health. (Although occupational and environmental factors probably do account for some racial and ethnic differences in health, we believe that they are unlikely to make a large contribution to the overall patterns found.) Much remains to be learned about both occupational and environmental health risks, and more rigorous studies of these risks across racial and ethnic groups will greatly improve our understanding of causal pathways for differences in health (Northridge and Shepard, 1997; Johnson and Coulberson, 1993; Institute of Medicine, 1999).

THE FUTURE

. . . with economic and industrial progress of the colored population its death-rate will gradually approach nearer to that of the White population.

—Trask, U.S. Public Health Service (1917)

. . . The prospect of improvement for Negro health that would result from changes in the economic and occupational environment is much less optimistic. It seems inescapable that low incomes derived from unskilled occupations will show a large degree of prevalence among Negroes for a long time.

—Tibbits, U.S. Public Health Service (1937)

Predicting the future trends of racial and ethnic differences in health in the United States has never been easy. So many variables come into play to complicate our predictions, and the health trends are affected by trends in every other dimension of life. The fundamental problem is that we do not understand the present very well. Key questions remain unanswered:

• Why are some Black mortality and morbidity rates so high, with Black infant mortality, in particular, seemingly so refractory to the usually mitigating effects of higher SEP?
• Why are American Indian mortality rates not worse than they are, given the historical and current deprivations suffered by Indian peoples?
• Why are Hispanic mortality rates so low, seemingly so refractory to the aggravating effects of low SEP?
• What are the intermediate steps that translate low SEP into poor health and do they vary among different racial and ethnic groups? How do psychological and social factors such as self-image and values interact with the more material aspects of deprivation?

Although we have speculated about the answers to some of these questions, definitive answers are at present beyond the reach of the scientific evidence. These are large, complex questions, and subsumed under them are hundreds of potential research questions that need to be asked and answered. Having looked back to the recent past, while we are reassured by general trends of improvements in health, perhaps the single most disturbing finding was the unprecedented downturn in life expectancy for Blacks during the 1980s. That downturn provides a cautionary lesson for future predictions: the health of racial and ethnic minorities in the United States will not inevitably improve with the mere passage of time. A multitude of factors, many outside of the control of the public health and medical communities, will interact to determine the trajectories, and the health of populations *can* deteriorate, as we have seen in recent years of transition in Russia (Walberg et al., 1998). Accepting our tenuous insight into current mechanisms of minority health status, it is nonetheless useful to look ahead.

Trends in Racial Differences in Socioeconomic Position Suggest Increases in Racial Health Disparities

Socioeconomic position will continue to play a large role in explaining many of the health differences among racial and ethnic groups, and evidence of growing socioeconomic inequality does not bode well for the future (Karoly, 1996; Wolff, 1998; Smith, Volume II, Chapter 4). Blacks, American Indians, and Hispanics all have high poverty rates and substantially lower levels of educational attainment than do Whites and Asians and Pacific Islanders. Moreover, inasmuch as educational attainment drives income in our society, the economic trajectory of these minority groups is worrisome as well. To the extent that disparities in economic resources and education increase, the health of racial and ethnic minorities who remain in a disadvantaged SEP will worsen. Particularly disturbing is the large number of minority children who live in poverty. The high rates of childhood poverty may be setting in place trajectories for a cohort of persons who will carry with them high risks for poor health if and when they reach middle and old age.

Hispanic Health May Worsen with Acculturation

The health status of Hispanics is of particular concern given their growing numbers in the population. The anomalous current combination of low SEP and relatively low death rates among Hispanics may amount to a form of "epidemiologic levitation." Hispanic high school completion rates are even lower than those for Blacks and American Indians. Because the acculturation literature suggests that the protective effect of recent immigration wears off with time, there is a real possibility that Hispanic health status could worsen.

Changing Definitions of Race and Ethnicity May Reshape Our Understanding of Racial Differences in Health

Another source of uncertainty is presented by the now familiar projection that by 2050 minorities will represent about half of the U.S. population. But the relatively high intermarriage rates for American Indians and Alaska Natives, Hispanics, and Asians and Pacific Islanders with the White population suggests that we will not have a mosaic of neatly partitioned racial and ethnic groups; rather, we will have what has been termed a "beige continuum" in which the lines among groups are quite unclear.

This projection for American Indians and Alaska Natives, Hispanics, and Asians and Pacific Islanders, however, contrasts with the likely scenario for Blacks. Blacks have a relatively low intermarriage rate, suggesting increased social partitioning for Blacks. Such a potential for a future nation divided into beige and Black will force us to reconsider our simplistic notions of race and ethnicity and its relationship to health (Lind, 1998).

Racial and Ethnic Groups Will Become More Heterogeneous

Minority elderly populations are growing at a rate faster than the White population, and larger numbers of racial and ethnic minorities will reach old age with distinctive life and health histories. The characteristics of immigrants will continue to change, each cohort bringing distinctive health and social characteristics. Similarly, as has happened throughout the history of this country, different cohorts of Blacks will have increasingly diverse race-related life experiences. The urban American Indian population may grow and present unique challenges. With the increasing heterogeneity within racial and ethnic groups, sweeping generalizations about a group's health will become of increasingly limited value as a means to explain causal pathways and promote better health outcomes.

The Research Agenda for the Future

As difficult as it is to predict future trends, it is equally difficult to determine the best course of action for reducing health disparities. What is clear is that more research is needed.

Study the Role of Culture in Determining Health

We know little about the processes underlying the acculturation of immigrants and other minority populations and the relationship between these processes and adoption of health-related behaviors. With the expectation that Hispanics will become the largest minority group during the early twenty-first century, how acculturation occurs may have a significant impact on the health of that population. Improved understanding of acculturation will be relevant not only for other immigrant populations such as Asians and Pacific Islanders but also for other groups including American Indians and Alaska Natives and Blacks.

Assess the Effectiveness of Public Health Interventions in Reducing Disparities

In completing this review, we were surprised by the dearth of literature that rigorously addresses the extent to which recent large public health initiatives have affected racial differences in health. For example, how much have the interventions to control blood pressure in Blacks contributed to recent improvements in cardiovascular mortality? Such analyses will provide essential information on which broad health interventions have an effect on disparities, why they do, and how; they will help in the planning of future efforts to reduce disparities. Recent efforts in Europe to understand the evidence on the effect of public health interventions on socioeconomic disparities in health may serve as a model (e.g., Arblaster et al., 1996)

Unify Research on Causal Factors and Their Biological Pathways

The overwhelming majority of the research on causal pathways for racial differences has been piecemeal, artificially separating groups of factors that are closely, and often causally, related to each other as well as to health outcomes. For example, it is unlikely education and income will change independent of nutrition and access to health care. The traditional, piecemeal approach limits our ability to assess the effectiveness of changing various factors to reduce disparities; more methodological and empirical work is needed to provide a more realistic understanding of the interactive effects of causal factors. This will likely require the development of a series of from-birth cohort study populations from diverse racial and ethnic groups. Similar cohorts in England and other European countries have greatly increased our understanding of how SEP affects health across the life cycle.

Policy Challenges

In the absence of changes in the social environment, isolated public health and medical interventions are unlikely to eliminate racial and ethnic disparities, especially in light of the importance of SEP in determining health (Marmot, 1998). Nevertheless, we have chosen to restrict our comments here to health-care policy options as traditionally defined.

Improve Health Care Access and Monitor Differences in Health-Care Quality

Differentials in access to health care play a role in perpetuating racial and ethnic differences in health, and recent initiatives aimed at improving access, especially for poor children, are likely to affect the trajectories of poor minority populations. Because access so heavily relies on health insurance, of particular concern is the high percentage of Hispanics, especially immigrants, who are uninsured. We also cannot ignore the evidence of racial and ethnic differences in quality of care delivered. Suggestions that race and ethnicity be among the variables included in efforts to monitor the quality of health care in managed care organizations warrant serious consideration (Smith, 1998; Lavizzo-Mourey and Mackenzie, 1996).

Promote Targeted Health Behavior Interventions

Although health-risk behaviors alone probably cannot account for the disparities in health among racial and ethnic groups, they likely contribute to the differences; and we can do something about them. A growing body of research is available on public health interventions that are most likely to work in increasing the adoption of health-promoting behaviors and the cessation of health-reducing behaviors. Certain trends warrant consideration for targeted public health interventions, in particular recent increases in smoking among Black and Hispanic adolescents.

Increase Minority Representation Among Health-Care Providers

The low educational attainment of Blacks and Hispanics serves as a powerful barrier to producing a diverse health professional and scientific workforce (Nickens et al., 1994). Higher education institutions have been able to admit substantial numbers of Hispanics, Blacks, and American Indians by engaging in affirmative action. However, that these groups score substantially lower than Whites and Asians on standardized tests has provided numerical ammunition for the opponents of affirmative action to assert that it is both unfair and admits unqualified students (Association of American Medical Colleges, 1998b). Critics of affirmative action have gone further, attacking the legitimacy of any minority-targeted programming, which complicates national ameliorative efforts. One of the issues that underlies the battle over affirmative action is a debate about the nature of race and ethnicity in contemporary America. Implicit in the arguments that race should not be a consideration in, for example, educational programming decisions, is an assertion that race no longer is determinative of life chances and thus is not a relevant way to distinguish among people or is not a suitable criterion on which to give minorities a "plus factor" in, for example, an admissions process. This general assertion that "race no longer matters" is not sustained by this review; with regard to health status, race and ethnicity remain important factors.

CONCLUSION

Future trends for racial and ethnic disparities are uncertain, but we see little evidence for optimism that disparities will be eliminated in the near future. Most of the research evidence suggests that the current relative health status of some minority groups is substantially "locked in" by poorly understood economic, social, educational, and medical structural disadvantages. The only viable key is an understanding of how all these variables interact and the national resolve to open the door to change.

ACKNOWLEDGMENTS

We are particularly grateful for the assistance of the following individuals: at the National Center for Health Statistics: Charlene Brock, Harnethia Cousar (Research Library); Dawn Hutcherson, Kathryn Porter, Yolanda Cowan (DHES); Anjum Hajat, Jacqueline Lucas, Ann Hardy (DHIS); Jeff Mauer (DVS); Diane Wagener, Elsie Pamuk, Diane Makuc (OAEHP); Jennifer Madans (DVHSS); and Ed Sondik, Director; at the Agency for Health Care Research and Quality: Jessica Vistnes; at the Association of American Medical Colleges: Willa Owens, Lois Bergeisen; and at other institutions: Jay Kaufman.

REFERENCES

Adler, N., T. Boyce, M. Chesney, S. Cohen, S. Folkman, R. Kahn, and S. Syme
  1994   Socioeconomic status and health: The challenge of the gradient. *American Psychologist* 49:15-24.
Aguirre-Molina, M., and R. Caetano
  1994   Alcohol use and alcohol-related issues. In *Hispanic Health in the United States: A Growing Challenge*, C. Molina and M. Aguirre-Molina, eds. Washington, D.C.: American Public Health Association.
Alaimo, K., R. Briefel, E. Frongillo, and C. Olson
  1998   Food insufficiency exists in the United States: Results from the Third National Health and Nutrition Examination Survey (NHANES III). *American Journal of Public Health* 88:419-426.

Aluli, N.
  1991 Prevalence of obesity in a native Hawaiian population. *American Journal of Clinical Nutrition* 53:1556-1560S.
Anderson, N., and C. Armstead
  1995 Toward understanding the association of socioeconomic status and health: A new challenge for the biopsychosocial approach. *Psychosomatic Medicine* 57:213-225.
Anderson, R., P. Sorlie, E. Backlund, N. Johnson, and G. Kaplan
  1997 Mortality effects of community socioeconomic status. *Epidemiology* 8:42-47.
Anderton, D., B. Anderson, J. Oakes, and M. Fraser
  1994 Environmental equity: The demographics of dumping. *Demography* 31(2):229-248.
Andrulis, D.
  1998 Access to care is the centerpiece of the elimination of socioeconomic disparities in health. *Annals of Internal Medicine* 129:412-416.
Angel, J., and D. Hogan
  1994 The demography of minority aging populations. In *Minority Elders: Five Goals Toward Building a Public Policy Base*. Washington, D.C.: Gerontological Society of America.
Antonovsky, A.
  1967 Social class, life expectancy, and overall mortality. *Milbank Memorial Fund Quarterly* 45:31-73.
Arblaster, L., M. Lambert, V. Entwistle, M. Forster, D. Fullerton, T. Sheldon, and I. Watt
  1996 A systematic review of the effectiveness of health services interventions aimed at reducing inequalities in health. *Journal of Health Services Research and Policy* 1(2):93-103.
Association of American Medical Colleges (AAMC)
  1998a *Minority Students in Medical Education: Facts and Figures XI*. Washington, D.C.: Association of American Medical Colleges.
  1998b *Questions and Answers on Affirmative Action in Medical Education*. Washington, D.C.: Association of American Medical Colleges.
Atlanta University
  1896 *Mortality Among Negroes in Cities*. Atlanta University Publications No. 1. Atlanta: Atlanta University Press.
  1906 *The Health and Physique of the Negro American*. Atlanta University Publications No. 11. Atlanta: Atlanta University Press.
Ayanian, J., B. Kohler, T. Abe, and A. Epstein
  1993 The relation between health insurance coverage and clinical outcomes among women with breast cancer. *New England Journal of Medicine* 329:326-331.
Baird, P.
  1994 The role of genetics in population health. In *Why Are Some People Healthy and Others Not? The Determinants of Health of Populations*, R. Evans, M. Barer, and T. Marmor, eds. New York: Aldine De Gruyter.
Barker, D.
  1994 *Mothers, Babies, and Disease in Later Life*. London: British Medical Journal Publishing Group.
Bell, C., N. Stout, T. Bender, C. Conroy, W. Crouse, and J. Myers
  1990 Fatal occupational injuries in the United States, 1980 through 1985. *Journal of the American Medical Association* 263:3047-3050.
Bell, R., E. Mayer-Davis, Y. Jackson, and C. Dresser
  1997 An epidemiologic review of dietary intake studies among American Indians and Alaska Natives: Implications for heart disease and cancer risk. *Annals of Epidemiology* 7:229-240.

Berk, M., A. Albers, and C. Schur
    1996 The growth of the U.S. uninsured population: Trends in Hispanic subgroups,
          1977-1992. *American Journal of Public Health* 86:572-575.
Berkman, L., and J. Mullen
    1997 How health behaviors and the social environment contribute to health differ-
          ences between Black and White older Americans. In *Racial and Ethnic Differences
          in the Health of Older Americans*, L. Martin and B. Soldo, eds. Washington, D.C.:
          National Academy Press.
Blane, D., E. Brunner, and R. Wilkinson, eds.
    1996 *Health and Social Organization: Toward a Health Policy for the 21st Century.* New
          York: Routledge.
Bloom, B., G. Simpson, R. Cohen, and P. Parsons
    1997 Access to health care. Part 2: Working-age adults. National Center for Health
          Statistics. *Vital Health Statistics* 10(197).
Braveman, P., G. Oliva, M. Miller, R. Reiter, and S. Egerter
    1989 Adverse outcomes and lack of health insurance among newborns in an eight-
          county area of California, 1982 to 1986. *New England Journal of Medicine* 321:508-
          513.
Braveman, P., V. Schaff, S. Egerter, T. Bennett, and W. Schecter
    1994 Insurance-related differences in the risk of ruptured appendix. *New England Jour-
          nal of Medicine* 331:444-449.
Brody, D., J. Pirkle, R. Kramer, K. Flegal, T. Matte, E. Gunter, and D. Paschal
    1994 Blood lead levels in the U.S. population. Phase 1 of the Third National Health and
          Nutrition Examination Survey (NHANES III, 1988 to 1991). *Journal of the American
          Medical Association* 272:277-283.
Broussard, B., A. Johnson, J. Himes, R. Fichtner, and F. Hauck, et al.
    1991 Prevalence of obesity in American Indians and Alaska Natives. *American Journal
          of Clinical Nutrition* 53:1535-1542S.
Bunker, J.
    1995 Medicine matters after all. *Journal of the Royal College of Physicians of London*
          29(2):105-112.
Bunker, J., D. Gomby, and B. Kehrer, eds.
    1989 *Pathways to Health—The Role of Social Factors.* Menlo Park, Calif.: Henry J. Kaiser
          Family Foundation.
Burstin, H., S. Lipsitz, and T. Brennan
    1992 Socioeconomic status and risk for substandard medical care. *Journal of the Ameri-
          can Medical Association* 268:2383-2387.
Caraballo, R., G. Giovino, T. Pechacek, and P. Mowery, et al.
    1998 Racial and ethnic differences in serum cotinine level of cigarette smokers. Third
          National Health and Nutrition Examination Survey 1988-1991. *Journal of the Ameri-
          can Medical Association* 280:135-139.
Carlisle, D., B. Leake, and M. Shapiro
    1995 Racial and ethnic differences in the use of invasive cardiac procedures among
          cardiac patients in Los Angeles County, 1986 through 1988. *American Journal of
          Public Health* 85(3):352-356.
Carrasquillo, O., D. Himmelstein, S. Woolhandler, and D. Bor
    1999 Going bare: Trends in health insurance coverage, 1989 through 1996. *American
          Journal of Public Health* 89:36-42.
Carter-Pokras, O., J. Pirkle, G. Chavez, and E. Gunter
    1990 Blood lead levels of 4-11-year-old Mexican American, Puerto Rican, and Cuban
          children. *Public Health Reports* 105:388-393.

Centers for Disease Control and Prevention (CDC)
    1992 *Chronic Disease in Minority Populations*. Atlanta: Centers for Disease Control and Prevention.
Chen, V.
    1993 Smoking and the health gap in minorities. *Annals of Epidemiology* 3:159-164.
Clark, D.
    1997 U.S. trends in disability and institutionalization among older Blacks and Whites. *American Journal of Public Health* 87:438-440.
Cleeland, C., R. Gonin, L. Baez, P. Loeher, and K. Pandya
    1997 Pain and treatment of pain in minority patients with cancer. *Annals of Internal Medicine* 127:813-816.
Cobas, J., H. Balcazar, M. Benin, V. Keith, and Y. Chong
    1996 Acculturation and low-birthweight infants among Hispanic women: A reanalysis of HHANES data with structural equation models. *American Journal of Public Health* 86:394-396.
Cockerham, W.
    1990 A test of the relationship between race, socioeconomic status, and psychological distress. *Social Science and Medicine* 31:1321-1326.
Cohen, R., B. Bloom, G. Simpson, and P. Parsons
    1997 Access to health care. Part 3: Older adults. National Center for Health Statistics. *Vital Health Statistics* 10(198).
Cooper, R., and C. Rotimi
    1994 Hypertension in populations of West African origin: Is there a genetic predisposition? *Journal of Hypertension* 12:215-227.
Corti, M., J. Guralnik, L. Ferrucci, G. Izmirlian, S. Leveille, M. Pahor, H. Cohen, C. Pieper, and R. Havlik
    1999 Evidence for a Black-White crossover in all-cause and coronary heart disease mortality in an older population: The North Carolina EPESE. *American Journal of Public Health* 89:308-314.
Cowie, C., M. Harris, R. Silverman, E. Johnson, and K. Rust
    1993 Effect of multiple risk factors on differences between Blacks and Whites in the prevalence of non-insulin dependent diabetes mellitus in the United States. *American Journal of Epidemiology* 137(7):719-732.
Cunningham, P., and C. Schur
    1991 Health care coverage: Findings from the Survey of American Indians and Alaska Natives. DHHS Pub. No. (PHS) 91-0027. National Medical Expenditures Survey Research Findings 8, Agency for Health Care Policy and Research. Rockville, Md.: Public Health Service.
Curtis, A., S. James, T. Raghunathan, and K. Alcser
    1997 Job strain and blood pressure in African Americans: The Pitt County Study. *American Journal of Public Health* 87(8):1297-1302.
David, R., and J. Collins
    1997 Differing birth weight among infants born of U.S.-born Blacks, African-born Blacks, and U.S.-born Whites. *New England Journal of Medicine* 337:1209-1214.
Davis, K., M. Lillie-Blanton, B. Lyons, F. Mullan, N. Powe, and D. Rowland
    1987 Health care for Black Americans: The public sector role. *Milbank Memorial Fund Quarterly* 65(Suppl 1):213-247.
DeJong, G., A. Batavia, and R. Griss
    1989 America's neglected health minority: Working-age persons with disabilities. *Milbank Memorial Fund Quarterly* 67(Suppl 2, Part 2):311-351.

Dorn, H.
  1940   *The Health of the Negro, A Research Memorandum. Carnegie-Myrdal Study.* New York: Schomburg Center for Research in Black Culture.
Dowd, J., and V. Bengston
  1978   Aging in minority populations: An examination of the double jeopardy hypothesis. *Journal of Gerontology* 33(3):427-436.
Dressler, W.
  1993   Health in the African American community: Accounting for health inequalities. *Medical Anthropology Quarterly* 7:325-345.
DuBois, W.E.B.
  1899   *The Philadelphia Negro: A Social Study.* Philadelphia: University of Pennsylvania Press.
English, P., M. Kharrazi, and S. Guendelman
  1997   Pregnancy outcomes and risk factors in Mexican Americans: The effect of language use and mother's birthplace. *Ethnicity and Disease* 7:229-240.
Erikson, P., R. Wilson, and I. Shannon
  1995   Years of healthy life. Statistical Notes No. 7. Hyattsville, Md.: Centers for Disease Control and Prevention, National Center for Health Statistics.
Escarce, J., K. Epstein, D. Colby, and J. Schwartz
  1993   Racial differences in the elderly's use of medical procedures and diagnostic tests. *American Journal of Public Health* 83:948-954.
Ettner, S.
  1996   New evidence on the relationship between income and health. *Journal of Health Economics* 15:49-66.
Evans, R., M. Barer, and T. Marmor, eds.
  1994   *Why Are Some People Healthy and Others Not? The Determinants of Health of Populations.* New York: Aldine De Gruyter.
Ewbank, D.
  1987   History of Black mortality and health before 1940. *Milbank Memorial Fund Quarterly* 5:100-128.
Fang, J., T. Madhavan, and M. Alderman
  1996   The association between birthplace and mortality from cardiovascular causes among Black and White residents of New York City. *New England Journal of Medicine* 335:1545-1551.
  1997   Nativity, race and mortality: Influence of region of birth on mortality of U.S.-born residents of New York City. *Human Biology* 69(4):533-544.
Farrer, L., L. Cupples, J. Haines, B. Hyman, and W. Kukull
  1997   Effects of age, sex, and ethnicity on the association between apolipoprotein E genotype and Alzheimer disease: A metaanalysis. *Journal of the American Medical Association* 278:1349-1356.
Feinstein, J.
  1993   The relationship between socioeconomic status and health—A review of the literature. *Milbank Memorial Fund Quarterly* 71:279-323.
Ferraro, K., and M. Farmer
  1996   Double jeopardy to health hypothesis for African Americans: Analysis and critique. *Journal of Health and Social Behavior* 37:27-43.
Fiscella, K.
  1995   Does prenatal care improve birth outcomes? A critical review. *American Journal of Obstetrics and Gynecology* 85(3):468-479.

Fiscella, K., and P. Franks
 1997 Does psychological distress contribute to racial and socioeconomic disparities in mortality? *Social Sciences and Medicine* 45:1805-1809.
Flegal, K., M. Carroll, R. Kuczmarski, and C. Johnson
 1998 Overweight and obesity in the United States: Prevalence and trends, 1960-1994. *International Journal of Obesity* 22:39-47.
Ford, E., and R. Cooper
 1995 Racial and ethnic differences in health care utilization of cardiovascular procedures: A review of the evidence. *Health Services Research* 30:237-251.
Franks, P., C. Clancy, and M. Gold
 1993a Health insurance and mortality. Evidence from a national cohort. *Journal of the American Medical Association* 270:737-741.
Franks, P., C. Clancy, M. Gold, and P. Nutting
 1993b Health insurance and subjective health status: Data from the 1987 National Medical Expenditure Survey. *American Journal of Public Health* 83:1295-1299.
Freeman, V., and L. Martin
 1998 Understanding trends in functional limitations among older Americans. *American Journal of Public Health* 88:1457-1462.
Friedman-Jimenez, G., and J. Ortiz
 1994 Occupational health. In *Hispanic Health in the U.S.: A Growing Challenge*, C. Molina and M. Aguirre-Molina, eds. Washington, D.C.: American Public Health Association.
Garber, A.
 1989 Pursuing the links between socioeconomic factors and health: Critique, policy implications, and directions for future research. In *Pathways to Health: The Role of Social Factors*, J. Bunker, D. Gomby, and B. Kehrer, eds. Menlo Park, Calif.: Henry J. Kaiser Family Foundation.
General Accounting Office (GAO)
 1983 *Siting of Hazardous Waste Landfills and Their Correlation with Racial and Ethnic Status of Surrounding Communities.* RCED-83-168. Washington, D.C.: General Accounting Office.
 1992 *Hispanic Access to Health Care: Significant Gaps Exist.* PEMD-92-6. Washington, D.C.: General Accounting Office.
Geronimus, A., J. Bound, T. Waidmann, M. Hillemeire, and P. Burns
 1996 Excess mortality among Blacks and Whites in the United States. *New England Journal of Medicine* 335:1552-1558.
Gibson, R.
 1991 Age-by-race differences in the health and functioning of elderly persons. *Journal of Aging and Health* 3:335-351.
Grossman, D., J. Krieger, J. Sugarman, and R. Forquera
 1994 Health status of urban American Indians and Alaskan Natives. *Journal of the American Medical Association* 271:845-850.
Guralnik, J., K. Land, D. Blazer, G. Fillenbaum, and L. Branch
 1993 Educational status and active life expectancy among older Blacks and Whites. *New England Journal of Medicine* 329:110-116.
Haan, M., and T. Camacho
 1987 Poverty and health: Prospective evidence from the Alameda County Study. *American Journal of Epidemiology* 125:989-998.
Haan, M., and G. Kaplan
 1985 The contribution of SEP to minority health. In *Report of the Secretary's Task Force on Black and Minority Health: Crosscutting Issues in Minority Health.* Washington, D.C.: U.S. Department of Health and Human Services.

Hahn, R., and S. Eberhardt
  1995   Life expectancy in four U.S. racial/ethnic populations: 1990. *Epidemiology* 6(4):350-355.
Halperin, E.
  1988   Desegregation of hospitals and medical societies in North Carolina. *New England Journal of Medicine* 318:58-63.
Hart, C., G. Smith, and D. Blane
  1998   Inequalities in mortality by social class measured at three stages of lifecourse. *American Journal of Public Health* 88:471-474.
Hayes-Bautista, D.
  1992   Latino health indicators and the underclass model: From paradox to new policy models. In *Health Policy and the Hispanic*, A. Furino, ed. Boulder, Colo.: Westview Press.
Haynes, S., C. Harvey, H. Montes, H. Nickens, and B. Cohen
  1990   Patterns of cigarette smoking among Hispanics in the United States: Results from the HHANES 1982-84. *American Journal of Public Health* 80(Suppl):47-54.
Hazuda, H., S. Haffner, M. Stern, and C. Eifler
  1988   Effects of acculturation and socioeconomic status on obesity and diabetes in Mexican Americans. *American Journal of Epidemiology* 128:1289-1301.
Holland, D., and G. Perrott
  1938   The health of the Negro. *Milbank Memorial Fund Quarterly* 16:5-38.
Hoyert, D., and H. Kung
  1997   Asian and Pacific Islander mortality, selected states, 1992. *Monthly Vital Statistics Report* 46(1 Suppl):1-63.
Hutchins, E., J. Reitman, and D. Klaub
  1967   Minorities, manpower, and medicine. *Journal of Medical Education* 42:809-821.
Idler, E., and Y. Benyamini
  1997   Self-rated health and mortality: A review of twenty-seven community studies. *Journal of Health and Social Behavior* 38:21-37.
Indian Health Service (IHS)
  1991   *Trends in Indian Health, 1991.* Rockville, Md.: Indian Health Service, U.S. Department of Health and Human Services.
  1996   *Trends in Indian Health, 1996.* Rockville, Md.: Indian Health Service, U.S. Department of Health and Human Services.
Institute of Medicine (IOM)
  1999   *Toward Environmental Justice: Research, Education, and Health Policy Needs.* Washington, D.C.: National Academy Press.
Jackson, J., T. Brown, D. Williams, M. Torres, S. Sellers, and K. Brown
  1996   Racism and the physical and mental health status of African Americans: A thirteen year national panel study. *Ethnicity and Disease* 6:132-147.
James, S.
  1994   John Henryism and the health of African Americans. *Culture, Medicine and Psychiatry* 18:163-182.
James, W., M. Nelson, A. Ralph, and S. Leather
  1997   The contribution of nutrition to inequalities in health. *British Medical Journal* 314:1545-1549.
Jarvik, G.
  1997   Genetic predictors of common disease: Apolipoprotein E genotype as a paradigm. *Annals of Epidemiology* 7:357-362.

John, R.
   1996   Demography of American Indian elders: Social, economic, and health status. In *Changing Numbers, Changing Needs: American Indian Demography and Public Health*, G. Sandefur, R. Rindfuss, and B. Cohen, eds. Washington, D.C.: National Academy Press.
Johnson, B., and S. Coulberson
   1993   Environmental epidemiologic issues and minority health. *Annals of Epidemiology* 3:175-180.
Kahn, K.L., M.L. Pearson, E.R. Harrison, K.A. Desmond, W.H. Rogers, L.V. Rubenstein, R.H. Brook, and E.B. Keeler
   1994   Health care for Black and poor hospitalized Medicare patients. *Journal of the American Medical Association* 271(15):1169-1174.
Karoly, L.
   1996   Anatomy of the U.S. income distribution: Two decades of change. *Oxford Review of Economic Policy* 12(1):77-96.
Kaufman, J., and R. Cooper
   1995   In search of the hypothesis. *Public Health Reports* 110:662-666.
Kaufman, J., R. Cooper, and D. McGee
   1997   Socioeconomic status and health in Blacks and Whites: The problem of residual confounding and the resiliency of race. *Epidemiology* 8:621-628.
Kaufman, J., A. Long, Y. Liao, R. Cooper, and D. McGee
   1998   The relation between income and mortality in U.S. Blacks and Whites. *Epidemiology* 9:147-155.
Keil, J., S. Sutherland, R. Knapp, and H. Tyroler
   1992   Does equal socioeconomic status in Black and White men mean equal risk of mortality? *American Journal of Public Health* 82:1133-1136.
Kennedy, B., I. Kawachi, K. Lochner, C. Jones, and D. Prothrow-Stith
   1997   (Dis)respect and Black mortality. *Ethnicity and Disease* 7:207-214.
Kessler, R., and H. Neighbors
   1986   A new perspective on the relationships among race, social class, and psychological distress. *Journal of Health and Social Behavior* 27:107-115.
Kington, R., D. Carlisle, D. McCaffrey, H. Myers, and W. Allen
   1998   Racial differences in functional status among elderly U.S. migrants from the south. *Social Sciences and Medicine* 47:831-840.
Kington, R., and J. Smith
   1997   Socioeconomic status and racial and ethnic differences in functional status associated with chronic diseases. *American Journal of Public Health* 87:805-810.
Kipen, H., D. Wartenberg, P. Scully, and M. Greenberg
   1991   Are non-Whites at greater risk for occupational cancer? *American Journal of Indian Medicine* 19:76-74.
Kochanek, K., J. Maurer, and H. Rosenberg
   1994   Why did Black life expectancy decline from 1984 through 1989 in the United States? *American Journal of Public Health* 84:938-944.
Komaromy M., K. Grumbach, M. Drake, K. Vranizan, N. Lurie, D. Keane, and A. Bindman
   1996   The role of Black and Hispanic physicians in providing health care for underserved populations. *New England Journal of Medicine* 334:1305-1310.
Kovar, M., and G. Poe
   1985   The National Health Interview Survey design, 1973-1984, and procedures, 1975-1993. Vital and Health Statistics. Series 1, No. 8. DHHS Pub. No. (PHS) 85-1320. National Center for Health Statistics. Washington, D.C.: U.S. Government Printing Office.

Krieger, N.
    1987   Shades of difference: Theoretical underpinnings of the medical controversy on Black/White differences in the United States, 1830-1870. *International Journal of Health Services* 17:259-278.
Krieger, N., and S. Sidney
    1996   Racial discrimination and blood pressure: The CARDIA study of young Black and White adults. *American Journal of Public Health* 86:1370-1378.
Krieger, N., D. Williams, and N. Moss
    1997   Measuring social class in U.S. public health research: Concepts, methodologies and guidelines. *Annual Review of Public Health* 18:341-378.
Kumanyika, S.
    1993   Special issues regarding obesity in minority populations. *Annals of Internal Medicine* 119:650-654.
Kunitz, S.
    1996   The history and politics of U.S. health care policy for American Indians and Alaskan Natives. *American Journal of Public Health* 86(10):1464-1473.
Kuo, J., and K. Porter
    1998   Health status of Asian Americans: United States, 1992-1994. Advance Data from Vital and Health Statistics; no. 298. Hyattsville, Md.: National Center for Health Statistics.
The Lancet
    1995   The unequal, the achievable, and the champion. *The Lancet* 345:1061-1062.
Lantz, P., J. House, J. Lepkowski, D. Williams, R. Mero, and J. Chen
    1998   Socioeconomic factors, health behaviors, and mortality. Results from a nationally representative prospective study of U.S. adults. *Journal of the American Medical Association* 279:1703-1708.
LaVeist, T.
    1994   Beyond dummy variables and sample selection: What health services researchers ought to know about race as a variable. *Health Services Research* 29(1):1-16.
Lavizzo-Mourey, R., and E. Mackenzie
    1996   Cultural competence: Essential measurements of quality for managed care organizations. *Annals of Internal Medicine* 124(10):919-921.
Lewontin, R.
    1972   The apportionment of human diversity. *Evolutionary Biology* 6:381-398.
Liao, Y., R. Cooper, G. Cao, R. Durazo-Arvizu, J. Kaufman, A. Luke, and D. McGee
    1998   Mortality patterns among adult Hispanics: Findings from the NHIS 1986-1990. *American Journal of Public Health* 88:227-232.
Libby, D., Z. Zhou, and D. Kindig
    1997   Will minority physician supply meet U.S. needs? *Health Affairs* 16:205-214.
Lillie-Blanton, M., P. Parson, H. Gayle, and A. Dievler
    1996   Racial differences in health: Not just Black and White, but shades of gray. *Annual Review of Public Health* 17:411-448.
Lind, M.
    1998   The Beige and the Black. *New York Times Magazine*, August 16: 38-39.
Loomis, D., and D. Richardson
    1998   Race and risk of fatal injury at work. *American Journal of Public Health* 88:40-44.
Lynch, J., G. Kaplan, and S. Shema
    1997   Cumulative impact of sustained economic hardship on physical, cognitive, psychological, and social functioning. *New England Journal of Medicine* 337(26):1889-1895.

MacDorman, M., and J. Atkinson
    1998 Infant mortality statistics from the linked birth/infant death data set—1995 period data. *Monthly Vital Statistics Report* 46(6/Suppl 2). Hyattsville, Md.: National Center for Health Statistics.
Malcolm S., G. VanHorne, Y. George, and C. Gaddy
    1998 *Losing Ground: Science and Engineering Graduate Education of Black and Hispanic Americans.* Washington, D.C.: American Association for the Advancement of Science.
Markides, K., and J. Coreil
    1986 The health of Hispanics in the southwestern United States: An epidemiologic paradox. *Public Health Reports* 3:253-265.
Marmot, M.
    1998 Improvement of social environment to improve health. *The Lancet* 351:57-60.
Marmot, M., H. Bosma, H. Hemingway, E. Brunner, and S. Stansfield
    1997 Contribution of job control and other risk factors to social variations in coronary heart disease incidence. *The Lancet* 350:235-239.
Marmot, M., M. Kogevinas, and M. Elston
    1987 Social/economic status and disease. *Annual Review of Public Health* 8:111-135.
May, P.
    1996 Overview of alcohol abuse epidemiology for American Indian populations. In *Changing Numbers, Changing Needs: American Indian Demography and Public Health,* G. Sandefur, R. Rindfuss, and B. Cohen, eds. Washington, D.C.: National Academy Press.
McBean, A., and M. Gornick
    1994 Differences by race in the rates of procedures performed in hospitals for Medicare beneficiaries. *Health Care Financing Review* 15:77-90.
McCord, C., and H. Freeman
    1990 Excess mortality in Harlem. *New England Journal of Medicine* 322:173-179.
McDonough, P., G. Duncan, D. Williams, and J. House
    1997 Income dynamics and adult mortality in the United States, 1972 through 1989. *American Journal of Public Health* 87:1476-1483.
McGarvey, S.
    1991 Obesity in Samoans and a perspective in its etiology in Polynesians. *American Journal of Clinical Nutrition* 53:1586-1594S.
McKeown, T.
    1979 *The Role of Medicine: Dream, Mirage or Nemesis?* Princeton: Princeton University Press.
McKinlay, J., and S. McKinlay
    1977 The questionable contribution of medical measures to the decline of mortality in the United States in the twentieth century. *Milbank Memorial Fund Quarterly* (Summer):405-428.
Medicaid Access Study Group
    1994 Access of Medicaid recipients to outpatient care. *New England Journal of Medicine* 330:1426-1430.
Menchik, P.
    1993 Economic status as a determinant of mortality among Black and White and older men—Does poverty kill? *Population Studies* 47:427-436.
Morbidity and Mortality Weekly Report (MMWR)
    1994 Prevalence of risk factors for chronic disease by education level in racial/ethnic populations—United States, 1991-1992. *Morbidity and Mortality Weekly Report* 43(48):894-899.

Moy E., and B. Bartman
    1995   Physician race and care of minority and medically indigent patients. *Journal of the American Medical Association* 273:1515-1520.
Mustard, C., and N. Roos
    1994   The relationship of prenatal care and pregnancy complications to birthweight in Winnipeg, Canada. *American Journal of Public Health* 84(9):1450-1457.
Myers, H., M. Kagawa-Singer, S. Kumanyika, B. Lex, and K. Markides
    1995   Behavioral risk factors related to chronic diseases in ethnic minorities. *Health Psychology* 14:613-621.
Nagi, S.
    1976   An epidemiology of disability among adults in the United States. *Milbank Memorial Fund Quarterly* (Fall):439-467.
National Center for Health Statistics (NCHS)
    1998   *Health, United States 1998 with Socioeconomic Status and Health Chartbook.* Hyattsville, Md.: Public Health Service.
National Research Council (NRC)
    1989   *Diet and Health: Implications for Reducing Chronic Disease Risk. Committee on Diet and Health.* Washington, D.C.: National Academy Press.
Neel, J.
    1997   Are genetic factors involved in racial and ethnic differences in late-life health? In *Racial and Ethnic Differences in the Health of Older Americans,* L. Martin and B. Soldo, eds. Washington, D.C.: National Academy Press.
Nickens, H.
    1991   Minorities in medicine. *The Association of Black Cardiologists Newsletter* 17:1,3.
Nickens, H., T. Ready, and R. Petersdorf
    1994   Project 3000 by 2000: Racial and ethnic diversity in U.S. medical schools. *New England Journal of Medicine* 331:472-476.
Norris, J., L. Harmack, S. Carmichael, T. Pouane, P. Wakimoto, and G. Block
    1997   U.S. trends in nutrient intake: The 1987 and 1992 National Health Interview Surveys. *American Journal of Public Health* 87:740-746.
Northridge, M., and P. Shepard
    1997   Comment: Environmental racism and public health. *American Journal of Public Health* 87:730-732.
O'Brien, T., W. Flanders, P. Decoufle, C. Boyle, F. DeStefano, and S. Teutsch
    1989   Are racial differences in the prevalence of diabetes in adults explained by differences in obesity? *Journal of the American Medical Association* 262:1485-1488.
Office of Management and Budget (OMB)
    1997   Revisions to the Standards for the Classification of Federal Data on Race and Ethnicity. *Federal Register* 62(210):58781-58790.
Olshanksy, S., and A. Ault
    1986   The fourth stage of the epidemiologic transition: The age of delayed degenerative diseases. *Milbank Memorial Fund Quarterly* 64(3):355-391.
Otten, M., S. Teutsch, D. Williamson, and J. Marks
    1990   The effect of known risk factors on the excess mortality of Black adults in the United States. *Journal of the American Medical Association* 263:845-850.
Palinkas, L., and S. Pickwell
    1995   Acculturation as a risk factor for chronic disease among Cambodian refugees in the United States. *Social Sciences and Medicine* 40(12):1643-1653.
Pappas, G., W. Hadden, L. Kozak, and G. Fischer
    1997   Potentially avoidable hospitalizations: Inequalities in rates between U.S. socioeconomic groups. *American Journal of Public Health* 87(5):811-816.

Pappas, G., S. Queen, W. Hadden, and G. Fisher
  1993 The increasing disparity in mortality between socioeconomic groups in the United States, 1960 and 1986. *New England Journal of Medicine* 329:103-109.
Peck, M.
  1994 The importance of childhood socio-economic group for adult health. *Social Sciences and Medicine* 39(4):553-562.
Perez-Stable, E., B. Herrera, P. Jacob, and N. Benowitz
  1998 Nicotine metabolism and intake in Black and White smokers. *Journal of the American Medical Association* 280:152-156.
Piani, A., and C. Schoenborn
  1993 Health promotion and disease prevention, United States, 1990. National Center for Health Statistics. *Vital Health Statistics* 10(185).
Popkin, B.
  1997 Correction and revision of conclusions: Dietary trends in the United States. *New England Journal of Medicine* 337:1846-1848.
Popkin, B., A. Siega-Riz, P. Haines
  1996 A comparison of dietary trends among racial and socioeconomic groups in the United States. *New England Journal of Medicine* 335:716-720.
Popkin, B., and J. Udry
  1998 Adolescent obesity increases significantly in second and third generation U.S. immigrants: The National Longitudinal Study of Adolescent Health. *Journal of Nutrition* 128:701-706.
Preston, S., I. Elo, I. Rosenwaike, and M. Hill
  1996 African-American mortality at older ages: Results of a matching study. *Demography* 33:193-209.
Preston, S., and P. Taubman
  1994 Socioeconomic differences in adult mortality and health status. In *Demography of Aging*, L. Martin and S. Preston, eds. Washington, D.C.: National Academy Press.
Reid, J.
  1986 Immigration and the future U.S. Black population. *Population Today* 14(2):6-8.
Ren, X., and B. Amick
  1996 Race and self-assessed health status: The role of socioeconomic factors in the U.S.A. *Journal of Epidemiology and Community Health* 50:269-273.
Robinson, J.
  1984 Racial inequality and the probability of occupation-related injury or illness. *Milbank Memorial Fund Quarterly* 62(4):567-590.
  1987 Trends in racial inequality and exposure to work-related hazards, 1968-1989. *Milbank Memorial Fund Quarterly* 65(Suppl. 2):404-420.
  1989 Exposure to occupational hazards among Hispanics, Blacks, and non-Hispanic Whites in California. *American Journal of Public Health* 79:629-630.
Rogers, R.
  1992 Living and dying in the U.S.A.—Sociodemographic determinants of death among Blacks and Whites. *Demography* 29:287-303.
Rosenbaum, M., R. Leibel, and J. Hirsch
  1997a Obesity. *New England Journal of Medicine* 337:396-407.
Rosenbaum, S., R. Serrano, M. Magar, and G. Stern
  1997b Civil rights in a changing health care system. *Health Affairs* 16:90-105.
Schneider, D., M. Greenberg, and L. Lu
  1997 Region of birth and mortality from circulatory diseases among Black Americans. *American Journal of Public Health* 87:800-804.

Schneider, R., F. Staggers, C. Alexander, M. Rainforth, K. Kondwani, S. Smith, and C. King
  1995 A randomized controlled trial of stress reduction for hypertension in older African Americans. *Hypertension* 26(5):820-827.
Schoenbaum, M., and T. Waidmann
  1997 Race, socioeconomic status, and health: Accounting for race differences in health. *Journal of Gerontology* 52B(Special Issue):61-73.
Schulman, K., J. Berlin, W. Harless, J. Kerner, S. Sistrunk, B. Gersh, R. Dibe, C. Taleghani, J. Burke, S. Williams, J. Eisenberg, and J. Escarce
  1999 The effect of race and sex on physicians' recommendations for cardiac catheterization. *New England Journal of Medicine* 340:618-626.
Shea, S., D. Misra, M. Ehrlich, L. Field, and C. Francis
  1992 Predisposing factors for severe uncontrolled hypertension in an inner-city minority population. *New England Journal of Medicine* 327:776-781.
Short, P., A. Monheit, and K. Beauregard
  1989 A profile of uninsured Americans. National Medical Expenditures Survey Research Finding 1. DHHS Pub. No. 89-3443. Rockville, Md.: National Center for Health Services Research and Health Care Technology Assessment.
Singer, B., and C. Ryff
  1997 Racial and ethnic inequalities in health: Environmental, psychosocial, and physiological pathways. In *Intelligence, Genes, and Success: Scientists Respond to the Bell Curve*, B. Devlin, S. Fienberg, D. Resnick, and K. Roeder, eds. New York: Springer-Verlag (Copernicus).
Smith, D.
  1998 Addressing racial inequities in health care: Civil rights monitoring and report cards. *Journal of Health Care Politics, Policy and Law* 23(1):75-105.
Smith, J., and R. Kington
  1997a Demographic and economic correlates of health in old age. *Demography* 34:159-170.
  1997b Race, socioeconomic status, and health in late life. In *Racial and Ethnic Differences in the Health of Older Americans*, L. Martin and B. Soldo, eds. Washington, D.C.: National Academy Press.
Sorlie, P., E. Backlund, N. Johnson, and E. Rogot
  1993 Mortality by Hispanic status in the United States. *Journal of the American Medical Association* 270:2464-2468.
Sorlie, P., E. Rogot, and N. Johnson
  1992a Validity of demographic characteristics of death certificate. *Epidemiology* 3:181-184.
Sorlie, P., E. Rogot, R. Anderson, N. Johnson, and E. Backlund
  1992b Black-White mortality differences by family income. *The Lancet* 340:346-350.
Strogatz, D., J. Croft, S. James, N. Keenan, S. Browning, J. Garret, and A. Curtis
  1997 Social support, stress, and blood pressure in Black adults. *Epidemiology* 8:482-487.
Tang, M., Y. Stern, K. Marder, K. Bell, B. Gurland, et al.
  1998 The apoE-ε4 allele and the risk of Alzheimer disease among African Americans, Whites, and Hispanics. *Journal of the American Medical Association* 279:751-755.
Thamer, M., C. Richard, A. Waldman, A. Casebeer, and N. Ray
  1997 Health insurance coverage among foreign-born U.S. residents: The impact of race, ethnicity, and length of residence. *American Journal of Public Health* 87:96-102.
Thomson, G.
  1997 Discrimination in health care. *Annals of Internal Medicine* 126:910-912.
Tibbits, C.
  1937 The socio-economic background of Negro health status. *Journal of Negro Education* 6:413-428.

Todd, K., N. Samaroo, and J. Hoffman
1993 Ethnicity as a risk factor for inadequate emergency department analgesia. *Journal of the American Medical Association* 269:1537-1539.

Trask, J.
1917 The significance of the mortality rates of the colored population of the United States. *American Journal of Public Health* 6:254-260.

United Church of Christ Commission for Racial Justice
1987 *Toxic Wastes and Race in the United States: A National Report on the Racial and Socioeconomic Characteristics of Communities with Hazardous Waste Sites.* New York: United Church of Christ.

U.S. Bureau of the Census (USBC)
1991 The Hispanic population in the United States, March 1991. Pp. 20-455 in *Current Population Reports.* Washington, D.C.: U.S. Government Printing Office Bureau of Indian Affairs.
1993 *We, the American Asians.* Washington, D.C.: U.S. Government Printing Office.
1994 *Census of Populations and Housing, 1990: Special Tabulations on Aging (STP 14).* Washington, D.C.: U.S. Government Printing Office.
1996 65+ in the United States. Pp. 23-190 in *Current Population Reports, Special Studies.* Washington, D.C.: U.S. Government Printing Office.
1999 *Estimates of the Population of States by Age, Sex, Race, and Hispanic Origin: 1990 to 1996.* Washington, D.C.: U.S. Government Printing Office.

U.S. Department of Health and Human Services (USDHHS)
1985 *Report of the Secretary's Task Force on Black and Minority Health.* Washington, D.C.: U.S. Department of Health and Human Services.
1988 *Nature and Extent of Lead Poisoning in Children in the United States.* Washington, D.C.: U.S. Department of Health and Human Services.
1990 *Healthy People 2000: National Health Promotion and Disease Prevention Objectives.* Washington, D.C.: U.S. Department of Health and Human Services.
1996 *Physical Activity and Health: A Report of the Surgeon General.* Atlanta, Ga.: U.S. Department of Health and Human Services, Centers for Disease Control and Prevention, National Center for Chronic Disease Prevention and Health Promotion.
1998 *Tobacco Use Among U.S. Racial/Ethnic Minority Groups—African Americans, American Indians and Alaska Natives, Asian Americans and Pacific Islanders, and Hispanics: A Report of the Surgeon General.* Atlanta, Ga.: U.S. Department of Health and Human Services, Centers for Disease Control and Prevention, National Center for Chronic Disease Prevention and Health Promotion, Office on Smoking and Health.

Valdez, R., H. Morgenstern, E. Brown, R. Wyn, C. Wang, and W. Cumberland
1993 Insuring Hispanics against the costs of illness. *Journal of the American Medical Association* 269:889-894.

Vistnes, J., and A. Monheit
1997 Health insurance status of the civilian noninstitutionalized population: 1996. MEPS Research Findings No. 1. AHCPR Pub. No. 97-0030. Rockville, Md.: Agency for Health Care Policy and Research.

Wagener, D., and D. Winn
1991 Injuries in working populations: Black-White differences. *American Journal of Public Health* 81:1408-1414.

Walberg, P., M. McKee, V. Shkolnikov, L. Chenet, and D. Leon
1998 Economic change, crime, and mortality crisis in Russia: Regional analysis. *British Medical Journal* 317(7154):312-318.

Waldron, I.
    1993   Recent trends in sex mortality ratios for adults in developed countries. *Social Sciences and Medicine* 36(4):451-462.
Wei, M., R. Valdez, B. Mitchell, S. Haffner, M. Stern, and H. Hazuda
    1996   Migration status, socioeconomic status, and mortality rates in Mexican Americans and non-Hispanic Whites: The San Antonio Heart Study. *Annals of Epidemiology* 6:307-313.
Weiner, H.
    1992   *Perturbing the Organism: The Biology of Stressful Experience.* Chicago: University of Chicago Press.
Wild, S., A. Laws, S. Fortmann, A. Varady, and C. Byrne
    1995   Mortality from coronary heart disease and stroke for six ethnic groups in California, 1985-1990. *Annals of Epidemiology* 5:432-439.
Wilkinson, R.
    1996   *Unhealthy Societies: The Afflictions of Inequality.* New York: Routledge.
Williams, D.
    1990   Socioeconomic differentials in health: A review and redirection. *Social Psychology Quarterly* 53(2):81-99.
    1994   The concept of race in health services research: 1966 to 1990. *Health Services Research* 29(3):261-274.
    1996   Race/ethnicity and socioeconomic status: Measurement and methodological issues. *International Journal of Health Services* 26:483-505.
Williams, D., and C. Collins
    1995   U.S. socioeconomic and racial differences in health: Patterns and explanations. *Annual Review of Sociology* 21:349-386.
Williams, D., R. Lavizzo-Mourey, and R. Warren
    1993   The concept of race and health status in America. Paper from the CDC-ATSDR Workshop on the Use of Race and Ethnicity in Public Health Surveillance. *Public Health Reports* 109:26-41.
Wolff, E.
    1998   Recent trends in the distribution of household wealth. *Journal of Economic Perspectives* 12(3):131-150.
Young, T.
    1994   *The Health of American Indians: Toward a Biocultural Epidemiology.* New York: Oxford University Press.
Yu, E., and W. Liu
    1992   U.S. national data on Asian Americans and Pacific Islanders: A research agenda for the 1990s. *American Journal of Public Health* 82:1645-1652.
Zambrana, R., S. Scrimshaw, N. Collins, and C. Dunkel-Schetter
    1997   Prenatal health behaviors and psychosocial risk factors in pregnant women of Mexican origin: The role of acculturation. *American Journal of Public Health* 87:1022-1026.
Zwerling, C., N. Sprince, R. Wallace, C. Davis, P. Whitten, and S. Heeringa
    1996   Risk factors for occupational injuries among older workers: An analysis of the Health and Retirement Study. *American Journal of Public Health* 86:1306-1309.

12

Racial and Ethnic Trends in Children's and Adolescents' Behavior and Development

Vonnie C. McLoyd and Betsy Lozoff

Behavioral and developmental problems are major challenges for U.S. children (Committee on Psychosocial Aspects of Child and Family Health, 1993). Psychosocial and developmental problems, and their interference with normal functioning, have been termed the "new morbidity" (Haggerty et al., 1975), and many of these problems appear to have a strong connection to race and ethnicity. In this chapter, we examine the prevalence of some of these problems in terms of race and ethnicity, and we assess whether and how the connection between race and ethnicity and these problems has changed over time. Addressed also is the concept of public policies as factors contributing to changes in prevalence in the general population, to race and ethnic differences in prevalence, and to race- and ethnic-related historical trends.

Our analysis focuses on two broad sets of indicators: (1) negative physical health conditions during infancy—i.e., iron deficiency, elevated lead levels, low birth weight, prenatal alcohol exposure; and (2) psychosocial problems salient during adolescence—i.e., assaultive violence and homicide, suicide, drug use. We selected these indicators because, historically, there have been striking ethnic and racial differences in their prevalence, and because their preventable nature and impact on society as well as the individual have led them to be major health concerns. The physical health indicators we examine are ones that consistently have been found to contribute to poorer school achievement and lower scores on tests of cognitive functioning.

While reading this chapter, there are three points of importance to note: (1) because race and poverty are closely intertwined, it is often impossible to separate racial trends from socioeconomic disadvantage; (2)

311

the short summaries in this paper are oversimplified and cannot do justice to the relevant controversies or the limitations of the available studies; and (3) we emphasize national data sets wherever possible, but nationally representative samples are not available for some important indicators.

CONDITIONS DURING INFANCY THAT AFFECT BEHAVIOR AND DEVELOPMENT

The lower scores on tests of cognitive functioning and poorer school achievement of many minority children have received considerable attention. Results from the Third National Health and Nutrition Examination Survey (NHANES III) show that Black and Mexican children, compared to Whites at all levels of family income, receive lower scores on subtests of an IQ scale and on reading and writing achievement tests (Figure 12-1) (Kramer et al., 1995). These test results, combined with their correlates in poor school achievement, mean that the country is losing important human capacity.

Perinatal problems and poor nutrition in infancy contribute to poorer behavioral and developmental outcomes. The rapid growth of the brain in the early years, and the development of fundamental mental and motor processes, make infancy a particularly vulnerable period. Despite the plasticity of the brain, children who experience early biologic insults and stressors are at higher risk for long-lasting behavioral and developmental disturbances. Although considerations of lower test scores and poorer school achievement may acknowledge the role of health and nutrition, specific information is often not incorporated into the discussion; yet this is an issue for which there is nationally representative data, showing major racial differences in the prevalence of common early biologic risks. For some of these problems, there is also evidence that dramatic changes can occur when the country identifies a problem, makes the commitment to improve the situation, and dedicates the necessary resources.

Iron Deficiency

On a worldwide basis, iron deficiency is the most common single-nutrient disorder. Dietary iron deficiency develops relatively slowly, and anemia is a late manifestation. Infants are at particularly high risk because they grow so rapidly and there are limited sources of iron in the infant diet. Approximately one in five babies (0 to 2 years old) in the world has iron-deficiency anemia, and an even higher percentage have iron deficiency without anemia (deMaeyer et al., 1985; Florentino and Guirriec, 1984).

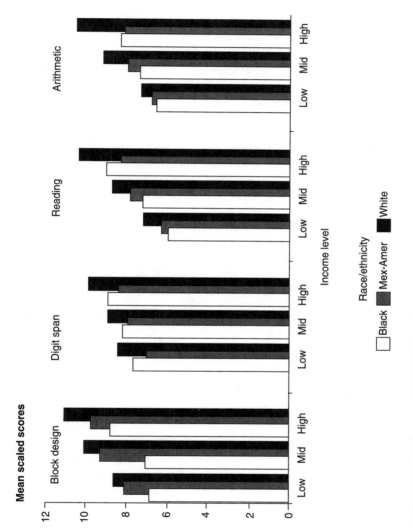

FIGURE 12-1 Mean scaled *WISC-R* and *WRAT-R* scores for children aged 6 to 16, by income level and race/ethnicity, 1988-1991. SOURCE: Kramer et al. (1995). Reprinted by permission.

Behavioral/Developmental Outcomes

Because iron is involved in neurotransmitter function and myelin formation, there is reason to worry about ill effects on brain and behavior. Iron-deficiency anemia in infancy is consistently associated with poorer scores on measures of behavior and development (Nokes et al., 1998). Roncagliolo et al. (1998) report direct evidence that iron deficiency adversely affects brain development in the human infant.

A full course of iron treatment does not appear to correct lower mental and motor test scores or behavioral differences in the majority of iron-deficient-anemic infants, despite correction of anemia (Nokes et al., 1998). At early school age (Lozoff et al., 1991), and in early adolescence (Lozoff et al., 1997), formerly iron-deficient children still test lower than peers. Thus, chronic, severe iron deficiency in infancy identifies children at risk for poorer outcome even 10 years after treatment.

Racial and Ethnic Differences in Prevalence

There are marked ethnic and socioeconomic differences in the prevalence of iron deficiency (with or without anemia) in U.S. infants (Ogden, 1998). Iron-deficiency anemia is observed in approximately 5 percent of poor Black and Mexican-American toddlers—twice the proportion found among poor Whites. Nonpoor Black and White infants are at considerably lower risk (1.6 percent and 0.9 percent, respectively), but iron-deficiency anemia is more common in nonpoor Mexican-American toddlers (3.4 percent). The pattern is generally similar for iron deficiency without anemia (Figure 12-2)—poor White infants are three to four times more likely to be iron deficient than nonpoor White infants, but iron deficiency remains more common among nonpoor Blacks. Mexican-American infants are at higher risk regardless of socioeconomic status; iron deficiency affects approximately 18 percent and 12 percent of poor and nonpoor Mexican American infants, respectively. There is also reason to be concerned about other immigrant groups and Alaska Natives. Racial and socioeconomic differences are thought to be largely the result of different dietary habits, although blood loss may be a factor in some groups (Petersen et al., 1996).

Historical Trends

There has been a marked drop in the prevalence of anemia in infants and children in the United States over the last several decades (Vazquez-Seoane et al., 1985; Yip et al., 1987). Iron-deficiency anemia used to be fairly common among poor U.S. infants (U.S. Department of Health and

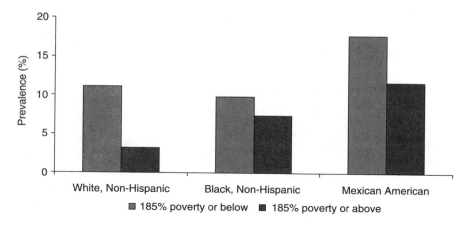

FIGURE 12-2 Iron deficiency among 1- to 2-year-old children by race and poverty status. SOURCE: Ogden, C., Centers for Disease Control and Prevention, unpublished analyses, Third National Health and Nutrition Examination Survey.

Human Services, 1982); it was reported to be 20.6 percent in NHANES II (1976-1980) (Life Sciences Research Office, 1984). NHANES III (1988-1991) reports an almost 10-fold reduction among poor White infants but only 4-fold among poor Black infants (Looker, 1997). Comparisons of change over time are not straightforward, however, because information combining ethnicity and poverty is readily available only for NHANES III (Ogden, 1998).

Impact of Public Policies

The declining prevalence of anemia among U.S. infants is compelling testimony that national health policy can have a major impact. About 30 years ago the American Academy of Pediatrics (AAP) started recommending the use of iron-fortified formula for bottle-fed babies (AAP Committee on Nutrition, 1969). The federal government's Women, Infants, and Children program began providing iron-fortified formula. In addition, the amount of ascorbic acid (which enhances iron absorption) was increased in the infant diet, breastfeeding was encouraged (the iron in breast milk is readily absorbed), and iron-fortified infant cereals are now readily available.

Elevated Lead Levels

In contrast to iron, which the body requires for normal function, there is no known role for lead. The neurotoxicity of lead, though recognized for centuries, has become a worldwide public health problem only relatively recently because of increasing lead levels in human blood, the result of exposures to lead-based paint and leaded gasoline, among others.

Behavioral/Developmental Outcomes

There is no question that high levels of lead can cause permanent neurologic damage or death. Research and controversy in the last 10 to 20 years has focused on the effects of lead exposure at lower levels (Banks et al., 1997; Pocock et al., 1994; National Research Council, 1993). Taken together, the studies find that children with increased lead burdens show a variety of cognitive and behavioral differences compared to children with lower lead burdens: slightly decreased scores on measures of intelligence, poorer school performance and achievement test scores, increased distractibility, short attention span, impulsiveness, etc. Separating the effects of lead from those of socioeconomic and family factors is challenging. However, congruent findings from studies of rodent and primate models suggest that similar behavioral processes underlie the poorer developmental outcome across species (Banks et al., 1997).

Racial and Ethnic Differences in Prevalence

As with iron deficiency, the most recent data (1988 to 1994) show marked differences in prevalence of elevated lead levels in young children of different ethnic and socioeconomic backgrounds (U.S. Department of Health and Human Services, 1982; Pirkle et al., 1994) (Figure 12-3). About 12 percent of children living in poverty have elevated lead levels compared to 2 percent of children in high-income families. This income gradient is observed in all ethnic groups but most markedly among Black children. In poor Black families, 22 percent of the children have elevated lead levels. Although the proportion among Black children in middle- or high-income families is much lower (6 percent), it is still higher than that among White and Mexican-American children, regardless of family income. These racial and socioeconomic differences seem to be largely related to housing—children who live in houses built before the 1960s, and currently concentrated in older inner city areas, are at highest risk (Mahaffey et al., 1982).

Historical Trends

As research on developmental outcomes has accumulated, the Centers for Disease Control and Prevention has progressively lowered the level of blood lead considered to be of concern—from 60 μg/dL in the

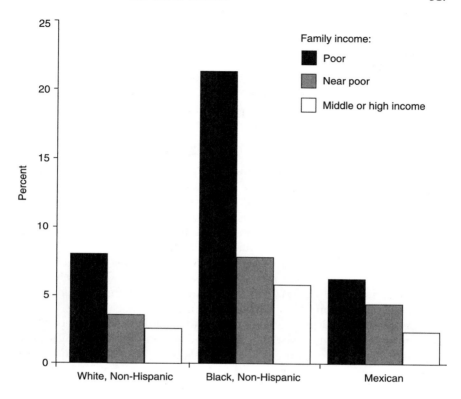

FIGURE 12-3 Elevated blood lead among children 1 to 5 years of age by family income, race, and Hispanic origin: United States, average annual 1988-1994. Notes: Elevated blood lead was defined as having at least 10 micrograms of lead per deciliter of blood.   SOURCE: Centers for Disease Control and Prevention, National Center for Health Statistics, Third National Health and Nutrition Examination Survey.

1950s to 10 µg/dL in 1991 (Centers for Disease Control and Prevention, 1991; Pirkle et al., 1994). At the same time, there has been a dramatic decline in lead levels in U.S. children, although national data are not available before NHANES II in the late 1970s. For children 1 to 4 years of age, blood-lead levels have declined even further in the last decade—from a mean of 16 µg/dL in NHANES II (Mahaffey et al., 1982) to less than 4 µg/dL in NHANES III (Pirkle et al., 1994). The decline has been observed in both Black and White children; however, Blacks were at higher risk in NHANES II and continue to be so in NHANES III.

Impact of Public Policies

The story of lead and public policy is one of both pride and shame. Despite opposition and delays from affected industries, federal regulations prohibiting lead in house paint and gasoline have had a tremendous public-health impact. The declining blood-lead levels of U.S. children provide compelling proof that public policy can protect children from harm.

Low Birth Weight

Low birth weight (LBW) babies, weighing ≤2,500 g at birth, are a heterogeneous group consisting of those born prematurely and term babies who did not grow optimally in utero. Survival of LBW babies, at lower and lower birth weights, has greatly improved with the advent of neonatal intensive care. Nonetheless, the United States has higher rates of LBW babies than many other industrial societies.

Although the vast majority of LBW children have normal outcomes, as a group they have higher rates of neurodevelopmental and behavioral problems (Hack et al., 1995). A small minority has severe disability, such as mental retardation, cerebral palsy, blindness, or deafness. A larger proportion show milder problems in cognition, attention, and neuromotor functioning during the school years and continuing into adolescence. There appears to be a gradient across levels of LBW: neurocognitive differences, observed at all levels of LBW (compared to babies with birth weight >2,500 g), are greater the lower the birth weight (Breslau et al., 1996).

Racial and Ethnic Differences in Prevalence

LBW births are more common among Blacks than among any other ethnic group (David and Collins, 1997; Foster, 1997); and LBW is a problem for Black infants regardless of the level of education (a proxy for socioeconomic status) the mother has attained (Foster, 1997). Conversely, among Whites there is a strong relationship between maternal education and LBW, such that the less education mothers have, the greater the proportion of LBW infants (National Center for Health Statistics, 1998; Guyer et al., 1997). No such gradient relationship is observed among Hispanic, American Indian or Alaska Native, or Asian or Pacific Islander mothers. All these groups have low rates of LBW births (Figure 12-4). The relatively low rates may be misleading, however. Altered glucose metabolism and diabetes during pregnancy, which occur at increased frequency in several of these groups (Balcazar et al., 1992; Kieffer et al., 1995), may lead to higher birth weight in relatively immature infants, with increased risks for poorer health and developmental outcome.

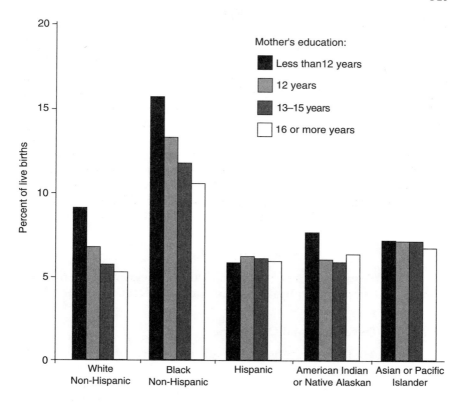

FIGURE 12-4 Low-birth-weight live births among mothers 20 years of age and over by mother's education, race, and Hispanic origin: United States, 1996. Note: Low birth weight refers to an infant weighing less than 2,500 grams at birth. SOURCE: Centers for Disease Control and Prevention, National Center for Health Statistics, National Vital Statistics System.

Historical Trends

The LBW rate declined during the 1970s and early 1980s but has risen 10 percent since then—from a low of 6.7 percent in 1984 to 7.4 percent in 1996 (National Center for Health Statistics, 1998). Some of the recent increase can be attributed to the rising proportion of multiple births among White mothers. Among births to Black mothers, LBW fell to the lowest rate reported since 1987, but the rate remains much higher than that among other ethnic groups. The decline is not the result of fewer very small babies because the level of babies weighing <1,500 g has remained stable among Black births since the late 1980s (about 3 percent).

Impact of Public Policies

In contrast to iron deficiency and environmental lead exposure, public policy has not been as focused or effective when it comes to LBW; yet a number of interventions have been shown to reduce LBW, including prenatal care, mother's good nutrition with adequate weight gain, control of hypertension, avoidance of long working hours and excessive physical exertion toward the end of pregnancy, etc. (Luke et al., 1995). Intervention can also improve later outcomes for LBW babies. For example, additional stimulation for the infant, and social support for families can benefit LBW babies, especially heavier LBW children of lower socioeconomic status families (Hack et al., 1995). Public laws now mandate services for infants with identified congenital disabilities, but much less progress has been made in serving LBW infants at biological and environmental risk.

Prenatal Alcohol Exposure

As with lead, alcohol can be toxic. During pregnancy, the mother's drinking can impair the physical and mental development of the fetus.

Behavioral/Developmental Outcomes

Fetal alcohol syndrome (FAS) is characterized by a distinctive pattern of biological effects—craniofacial changes, growth retardation, and central nervous system impairment including mental retardation and/or hyperactivity (Committee on Substance Abuse and Committee on Children with Disabilities, 1993; Institute of Medicine, 1996). Deficits in growth and development are also found in non-FAS children of nonalcoholic women who drink at moderate-to-heavy levels during pregnancy (Streissguth et al., 1996).

Racial and Ethnic Differences in Prevalence

As yet, there are no comprehensive national data sets for effects of alcohol on fetuses. However, relevant information on alcohol consumption is available. In the 1988 National Maternal and Infant Health Survey (Faden et al., 1997), only a small proportion of women reported heavy alcohol consumption after finding out they were pregnant, but Black women (1.2 percent) and American Indian and Alaska Native (2.2 percent) women were 3 to 4 times more likely than White (0.4 percent), Hispanic (0.3 percent), or Asian and Pacific Islander (0.7 percent) women to report consuming six or more drinks per week (Figure 12-5) (Faden et al., 1997). The incidence of FAS births is approximately 10 times higher

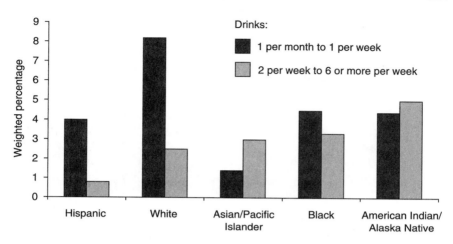

FIGURE 12-5 Alcohol consumption after finding out about pregnancy: Expectant mothers in the United States, 1988. SOURCE: Faden et al. (1997). Reprinted by permission.

among Blacks than Whites (Abel, 1995). Incidence figures are not available for a national sample of American Indian and Alaska Natives, but a surveillance project in four communities estimated that the rate may be 3 to 4 times higher than among Blacks and 30 to 40 times higher than among Whites (Duimstra et al., 1993). FAS is also 10 times more common among women of low socioeconomic status compared to women of middle and high socioeconomic status (Abel, 1995). The effects of alcohol on the fetus worsen with successive pregnancies so that women who are moderate-to-heavy drinkers are at increased risk of giving birth to a child affected by alcohol with each succeeding pregnancy (Jacobson et al., 1996).

Historical Trends

FAS was only recognized 30 years ago. Although obtaining accurate information about alcohol consumption during pregnancy is challenging, national surveys are now starting to include alcohol-consumption related questions. Data show that the proportion of women who consume alcohol during pregnancy decreased after the mid-1980s (Serdula et al., 1991). Much of the decline, however, is the result of changed habits of light drinkers; there has been little decrease in heavy drinking (Serdula et al., 1991; Hankin et al., 1993), which poses the greatest risk to the fetus. In 1995 (the most recent year for which data are available), the Centers for Disease Control found that the incidence of drinking at levels that put the fetus at risk for neurobehavioral impairment was 3.5 percent, with binge drinking the predominant pattern (87 percent of the cases) (Ebrahim et al., 1998). There are no national data on racial trends over time.

Impact of Public Policies

Public health warnings about the risks of drinking during pregnancy may have contributed to the decline observed in the number of pregnant women drinking alcohol. Women who drink heavily, however, present different challenges because of associated chemical dependency (more smoking and other drug use in addition to alcohol consumption), poor nutrition, depression, abusive relationships, domestic violence, etc. Inadequate societal commitment to providing alcohol-treatment programs for pregnant women has undoubtedly adversely affected the offspring of moderate-to-heavy drinkers. The intermittent heavy drinker, who may pose a great risk to her baby, has been virtually neglected.

BEHAVIORAL AND MENTAL HEALTH PROBLEMS AMONG ADOLESCENTS

A vast number of indicators are available that can inform us about the behavioral and psychological health of adolescents. Because of our interest in historical trends, we limit our discussion to major indicators that have been tracked over several years in nationally representative samples or by the federal statistical system. In addition, the data had to be reliably and consistently measured over time and disaggregated by race and/or ethnicity. Three indicators of internalizing and externalizing symptoms met these criteria—specifically, homicide and assaultive violence, suicide, and drug use. This small corpus of indicators reflects the scarcity of measures of mental health in regularly repeated national surveys of youth.

Our focus on homicide and assaultive violence, suicide, and drug use also reflects the bias in regularly repeated national surveys of youth toward problematic functioning, rather than well-being and resilience. We call attention to this bias because focusing on indicators of problematic functioning may result in a more pessimistic picture of adolescents' overall psychological and behavioral well-being than is, in fact, the case (U.S. Department of Health and Human Services, 1997). We fully endorse the view that successful development is more than the absence of problematic behaviors, and that research documenting the prevalence and determinants of behavioral and psychological well-being should be pursued with a vigor that rivals that devoted to understanding problematic development (McLoyd, 1998a).

The causal role of public policies in historical trends in adolescents' mental health functioning is less clear cut and dramatic than is the case for some of the physical health conditions relevant to infancy. Here, we briefly note some of these policies; we give relatively more attention to intervention programs that aim to prevent or reduce high-risk behaviors in adolescents. Research on the efficacy of these programs provides important information needed to guide policy formulation and service delivery.

Homicide and Assaultive Violence

Homicide is the second leading cause of death among children and adolescents in the United States. The homicide rate for adolescents age 15 to 19 more than doubled between 1970 and 1994, increasing from 8 per 100,000 in 1970 to 20.3 per 100,000 in 1994. Virtually all of this increase occurred after 1985 (U.S. Department of Health and Human Services, 1997). Both murders and assaults of adolescents older than 12 years tend to be committed by same-age peers who are acquainted with their victims (Christoffel, 1990). In general, the incidence of fatal violence for Hispanic, American Indian and Alaska Native, and Black adolescents far exceeds that for White adolescents (Allen and Mitchell, 1998). For several years during the past two decades, homicide has been the leading cause of death for both Black males and females age 15 to 24 (Allen and Mitchell, 1998; Hammond and Yung, 1993).

Historical Trends by Race

Unfortunately, national data spanning several years are not available for Hispanics, Asian and Pacific Islanders, and American Indian and Alaska Natives. Scholars interested in comparative homicide data for specific non-Black minority populations typically must rely on studies of murder rates conducted in specific regions or cities with sizable concentrations of these ethnic minority groups (Hammond and Yung, 1993). Our discussion of historical trends in homicide rates is limited to Black and White adolescents because national data spanning several years are more readily available for these two groups.

For several decades, the rate of death from homicide has been higher for Black male adolescents than White adolescents. This racial gap markedly increased between 1985 and 1994 (Figure 12-6). Whereas in 1985 Black males age 15 to 19 had a homicide rate of 47 per 100,000, by 1994, the rate had tripled to 136 per 100,000, a rate nearly nine times that for White males of the same age group. For Black males this period also marked a sharp increase in the rate of homicides in which firearms were used (Figure 12-7). Since 1985, the homicide rate for White males doubled (from 7.2 to 15.4 per 100,000). It is noteworthy that the homicide rate for Black

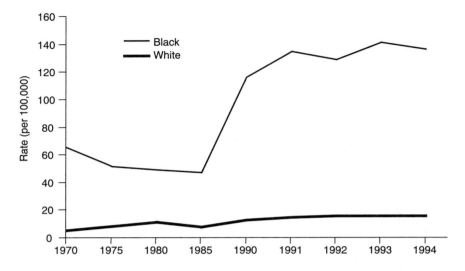

FIGURE 12-6 Rates for adolescent male homicides, age 15 to 19, by race, 1970-1994. SOURCE: U.S. Department of Health and Human Services (1997).

males in this age group actually declined nearly 30 percent from 1970 to 1985 but rose again after 1985 (U.S. Department of Health and Human Services, 1997).

Homicide rates for females age 15 to 19 of both races are much lower than those for males in this age group. The gender disparity is larger among Blacks than Whites (e.g., in 1994, the homicide rate for Black females age 15 to 19 was approximately one-ninth the rate for Black males, whereas the rate for White females in this age group was approximately one-fifth the rate for White males). As with males, the adolescent-homicide rate for Black females has long been higher than the rate for White females. Since 1985, rates for Black females increased by nearly half, whereas the rates for White females remained stable. Assaultive violence not resulting in death generally follows historical patterns similar to those for homicide (U.S. Department of Health and Human Services, 1997).

There has been considerable debate about whether racial and ethnic differences in homicide rates are largely the result of socioeconomic status (SES). Some researchers find differences along racial and ethnic lines even when poverty or SES is taken into account. Extreme poverty, however, is a stronger predictor of homicide than is race or ethnicity. In any case, as Hammond and Yung (1993:148) point out, " . . . the practical effects of excessive risk remain for young Black men because they are

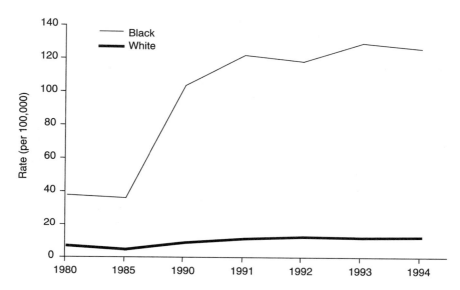

FIGURE 12-7 Homicide rates for male adolescents, age 15 to 19, resulting from the use of firearms, 1980-1994. SOURCE: U.S. Department of Health and Human Services (1997:17).

overrepresented in the population of families with incomes below the poverty level."

Drawing on existing research findings, Hammond and Yung (1993) proposed a tripartite conceptual framework for understanding the markedly higher rates of homicide and assaultive violence among Blacks. This framework emphasizes etiological roles:

1. Host-related factors—e.g., a propensity to believe that any physical, verbal, or social offense is deliberate and malicious or that an aggressive response to a perceived provocation is legitimate; exposure to violent role models within families of origin.

2. Agent-related factors—e.g., a weapon is used to commit the act.

3. Environment-related factors—e.g., stress caused by poverty and the constellation of poverty-related factors such as joblessness, community disorganization, high population density.

Many of these factors have been shown in empirical research to be risk factors or mediators of aggressive and violent behavior (Coie and Dodge, 1998). For example, Sampson et al. (1997) found that neighborhood disadvantage (e.g., high rates of poverty, unemployment, welfare receipt, and residential instability) increases violent crime and homicide partly by reducing collective efficacy (i.e., social cohesion among neighbors, combined with their willingness to intervene on behalf of the common good); however, extant data are inadequate to determine the relative contribution of these factors to race differences in aggression and violent behavior.

Nonetheless, it is clear that the sharp rise in rates of homicide and assaultive violence among Black male adolescents that began in 1985 was accompanied by increases in a cluster of various forms of disadvantage among Blacks. First, between 1980 and 1990, concentrated poverty among Blacks in metropolitan areas grew, both in terms of the absolute number and the percentage of the Black population living in neighborhoods of concentrated poverty—i.e., neighborhoods in which 40 percent or more of the residents are poor. Links have been found between increasing concentrations of the poor in certain cities and increases in violence (Gephart, 1997). The increase in these disadvantage factors may have weakened social and cultural norms that inhibit violent behavior.

Second, Black male adolescents experienced profound economic attrition during the 1970s and 1980s because of their increased vulnerability to structural changes in the economy (Fusfeld and Bates, 1984; James, 1985; Wilson, 1987). Between 1973 and 1986, real annual earnings of Black civilian males age 20 to 24 dropped 46 percent, more than two times the decline among comparable White males. During roughly the same period, the percentage of young (20 to 24 years old) male Black high school dropouts with no reported earnings whatsoever increased from 12 percent to 23 percent (William T. Grant Foundation Commission on Work, Family and Citizenship, 1988). Third, in the mid- to late-1980s there was a remarkable increase in the trafficking and use of crack cocaine in Black communities (Massing, 1998). Fourth, unemployment and diminished life prospects caused by economic downturns, which occurred at roughly the same time, are associated with the emergence of drug dealing among urban gangs as entrepreneurial enterprises offering economic maintenance for young men with limited resources for other employment. It is important to point out, however, that incidents involving drug trafficking and gang-related activity account for only a small portion of the violence among Black youth nationally, though they account for a much larger portion in large cities (Hammond and Yung, 1993).

Impact of Public Policies and Programs

Historical research lends credence to the claim that federal and local urban and economic policies (e.g., subsidization of interstate highways and freeways, urban renewal and public housing policies), by contributing to the concentration of poverty and by failing to stem economic disinvestment and withdrawal of services in cities, played a significant role in the economic decline of inner cities and their residents and, ultimately, in community disorganization and crime (Gephart, 1997). In addition, the dismantling during the early 1980s of a national drug policy that gave priority to reducing the demand for drugs through education and treatment rather than through law enforcement interventions is thought to have fueled the drug epidemic and its attendant violence during the late 1980s. During the Reagan administration (1981 to 1988), the amount spent for drug treatment in real dollars fell to less than a quarter of what had been provided during the Nixon administration (Massing, 1998).

Intervention programs for antisocial adolescents have not proved to be highly effective. At best, they produce short-term effects that are lost within a year or two of treatment termination. For preadolescents, however, successful intervention appears to be possible, especially via those programs more comprehensive in approach that include parent training, child social-skills training, and academic support and remediation (Patterson, 1986). Several education-oriented preschool interventions for poor children have produced reductions in aggression, acting out, and antisocial behavior during adolescence (Lally et al., 1988; Johnson, 1988; Seitz et al., 1985). Some have been effective in reducing the number of probation cases, number of months on probation or parole, number of lifetime (juvenile and adult) criminal arrests (including drug-related, property, and personal-violence crimes), and number of frequent offenders (Lally et al., 1988; Schweinhart et al., 1993). Most of these numbers are large enough to be socially meaningful, with "number of frequent offenders" being especially important given that most crimes are committed by frequent offenders (Wilson and Herrnstein, 1985).

Preschool interventions that produce such effects typically are family-focused, whereby preschool education is accompanied by various core services to parents and other family members (e.g., parenting education, assistance with housing and legal problems). These programs appear to attenuate aggressive and delinquent behavior by reducing multiple risk factors associated with these outcomes (e.g., cognitive deficits, impaired socioemotional functioning in early life, low parental involvement with children, hostile or rejecting parenting, low levels of schooling and earnings during late adolescence). With rare exception (Schweinhart et al., 1993), these hypothesized pathways have not been directly tested, but they are consistent with an extensive body of research on the precursors of delinquent and externalizing behaviors (Zigler et al., 1992; Yoshikawa, 1994). Evidence of the efficacy of these programs lends support to the call for universal preschool education and complementary family support services for poor children and families (McLoyd, 1998b). In addition to evidence that broad-based interventions at the individual level can reduce violence, persuasive data show that agent-centered interventions, such as more stringent gun control and education about the importance of gun storage and trigger-locking mechanisms, would reduce fatalities and serious levels of injury (Hammond and Yung, 1993).

Illicit Drug Use

Drug use among adolescents contributes to crime, decreases economic productivity, and increases the rate at which individuals use health-care services because of the adverse effects illicit drug use has on health. Chronic marijuana use, for example, is associated with damage to pulmonary functions, whereas cocaine is linked to eating disorders, heart attack, and stroke. Consumption of alcohol increases adolescents' risk of motor vehicle crashes and deaths, difficulties in school and the workplace, violence, criminal behavior, and suicide. Cigarette smoking is a significant risk factor for emphysema, heart disease, stroke, birth defects, and unintentional fires (Bachman and Wallace, 1991).

During the past two decades, marijuana has consistently been used (30-day and annual prevalence) by higher percentages of 10th and 12th graders than any of the other illicit drugs typically tracked in national surveys (e.g., cocaine, hallucinogens). Since the peak of the epidemic in the late 1970s, illicit drug use declined steadily and markedly until 1992, when data show increases in the use of all illicit drugs tracked in regularly repeated national surveys, with the most pronounced increases occurring in marijuana use (see Figure 12-8 A-D). The annual prevalence of marijuana use among 12th graders, for example, almost doubled between 1992 (22 percent) and 1997 (39 percent). Parallel increases were also observed for 8th and 10th graders. A substantial increase in the prevalence of daily cigarette smoking and a modest rise in the prevalence of binge drinking also occurred during this period (Johnston et al., 1998).

Prevalence and Historical Trends by Race and Ethnicity

Compared to Hispanic and White adolescents, Black adolescents participating in annual national surveys during the past two decades consistently report the lowest level of usage of marijuana (Figure 12-8A), the lowest prevalence of alcohol use and binge drinking (Figure 12-8B and C), and the lowest level of cigarette smoking (Figure 12-8D). The subgroup differences tend to be substantial. For example, in 1997, the percentage of Black, Hispanic, and White 12th graders in the Monitoring the Future national survey who reported binge drinking was 13 percent, 28 percent,

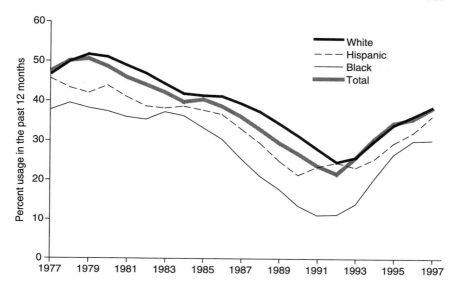

FIGURE 12-8A Marijuana: Trends in marijuana, alcohol, and cigarette usage from 1977 to 1997 among Black, Hispanic, and White 12th graders. Percentage of use during 1-year periods. SOURCE: Institute for Social Research (1997).

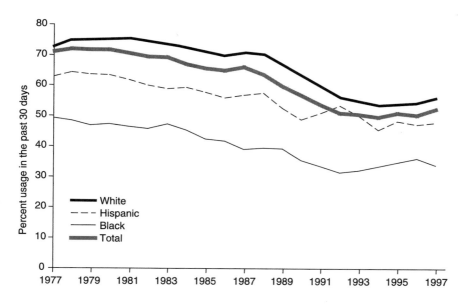

FIGURE 12-8B Alcohol: Trends in use among 12th graders during 30-day periods. SOURCE: Institute for Social Research (1997).

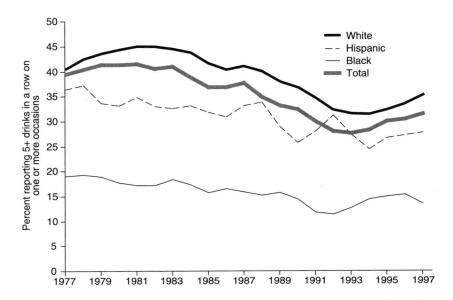

FIGURE 12-8C Binge drinking: Trends in percentage of 12th graders reporting five or more drinks in a row during two-week periods. SOURCE: Institute for Social Research (1997).

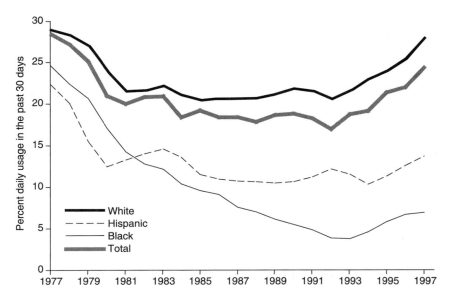

FIGURE 12-8D Cigarettes: Trends in percentage of 12th graders reporting use during 30-day periods. SOURCE: Institute for Social Research (1997).

and 35 percent, respectively (Johnston et al., 1998). Rates of use of alcohol, cigarettes, and other drugs for Hispanic adolescents typically fall between those for White and Black adolescents, with the exception that Hispanic adolescents tend to report the highest rates for cocaine use. Race and ethnic differences in levels of drug use notwithstanding, trends in drug use during the past two decades are fairly similar for all three groups. The one notable exception is that, during the 1990s, frequent cigarette smoking declined among Black female students in grades 9 to 12, while increasing among all other ethnic and gender subgroups (U.S. Department of Health and Human Services, 1997).

An extensive literature exists concerning possible reasons for the relatively low self-reported prevalence of drug use among Black and Hispanic adolescents. Explanations offered include:

1. Minority youth are less likely than White youth to report their drug use truthfully.

2. Minority youth, especially Hispanics, may be more likely than White youth to abstain from the use of most drugs, but those who do use drugs are more likely than their White counterparts to use heavily, resulting in a disproportionate share of drug-related problems.

3. Large within-group gender differences exist, such that the significant numbers of females who do not use drugs cause the overall prevalence rates for minority youth to be disproportionately low relative to those for White youth.

4. School-based surveys underestimate drug use by Black and Hispanic youth because of the higher dropout rates among minorities (and hence, minority drug users) compared to White youth (Wallace et al., 1995).

Wallace and his colleagues have creatively used various data-based approaches to test these hypotheses. Their investigations suggest that some of the differences in reported drug use between White and Hispanic samples of high school seniors can be explained by higher school dropout rates among Hispanic youth. None of the hypotheses, however, adequately accounts for the substantial gap between Black and White youth. They conclude that the general patterns of racial and ethnic differences found in their work and that of others are, on the whole, valid (Wallace and Bachman, 1991, 1993; Wallace et al., 1995).

Wallace and his colleagues suggest that Black youth may be less likely than White youth to use drugs because they have less exposure to peer or adult drug users, and given equal exposure are less vulnerable to users than are White youth. The highest rates of drug use among Black and other minority youth likely occur in segregated, high-poverty, and high-crime areas; and inner-city Black youth are underrepresented in both the Monitoring the Future Survey and the National Survey of Drug Abuse, the two national surveys that are the major sources of data on substance use by adolescents. Findings from inner-city areas are, in fact, not well-represented in most general population surveys and probably are not generalizable to the larger population of minority youth (Dryfoos, 1990). Wallace and his colleagues also hypothesize that race differences in drug use are partially accounted for by differential levels of religiosity. Research indicates that Black youth are more religious than White youth and that religiosity is negatively related to drug use (Wallace et al., 1995).

Another important issue needing explanation is the apparent discrepancy between the relatively low self-reports of drug use by minority youth and the relatively high prevalence of drug-related problems among minority adults. Findings from the literature on alcohol consumption may be instructive in this regard. Studies indicate that alcohol use begins later among Blacks than among Whites, but once initiated, heavy use continues for a longer period of time among Blacks. This pattern of later initiation but longer and heavy use is consistent with both the lower self-reports of use among Black youth and the higher prevalence of drug-related problems among Black adults. Wallace et al. (1995:77) speculate that "Witnessing the drug-related problems of adults might deter many black youth from using drugs until they are faced with the realities of adulthood (e.g., racism, poverty, unemployment, bad relationships) that lead some of the adults around them to use drugs."

At the same time, it is important to underscore problems of "objective" data sources (e.g., Drug Abuse Warning Network [DAWN] data on drug-related emergency room visits, data on juvenile arrests for drug abuse violations, data on drug-related mortality and morbidity among adults), all of which tend to yield race-related differences opposite those found with self-report data. Until recently, DAWN data were collected from hospital emergency rooms and medical examiner facilities in metropolitan areas such as Detroit, Atlanta, and Miami—selected specifically because those areas were believed to have higher rates of problem drug use. The residents of these targeted areas are disproportionately Black and Hispanic; hence, minorities are disproportionately overrepresented in drug-related emergency room incidents as tracked by DAWN. Second, it is unclear whether Black youth are disproportionately arrested for illicit drug violations because they are actually more involved in drug-related activity, or because of heavy policing of poor, predominantly Black neighborhoods, or because of bias toward detection and arrest of certain groups (e.g., Black male adolescents). Furthermore, arrest data may not be a valid indicator of adolescent drug use because drug dealers and drug users may be different populations (Wallace et al., 1995).

Finally, skeptics point out that the overrepresentation of minority group members in public drug treatment facilities may not reflect race differences in drug abuse in the general population for two reasons: (1) these centers tend to be located in inner cities and (2) many minority group members lack money and insurance coverage to seek private treatment. In any case, extrapolating from drug-related mortality and morbidity among adults to patterns of use among youth is problematic because these two groups represent different age cohorts with different historical experiences (Wallace et al., 1995).

Impact of Public Policies and Programs

Historical trends in adolescents' drug use cannot be linked definitively to particular public policies, but a strong case can be made for their indirect effects on use of certain drugs through their impact on public attitudes. The decline in cigarette smoking among adolescents and adults that occurred in the 1970s has been attributed to drastic shifts in public opinion about its social acceptability and safety following the release of the Surgeon General's reports in 1967 and 1971 documenting the negative health consequences of smoking. The large-scale initiation of smoking prevention programs in schools in the early 1980s probably helped to sustain this downward trend among adolescents (Dryfoos, 1990). The rise in the 1990s in cigarette smoking among adolescents is generally thought to be a consequence of increased advertising and marketing by tobacco companies aimed at adolescents (e.g., the fashionable demeanor and attire of Joe Camel in Camel cigarette advertisements, the introduction of coupon programs offering Marlboro Gear and Camel Cash, the decline in the real price of cigarettes) (Rosenbaum, 1998; Shane, 1998).

Declines during the 1980s in the use of illicit drugs such as marijuana and cocaine among adolescents have been attributed to changing perceptions among adolescents about the risks of using these drugs. Conversely, increases in the use of marijuana since 1992 correspond with a decline from 1991 to 1996 in its perceived harmfulness by students across all grade levels (U.S. Department of Health and Human Services, 1997). The 1980s were marked by increasing involvement of the American public in stopping the "drug epidemic," provoked by highly publicized evidence that age of first use of illicit drugs was getting lower and lower. During this period, more than 7,000 local groups with concerns about adolescent drug use were organized around the country—National Federation of Parents for Drug-Free Youth, Parent Resources and Information on Drug Education, Mothers Against Drunk Driving. Most of these groups were comprised of suburban middle-class families. School systems, working in concert with these groups, became the central agency for substance abuse prevention programs. Two federal agencies, the National Institute on Drug Abuse and the National Institute on Alcohol Abuse and Alcoholism, played major roles in developing and implementing drug prevention demonstration projects (Dryfoos, 1990). Another deterrent, to marijuana use in particular, may have been the shift in focus of federally supported drug programs from heroin to marijuana during the latter half of the Carter administration (1977 to 1980), in response to increased complaints by parents (Massing, 1998).

Substance abuse prevention programs tend to be school-based and addressed to the general school population. These programs are more successful at changing knowledge than decreasing or preventing drug use. Among the strategies that stand out as unsuccessful in decreasing rates of drug use are programs that use only information or cognitive approaches, self-esteem enhancement or affective methods, scare tactics, and "Just Say No" media campaigns (Dryfoos, 1990). These generalized programs overlook the fact that the most intense need is among the population of adolescents with risk markers for later substance abuse, such as a history of use of any substances during preadolescence, poor academic performance, family problems, consorting with peers who use substances, and/or personality characteristics such as being a nonconformist or rebellious.

Three types of programs appear to be the most successful in preventing nonuser students from initiating drug use and convincing user students to reduce or stop use: (1) school-based social-skills curricula, (2) school-based counseling services, and (3) multicomponent collaborative community programs. The most effective curricula emphasize coping skills for dealing with anxiety, social-skills training for resisting peer pressure, and decision-making skills to foster critical thinking and formulation of counter-arguments to advertising appeals. Programs (especially those using older students as teachers and role models for younger students) tend to be more successful than teacher- or counselor-led efforts. School-based counseling services focus on individual counseling by social workers, school liaison workers, and "skilled listeners," who work collaboratively with school-based psychologists, guidance counselors, and teachers. Successful models of collaborative community programs include a wide range of training and educational approaches (e.g., school-based social-skills curricula) both within schools and in the community. Principals and teachers are key in these efforts and in programs that attempt to change school climate. Parental involvement is achieved through advisory committees, school teams, and parent education (Dryfoos, 1990).

Suicide

Suicide is the third leading cause of death among adolescents age 15 to 19. Since 1990, the rate for this segment of the population stabilized at approximately 11 deaths per 100,000 (U.S. Department of Health and Human Services, 1997). But it had nearly doubled since the 1970s, going from 5.9 percent of deaths per 100,000 adolescents in 1970 to 11 percent of deaths per 100,000 in 1994, increasing much more dramatically than in the general population. The increase has been attributed to several factors: increased rates of drug and alcohol abuse, increased psychosocial stressors and negative life events experienced by youth (e.g., parental separation and divorce, change in caretaker and living situation), increased accessibility to and use of firearms, increased pressure on children to achieve and be responsible at an early age, and increased coverage of suicide in the mass media, which, reportedly, encourages social imitation and diminishes the taboo against this act.

Empirical research provides indirect support for several of these hypotheses. Data on suicide rates in Europe, for example, indicate that the percentage change in alcohol consumption had the highest correlation with changes in suicide rates. Data also indicate that adolescents who attempt suicide experience more familial turmoil and increased social instability in the year before the suicide attempt, compared with depressed but nonsuicidal adolescents and a normal sample of adolescents. The number of firearms per 100 Americans has increased dramatically over the past several decades, and the rate of suicide by firearm has increased three times faster than the rates of all other methods for 15- to 19-year olds (for a detailed discussion of this research, see Garland and Zigler, 1993).

Prevalence and Historical Trends by Race and Ethnicity

Black youth have long had substantially lower suicide rate than White youth. Early explanations of this disparity were based on a reciprocal model for suicide and homicide—i.e., some groups were more likely to express frustration and aggression inwardly, whereas others were more likely to express them outwardly. Extant research lends little support to this model. Most studies report high correlations between outwardly aggressive behavior and suicidal behavior and the coexistence of internalized and externalized rage among adolescents who have attempted suicide. More recently, scholars have speculated that suicidal behavior is inhibited among Blacks by factors such as extended social support networks that serve as buffers against extreme stress and the effects of discrimination, and by cultural values that proscribe suicide (Garland and

Zigler, 1993; Rutledge, 1990). For example, traditional Black religion teaches that suicide is the one sin that is not forgiven and that "heavenly rewards will be given for earthly sufferings" (Rutledge, 1990:346). However, whether differences in exposure to such religious teachings explain race differences in rates of suicide remains unclear because most studies have research designs that are inadequate to address this question (e.g., studies that focus exclusively on African Americans or on European Americans). A recent study of this issue yielded findings that appear contrary to common perception. Stack and Wasserman's (1995) investigation based on a national probability sample found that church attendance lowered pro-suicide ideology more among European Americans than African Americans.

In spite of this long-standing disparity, the racial gap in the adolescent suicide rate has narrowed in recent years, especially among males, who have markedly higher suicide rates than females (Figure 12-9). In 1970, White males age 15 to 19 were twice as likely as Black males to commit suicide (9.4 percent versus 4.7 percent per 100,000), but by 1994, the rates were 18.7 percent for Whites and 16.6 percent for Blacks. This trend is particularly pronounced for the period between 1985 and 1994, when the suicide rate among Black males more than doubled, going from 8.2 percent to 16.6 percent. The suicide rate among White males during this period remained relatively stable (U.S. Department of Health and Human Services, 1997).

Race differences in suicide rates among females have shifted over time; however, suicide is infrequent among females. In 1970, among females age 15 to 19, Black and White females were equally likely to commit suicide (2.9 percent per 100,000 in each group). In 1975, however, the suicide rate for White females in this age group was twice that of their Black counterparts (3.1 versus 1.6 percent, respectively). This trend held until 1994 when the suicide rate for White females in this age category was 3.5 percent compared to 2.4 percent for Black females. Though substantially lower, suicide rates for youths age 10 to 14 have followed similar trends in terms of both race and sex differences as well as historical trends (U.S. Department of Health and Human Services, 1997).

Several hypotheses have been offered to account for the sharp rise in suicide rates among Black adolescents and, correspondingly, the narrowing of the racial gap; but none of these hypotheses has been adequately tested. Drawing on Gibbs and Martin's (1964) status integration theory of suicide, scholars have suggested that the rise to middle-class status is accompanied by a splintering of community and family support networks, a weakening of bonds to religion, and psychological distress resulting from efforts to compete in historically White-dominated social circles (Belluck, 1998). These factors can lead to internal alienation that ulti-

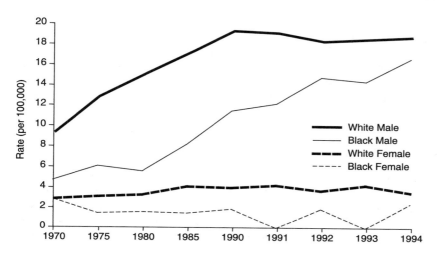

FIGURE 12-9 Adolescent (age 15 to 19) suicides: Selected years, 1970-1994. SOURCE: U.S. Department of Health and Human Services (1997:119).

mately results in self-destruction—i.e., suicide (Rutledge, 1990). There also is speculation that with greater assimilation and contact with White counterparts, Black adolescents may increasingly adopt or model some of White adolescents' strategies for coping with depression and other forms of psychological distress. Others have attributed the increase in suicide rates among Black adolescents to a growing paucity of mental health services in many Black communities and to increased availability of firearms (Belluck, 1998).

Unfortunately, national statistics on adolescent suicide rates are not separated by social class within race. It is noteworthy, however, that a recent study of adolescent suicide in the New York metropolitan area found that unlike White and Hispanic adolescents, Black adolescents who committed suicide tended to come from higher socioeconomic backgrounds than Blacks in the general population (Belluck, 1998).

American Indian and Alaska native adolescents have the highest suicide rates of any ethnic group in the United States. Suicide is the second leading cause of death in this group, although there is considerable variability across tribes. For example, the Navajo and Chippewa have rates close to the national average, whereas some Apache groups have rates four or more times higher. Research suggests that, in general, less traditional tribes have higher rates of suicide, in part because they lack a sense of belonging and support (Garland and Zigler, 1993; Wyche and

Rotheram-Borus, 1990; Wyche et al., 1990). Alcohol abuse is a major risk factor associated with suicidal behavior among Native American adolescents and adults, with some research reporting that as many as 80 percent of Native American suicide attempters also have alcohol abuse problems (Wyche and Rotheram-Borus, 1990; Young, 1988). Few studies report suicide rates for Hispanic adolescents, and substantial discrepancies exist in the data that are reported (Wyche and Rotheram-Borus, 1990).

Impact of Programs

The most common types of suicide prevention programs are crisis intervention services; telephone hotlines are the most popular. Empirical research suggests, however, that suicide hotlines are minimally effective in reducing suicidal behavior. Positive effects tend to be limited to White women, who also tend to be the most frequent users of suicide prevention services (Garland and Zigler, 1993).

An increasingly popular approach to suicide prevention involves curriculum-based prevention or education programs. Directed by mental-health professionals or educators, these programs typically train interventionists by (1) raising their awareness of the problem of adolescent suicide, (2) teaching them to identify adolescents at risk for suicide, and (3) educating them about community mental health resources and referral techniques. Unfortunately, only a few evaluation studies have been published, and most of these are poorly designed, having no control group. Other criticisms of these programs include failure to formulate the curriculum on the basis of current empirical knowledge of the risk factors of adolescent suicide, a tendency to exaggerate the incidence of adolescent suicide in an attempt to increase awareness and concern about the problem, and a lack of focus on those adolescents most at risk of suicide— e.g., incarcerated and runaway youth and dropouts (Garland and Zigler, 1993; Rotheram-Borus, 1993).

There is growing consensus that rather than adopt a narrow approach to the specific problem of adolescent suicide, efforts should be made to reduce the prevalence of risk factors of suicide—depression, lack of social support, poor problem-solving skills, and low self-efficacy. These are also risk factors for major social problems such as delinquency, substance abuse, dropping out of school, and adolescent pregnancy. Primary prevention efforts would seek to enhance adolescents' social competence, problem-solving skills, and basic mental health; schools probably are the most appropriate setting for their implementation.

Stricter gun control laws also have been proposed as a suicide-prevention strategy. Tentative evidence suggests that states with stricter laws have lower suicide rates among males and show a smaller increase in suicide rates than states with less strict laws (Garland and Zigler, 1993). Other proposals include public awareness campaigns about the importance of storing guns and ammunition in separate, locked areas, requirements that gun dealers provide buyers with trigger locks, and making the unsafe storage of weapons a felony.

PRIORITIES FOR FUTURE RESEARCH

Conditions During Infancy

Iron Deficiency

Several unanswered questions and puzzling observations concerning iron deficiency warrant further research. Blacks consistently have lower hemoglobin levels than Whites; but differences in iron status do not seem to explain the differences in hemoglobin, at least in older children and adults (Perry et al., 1992). The high prevalence of iron deficiency in Mexican-American infants urgently requires further study. It will also be important to identify other ethnic and immigrant groups with infant dietary patterns that provide poor sources of iron. There needs to be further study of the optimal level of iron fortification of infant formula to prevent iron deficiency without adding more iron than is needed. Applying new neuroscience research methods should make it possible for the first time to determine directly how iron deficiency affects the developing brain in humans. There also continue to be unanswered questions about the effects of iron deficiency when not severe enough to cause anemia. Sensitive measures of behavior and development, guided by recent basic science research on iron's role in the brain, could be used to shed new light on this crucial issue.

Elevated Lead Levels

Recent advances will afford science the chance for a better understanding of how lead affects the developing brain. This understanding may guide specific remediation treatments in children with elevated blood lead levels. The higher prevalence of elevated lead levels among Black children, even of middle- and high-income families, demands further investigation.

Low Birth Weight

The high proportion of LBW infants among Black women, regardless of educational level, remains one of the most important puzzles to be solved (Foster, 1997). Higher teen pregnancy rates among Blacks do not explain race differentials in LBW; although the very youngest teens have higher rates of LBW babies (Leland et al., 1995), LBW actually increases with advancing age in Black women (Geronimus, 1999). The hypothesis that the explanation is genetic has also been challenged. A recent study of West African immigrant women shows that their babies were similar in weight distribution to U.S. Whites (David and Collins, 1997). Thus, it appears that environmental and behavioral factors are adversely affecting the pregnancies of U.S.-born Black women. The contribution of altered glucose metabolism and diabetes during pregnancy to the rates of LBW among some ethnic groups is another important area of research.

Prenatal Alcohol Exposure

There is considerable evidence that undernutrition, hypoxia, intra-uterine growth retardation, and altered iron transport are important underlying or contributing factors to some ill effects of prenatal alcohol exposure. Determining the interconnections among these factors and others should increase understanding of the mechanisms by which alcohol affects the developing fetus. There is clearly an urgent need for effective treatment programs for pregnant women with drinking problems, with special approaches needed to reach Black and American Indian and Alaska Native women. Protecting the developing fetus from the harmful effects of alcohol should be a high national priority

Behavioral and Mental Health Problems Among Adolescents

As we have documented, poor children from racial minority backgrounds are more likely to start life with biologic insults and stressors that adversely affect behavior and development. We need more systematic study of whether these biologic risks increase children's vulnerability to behavioral and developmental ill effects of other disadvantages they face in growing up, such as financial stress, poor schools, dangerous neighborhoods, family violence, maternal depression, etc.

Homicide and Assaultive Violence

There is some evidence that the risk factors for violence vary among different ethnic groups, but knowledge in this area needs considerable expansion. Especially needed is evidence about which childhood experiences and behaviors, as well as social, economic, and cultural factors, are most predictive of future aggression or victimization among Black, Hispanic, and American Indian and Alaska Native males. Priority also should be given to understanding the factors that prevent as well as buffer the effects of violence among individuals in high risk groups. Although young men are at higher risk of committing and being the victims of assaultive violence, the correlates, precipitants, and buffers of violence among young ethnic minority women also warrant systematic study. Research is also needed to determine the effectiveness of different violence prevention approaches and techniques for different ethnic groups (Hammond and Yung, 1993).

Drug Use

The apparent discrepancy between the relatively low self-reports of drug use by Black youth and the relatively high prevalence of drug-related problems among Black adults is among the most challenging issues beckoning empirical study. Research has identified several risk factors of adolescent drug use, but we possess far less knowledge about the link between these factors and the precursors of drug abuse during adulthood. We need to understand, for different ethnic groups, what factors determine the probability that individuals who used drugs to varying degrees during adolescence experience drug-related problems as adults.

Suicide

Empirical study of the factors contributing to the rise in suicide among Black males is crucial, as is the development of intervention programs based on these etiologic data. Research is needed regarding racial and ethnic group disparities in the availability, use, and effectiveness of suicide prevention programs.

Future Data Needs

Social class and income are highly interwoven with race and ethnicity. Consequently, more precise specification of racial and ethnic trends over time requires data that are disaggregated by social class or income within racial and ethnic groups. Rarely are national data presented in this manner.

Also glaring and in need of redress is the lack of across-time nationally representative epidemiological studies of depression in adolescents from different racial and ethnic backgrounds (U.S. Department of Health and Human Services, 1997). Studies of community samples indicate that depressive mood syndromes and disorders increase dramatically in adolescence compared to childhood and that they often occur in tandem with other symptoms and disorders such as anxiety, conduct disorders, suicidal ideation, and drug use. Moreover, preadolescent or adolescent onset of clinical depression appears to be a major risk factor for adult depression and other major mental disorders (Petersen et al., 1993). Our ability to address these questions will be enhanced greatly by the recently initiated National Longitudinal Study of Adolescent Health, which includes methodology to measure depressive symptoms.

In addition, nationally repeated surveys need to include more measures of positive functioning in adolescents, as well as more indicators that may constitute precursors of behavioral and psychological outcomes during adolescence—e.g., parenting behavior of both mothers and fathers, neighborhood characteristics, and characteristics of peer groups.

Tracking the Impact of Welfare Reform

The Welfare Reform Act of 1996 stands out as the single social policy adopted in recent years with the potential to disproportionately and profoundly affect ethnic minority families and children. This law mandated large reductions in the food stamp program; decreased assistance to legal immigrants; cuts in benefits to adult welfare recipients who do not find work after two years; and a five-year lifetime limit on assistance in the form of cash aid, work slots, or noncash aid such as vouchers to poor children and families, regardless of whether parents can find employment. Exercising the vast discretion given to them under the new welfare law, many states are adopting stricter work requirements and shorter time limits for public assistance than Congress envisioned. In addition, many states will no longer increase payments to women who have additional children while receiving public assistance, on the theory that increased payments create an economic incentive for parents to have more children whom they cannot support (Pear, 1997; Super et al., 1996).

The new welfare reform law voids the long-standing principle of entitlement for poor children and adults alike, such that neither the federal government nor the states, in fact, have a duty to provide assistance to the poor for any period of time. The end of entitlement is signaled most glaringly by two aspects of the policy. (1) There is no longer a federal definition of who is eligible for assistance and, therefore, no guarantee of assistance to anyone; each state can decide whom to exclude in any way it wants, as long as it does not violate the Constitution. (2) Each state will get a fixed sum of federal money each year, irrespective of whether a recession or a local calamity causes a state to run out of federal funds before the end of the year (Temporary Assistance to Needy Families [TANF] block grant). Furthermore, although waivers will be granted for some, in most cases federally supported help will end after five years, even if a family has done everything that was asked of it and even if it is still needy (Greenberg, 1996).

In light of race and ethnic disparities in residential patterns, employment, housing, and other economic-related factors, it is supremely important to determine whether the effects of welfare reform are less positive or more adverse for minority children and families than majority families and the factors responsible for these disparities. Poor Blacks and Hispanics are more likely than poor Whites to reside in economically depressed, societally isolated, urban neighborhoods where jobs are scarce and growth in entry level jobs is unlikely, and high-quality day care and health care are less accessible—all of which are available and accessible in most suburbs and nonmetropolitan areas. Poor Blacks and Hispanics also hold jobs with higher rates of displacement and lower rates of reemployment following layoffs (Fusfeld and Bates, 1984; James, 1985; Jargowsky, 1994; Simms, 1987; Wilson, 1996). These differences in context and economic prowess would appear to put Blacks and Hispanics at a distinct disadvantage in terms of their ability to comply and cope effectively with some of the new welfare provisions such as finding employment and staying afloat following cutoffs of welfare assistance.

Relevant research has not yet been completed, but it is clear that there is the potential for all of the major domains of child outcomes to be affected by welfare reform. The indicators examined in this paper are only some of the relevant markers that need to be tracked. In addition to assessing the effects on these outcomes, it is important to document the effect of welfare reform on the broader ecological context within which children develop. Individual and aggregate level data on the following indicators are of particular interest:

- homelessness,
- malnutrition,
- crime,
- infant morbidity and mortality,
- drug and alcohol abuse,
- family and community violence,
- child abuse and placement of children in foster care, and
- use of mental health services.

Questions that must be answered include:

- Will negative indicators of family, infant, and child functioning increase shortly after the time limits take effect?
- Over time, will these indicators return to their previous levels as families adapt?

- Are variations in welfare programs across states related to what fortunes or misfortunes befall families and children following cutoffs?
- Are welfare cutoffs and the events they trigger more detrimental if they occur during the infancy and preschool years, as opposed to middle-childhood and adolescence?
- Under what conditions do particular sets of welfare provisions have negative effects versus positive effects on children's development?

Researchers will need to be able to identify pathways of influence and intervening variables before they can answer these questions and speak with authority in policy arenas about how welfare programs might be modified to enhance children's development, or at least be rendered less damaging. Welfare provisions may influence children through their impact on a variety of variables, including household or family income, maternal employment, maternal education, maternal physical and psychological well-being, parenting and the home environment, and child care (Zaslow et al., 1995).

The multitude of questions that need to be addressed in light of welfare reform are amenable to a variety of research methodologies ranging from large-scale surveys to small-scale ethnographic studies. Data collection options include administrative records, in-home and telephone interviews, direct child assessments, self-administered questionnaires, teacher surveys, and in-home observations. Some effects can be estimated by tracking age cohorts of children within state, across time using data from various national longitudinal studies that follow children throughout childhood and into adulthood—e.g., the National Longitudinal Survey of Youth. Others may be assessed in ongoing, more rigorous within-state experimental evaluations of the effects of welfare reform demonstrations made possible by federal waivers granted to states (Collins and Aber, 1996). Still others can be addressed by across-state comparisons. Obviously, high-quality research on these issues will require creative research designs that draw on the expertise of child developmentalists, working collaboratively with sociologists, economists, social workers, and researchers from allied disciplines.

REFERENCES

Abel, E.
1995 An update on incidence of FAS: FAS is not an equal opportunity birth defect. *Neurotoxicolology Teratology* 17:437-443.

Allen, L., and C. Mitchell
    1998   Racial and ethnic differences in patterns of problematic and adaptive develop-
            ment: An epidemiological review. Pp. 29-54 in *Studying Minority Adolescents: Con-
            ceptual, Methodological, and Theoretical Issues*, V. McLoyd and L. Steinberg, eds.
            Mahwah, N.J.: Erlbaum Associates.
American Academy of Pediatrics Committee on Nutrition
    1969   Iron balance and requirements in infancy. *Pediatrics* 43:134-142.
Bachman, J., and J. Wallace
    1991   The "drug problem" among adolescents: Getting beyond the stereotypes. *Ethnicity
            and Disease* 1:315-319.
Balcazar, H., G. Cole, and J. Hartner
    1992   Mexican Americans' use of prenatal care and its relationship to maternal risk
            factors and pregnancy outcome. *Journal of Preventive Medicine* 8:1-7.
Banks, E., L. Ferretti, and D. Shucard
    1997   Effects of low level lead exposure on cognitive function in children: a review of
            behavioral, neuropsychological and biological evidence. *Neurotoxicology* 18:237-
            282.
Belluck, P.
    1998   Black youths' rate of suicide rising sharply, studies find. *New York Times* (March
            20):A1, A16.
Breslau, N., H. Chilcoat, J. DelDotto, P. Andreski, and G. Brown
    1996   Low birth weight and neurocognitive status at six years of age. *Biological Psychia-
            try* 40:389-397.
Centers for Disease Control and Prevention
    1991   *Preventing Lead Poisoning in Young Children: A Statement by the Centers for Disease
            Control and Prevention*. Atlanta: Centers for Disease Control and Prevention.
Christoffel. K.
    1990   Violent death and injury in U.S. children and adolescents. *American Journal of
            Diseases of Childhood* 144:697-706.
Coie, J., and K. Dodge
    1998   Aggression and antisocial behavior. In *Handbook of Child Psychology: Social, Emo-
            tional, and Personality Development* (Vol. 3), W. Damon (Series ed.), and N.
            Eisenberg (Volume ed.). New York: John Wiley and Sons.
Collins, A., and L. Aber
    1996   *State Welfare Waiver Evaluations: Will They Increase Our Understanding of the Impact
            of Welfare Reform on Children?* New York: Columbia University National Center
            for Children in Poverty.
Committee on Psychosocial Aspects of Child and Family Health
    1993   The pediatrician and the "new morbidity." *Pediatrics* 92:731-733.
Committee on Substance Abuse and Committee on Children with Disabilities
    1993   Fetal alcohol syndrome and fetal alcohol effects. *Pediatrics* 91:1004-1006.
David, R., and J. Collins, Jr.
    1997   Differing birth weight among infants of U.S.-born Blacks, Africa-born Blacks, and
            U.S.-born Whites. *New England Journal of Medicine* 337:1209-1214.
deMaeyer, E., and M. Adiels-Tegman
    1985   The prevalence of anaemia in the world. *World Health Statistics Quarterly* 38:302-
            316.
Dryfoos, J.
    1990   *Adolescents at Risk: Prevalence and Prevention*. New York: Oxford University Press.
Duimstra, C., D. Johnson, C. Kutsch, B. Wang, M. Zentner, S. Kellerman, and T. Welty
    1993   A fetal alcohol syndrome surveillance pilot in American Indian communities in
            the northern plains. *Public Health Reports* 108:225-229.

Ebrahim, S., E. Luman, R. Floyd, C. Murphy, E. Bennett, and C. Boyle
    1998   Alcohol consumption by pregnant women in the United States during 1988-1995.
            Obstetrics and Gynecology 92:187-192.
Faden, V., B. Graubard, and M. Dufour
    1997   The relationship of drinking and birth outcome in a U.S. national sample of ex-
            pectant mothers. *Paediatric and Perinatal Epidemiology* 11:167-180.
Florentino, R., and R. Guirriec
    1984   Prevalence of nutritional anemia in infancy and childhood with emphasis on
            developing countries. Pp. 61-74 in *Iron Nutrition in Infancy and Childhood*, A.
            Steckel, ed. New York: Raven Press.
Foster, H.
    1997   The enigma of low birth weight and race. *New England Journal of Medicine*
            337:1232-1233.
Fusfeld, D., and T. Bates
    1984   *The Political Economy of the Urban Ghetto*. Carbondale: Southern Illinois University
            Press.
Garland, A., and E. Zigler
    1993   Adolescent suicide prevention: Current research and social policy implications.
            American Psychologist 48:169-182.
Gephart, M.
    1997   Neighborhoods and communities as contexts for development. Pp. 1-43 in *Neigh-
            borhood Poverty: Context and Consequences for Children* (Vol. 1), J. Brooks-Gunn, G.
            Duncan, and L. Aber, eds. New York: Russell Sage.
Geronimus, A.
    1999   Black/White differences in the relationship of maternal age to birthweight: A
            population-based test of the weathering hypothesis. *Social Science Medicine* 42:589-
            597.
Gibbs, J., and W. Martin
    1964   *Status Integration and Suicide: A Sociological Study*. Eugene: University of Oregon.
Greenberg, M.
    1996   *No Duty, No Floor: The Real Meaning of "Ending Entitlements."* Washington, D.C:
            Center for Law and Social Policy.
Guyer, B., J. Martin, M. MacDorman, R. Anderson, and D. Strobino
    1997   Annual summary of vital statistics—1996. *Pediatrics* 100:905-918.
Hack, M., N. Klein, and G. Taylor
    1995   Long-term developmental outcomes of low birth weight infants. Pp. 176-196 in
            The Future of Children—Low Birth Weight, R. Behrman, ed. Los Angeles: The Cen-
            ter for the Future of Children, The David and Lucile Packard Foundation.
Haggerty, R., K. Roghmann, and I. Pless
    1975   *Child Health and the Community*. New York: John Wiley and Sons.
Hammond, W., and B. Yung
    1993   Psychology's role in the public health response to assaultive violence among
            young African American men. *American Psychologist* 48:142-154.
Hankin, J., J. Sloan, I. Firestone, J. Ager, R. Sokol, and S. Martier
    1993   A time series analysis of the impact of the alcohol warning label on antenatal
            drinking. *Alcohol and Clinical Experimental Research* 17:284-289.
Institute of Medicine
    1996   *Fetal Alcohol Syndrome*. K. Stratton, C. Howe, and F. Battaglia, editors. Washing-
            ton, D.C.: National Academy Press.

Institute for Social Research
  1997   *National Survey Results on Drug Use from the Monitoring the Future Study, 1975-1997*. Vol. 1. Institute for Social Research, University of Michigan, Ann Arbor, Michigan. Washington, DC: U.S. Department of Health and Human Services.
Jacobson, J., S. Jacobson, and R. Sokol
  1996   Increased vulnerability to alcohol-related birth defects in the offspring of mothers over 30. *Alcohol and Clinical Experimental Research* 20:359-363.
James, S.
  1985   *The Impact of Cybernation Technology on Black Automobile Workers in the United States.* Ann Arbor: University of Michigan Research Press.
Jargowsky, P.
  1994   Ghetto poverty among Blacks in the 1980s. *Journal of Policy Analysis and Management* 13:288-310.
Johnson, D.
  1988   Primary prevention of behavior problems in young children: The Houston Parent-Child Development Center. Pp. 44-45 in *14 Ounces of Prevention: A Casebook for Practitioners,* R. Price, E. Cowen, R. Lorion, and J. Ramos-McKay, eds. Washington, D.C.: American Psychological Association.
Johnston, L., P. O'Malley, and J. Bachman.
  1998   *National Survey Results on Drug Use from the Monitoring the Future Study, 1975-1997* (Vol. 1: Secondary School Students). Rockville, Md.: U.S. Department of Health and Human Services.
Kieffer, E., G. Alexander, and J. Mor
  1995   Pregnancy outcomes of Pacific Islanders in Hawaii. *American Journal of Epidemiology* 141:674-679.
Kramer, R., A. LaRue, and P. Gergen
  1995   Health and social characteristics and children's cognitive functioning: Results from a national cohort. *American Journal of Public Health* 85:312-318.
Lally, J., P. Mangione, and A. Honig
  1988   The Syracuse University Family Development Research Program: Long-range impact on an early intervention with low-income children and their families. Pp. 79-104 in *Advances in Applied Developmental Psychology. Parent Education as Early Childhood Intervention: Emerging Directions in Theory, Research, and Practice* (Vol. 3), I. Sigel (series ed.) and D. Powell (volume ed.). Norwood, N.J.: Ablex.
Leland, N., D. Petersen, M. Braddock, and G. Alexander
  1995   Variations in pregnancy outcomes by race among 10- to 14-year-old mothers in the United States. *Public Health Reports* 110:53-58.
Life Sciences Research Office
  1984   *Assessment of the Iron Nutrition Status of the U.S. Population Based on Data Collected in the Second National Health and Nutrition Survey, 1976-1980.* Bethesda, Md.: Federation of American Societies for Experimental Biology.
Looker, A., P. Dallman, M. Carroll, E. Gunter, and C. Johnson
  1997   Prevalence of iron deficiency in the United States. *Journal of the American Medical Association* 277:973-976.
Lozoff, B., E. Jimenez, and A. Wolf
  1991   Long-term developmental outcome of infants with iron deficiency. *New England Journal of Medicine* 325:687-694.
Lozoff, B., A. Wolf, E. Mollen, and E. Jimenez
  1997   Functional significance of early iron deficiency (Abstract). *Pediatric Research* 41:15A.

Luke, B., N. Mamelle, L. Keith, F. Munoz, J. Minogue, E. Papiernik, and T. Johnson
  1995   The association between occupational factors and pre-term birth: A United States nurses' study. *American Journal of Obstetrics and Gynecology* 173:849-862.
Mahaffey, K., J. Annest, J. Roberts, and R. Murphy
  1982   National estimates of blood lead levels: United States, 1976-1980: Association with selected demographic and socioeconomic factors. *New England Journal of Medicine* 307:573-579.
Massing, M.
  1998   *The Fix*. New York: Simon and Schuster.
McLoyd, V.
  1998a   Changing demographics in the American population: Implications for research on minority children and adolescents. Pp. 3-28 in *Studying Minority Adolescents: Conceptual, Methodological, and Theoretical Issues*, V. McLoyd and L. Steinberg, eds. Mahwah, N.J.: Erlbaum Associates.
  1998b   Socioeconomic disadvantage and child development. *American Psychologist* 53:185-204.
National Center for Health Statistics
  1998   Health, United States, 1998 with Socioeconomic Status and Health Chartbook. Hyattsville, Md.: U.S. Department of Health and Human Services.
National Research Council
  1993   *Measuring Lead Exposure in Infants, Children, and Other Sensitive Populations*. Washington, D.C.: National Academy Press.
Nokes, C., C. van den Bosch, and D. Bundy
  1998   *The Effects of Iron Deficiency and Anemia on Mental and Motor Performance, Educational Achievement, and Behavior in Children*. Washington, D.C.: International Nutritional Anemia Consultative Group.
Ogden, C.
  1998   Third National Health and Nutrition Examination Survey. (unpublished analysis). Atlanta: Centers for Disease Control and Prevention.
Patterson, G.
  1986   Performance models for antisocial boys. *American Psychologist* 41:432-444.
Pear, R.
  1997   Rewards and penalties vary in states' welfare programs. *The New York Times*, February 23, p. 26.
Perry, G., T. Byers, R. Yip, and S. Margen
  1992   Iron nutrition does not account for hemoglobin differences between Blacks and Whites. *Journal of Nutrition* 122:1417-1424.
Petersen, A., B. Compas, J. Brooks-Gunn, M. Stemmler, S. Ey, and K. Grant
  1993   Depression in adolescence. *American Psychologist* 48:155-168.
Petersen, K., A. Parkinson, E. Nobmann, L. Bulkow, R. Yip, and A. Mokdad
  1996   Iron deficiency anemia among Alaska natives may be due to fecal loss rather than inadequate intake. *Journal of Nutrition* 126:2774-2783.
Pirkle, J., D. Brody, E. Gunter, R. Kramer, D. Paschal, K. Flegal, and T. Matte
  1994   The decline in blood lead levels in the United States. *Journal of the American Medical Association* 272:284-291.
Pocock, S., M. Smith, and P. Baghurst
  1994   Environmental lead and children's intelligence: A systematic review of the epidemiological evidence. *British Medical Journal* 309:1189-1197.
Roncagliolo, M., M. Garrido, T. Walter, P. Peirano, and B. Lozoff
  1998   Evidence of altered central nervous system development in young iron-deficient anemic infants: Delayed maturation of auditory brain stem responses. *American Journal of Clinical Nutrition* 68:683-690.

Rosenbaum, D.
  1998 Smoking by college students is on the rise, research finds. *The New York Times* (November 18):A18.
Rotheram-Borus, M.
  1993 Suicidal behavior and risk factors among runaway youths. *American Journal of Psychiatry* 150:103-107.
Rutledge, E.
  1990 Suicide among Black adolescents and young adults: A rising problem. Pp. 351-352 in *Ethnic Issues in Adolescent Mental Health*, A. Stiffman and L. Davis, eds. Newbury Park, Calif.: Sage.
Sampson, R., S. Raudenbush, and F. Earls
  1997 Neighborhoods and violent crime: A multilevel study of collective efficacy. *Science* 277:918-924.
Schweinhart, L., H. Barnes, and D. Weikart
  1993 Significant benefits: The High/Scope Perry Preschool study through age 27. *Monographs of the High/Scope Educational Research Foundation*. Ypsilanti, Mich.: High/Scope Press.
Seitz, V., L. Rosenbaum, and N. Apfel
  1985 Effects of family support intervention: A ten-year follow-up. *Child Development* 56:376-391.
Serdula, M., D. Williamson, J. Kendrick, R. Anda, and T. Byers
  1991 Trends in alcohol consumption by pregnant women. *Journal of the American Medical Association* 265:876-879.
Shane, S.
  1998 Anti-smoking message not working with teens. *Ann Arbor News* (November 30):A1, A12.
Simms, M.
  1987 How loss of manufacturing jobs is affecting blacks. *Focus: The Monthly Newsletter of the Joint Center for Political Studies* 15:6-7.
Stack, S., and I. Wasserman
  1995 The effect of marriage, family, and religious ties on African American suicide ideology. *Journal of Marriage and the Family* 57:215-222.
Streissguth, A., F. Bookstein, and H. Barr
  1996 A dose-response study of the enduring effects of prenatal alcohol exposure, birth to fourteen years. Pp. 141-168 in *Alcohol, Pregnancy, and the Developing Child*, H. Spohr and H. Steinhausen, eds. Cambridge: Cambridge University Press.
Super, D., S. Parrot, S. Steinmetz, and C. Mann
  1996 *The New Welfare Law*. Washington, D.C.: Center on Budget and Policy Priorities.
U.S. Department of Health and Human Services
  1982 *Vital and Health Statistics: Diet and Iron Status, A Study of Relationships: United States, 1971-1974*. Hyattsville, Md.: Public Health Service.
  1997 *Trends in the Well-Being of America's Children and Youth*. Washington, D.C.: Child Trends.
Vazquez-Seoane, P., R. Windom, and H. Pearson
  1985 Disappearance of iron-deficiency anemia in a high-risk infant population given supplemental iron. *New England Journal of Medicine* 1239-1240.
Wallace, J., and J. Bachman
  1991 Explaining racial/ethnic differences in adolescent drug use: The impact of background and lifestyle. *Social Problems* 38:333-357.

1993   Validity of self-reports in student-based studies on minority populations: Issues and concerns. Pp. 167-200 in *Drug Abuse Among Minority Youth: Advances in Research and Methodology*, M. La Rosa and J. Adrados, eds. Rockville, Md.: U.S. Department of Health and Human Services.

Wallace, J., J. Bachman, P. O'Malley, and L. Johnston
1995   Racial/ethnic differences in adolescent drug use. Pp. 59-80 in *Drug abuse prevention with multiethnic youth*, G. Botvin, S. Schinke, and M. Orlandi, eds. Thousand Oaks, Calif.: Sage.

William T. Grant Foundation Commission on Work, Family and Citizenship
1988   *The Forgotten Half: Pathways to Success for America's Youth and Young Families.* Washington, D.C.: William T. Grant Foundation.

Wilson, J., and R. Herrnstein
1985   *Crime and Human Nature.* New York: Simon and Schuster.

Wilson, W.
1987   *The Truly Disadvantaged: The Inner City, the Underclass, and Public Policy.* Chicago: University of Chicago Press.
1996   *When Work Disappears: The World of the New Urban Poor.* New York: Knopf.

Wyche, K., and M. Rotheram-Borus
1990   Suicidal behavior among minority youth in the United States. Pp. 323-338 in *Ethnic Issues in Adolescent Mental Health*, A. Stiffman, and L. Davis, eds. Newbury Park, Calif.: Sage.

Wyche, K., N. Obolensky, and E. Glood
1990   American Indian, Black American, and Hispanic American youth. Pp. 355-389 in *Planning to Live: Evaluating and Treating Suicidal Teens in Community Settings*, M. Rotheram-Borus, J. Bradley and N. Obolensky, eds. Tulsa: University of Oklahoma Press.

Yip, R., N. Binkin, L. Fleshood, and F. Trowbridge
1987   Declining prevalence of anemia among low-income children in the United States. *Journal of the American Medical Association* 258:1619-1623.

Yoshikawa, H.
1994   Prevention as cumulative protection: Effects of early family support and education on chronic delinquency and its risks. *Psychological Bulletin* 115:28-54.

Young, T.
1988   Substance abuse and abuse among Native Americans. *Clinical Psychology Review* 8:125-138.

Zaslow, M., K. Moore, D. Morrison, and M. Coiro
1995   The Family Support Act and children: Potential pathways of influence. *Children and Youth Services Review* 17:231-249.

Zigler, E., C. Taussig, and K. Black
1992   Early childhood intervention: A promising preventative for juvenile delinquency. *American Psychologist* 47:997-1006.

13

The Health of Minority Children in the Year 2000: The Role of Government Programs in Improving the Health Status of America's Children

Renée R. Jenkins

T he health status of the children of a society is a reflection of that society's vision and desire to ensure the safety of its future. Children's health status makes a statement about the investment a society is willing to make in its youngest members in the face of multiple competing constituencies of its other members. What occurs or does not occur during the early formative years has an impact on adult potential, both physical and cognitive. That potential is also shaped—either re-stricted or expanded—by environmental, familial, and individual limita-tions and resources. Thus, the overall health of a child has a direct impact on the probability of that child achieving his or her optimal developmen-tal competency. The challenge before us—improving the health status of all children and reducing racial disparities in their health care—will be informed by understanding both promoting and inhibiting factors related to that goal, which exist in the environment, the family, and the cultural milieu. That challenge should be driven by our need to ensure America's future.

This paper addresses selected health-status indicators and goals from the federal government's Healthy People 2000 initiative (National Center for Health Statistics, 1996), noting trends, factors that influence the indica-tors, programs or policies designed to improve health outcomes, and con-siderations for future research as it relates to minority children. The goals of Healthy People 2000 are widely accepted as nationally critical mea-sures that reflect the effectiveness of preventive health systems in ad-dressing the mental and physical health status of the American people.

The goals also set national benchmarks for state- and community-level assessments and evaluations. The agenda for health services research often incorporates these goals as outcome measures for health status.

Access to health care is directly associated with good health status. Some policies are in place, and others are evolving, to improve access to health care specifically for pregnant women and children. It will be important to examine health outcomes as part of evaluating the programs emanating from these policies. Findings from the evaluations will help researchers adapt the successful models and develop improved models that will take us further in identifying and removing barriers to high-quality health care. As the percentage of minority children in this country grows, the persistence of disparities in attaining optimal health and development will threaten the foundation on which we are building future contributing citizens, workers, and leaders. The question is whether we, as a society, have the will and commitment to invest our resources in reversing negative trends and accelerating positive ones.

THE CHANGING CHILD POPULATION AND FAMILY STRUCTURE

Although the percentage of the population made up of children younger than age 18 has decreased since 1950, the actual number of children in that age group increased, simply because the numbers increased proportionately for all age groups. In 1950, 31 percent of the U.S. population was children younger than 18 years old, compared to 26 percent in 1990. In 1950, the total number of children in that age group was 47.3 million, compared to 63.6 million in 1990. The Census Bureau projects the percentage of children will plateau by 2010; at that time, the actual number is projected to be 73.6 million. By 2010, the number of Hispanic children is expected to exceed the number of Black children, making Hispanic children, at 18 percent of children, the most populous minority children group (Table 13-1). Asians and Pacific Islanders will be the most rapidly growing population, projected to increase from 2 percent of the population in 1980 to 8 percent in 2020.

Since 1960, Americans in all ethnic groups have been having smaller families. The drop was most precipitous for Black families, going from 19 percent of families having four or more children in 1970 to 5 percent in 1994. Whites were more likely than Blacks and Hispanics to live in families with no minor children. From 1950 to 1994, the percentage of children living in female-headed households quadrupled, going from 6 percent to 24 percent. Black children were most affected; more than half lived in single-parent, female-headed households in 1994. Only 28 percent of Hispanic and 18 percent of White children lived in female-headed house-

TABLE 13-1 Percent Distribution of U.S. Children Under 18 by Race/Ethnicity, 1960 to 2020

	1960	1970	1980	1990	1995	2000	2010	2020
White[a]	86	85	74	69	67	64	58	54
Black	13	14	15	15	16	16	17	18
Hispanic[b]	NA	NA	9	12	14	15	18	21
Asian American	NA	NA	2	3	4	5	7	8
Native American	NA	NA	1	1	1	1	1	1

NA, data not available.

[a]After 1980, this Census category is "White, Non-Hispanic."
[b]Hispanics can be either Black or White.

SOURCE: For projections 1995-2020: Day, Jennifer Cheeseman, "Population Projections of the United States, by Age, Sex, Race, and Hispanic Origin: 1993-2050," U.S. Bureau of the Census, Current Population Reports, Series P25-1104, U.S. Government Printing Office, Washington, D.C. 1993.
For 1980 and 1990 estimates: "The Challenge of Change: What the 1990 Census Tells Us About Children." Prepared by the Population Reference Bureau for the Center for the Study of Social Policy.
For 1960 and 1970 estimates: Hernandez, Donald J., "Population change, the family environment of children, and statistics on children." In Trends in the Well-being of America's Children and Youth, U.S. Department of Health and Human Services, Washington, DC, 1996.

holds (Figure 13-1). Even though family size decreased, the change from two-parent to single-parent households, with fewer economic resources, increased the likelihood of poverty for those single parents and their children.

Childhood poverty and race are intricately interwoven, and young children are most adversely affected by poverty. Even though a higher proportion of minority children are poor, the greatest number of poor children are White, because they are the largest population group. More than 50 percent of children younger than age 6 living in poverty are children of color, but young White children represented 2.5 million poor, young Black children represented 2 million poor, and young Hispanic children represented 1.3 million poor in 1994 (Li and Bennett, 1994). Over-all, from 1975 (Figure 13-2A) to 1993 (Figure 13-2B), the percentage of children who lived in households with annual incomes less than 150 per-cent of the poverty level[1] rose for all ethnic groups; however, the most disturbing trend was the flow of children to the bottom rungs of extreme poverty (annual household income less than 50 percent of the poverty level).

CHANGES IN INDICATORS OF HEALTH STATUS AND EXPECTATIONS FOR HEALTHY CHILDREN 2000

Observing the progress made toward the Healthy People 2000 goals, it would seem that areas in which interventions have had some success are not the areas most in need of the attention of the health service re-search community. Infant mortality and child immunizations, the indica-tors chosen for discussion here, are among those highlighted in the President's Initiative to end racial disparity in health status for children. Two more indicators, teen births and violent injuries in youth, were se-lected based on marked discrepancies in the prevalence of these health risk behaviors or conditions between minority youth, particularly Black, and nonminority youth.

Infant Mortality

Infant mortality has been accepted over the years as an indicator of the well-being of medical and social systems within a country. Although America's infant mortality rate[2] has decreased dramatically since 1960, it

---

[1]The poverty level in 1999 was $16,700 per year for a family of four.

[2] Rate of death per 100,000 of children less than 1 year old

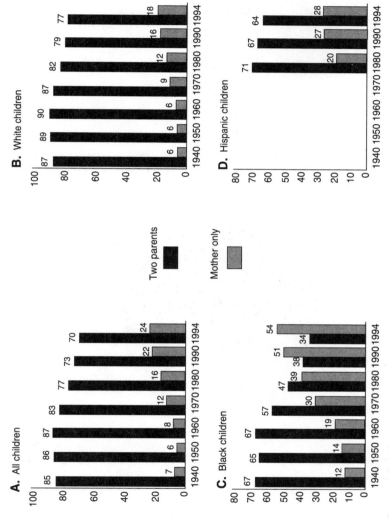

FIGURE 13-1 Percent distribution of U.S. children younger than age 18 living with one or two parents in household, by race/ethnicity: 1940-1994. (A) All children. (B) White children. (C) Black children. (D) Hispanic children. SOURCE: Adapted from Hernandez (1993). Tabulations for 1994 by Child Trends, Inc., from March 1994 *Current Population Survey*.

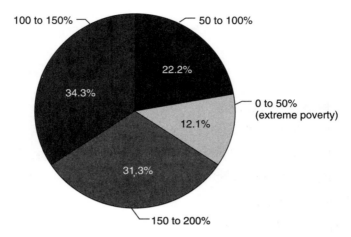

FIGURE 13-2A Percentage of children under age 18 in families whose household income is below or near the poverty line, 1975. SOURCE: U.S. Bureau of the Census, Series P-60, No. 188.

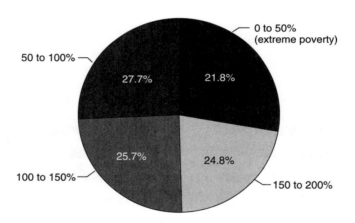

FIGURE 13-2B Percentage of children under age 18 in families whose household income is below or near the poverty line, 1993. SOURCE: U.S. Bureau of the Census, Series P-60, No. 188.

remains one of the country's most glaring indicators of child health status, displaying a wide disparity between Whites and minorities. Infant mortality rates are quite diverse, however, when one also examines rates for other ethnic minorities, especially when one factors in the components of infant mortality—i.e., neonatal mortality (death within the first 27 days of life) and postneonatal mortality (death from day 28 through age 1 year). Hispanics have infant mortality rates very similar to Whites; American Indians and Alaska Natives have rates midway between Whites and Blacks; Asians and Pacific Islanders have the lowest rates. The neonatal mortality rates for American Indians and Alaska Natives approach those of Whites and Hispanics, while postneonatal mortality rates are more similar to those for Blacks. American Indians and Alaska Natives seem particularly vulnerable to sudden infant death syndrome. Among the Hispanic subpopulations, Puerto Rican infants have the highest mortality rate, 8.9 per 1,000.

Healthy People 2000 goals for infant mortality for the total population were set at 7 per 1,000. Based on estimated data for 1996 (7.3 per 1,000), it seems likely that target will be met. To date, however, the target for Blacks (11 per 1,000), appears unlikely to be met considering the 1995 statistics were 14.6 per 1,000. The goals set for American Indians and Alaska Natives, 8.5 per 1,000, and Puerto Ricans, 8 per 1,000, are very likely to be met, based on reports of 9 per 1,000 and 8.9 per 1,000, respectively, in 1995.

Children's Immunizations

Immunization rates are considered to be a measurable component of the delivery of preventive health services to children and adolescents. Being fully immunized has been demonstrated to correlate highly with other primary-care prevention measures such as screening for anemia, tuberculosis, and lead poisoning (Rodewald et al., 1995). Because this indicator is particularly sensitive for preschool children who are less likely to have received the immunizations as a requirement of school entry, the extent of immunization coverage for children age 19 to 35 months is the standard for comparison between populations.

Several major outbreaks of measles occurred from 1989 to 1991 and prompted the Centers for Disease Control and Prevention (CDC) to refocus its efforts on immunizations. Frequent adjustments in the vaccine schedule prevent extended annual comparisons; however, data are available for two sets of annual measures of the combined vaccinations series. The combination series measure is a more stringent measure than the individual vaccine measure. Comparing the 4:3:1 vaccine regimen (four doses of DTP, three doses of poliovirus [Opv], and one dose of measles-mumps-rubella [MMR]) from 1991 to 1993 (Figure 13-3), there were dramatic improvements in the rates of vaccination for Blacks and other minorities as well as all children living below the poverty level. The change for Blacks was an increase from 20.8 percent to 61.8 percent and for poor children, from 23.8 percent to 58.7 percent. In 1994, the hemophilus vac-

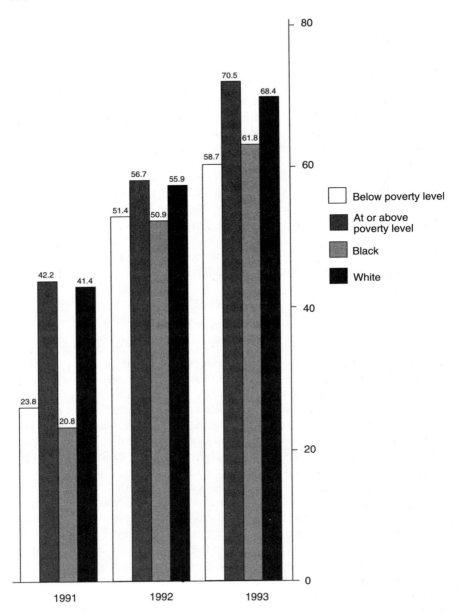

FIGURE 13-3 Percent of children 19-35 months who received the combined series immunizations (4:3:1:3*), by race, Hispanic origin, and poverty status. *4:3:1:3, Four doses of DTP, three doses of poliovirus, one dose of measles-mumps-rubella vaccine, and three doses of Haemophilus influenza type b (Hib) vaccine. SOURCE: U.S. Department of Health and Human Services (1996).

cine was added to the required combination, making it the 4:3:1:3 vaccine regimen (four doses of DTP, three doses of Opv, one dose of MMR, and three doses of hemophilus influenza type b [Hib]). From 1994 to 1996, there continued to be improvement in the rates (Figure 13-4), up to a total of 74 percent for Black children and 78 percent for Asian and Pacific Islander children (a 23 percent increase).

American Indians and Alaska Natives had the highest completion rates of all the minority groups measured. Poor children reached a maximum of 69 percent. The Healthy People 2000 goal is 90 percent for the basic immunization series. If the annual incremental gains continue at their current pace, Asian and Pacific Islander children may reach the target; however, other ethnic groups, including Whites and poor children, would have to accelerate their gains significantly to reach the goal.

Teen Births

Teen births have been linked to increased vulnerability to adverse social, economic, and psychosocial risks for both the mothers and their children. Teen birth rates reached an all-time low in the mid-1980s, only to climb and peak again in 1991 (Figure 13-5). The rates have dropped since 1991, but they have yet to reach their nadir of the mid-1980s. Although the rates dropped most precipitously for Black teens (21 percent from 1991 to 1996) compared to the 5- to 12-percent drop for other groups, there is still a wide disparity between Black, Hispanic, and American Indian and Alaska Native girls compared to White and Asian and Pacific Islander girls. Healthy People 2000 goals for teens are framed in terms of teen pregnancies rather than teen births. "Teen pregnancies" is a combination of the birth rate along with estimates of induced abortions and fetal losses. For example, although the teen birth rate in 1994 was 58.9 per 1,000, the pregnancy rate was 108 per 1,000 (Ventura et al., 1998).

The goals for teen pregnancy were set at rates that are extremely unlikely to be met, given that the birth rate alone approximates the pregnancy targets of 50 per 1,000 for the total population and 120 and 105 per 1,000 set for Blacks and Hispanic teens, respectively. It appears as though those targeted goals were very unrealistic; theory-driven estimates should be recalculated and reconsidered for the 2010 projections.

Violent Injuries

From 1983 to 1993, the homicide-with-the-use-of-firearms rate more than tripled, from 5 to 18 per 100,000. Since 1993, the rates of fatal and nonfatal firearm injuries declined; but from 1993 to 1995, the estimated case-fatality rate increased among males age 15 to 24 years, suggesting

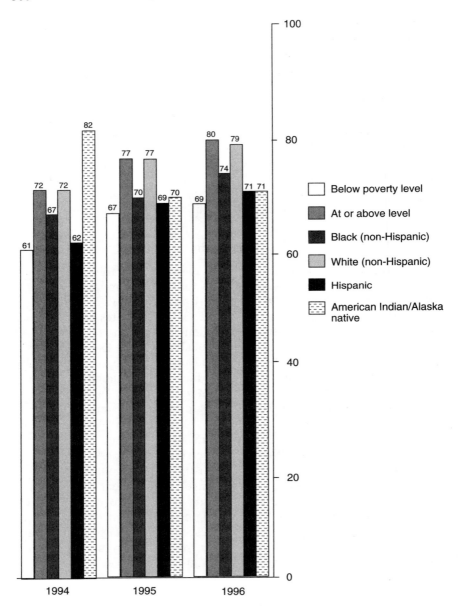

FIGURE 13-4 Percent of children 19-35 months who received the combined series immunizations (4:3:1*), by race and poverty status. *4:3:1, Four doses of DTP, three doses of poliovirus, one dose of measles-mumps-rubella vaccine. SOURCE: U.S. Department of Health and Human Services (1996).

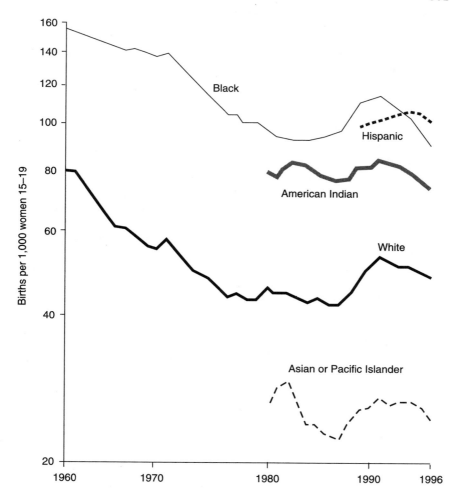

FIGURE 13-5 Birth rate for teenagers 15-19 years by race and Hispanic origin: United States. SOURCE: National Center for Health Statistics.

that the use of higher-powered, semiautomatic handguns increased the lethality of firearm injuries. Males are much more likely to be represented in fatal and nonfatal firearm injuries; however, compared to women in other age groups, 15- to 24-year-old women are the age group with the highest percentage of injuries. Black males age 15 to 19 years old are twice as likely as Hispanic males and six times more likely than White non-Hispanic males to be killed with a firearm (Figure 13-6).

The Youth Risk Behavior Surveillance System (Kahn et al., 1996) reports that in 1995, 20 percent of students (31 percent male and 8 percent female) carried a weapon, such as a gun, knife, or club, within the 30 days preceding a survey. Compared to the baseline survey done in 1991, however, weapon carrying had decreased. The survey also showed that whereas 39 percent of students reported having been in a fight in the past year in 1993, rates for this indicator also declined, from 137 per 100 students per 12 months in 1993 to 128 in 1995. Black and Hispanic youth were more likely to carry a weapon, be involved in fights, and be victimized by others (Anglin, 1997).

The Healthy People 2000 goals for violence reduction are highly likely to be met in some areas but not in others. The overall goal of a homicide mortality rate of 7.2 per 100,000 is very much on its way to being met, with an unadjusted rate of 7.9 reported for 1996. The target rate of 42.5 per 100,000 for Hispanic males age 15 to 34 is also likely to be met considering the 1996 rate was 48.9, balanced by a 31.2 rate for 25 to 34 year olds. By comparison, the target rate of 72.4 for Black males seems fairly distant from the 1996 report of 123.1 for 15 to 24 year olds and 89.5 for 25 to 34 year olds (U.S. Department of Health and Human Services, 1991; National Center for Health Statistics, 1998).

The risk-reduction objectives for physical fighting and weapon carrying for 14 to 17 year olds are set at 20 percent lower than the 1991 baseline survey. By the first follow up in 1995, weapon-carrying reports for the total population and for Blacks had reached or surpassed the goal. The percentages for Hispanics had decreased but lagged behind in the percentage reduction necessary to meet the goal. Findings showed less success in reaching targeted goals for physical fighting, but the trend is still toward improvement for the total population and for Blacks. Hispanic youth reported an increase in physical fighting from 41.3 percent in 1991 to 47.9 percent in 1995. Rates for these behaviors vary by geographic area; therefore, comparisons from survey to survey must take into account any variations in participating sites when estimating changes over time.

Summary

The likelihood of the Healthy People 2000 goals, as stated above, being met varies considerably by goal and ethnic group. The overall infant mortality goal will probably be met, as will the targets for Puerto Rican and American Indian and Alaska Native infants. The target is unlikely to be met for Black infants, however. Immunization goals will be met for Asian and Pacific Islander children but are unlikely to be met for other groups. Although the decreasing number of births (and abortions)

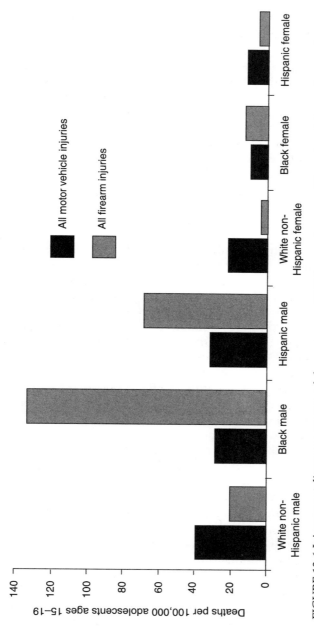

FIGURE 13-6 Injury mortality rates among adolescents ages 15-19 by gender, race, Hispanic origin, and type of injury, 1994-1995. SOURCE: Indicators of Children's Well-being: Health, 1997.

is encouraging, the teen pregnancy reduction goals are completely unrealistic. Violent deaths, specifically overall homicide rates, will likely be reduced to the overall target goals; and it is likely the goals for Hispanic males will also be met. It is highly unlikely that the goal set for the Black male population will be achieved. Weapon carrying among all teens decreased significantly and target goals will likely be met; however, reports of physical fighting for Hispanic male adolescents have increased.

If intervention strategies designed to improve outcomes that fall short of the Healthy People 2000 goals are to be effective, they must focus on factors unique to the specific indicators and populations as well as factors that are similar for several indicators and populations across family, community, and health system variables.

STRATEGIES ADDRESSING THE DISPARITY GAP

Infant Mortality

The public health community has struggled over the past decade to reduce infant mortality, meeting some success in reducing the rate overall, but frustrated by persistently high rates in comparison to other industrialized nations and by the rates in minority populations and in large urban areas. The Healthy Start Initiative is the most recent federal program directed toward reducing infant mortality at the community level. During the initial phase of the program, which began in 1991, the Health Resources Service Administration funded five-year demonstration projects in 15 communities with the ambitious goal of reducing infant mortality rates by 50 percent within the five-year project period. Strategies were to be unique to each community, and the issue of medical intervention was to be addressed as were issues related to poverty, inadequate community services, and educational factors. The community sites were expected to demonstrate innovation, community commitment and involvement, increased access to care, service integration, and personal responsibility. Additional "special projects" and 41 new community sites have been funded since 1997 (U.S. General Accounting Office, 1998). Minority groups were well represented in the targeted communities; the original demonstration grants included two sites that served American Indian and Alaska Native mothers.

Evaluation of the demonstration projects is still under way; however, issues related to ethnic identity have arisen that may influence the interpretation of the evaluation data. Mothers who note their baby's race for birth records may identify race differently than hospital personnel who categorize the race or ethnicity of babies who die; hence, vital record identifiers may not match. A special U.S. Department of Health and

Human Services Secretarial Task Force on Racial Disparities is addressing this issue, as well as others, in a focused effort to have Healthy Start evaluation data contribute to successful strategies to reduce racial disparities.

Children's Immunization

Access is one of the key issues being addressed by Healthy Start and other initiatives to improve infant health, such as the State Child Health Insurance Program (SCHIP). Adult as well as child health data show economic barriers to be the primary impediments blocking poor, minority patients from access to health care, particularly nonurgent, preventive care (Andrulis, 1998; Newacheck et al., 1996). Poverty, minority status, and lack of health insurance exerted independent effects on access to and use of primary care. Poor children, minority children, and uninsured children were twice as likely as children in the mainstream to lack a usual source of care, to wait longer at the site of care, and to receive fewer physician services after controlling for health status (Newacheck et al., 1996). Although SCHIP is in the early stages of national implementation, many states had already begun special programs for uninsured children and are able to demonstrate successful outcomes in many of the areas of deficiency noted in the baseline studies. One such model, in western Pennsylvania, reported that after 12 months of their program, 99 percent of the children had a regular source of care and 85 percent had a regular dentist, compared to 89 percent and 60 percent, respectively, at baseline; reports of unmet need or delayed care in the past 6 months were reduced from 57 percent to 16 percent at 12 months. During this same period emergency department visits decreased from 22 percent to 17 percent, suggesting more appropriate use of services by the newly insured. Although these data are reported for a predominantly White population (94.4 percent), they are encouraging and provide a methodology for evaluation of strategies in other communities with more ethnically diverse populations (Lave et al., 1998). The usefulness of these data is limited because it is too soon to link them to immunization rates and other health-screening procedures. The challenge will be for those implementing SCHIP in the different states to provide data via commonly accepted indicator measures.

Teen Births

Decreases in the teen birth rate are attributed to five major factors: (1) a greater emphasis on delaying sexual activity; (2) more conservative attitudes among teenagers about casual sex and out-of-wedlock child-bearing; (3) fear of sexually transmitted diseases, especially HIV and AIDS; (4) increased use of long-acting contraceptive methods; and (5) a strong national economy with better job prospects for young people (Donovan, 1998). The program strategies have varied widely from concentrating on delaying sexual activity in young teens through comprehensive approaches to addressing academic skills, social skills, and contraceptive knowledge, to offering family planning and counseling services in school settings or adjacent to schools.

Violent Injury

The CDC has led the major research effort in community interventions for violence prevention programs. The strategy for selecting potentially successful interventions has been as follows:

> Interventions must encompass individual and social factors. Violent behaviors are influenced not only by characteristics of individuals, but also by—moving out from the individual—characteristics of families, such as cohesion and parent practices; characteristics of peers, such as delinquent behaviors; characteristics of schools, such as teacher practices and school atmosphere; characteristics of community organization, such as the frequency and type of youth activities; and characteristics of the larger society, such as economic opportunity, misuse of firearms, or media exposure. Violence-prevention efforts to date have emphasized individually oriented strategies, directed toward students in school or patients in clinical settings. These approaches should be continued, but need to be complemented by activities designed to modify exposures at the family, peer, community, and society level (Satcher et al., 1996, v-vi).

RESEARCH CHALLENGES FOR REACHING 2010 GOALS

Broad Institutional and System Issues

Reducing the health disparity gap can be addressed at national, community, and individual levels. Health services research models can take into account policy as well as program impact within and across settings—e.g., the impact of changes in eligibility for a state Medicaid program on immunization rates. Using national data, research can be conducted on how policy changes that affect a family's financial resources in turn affect access to quality health care, because national data provide the complexity of detail necessary for ethnic subgroup analysis—i.e., the full demographic variation that is not possible with smaller population studies.

Community-based studies, particularly research interventions, use innovative models to involve communities in creating the solutions to their problems. These interventions often employ community residents as project staff. These smaller studies can collect more individualized health and laboratory data. This level of data collection is preferable for examining relationships between biochemical markers and behavioral measures, such as the work being done that associates (α-feto protein with preterm delivery and stress and support issues.

Specific Applications

Although limited, the set of program interventions offered above as examples demonstrates the approaches that enhance successful strategies—the kind that move us further toward reducing racial disparities in child and adolescent health status. When the data set allows, specific ethnic subgroup analysis is preferable in Hispanic and Asian and Pacific Islander populations, given the differing baseline and outcome data that may emerge in such subpopulations. Poverty has been so inextricably linked to minority groups, because of the disproportionate representation of minority families with annual incomes below the poverty level, that intragroup studies with more middle-income representation should be considered when "teasing" out effects of financial as well as nonfinancial barriers to access and changes in health behavior. It appears as though the most recent intervention programs have been "reawakened" to the importance of enlisting the community as collaborators in seeking solutions to health problems prevalent in their midst. The Healthy Start as well as the CDC Violence Prevention programs have taken on this approach.

The impact of racism and discrimination in the health-care delivery system as sources of stress and adverse health experiences has not been successfully addressed. Ethnic identity has begun to appear as a variable in research addressing youth violence. As more minority researchers, with their own personal experiences in these issues, become part of the investigator cadre, one hopes that the issues of stress and racism will be included more consistently. On the other end of the spectrum, more research on positive constructs, such as "social capital" (personal relations and network of relations—e.g., church), which identifies supportive elements for resilient individuals and families, is essential to formulating more proactive, as compared to corrective, interventions (Runyan et. al, 1998).

A model in which the contextual issues of racism and discrimination were included was recently introduced by a multidisciplinary group of investigators looking at developmental competencies in Black and His-

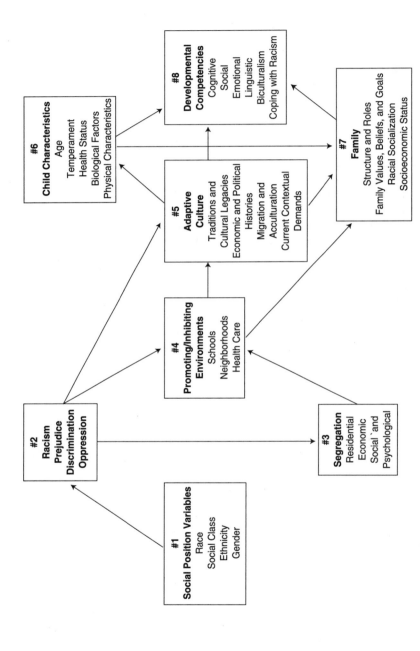

FIGURE 13-7 Integrative model for the study of developmental competencies in minority children. SOURCE: García-Coll et al., 1996. Reprinted with permission from the Society for Research in Child Development, Ann Arbor, Mich.

panic children (García-Coll et al., 1996). The model, though complex at first sight, does allow one the overall contextual setting for contributory factors in the developmental process. It may be useful for investigators—those seeking to move to more population-specific dynamics—to understand and operationalize noneconomic residuals that remain, should the public health community be successful in removing the economic barriers to health care.

CONCLUSION

Having a set of agreed upon goals for health status that are tracked at national and state levels creates an excellent opportunity for health services research. The impact of health policies at state and national levels can create the context for the examination of a myriad of indicators used to measure many of the adverse trends in these goals that disproportionately affect minority children and youth (Figure 13-7). The four addressed in this paper—infant mortality, childhood immunization, teen pregnancy, and youth violence—are among the most glaring at the national level, but others may be more evident in differing communities. The work that continues to be done for the next iteration of Healthy People, the goals for 2010, is to set forth a process that promotes wide dissemination in a manner that allows researchers and policy makers to help shape these new targets. The challenge to the community of researchers is to use those goals in a focused effort to reduce racial disparities and to benefit the most needy of the population.

REFERENCES

Andrulis, D.
   1998   Access to care is the centerpiece in the elimination of socioeconomic disparities in health. *Annals of Internal Medicine* 129(5):412-416.
Anglin, T.
   1997   The medical clinician's roles in preventing adolescent involvement in violence. *Adolescent Medicine: State of the Art Reviews* 8(3):501-515.
Donovan, P.
   1998   Falling teen pregnancy, birthrates: What's behind the declines? *Guttmacher Report on Public Policy* (October).
García-Coll, C., G. Lamberty, R. Jenkins, H. McAdoo, K. Crnic, B. Wasik, and H. Vasquez
   1996   An integrative model for the study of developmental competencies in minority children. *Child Development* 67(5):1891-1914.
Hernandez, Donald J.
   1993   *America's Children, Resources for Family, Government and the Economy.* New York: Russell Sage Foundation.
   1996   Population change, the family environment of children, and statistics on children. In *Trends in the Well-Being of America's Children and Youth,* U.S. Department of Health and Human Services, Washington, D.C.

Kahn L, C. Warren, W. Harris, J. Collins, B. Williams, J. Ross, and L. Kolbe
  1996   Youth risk behavior surveillance—United States, 1995. *MMWR* 45(SS04):1-83.
Lave, J., C. Keane, C. Lin, E. Ricci, G. Amersbach, and C. LaVallee
  1998   Impact of a children's health insurance program on newly enrolled children. *Journal of the American Medical Association* 279(22):1820-1825.
Li, J., and N. Bennett
  1994   *Young Children in Poverty: A Statistical Update.* New York: National Center for Children in Poverty.
National Center for Health Statistics (NCHS)
  1996   *Healthy People 2000 Review, 1995-1996.* Hyattsville, Md.: U.S. Public Health Service.
  1998   *Health, United States, 1998 with Socioeconomic Status and Health Chartbook.* Hyattsville, Md.: U.S. Public Health Service.
Newacheck, P., D. Hughes, and J. Stoddard
  1996   Children's access to primary care: Differences by race, income, and insurance status. *Pediatrics* 97(1):26-32.
Rodewald, L., P. Szilagyi, T. Shiuh, S. Humiston, C. LeBaron, and C. Hall
  1995   Is underimmunization a marker for insufficient utilization of preventive and primary care? *Archives of Pediatric & Adolescent Medicine* 149:393-397.
Runyan, D., W. Hunter, R. Socolar, L. Amaya-Jackson, D. English, J. Landsverk, H. Dubowitz, D. Browne, S. Bangdiwala, and R. Mathew
  1998   Children who prosper in unfavorable environments: The relationship to social capital. *Pediatrics* 101(1):12-18.
Satcher D., K. Powell, J. Mercy, and M. Rosenberg
  1996   Opening commentary: Violence prevention is as American as apple pie. *American Journal of Preventive Medicine* 12(5):v.
U.S. Department of Health and Human Services
  1991   *Healthy Children 2000: National Health Promotion and Disease Prevention Objectives Related to Mother, Infants, Children, Adolescents, and Youth.* National Maternal and Child Health Clearinghouse.
  1996   *Trends in the Well-Being of America's Children and Youth.* Washington, D.C.
U.S. General Accounting Office (GAO)
  1998   *Report to Congressional Requesters, Healthy Start—Preliminary Results from National Evaluation Are Not Conclusive: Preliminary Evaluation of Healthy Start.* June.
Ventura, S., S. Curtin, and T. Mathews
  1998   *Teenage Births in the United States: National and State Trends, 1990-1996.* National Vital Statistics System. Hyattsville, Md.: National Center for Health Statistics.

14

Racial Variations in
Adult Health Status:
Patterns, Paradoxes, and Prospects

David R. Williams

I n compliance with Article One of the U.S. Constitution, the first U.S. census, conducted in 1790, enumerated Whites, Blacks (as three-fifths of a person), and only those Indians who paid taxes. Over time racial categories have been added and altered to track new immigrants. Guidelines laid out by the federal government's Office of Management and Budget (OMB) for categorizing race and ethnicity currently stipulate five racial categories—White, Black, American Indian or Alaska Native, Asian, Native Hawaiian, or other Pacific Islander—and one ethnic category—Hispanic (Tabulation Working Group, 1999). These categories do not capture race in any biological sense; they are socially constructed (American Association of Physical Anthropology, 1996; Williams, 1997) and reflect, in fact, ethnicity: common geographic origins, ancestry, family patterns, language, values, cultural norms, and traditions. "Race," however, as it is popularly understood, does predict variations in health status in the United States.

This paper provides a brief overview of racial differences in health trends in the United States based on selected health-status indicators. The emphasis is on trends in specific causes of death because of the availability of national data for the major racial groups. Discussed are the limitations of the available data and priorities for research; outlined are possible future trends based on current racial data. Given the arbitrary nature of racial categorization, in the interest of economy of presentation, I will use the term "race" to refer to all six OMB categories.

In many of the tables provided in this chapter, the basis for comparison will be Whites. It should be noted, however, that U.S. Whites do not have optimal or ideal levels of health either. International comparisons of infant mortality and life expectancy rates show that the White population of the United States lags behind populations of most major industrialized countries on these health-status indicators—e.g., in 1994, life expectancy for White females in the United States ranked behind that of women in 15 other countries (National Center for Health Statistics, 1998). Nevertheless, because we live in a racially stratified, color-conscious society, where being White can confer significant privileges that non-Whites do not have, Whites can serve as an appropriate, if imperfect, group for comparison with more socially disadvantaged groups.

RACIAL DIFFERENCES IN HEALTH STATUS

This section considers differences in age-adjusted death rates from major chronic diseases, infectious diseases, and external causes (murder and suicide) for the various racial groups. For Blacks and Whites, data are available from approximately 1950 to the present, 1980 for American Indians or Alaska Natives and a combined Asian and other Pacific Islander category, and 1985 for Hispanics. Despite the usefulness of mortality data, it must be remembered that they do not provide the same information as data for disease incidence (the number of new cases in a given period) and prevalence (the total number of cases at a given time). Moreover, death certificates are not uniformly accurate in recording either the cause of death or the race of the deceased.

Major Chronic Diseases

Heart Disease

Heart disease is the leading cause of death in the United States. In 1996, it claimed the lives of 733,361 U.S. citizens. Table 14-1A presents age-adjusted death rates[1] by race for heart disease between 1950 and 1995. Other than Blacks, all racial groups had death rates lower than those of Whites; Asians and other Pacific Islanders had the lowest rates. Since 1950, there has been a consistent pattern of declining rates from coronary heart disease for both Blacks and Whites. A similar pattern is

---

[1]Age-adjusted rate: weighted average for age-specific rates, where the weights represent the fixed population proportionate by age. For example, comparing the 1980 death rates for Whites and Blacks, the age-adjusted formula would account for the fact that a certain percentage of Whites were 75 years of age or older, where significantly fewer Blacks were in that age group.

TABLE 14-1 Trends in Heart Disease Mortality, 1950-1995

	1950	1960	1970	1980	1985	1990	1995
A. Age-Adjusted Death Rates per 100,000 Population							
White	300.5	281.5	249.1	197.6	176.6	146.9	133.1
Black	379.6	334.5	307.6	255.7	240.6	213.5	198.8
American Indian	—	—	—	131.2	119.6	107.1	104.5
Asian or PI	—	—	—	93.9	88.6	78.5	78.9
Hispanic	—	—	—	—	116.0	102.8	92.1
B. Minority/White Ratios							
B/W	1.26	1.19	1.23	1.29	1.36	1.45	1.49
Am. Indian/W	—	—	—	0.66	0.68	0.73	0.79
Asian or PI/W	—	—	—	0.48	0.50	0.53	0.59
Hispanic/W	—	—	—	—	0.66	0.70	0.69

SOURCE: NCHS (1998).

evident in available data for the other racial groups. With the exception of Asians and other Pacific Islanders between 1990 and 1995, heart disease mortality declined for all racial groups.

Table 14-1B shows the minority/White ratios for heart disease. In 1950, Blacks were 1.3 times more likely than Whites to die of heart disease compared to 1.5 times more likely in 1995. Thus, although rates declined for both groups, Whites experienced a more rapid decline than Blacks, so that the gap between the two groups widened. In fact, the reduction in heart disease rates for Whites has been relatively larger than that for all other racial groups. Although these groups still have markedly lower rates of heart disease than Whites, the gap was narrower in 1995 than in the first year for which data were available.

Cancer

Cancer is the second leading cause of death in the United States. In 1996, 539,533 people died from cancer. Table 14-2A presents trends in age-adjusted cancer death rates. Similar to the pattern observed for heart disease, Blacks had the highest death rates from all cancers in 1995. All the other racial groups had cancer death rates that were about 35 percent lower than Whites. Unlike the pattern for heart disease, however, for which there was a general trend of declining rates for all groups, data in Table 14-2A show that through 1990, cancer death rates had been rising for all racial groups. There was a slight downturn between 1990 and 1995 for the White, Black, and Hispanic populations, while there was a consistent upward trend for the Native American or Alaska Native and Asian

TABLE 14-2 Trends in Cancer Mortality, 1950-1995

	1950	1960	1970	1980	1985	1990	1995
A. Age-Adjusted Death Rates per 100,000 Population							
White	124.7	124.2	127.8	129.6	131.2	131.5	127.0
Black	129.1	142.3	156.7	172.1	176.6	182.0	171.6
American Indian	—	—	—	70.6	72.0	75.0	80.8
Asian or PI	—	—	—	77.2	80.2	79.8	81.1
Hispanic	—	—	—	—	75.8	82.4	79.7
B. Minority/White Ratios							
B/W	1.04	1.15	1.23	1.33	1.35	1.38	1.35
Am. Indian/W	—	—	—	0.54	0.55	0.57	0.64
Asian or PI/W	—	—	—	0.60	0.61	0.61	0.64
Hispanic/W	—	—	—	—	0.58	0.63	0.63

SOURCE: NCHS (1998).

or Pacific Islander populations. Table 14-2B data show that, although Black-White differences in cancer were negligible in 1950, they became more marked over time. That is, the cancer death rate for Whites increased only slightly, while the rate for Blacks increased greatly. Although the changes are less marked, available data for the other racial groups show a similar pattern of more rapid increases in cancer deaths than the White population, with a correspondingly narrower differential in 1995 than in the earliest available data.

Diabetes

Diabetes mellitus describes a group of diseases characterized by high blood-sugar levels resulting from defects in insulin secretion, insulin action, or both. In 1996, diabetes was the seventh leading cause of death in the United States, claiming 61,767 lives. Table 14-3A shows that in 1995 Blacks, Native Americans or Alaska Natives, and Hispanics had higher death rates than Whites, and the rate for Asians or Pacific Islanders was slightly lower than that of Whites. Mortality rates for Whites were fairly stable over time, declined in the 1980s, then increased in the 1990s. Rates for the Black population rose between 1950 and 1970, and, after a slight decline in the 1980s, began to rise in the 1990s, going from 17.2 per 100,000 in 1950 to 28.5 per 100,000 in 1995. Rates for Native Americans or Alaska Natives, Asians or Pacific Islanders, and Hispanics also show a pattern of rising rates in recent years. Increases for the Black, Native American or Alaska Native, and Hispanic populations were somewhat higher than

TABLE 14-3 Trends in Diabetes Mortality, 1950-1995

	1950	1960	1970	1980	1985	1990	1995
A. Age-Adjusted Death Rates per 100,000 Population							
White	13.9	12.8	12.9	9.1	8.6	10.4	11.7
Black	17.2	22.0	26.5	20.3	20.1	24.8	28.5
American Indian	—	—	—	20.0	18.7	20.8	27.3
Asian or PI	—	—	—	6.9	6.1	7.4	9.2
Hispanic	—	—	—	—	12.8	15.7	19.3
B. Minority/White Ratios							
B/W	1.24	1.72	2.05	2.23	2.34	2.38	2.44
Am. Indian/W	—	—	—	2.20	2.17	2.00	2.33
Asian or PI/W	—	—	—	0.76	0.71	0.71	0.79
Hispanic/W	—	—	—	—	1.49	1.51	1.65

SOURCE: NCHS (1998).

increases for the White population, leading to a larger overall minority/ White ratio in 1995. Table 14-3B shows that the Black/White ratio in 1995 was 2.44:1 compared to 1.24:1 in 1950, the Native American or Alaska Native/White ratio was 2.33:1 in 1995 compared to 2.20:1 in 1980, and the Hispanic/White ratio was 1.65:1 in 1995 compared to 1.49:1 in 1985.

Liver Disease/Cirrhosis

Chronic liver disease, or cirrhosis (a term used to describe a number of different liver disorders), was the tenth leading cause of death in the United States in 1996, accounting for some 25,047 deaths. In 1950, the death rate from cirrhosis was higher for Whites than for Blacks. By 1995, the rate was slightly lower for Whites, but rates for this group had changed little during this period. Table 14-4A shows that in 1995, Blacks, Native Americans or Alaska Natives, and Hispanics all had higher age-adjusted death rates than Whites. Asians or Pacific Islanders had rates that were markedly lower than all other groups, whereas Native Americans or Alaska Natives had rates that were markedly higher. Their rates declined between 1980 and 1990, but an upward trend was evident from 1990 to 1995. Asian or Pacific Islander and Hispanic populations show a small but consistent decline in cirrhosis rates over time. In 1995 the Native American or Alaska Native and the Hispanic rates were slightly lower than at the earliest noted time points for each, and the advantage of Asian or Pacific Islanders over Whites slightly increased. The rate for Blacks increased remarkably from 1960 to 1970, but began to decrease thereafter; in 1995, it was slightly higher than in 1950.

TABLE 14-4 Trends in Cirrhosis Mortality, 1950-1995

	1950	1960	1970	1980	1985	1990	1995
A. Age-Adjusted Death Rates per 100,000 Population							
White	8.6	10.3	13.4	11.0	8.9	8.0	7.4
Black	7.2	11.7	24.8	21.6	16.3	13.7	9.9
American Indian	—	—	—	38.6	23.6	19.8	24.3
Asian or PI	—	—	—	4.5	4.2	3.7	2.7
Hispanic	—	—	—	—	16.3	14.2	12.9
B. Minority/White Ratios							
B/W	0.84	1.14	1.85	1.96	1.83	1.71	1.34
Am. Indian/W	—	—	—	3.51	2.65	2.48	3.28
Asian or PI/W	—	—	—	0.41	0.47	0.46	0.36
Hispanic/W	—	—	—	—	1.83	1.78	1.74

SOURCE: NCHS (1998).

Infectious Diseases

Pneumonia/Influenza

Pneumonia/influenza was the sixth leading cause of death in the United States in 1996, accounting for 83,727 lives. Table 14-5 shows that Blacks and Native Americans or Alaska Natives had higher pneumonia/influenza death rates in 1995 than Whites, while Asian or Pacific Islander and Hispanic groups had lower rates. Between 1950 and 1980, there were

TABLE 14-5 Trends in Flu and Pneumonia Mortality, 1950-1995

	1950	1960	1970	1980	1985	1990	1995
A. Age-Adjusted Death Rates per 100,000 Population							
White	22.9	24.6	19.8	12.2	12.9	13.4	12.4
Black	57.0	56.4	40.4	19.2	18.8	19.8	17.8
American Indian	—	—	—	19.4	14.9	15.2	14.2
Asian or PI	—	—	—	9.1	9.1	10.4	10.8
Hispanic	—	—	—	—	12.0	11.5	9.9
B. Minority/White Ratios							
B/W	2.49	2.29	2.04	1.57	1.46	1.48	1.44
Am. Indian/W	—	—	—	1.59	1.16	1.13	1.15
Asian or PI/W	—	—	—	0.75	0.71	0.78	0.87
Hispanic/W	—	—	—	—	0.93	0.86	0.80

SOURCE: NCHS (1998).

marked declines in rates for both Blacks and Whites, but fluctuations occurred after 1980 for both groups. In 1995, the rate for Whites was slightly higher than it was in 1980, but the rate for Blacks was slightly lower. The overall pattern of Black-White rates from 1950 to 1995 shows a decline, and more rapid declines for Blacks than Whites. Data for Native Americans or Alaska Natives and Hispanics also show a general pattern of declining rates, with the Native American or Alaska Native/White ratio in 1995 (1.15:1) smaller than it was in 1980 (1.59:1). For Hispanics the rate of decline between 1985 and 1995 was greater than for the White population, so that the Hispanic advantage over Whites increased during 1980 to 1995. For Asians or Pacific Islanders, mortality rates from the flu and pneumonia were considerably lower than for Whites throughout 1980 to 1995, but the rates increased so that the Asian or Pacific Islander/White ratio was closer to parity in 1995 (0.87:1) than in 1980 (0.75:1).

HIV/AIDS

In recent years, acquired immune deficiency syndrome (AIDS), and the human immunodeficiency virus (HIV) that causes AIDS, emerged as a major infectious disease—the eighth leading cause of death in the United States. In 1996, it claimed 31,130 lives. Table 14-6 presents age-adjusted death rates from HIV/AIDS for selected years between 1990 and 1996. For Whites, during 1993 through 1995, death rates increased from the 1990 level; but 1996 shows a decrease—7.2 per 100,000 as opposed to 8.0

TABLE 14-6 Trends in HIV/AIDS Mortality, 1990-1995

	1990	1993	1994	1995	1996
A. Age-Adjusted Death Rates per 100,000 Population					
White	8.0	10.5	11.2	11.1	7.2
Black	25.7	41.6	49.4	51.8	41.4
American Indian	1.8	4.6	5.4	7.0	4.2
Asian or PI	2.1	2.8	3.5	3.1	2.2
Hispanic	15.5	20.1	23.6	23.9	16.3
B. Minority/White Ratios					
B/W	3.21	3.96	4.41	4.67	5.75
Am. Indian/W	0.23	0.44	0.48	0.63	0.58
Asian or PI/W	0.26	0.27	0.31	0.28	0.31
Hispanic/W	1.94	1.91	2.11	2.15	2.26

SOURCE: NCHS (1998).

per 100,000 in 1990. Data show a pattern of increasing death rates between 1990 and 1995 for the other racial groups as well, and for them, also, a decrease in 1996. Rates for Blacks and Hispanics, however, are considerably higher than those for Whites, while rates for Native Americans or Alaska Natives and Asians or Pacific Islanders are considerably lower. In 1996, the Black/White death rate ratio for HIV/AIDS deaths was 5.75:1 and the Hispanic/White ratio was 2.26:1, both considerably higher than they were in 1990. The impact of AIDS on the Black population is revealed by the fact that in 1996, while HIV was the eighth leading cause of death in the United States overall, it was the fourth leading cause of death in the Black population and the third leading cause of death among Black males.

External Causes

Homicide

In 1996, homicide was the eleventh leading cause of death for the U.S. population overall, but it was the seventh leading cause of death for Blacks and Hispanics, the ninth leading cause of death for Asians or Pacific Islanders, and the tenth leading cause of death for Native Americans or Alaska Natives (National Center for Health Statistics, 1998). Among males, homicide is the fifth leading cause of death for Blacks and Hispanics and the ninth leading cause of death for Native Americans or Alaska Natives and Asians or Pacific Islanders. In 1996, firearms were used in 70 to 80 percent of homicides of White, Black, and Hispanic men age 25 to 44 and between 50 and 60 percent of homicides of women (National Center for Health Statistics, 1998). Age-adjusted death rates from homicide in Table 14-7A show that in 1995, Blacks, Hispanics, and Native Americans or Alaska Natives had mortality rates considerably higher than those of Asians or Pacific Islanders and Whites. For Whites, homicide death rates rose progressively between 1950 and 1980, then declined slightly but remained relatively stable between 1985 and 1995; however, the rate in 1995 was 2.5 times higher than it was in 1950. Homicide rates for Blacks were 11 times higher than rates for Whites in 1950 and rose to a peak of 46.1 per 100,000 in 1970. Between 1970 and 1980, rates declined for Blacks but increased for Whites. By 1995, the homicide death rate for Blacks (33.4 per 100,000) was six times higher than it was for Whites. Homicide rates for Native Americans or Alaska Natives declined from 1980 to 1995 to a rate 2.16 times higher than that of Whites. Homicide rates for Asians or Pacific Islanders fluctuated between 1980 and 1995, with the 1995 rate being very close to that of the White population. Homicide death rates for Hispanics hovered at around three times higher than those of Whites, with the rate in 1995 only slightly lower than it was in 1985.

TABLE 14-7 Trends in Homicide, 1950-1995

	1950	1960	1970	1980	1985	1990	1995
A. Age-Adjusted Death Rates per 100,000 Population							
White	2.6	2.7	4.7	6.9	5.4	5.9	5.5
Black	30.5	27.4	46.1	40.6	29.2	39.5	33.4
American Indian	—	—	—	16.0	12.2	11.1	11.9
Asian or PI	—	—	—	5.6	4.2	5.2	5.4
Hispanic	—	—	—	—	15.7	17.7	15.0
B. Minority/White Ratios							
B/W	11.73	10.15	9.81	5.88	5.41	6.69	6.07
Am. Indian/W	—	—	—	2.32	2.26	1.88	2.16
Asian or PI/W	—	—	—	0.81	0.78	0.88	0.98
Hispanic/W	—	—	—	—	2.91	3.00	2.73

SOURCE: NCHS (1998).

Suicide

Suicide was the ninth leading cause of death in the United States in 1996, claiming some 30,903 lives that year. Table 14-8 shows that, in 1995, Native Americans or Alaska Natives had a suicide rate slightly higher than that of Whites, with Blacks, Asians or Pacific Islanders, and Hispanics having rates considerably lower. The table also shows that there was remarkable consistency in suicide rates over time for the White population, with the rate changing from 11.6 in 1950 to 11.9 in 1995. The highest

TABLE 14-8 Trends in Suicide, 1950-1995

	1950	1960	1970	1980	1985	1990	1995
A. Age-Adjusted Death Rates per 100,000 Population							
White	11.6	11.1	12.4	12.1	12.3	12.2	11.9
Black	4.2	4.7	6.1	6.4	6.4	7.0	6.9
American Indian	—	—	—	12.8	12.1	12.4	12.2
Asian or PI	—	—	—	6.7	6.4	6.0	6.6
Hispanic	—	—	—	—	6.1	7.3	7.2
B. Minority/White Ratios							
B/W	0.36	0.42	0.49	0.53	0.52	0.57	0.58
Am. Indian/W	—	—	—	1.06	0.98	1.02	1.03
Asian or PI/W	—	—	—	0.55	0.52	0.49	0.55
Hispanic/W	—	—	—	—	0.50	0.60	0.61

SOURCE: NCHS (1998).

rate (12.4) was in 1970. Rates were similarly high, and stable, for Native American or Alaska Native populations. In contrast, for Asians or Pacific Islanders, Blacks, and Hispanics, the pattern was of lower but generally increasing rates of suicide. Accordingly, although Asians or Pacific Islanders, Blacks, and Hispanics consistently had lower rates of suicide than Whites and Native Americans or Alaska Natives, rates were closer in 1995 than they were in the earliest available data.

Summary

The tables provided in this section show that the association between race and health is complex, and varies with the health-status indicator and the particular racial group under consideration. With the exception of suicide, Blacks consistently have higher death rates than Whites for the leading causes of death in the United States. Asians or Pacific Islanders consistently have lower death rates than Whites. Native Americans or Alaska Natives and Hispanics generally have lower death rates than Whites for the two leading causes of death in the United States (coronary heart disease and cancer) but higher death rates from several other causes.

Because there are extensive data for Blacks and Whites, trends become evident in comparisons of differences over time; and it is easy to see that among the groups considered, overall, Black-White differences are the most pronounced. For multiple causes of death (heart disease, cancer, cirrhosis of the liver, diabetes) the Black-White gap was wider in 1990 than in 1950. For heart disease, the Black-White difference has widened as a result of more rapid improvements in the health of the White population compared to that of the Black population. For cancer and diabetes, there were stable or declining rates for Whites but increasing rates for Blacks. For cirrhosis of the liver, between 1950 and 1970, there were increases for both Blacks and Whites, but more rapid increases for Blacks. For influenza and pneumonia, the Black-White difference narrowed as a result of more rapid improvements in the health of Blacks compared to Whites. Declines in influenza and pneumonia deaths for Blacks were especially significant between 1960 and 1980; these declines coincided with the heyday of some of the gains of the Civil Rights Movement. Evidence suggests that the Civil Rights Movement had a positive effect on the health of the Black population overall (Mullings, 1989). One study found that Blacks experienced a more significant decline in mortality rates than Whites, both on a percentage basis and an absolute basis, between 1968 and 1978 (Cooper et al., 1981a). We need a better understanding of the reasons for this success.

Patterns, Caveats, and Limitations

Patterns

To put these data into perspective, several issues must be considered. First, the lower rate of suicide for Blacks compared to Whites is consistent with other mental health data and reflects a well-documented paradox in the health literature. Blacks tend to rate higher than Whites on indicators of physical health problems, and Blacks rate lower than Whites on indicators of subjective well-being, such as life satisfaction and happiness (Hughes and Thomas, 1998); but Blacks have comparable or better rates than Whites on other indicators of mental health. Community-based studies using measures of psychological distress show an inconsistent pattern of Black-White differences. Some studies show that Blacks have higher rates of distress compared to Whites, while other studies show higher rates of psychological distress for Whites compared to Blacks (Dohrenwend and Dohrenwend, 1969; Neighbors, 1984; Williams, 1986; Vega and Rumbaut, 1991; Williams and Harris-Reid, 1999).

The Epidemiologic Catchment Area study (ECA), the largest study of psychiatric disorders ever conducted in the United States, is based on interviews of some 20,000 adults in five communities. ECA estimated the prevalence and incidence of specific psychiatric disorders in the general population in the five communities—people both in treatment and not in treatment (see Table 14-9; Robins and Regier, 1991). Data show that there are few differences among the groups in rates of either current or lifetime psychiatric disorders. Especially striking is the absence of a substantial racial difference in drug-use history or alcohol and drug abuse. On the other hand, anxiety disorders, especially phobias, stand out as one area in

TABLE 14-9 Rates of Psychiatric Disorder for Blacks, Whites, and Hispanics: Epidemiologic Catchment Area Study

Disorders	Current			Lifetime		
	Black	White	Hispanic	Black	White	Hispanic
Affective disorder	3.5	3.7	4.1	6.3	8.0	7.8
Alcohol abuse	6.6	6.7	9.1	13.8	13.6	16.7
Drug history	—	—	—	29.9	30.7	25.1
Drug abuse	2.7	2.7	1.9	5.4	6.4	4.3
Schizophrenia	1.6	0.9	0.4	2.1	1.4	0.8
Generalized anxiety	6.1	3.5	3.7	—	—	—
Phobic disorder	16.2	9.1	8.1	23.4	9.7	12.2

SOURCE: Robins and Regier (1991). Reprinted by permission.

TABLE 14-10 Rates of Psychiatric Disorders and Black/White, Hispanic/White Ratios: National Comorbidity Study

Disorder	Percentage	B/W Ratio	H/W Ratio
Any affective disorder	11.3	0.78	1.38
Any anxiety disorder	17.1	0.90	1.17
Any substance abuse/dependence	11.3	0.47	1.04
Any disorder	29.5	0.70	1.11

SOURCE: Kessler et al. (1994). Reprinted by permission

which Blacks had considerably higher rates than Whites or Hispanics. Compared to Blacks and Whites, Hispanics had a lower rate of drug-use history and lower current and lifetime rates of schizophrenia and drug abuse, but higher current rates of alcohol abuse and affective disorder. Hispanic data, however, were limited to a sample drawn from the Los Angeles area.

Findings from the National Comorbidity Survey (NCS), the first to use a national probability sample to assess psychiatric disorders in the United States, are generally consistent with those of the ECA (see Table 14-10; Kessler et al., 1994). These data show that Blacks do not have higher rates than Whites for any of the major classes of disorders. Instead, lower rates for Blacks are especially pronounced for the affective disorders (depression) and the substance abuse disorders (alcohol and drug abuse). In NCS, Hispanics had higher rates of disorder than Whites. These data should be interpreted with caution because of the relatively small sample of Hispanics ($n = 737$). Large epidemiological surveys like ECA and NCS provide no data on the mental health problems of Asians or Pacific Islanders or Native Americans or Alaska Natives.

It is also important to attend to racial differences in the severity and course of disease. Mortality rates in a given year are a function not only of the number of persons who die because of a disease but also of the severity and the progression of that disease. Higher death rates for minority populations tend to reflect both higher levels of ill health and greater severity of disease. Higher rates may also reflect differences in access to medical care and racial disparities in the modalities of treatment. Data in Table 14-11 illustrate the pattern in differential outcomes of cancer survival. Five-year survival rates are shown for all sites and for the three most common cancers for both genders and for Blacks and Whites from 1974 to 1994 (National Center for Health Statistics, 1998). For males, the data indicate that during 1974 to 1979, 43 percent of White males had a five-year survival rate compared to 32 percent of Black males. Over time the level of survival has increased for both Blacks and Whites, but the increase has been more rapid for Whites than Blacks; thus, the racial disparity has widened. White males, during 1989 to 1994, had a 60 percent survival rate compared to 45 percent of Black males. There is some variation by specific type of cancer, with the racial disparity being greater for colon and prostate cancer than for lung cancer.

The racial difference in cancer survival for females is similar to that observed for males. During 1974 to 1979, there was a 10-point difference in cancer survival, which increased to a 14-point difference during 1989 to 1994. During the latter period, Black females had a 49 percent, five-year survival rate compared to 63 percent for White females. This pattern is similar to that of males, both in the magnitude of the difference and the widening gap in survival rates over time. Also, mirroring the pattern observed for males, Black females have a very small survival rate difference for lung cancer, with much larger differences for colon and breast cancer. The increasing racial disparity in survival is especially striking for colon cancer, with the Black-White difference being almost three times as large in the early 1990s as it was in the 1970s. The racial difference in survival rate for breast cancer is also instructive. Breast cancer stands out as one of the few physical health outcomes for which the incidence rate is higher for Whites than for Blacks. Yet in spite of the fact that Black females are less likely to get breast cancer, they are more likely to die from it. It is well documented that there are racial differences in cancer staging, with Black females more likely to have more advanced cancer at the time of detection than White females. Some research suggests that Black females have even poorer stage-specific survival rates than their White counterparts (Hunter et al., 1993).

Caveats

A third factor that needs to be kept in mind, to put these data into perspective, is the dramatic heterogeneity that exists within each of the major racial categories. Subgroup variations within the major racial categories tend to predict variation in sociodemographic and socioeconomic characteristics in access to and use of medical care and in health status.

For example, the Native American or Alaska Native category consists of more than 250 federally recognized tribes; 209 Alaska Native villages; 65 communities that have been recognized as tribes by the states in which they are located, but not by the federal government; and several dozen other communities that have not received any formal recognition (Norton and Manson, 1996). Although these tribes and communities share a common history of exploitation and oppression, there is great diversity in cultures, socioeconomic circumstances, and health. The Indian Health

TABLE 14-11 Five-Year Relative Cancer Survival Rates for Blacks and Whites: SEER Cancer Registry

| | Percent of Patients Surviving | | | | | |
| | All Sites | | | Colon | | |
Years	White	Black	Diff.	White	Black	Diff.
Males						
1974-1979	43.3	31.9	−11.4	50.8	44.9	−5.9
1980-1982	46.6	32.4	−14.2	56.0	46.4	−9.6
1983-1985	49.1	34.7	−14.4	59.9	48.3	−11.6
1986-1988	52.8	37.7	−15.1	64.1	52.0	−12.1
1989-1994	60.0	45.1	−14.9	64.6	51.4	−13.2
Females						
1974-1979	57.2	46.7	−10.5	52.4	48.6	−3.8
1980-1982	57.0	45.9	−11.1	55.4	51.3	−4.1
1983-1985	59.1	45.5	−13.6	58.5	50.0	−8.5
1986-1988	61.9	47.8	−14.1	61.7	53.4	−8.3
1989-1994	63.1	48.8	−14.3	63.1	53.1	−10.0

[a]For men, prostate cancer; for women, breast cancer.

Service (IHS) is a federal agency responsible for providing medical care to those who live on or near reservations. IHS estimates that it serves about 60 percent of the Native American or Alaska Native population. IHS data reveal that death rates for this population vary considerably from state to state, with rates being higher in states that have larger concentrations of Native Americans or Alaska Natives (IHS, 1997). In addition, there is considerable tribal-specific variation within a given state.

Similarly, the Hispanic category consists of more than 25 national-origin groups that share a common language, religion, and traditions, but vary dramatically in terms of the timing of immigration, regional concentration, incorporation experiences, and socioeconomic status. It is not surprising that there is also considerable variation in health status within the Hispanic group (Sorlie et al., 1993; Vega and Amaro, 1994).

The Asian or Pacific Islander population in the United States consists

Lung			Gender-Specific[a]		
White	Black	Diff.	White	Black	Diff.
11.6	9.9	−1.7	70.0	60.5	−9.5
12.2	11.0	−1.2	74.5	64.7	−9.8
12.2	10.4	−1.8	77.7	64.0	−13.7
12.7	11.9	−0.5	85.2	69.2	−16.0
13.0	9.7	−3.3	95.1	81.2	−13.9
16.7	15.4	−1.3	75.2	63.1	−12.1
16.2	15.4	−0.8	77.1	65.9	−11.2
17.1	14.2	−2.9	79.7	63.7	−16.0
15.9	11.6	−4.3	84.6	69.6	−15.0
16.5	13.9	−2.6	86.7	70.6	−16.1

of persons from some 28 Asian countries and 25 Pacific Island cultures (Lin-Fu, 1993). Each of these subgroups has its own distinctive history, culture, and language. Table 14-12 presents 1990 census data that show percentages of poverty and median income levels for subgroups of the Asian or Pacific Islander population (U.S. Bureau of the Census, 1993). Overall median income and aggregate poverty level mask the tremendous heterogeneity within that population, and it is these differences that predict variations in health status. Table 14-13 presents incidence rates for four frequently diagnosed cancers among females in Asian or Pacific Islander subgroups (Miller et al., 1996). (Rates for Blacks and Whites are included for comparison purposes.) These data reveal that there is considerable variation in cancer incidence rates for the six ethnic groups considered and that the risk of cancer varies by group and by cancer site.

The considerable cultural and ethnic diversity of the Black population

TABLE 14-12 Selected Socioeconomic Indicators for Asians in the United States, 1990

Ethnic Groups	Median Family Income, 1989	Percentage Persons in Poverty
Asian	$41,583	14.0
Japanese	$51,550	7.0
Chinese	$41,316	14.0
Filipino	$46,698	6.4
Korean	$33,909	13.7
Asian Indian	$49,309	9.7
Vietnamese	$30,550	25.7
Cambodian	$18,126	42.6
Hmong	$14,327	63.6
Laotian	$23,101	34.7

SOURCE: U.S. Bureau of the Census (1993).

TABLE 14-13 Age-Adjusted Incidence Rates (per 100,000 population) for Select Cancers Among Females, 1988-1992

Group	Breast	Cervix	Colo-Rectal	Lung
Chinese	55.0	7.3	33.6	25.3
Filipino	73.1	9.6	20.9	17.5
Hawaiian	105.6	9.3	30.5	43.1
Japanese	82.3	5.8	39.5	15.2
Korean	28.5	15.2	21.9	16.0
Vietnamese	37.5	43.0	27.1	31.2
Black	95.4	8.7	45.5	44.2
White	111.8	13.2	38.3	41.5

SOURCE: SEER Cancer Registry; Miller et al. (1996).

is an important factor to consider in health outcomes, also. Distinctive cultural and geographical regions predict variations in the economic and social experience of Blacks (Green, 1978). Health researchers have documented variations in morbidity and mortality based on region of birth (Fang et al., 1997). Considerable ethnic variation also exists among Black immigrants from the Caribbean region and the African mainland and islands in terms of both culture and language. For example, a Black person born and raised in the U.S. South, a Kenyan, a Jamaican, a Haitian, and a Black person born and raised in the U.S. North are likely to differ in beliefs, behaviors, and even biology. Some limited research suggests that ethnicity predicts variations in health within the Black population (David and Collins, 1997; Fruchter et al., 1985).

The U.S. census also collects data on White ethnic subgroups, but the extent to which ethnicity predicts variations in health for the White population has not been systematically explored in recent health research.

Limitations

In creating mortality statistics, the numerator for death rates for any given group comes from absolute counts based on death certificates. An undercount in the numerator suppresses death rates for the subject group. A growing body of evidence indicates that funeral home directors and other officials who record racial status on death certificates misclassify a relatively high proportion of Native Americans or Alaska Natives, Hispanics, and Asians or Pacific Islanders as White. This has serious implications for the quality and accuracy of mortality data trends for these populations (Hahn, 1992). Miscategorization undercounts death rates for these groups and slightly inflates rates for Whites.

Sorlie et al. (1992) compared race as self-reported during personal interviews for the Current Population Survey with race as recorded on the self-reporter's death certificate. They found very high agreement for Blacks and Whites; however, 26 percent of Native Americans or Alaska Natives, 18 percent of Asians or Pacific Islanders, and 10 percent of Hispanics were classified as another racial category on the death certificate; most were classified as White. A study of mortality data for American Indian infants found that 28 percent were misclassified as another race on the death certificate (Kennedy and Deapen, 1991). Another study of data in a cancer surveillance registry found that 40 percent of cancer patients registered with IHS as Native Americans or Alaska Natives were identified as another race in the registry (Frost et al., 1992). For Native Americans or Alaska Natives, misclassification on the death certificate also appears to vary by cause of death; Native Americans or Alaska Natives who die alcohol-related deaths are more likely to be correctly coded than those who die as a result of some other major chronic illness (Frost et al., 1994).

The denominator for mortality statistics comes from census data. Obviously, inaccuracy in those data also limits the quality of these health-related statistics (Notes and Comments, 1994). A denominator based on an undercount inflates the rate in exact proportion to the undercount. Although the overall undercount for the U.S. population is relatively small, it is much higher for Blacks than it is for Whites. Evaluations based on demographic analyses suggest that there is a net census undercount of 11 to 13 percent for all of the 10-year age groups for Black males between the ages of 25 and 64 (National Center for Health Statistics, 1994a). Thus, all the officially reported morbidity and mortality rates for Black males in these age groups are 11 to 13 percent too high. For the 1990 census, in addition to demographic analysis, the Bureau of the Census conducted a postcensus enumeration survey (PES) in which the undercount was estimated on a case-by-case matching of census records with those obtained by PES of 165,000 households. According to PES, the undercount rates for Hispanics and for American Indians residing on reservations were even higher than the undercount for Blacks (Hogan, 1993). Future research must give greater attention to the magnitude and size of the undercount and of its impact on the quality of health data.

UNDERSTANDING THE SOURCES OF RACIAL DIFFERENCES IN HEALTH STATUS

Health is socially embedded in the larger conditions in which individuals and groups live and work (Amick et al., 1995; Engels, 1984). Biological differences do exist between human population groups, but the existing racial categories do not capture those differences (American Association of Physical Anthropology, 1996; Montagu, 1965). About 75 percent of known genetic factors are innate and identical in all humans; about 95 percent of human genetic variation exists within racial groups (Lewontin, 1974, 1982). Thus, there is more genetic variation within races than between them, and, at best, genetic and biological differences play a minor role in accounting for the observed racial disparities in health (Kaufman and Cooper, 1995).

A prominent hypothesis in the health literature is that racial differences in socioeconomic status (SES) account for the racial variations in health. A robust inverse association persists between SES and health across a broad range of health outcomes in both the industrialized and the developing worlds (Antonovsky, 1967; Bunker et al., 1989; Williams, 1990). Moreover, some research suggests there is a stepwise progression of diminished risk with each higher level of SES (Adler et al., 1993; Marmot et al., 1991). Race is strongly associated with SES, and adjusting Black-White disparities in health for SES sometimes eliminates, but always substantially reduces, these differences (Williams and Collins, 1995; Lillie-Blanton et al., 1996). It is frequently found, however, that even when education and income level are held constant, Blacks have higher levels of ill health than Whites (Williams, 1996b). Some studies find that Black-White differences in health status actually increase with rising SES (Schoendorf et al., 1992; Singh and Yu, 1995).

Greater attention to the construct of racism can serve to inform and structure our understanding of racial inequalities in health (Cooper et al., 1981b; Hummer, 1996; Krieger et al., 1993; LaVeist, 1996; Williams, 1996c,

1997). "Races" are socially meaningful groupings linked to the structure of society; different races have differential access to societal resources and rewards. Although there is considerable overlap between race and SES, race reflects more than SES; and fully understanding racial differences in health will require researchers to explicitly consider the role of racism in health and society. Racism incorporates ideologies of superiority, negative attitudes and beliefs toward racial outgroups, and differential treatment of members of those groups both by individuals and by social institutions. Racism has been a fundamental organizing principle within American society and has played a major role in shaping major social institutions and policies (Omi and Winant, 1986; Quadagno, 1994).

Table 14-14 presents data from the 1990 General Social Survey (GSS) based on White Americans' prejudgments and perceptions about other White and non-White groups—Blacks, Hispanics, Asians, Jews, and Southern Whites (Davis and Smith, 1990). The Black column indicates that substantial proportions of Whites endorsed negative stereotypes of Blacks. Forty-four percent of the White population responding to the survey believe that most Blacks are lazy; 56 percent believe most Blacks prefer to live off welfare, and 50 percent believe most Blacks are prone to violence. Relatively small percentages of Whites were willing to endorse positive stereotypes of Blacks. Only 17 percent believe most Blacks are hard working, only 20 percent believe most Blacks are intelligent, only 13 percent believe most Blacks prefer to be self-supporting, and only 15 percent believe most Blacks are not prone to violence. Twenty-eight to 45 percent opted for the "Neither" category for each choice. It is impossible to know the extent to which the desire to give socially acceptable and nonracist answers contributed to this pattern of response. It is instructive, though, that a large percentage of Whites view Blacks so much more negatively than they view themselves. Hispanics tend to be viewed twice as negatively as Asians; Jews tend to be viewed more positively than Whites in general; and southern Whites tend to be viewed more negatively than non-southern Whites. In general, the data show that a significant percentage of Whites view other groups more negatively than themselves and view Blacks more negatively than any other group.

Historically, ideologies and attitudes about racial groups have been translated into policies and societal arrangements that limit the opportunities and life chances of stigmatized groups. The disproportionate representation of minority groups at the low end of the socioeconomic spectrum in the United States reflects the successful implementation of social policies designed to limit societal benefits to socially marginalized groups.

TABLE 14-14 White Americans' Stereotypes: Percent Agreeing That Most Group Members . . .

	Blacks	Whites	Hispanics	Asians	Jews	Southern Whites
Are Unintelligent						
Unintelligent	28.8	6.1	29.1	13.2	7.0	14.3
Neither	45.0	33.3	42.6	38.0	25.9	44.9
Intelligent	20.0	55.4	18.4	37.3	58.8	31.5
DK/NA	6.2	5.2	9.8	11.5	8.3	9.4
Are Lazy						
Lazy	44.3	4.9	33.5	15.0	4.7	17.9
Neither	34.0	36.4	33.7	27.7	21.9	41.2
Hardworking	16.8	54.5	23.9	47.2	65.5	32.0
DK/NA	4.9	4.2	9.0	10.1	7.9	8.9
Prefer to Live Off Welfare						
Prefer welfare	56.1	3.7	41.6	16.3	2.4	12.9
Neither	26.5	21.5	30.5	31.6	14.6	35.2
Prefer self-support	12.7	70.5	18.3	40.6	75.7	41.4
DK/NA	4.7	4.3	9.7	11.5	7.3	10.5
Are Prone to Violence						
Violence prone	50.5	15.7	38.3	17.2	10.1	17.9
Neither	28.3	42.3	34.0	41.1	33.3	45.5
Not violence prone	15.2	36.6	17.8	29.6	46.6	25.9
DK/NA	5.9	5.5	9.8	12.1	10.0	10.7

Note: DK/NA-don't know or no answer.

SOURCE: Davis and Smith (1990).

Institutional Discrimination and Health

SES is one of the strongest known predictors of variations in health; and racial differences in SES reflect, in part, the impact of economic discrimination produced by large-scale societal structures. Residential de facto segregation has been a primary mechanism by which racial inequality has been created and reinforced. Racial segregation has limited access to educational and employment opportunities, which has led to truncated socioeconomic mobility for Blacks and Native Americans or Alaska Natives (Jaynes and Williams, 1987; Massey and Denton, 1993). Moreover, racism skews the value of SES indicators, making them nonequivalent across racial groups. This makes it difficult to truly adjust racial differences in health for SES (Kaufman et al., 1997). For example, there are racial differences in the quality of education, income returns for a given level of education or occupational status, wealth or assets associated with a given level of income, purchasing power of income, stability of employment, and health risks associated with occupational status (Williams and Collins, 1995; Kaufman et al., 1997).

Evidence suggests that some White employers use racial group membership and residence in undesirable neighborhoods as criteria for refusing to hire some urban residents (Kirschenman and Neckerman, 1991). Thus, beliefs based on stereotypes are combined with Blacks' geographic concentration to systematically reduce their employment opportunities. Empirical evidence suggests corporate executives use beliefs about minority group inferiority and data on minority group concentration to move firms away from areas that are likely to have a high proportion of minority group workers. A *Wall Street Journal* analysis of the Equal Employment Opportunity Commission reports of more than 35,000 U.S. companies revealed that during the economic downturn of 1990-1991, Blacks were the only group that experienced a net job loss—59,500 jobs—compared to net job *gains* of 71,100 for Whites, 60,000 for Hispanics, and 55,100 for Asians (Sharpe, 1993). Blacks lost a disproportionately high share of the jobs that were cut and gained a disproportionately low share of the jobs that were added.

Corporate America indicated that these job losses were the result of restructuring, relocating, and downsizing. Sears moved distribution centers from the central city to the suburbs to facilitate more convenient routing of its truck fleet. Coca Cola reduced its workforce to maintain profits, but 42 percent of those laid off were Black, even though Blacks were only 18 percent of its workforce. General Electric stopped production in two plants—39 percent of employees in one were Black, in the other, 80 percent. Clearly there are a number of structural forces driving the movement of high-pay, low-skill jobs from the urban areas where

Blacks live to the suburbs (Wilson, 1987; Kasarda, 1993); consciously or subconsciously, beliefs about racial groups and explicit racial discrimination may reinforce and accentuate these larger patterns (Hajnal, 1995). If one believes that a potential workforce is likely to be disproportionately unintelligent and lazy, it is a fairly rational decision to take initiatives to avoid such undesirable workers.

In addition to its effects on individual health and economic well-being, segregation can also create pathogenic neighborhood and community conditions. Residential segregation creates communities characterized by unequal access to municipal services and medical care, lower levels of social participation, higher levels of undesirable land uses, higher rates of crime, and poor housing quality (Alba and Logan, 1993; Roberts, 1997; Shihadeh and Flynn, 1996; LeClere et al., 1997; Greenberg and Schneider, 1994). Studies have found a correlative association between residential segregation and mortality for Blacks, independent of measures of SES (Polednak, 1997; LaVeist, 1989). One recent study found that cities high on two indices of segregation have higher levels of mortality for both Blacks and Whites compared to cities with lower indices of segregation (Collins and Williams, 1999). Thus, beyond some threshold of poor living conditions, residential segregation appears to be costly for Whites as well as for Blacks.

Institutional discrimination can also affect health by determining exposure to environmental pollution, toxins, and pathogens in both residential and occupational contexts. Even after adjusting for job experience and training, Blacks are more likely than Whites to be exposed to occupational hazards and carcinogens at work (Robinson, 1984). Research on the location of hazardous waste sites indicates they are more likely to be located in poor, minority urban and rural communities than in other residential areas (United Church of Christ Commission for Racial Justice, 1987). Exposure to lead poisoning and other toxic materials is also disproportionately high for racial minorities.

Discrimination and Medical Care

Institutional discrimination affects access to desirable goods and services in society, and health care is no exception. Given the link between employment and health insurance, the high levels of unemployment, instability of employment, and the overrepresentation of racial minorities in jobs that do not provide adequate benefits, Blacks and Hispanics have lower levels of health insurance coverage than Whites. National data reveal that Blacks and Hispanics are disadvantaged compared to Whites on indicators of both access to ambulatory medical care and the quality of care received (Blendon et al., 1989; Council on Ethical and Judicial Affairs,

1990; Anderson et al., 1986; Trevino et al., 1991). Dental services are not covered well by most insurance policies, and minority access to dental care is especially problematic. Although the use of dental services has increased over time for all racial groups, the absolute percentages of persons who see a dentist in a given year is still unacceptably low. In 1993, for example, among persons 25 years of age and over, only 64 percent of Whites, 47 percent of Blacks, and 46 percent of Hispanics had visited a dentist within the previous year (National Center for Health Statistics, 1998).

Research also reveals there are large and systematic racial differences in the quality of medical care provided, which reflects, at least in part, the role of racism. Louis Sullivan, the former Secretary of Health and Human Services, concluded that "There is clear, demonstrable, undeniable evidence of discrimination and racism in our health-care system" (Sullivan, 1991). Evidence of discrimination comes from studies that have examined Black-White differences in access to a broad range of specific medical procedures. These studies reveal that, even after adjustment for health insurance and clinical status, Whites are more likely than Blacks to receive coronary angiography, bypass surgery, angioplasty, chemodialysis, total-knee arthroplasty for osteoarthritis, intensive care for pneumonia, and kidney transplants (Giles et al., 1995; Council on Ethical and Judicial Affairs, 1990; Wilson et al., 1994). Blacks are less likely than Whites to be on the waiting list for kidney transplants and once on the list, are likely to wait twice as long to receive a kidney (Sullivan, 1991).

A recent analysis of 1.7 million inpatient discharge abstracts from a national sample of 500 hospitals revealed that for almost half (48 percent) of a broad range of disease conditions, Blacks were less likely than Whites to receive major therapeutic procedures (Harris et al., 1997). Studies of specific health conditions also document racial differences in the intensity of medical care for comparable conditions. A cohort study of 8,406 Black and White men with prostate cancer found that, with comparable disease, Black men were 2.2 times less likely than their White peers to receive aggressive therapy (Schapira et al., 1995). Similarly, a national study using randomly selected hospitals found that among patients with pneumonia, non-Whites (mainly Blacks) compared to Whites, received fewer hospital services than expected on the basis of their health status and had longer than expected hospital lengths of stay (Yergan et al., 1987). It is important to note that these racial differences were apparent not only in the aggregate, but also within individual hospitals.

Especially striking are racial differences in the Veterans Health Administration (VHA) system and the Medicare program. Among inpatients in these two large federal programs, racial differences should be eliminated by the absence of differences in insurance coverage; yet, racial differences in the use of cardiovascular procedures have been documented among VHA patients (Whittle et al., 1993; Peterson et al., 1994). Similarly, a large national study of almost 10,000 Medicare patients found that patients who were Black or resided in poor neighborhoods received poorer inpatient medical care and had greater instability at discharge than other patients (Kahn et al., 1994). These differences were evident in all types of hospitals, but less pronounced in urban teaching hospitals than in rural and urban nonteaching institutions. An analysis of all inpatient Medicare reimbursement claims for 1992 revealed that Blacks were less likely than Whites to receive all of the 16 most commonly received procedures by Medicare beneficiaries (McBean and Gornick, 1994). The racial differences were especially large for the newer, elective, and referral-sensitive procedures.

These racial differences in medical care are consequential and in some cases life threatening. Among the 1992 Medicare beneficiaries, Blacks had a higher 30-day postadmission mortality rate than Whites for most of the procedures (McBean and Gornick, 1994). Moreover, additional analyses of the Medicare files revealed four procedures that Black beneficiaries received more frequently than their White counterparts—all four procedures reflect delayed diagnosis, delayed initial treatment, or failure in the management of chronic disease.

1. Amputation of part of the lower limb, usually as a consequence of poor management of diabetes, was 3.6 times more likely to be performed on Blacks compared to Whites.

2. Excisional debridement, the removal of tissue usually related to poor and infrequent medical care that leads to decubitus ulcers and skin infections, was performed 2.7 times more frequently on Black than on White patients.

3. Arterial venostomy, the implantation of shunts for chronic renal dialysis, often reflective of the failure of the management of end-stage renal disease, was 5.2 times more likely to be performed on Black patients than on White.

4. Bilateral orchiectomy, removal of both testes, often reflective of delayed diagnosis or initial treatment in the case of prostate cancer, was 2.2 times more likely to be performed on Black men than on White men.

Further evidence of the potential adverse effects of racial differences in medical care comes from two more recent studies. Peterson et al. (1997) studied 12,402 patients who underwent their first cardiac catherization. After adjusting for demographic factors, severity of disease, coexisting medical conditions, and access to subspeciality cardiology care, Blacks were only slightly less likely to receive coronary angioplasty but markedly less likely to undergo bypass surgery. The racial difference was largest among patients with severe disease—those who would benefit the most. Moreover, compared to Whites, Blacks had a higher five-year mortality rate, which was partly explained by differences in treatment. Hannan et al. (1999) followed for three months a random sample of 4,905 patients undergoing angiography to determine racial differences in the receipt of coronary artery bypass graft (CABG) surgery. They found that among patients judged as appropriate for CABG using rigorous criteria, Black and Hispanic patients were about 1.6 times less likely than non-Hispanic Whites to receive the surgery, even after adjustment for age, gender, insurance status, and vessels diseased. Moreover, Blacks, but not Hispanics, were 1.6 times less likely than Whites to receive the surgery among patients for whom CABG surgery was judged to be necessary. In addition, the study interviewed the gatekeeper physician for a random sample of patients appropriate for CABG surgery who did not receive it. For 90 percent of this group, the physician indicated that he/she had not recommended surgery. Among those patients who were not recommended for CABG surgery, in 9 percent of the cases, the patient preferred another intervention; in 8 percent, the physician preferred another intervention first. Thus, patient preference did not play a major role in accounting for racial differences in CABG surgery.

Taken together, the research on racial differences in medical care raises uncomfortable questions about the prevalence of racial bias among America's physicians. Health-care providers are a part of society and share, to some degree, prevailing negative beliefs about Blacks and other racial groups, as reflected in the stereotype data reviewed in Table 14-14. Consciously or unconsciously, race appears to influence the practice of medicine. In a world of finite medical resources, larger societal beliefs about the intellectual capacities, violent nature, and laziness of racial groups may creep into clinical decision making to establish the worthiness, or lack thereof, of some patients for the receipt of medical care. More research is clearly needed on provider attitudes and behaviors (King, 1996). More important is the urgent need for the organizations responsible for medical education, training, and licensure to develop and implement strategies to eradicate racial inequities in medical care. They should also establish strong countervailing influences to combat tendencies toward racial prejudice and bias (Williams, 1998).

The Subjective Experience of Racism and Health

A small but growing body of research also indicates that chronic and acute experiences of discrimination in the lives of minority group members is a source of stress that adversely affects their physical and mental health. Laboratory studies reveal that exposure to discrimination leads to cardiovascular and psychological reactivity (Anderson, 1989; Armstead et al., 1989; Dion, 1975; Pak et al., 1991). Two studies of Hispanic females note that self-reported experiences of discrimination are positively related to psychological distress (Amaro et al., 1987; Salgado de Snyder, 1987). Epidemiologic studies indicate that, at least under some conditions, racial discrimination is positively related to blood pressure among Blacks (Krieger, 1990; Krieger and Sidney, 1996). Similarly, two studies using national probability samples found that self-reports of discrimination are adversely related to both physical and psychological distress (Williams and Chung, in press; Jackson et al., in press). One recent study of a major metropolitan area found that discrimination made more of an incremental contribution to racial disparities in health than SES and, in combination with SES, completely explained racial differences in physical health (Williams et al., 1997).

Widespread negative societal stereotypes can adversely affect the health status of minority group members in that the stigma of inferiority can, for some, create certain expectations, anxieties, and reactions that affect motivation, performance, and psychological well-being. Research across a broad range of societies reveals that groups that are socially unequal have lower scores on standardized tests (Fischer et al., 1996). U.S.-based studies reveal that the performance of Black students on an exam is adversely affected when the stereotype of Black intellectual inferiority is made salient (Steele, 1992). This phenomenon is so robust that the performance of females is adversely affected when told in advance that they perform more poorly than men, and White men's performance is negatively affected when they are contrasted with Asians (Fischer et al., 1996). Health researchers have also documented that among Blacks, there is a correlative relationship between mental and physical health problems and the endorsement of the dominant society's negative stereotypes of Blacks. Taylor found that Blacks who believe that Blacks are inferior have higher levels of psychological distress and alcohol use (Taylor and Jackson, 1990; Taylor et al., 1991). Analyses of data from the National Study of Black Americans revealed that Blacks who endorse negative stereotypes of Blacks as accurate were more likely to report poorer physical and mental health than those who rejected those stereotypes (Williams and Chung, in press).

RESEARCH NEEDS

Research is needed to identify the mechanisms and processes that link location in social structure to health outcomes. *Healthy People: The Surgeon General's Report on Health Promotion and Disease Prevention* (U.S.

Department of Health, Education, and Welfare, 1979) indicated that health behaviors and lifestyle account for more of the variation in health than medical care and genetic factors combined. Similarly, the *Report of the Secretary's Task Force on Black and Minority Health* (U.S. Department of Health and Human Services, 1985) concluded that most of the major risk factors responsible for the excess level of disease and death within Black and minority populations are behavioral, and thus potentially preventable. Behavioral risk factors are typically measured at the individual level; and much research on health behaviors views them simply as individual characteristics. Research is needed that would seek to understand the constraints on individual choice and the ways in which the larger social environment is consequential in the initiation and maintenance of unhealthy practices (McKinlay, 1990; Williams, 1990).

For example, cigarette smoking and alcohol use were risk factors in five of the six causes of death responsible for the 60,000 annual excess deaths in the Black population compared to the White population (U.S. Department of Health and Human Services, 1985). Alcohol and tobacco are mood altering substances frequently used to alleviate stressful working and living conditions created by social structures and processes. Research is needed that would elucidate the ways in which the cooperative efforts of governmental and commercial interests to initiate and maintain the use of these substances within disadvantaged populations combine with their adverse living and working conditions to produce particular patterns of risk behavior. Research is also needed to rigorously assess the relative contribution of behavioral factors to racial disparities in health. One study using a national sample found that although health behaviors varied by SES, individual behaviors played only a minimal role in accounting for SES differences in mortality (Lantz et al., 1997). Some limited research suggests that although behavioral factors are related to race and SES and to health status, modification of these risk factors without changes in the larger social institutions that drive them will give rise to new intervening factors that will maintain social inequalities in health (Williams, 1997).

Research on social support and other psychosocial factors that can affect health also needs to attend to the ways in which these characteristics are shaped by social conditions. For example, marital status is a powerful predictor of health; married persons enjoy lower levels of ill health and lower rates of mortality than unmarried persons. Marriage rates, however, are shaped by economic conditions. Unemployment, declines in income, and high job turnover are all associated with increased rates of marital dissolution; female-headed households decline when male earnings rise and rise when male unemployment increases (Bishop, 1977). Rates of female-headed households within the Black population are inversely related to employment opportunities for Black males (Wilson, 1987). Lack of meaningful and adequately compensated employment can create frustration and hostility, which have emerged as important risk factors for coronary heart disease, obesity, and other health conditions. Levels of hostility, however, are patterned by SES; and residence in poor living conditions predicts the higher likelihood of hostile responses (Harburg et al., 1973).

As the findings on race and mental health status suggest, research is also critically needed to identify the reason why Blacks have lower rates than Whites on indicators of subjective well-being but comparable or better rates than Whites on other indicators of mental health. More attention needs to be focused on the resources and cultural strengths within minority communities. High levels of religious involvement, family and kin support systems, psychological resources, such as John Henryism and racial identity, and processes of attribution have all been identified as potential adaptive resources within minority populations (James, 1993, 1994; Neighbors et al., 1996; Williams, 1998).

Future research must give greater attention to comprehensively assessing racial minority status and including identifiers for ethnic variation within each of the five OMB categories. The availability of adequate data for Native Americans or Alaska Natives, Hispanics, and Asians or Pacific Islanders is still a major problem. Because of the relatively small sizes of some of these groups and their geographic distribution, standard sampling strategies for national populations do not yield adequate sample sizes to provide reliable estimates for the distribution of diseases in these groups or to explore heterogeneity within a given racial group. Surveys focused on a particular geographic area with a high concentration of a racial subgroup, as opposed to national ones, are necessary to provide data for these groups. Combining multiple years of data in ongoing surveys is another useful strategy for obtaining health information for small population groups.

Researchers also need to be more self-critical about the collection, analysis, and interpretation of racial data. Greater consideration must be given to why race/ethnicity identification is being collected, the limitations of racial data, and how the findings should be interpreted. Data on racial differences should routinely be stratified by SES within racial groups. Failure to do this may misspecify complex health risks and even lead to harmful social stereotypes and consequences. Whenever feasible, additional information that captures these characteristics should be collected. This will include the assessment of SES, acculturation, and economic and noneconomic aspects of discrimination (Williams, 1997). There are limited opportunities to collect additional information in vital-statistics systems and in record-based surveys. Even in these contexts, however, years of formal education, nativity status, and years of residence in the United States can be ascertained.

FUTURE TRENDS

A number of factors are likely to affect future patterns in the health status of racial minority populations in the United States. One likely trend is that increasing length of stay and greater acculturation of Hispanic and Asian or Pacific Islander populations will lead to worsening health for them (Hernandez and Charney, 1998). Across a broad range of health-status indicators, research indicates that foreign-born Hispanics have a better health profile than their counterparts born in the United States. Rates of infant mortality, low birth weight, cancer, high blood pressure, adolescent pregnancy, and psychiatric disorders increase with length of stay in the United States (Vega and Amaro, 1994). As groups migrate from one culture to another, immigrants often adopt the diet and behavior patterns of the new culture—e.g., decreased fiber consumption; decreased breast feeding; increased use of cigarettes and alcohol, especially among young females; driving under the influence of alcohol; and increased use of illicit drugs (Vega and Amaro, 1994). Early studies of acculturation found that the rate of heart disease among Japanese increased progressively as Japanese moved from Japan to Hawaii to the U.S. mainland (Marmot and Syme, 1976). The association between acculturation and length of stay in the United States and the prevalence of disease, however, is complex. Migration studies of Chinese and Japanese people show that rates of some cancers, such as prostate and colon, increase when these populations migrate to the United States, while the rates of other cancers, such as liver and cervical, decrease (Jenkins and Kagawa-Singer, 1994).

A second trend that may have implications for health is the growing income inequality in the United States between the very rich and everyone else. Since the mid-1970s there has been a growing concentration of wealth among the highest income groups and worsening economic conditions for a substantial proportion of the population (Danziger and Gottschalk, 1993). Research from both Western Europe and the United States suggests that widening health-status disparities parallel widening economic disparities (Williams and Collins, 1995). To the extent that racial minority group members are overrepresented among lower-income groups, worsening health status linked to economic inequalities will disproportionately affect these populations. The data cited earlier, and other data showing the widening of the health gap between Blacks and Whites during the 1980s, are consistent with this hypothesis (National Center for Health Statistics, 1994b; Williams and Collins, 1995).

A third factor that is likely to affect future trends in minority health is the high rate of childhood poverty. National data suggest that the rate of childhood poverty is disconcertingly high in the United States. One in five U.S. children, and two in five Black and Hispanic children under the age of 18, live in poverty (National Center for Health Statistics, 1998); children of the poor[2] and the near poor[3] combined represent 43 percent—nearly half—of all children in the United States—31 percent White, 41 percent Asian or Pacific Islander, 68 percent Black, and 73 percent Hispanic.

Health status is affected not only by current SES but by exposure to economic deprivation over one's life course. Several studies reveal that early-life economic and health conditions have long-term adverse consequences for adult health (see, e.g., Elo and Preston, 1992). For example, some studies suggest that growth retardation during the fetal period, leading to low birth weight, is associated with elevated risk of high blood pressure in adulthood (Elo and Preston, 1992). Rates of low birth weight are twice as high for Blacks as for Whites, and rates of hypertension during adulthood are also considerably higher for Black than White populations. However, the contribution, if any, of low birth weight to the elevated rates of hypertension among Blacks has not been systematically studied.

Finally, the persistence of racism suggests the disparities in minority health may linger for some time. National data reveal that Whites are more opposed to race-targeted policies than to similar poverty-targeted policies (Bobo and Kluegel, 1993). Current debates about affirmative action reveal the absence of a reservoir of sympathy for the economic disadvantages of minority group members, despite the fact that data suggest that challenges for the Black population may be distinctive and greater than those of other minority groups. Although racial relations in the United States are much more complex than Black and White, Black-White relations have historically anchored U.S. race relations. In light of that, factors shaping future trends for Blacks in particular are not hopeful.

1. Blacks continue to be the group most discriminated against in terms of residential segregation (Massey and Denton, 1993) and continue to have the greatest difficulties finding opportunities for socioeconomic mobility (Lieberson, 1980). The high level of segregation is not self-

---

[2]Households for which the annual income is at or below the poverty level—$16,000/year for a family of four.

[3]Households for which the annual income is just above but less than 200 percent of the poverty level.

imposed; Blacks reflect the highest support for residence in integrated neighborhoods (Bobo and Zubrinsky, 1996). Available evidence suggests, however, that instead of greater ethnic diversity leading to greater acceptance of Blacks as neighbors, greater diversity adds to the climate of resistance toward Blacks. One Los Angeles study found that Hispanics were as hostile as Whites to Black neighbors, while Asians were more hostile than Whites (Bobo and Zubrinsky, 1996).

2. The 1990 General Social Survey (see Table 14-14) indicated that, although Whites tend to view all minority populations more negatively than they view other Whites, Blacks tended to be viewed more negatively than other minority groups. A key characteristic of racial prejudice has been an explicit desire to maintain social distance from defined outgroups; and with 25 to 44 percent of Hispanics and 25 to 50 percent of Asian or Pacific Islander subgroups marrying persons of other races (primarily White) (Rumbaut, 1994), the future trend is that Blacks are likely to be further marginalized. However, rates of Black-White intermarriage have been increasing in recent years—6 percent in 1990 compared to 2 percent in 1970.

3. Data from around the world indicate that in virtually all cultures, the color black is associated with negative attributes (Franklin, 1968), and Blacks are darker in skin color than any other racial group. National data on Blacks reveal that skin color is a stronger predictor of adult occupation and income than is parental socioeconomic status (Keith and Herring, 1991). National data on Mexicans reveal that those who were darker in skin color and more Indian in appearance experienced higher levels of discrimination than those who were lighter in skin color and more European in appearance (Arce et al., 1987). Similarly, studies of Sephardic Jews in the United States, Israel, and Australia reveal that they experience higher levels of discrimination than their lighter-skinned peers (Rosen, 1982; Kraus and Koresh, 1992; Gale, 1994). Some research also suggests that darker skin color predicts higher levels of morbidity among Blacks (Klag et al., 1991; Dressler, 1996). Thus, although many groups have suffered and continue to experience prejudice and discrimination in the United States, Blacks have always been at the bottom of the racial hierarchy; and the social stigma associated with this group is probably greatest. The resultant unique challenges to socioeconomic mobility and, thus, health status, are likely to persist.

CONCLUSION

This chapter documents that there is a complex but persistent pattern of racial differences in health. On virtually all indicators of physical health status, at least one racial minority population experiences worse health status than the White population. These differences should not be ignored for at least two reasons. First, some evidence suggests that because of the economic links tying various communities together, health problems that initially are more prevalent in minority communities eventually spread to other areas and populations (Wallace and Wallace, 1997). If unaddressed, the health problems of minority populations will eventually become the health problems of the larger society. Second, given current patterns of population growth, the health problems of minority populations may soon become the statistical norm. The Bureau of the Census' 1997 estimate of the population indicates that minority populations comprised 27 percent of the U.S. population and an even higher proportion in the most populous states—49 percent of California, 44 percent of Texas, 34 percent of New York, and 31 percent of Florida. Given current demographic trends, minority racial groups will increasingly become a larger share of the U.S. population. Thus, taking action to improve the health and social conditions of marginalized population groups is investing in our mutual future and likely to have positive health consequences for the entire society.

ACKNOWLEDGMENTS

Preparation of this paper was supported in part by grant 1 RO1 MH57425 from the National Institute of Mental Health and by the John D. and Catherine T. MacArthur Foundation Research Network on Socioeconomic Status and Health. I wish to thank Car Nosel, Clara Kawanishi, Colwick Wilson, and Scott Wyatt for assistance with the preparation of the manuscript.

REFERENCES

Adler, N., T. Boyce, M. Chesney, S. Folkman, and S. Syme
    1993   Socioeconomic inequalities in health: No easy solution. *Journal of the American Medical Association* 269:3140-3145.
Alba, R., and J. Logan
    1993   Minority proximity to Whites in suburbs: An individual-level analysis of segregation. *American Journal of Sociology* 98(6):1388-1427.
Amaro, H., N. Russo, and J. Johnson
    1987   Family and work predictors of psychological well-being among Hispanic women professionals. *Psychology of Women Quarterly* 11:505-521.
American Association of Physical Anthropology (AAPA)
    1996   AAPA statement on biological aspects of race. *American Journal of Physical Anthropology* 101:569-570.
Amick III, B., S. Levine, D. Walsh, and A. Tarlov, eds.
    1995   *Society and Health*. New York: Oxford University Press.

Anderson, N.
1989   Racial differences in stress-induced cardiovascular reactivity and hypertension: Current status and substantive issues. *Psychological Bulletin* 105:89-105.
Anderson, R., A. Giachello, and L. Aday
1986   Access of Hispanics to health care and cuts in services: A state-of-the-art overview. *Public Health Reports* 101:238-252.
Antonovsky, A.
1967   Social class, life expectancy and overall mortality. *Milbank Memorial Fund Quarterly* 45:31-73.
Arce, C., E. Murguia, and W. Frisbie
1987   Phenotype and life chances among Chicanos. *Hispanic Journal of Behavioral Sciences* 9:19-32.
Armstead, C., K. Lawler, G. Gordon, J. Cross, and J. Gibbons
1989   Relationship of racial stressors to blood pressure responses and anger expression in Black college students. *Health Psychology* 8:541-556.
Bishop, J.
1977   *Jobs, Cash Transfers, and Marital Instability: A Review of the Evidence.* Madison: Institute for Research on Poverty, University of Wisconsin.
Blendon, R., L. Aiken, H. Freeman, and C. Corey
1989   Access to medical care for Black and White Americans. *Journal of the American Medical Association* 261:278-281.
Bobo, L., and J. Kluegel
1993   Opposition to race-targeting: Self-interest, stratification ideology, or racial attitudes. *American Sociological Review* 58:443-464.
Bobo, L., and C. Zubrinsky
1996   Attitudes on residential integration: Perceived status differences, mere in-group preference, or racial prejudice? *Social Forces* 74(3):883-909.
Bunker, J., D. Gomby, and B. Kehrer, eds.
1989   *Pathways to Health: The Role of Social Factors.* Menlo Park, Calif.: Henry J. Kaiser Family Foundation.
Collins, C., and D. Williams.
1999   Segregation and mortality: The deadly effects of racism. *Sociological Forum* 14(3):493-521.
Cooper, R., M. Steinhauer, A. Schatzkin, and W. Miller
1981a   Improved mortality among U.S. Blacks, 1968-1978: The role of antiracist struggle. *International Journal of Health Services* 11:511-522.
Cooper, R. , M. Steinhauer, W. Miller, R. David, and A. Schatzkin
1981b   Racism, society, and disease: An exploration of the social and biological mechanisms of differential mortality. *International Journal of Health Services* 11(3):389-414.
Council on Ethical and Judicial Affairs
1990   Black-White disparities in health care. *Journal of the American Medical Association* 263:2344-2346.
Danziger, S., and P. Gottschalk, eds.
1993   *Uneven Tides: Rising Inequality in America.* New York: Russell Sage.
David, R., and J. Collins, Jr.
1997   Differing birth weight among infants of U.S.-born Blacks, African-born Blacks, and U.S.-born Whites. *New England Journal of Medicine* 337(17):1209-1214.
Davis, J., and T. Smith
1990   *General Social Surveys, 1972-1990 NORC Edition.* Chicago: National Opinion Research Center.

Dion, K.
  1975 Women's reactions to discrimination from members of the same or opposite sex. *Journal of Research in Personality* 9:294-306.
Dohrenwend, B., and B. Dohrenwend
  1969 *Social Status and Psychological Disorder: A Casual Inquiry*. New York: Wiley.
Dressler, W.
  1996 Social identity and arterial blood pressure in the African-American community. *Ethnicity and Disease* 6:176-190.
Elo, I., and S. Preston
  1992 Effects of early-life conditions on adult mortality: A review. *Population Index* 58:186-212.
Engels, F.
  1984 *The Condition of the Working Class in England*. Chicago: Academy Chicago.
  [1844]
Fang, J., S. Madhavan, and M. Alderman
  1997 Nativity, race, and mortality: Influence of region of birth on mortality of U.S.-born residents of New York City. *Human Biology* 69(4):533-544.
Fischer, C., M. Hout, M. Jankowski, S. Lucas, A. Swidler, and K. Voss
  1996 *Inequality by Design: Cracking the Bell Curve Myth*. Princeton: Princeton University Press.
Franklin, J.
  1968 *Color and Race*. Boston: Houghton Mifflin.
Frost, F., V. Taylor, and E. Fries
  1992 Racial misclassification of Native Americans in a surveillance, epidemiology, and end results cancer registry. *Journal of the National Cancer Institute* 84:957-962.
Frost, F., K. Tollestrup, A. Ross, E. Sabotta, and E. Kimball
  1994 Correctness of racial coding of American Indians and Alaska Natives on the Washington State death certificate. *American Journal of Preventive Medicine* 10:290-294.
Fruchter, R., C. Wright, B. Habenstreit, J. Remy, J. Boyce, and P. Imperato
  1985 Screening for cervical and breast cancer among Caribbean immigrants. *Journal of Community Health* 10(3):121-135.
Gale, N.
  1994 A case of double rejection: The immigration of Sephardim to Australia. *New Community* 20:269-286.
Giles, A., R. Anda, M. Casper, L. Escobedo, and H. Taylor
  1995 Race and sex differences in rates of invasive cardiac procedures in U.S. hospitals. *Archives of Internal Medicine* 155:318-324.
Green, V.
  1978 The Black extended family in the United States: Some research suggestions. Pp. 378-387 in *The Extended Family in Black Societies*, D. Shimkin, E. Shimkin, and D. Frate, eds. The Hague, The Netherlands: Mouton DeGruyter.
Greenberg, M., and D. Schneider
  1994 Violence in American cities: Young Black males is the answer, but what is the question? *Social Science and Medicine* 39:179-187.
Hahn, R.
  1992 The state of federal health statistics on racial and ethnic groups. *Journal of the American Medical Association* 267(2):268-271.
Hajnal, Z.
  1995 The nature of concentrated urban poverty in Canada and the United States. *Canadian Journal of Sociology* 20(4):497-528.

Hannan, E., M. van Ryn, J. Burke, D. Stone, D. Kumar, D. Arani, W. Pierce, S. Rafii, T. Sanborn, S. Sharma, J. Slater, and B. DeBuono
  1999 Access to coronary artery bypass surgery by race/ethnicity and gender among patients who are appropriate for surgery. *Medical Care* 37(1):68-77.
Harburg, E., J. Erfurt, C. Chape, L. Havenstein, W. Schull, and M. Schork
  1973 Socioecological stressor areas and Black-White blood pressure: Detroit. *Journal of Chronic Disease* 26:595-611.
Harris, D., R. Andrews, and A. Elixhauser
  1997 Racial and gender differences in use of procedures for Black and White hospitalized adults. *Ethnicity and Disease* 7:91-105.
Hernandez, D., and E. Charney, eds
  1998 *From Generation to Generation; The Health and Well-Being of Children in Immigrant Families.* Washington, D.C.: National Academy Press.
Hogan, H.
  1993 The 1990 post-enumeration survey: Operations and results. *Journal of the American Statistical Association* 88:1047-1057.
Hughes, M., and M. Thomas
  1998 The continuing significance of race revisited: A study of race, class, and quality of life in America, 1972 to 1996. *American Sociological Review* 63:785-795.
Hummer, R.
  1996 Black-White differences in health and mortality: A review and conceptual model. *Sociological Quarterly* 37(1):105-125.
Hunter, C., C. Redmond, V. Chen, D. Austin, R. Greenberg, P. Correa, H. Muss, M. Forman, M. N. Wesley, R. Blacklow, R. Kurman, J. Digman, B. Edwards, and S. Shapiro
  1993 Breast cancer: Factors associated with stage at diagnosis in Black and White women. *Journal of the National Cancer Institute* 85(14):1129-1137.
Indian Health Service (IHS)
  1997 *Regional Differences in Indian Health.* Rockville, Md.: U.S. Department of Health and Human Services.
Jackson, J., D. Williams, and M. Torres
  In   Perceptions of discrimination: The stress process and physical and psychological
  press health. In *Social Stressors, Personal and Social Resources and Their Mental Health Consequences*, A. Maney, ed. Washington, D.C.: National Institute for Mental Health.
James, S.
  1993 Racial and ethnic differences in infant mortality and low birth weight: A psychosocial critique. *Annals of Epidemiology* 3(2):131-136.
  1994 John Henryism and the health of African Americans. *Culture of Medicine and Psychiatry* 18:163-182.
Jaynes, G., and R. Williams, Jr., eds.
  1987 *A Common Destiny: Blacks and American Society.* Washington, D.C.: National Academy Press.
Jenkins, C., and M. Kagawa-Singer
  1994 Cancer. Pp. 105-147 in *Confronting Critical Health Issues of Asian and Pacific Islander Americans*, N. Zane, D. Takeuchi, and K. Young, eds. Thousand Oaks, Calif.: Sage.
Kahn, K., M. Pearson, E. Harrison, K. Desmond, W. Rogers, L. Rubenstein, R. Brook, and E. Keeler
  1994 Health care for Black and poor hospitalized Medicare patients. *Journal of the American Medical Association* 271(15):1169-1174.
Kasarda, J.
  1993 Urban industrial transition and the underclass. Pp. 43-64 in *The Ghetto Underclass*, W. Wilson, ed. Newberry Park, Calif.: Sage.

Kaufman, J., and R. Cooper
    1995 In search of the hypothesis. *Public Health Reports* 110:662-666.
Kaufman, J., R. Cooper, and D. McGee
    1997 Socioeconomic status and health in Blacks and Whites: The problem of residual confounding and the resiliency of race. *Epidemiology* 8:621-628.
Keith, V., and C. Herring
    1991 Skin tone and stratification in the Black community. *American Journal of Sociology* 97(3):760-778.
Kennedy, R., and R. Deapen
    1991 Differences between Oklahoma and Indian infant mortality and other races. *Public Health Reports* 106:97-99.
Kessler, R., K. McGonagle, S. Zhao, C. Nelson, M. Hughes, S. Eshleman, H. Wittchen, and K. Kendler
    1994 Lifetime and 12-month prevalence of DSM-III-R psychiatric disorders in the United States. *Archives of General Psychiatry* 51:8-19.
King, G.
    1996 Institutional racism and the medical/health complex: A conceptual analysis. *Ethnicity and Disease* 6(1,2):30-46.
Kirschenman, J., and K. Neckerman
    1991 "We'd love to hire them, but . . ." : The meaning of race for employers. Pp. 203-232 in *The Urban Underclass*, C. Jencks and P. Peterson, eds. Washington, D.C.: The Brookings Institution.
Klag, M., P. Whelton, J. Coresh, C. Grim, and L. Kuller
    1991 The association of skin color with blood pressure in U.S. Blacks with low socioeconomic status. *Journal of the American Medical Association* 265:599-602.
Kraus, V., and Y. Koresh
    1992 The course of residential segregation: Ethnicity, socioeconomic status, and suburbanization in Israel. *Sociological Quarterly* 33:303-319.
Krieger, N.
    1990 Racial and gender discrimination: Risk factors for high blood pressure? *Social Science and Medicine* 30(12):1273-1281.
Krieger, N., D. Rowley, A. Herman, B. Avery, and M. Phillips
    1993 Racism, sexism, and social class: Implications for studies of health, disease, and well-being. *American Journal of Preventive Medicine* 9(6 suppl):82-122.
Krieger, N., and S. Sidney
    1996 Racial discrimination and blood pressure: The CARDIA study of young Black and White adults. *American Journal of Public Health* 86:1370-1378.
Lantz, P., M. Weigers, and J. House
    1997 Education and income differentials in breast and cervical cancer screening: Policy implications for rural women. *Medical Care* 35:219-236.
LaVeist, T.
    1989 The political empowerment and health status of African Americans: Mapping a new territory. *American Journal of Sociology* 97:1080-1095.
    1996 Why we should continue to study race . . . but do a better job: An essay on race, racism and health. *Ethnicity and Disease* 6(1,2):21-29.
LeClere, F., R. Rogers, and K. Peters
    1997 Ethnicity and mortality in the United States: Individual and community correlates. *Social Forces* 76(1):169-198.
Lewontin, R.
    1974 *The Genetic Basis of Evolutionary Change.* New York: Columbia University Press.
    1982 *Human Diversity.* New York: Scientific American Books.

Lieberson, S.
    1980   *A Piece of the Pie: Black and White Immigrants Since 1880.* Berkeley: University of California Press.
Lillie-Blanton, M., P. Parsons, H. Gayle, and A. Dievler
    1996   Racial differences in health: Not just Black and White, but shades of gray. *Annual Review of Public Health* 17:411-448.
Lin-Fu, J.
    1993   Asian and Pacific Islander Americans: An overview of demographic characteristics and health care issues. *Asian and Pacific Islander Journal of Health* 1:20-36.
Marmot, M., D. Smith, S. Stansfeld, C. Patel, F. North, et al.
    1991   Health inequalities among British civil servants: The Whitehall II study. *Lancet* 337:1387-1393.
Marmot, M., and S. Syme
    1976   Acculturation and coronary heart disease in Japanese-Americans. *American Journal of Epidemiology* 104:225-247.
Massey, D., and N. Denton
    1993   *American Apartheid: Segregation and the Making of the Underclass.* Cambridge: Harvard University Press.
McBean, A., and M. Gornick
    1994   Differences by race in the rates of procedures performed in hospitals for Medicare beneficiaries. *Health Care Financing Review* 15(4):77-90.
McKinlay, J.
    1990   A case for refocusing upstream: The political economy of illness. Pp. 502-516 in *The Sociology of Health and Illness: Critical Perspectives*, P. Conrad and R. Kern, eds. New York: St. Martin's Press.
Miller, B., L. Kolonel, L. Bernstein, J. Young Jr., G. Swanson, D. West, D. Key, J. Liff, C. Glover, and G. Alexander et al., eds.
    1996   *Racial/Ethnic Patterns of Cancer in the United States 1988-1992* (NIH Pub. No. 96-4101). Bethesda, Md.: National Cancer Institute.
Montagu, A.
    1965   *The Concept of Race.* New York: Free Press.
Mullings, L.
    1989   Inequality and African-American health status: Policies and prospects. Pp. 154-182 in *Twentieth Century Dilemmas—Twenty-First Century Prognoses*, W. VanHome and T. Tonnesen, eds. Madison: University of Wisconsin Institute on Race and Ethnicity.
National Center for Health Statistics (NCHS)
    1994a   *Excess Deaths and Other Mortality Measures for the Black Population: 1979-81 and 1991.* Hyattsville, Md.: Public Health Service, U.S. Department of Health and Human Services.
    1994b   *Vital Statistics of the United States, 1990, Vol. 11, Mortality, Part A.* Washington, D.C.: Public Health Service, U.S. Department of Health and Human Services.
    1998   *Health, United States, 1998 With Socioeconomic Status and Health Chartbook.* Hyattsville, Md.: Public Health Service, U.S. Department of Health and Human Services.
Neighbors, H.
    1984   The distribution of psychiatric morbidity in Black Americans. *Community Mental Health Journal* 20:169-181.
Neighbors, H., J. Jackson, C. Broman, and E. Thompson
    1996   Racism and the mental health of African Americans: The role of self and system blame. *Ethnicity and Disease* 6(1,2):167-175.

Norton, I., and S. Manson
    1996   Research in American Indian and Alaska Native communities: Navigating the
            cultural universe of values and process. *Journal of Consulting and Clinical Psychol-
            ogy* 65(5):856-860.
Notes and Comments
    1994   Census undercount and the quality of health data for racial and ethnic popula-
            tions. *Ethnicity and Disease* 4(1):98-100.
Omi, M., and H. Winant
    1986   *Racial Formation in the United States from the 1960s to the 1980s.* New York:
            Routledge.
Pak, A., K. Dion, and K. Dion
    1991   Social-psychological correlates of experienced discrimination: Test of the double
            jeopardy hypothesis. *International Journal of Intercultural Relations* 15:243-254.
Peterson, E., L. Shaw, E. DeLong, D. Pryor, R. Califf, and D. Mark
    1997   Racial variation in the use of coronary-revascularization procedures—Are the
            differences real? Do they matter? *New England Journal of Medicine* 336(7):480-486.
Peterson, E., S. Wright, J. Daley, and G. Thibault
    1994   Racial variation in cardiac procedure use and survival following acute myocar-
            dial infarction in the Department of Veterans Affairs. *Journal of the American Medi-
            cal Association* 271:1175-1180.
Polednak, A.
    1997   *Segregation, Poverty, and Mortality in Urban African Americans.* New York: Oxford
            University Press.
Quadagno, J.
    1994   *The Color of Welfare: How Racism Undermined the War on Poverty.* New York: Ox-
            ford University Press.
Roberts, E.
    1997   Neighborhood social environments and the distribution of low birthweight in
            Chicago. *American Journal of Public Health* 87:597-603.
Robins, L., and D. Regier
    1991   Psychiatric disorders in America, in *The Epidemiologic Catchment Area Study.* New
            York: Free Press.
Robinson, J.
    1984   Racial inequality and the probability of occupation-related injury or illness.
            Milbank Memorial Fund Quarterly 62:567-593.
Rosen, S.
    1982   Intermarriage and the blending of exiles in Israel. *Research in Race and Ethnic
            Relations* 3:79-102.
Rumbaut, R.
    1994   The crucible within: Ethnic identity, self-esteem, and segmented assimilation
            among children of immigrants. *International Migration Review* 28:748-794.
Salgado de Snyder, V.
    1987   Factors associated with acculturative stress and depressive symptomatology
            among married Mexican immigrant women. *Psychology of Women Quarterly*
            11:475-488.
Schapira, M., T. McAuliffe, and B. Nattinger
    1995   Treatment of localized prostate cancer in African-American compared with Cau-
            casian men. *Medical Care* 33(11):1079-1088.
Schoendorf, K., C. Hogue, J. Kleinman, and D. Rowley
    1992   Mortality among infants of Black as compared with White college-educated par-
            ents. *New England Journal of Medicine* 326(23):1522-1526.

Sharpe, R.
   1993   In latest recession, only Blacks suffered net employment loss. *Wall Street Journal* LXXIV(233).
Shihadeh, E., and N. Flynn
   1996   Segregation and crime: The effect of Black social isolation on the rates of Black urban violence. *Social Forces* 74(4):1325-1352.
Singh, G., and S. Yu
   1995   Infant mortality in the United States: Trends, differentials, and projections, 1950 through 2010. *American Journal of Public Health* 85:957-964.
Sorlie, P., E. Backlund, N. Johnson, and E. Rogot
   1993   Mortality by Hispanic status in the United States. *Journal of the American Medical Association* 270:2464-2468.
Sorlie, P., E. Rogot, and N. Johnson
   1992   Validity of demographic characteristics on the death certificate. *Epidemiology* 3:181-184.
Steele, C.
   1992   Race and the schooling of Black Americans. *Atlantic Monthly* 269:68ff.
Sullivan, L.
   1991   Effects of discrimination and racism on access to health care. *Journal of the American Medical Association* 266:2674.
Tabulation Working Group, Interagency Committee for the Review of Standards for Data on Race and Ethnicity
   1999   *Draft Provisional Guidance on the Implementation of the 1997 Standards for the Collection of Federal Data on Race and Ethnicity* (February 17:65). Washington, D.C.: Executive Office of the President, Office of Management and Budget.
Taylor, J., D. Henderson, and B. Jackson
   1991   A holistic model for understanding and predicting depression in African American women. *Journal of Community Psychology* 19:306-320.
Taylor, J., and B. Jackson
   1990   Factors affecting alcohol consumption in Black women, part II. *The International Journal of Addictions* 25(12):1415-1427.
Trevino, F., M. Moyer, R. Valdez, and C. Stroup-Benham
   1991   Health insurance coverage and utilization of health services by Mexican Americans, mainland Puerto Ricans, and Cuban Americans. *Journal of the American Medical Association* 265:2233-2237.
United Church of Christ Commission for Racial Justice
   1987   *Toxic Wastes and Race in the United States: A National Report on the Racial and Socioeconomic Characteristics of Communities with Hazardous Waste Sites*. New York: United Church of Christ.
U.S. Bureau of the Census (USBC)
   1993   *U.S. Census of Population 1990, Social and Economic Characteristics* (CP-2-1). Washington, D.C.: U.S. Government Printing Office.
U.S. Department of Health, Education, and Welfare (USDHEW)
   1979   *Healthy People: The Surgeon General's Report on Health Promotion and Disease Prevention*. (DHEW Pub. No. PHS 79-55071). Washington, D.C.: U.S. Government Printing Office.
U.S. Department of Health and Human Services (USDHHS)
   1985   *Report of the Secretary's Task Force on Black and Minority Health*. Washington, D.C.: U.S. Government Printing Office.

Vega, W., and H. Amaro
    1994   Latino outlook: Good health, uncertain prognosis. *Annual Review of Public Health* 15:39-67.
Vega, W., and R. Rumbaut
    1991   Ethnic minorities and mental health. *Annual Review of Sociology* 17:351-383.
Wallace, R., and D. Wallace
    1997   Socioeconomic determinants of health: Community marginalisation and the diffusion of disease and disorder in the United States. *British Medical Journal* 314:1341-1345.
Whittle, J, J. Conigliaro, C. Good, and R. Lofgren
    1993   Racial differences in the use of invasive cardiovascular procedures in the Department of Veterans Affairs. *New England Journal of Medicine* 329:621-626.
Williams, D.
    1986   The epidemiology of mental illness in Afro-Americans. *Hospital and Community Psychiatry* 37:42-49.
    1990   Socioeconomic differentials in health: A review and redirection. *Social Psychology Quarterly* 53(2):81-99.
    1996a   The health of the African American population. Pp. 404-416 in *Origins and Destinies: Immigration, Race, and Ethnicity in America*, S. Pedraza and R. Rumbaut, eds. Belmont, Calif.: Wadsworth Health Sciences.
    1996b   Race/ethnicity and socioeconomic status: Measurement and methodological issues. *International Journal of Health Services* 26(3):483-505.
    1996c   Racism and health: A research agenda. *Ethnicity and Disease* 6(1,2):1-6.
    1997   Race and health: Basic questions, emerging directions. *Annals of Epidemiology* 7(5):322-333.
    1998   African-American health: The role of the social environment. *Journal of Urban Health Bulletin of the New York Academy of Medicine* 75:300-321.
Williams, D., and A. Chung
    In   Racism and health. In *Health in Black America*, R. Gibson and J. Jackson, eds.
    press   Thousand Oaks, Calif.: Sage Publications.
Williams, D., and C. Collins
    1995   U.S. socioeconomic and racial differences in health. *Annual Review of Sociology* 21:349-386.
Williams, D., and M. Harris-Reid
    1999   Race and mental health: Emerging patterns and promising approaches. Pp. 295-314 in *A Handbook for the Study of Mental Health: Social Contexts, Theories, and Systems*, A. Horwitz and T. Scheid, eds. New York: Cambridge University Press.
Williams, D., Y. Yu, J. Jackson, and N. Anderson
    1997   Racial differences in physical and mental health: Socioeconomic status, stress, and discrimination. *Journal of Health Psychology* 2(3):335-351.
Wilson, W.
    1987   *The Truly Disadvantaged*. Chicago: University of Chicago Press.
Wilson, M., D. May, and J. Kelly
    1994   Racial differences in the use of total knee arthroplasty for osteoarthritis among older Americans. *Ethnicity and Disease* 4:57-67.
Yergan, J., A. Flood, J. Logerfo, and P. Diehr
    1987   Relationship between patient race and the intensity of hospital services. *Medical Care* 25(7):592-603.

15

Health-Care Use in the Veterans Health Administration: Racial Trends and the Spirit of Inquiry

Eugene Z. Oddone, Laura A. Petersen, and Morris Weinberger

Throughout its history, the United States has provided some degree of health care to its current and post-service military personnel, particularly those injured while serving (Kizer, 1996). Prior to World War II, a relatively small-scale, loosely organized system existed to provide such care (Hollingsworth and Bondy, 1990). After World War II, the federal government recognized that the existing system was ill equipped to provide adequate care for the increasing number of veterans with severe disabilities (Hollingsworth and Bondy, 1996; Iglehart, 1996). The government established a largely inpatient-based health-care system for veterans (Iglehart, 1996), which was the genesis for the Veterans Health Administration (VHA), now the largest integrated health-care system in the United States (Kizer, 1996).

RESEARCH ON RACIAL VARIATIONS IN THE PROVISION OF CARE IN THE VETERANS HEALTH ADMINISTRATION

To understand VHA research to date regarding racial variations in health care, two issues must be emphasized. First, because virtually all studies have been limited to veterans who receive care in VHA, findings are not immediately generalizable. There is overwhelming evidence that veterans who use VHA have significantly fewer financial resources and less, if any, supplemental health insurance (Wolinsky et al., 1985; Randall et al., 1987); report meaningfully lower scores on health related quality-of-life measures (Kazis et al., 1997; Weinberger et al., 1996); and have

411

significantly less experience with the traditional doctor-patient relationship (Inui et al., 1984). These data clearly indicate that veterans receiving care within VHA are more medically and socioeconomically vulnerable than either nonveterans or veterans who do not use VHA.

Second, published VHA studies rely on information available in the Patient Treatment File (PTF), a national administrative database that contains a record for each admission to a VA hospital since the 1970s (Lamoreaux, 1996). PTF was developed to provide information about health-care use to VHA policy makers and managers. It does not, however, contain clinical data. Without valid clinical data, any relationship between race and health must be seen as theoretical. The nature of administrative data sets limits investigators' ability to reach cause-and-effect conclusions about observed racial variations. On the other hand, primary data are needed for prospective studies designed to better understand whether observed racial variations can be accounted for by factors such as patients' clinical characteristics, health/functional status, preferences for treatment options, or racism.

Given the above limitations, why should we nevertheless pursue studies examining the relationship between race and health among veterans receiving care within VHA? First, from a policy point of view, Kenneth W. Kizer, VHA Undersecretary for Health, has stated that one goal of VHA is to document that the quality of care it provides is equal to, or better than, care available in the private sector (Kizer, 1998). The Undersecretary specifically addressed actions needed to increase the accessibility of VA services. Second, VHA provides a functional safety net for a group for whom investigations about race and health may be most important—the most socioeconomically vulnerable veterans (Iglehart, 1996; Wilson and Kizer, 1997). Third, from the standpoint of research, because access to health care for eligible veterans is not limited by income, well-designed prospective studies can separate the effects of race and income. This factor is unique to studies conducted in VHA. Fourth, the veteran population contains a greater proportion of underrepresented minorities than exists in the country overall. The percentage of Blacks among all veterans is growing: they comprise 6.1 percent of World War II veterans, 8.3 percent Korean Conflict veterans, 8.6 percent of Vietnam Era veterans, and 17.1 percent of post-Vietnam veterans. The number of Hispanic veterans has also grown since World War II, from 3.4 percent to 5.7 percent (Heltman and Bonczar, 1990). Finally, research based on data from the PTF database is limited to vital statistics, as is research based on data from most administrative databases. The limitations of these data give emphasis to the critical need to supplement PTF with primary (clinical) data collection.

PLAUSIBLE PARADIGMS FOR STUDYING RACIAL VARIATIONS

At least four areas of inquiry have been advanced as plausible explanations for observed racial differences in health-care use outcomes. First, observed racial variation may result from underlying differences in clinical factors related to the disease—e.g., etiology or severity—which would affect appropriateness of procedures taken. If there are racial variations in clinical factors, observed differences may be appropriate for those cases, if all patients receive the tests and procedures needed (Chassin et al., 1987). Without an understanding of the clinical issues, one does not know whether Blacks received too few, or Whites too many, tests and procedures. The paradigm shifts from simply counting who did or did not receive a test or procedure to understanding the "appropriateness" of that procedure. Using the appropriateness paradigm regarding health-care use, both over-use by one group and under-use by another can be identified.

A second area of inquiry examines whether racial differences in health-care use are a function of patients' ability to pay for care—i.e., an economic paradigm. Indeed, economic factors are important determinants in many health-care decisions. For example, more Whites than Blacks supplement Medicare coverage with private insurance to cover the deductible and copayment requirements of Medicare (Rice and McCall, 1985); better Medicare coverage might have given older veterans more options for care (Ashton et al., 1994). In addition, changes in eligibility or financial barriers to either Medicare or VHA care influence veterans' decisions about where to seek care (Fleming et al., 1992).

Examining the economic factor as a paradigm for racial variation necessitates equating racial variations with socioeconomic status. Studies in this paradigm are often hampered by the need to use proxy variables, such as insurance status or zip-code-averaged income per household, because individual information is not available. Studies conducted in VHA do not have this problem because all eligible veterans (defined as those with an honorable discharge from U.S. military service) have specified and equal access to health care protected by congressional mandate. Although there are standards for complete versus partial eligibility, the vast majority of veterans cared for in VHA are eligible for unrestricted access to care with no payments required and no need for supplemental insurance. Furthermore, physicians who provide care in VHA are salaried and therefore have no financial reasons to provide or deny care for patients. This makes VHA an ideal setting for studying racial variation; here researchers can separate the effects of race and income, at least as they relate to ability to pay for care (Horner et al., 1997).

The third and emerging line of research deals with patients' preferences regarding the health care they receive—either preferences for care within the scope of traditional health-care options or preferences for alternative strategies, such as spirituality or nonallopathic medicine. Evidence suggests that patients' preferences reflect standards and mores of their cultures. Thus, some observed racial variations in the use or nonuse of traditional health-care procedures may reflect patients' preferences rather than bias on the part of the health-care system or health-care providers. The patient-preference paradigm requires prospectively asking patients about their preferences. This requires time, funding, and validated measures of critical constructs, such as religiosity, trust in the health-care system or an individual provider, or patients' preferences for a particular health-care strategy.

The fourth and last major line of inquiry is that observed differences in health-care outcomes reflect true racial bias (either conscious or unconscious) on the part of the health-care system or individual clinicians. Hypothesizing that racial bias accounts for differences in the use or receipt of certain health-care strategies mandates an understanding of racial prejudice or lack of cultural tolerance. Such biases are perhaps more difficult to measure than patient preferences or trust. It may be that true bias may never be accurately assessed. One tactic researchers have used is to try to explain observed differences in terms of some measurable construct—e.g., ability to pay, appropriateness of care, or patient preference. Then, if differences in care still remain after accounting for these other factors, it is considered that bias may be the explanation.

Paradigm 1. Disease Severity as an Explanation for Racial Differences in Care

Racial Differences in the Use of Cardiovascular Procedures

Chronic ischemic heart disease and its complications are the most prevalent disorders treated in VHA medical centers (National Center for Veterans Analysis, 1993). In addition, coronary artery disease is the leading cause of death for Blacks in the United States (Gillum and Liu, 1984). Thus, many of the studies of racial variation in health-care use have focused on cardiovascular diagnoses.

Invasive cardiovascular procedures such as percutaneous transluminal coronary angioplasty (PTCA) and coronary artery bypass graft (CABG) surgery have been shown to delay death and relieve symptoms for selected groups of patients with coronary artery disease (Ryan et al., 1996). Despite the potential benefits of these procedures in treating coronary artery disease, Black veterans and nonveterans receive fewer of these procedures in a variety of settings. Compared to Blacks, Whites are 1.3 to

1.4 times more likely to receive cardiac catheterization, 1.5 to 2.5 times more likely to receive PTCA, and 1.9 to 2.2 times more likely to receive CABG (Whittle et al., 1993; Wenneker and Epstein, 1989). With respect to differences in the use of CABG, differences persist even after accounting for clinical appropriateness of the procedure (Hannan et al., 1998). Racial differences also occur with respect to the use of certain medications deemed to be important in preventing heart attacks (Allison et al., 1996).

Can the observed racial difference be attributable to Blacks having a lower burden of atherosclerotic blockage? Peterson et al. (1997) studied PTCA and CABG procedures in Blacks and Whites. After adjusting for disease severity and other characteristics, they reported that Blacks remained 13 percent less likely than Whites to undergo PTCA and 32 percent less likely to undergo CABG. Racial differences in rates of CABG persisted even among those with severe symptoms and among those predicted to have the greatest survival benefit—i.e., those with the most extensive blockage. Hannan et al. (1998) examined a racially diverse group of New York residents who received coronary angiography. Using detailed information to assess the clinical appropriateness of the procedure, they found that Blacks and Hispanics were approximately 40 percent less likely to receive CABG after they were deemed appropriate for the procedure. Findings suggest that differential use of these procedures persists even after accounting for disease severity. This implies that disease biology is not the underlying factor explaining differences in procedure rates, at least as it relates to cardiovascular disease.

Racial Differences in the Use of Cerebrovascular Procedures

Stroke is the third leading cause of death and a leading cause of disability among adults in the United States (American Heart Association, 1997). Blacks are at higher risk of stroke than Whites, and current reports indicate that stroke mortality among Blacks may be rising (Kaplan, 1991). Because of limitations in effectively treating disabilities caused by acute stroke, stroke prevention practices are important. Carotid endarterectomy (CE) is known to be effective in preventing stroke for a wide variety of patients. Despite their higher risk for stroke, Blacks are only one-third to one-fourth as likely to receive CE as a preventive procedure (Oddone et al., 1993; Maxwell et al., 1989).

From a clinical perspective, the most likely explanation for this is a racial difference in the degree of atherosclerotic blockage. To be effective, CE must be performed on patients with more than 70 percent blockage of a carotid artery in an operable location. Other relevant clinical factors include the patient's symptoms, estimated operative risk, and the number and type of comorbid illnesses present. Pathophysiological studies show that, in relation to Whites, some Black patients have lower degrees of blockage in the portion of the carotid artery that is amenable to surgery (Aronow and Schoenfeld, 1993; Prisant et al., 1993). These differences may render Blacks potentially less appropriate candidates for CE.

Based on ratings of expert clinicians (Matchar et al., 1992), CE is an appropriate procedure when the expected health benefits—e.g., increased life expectancy, pain relief, and improved functional capacity—exceed the expected health risks—e.g., procedure-related mortality and morbidity. The appropriateness of CE is adjudicated based on the degree of ipsilateral and contralateral carotid artery stenosis, the constellation of patient symptoms at presentation, and the patient's surgical risk. To date there are no studies that document racial differences in appropriateness of care for patients eligible for, or those who have received, CE. Brook et al. (1990) found that the proportion of appropriate CE was similar for Whites and non-Whites in a sample of Medicare patients who received the procedure. In a large sample of veterans deemed eligible for CE, we found no difference in clinical appropriateness between a racially stratified sample of Whites and Blacks (Oddone et al., 1997). However, this analysis fails to account for any differences in the diagnostic evaluation process prior to receipt of carotid angiography. What has yet to be determined is whether a similar proportion of White and Black patients receive the necessary evaluation to determine appropriateness.

Paradigm 2. Economic Factors as an Explanation for Differences in Care Provided

Because race and socioeconomic status are closely associated in U.S. society, it is possible that observed patterns of usage of expensive diagnostic or therapeutic procedures reflect the ability to pay for care. Blacks represent between 2 and 4 percent of patients who receive CE (Maxwell et al., 1989; Brook et al., 1990; Oddone et al., 1993). Regardless of adjustment for income, the relative odds of Whites versus Blacks undergoing CE are approximately 3 to 1. Moreover, this degree of variation is found across hospitals with different reimbursement arrangements—in private-sector hospitals, where fee-for-service reimbursement predominates, and in VHA hospitals, where hospital budgets are capitated, physicians are salaried and have no financial incentive to perform unnecessary procedures, and patients do not have to pay for care. Thus, among hospitalized patients, "ability to pay" does not appear to explain the significant racial variation in the use of CE.

Another point is that available studies in this area only report the experiences of hospitalized patients—i.e., those who have already gained access to the system. If racial bias plays a significant role in evaluation as well as treatment of patients, it may be a particularly important factor in the outpatient setting where presenting signs and symptoms are ostensibly more subtle and, thus, the approach to clinical management is less clear. Consequently, the experience of hospitalized patients may not be generalizable to patients prior to hospitalization. There have been no studies to address this issue for patients with cerebrovascular disease.

Paradigm 3. Patient Preference as an Explanation for Racial Differences in Care Provided

In this era of informed consent and increased recommendations for patients to advocate for themselves, patients' own beliefs and preferences have become an increasingly important influence in the course of health-care decisions.

Patient Perceptions of Their Own Health

In self-report surveys, Blacks consistently report poorer health status than Whites (Bergner, 1993; Rogers, 1992), and self-reported health status is an important predictor of mortality regardless of race or ethnicity. But the relationship of provision of care to self-reported health status and to comorbid illness or disease severity is difficult to determine. Previous studies based on self-report of outcomes among selected patient groups provide conflicting results. Blustein et al. (1995) report that among stroke patients, Blacks reported worse physical impairment than did Whites; on the other hand, Dignan et al. (1986) found no racial differences in activities of daily living. Among dialysis patients, Tell et al. (1995) noted that Blacks reported better quality of life than did Whites. Johnson et al. (1993) found Black patients presenting with chest pain had worse health-related quality of life; but when results were adjusted for sociodemographic factors, comorbid illness, and functional status, no differences remained.

Some research has also pointed to racial differences in perceptions of symptoms. This factor may influence differential use of health-care services for cardiovascular disease as well as other illnesses (Strogatz, 1990). To the extent that Blacks perceive their symptoms to be less severe (Raczynski et al., 1994), have less access to health care (Blendon et al., 1989), or believe the health-care system to be less responsive to them once they do seek care (Weddington and Gabel, 1991), they may be less likely to consider medical intervention as either obtainable or beneficial. Ren and Amick (1996) suggest that differences they observed between Blacks and Whites, in both self-perceived health and functional status, may result from cultural factors as well as institutional racism. Differences noted in these studies are not simply a matter of self-report; they are corroborated by mortality rates, which also are associated with race (Nickens, 1995).

Most studies that attempt to explain racial variations in cardiac procedures use administrative data and, thus, have no data on patients' preferences that might explain such variations. Whittle et al. (1997), however, surveyed a sample of VA in- and outpatients, who may or may not have had coronary artery disease, regarding their willingness to undergo heart bypass surgery, should such surgery be recommended. Black patients indicated less willingness to undergo surgery; but regardless of race, those who were less familiar with the procedure were less willing to undergo the surgery. These results suggest that race may be differentially associated with certain beliefs about cardiac procedures, but this needs to be tested in samples of patients who are actually eligible for such procedures.

Patient Preferences

Although racial variation in the delivery of cardiac procedures was first documented more than a decade ago, the etiology of this disparity remains unclear. As summarized above, data from some studies suggest that neither disease severity nor access to health care completely explains observed differences (Whittle et al., 1993; Ford and Cooper, 1995). Most prior research examining this issue has used administrative data, so detailed information about patients' experiences of and perspectives about the cardiac treatment decision-making process was not available. Notably, one study (Maynard et al., 1986) showed that Black patients are more likely to decline recommended cardiac procedures, and White patients are more likely to request such procedures, even when only medical therapy is recommended. Preferences for information and involvement in the decision-making process regarding health care vary significantly, but female, White, younger, and better-educated patients generally desire more involvement in decision making (Ende et al., 1989). Studies have also found that patients who participate more in their treatment decisions have better subsequent health outcomes (Kaplan et al., 1989; Greenfield et al., 1985). The VA is currently funding studies incorporating patient-preference data.

It may be that the amount of information patients have about their disease and their treatment options, and their appraisal of the risks and benefits, affect the likelihood of undergoing particular treatments. Intervention studies with cancer patients have shown that although it is important to match the provision of information to the patient's interest in receiving such information, patients who are provided information and offered a choice about treatment options experience less anxiety and depression after cancer surgery (Morris and Royle, 1987).

Perceived Barriers to Care

The perception of having received high-quality care, and satisfaction with the process, is the "ultimate validator of the quality of health care" (Donabedian, 1966); but patients' beliefs drive their usage of health care. Luft et al. (1990) found that patients choose a hospital based on their perceptions of the quality of that hospital. Wolinsky and Steiber (1982) found that individuals with lower socioeconomic status, but better access to medical care, focus more on the cost of a visit when choosing a new physician.

Patient satisfaction is an important element in the delivery of health care for a number of reasons. Patients who are dissatisfied with their health care change health-care providers or "doctor-shop" more frequently, disenroll from prepaid health plans more frequently, adhere less well to medical regimens prescribed by their doctors, and recall less about what their doctor has told them or advised them to do. Studies have documented that Black patients in general are less satisfied with their health care (Blendon et al., 1989). It is surprising then, that little attention has been paid to racial differences in many patient satisfaction studies. In fact, one meta-analysis of the patient satisfaction literature noted that only 58 percent of the studies even included race as an independent variable (Hall and Dornan, 1990).

Trust in the System

In the past few decades, discrimination in the health-care environment has been a subject of particular scrutiny (Gamble, 1995; Blendon et al., 1995). Since the 1972 exposure of the U.S. Public Health Service Tuskegee Syphilis Study on Untreated Syphilis in the Negro Male, during which available treatment was withheld from several hundred Black men with syphilis, it has been widely thought that Blacks remain distrustful of the medical establishment (Gamble, 1993). It has also been argued that Black distrust of the medical establishment predated the Tuskegee experiment, and that the experiment simply verified for Blacks the existence of long-standing racist attitudes in health-care provision (Gamble, 1995). Although a considerable amount has been written about the long-lasting effects of the Tuskegee study on the Black community, most of this work has been from a legal, ethical, or historical perspective. There is little empirical documentation of minorities' trust or mistrust of their physician(s) and health-care institutions when facing clinical decisions or undergoing diagnosis and treatment. The "Tuskegee effect" may or may not translate into distrust when the respondent is a patient. Furthermore, without specific data, it is difficult to determine whether measures of satisfaction and dissatisfaction also reflect the element of trust.

Despite VA's long history of serving veterans, Black veterans may have concerns about racial discrimination in the VA health-care setting inasmuch as many ethnic minority servicemen and -women had difficult and alienating experiences in the military (Parson, 1985; Terry, 1984). Findings from the National Vietnam Veterans Readjustment Study indicated that Hispanics and Blacks experienced more negative effects from their military service than did their White comrades (Kulka et al., 1990). For many minority veterans, wartime experiences led to extensive and continued distrust (Allen, 1986). Indeed, earlier this century VHA itself provided a reason for possible distrust among Blacks when it attempted to segregate Black veterans in a separate hospital, in Tuskegee, Alabama, rather than serve them in the same facilities where White veterans were served (Blendon et al., 1989).

Paradigm 4. Racism as an Explanation for Differences in the Provision of Health Care

There is evidence that Blacks receive a poorer quality of care in some health-care settings than do Whites (Escarce et al., 1993; Gornick et al., 1996). Further, research has demonstrated that Blacks have less access to certain elements of health care than do Whites (Blendon et al., 1989; Escarce et al., 1993). Even when generalized access is equal, wide disparities in access to particular medical services persist. One recent analysis of Medicare data found that Black and low-income patients were less likely to have ambulatory physician's visits, mammograms, and influenza immunizations, and that such individuals were more likely to be hospitalized or die from the lack of such services (Gornick et al., 1996). Similarly, Escarce and colleagues (1993) found that elderly Whites were more likely than elderly Blacks to receive 23 different procedures and tests, with more Whites receiving services incorporating new types of technologies.

Other research into the processes of health care has shown that ethnic minority patients receive less empathy, attention, and information from their doctors (Kaplan et al., 1995). A separate study found racial differences in the use of pain medication for patients treated in an emergency room, with Hispanic patients receiving less analgesia than Whites (Todd et al., 1993). It has been hypothesized that such experiences relate to greater distrust of the medical care system on the part of Blacks and result in decreased health-care use (Blendon et al., 1995).

In a study of patients treated for posttraumatic stress disorder in VHA, Black veterans received less treatment by several measures than Whites. When the authors examined clinician-veteran racial pairings, they concluded that variation in treatment provided was at least partially explained by the pairing of White clinicians with Black veterans (Rosenheck et al., 1995). Similarly, in another study assessing reactions to hypothetical patients, White clinicians judged Black patients to be less appropriate candidates for psychotherapy and expected more adverse reactions to treatment (Geller, 1988).

Two studies have demonstrated that Black patients are less likely to have surgery recommended to them, and that those who receive such recommendations are less likely to accept them (Maynard et al., 1986; Sedlis et al., 1997). Sedlis et al. (1997) studied postcardiac catheterization VHA patients who were all considered to be potential candidates for CABG or PTCA. They found that fewer Black than White patients were offered procedures (64.3 percent versus 72.9 percent), but of those given the option of a procedure, almost twice as many Black patients declined (Sedlis et al., 1997). These results emphasize the importance of including physician behavior and access to care as explanatory variables in studies of racial variation.

Providing detailed information about potential race-related differences in patients' understanding of treatment options, perceptions of the quality of VHA health care, and general preferences for care is a crucial first step toward improving health care in both VHA and non-VHA health-care settings. For example, curricula for mental health providers designed to help White clinicians overcome their own negative feelings when the issue of race emerges in the clinical setting have been described (e.g., Bradshaw, 1978), but their effectiveness has not been rigorously tested. Evidence from intensive courses in the patient-physician relationship given as part of residency training programs has shown that residents' knowledge and skills in interviewing can be improved, though the effect sizes between patient groups were too small to assess patient satisfaction and well-being.

THE VETERANS HEALTH ADMINISTRATION'S COMMITMENT TO UNDERSTANDING THE REASONS FOR RACIAL DIFFERENCES IN HEALTH CARE

VHA research has engaged in a focused program to determine the reasons for ethnic and cultural variations in the delivery of VA health services. Based on early research results, VHA acknowledged that variations were evident for a wide spectrum of invasive diagnostic and treatment procedures including cardiac catheterization and coronary artery

TABLE 15-1 Summary of Studies Funded by the Department of Veterans Affairs Health Services and Research Service That Address Important Initiatives in Understanding Racial and Ethnic Variation in Health Care Services

Study	Title	Principal Investigator	Main Objectives	Study Period
ECV 97-005	Delivery of mental health services to American Indians and Hispanic Americans	Joseph Westermeyer, M.D., Ph.D.; Minneapolis VAMC	1. Identify patient characteristics related to underuse of mental health 2. Develop interventions to improve use 3. Study patient outcomes associated with interventions	1997-1999
ECV 97-009	Cultural factors in adaptation to chronic illness	Murray Katz, M.D.; Tucson VAMC	Develop a clinically useful measure of cultural factors impacting health for patients with chronic disease	1997-1999
ECV 97-014	Ethnic/cultural variations in the care of veterans with osteoarthritis	Kenneth Covinsky, M.D.; Cleveland VAMC	1. Measure ethnic variation in pathways leading from joint destruction to impaired quality of life 2. Understand the relationship between cultural attitudes and treatment choices	1997-2001
ECV 97-020	Race, patient preferences and stroke risk reduction	Eugene Oddone, M.D.; Durham VAMC	1. Measure relationship between patient's aversion to surgery and use of carotid endarterectomy 2. Measure interaction between provider recommendation and patient choice	1997-2000

ECV 97-022	Racial differences in cardiac procedures: do health beliefs matter?	Nancy Dressin, Ph.D., Bedford VAMC	Assess racial differences in beliefs regarding use of invasive procedures controlling for clinical appropriateness	1998-2001
ECV 97-026	Educational efforts to reduce the cultural and ethnic variation in cardiac procedure use	Joseph Conigliaro, M.D., Pittsburgh VAMC	Assess racial differences in knowledge, attitudes, and acceptance of CABG and PTCA	1997-1999
ECV 97-028	Ethnicity and veteran identity as determinants of VA ambulatory care use	Nancy Harada, Ph.D.; West Los Angeles VAMC	Identify factors related to ethnicity and veteran identity that influence use of outpatient care	1997-2001
ECV 97-081	Prostate cancer outcome measures: age and race effects	Jack Clark, Ph.D.	Define the dimensions of quality of life related to prostate cancer with respect to age and racial differences	1998-2000

Note: ECV, Ethnic and Cultural Variation (term of specific request for proposals initiated by VA Health Services Research Service).

bypass surgery (Whittle et al., 1993; Peterson et al., 1994) and carotid endarterectomy (Oddone et al., 1993). In all areas, these trends were mirrored in Medicare and general populations (Gornick et al., 1996).

The first level of studies sought to understand whether racial differences in rates for certain procedures were attributable to over-use in one group or under-use in the other. To answer that question, however, rigorous assessment of medical records coupled with primary (clinical) data collection that goes beyond the traditional administrative database studies was necessary.

VHA research adopted an aggressive tactic by soliciting research proposals designed to understand the underpinnings of the observed racial differences. In 1996 VHA research developed an independent committee of experts to oversee racial variation research. This group solicited grants designed to go beyond the subjective grouping of individuals into arbitrary classifications, and encouraged research that incorporates self-identity and individual perceptions of self and others that may influence the delivery of health care. They mandated that research projects go beyond prior methodology, which to date had used retrospective analyses of information from large databases—all of which lack the level of detail required to fully understand existing differences. To be funded, research projects needed to collect prospective information, identify causes of systematic variation, and use innovative measures.

Eight studies were funded (Table 15-1), committing more than 7 million dollars to this innovative research agenda. The fruits of this extensive endeavor have yet to be realized; however, the results of these studies, perhaps more so than any other focused effort in racial variation research, will allow us to truly understand some of the root causes of current racial variation in health care and, thereby, allow us to better manage patient care in all of its complexities.

REFERENCES

Allen, I.
  1986   Posttraumatic stress disorder among Black Vietnam veterans. *Hospital Community Psychiatry* 37:55-61.
Allison, J., C. Kiefe, R. Centor, J. Box, and R. Farmer
  1996   Racial differences in the medical treatment of elderly Medicare patients with acute myocardial infarction. *Journal of General Internal Medicine* 11(12):736-743.
American Heart Association
  1997   *Heart and Stroke Statistical Update.* Dallas: American Heart Association Publications.
Aronow, W., and M. Schoenfeld
  1993   Prevalence of atherothrombotic brain infarction and extracranial carotid arterial disease, and their association in elderly blacks, Hispanics and whites. *American Journal of Cardiology* 71(11):999-1000.

Ashton, C., T. Weiss, N. Petersen, N. Wray, T. Menke, and R. Sickles
   1994   Changes in VA hospital use 1980-1990. *Medical Care* 32(5):447-458.
Bergner, L.
   1993   Race, health, and health services. *American Journal of Public Health* 7:939-941.
Blendon, R., L. Aiken, H. Freeman, and C. Corey
   1989   Access to medical care for Black and White Americans. *Journal of the American Medical Association* 261(2):278-281.
Blendon, R., A. Scheck, K. Donelan, C. Hill, M. Smith, D. Beatrice, and D. Altman
   1995   How White and African Americans view their health and social problems. *Journal of the American Medical Association* 273(4):341-346.
Blustein, J., R. Arons, and S. Shea
   1995   Sequential events contributing to variations in cardiac revascularization rates. *Medical Care* 33(8)864.
Bradshaw, W.
   1978   Training psychiatrists for working with Blacks in basic residency programs. *American Journal of Psychiatry* 135:1520-1524.
Brook, R., R. Park, M. Chassin, D. Solomon, J. Keesey, and J. Kosecoff
   1990   Predicting the appropriate use of carotid endarterectomy, upper gastrointestinal endoscopy, and coronary angiography. *New England Journal of Medicine* 323(17): 1173-1177.
Chassin, M., J. Kosecoff, and R. Park
   1987   Does inappropriate use explain geographic variations in the use of health care services? *Journal of the American Medical Association* 258:2533-2537.
Dignan, M., G. Howard, J. Toole, C. Becker, and K. McLeroy
   1986   Evaluation of the North Carolina stroke care program. *Stroke* 17:382-386.
Donabedian, A.
   1966   Evaluating the quality of medical care. *Milbank Memorial Fund Quarterly: Health and Society* 44:166.
Ende, J., L. Kazis, A. Ash, and M. Moskowitz
   1989   Measuring patients' desire for autonomy: Decision making and information-seeking preferences among medical patients. *Journal of General Internal Medicine* 4:23-30.
Escarce, J., A. Kenneth, R. Epstein, D. Colby, and J. Schwartz
   1993   Racial differences in the elderly's use of medical procedures and diagnostic tests. *American Journal of Public Health* 83(7):948-954.
Fleming, C., E. Fisher, C. Chang, T. Bubolz, and D. Malenka
   1992   Studying outcomes and hospital utilization in the elderly. The advantages of a merged data base for Medicare and Veterans Affairs hospitals. *Medical Care* 30(5):377-391.
Ford, E., and R. Cooper
   1995   Implications of race/ethnicity for health and health care use: Racial/ethnic differences in health care utilization of cardiovascular procedures: A review of the evidence. *Health Services Research* 30:1.
Gamble, V.
   1993   A legacy of distrust: African Americans and medical research. *American Journal of Preventive Medicine* 9(Suppl. 6):35-38.
   1995   *Making a Place for Ourselves: The Black Hospital Movement, 1920-1945.* New York: Oxford University Press.
Geller, J.
   1988   Racial bias in the evaluation of patients for psychotherapy. In *Clinical Guidelines in Cross-Cultural Mental Health,* L. Diaz and E. Griffith, eds. New York: Wiley and Sons.

Gillum, R., and K. Liu
    1984   Coronary heart disease mortality in United States Blacks, 1940-1978: Trends and
            unanswered questions. *American Heart Journal* 108(3, Part II):728-732.
Gornick, M., P. Eggers, T. Reilly, R. Mentnech, L. Fitterman, L. Kucken, and B. Vladeck
    1996   Effects of race and income on mortality and use of services among Medicare
            beneficiaries. *New England Journal of Medicine* 335(11):791-799.
Greenfield, S., S. Kaplan, and J. Ware, Jr.
    1985   Expanding patient involvement in care. *Annals of Internal Medicine* 102:520-528.
Hall, J., and M. Dornan
    1990   Patient sociodemographic characteristics as predictors of satisfaction with medi-
            cal care: A meta-analysis. *Social Science and Medicine* 30(7):811-818.
Hannan, E., A. Popp, B. Tranmer, P. Fuestel, J. Waldman, and D. Shah
    1998   Relationship between provider volume and mortality for carotid endarterecto-
            mies in New York state. *Stroke* 29(11):2292-2297.
Heltman, L., and T. Bonczar
    1990   *Estimates and Projections of the Veteran Population:1980-2040.* Washington, D.C.:
            U.S. Government Printing Office.
Hollingsworth, J., and P. Bondy
    1990   The role of Veterans Affairs hospitals in the health care system. *New England
            Journal of Medicine* 322:1851-1857.
Horner, R., H. Hoenig, R. Sloane, L. Rubenstein, and K. Kahn
    1997   Racial differences in the utilization of inpatient rehabilitation services among el-
            derly stroke patients. *Stroke* 28(1):19-25.
Iglehart, J.
    1996   Reform of the Veterans Affairs health care system. *The New England Journal of
            Medicine* 335(18):1407-1411.
Inui, T., B. Lipsky, and R. Pecoraro
    1984   Patients, clinicians and problems in the VA's ambulatory care system. *VA Practi-
            tioner* 1:45-49.
James, S., E. Wagner, D. Strogatz, S. Beresford, D. Kleinbau, C. Williams, L. Cutchin, and M.
    Ibrahim
    1984   The Edgecombe County (North Carolina) high blood pressure control program:
            II. Barriers to the use of medical care among hypertensives. *American Journal of
            Public Health* 74:468-472.
Johnson, P., T. Lee, E. Cook, G. Rouan, and L. Goldman
    1993   Effect of race on the presentation and management of patients with acute chest
            pain. *Annals of Internal Medicine* 118:593-601.
Kaplan, L.
    1991   Cardiovascular disease and stroke in African Americans. *Circulation* 83:1469-1471.
Kaplan, S., B. Gandek, S. Greenfield, W. Rogers, and J. Ware
    1995   Patient and visit characteristic related to physicians' participatory decision-mak-
            ing style: Results from the medical outcome study. *Medical Care* 33(12):1176-1187.
Kaplan, S., S. Greenfield, and J. Ware, Jr.
    1989   Assessing the effects of physician-patient interactions in the outcomes of chronic
            disease. *Medical Care* 27(Suppl):S110-S127.
Kasprow, W., and R. Rosenheck
    1998   Substance use and psychiatric problems of homeless Native American veterans.
            Psychiatric Services 49(3):345-350.

Kazis, L., D. Miller, J. Clark, K. Skinner, A. Lee, W. Rogers, A. Spiro, S. Payne, G. Fincke, A. Selim, and M. Linzer
  1997   Health-related quality of life in patients served by the Department of Veterans Affairs: Results from the Veterans Health Study. *Archives of Internal Medicine* 158:626-632.

Kizer, K.
  1996   Transforming the Veterans health care system—the new VA. *Journal of the American Medical Association* 275:1069.
  1998   Statement on the Future of the Veterans Healthcare System before the Committee on Veterans Affairs' Subcommittee on Health, U.S. House of Representatives, June 17, 1998.

Kulka, R., W. Schlenger, J. Fairbank, R. Hough, B. Jordan, C. Marmar, and D. Weiss
  1990   *Trauma and the Vietnam War Generation Report of Findings from the National Vietnam Veterans Readjustment Study.* New York: Brunner/Mazel.

Lamoreaux, J.
  1996   The organizational structure for medical information management in the Department of Veterans Affairs. *Medical Care* 34:MS31-MS44.

Luft, H., D. Garnick, D. Mark, D. Peltzman, C. Phibbs, E. Lichtenberg, and S. Mcphee
  1990   Does quality influence choice of hospital? *Journal of the American Medical Association* 263(21):2899-2906.

Matchar, D., G. Divine, A. Heyman, and J. Feussner
  1992   The influence of hyperglycemia on outcome of cerebral infarction. *Annals of Internal Medicine* 117(6):449-456.

Maxwell, J., E. Rutherford, D. Covington, T. Clancy, A. Tackett, N. Robinson, and G. Johnson Jr.
  1989   Infrequency of Blacks among patients having carotid endarterectomy. *Stroke* 20:22-26.

Maynard, C., L. Fisher, E. Passmani, and T. Pullum
  1986   Blacks in the Coronary Artery Surgery Study (CASS): Race and clinical decision making. *American Journal of Public Health* 76(12):1446-1448.

Morris, J., and G. Royle
  1987   Cancer: Pre- and postoperative levels of clinical anxiety and depression in patients and their husbands. *British Journal of Surgery* 74:1017-1019.

National Center for Veteran Analysis
  1993   *National Survey of Veterans.* Washington, D.C.: National Center for Veteran Analysis.

Nickens, H.
  1995   The role of race/ethnicity and social class in minority health status. *Health Services Research* 30:1,151-161.

Oddone, E., R. Horner, S. Diem, L. McIntyre, et al.
  1997   Understanding racial variation in utilization of CE: Role of clinical factors. *Journal of General Internal Medicine* 12(9):122.

Oddone, E., R. Horner, M. Monger, and D. Matchar
  1993   Racial variations in the rates of carotid angiography and endarterectomy in patients with stroke and transient ischemic attack. *Archives of Internal Medicine* 153:2781-2786.

Parson, E.
  1985   The intercultural setting: Encountering Black Vietnam veterans. In *The Trauma of War: Stress and Recovery in Vietnam Veterans.* Washington, D.C.: American Psychiatric Press.

Peterson, E.D., S.M. Wright, J. Daley, and G.E. Thibault
    1994   Racial variations in cardiac procedures use and survival following acute myocar-
            dial infarction in the Department of Veteran Affairs. *Journal of the American Medi-
            cal Assocation* 271:1175-1180.
Peterson, E., L. Shaw, E. DeLong, D. Pryor, R. Califf, and D. Mark
    1997   Racial variation in the use of coronary revascularization procedures. Are the dif-
            ferences real? Do they matter? *New England Journal of Medicine* 336:480-486.
Prisant, L., P. Zemel, F. Nichols, M. Zemel, J. Sowers, A. Carr, W. Thompson, and M. Bond
    1993   Carotid plaque associations among hypertensive patients. *Archives of Internal
            Medicine* 153(4):501-506.
Raczynski, J., H. Taylor, G. Cutter, M. Hardin, N. Rappaport, and A. Oberman
    1994   Diagnoses, symptoms, and attribution of symptoms among Black and White in-
            patients admitted for coronary heart disease. *American Journal of Public Health*
            84(6):951-956.
Randall, M., K. Kilpatrick, J. Pendergast, K. Jones, and W. Vogel
    1987   Differences in patient characteristics between Veterans Administration and com-
            munity hospitals. *Medical Care* 25:1099-1104.
Ren, X., and B. Amick
    1996   Racial and ethnic disparities in self-assessed health status: Evidence from the
            national survey of families and households. *Ethnicity and Health* 1(3):293-303.
Rice, T., and N. McCall
    1985   The extent of ownership and the characteristics of Medicare supplemental poli-
            cies. *Inquiry* 22:188-200.
Rogers, R.
    1992   Living and dying in the USA: Sociodemographic determinants of death among
            Blacks and Whites. *Demography* 2:287-303.
Rosenheck, R., A. Fontana, and C. Cottrol
    1995   Effect of clinician-veteran racial pairing in the treatment of posttraumatic stress
            disorder. *American Journal of Psychiatry* 152(4):555-563.
Ryan, T., J. Anderson, E. Antman, B. Braniff, N. Brooks, R. Califf, L. Hillis, L. Hiratzka, E.
        Rapaport, B. Riegel, R. Russell, E. Smith III, and W. Weaver
    1996   ACC/AHA guidelines for the management of patients with acute myocardial
            infarction: A report of the American College of Cardiology/American Heart As-
            sociation Task Force on Practice Guidelines (Committee on Management of Acute
            Myocardial Infarction). *Journal of the American College of Cardiology* (28):1328-1428.
Sedlis, S., V. Fisher, D. Tice, R. Esposito, L. Madmon, and E. Steinberg
    1997   Racial differences in performance of invasive cardiac procedures in a Department
            of Veterans Affairs medical center. *Journal of Clinical Epidemiology* 50(8):899-901.
Strogatz, D.
    1990   Use of medical care for chest pain: Differences between Blacks and Whites. *Ameri-
            can Journal of Public Health* 80:290-294.
Tell, G., M. Mittelmark, B. Hylander, S. Shumaker, G. Russel, and J. Burkart
    1995   Social support and health-related quality of life in Black and White dialysis pa-
            tients. *Per Medline Anna Journal* 22(3):301-308.
Terry, W.
    1984   *Bloods: An Oral History of the Vietnam War by Black Veterans.* New York: Random
            House.
Todd, K., N. Samaroo, and J. Hoffman
    1993   Ethnicity as a risk factor for inadequate emergency department analgesia. *Journal
            of the American Medical Association* 269:1527-1539.

Weddington, W., and L. Gabel
1991 Racial differences in physicians' and patients' relationship to quality of care. *Journal of the National Medical Association* 83(7):569-572.

Weinberger, M., E. Oddone, G. Samsa, and P. Landsman
1996 Are health related quality of life measures affected by mode of administration? *Journal of Clinical Epidemiology* 49(2)135-140.

Wenneker, M., and A. Epstein
1989 Racial inequalities in the use of procedures for patients with ischemic heart disease in Massachusetts. *Journal of the American Medical Association* 261(2):253-257.

Whittle, J., J. Conigliaro, C. Good, and M. Joswiak
1997 Do patient preferences contribute to racial differences in cardiovascular procedure use? *Journal of General Internal Medicine* 12:267-273.

Whittle, J., J. Conigliaro, C. Good, and R. Lofgren
1993 Racial differences in the use of invasive cardiovascular procedures in the Department of Veterans Affairs medical system. *New England Journal of Medicine* 329(9):621-627.

Wilson, N., and K. Kizer
1997 The VA health care system: An unrecognized national safety net. *Health Affairs* 16:200-204.

Wolinsky, F., R. Coe, R. Mosely 2d., and S. Homan
1985 Veterans' and non-veterans' use of health services: A comparative analysis. *Medical Care* 23(12):1358-1371

Wolinsky, F., and S. Steiber
1982 Salient issues in choosing a new doctor. *Social Science and Medicine* 16:759-767.

APPENDIX
A

Acronyms

AAP	American Academy of Pediatrics (McLoyd)
AFDC	Aid to Families with Dependent Children (Moffitt)
AFQT	Armed Forces Qualification Test (Conrad)
BRFSS	Behavioral Risk Factor Surveillance System (Kington)
CBO	Characteristics of Business Owners (Boston)
CPS	Current Population Survey (Zhou, Conrad, Smith)
ECA	Epidemiologic Catchment Area Study (Williams)
EEO	Equal Employment Opportunity (Holzer)
EPESE	Established Populations for Epidemiologic Studies of the Elderly (Kington)
ETS	Educational Testing Service (Ferguson)
FAS	fetal alcohol syndrome (McLoyd)
HDS	Housing Discrimination Study (Massey)
HHNES	Hispanic Health and Nutrition Examination Survey (Kington)
HRS	Health and Retirement Study (Oliver/Shapiro)
HUD	U.S. Department of Housing and Urban Development (Pastor)
IHS	Indian Health Service (USDHHS) (Kington, Williams)

JTPA	Job Taining Partnership Act (Moffitt)
LBW	low birth weight (Kington, Jenkins)
LFPR	labor-force participation rate (Conrad)
LULUs	locally undesirable land uses (Pastor)
NAEP	National Assessment of Educational Progress (Ferguson)
NCES	National Center for Education Statistics (Ferguson)
NCHS	National Center for Health Statistics (Kington, Williams)
NCS	National Comorbidity Survey (Williams)
NHANES III	Third National Health and Nutrition Examination Survey (McLoyd)
NHIS	National Health Interview Survey (Kington)
NICHHD	National Institute of Child Health and Human Development (Smith)
NLMS	National Longitudinal Mortality Survey (Kington)
NLSAH	National Longitudinal Study of Adolescent Health (McLoyd)
NLSY	National Longitudinal Survey of Youth (Holzer, Conrad)
NMES	National Medical Expenditures Survey (Kington)
OMB	U.S. Office of Management and Budget (Kington, Williams)
PRWORA	Personal Responsibility and Work Reconciliation Act (Moffitt)
PSID	Panel Study of Income Dynamics (Smith, Oliver/Shapiro)
PUMAs	Public Use Microdata Areas (in Los Angeles) (Pastor)
PUMS	Public Use Micro Samples (Conrad)
SCF	Survey of Consumer Finances, Federal Reserve Board (Oliver/Shapiro)
SEP	socioeconomic position (Kington)
SES	socioeconomic status (Williams, McLoyd)
SIE	Survey of Income and Education (Conrad)
SIPP	Survey of Income and Program Participation (Oliver/Shapiro)
SMOBE	Survey of Minority-Owned Business Enterprises (Boston)

SMSAs	Standard Metropolitan Statistical Areas (Sandefur)
SNC	The State of the Nation's Cities (Pastor)
SSI	Supplemental Security Income (Moffitt)
SSRC	Social Science Research Council (Massey)
TANF	Temporary Assistance to Needy Families, was AFDC until 1996 (Moffitt)
TSDFs	toxic storage and disposal facilities (Pastor)
UCLA	University of California, Los Angeles (Kington)
USBC	U.S. Bureau of the Census (Kington, Williams, Boston)
USDHHS	U.S. Department of Health and Human Services (Kington, Williams)
WIC	Women, Infants, and Children (McLoyd)

APPENDIX
B
Agenda:
Research Conference on Racial Trends in the United States

National Academy of Sciences Auditorium
October 15-16, 1998

October 15

8:30   *Opening Remarks*
         Bruce Alberts, Chairman, National Research Council
      and Conference Chairs
         Neil Smelser (CASBS), William Julius Wilson (Harvard)

9:00   *History and Future*
         Christopher Edley (Harvard)
      Changing America: Indicators of Well-Being by Race
         Rebecca Blank (Council of Economic Advisers)

9:45   *Group Discussion of Demographic and Immigration Trends*

      Discussion Leaders:
         Reynolds Farley (Russell Sage)
         Mary Waters (Harvard)

      Paper Authors:
         Gary Sandefur (Wisconsin): "An Overview of Racial and
            Ethnic Demographic Trends"
         Min Zhou (UCLA): "America Becoming: Contemporary
            Immigration and the Dynamics of Race and Ethnicity"

10:45 *Selected Questions and Comments from the Audience*

11:00 *Group Discussion of Income, Wealth, and Welfare Trends*

Discussion Leaders:
Gerald Jaynes (Yale)
Sanders Korenman (Baruch College)
Paper Authors:
James Smith (RAND): "Race and Ethnicity in the Labor
Market: Trends Over the Short and Long Run "
Thomas Shapiro (Northeastern) & Melvin Oliver (Ford):
"Wealth and Racial Stratification"
Robert Moffitt (Johns Hopkins) & Peter Gottschalk
(Boston College): "Ethnic and Racial Differences in
Welfare Receipt in the United States"

12:00 *Selected Questions and Comments from the Audience*

1:15 *Group Discussion of Education Trends*

Discussion Leader:
Thomas Kane (Harvard)
Paper Authors:
Ronald Ferguson (Harvard): "Racial Test-Score Trends
1971-1996, Popular Culture and Community Academic
Standards"
Daryl Smith (Claremont): "Racial Trends in Higher
Education Policy and Research Implications"
Sharon Robinson (ETS): "Assessment and Learning
Trends in Group Test Score Differences"

2:00 *Selected Questions and Comments from the Audience*

2:15 *Group Discussion of Labor Force Trends*

Discussion Leaders:
Kenneth Chay (Berkeley)
Marcus Alexis (Northwestern)
Paper Authors:
Harry Holzer (MSU): "Racial Differences in Labor Market
Outcomes Among Men"
Cecilia Conrad (Pomona): "Racial Trends in Labor Market
Access and Wages: Women"

John Sibley Butler (Texas) & Charles Moskos (Northwestern):
"Labor Force Trends: The Military as Data"
Thomas Boston (Georgia Tech): "Trends in Minority-Owned
Businesses"

3:30   *Selected Questions and Comments from the Audience*

3:45   *Group Discussion of Neighborhood and Geographic Trends*

Discussion Leaders:
Roberto Fernandez (Stanford)
Paul Jargowsky (Texas)
Paper Authors:
Douglas Massey (Penn): "Residential Segregation and
Neighborhood Conditions in U.S. Metropolitan Areas"
Manuel Pastor (UC Santa Cruz): "Geography and
Opportunity"

4:45   *Selected Questions and Comments from the Audience*

5:00   *Adjourn*

October 16

8:30   *Group Discussion of the Meaning of Race and International
Comparisons*

Discussion Leaders:
Anthony Marx (Columbia)
Richard Alba (SUNY Albany)
Paper Authors:
Michael Omi (Berkeley): "The Changing Meaning of Race"

9:30   *Selected Questions and Comments from the Audience*

9:45   *Group Discussion of Trends Among Asians, Latinos, and
Native Americans*

Discussion Leaders:
Rodolfo de la Garza (Texas)
Matthew Snipp (Stanford)

Paper Authors:
    Albert Camarillo (Stanford) & Frank Bonilla (Hunter):
    "Latinos in a Multiracial Society: A New American
    Dilemma?"
    Don Nakanishi (UCLA): "Beyond the Campaign Finance
    Controversy: Trends and Issues of the New Asian Pacific
    American Population"
    Russell Thornton (Stanford): "Recent Trends Among Native
    Americans in the United States"

10:45   *Selected Questions and Comments from the Audience*

11:00   *Group Discussion of Racial Attitudes, Affirmative Action,
and Political Participation*

Discussion Leaders:
    James Jones (Delaware)
    Jennifer Hochschild (Princeton)
Paper Authors:
    Lawrence Bobo (Harvard): "Overview of Racial Attitudes
    and Beliefs"
    Carol Swain (Stanford):"Affirmative Action: A Search for
    Consensus"

12:00   *Selected Questions and Comments from the Audience*

1:15   *Group Discussion of Justice Trends*

Discussion Leaders:
    Alfred Blumstein (Carnegie-Mellon)
    Darnell Hawkins (Illinois)
Paper Authors:
    Randall Kennedy (Harvard): "Overview of Racial Trends in
    the Administration of Criminal Justice"

2:00   *Selected Questions and Comments from the Audience*

2:15   *Group Discussion of Health Trends*

Discussion Leaders:
    James S. Jackson (Michigan)
    Beverly Coleman-Miller (HSPH)

Paper Authors:
Raynard Kington (NCHS) & Herbert Nickens (AAMC):
"Racial and Ethnic Differences in Health: Recent Trends,
Current Patterns, Future Directions"
Vonnie McLoyd (Michigan) & Betsy Lozoff (Michigan):
"Behavior and Development in Children and Adolescents"
Renee Jenkins (Howard): "Physical Health Issues in Children
and Adolescents"
David Williams (Michigan): "Racial Variations in Adult
Health Status: Patterns, Paradoxes, and Prospects"
Eugene Oddone (VA), Laura Petersen (VA), Morris
Weinberger: "Health Care Use in the Veterans Health
Administration: Racial Trends and the Spirit of Inquiry"

3:45   *Selected Questions and Comments from the Audience*

4:00   *Concluding Discussion of Racial Trends and Research Needs*
William Julius Wilson, Neil Smelser

4:30   *Selected Questions and Comments from the Audience*

5:00   *Adjourn*

Biographical Sketches

REBECCA M. BLANK is Dean of the Gerald R. Ford School of Public Policy, Henry Carter Adams Collegiate Professor of Public Policy, and Professor of Economics at the University of Michigan. Prior to going to Michigan, she served as a Member of the President's Council of Economic Advisers from 1997-1999. Professor Blank's research has focused on the interaction between the macroeconomy, government anti-poverty programs, and the behavior and well-being of low-income families.

ALFRED BLUMSTEIN is a University Professor and the J. Erik Jonsson Professor of Operations Research, and former Dean of the H. John Heinz III School of Public Policy and Management, of Carnegie Mellon University. His research related to crime and punishment has covered issues of criminal careers, deterrence and incapacitation, sentencing, incarceration practice and policy, racial disproportionality, youth violence, and demographic trends. He was elected to the National Academy of Engineering in 1998.

LAWRENCE D. BOBO is Professor of Sociology and Afro-American Studies at Harvard University. Prior to joining the faculty at Harvard he was Professor of Sociology at the University of California, Los Angeles, where he directed the Center for Research on Race, Politics & Society. He is coauthor of *Racial Attitudes in America: Trends and Interpretations*, which won the 1986 Scholarly Achievement Award of the North Central Sociological Association. His research interests include racial attitudes and relations, social psychology, public opinion, and political behavior.

FRANK BONILLA is Thomas Hunter Professor of Sociology, Emeritus, at Hunter College of the City University of New York. From 1973 to 1993 Dr. Bonilla was the director of C.U.N.Y.'s Centro de Estudios Puertorriquenos and Professor in C.U.N.Y.'s Ph.D. Programs in Sociology and Political Science. Professor Bonilla's current research, writing, and advocacy efforts are focused on promoting a vitalization of Latino academic and policy research capabilities.

THOMAS D. BOSTON is a Professor of Economics in the School of Economics at Georgia Institute of Technology in Atlanta and the owner of Boston Research Group, an Atlanta-based consulting company. Dr. Boston has consulted for dozens of public agencies and private companies and is recognized as one of the country's most knowledgeable experts on minority business issues.

JOHN SIBLEY BUTLER holds The Gale Chair in Entrepreneurship and Small Business in the Graduate School of Business (Department of Management) at the University of Texas. He is Chair of the Management Department and holds a joint appointment in Organizational Behavior in the College of Liberal Arts (Sociology). His research is in the areas of organizational behavior, entrepreneurship/new ventures, and general race relations.

ALBERT CAMARILLO is a Professor of American History and Director of the Center for Comparative Studies in Race and Ethnicity at Stanford University. He is a past director of the Inter-University Program for Latino Research and the Stanford Center for Chicano Research. In his research, Professor Camarillo has examined the origins of the Chicano civil rights movement, as well as settlement, labor, and immigration patterns in urbanized populations.

CECILIA A. CONRAD is an Associate Professor of Economics at Pomona College in Claremont, California. Prior to joining the faculty at Pomona, Professor Conrad taught at Duke University in Durham, North Carolina, and at Barnard College, Columbia University, New York. Her research focuses on the economics of inequality and of the family.

CHRISTOPHER EDLEY, JR, is a Professor at Harvard Law School and the Co-Diretor of the Harvard Civil Rights Project. He served as Senior Advisor to President Clinton for the Race Initiative. His acaemic work is primarily in administrative law, but has also included civil rights, federalism, budget policy, and national security law.

RONALD F. FERGUSON is Lecturer in Public Policy at the John F. Kennedy School of Government, Harvard University, and Senior Research Associate at the Wiener Center for Social Policy, Harvard University. He is also currently a Visiting Scholar at the College Board.. His research and publications include the effects of teacher quality and other school resources on test scores in public primary and secondary schools; the effects of school quality, parenting practices, and youth culture on the Black-White achievement gap; the influence of technology and other factors on changes in the demand for low-skilled workers; and various other issues related to the quality of life in cities.

PETER T. GOTTSCHALK is Professor of Economics at Boston College. He is currently a Research Affiliate at the Institute for Research on Poverty at the University of Wisconsin, Madison, and was previously a Russell Sage Foundation Visiting Scholar and a Brookings Economic Policy Fellow. Professor Gottschalk's main area of research is labor economics, with a special emphasis on income distribution and poverty issues.

DARNELL F. HAWKINS is Professor of African-American Studies, Sociology, and Criminal Justice at the University of Illinois in Chicago. He has conducted research on racial disproportionality in the American prison system, homicide patterns and violence as a public-health problem, and public perceptions of crime and punishment.

HARRY J. HOLZER is Professor of Public Policy at Georgetown University. He is also a Senior Affiliate of the Joint Center for Poverty Research (University of Chicago and Northwestern University), Research Affiliate of the Institute for Research on Poverty (University of Wisconsin), and a former Chief Economist at the U.S. Department of Labor. Dr. Holzer has written extensively on the labor market problems of minorities and the urban poor.

RENÉE R. JENKINS is a Professor and the Chairman of the Department of Pediatrics and Child Health at Howard University. Dr. Jenkins was the first director of Adolescent Medicine in the Department of Pediatrics and Child Health at Howard University and is a past President of the Society for Adolescent Medicine. Her publications and presentations range from adolescent health and sexuality to violence prevention and health issues of minority children.

RANDALL KENNEDY is a Professor at Harvard Law School, where he teaches courses on contracts, freedom of expression, and the regulation of race relations. His recent book, *Race, Crime and the Law*, won the 1998 Robert F. Kennedy Book Prize.

RAYNARD S. KINGTON is a Research Medical Officer at the National Center for Health Statistics (N.C.H.S.), where he works primarily on the National Health and Nutrition Examination Survey. Prior to joining N.C.H.S. in 1997, he was a Senior Scientist in the Social Policy Department at RAND. Dr. Kington's research has focused on the relationships between race, socioeconomic position, and health status, especially in older populations.

BETSY LOZOFF, a behavioral pediatrician, is Director of the Center for Human Growth and Development and Professor of Pediatrics and Communicable Diseases at the University of Michigan. Her research, teaching, and patient care use a cross-cultural perspective to understand common pediatric issues related to behavior and development. Her major research focus is on iron deficiency and infant development.

ANTHONY MARX is Associate Professor of Political Science at Columbia University. His research focuses on comparative race relations and includes extensive work in South Africa, Brazil, and the U.S. South. Professor Marx's book, *Making Race and Nation*, won the 1999 Ralph Bunche Award of the American Political Science Association and the 2000 Barrington Moore Prize of the American Sociological Association.

DOUGLAS S. MASSEY is the Dorothy Swaine Thomas Professor of Sociology at the University of Pennsylvania and Chair of its Sociology Department. He is co-author of the book *American Apartheid: Segregation and the Making of the Underclass,* which won the Distinguished Publication Award of the American Sociological Association, the Otis Dudley Duncan Award of the Section on the Sociology of Population, and the Critics' Choice Award of the American Educational Studies Association. Professor Massey has also published extensively on U.S.-Mexico migration. He is a member of the National Academy of Sciences and the American Academy of Arts and Sciences.

VONNIE C. McLOYD is a Professor in the Department of Psychology at the University of Michigan in addition to holding a research scientist appointment in the Center for Human Growth and Development. Dr. McLoyd is a developmental psychologist whose primary research objective is to develop and test models of the processes by which economic hardship (i.e., poverty, parental job loss, parental income loss) affects children's development, with a special focus on development in African

American children. She received a MacArthur "Genius" Fellowship in 1996.

FAITH MITCHELL is Director of the Division on Social and Economic Studies of the Commission on Behavioral and Social Sciences and Education. She is co-editor of *Premature Death in the New Independent States* (National Academy Press, 1997) and *Governance and Opportunity in Metropolitan America* (National Academy Press, 1999).

ROBERT A. MOFFITT is Professor of Economics at Johns Hopkins University. He is affiliated with the Institute for Research on Poverty, the Joint Center on Poverty Research, and the Harvard Program on Inequality and Social Policy. He currently chairs the NRC Panel on Data and Methods for the Evaluation of Welfare Reform and is a member of CBASSE. He is a co-Principal Investigator of the Three-City Study, a major interdisciplinary study of welfare reform. His research focuses on the effects of the U.S. welfare system on employment, income, family structure, and other behaviors, and on the economics of the low-income population in general

CHARLES MOSKOS is a Professor of Sociology at Northwestern University. His current research deals with race relations in the Army and what lessons that experience may have for civilian society.

DON T. NAKANISHI is a Professor and the Director of the U.C.L.A. Asian American Studies Center. He is the author of numerous books, articles, and policy reports that have focused on topics of access, representation, and influence of Asian Pacific Americans and other ethnic and racial groups in American political, educational, and social institutions. He was appointed by President Clinton to the Civil Liberties Public Education Board.

HERBERT W. NICKENS was Vice-President and Director of the Division of Community and Minority Programs at the Association of American Medical Colleges when he died in 1999.

EUGENE Z. ODDONE is Director of the Center for Health Services Research in Primary Care at the Veterans Affairs Medical Center in Durham, North Carolina; Chief of the Division of General Internal Medicine at Duke University Medical Center; and Associate Director of Epidemiology Research and the Information Center at V.A.M.C. His research interests include evaluation of the effectiveness and delivery of ambulatory care with emphasis on hospital readmission and health care cost, assessing the reason for racial disparities in the use and outcomes of health care, evaluation of house staff training, and primary care for H.I.V.-infected patients.

MELVIN L. OLIVER is Vice President of the Asset Building and Community Development Program at the Ford Foundation. From 1978 to 1996 he was a member of the faculty at U.C.L.A., teaching at both the graduate and undergraduate levels. An expert on racial and urban inequality and poverty, Dr. Oliver is the author (with Thomas M. Shapiro) of *Black Wealth/White Wealth: A New Perspective on Racial Inequality*, which has received the Distinguished Scholarly Publication Award from the American Sociological Association, the C. Wright Mills Award from the Society for the Study of Social Problems, and the award for the Outstanding Book on the subject of human rights from the Gustavus Myers Center for the Study of Human Rights in North America.

MICHAEL A. OMI is Professor of Comparative Ethnic Studies at the University of California, Berkeley. He has written about racial theory and politics, Asian Americans and race relations, right-wing political movements, and race and popular culture.

MANUEL PASTOR is Professor of Latin American and Latino Studies and Director of the Center for Justice, Tolerance, and Community at UC Santa Cruz. He has conducted research on Latin American economic issues and U.S. urban issues, and is currently involved in a multi-year project on community-based environmental justice movements.

LAURA A. PETERSEN is a health care researcher at the Houston Center for Quality of Care and Utilization Studies and the Center to Study Racial and Ethnic Variations in Medical Interactions at the Houston Veterans Affairs Medical Center (funded by the Agency for Health Care Research and Quality and the National Institutes of Health Office of Minority Health). Her research interests include racial disparities in the use and outcomes of cardiovascular care, as well as the relationship between health care financing mechanisms and acess to health care.

GARY D. SANDEFUR is Professor of Sociology and member of the Center for Demography and Ecology at the University of Wisconsin, Madison. Most of his publications deal with issues at the intersection of race and ethnicity, social demography, and public policy. His co-authors, Molly Martin, Jennifer Eggerling, Susan Mannon, and Ann Meier are graduate students in sociology at the University of Wisconsin, Madison. Martin has interests in social demography, poverty, and welfare policy; Eggerling specializes in race and ethnicity and social psychology; Mannon studies agricultural development and change in Central America; and Meier studies social capital and family and education outcomes.

THOMAS M. SHAPIRO is Professor of Sociology and Anthropology at Northeastern University. His primary interest is in racial inequality. With Dr. Melvin Oliver, he wrote *Black Wealth/White Wealth*, which was awarded the 1995 C. Wright Mills Award by the Society for the Study of Social Problems, named an Outstanding Book of 1996 by the Gustavus Myers Center for the Study of Human Rights in North America, and received the 1997 Distinguished Scholarly Publication Award from the American Sociological Association.

NEIL J. SMELSER is Director of the Center for Advanced Study in the Behavioral Sciences, Stanford, California. From 1958 to 1994 he was on the faculty of Sociology of the University of California, Berkeley, serving as University Professor since 1971. He is a member of the American Academy of Arts and Sciences, the American Philosophical Society, and the National Academy of Sciences.

JAMES P. SMITH holds the RAND Chair in Labor Markets and Demographic Studies and was the Director of RAND's Labor and Population Studies Program from 1977 to 1994. He has led numerous projects, including studies of immigration, the economics of aging, Black-White wages and employment, the effects of economic development on labor markets, wealth accumulation and savings behavior, and the interrelation of health and economic status among the elderly.

CAROL M. SWAIN is Professor of Law and Professor, Political Science at Vanderbilt University. She is the author of *Black Faces, Black Interests: The Representation of African Americans in Congress*, which was selected by *Library Choice Journal* as one of the seven outstanding academic books of 1994, was the winner of the 1994 Woodrow Wilson prize given to "the best book published in the United States during the prior year on government, politics or international affairs," co-winner of the V.O. Key Award for the best book published on southern politics, and the winner of the 1995 D.B. Hardeman prize for the best scholarly work on the U.S. Congress during a biennial period.

RUSSELL THORNTON is Professor of Anthropology at the University of California at Los Angeles. Born and raised in Oklahoma, he is a registered member of the Cherokee Nation of Oklahoma. Since 1990 he has been chair of the Smithsonian Institution's Native American Repatriation

Review Committee. He has published six books and some 60 articles and book chapters.

MORRIS WEINBERGER is Director of Health Services Research at Roudebush Veterans' Affairs Medical Center. He is also a Professor of Medicine at the Indiana University School of Medicine and a Senior Investigator at the Regenstrief Institute for Health Care. His research interests include improved treatment of chronic medical conditions.

DAVID R. WILLIAMS is a Professor of Sociology, a Senior Research Scientist at the Institute for Social Research, and a Faculty Associate in the African American Mental Health Research Center and the Center for Afro-American and African Studies at the University of Michigan. His research focuses on socioeconomic status and health, and the health of the African American population. His publications examine how racism, social support, religious involvement, and health behaviors can affect health. His current research is examining the ways in which experiences of discrimination affect both physical and mental health.

WILLIAM JULIUS WILSON is Lewis P. and Linda L. Geyser University Professor at Harvard University. He is a member of the National Academy of Sciences, the American Academy of Arts and Sciences, the National Academy of Education, and the American Philosophical Society, and a fellow of the American Academy of Political and Social Science. Professor Wilson is a member of numerous national boards and commissions, including the President's Commission on White House Fellowships, The Center for Advanced Study in the Behavioral Sciences, and the Century Foundation. His book, *When Work Disappears: The World of the New Urban Poor*, was selected as one of the notable books of 1996 by the editors of the New York Times Book Review, and received the Sidney Hillman Foundation Award. He received the National Medal of Science in 1998.

MIN ZHOU is Professor of Sociology at the University of California, Los Angeles. Her main areas of research are immigration and immigrant adaptation, race/ethnicity, ethnic economies, the community, and urban sociology. Currently, she is doing research in immigrant communities in downtown Los Angeles examining how neighborhood environment influences parent-child and peer-group relations, children's after-school life, and their current academic and future occupational aspirations.

Index

I and II indicate the respective volumes to
which the page numbers refer.

447